DERIVATIVES

DERIVATIVES

Valuation and Risk Management

David A. Dubofsky
Thomas W. Miller, Jr.

New York   Oxford
OXFORD UNIVERSITY PRESS
2003

Oxford University Press

Oxford   New York
Auckland   Bangkok   Buenos Aires   Cape Town   Chennai
Dar es Salaam   Delhi   Hong Kong   Istanbul   Karachi   Kolkata
Kuala Lumpur   Madrid   Melbourne   Mexico City   Mumbai   Nairobi
São Paulo   Shanghai   Singapore   Taipei   Tokyo   Toronto

and an associated company in Berlin

Published by Oxford University Press, Inc.
198 Madison Avenue, New York, New York, 10016
http://www.oup-usa.org

Library of Congress Cataloging-in-Publication Data

Dubofsky, David A.
    Derivatives: valuation and risk management / by David A. Dubofsky and Thomas W.
Miller, Jr.
        p. cm.
    Includes bibliographical references and index.
    ISBN 0-19-511470-1 (alk. paper)
    1. Derivative securities. 2. Risk management. I. Miller, Thomas W., 1955- II. Title.

HG6024.A3 D828 2002
332.63′2–dc21
                                                                        2001133061

Printing number: 9 8 7 6 5 4 3 2 1

Printed in the United States of America
on acid-free paper

To
My wife Paulette
The memory of my parents, Harry and Celia
D.A.D

To
My wife Carolyn
My parents, Tom and Kathy Miller
#21, Thomas W. Miller, III
T.W.M., Jr.

CONTENTS

PREFACE

We are all in the thick of a financial revolution. Over the past 25 years, the use of financial derivatives to manage risk has evolved from an exotic practice to a commonplace occurrence. This explosive growth in derivative securities mandates that all financial managers acquire a working knowledge of these important risk management instruments. Although this book is intended for a wide range of readers, it is more than just an introduction to derivative financial securities. A first reading of this book will yield a strong working knowledge of derivative securities. A mastery of the material, however, will guarantee a thorough understanding of the substantive elements in the burgeoning field of financial derivatives.

In this book, we concentrate on four classes of derivative security contracts. These classes are forward contracts, futures contracts, swap contracts, and option contracts. The focus of this book is on using forwards, futures, swaps, and options to manage price risk. However, it is important to realize that calculating the value of a derivative is also a crucial component of risk management. Fortunately, the field of finance has just the right paradigm to allow us to study how competitive markets set prices for derivative securities. Throughout this book, we detail the use of the 'absence of arbitrage' paradigm to calculate these prices.

Studying derivative securities can often be nettlesome because the material demands that the reader have a solid understanding of concepts in several fields, namely: finance, economics, elementary probability and statistics, and, of course, mathematics. For example, in writing this book, we have assumed that the reader is familiar with basic financial topics such as the term structure of interest rates, the workings of equity and fixed income markets, and the time value of money. Then, to understand the valuation of derivatives and their use in risk management, the student of financial derivatives must be able to mix these concepts with intuition and the "absence of arbitrage" paradigm.

Undeniably, the valuation concepts presented in this book are essential underpinnings for risk management. However, the actual process of valuing derivatives, especially as they grow in complexity, is also important. Although most textbooks on derivative securities use software to help the reader understand the vagaries of these markets, we provide a unique opportunity to acquaint readers with a software product used by practitioners, FinancialCAD.*

We are excited by our alliance with FinancialCAD. Purchasers of this book will be allowed to use this sophisticated, wide-ranging derivative valuation package. FinancialCAD is an industry leader, used by 2700 companies in over 60 countries. We have scattered many examples using FinancialCAD throughout this book. Our approach is first to demonstrate 'the long way' how to solve a valuation or pricing problem. Then, we show how FinancialCAD solves it, obtaining the same answer. With this approach, FinancialCAD is not a 'black box' software package. The student should know and understand how the software package solved the problem. After an introduction to FinancialCAD, students and instructors can explore the vast capability of FinancialCAD on their own, an undertaking that will allow them to discover fascinating aspects of derivative securities. Because it is an Excel add-in, FinancialCAD easily integrates into proprietary programs used to price and hedge derivative securities. Thus, using FinancialCAD with this book affords students a chance to acquire "real-life" skills. In the competitive job market facing business school graduates, this distinction is significant.

We have written this book so that it can be used in elective courses taken by undergraduate juniors and seniors as well as in courses taken by graduate students. We believe this book can be used as the main reading material in a derivatives course or serve as a dependable companion to more mathematically focused books. While we tried to make the mathematical level "manageable," this material requires a basic understanding of calculus and a solid ability to manipulate equations algebraically.

We are zealously attached to the study of derivative securities. In particular, we want our readers to acquire a deep understanding and appreciation for how markets in these securities can be used to shift risk, either away from the user or toward the user. Of course, we are also aware of the risk–return trade-off. Unfortunately, however, this book will not tell you how to get rich using derivative securities to acquire risk. Such an accomplishment relies on having an accurate and reliable method to predict future prices. If you are in possession of such a method, it is our hope that you share it with us, because we have toiled long to bring you an understanding of derivative markets. (By the way, after you share your secret, we promise that we will not tell anyone else.)

ORGANIZATION AND CONTENT

Part 1 of this book provides an important broad overview and framework for the remaining parts of the book. In Chapter 1, we discuss the four classes of derivatives securities we cover in the text: futures, forwards, swaps, and options. In this chapter, we present the first lesson in derivatives securities: The term "derivative" stems from the fact that the value of any such security depends on the value of another security. That is, their value is "derived" from the price of an "underlying" asset. We also stress the importance of studying derivatives. In Chapter 2, we discuss risk and how it is measured. Here, we also provide reasons firms should and should not manage risk. We also discuss the second lesson in derivatives. That is, it is possible to combine derivatives with underlying assets to form portfolios with a wide variety of risk profiles, ranging from zero risk to "way risky." We conclude Chapter 2 with an overview and discussion of Financial Accounting Standard No. 133, 'Accounting for Derivative Instruments and Hedging Activities' (FAS 133).

We introduce forward and futures contracts in Part 2. This section of the book contains a considerable amount of industry jargon as well as institutional details. It has been our experience that students really want to learn the language of derivative contracts. We begin the section with an introduction to forward contracts in Chapter 3. In part, we do this because students encounter forward contracts in their everyday life. As such, they are a bit more at ease with forward contracts. This chapter contains example using the new euro, €. We follow up with an entire chapter devoted to using forward contracts to manage risk, Chapter 4. This allows us to introduce concepts of risk management that we present later in the text when we discuss risk management with futures (Chapter 7), risk management with swaps (Chapter 12), and risk management with options (Chapter 19). We separate introductory chapters on forwards (Chapter 3) from futures (Chapter 6) to emphasize that these contracts have important differences concerning default risk and contract specifications. However, we bring them together in Chapter 5 when we present and prove the all-important cost-of-carry model. Chapter 8 focuses on stock index futures and their pricing. We believe Chapters 9 and 10 to be extremely valuable to those contemplating studying for the Chartered Financial Analyst (CFA) exam. In Chapter 9, we cover the Treasury note and Treasury bond futures markets. We discuss in detail how these futures contracts are priced, paying particular attention to determining the cheapest-to-deliver contracts. In Chapter 10, we present Treasury bill and Eurodollar futures contracts, paying particular attention to hedging interest rate risk with these contracts. We cover the material on the long bonds first because a grounding in Eurodollar futures is important in understanding how financial managers use swaps to shift risk.

Part 3 of the text concerns swaps. Chapter 11 is an introduction to swaps. In this chapter, we begin with a discussion of plain vanilla interest rate swaps. This chapter also contains material on currency swaps, commodity swaps, and equity index swaps. Chapter 12 is devoted to using these various swap contracts to manage risk. We conclude this section with a chapter on pricing swaps and valuing swaps after origination. We felt that if this chapter were to be left out of a semester-long course that must cover forwards, futures, swaps, and options (which it often is), then it is best to place it at the end, rather than in the middle, of the section.

Part 4 of the book deals with options. As with the other sections, we begin with an introductory chapter, Chapter 14. Then we turn our attention to option strategies and profit diagrams in Chapter 15. Our experience is that students really like this material. Chapter 16 contains important material on arbitrage restrictions on option prices, including the important put–call parity relationship. We find that we must continually stress to students that option prices, like all derivative prices, must obey the "absence of arbitrage" rule. Further, most students in an advanced derivatives course have heard of option pricing models, most likely the celebrated Black–Scholes model. As a result, they are surprised, at times, to learn that option prices can violate the Black–Scholes model but not the pricing conditions presented in Chapter 16. Chapter 17 presents the single- and multi-period binomial option pricing model. Continuous time option pricing models, including a detailed examination of the Black–Scholes model, are covered with as little complex mathematics as possible, in Chapter 18. Chapter 19 covers risk management using options. Students generally enjoy learning about the Greeks and their role in portfolio management.

We conclude the book with Part 5, a chapter on current topics in risk management. Because we wanted to present a vast array of introductory, intermediate, and advanced material in Parts 1–4, we felt that it best to limit the final section to one chapter. To get the most from this chapter, we divided it into three nonoverlapping parts. In this way, the instructor is afforded maximum flexibility in deciding what to cover. In fact, we suggest that the material on value at risk (VaR) in this chapter can easily be incorporated with the material in Chapter 2 that deals with risk and risk management. Also, the material in this chapter on credit derivatives and options on debt instruments can assist with making the material on swaps a bit deeper. Exotic options form the third part of Chapter 20. Students do tend to like this material, especially after it follows the, at times, difficult material in Chapter 18.

Throughout the text, we have incorporated numerous examples. The instructor's manual (for instructors only) provides solutions to end-of-chapter Problems.

ACKNOWLEDGMENTS

Several individuals reviewed early drafts of this book. We especially thank Jerald Pinto; W. Brian Barrett, University of Miami; Anthony Herbst, University of Texas—El Paso; and Avraham Kamara, University of Washington, for their valuable suggestions. We also thank Charles Corrado, University of Auckland; Mike Hemler, University of Notre Dame; and Bradford D. Jordan, University of Kentucky. We thank students who have volunteered their time to read this book and provide feedback, notably Scott Beyer, Lindsey Miller, Al Pennington, Rick Wienrank, and I. C. Wu. We thank our many undergraduate and MBA students who have taken derivatives courses from us. We appreciate their good cheer and willingness to work with a beta version of a textbook. We certainly value their feedback and error-tracking ability. Of course, we take full responsibility for any remaining errors. However, we appreciate hearing of any remaining errors or welcome comments concerning the book, because we hope there will be a second edition. We greatly appreciate the efforts of Greg Thomas, at FinancialCAD; and Ken MacLeod, Paul Donnelly, and Alfredo Tauriello of Oxford University Press. Most of all, we thank our wives, Paulette Dubofsky and Carolyn Miller, for making many sacrifices during the several years it took to complete this book.

ABOUT THE AUTHORS

David A. Dubofsky is Professor of Finance at Virginia Commonwealth University. From 1997 to 2002, he served as the chair of VCU's Department of Finance, Insurance, and Real Estate. He came to VCU from Texas A&M University, where he worked for sixteen years. He is the author of over twenty-five articles in refereed journals, including *The Journal of Finance, The Journal of Financial and Quantitative Analysis, Financial Management,* and *The Journal of Money, Credit, and Banking*. Dr. Dubofsky received his B.E. in Chemical Engineering from the City College of New York, his M.B.A. from the University of Houston, and his Ph.D. in Finance from the University of Washington. He is a CFA charterholder.

Thomas W. Miller, Jr., is an Associate Professor of Finance at the University of Missouri, where he has been honored with numerous research and teaching awards. He is currently visiting at Washington University in St. Louis. He has also taught in the CIU summer program, located in Paderno del Grappa, Italy. Dr. Miller has published articles in The *Journal of Financial and Quantitative Analysis, The Journal of Banking and Finance, The Journal of Futures Markets,* and *RISK*. He received his B.S. and M.S. degrees in Economics from Montana State University and his Ph.D. in Finance from the University of Washington.

PART 1

INTRODUCTION TO DERIVATIVES AND RISK MANAGEMENT

CHAPTER 1

An Overview of Derivative Contracts

A derivative is a financial contract whose value is "derived from," or depends on, the price of some underlying asset. Equivalently, the value of a derivative changes when there is a change in the price of an underlying related asset. This chapter provides a broad overview of the four classes of derivative contracts: forwards, futures, swaps, and options. However, because forwards, futures, and swaps are very similar types of contract, many believe that there are really only two types of derivative: options and forwards. While other derivative contracts exist, a careful analysis of their characteristics will reveal that they are merely variations of one (or more) of these major classes.

Mark Rubinstein (1976) was perhaps the earliest author to use "derivative" in a financial contract context; in this particular article, he used the term to refer to options. A computerized search found that it wasn't until 1981 that an article in the popular press *Business Week* (1981) used the term, with quotation marks around it. This article expressed the fear that trading in options and futures (derivatives) detrimentally affects the markets of the underlying assets. It also raised the issue of who—the Securities and Exchange Commission (SEC) or the Commodity Futures Trading Commission (CFTC)—should regulate trading in derivatives. Currently, "derivatives" is routinely used in business communication and all forms of media, and textbooks and college courses are devoted to the study of the subject.

Individuals of many types use derivatives. Speculators who think they know the future direction of prices use derivatives to try to profit from their beliefs. Arbitrageurs trade derivatives to take advantage of times during which prices are "out of sync": that is, one asset or derivative contract is mispriced relative to another. Hedgers face the risk that a change in a price will hurt their financial status; they use derivatives to protect, hedge, or insure themselves against such harmful movement in prices. Of particular interest is the current indispensability of derivatives for accomplishing many tasks necessary to the successful management of corporations, governments, and large pools of money in general: managing exposure to price risk, lowering interest expense, altering the structure of assets, liabilities, revenues, and costs, reducing taxes, circumventing unwieldy regulations that make transactions difficult, and arbitraging price differentials.

We can characterize derivatives by the structures of the markets in which they trade. Some derivatives trade on organized exchanges. In particular, there are options and futures exchanges in existence all over the world.[1] These exchanges allow virtually anyone who meets some set of financial criteria (e.g., the individual's net worth or income) to trade these contracts. Price and trade information are readily available, and at any point in time, the prices at which they can be bought do not appreciably differ from the prices at which they can be sold. Other derivative contracts actively trade in liquid and well-established over-the-counter (OTC) markets. These markets are open only to large, financially sound corporations, governments, and other institutions.

Large, well-capitalized financial institutions such as Morgan Stanley Dean Witter, Goldman Sachs, and Deutsche Bank quote prices for these contracts; the bid–ask quotes are characterized by having narrow spreads, and trading is often quite active. Finally, many derivatives are custom made by these financial institutions for a specific end user. Generally, the party desiring such unique derivative contracts enters into the agreement with the intent of keeping the position until it matures. In general, all derivatives that do not trade on an exchange are called OTC contracts.

For many assets, the size of the derivatives markets is many times larger than the size of the cash market. Indeed, 3 trillion futures and options contracts traded on organized exchanges in 2000, an increase of over 24% from 1999 (Burghardt, 2001, p. 34). The Bank for International Settlements (BIS) reported in its November 13, 2000, press release (www.bis.org/) that the total notional principal[2] of outstanding OTC derivatives as of June 30, 2000 was $94 *trillion*! The sizes of the individual markets will be noted in the following overviews of the four different types of derivative. More detailed analyses of the contracts are contained in subsequent chapters.

1.1 FORWARD CONTRACTS AND FUTURES CONTRACTS

A forward contract gives the owner the right and obligation to buy a specified asset on a specified date at a specified price. The seller of the contract has the right and obligation to sell the asset on the date for that specified price. At delivery, ownership of the good is transferred and payment is made. In other words, whereas the forward contract is executed today, and the price is agreed upon today, the actual transaction in which the underlying asset is traded does not take place until a later date.

Typically, no money changes hands on the origination date of a forward contract. However, because forwards contain a promise to exchange the good for cash at a later date, each party wants some form of assurance that the counterparty will strictly observe the terms of the contract. Therefore, it is not unusual for the more creditworthy party to demand that the less creditworthy party put up some collateral, or take other actions to reduce the possibility of default risk.

You have probably engaged in many forward transactions in your life. For example, if you call your barber to set up an appointment for a haircut, you have transacted in a forward market. Many major purchases of items such as cars are forward transactions, and sometimes, the seller will ask for a down payment. Usually, in these informal forward contracts, a party will not take legal action if the other party defaults. Imagine how you would feel if you made a reservation at a restaurant (which is a forward contract to purchase a meal, and pay for it, at a later date), failed to appear on time (or at all), and the restaurant brought legal action against you. On the other hand, many hotels will charge you for a room if you fail to show up on time after "taking on a long position in a forward contract" that obligates you to buy the use of a room for the period specified.

Defaults on derivatives, including forwards, are taken very seriously in the financial markets. A party that loses because its counterparty defaulted will typically take legal action. Furthermore, the defaulting party's reputation will be tarnished, likely making it difficult or impossible for the defaulter to engage in future derivative transactions. It is interesting to note that only one party at any time will have the incentive to default: the party that is losing as of that date. It would most certainly *not* be in the best interest of the other party, which has unrealized profits on its positions, to walk away from its obligations, since by doing so it would be giving up its rights to a likely future cash inflow.

A **futures contract** is similar to a forward contract; the differences will be presented in Chapter 6. Until then, think of a futures contract as a standardized forward contract[3] that can be easily traded. Futures and forwards both obligate the buyer (the party with a long position in the contract) to take delivery of the underlying asset at a future date and to pay for it upon delivery; both contracts give the seller the obligation to deliver the good, asset, or service at a future date. Money typically changes hands on the delivery date.

Default risk is lower on futures than on forwards for several reasons: (a) the counterparty to all futures trades is actually the clearinghouse of the futures exchange, which guarantees that all payments will be made; (b) futures contracts are marked to market daily (daily resettlement), which means that any change in the value of the contract is realized as a profit or loss every day; and (c) initial margin, which serves as a performance bond, is required when trading futures. In contrast, because they are not marked to market, forward contracts can build up large unrealized profits for one party and equally large unrealized losses for the other party.

For example, suppose that today you sell a *forward* contract that commits you to sell one barrel of oil at $21/barrel. Then on each of the next five days, the forward price rises by $1/barrel per day. After five days, you have an unrealized loss of $5. Had you instead sold a *futures* contract, you would have been forced to pay $1 each day to the holder of the long position in this contract. In other words, the futures contract is settled up daily. Profits and losses are realized each day in the futures market, but they are realized only upon delivery in the forward market.

Because they are marked to market daily, a futures contract is like a portfolio (a time series) of forward contracts. Put another way, a futures contract with a delivery date one month (30 days) hence is equivalent to 30 forward contracts. The first forward contract originates today and is cash settled on its delivery date, which is tomorrow. The second contract originates tomorrow, and is cash settled the day after that. The last (the 30th) forward contract originates 29 days hence, and its delivery date is 30 days hence.

The profit diagrams for forwards and futures are identical. If the spot price of the underlying asset on the delivery date is above the forward price that was agreed upon when the contract was originated, the party who is long profits. All derivatives are zero-sum games. Whatever amount of money one party gains must equal the amount of money the other party loses. Alternatively, you can think in terms of changes in the forward price. Suppose that today is June 3, 2000, and today's forward price for buying gold on February 3, 2001, is $285/oz. Then, suppose on December 3, 2000, the forward price for buying gold on February 3, 2001 is $245/oz. The party that is short the forward contract has a profit of $40/oz. (this profit will still be unrealized as of December 3), and the party that is long the forward contract has a loss of $40/oz. These concepts are illustrated in Figure 1.1.

The concept of forward delivery, with contracts stating what is to be delivered for a fixed price at a specified place on a specified date, existed in ancient Greece and Rome.[4] Perhaps the first organized commodity exchange on which forward contracts traded was doing business in Japan in the early 1700s. The first formal commodities exchange in the United States for spot and forward contracting was formed in 1848: the Chicago Board of Trade (CBOT). Futures contracts began trading on the CBOT in the 1860s. The Chicago Mercantile Exchange (CME) was formed in 1919, though it essentially existed before that date under other names.

In an article published four years before he and two other Americans were awarded the 1990 Nobel Prize in economic science, Merton Miller wrote, "my nomination for the most significant financial innovation of the last twenty years is: financial futures—the futures exchange style trading of financial instruments" (Miller, 1986, p. 463).

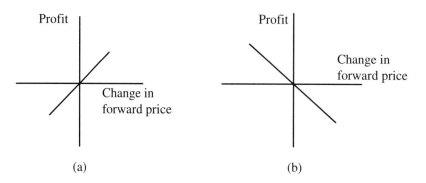

Figure 1.1 Profit diagrams for (*a*) a long forward position and (*b*) a short forward position.

The first financial futures contracts were the foreign currency futures contracts that began trading on May 16, 1972, on the International Monetary Market (IMM), a division of the CME[5]; 400 contracts were traded on the first day of operations. The first interest rate futures contracts that traded were the GNMA (Government National Mortgage Association) futures contracts,[6] on the CBOT, on October 20, 1975. The Eurodollar Time Deposit futures contract was the first "cash settled"[7] contract, and it began trading on the IMM on December 9, 1981. Another significant innovation occurred on February 24, 1982, when futures contracts on a stock index, the Value Line Index, began trading on the Kansas City Board of Trade; 1768 contracts traded on its opening day.

On September 7, 1984, the Singapore International Monetary Exchange (SIMEX) and the CME formed a trading link that permits investors to trade some contracts interchangeably on the two exchanges (this is called "mutual offset"). This was the first of several networks and systems that are leading to a globalized and increasingly automated world of 24-hour-a-day trading of securities.

Trading in energy futures commenced in the late 1970s and is now one of the most heavily traded sectors in the futures market. The New York Mercantile Exchange (NYMEX) introduced trading in No. 2 heating oil futures in November 1978. Gasoline trading began in 1981 and crude oil trading in 1983. Energy futures trade on many exchanges all over the world.

Figure 1.2 depicts how futures trading in the United States has exploded since the late 1960s. Much of the increase from 14.6 million contracts in 1971 to over 400 million contracts in 1994 and 1995 came from financial futures contracts, including futures on interest rate instruments, stock indexes, and foreign exchange. In 2000, 491.5 million futures contracts traded in the United States and another 952.6 million futures contracts traded outside the country (Burghardt, 2001). The notional principal of all the exchange traded derivatives (futures and options) traded in the world in 2000 was estimated to be $383 trillion (see the March 2001 BIS Quarterly Review, which can be viewed at www.bis.org/publ/); this was up 9.4% from the 1999 figure. Table 1.1 presents the actual number of futures contracts traded in the United States in several recent years. Table 1.2 breaks down volume in the recent past by the U.S. exchange on which the contracts traded.

It is interesting that futures trading, expressed in terms of number of contracts traded, peaked in 1998, followed by drops in 1999 and 2000. This occurred for two reasons. First, 1998 was a chaotic year in which Russia effectively defaulted on its debt and the currencies of many emerging market nations plummeted in value. These events led to considerable derivatives trading in general

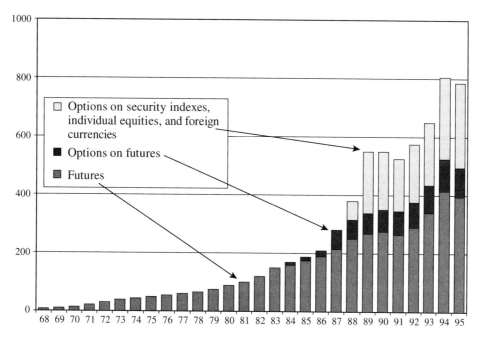

Figure 1.2 Volume of futures and options trading on U.S. futures and securities exchanges, 1968–1995. *Source:* © October/November 1996, reprinted with permission from *Futures* Industry.

TABLE 1.1 Average Estimated Number of Futures Contracts Traded, All U.S. Markets Combined: FY 1990–FY 2000

Fiscal Year	Total Contracts Traded
1990	272,306,699
1991	261,422,699
1992	289,453,855
1993	325,515,261
1994	411,056,929
1995	409,420,426
1996	394,182,422
1997	417,341,601
1998	500,562,510
1999	491,137,790
2000	477,834,609

Source: CFTC website at www.cftc.gov/.

in 1998. Second, 1999 and 2000 were much calmer years. Also, the euro was not a traded currency in 1998, so in 1998 there was trading in French francs, German marks, Italian lira, and so on. All the trading in the different "Euroland" currencies consolidated into euro-trading in 1999.

Futures trading takes place on a huge scale internationally. Table 1.3 summarizes trading activity for the most active exchange-traded futures and options contracts traded in the world

TABLE 1.2 Estimated Number of Futures Contracts Traded in U.S. Markets for Fiscal Years Ending 9/30/99 and 9/30/00

Exchange	Volume of Trading (number of contracts)		Underlying Asset of Most Actively Traded Contracts
	1998–1999	**1999–2000**	**(1999–2000 volume)**
Chicago Board of Trade (CBT)	203,662,672	187,048,113	U.S. Treasury bonds 67,008,924 contracts U.S. 10-year Treasury notes 42,769,912 contracts
Kansas City Board of Trade (KCBT)	2,378,920	2,345,727	Wheat 2,324,744 contracts
Minneapolis Grain Exchange (MGE)	1,180,573	967,504	Wheat 963,054 contracts
MidAmerica Commodity Exchange (MCE)	2,586,219	1,913,154	U.S. Treasury bonds 763,334 contracts
Chicago Mercantile Exchange (CME) and International Monetary Market (IMM)	175,488,669	181,852,421	Three-month Eurodollars 100,452,601 contracts
New York Mercantile Exchange (NYMEX) and Commodity Exchange Inc. (COMEX)	89,869,532	87,753,321	Crude oil, light "sweet" 37,526,345 contracts
New York Board of Trade (NYBT), New York Cotton Exchange (NYCE), New York Futures Exchange (NYFE), Coffee, Sugar & Cocoa Exchange (CS&CE), and Cantor Exchange (CFFE)	16,070,698	15,954,369	Sugar no. 11 5,819,141 contracts
Total, all markets	491,137,790	477,834,609	

Source: CFTC website at www.cftc.gov/.

during the first eight months of 2000. Table 1.4, which lists volume figures for the leading international futures exchanges during 2000, illustrates the international importance of futures trading.

1.2 SWAPS

In a swap contract, two parties agree to exchange cash flows at future dates according to a prearranged formula. Like a futures contract, a swap is also equivalent to a portfolio of forward contracts. However, whereas a futures contract is akin to a time series of one-day forwards, a swap is like a portfolio of forwards, all of which originate today and all of which have different delivery dates. Figure 1.3a illustrates the difference, using a futures contract with a delivery day (at time 4) four days after origination (the origination day is on day 0), and a four-period swap.

TABLE 1.3 Most Actively Traded Futures and Options Contracts for the Eight-Month Period Ending August 30, 2000

Contract	Exchange	Volume (number of contracts) January 1, 2000–August 31, 2000
Euro-BUND	EUREX-Frankfurt	105,736,279
KOSPI 200 Options	KSE, Korea	96,153,236
Eurodollars	CME, U.S.	72,920,253
CAC 40 Index Options	MONEP, France	54,795,638
U.S. Treasury Bonds	CBOT, U.S.	45,006,113
Euro-BOBL	EUREX-Frankfort	42,061,463
Three-month Euribor	LIFFE, UK	38,689,860
Euro-notional bond	Euronext Paris, France	33,049,313
U.S. T-bond options	CBOT, U.S.	31,270,050
Euro-SCHATZ	EUREX-Frankfurt	26,927,236

The exchanges are as follows: CBOT, Chicago Board of Trade (www.cbot.com); CME, Chicago Mercantile Exchange (www.cme.com); EUREX, Eurex (www.eurexchange.com/); KSE, Korea Stock Exchange (www.asiadragons.com/korea/finance/stock_market/); MONEP, Marché des Options Negociables de Paris (www.monep.fr/english/defaultuk.html); Euronext Paris (www.euronext.com); LIFFE, London International Financial Futures and Options Exchange (www.liffe.com).

Source: © October/November 2000, *Futures Industry*. Adapted with permission.

TABLE 1.4 Top Ten International Futures Exchanges in Terms of Number of Contracts Traded in 2000

Exchange	1999	2000
EUREX (Germany and Switzerland)	244,686,104	289,952,183
Chicago Mercantile Exchange (CME, U.S.)	168,013,354	195,106,383
Chicago Board of Trade (CBOT, U.S.)	195,147,279	189,662,407
London International Financial Futures and Options Exchange (LIFFE, U.K.)	97,689,714	105,712,717
New York Mercantile Exchange (NYMEX, U.S.)	92,415,006	86,087,640
Bolsa de Mercadorias & Futuros (BM&F, Brazil)	52,797,466	80,073,865
Paris Bourse SA (France)	35,129,074	62,968,653
London Metal Exchange (LME, U.K.)	57,563,009	61,413,076
Tokyo Commodity Exchange (Japan)	48,442,161	50,851,882
Euronext Brussels Derivatives Market (Belgium)	5,711,482	30,299,351

Source: © February/March 2001, *Futures Industry*. Reprinted with permission.

A simple, plain vanilla, interest rate swap illustrates how a formula is applied to the notional principal[8] amount to determine the cash flows that are paid by one party to the other. In this swap, I agree to pay you 8% of $40 million each year for the next five years. You agree to pay me whatever one-year LIBOR is (times $40 million) for each of the next five years.[9] The net payments are therefore:

if LIBOR > 8%, you pay me (LIBOR − 8%) × $40 million

if LIBOR < 8%, I pay you (8% − LIBOR) × $40 million

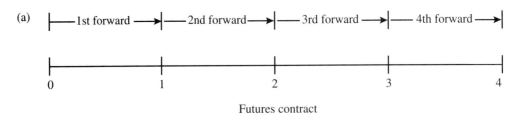

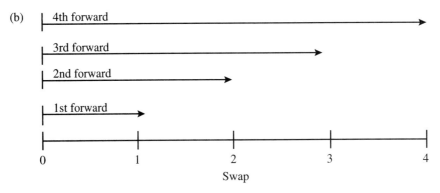

Figure 1.3 (*a*) A futures contract is like a time series of one-day forward contracts. (*b*) A swap is like a portfolio of forward contracts, all of which originate on the swap origination day (day 0), and all of which have different delivery dates.

Equivalently, I am long forward rate agreements, with delivery dates at the end of each of the next five years. As long as LIBOR is above 8%, I will profit.

The size of the swaps market has grown enormously since the first swap was transacted 1976. Continental Illinois, Ltd. and Goldman, Sachs arranged that first swap, which was a currency swap, between a Dutch company (Bos Kalis Westminster) and a British firm (ICI Finance). The currencies swapped were Dutch florins and British pounds. The first interest rate swaps took place in 1981.[10]

The growth in the swaps market is illustrated in Table 1.5, which shows that in terms of notional principal, interest rate swap trading activity expanded from $387.8 billion in 1987 to $17.1 trillion in 1997. The notional principal of interest rate swaps outstanding has grown from $682.8 billion at the end of 1987 to $48 trillion as of June 30, 2000. Trading activity of currency swaps grew from $85.8 billion in 1987 to $1.1 trillion in 1997, while the notional principal outstanding of currency swaps grew from $182.8 billion at the end of 1987 to $2.605 trillion in June 2000. The Bank for International Settlements (BIS) reported that outstanding OTC derivatives, including swaps, forwards, and OTC options, had grown to $94 trillion in notional principal on June 30, 2000 (see the press release at www.bis.org/publ/).

Table 1.5 also illustrates the expansion in the OTC interest rate options market. The amount outstanding increased from $327.3 billion to almost $8 trillion between the end of 1988 and the end of 1998. The BIS reports the size of the entire (foreign exchange, interest rates, equity-linked, and commodity) OTC options market to be $13.2 trillion as of June 30, 2000 (www.bis.org).

TABLE 1.5 Swaps: Annual Activity and Outstanding (U.S. $ billions of notional principal)

Year Ending	Interest Rate Swaps		Currency Swaps		Interest Rate Options		Totals	
	Activity	Outstandings	Activity	Outstandings	Activity	Outstandings	Activity	Outstandings
1987	$387.8	$682.80	$85.8	$182.80			$473.6	$865.6
1988	$568.1	$1,010.20	$122.6	$316.80		$327.30	$690.7	$1,654.3
1989	$833.6	$1,502.60	$169.6	$434.80	$335.5	$537.30	$1,338.7	$2,474.7
1990	$1,264.3	$2,311.50	$212.7	$577.50	$292.3	$561.30	$1,769.3	$3,450.3
1991	$1,621.8	$3,065.10	$328.4	$807.20	$382.7	$577.20	$2,332.9	$4,449.5
1992	$2,822.6	$3,850.80	$301.9	$860.40	$592.4	$634.50	$3,716.9	$5,345.7
1993	$4,104.6	$6,177.30	$295.2	$899.60	$1,117.0	$1,397.60	$5,516.8	$8,474.5
1994	$6,240.9	$8,815.60	$379.3	$914.80	$1,513.2	$1,572.80	$8,133.4	$11,303.2
1995	$8,698.8	$12,810.70	$454.1	$1,197.40	$2,015.4	$3,704.50	$11,169.3	$17,712.6
1996	$13,678.2	$19,170.90	$759.1	$1,559.60	$3,337.2	$4,722.60	$17,774.5	$25,453.1
1997	$17,067.1	$22,291.30	$1,135.4	$1,823.60	$3,978.4	$4,920.10	$22,180.9	$29,035.0
1998		$36,262.00		$2,253.00		$7,997.00		$46,512.0
1999		$43,936.00		$2,444.00		$9,380.00		$55,760.0

Sources: Reprinted with permission of the International Swaps and Derivatives Association, Inc. (ISDA) (www.isda.org/d6.html) from sources including the Bank for International Settlements (BIS) (www.bis.org/publ/).

TABLE 1.6 The Global OTC Interest Rate Derivatives Market Amounts Outstanding (billions of U.S. dollars)[1]

	By Currency		
	December 31, 1998	**December 31, 1999**	**June 30, 2000**
U.S. dollar	$13,763	$16,510	$17,606
Euro	$16,461	$20,692	$22,948
Japanese yen	$9,763	$12,391	$12,391
Pound sterling	$3,911	$4,588	$4,741
Swiss franc	$1,320	$1,414	$1,409
Canadian dollar	$747	$825	$846
Swedish krona	$939	$1,373	$1,255
Other	$3,113	$2,298	$2,558
	By Maturity[2]		
Up to one year	$18,185	$24,874	$25,809
Between one and five years	$21,405	$23,179	$24,406
Over five years	$10,420	$12,038	$13,910
Total contracts	$50,015	$60,091	$64,125

[1] All figures are adjusted for double-counting. Notional amounts outstanding have been adjusted by halving positions vis-à-vis other reporting dealers.

[2] Residual maturity.

Source: Press release dated November 13, 2000 (www.bis.org). Reprinted with permission of the Bank for International Settlements.

A more detailed breakdown, by currency and maturity, of recent OTC derivatives activity is provided in Tables 1.6 and 1.7. Table 1.6 presents the notional amount outstanding of interest rate derivatives, most of which are interest rate swaps. Table 1.7 shows the same information for foreign exchange derivatives, most of which are currency swaps. The tables show that interest rate derivatives involving the euro (i.e., the formulas were expressed in terms of euro-denominated interest rates, and all cash flows were in euros) is the largest market, with U.S.$22.9 trillion amount outstanding as of June 30, 2000. Another $17.6 trillion of OTC interest rate derivatives involved the U.S. dollar. The third most popular currency for interest rate derivatives is the Japanese yen. Foreign exchange derivatives involving the U.S. dollar (and some other currency) comprise the largest market in terms of currencies. The size of the U.S. dollar foreign exchange derivatives market, in terms of notional principal amount outstanding, was $14 trillion, which was 45.1% of the total market.

Other tables in the BIS report show that 40.2% of all interest rate derivatives had a maturity of less than one year, and another 38.1% matured in one to five years. Eighty-five percent of all outstanding currency swaps had a maturity of less than one year.

The BIS data indicated that the total notional principal of outstanding privately negotiated (OTC) interest rate swaps and currency swaps as of June 30, 2000 stood at $50.6 trillion.

Swap dealers have regretted that they express the sizes of their markets in terms of notional principal. The regret arises when government legislators and others voice alarm at the size of this unregulated (by the U.S. government) market. Upon hearing the size of this market: $94 trillion (in notional principal), a naïve person would fret over what would happen to the world's financial system if trading abuses and/or massive defaults occurred. One party might not abide by the terms

TABLE 1.7 The Global OTC Foreign Exchange Derivatives Market Amounts Outstanding in Billions of U.S. dollars[1,2]

	By Currency		
	December 31, 1998	**December 31, 1999**	**June 30, 2000**
U.S. dollar	$15,810	$12,834	$13,178
Euro	$7,758	$4,667	$5,863
Japanese yen	$5,319	$4,236	$4,344
Pound sterling	$2,612	$2,242	$2,479
Swiss franc	$937	$880	$906
Canadian dollar	$594	$647	$605
Swedish krona	$419	$459	$451
Other	$2,674	$2,723	$2,380
	By Maturity[3]		
Up to one year	$15,791	$12,140	$13,178
Between one and five years	$1,624	$1,539	$1,623
Over five years	$592	$666	$693
Total contracts	$18,011	$14,344	$15,494

[1] All figures are adjusted for double-counting. Notional amounts outstanding have been adjusted by halving positions vis-à-vis other reporting dealers.

[2] Counting both currency sides of every foreign exchange transaction means that the currency breakdown sums to 200% of the aggregate.

[3] Residual maturity.

Source: Press release dated November 13, 2000 (www.bis.org). Reprinted with permission of the Bank for International Settlements.

of its contracts, and this in turn would cause a second party to default, and so on. Some fear that such a domino effect would result in the collapse of our entire financial system and economy!

These fears are largely unfounded for several reasons.

1. Stating the market in terms of notional principal overstates the size of the market. The Government Accounting Office (GAO) has estimated that the present value of expected payments on existing swaps is only 1% of the notional principal amounts. The Bank for International Settlements (BIS) estimates that the estimated gross market value of all global OTC interest rate derivatives is only 2.2% of the reported notional amounts, and for OTC foreign exchange derivatives, its only 4.6%. These figures exclude netting (see item 2) and other risk-reducing arrangements. It is only this present value of expected swap cash flows that is at risk, since the notional principal is never exchanged. To illustrate, contrast an ordinary bond issue in the amount of $40 million (a fixed-income debt instrument) to a swap with a notional principal of $40 million. The principal amount of a bond is initially exchanged from the lenders to the borrower. At this time, the amount exposed to default risk is actually $40 million, which equals the present value of the remaining cash flows that the borrower is contractually obliged to repay the investors. If interest rates remain unchanged, and if no principal is ever retired, the amount exposed to default risk remains at $40 million. But now, consider the plain vanilla interest rate swap example we discussed just a bit earlier, in which I agreed to pay you 8% of $40 million each year and you agreed to pay me one-year LIBOR times $40 million. The $40 million notional principal is never exchanged. If LIBOR is expected to remain at 8% for the entire term of the swap, the present value of the expected swap cash flows is zero! And if one of the parties defaulted at any time that LIBOR was expected to stay at 8%, there would be virtually no economic impact caused by the default.

2. Only one party to a given swap has the incentive to default at any time. This party is the one that *expects* to make most of the remaining swap payments. Thus, a party to a swap may actually go bankrupt because of events external to the swap contract. But if this party expects its swap cash flows to be positive, it will not default on its swap obligations. Furthermore, most, if not all, swaps that originate now have bilateral netting agreements. This arrangement means that if a party defaults on one swap, then all other swaps to which it is a party and which have a positive value (the defaulting party expects to be receiving future cash flows) are also closed out. This prevents a party from defaulting only on the swaps on which it is losing money.

3. Many swaps are marked to market daily, so that there is never a large buildup of unrealized losses that would provide an incentive to default.

4. The less creditworthy parties to many swaps are required to post collateral.

1.3 OPTIONS

A **call** option is a contract that gives the owner the right, but not the obligation, to buy an underlying asset, at a fixed price, on (or before) a specific day. The call seller (usually known as the "writer") is obligated to deliver the underlying asset. Thus, options separate rights (option owners have rights) from obligations (option writers have the obligation to respond if the owner exercises his or her option).

The fixed price of an option is called the *strike price*, or the *exercise price*, and is symbolically denoted with the letter K. When an option can be exercised only on a specific day, it is called a European option. If it can be exercised at any time up to and including the expiration day, then the option is American. Options have value for the owner. At worst, the owner of a worthless option can throw it away, since he or she is not obligated to do anything with it.

A **put** option is a contract that gives the owner the right but not the obligation to *sell* the underlying asset at the strike price. The put seller (writer) is obligated to purchase the underlying asset, and pay the strike price for it. But the put seller will be forced to buy the underlying asset if and only if the put owner exercises the option.

Whereas forwards, futures (which are just portfolios of forwards), and swaps (which are also just portfolios of forwards) provide profit diagrams that are just 45° straight lines, option profit diagrams consist of kinked, piecewise linear portions. If there are kinks, they will always exist at the strike prices. Before we illustrate the profit diagrams for call options, let's define a set of new terms: in, out of, and at the money. If S denotes the price of the underlying asset, and K denotes the strike price, then a call is:

In the money if $S > K$

Out of the money if $S < K$

At the money if $S \sim K$ (i.e., S is close to K)

Deep in (out of) the money if $S >> K$ ($S << K$)

The payoff diagram of an option illustrates the cash flows that occur on the expiration day of the option. Figure 1.4 is the payoff diagram for the owner of a call option. If the call finishes out of the money, then it has expired worthless, the call owner will not exercise her option, and there is no expiration day cash flow. If, on the other hand, the option finishes in the money, the option owner will exercise her option and buy the underlying asset for $\$K$. The asset itself is worth $\$S_T$. So, the option owner is purchasing something for less than it is worth. Because the call is in the money at expiration, $S_T > K$, and the expiration day payoff to the owner of the call is $S_T - K$.

To generate a profit diagram, we now only need to account for the initial requirement that the owner pay for that option. Figure 1.5 shows that the payoff diagram is just uniformly lowered by the amount the call buyer originally paid for the option. Denote this initial cost (it is frequently called the option "premium") as C_0.

Calls are one type of options. Puts are the other type.

Figure 1.6 is the payoff diagram for a long put position, and Figure 1.7 is the profit diagram for the long put. A long position refers to the owner of the put.

You have used options many times and probably did not even realize it. If you own a home, you have probably borrowed money, perhaps for 15 or 30 years, to make the purchase. You also know that if you sell your house, or if interest rates drop sharply, you can pay your loan off early. This is called a *prepayment option*. A floating-rate mortgage, which has limits on how much the interest rate can rise or fall each year, is another example of an option; these limits are caps and floors, which are interest rate options. You have entered into an option agreement if you ever rented furniture or a car, with an option (a call) to buy. Perhaps you have purchased

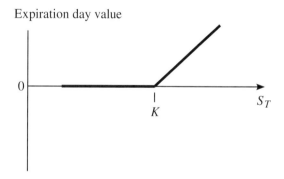

Figure 1.4 Payoff (at expiration) diagram for a long call.

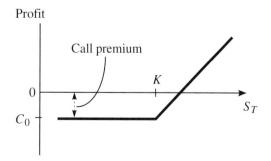

Figure 1.5 Profit diagram for a long call obtained by lowering the payoff diagram (Figure 1.4) by the call premium.

Expiration day value

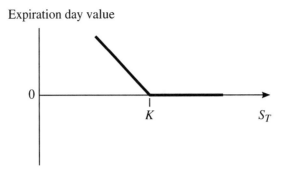

Figure 1.6 Payoff diagram for a long put.

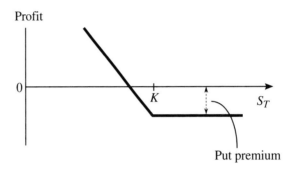

Figure 1.7 Profit diagram for a long put, obtained by lowering the payoff diagram (Figure 1.6) by the put premium.

options to get preferred seating at concerts and/or shows. When you purchase goods covered by a warranty, you have the option (a put) of returning the items within a specified period if you are unsatisfied in any way.

Options are often called "contingent claims" because their payoffs are contingent on some event. For example, option payoffs are contingent on whether they finish in the money or out of the money.

Options trading has a long history.[11] The concept of an option existed in ancient Greece and Rome. Options were used by speculators in the tulip craze of seventeenth-century Holland.[12] Unfortunately, there was no mechanism to guarantee the performance of the options' terms, and when the tulip craze collapsed in 1636, many speculators were wiped out. In particular, put writers would not take delivery of the tulip bulbs and refused to pay the high prices they had originally agreed to pay. Puts and calls, mostly on agricultural commodities, were traded in the nineteenth century in England and in the United States. Options on shares of common stock were available in the United States on the OTC market only until April 1973. The terms of these OTC options were negotiated by the buyer and seller, with a member of the Put and Call Brokers and Dealers Association serving as an intermediary or as one party to the contract. Thus an investor could buy a call option on 250 shares of AAA Corp. at a specified price of $26.125 per share, with an expiration date of the next April 30. Liquidity was lacking for these "custom-made" contracts, and each party had reason to be concerned about the other's ability to conform to the terms of the contract.

After five years of development that cost $2.5 million, the Chicago Board Options Exchange (CBOE) opened on April 26, 1973, in an old lunchroom at the Chicago Board of Trade.

Initially, 16 standardized call option contracts on individual stocks were listed on the exchange, and first-day volume totaled 911 contracts. Each founding member of the CBOE paid $10,000 for a seat (in 2001, the price of a seat was around $370,000). Put options began trading on the CBOE and four other options exchanges on June 3, 1977. On March 11, 1983, the first index option began trading on the CBOE; it was originally called the CBOE 100 Index, and later renamed the S&P 100 Index, or OEX (its ticker symbol). Options on futures contracts, which were temporarily banned by Congress in 1978,[13] were reintroduced to the marketplace on October 1, 1982. The first contracts were options on Treasury bond futures contracts (4080 T-bond futures options traded that day) on the CBOT, and sugar futures options on the New York Coffee, Sugar, and Cocoa Exchange.

The Bank for International Settlements estimated that at the end of 2000, the notional principal of the assets underlying outstanding exchange-traded options was $5.9 trillion. Actual trading activity of these options came to $66 trillion (notional principal) in 2000. Burghardt (2001) reports that in 2000, 156.9 million option contracts traded in the United States, and another 421.2 million contracts traded outside the country; these figures do *not* include options on individual stocks. Another 970 million option contracts on individual equities traded globally in 2000. A total of 578 million option contracts actually traded in 2000. The market for options that are created by securities dealers in the OTC market is even larger: the BIS reported that the notional principal of the OTC options market was $13.2 trillion at the end of June 2000.

1.4   WHY IS IT IMPORTANT TO LEARN ABOUT DERIVATIVES?

One obvious motivation (at least to the authors) for learning about derivatives is the sheer size of the market. It is difficult to justify ignorance about a market that, as of the end of 1999, was estimated to be $88 trillion.

Certainly, any student who hopes to work in the financial marketplace should have some knowledge about derivatives and how she might be able to use these products in her job. These contracts can be used to control risk exposures or to speculate on future price movements. Firms, institutions, and governments can all use derivatives to manage risk and/or to increase profitability. The prices of many commodities, interest rates, currencies, and equities have become increasingly volatile at times in the recent past. Price volatility can result in financial hardship, even bankruptcy, for some firms. Derivatives allow the user to transfer these risks to other parties who are willing and able to accept them. Everyone who works in the world of finance must understand how derivatives work.

Derivatives can have a tremendous impact on spot markets, and this is yet another reason for reading this book. Hardly a week passes that financial commentators in the media do not attribute the stock market's price movements to **program trading**. A program trade is an order, usually placed by a large institution, to buy or sell large amounts of stock of many different companies. Put another way, it is the trade of a large portfolio of stocks as a group. Many program trades also involve options and/or futures. Indeed, many program trades are performed to arbitrage small price discrepancies that exist between the spot, options, and/or futures markets. The actions of derivatives traders affects stock prices, interest rates and the prices of foreign currencies.

Options and futures trading has been blamed for almost every large stock market move since 1987, including the stock market crash of October 19, 1987, when the Dow Jones Industrial Average fell an unprecedented 508 points, down 22.6% on one day. If derivatives trading exists for a given commodity, then at times, that trading will almost certainly affect the spot price of that commodity. Thus options and futures trading has an impact on the lives of all consumers and suppliers of products and services, and on the experiences of all investors.

Last, but hardly least, you should understand futures and options to be able to protect yourself. Only if you understand derivatives can you decide intelligently whether you should ever use them. You will also be better able to avoid being defrauded or cheated.

Many investors lost huge amounts of money in the stock market crash of October 1987 because they listened to stockbrokers who advised that a particular strategy—writing naked puts—was a low risk route to profits.[14] Others have lost their life savings by speculating in futures, after being fast-talked into futures trading by high-pressure brokers, or by doing business with unscrupulous members of the futures industry. Individuals are not alone. Very large corporations (e.g., Procter & Gamble), financial institutions (e.g., Barings), and governments (e.g., Orange County, California) lost billions of dollars by using derivatives. By studying the material in this book, you will be better educated about such risks. You will also be better able to gauge the knowledge of any derivatives salespeople with whom you might do business.

Derivatives are not mere financial curiosities—the explosive growth in their number and usage is a direct result of their value in managing risks and returns. **Financial engineers** use derivative securities to manage risk and exploit opportunities to enhance returns. They create derivatives of different types that possess payoff patterns that meet investment or risk management needs, just as "typical" engineers create structures (manufacturing plants, bridges, roads, circuit boards) that meet the needs of the user.

In recent years, managing traditional price risks has mushroomed into managing the total risks of the firm. Financial engineers now have their own professional group, The International Association of Financial Engineers (www.iafe.org/). Risk managers also have a professional group, known as GARP, the Global Association of Risk Professionals (www.garp.com).

1.5   SUMMARY

In today's increasingly complex world of finance, both investors and financial managers must be aware of options and futures. They are important as speculative vehicles, and as risk management tools. This book takes the view that it is important for users of options and futures to know the principles of valuation and to learn how they can be used to manage price risk.

Speculators use derivatives (usually futures and options) to attempt to profit from expected price changes. Because derivatives are usually highly levered assets, huge profits can be realized if a speculator's prediction of the direction and amount of price change is correct. Consistent with the central concept that greater expected returns exist only where greater risks exist, it must be noted that many speculators have lost huge sums of money by being wrong about future price movements. Still, derivatives allow investors to establish, at low cost, return distributions that match up with their levels of risk aversion.

Hedgers use these contracts to control the risks they face regarding price changes. Hedgers include individuals, corporations, financial institutions, traders, and other entities facing the possibility that a price change will reduce the value of their net worth. Under ideal conditions, hedgers might be able to reduce the price risks they face to almost zero. Other hedgers might prefer the purchase of insurance, using options, rather than shrinking the range of possible future outcomes. Derivatives facilitate hedging and insuring. To successfully use these contracts, the basics of valuation and the principles of how derivatives can be used to manage risk must both be thoroughly understood, and this text attempts to promote such understanding.

References

Burghardt, Galen 2001. "Whassup?" *Futures Industry*, Vol. 11, No. 1, February/March, 2001, pp. 33–41.

Business Week. 1981. "An Explosion of Options and Futures," Vol. 62, No. 9, March 23, pp. 88–90.

Chicago Board of Trade. 1985. *Commodity Trading Manual*, Chicago: CBOT.

Das, Satyajit. 1994. *Swap and Derivative Financing*, rev. ed. Burr Ridge, IL, Irwin Professional Publishing.

Garber, Peter M. 1989. "Tulipmania." *Journal of Political Economy*, Vol. 97, No. 3, June, pp. 535–560.

Gastineau, Gary L. 1988. *The Stock Options Manual*, 3rd ed. New York: McGraw Hill.

Johnston, Elizabeth Tashjian, and John J. McConnell. 1989. "Requiem for a Market: An Analysis of the Rise and Fall of a Financial Futures Contract." *Review of Financial Studies*, Vol. 2, No. 1, pp. 1–23.

Miller, Merton H. 1986. "Financial Innovation: The Last Twenty Years and the Next." *Journal of Financial and Quantitative Analysis*, Vol. 21, No. 4, December, pp. 459–471.

Options Institute, ed. 1990. *Options: Essential Concepts and Trading Strategies*. Homewood, IL: Business One, Irwin.

Rubinstein, Mark. 1976. "The Valuation of Uncertain Income Streams and the Pricing of Options." *Bell Journal of Economics*, Vol. 7, No. 2, Autumn, pp. 407–425.

Notes

[1] *Futures Industry* lists 58 futures and options exchanges in existence in 26 different countries in 2000 (Burghardt, 2001, pp. 40–41).

[2] The notional principal is just the amount of money that is used to determine the cash flows of a swap. When the principal amount is notional, it is not actually exchanged; it simply represents the amount to which a formula is applied so that periodic cash flows can be computed.

[3] A standardized contract has terms that are identical to those of all other contracts. In other words, it specifies an exact amount of a good, the quality of the good, where and when it is to be delivered, and so on. All the contract's terms are stated, except the price. Thus, every gold futures contract that calls for delivery in a given month is identical to every other gold futures contract for that month. Standardization of futures contracts contributes to their liquidity.

[4] Much of the following history of forward transacting and futures trading is drawn from the Chicago Board of Trade's *Commodity Trading Manual*, (1985).

[5] Actually, foreign exchange futures began trading on the International Commercial Exchange (ICE), which was part of the New York Produce Exchange, in 1970. This venture failed after the IMM commenced operations, perhaps because of high initial margin requirements at the ICE, and perhaps because the ICE failed to adequately promote and market itself.

[6] A GNMA certificate is a security that is backed by a pool of mortgages. Investors in GNMAs receive the interest and principal that are paid by the homeowners, less some fees. The U.S. government guarantees these payments of interest and principal. The values of GNMAs rise as interest rates fall and decline as rates rise.

Volume in GNMA futures rose sharply in the early years of trading, reaching more than 9000 contracts per day in 1980. However, the contract's terms were complex, and other interest rate futures contracts became much more popular. Trading volume shrunk and in January 1988, the GNMA futures contract (in its original form, at least) ceased to exist. See Johnston and McConnell (1989) for an analysis on what contributed to the contract's failure.

[7]By "cash-settled," we mean that no delivery of the underlying good ever takes place. At delivery, all profits and losses are received and paid in cash.

[8]See note 2 in this chapter.

[9]LIBOR is the acronym for the London interbank offer rate. U.S. dollar LIBOR is the rate at which major London banks lend Eurodollar deposits. There is a LIBOR for each different maturity and for different currencies. Thus, we can speak of 3-month U.S. dollar LIBOR, and 6-month Japanese yen (JPY) LIBOR. "Eurodollars" is the term used for dollars that are borrowed and lent outside of the United States. Any dollars deposited in *any* bank located outside the United States (even if that bank is in Asia) are called Eurodollars. A more general term is **Eurocurrency**, which refers to any currency that is deposited in a bank located outside its country of origin (e.g., Euroyen are yen that are deposited in any bank outside of Japan).

[10]Das (1994, Chap. 1) provides a history of the swap markets.

[11]See Chapter 3 of Gastineau (1988), and Chapter 1 in *Options: Essential Concepts and Trading Strategies*, edited by the Options Institute (1990) for more details on the history of options.

[12]See Garber (1989) for details on the tulip bulb speculative bubble.

[13]In the 1970s, futures options were not traded on exchanges, but were instead often promoted by "boiler room" sales people, who pressured naive investors into buying the contracts. Furthermore, there was frequently no seller of the futures option, and by the time an investor tried to sell his option, the salesman and his operation had disappeared. Later, having introduced a stringent set of regulations and disclosure requirements, the Commodity Futures Trading Commission was able to persuade Congress to rescind the ban. Option contracts had been temporarily banned in England for several periods, beginning in 1733, when Bernard's Act was passed, until the 1950s.

[14]A front-page article in the December 2, 1987, issue of *The Wall Street Journal* recounts some of these horror stories.

PROBLEMS

1.1 On July 10, party A buys a forward contract from party B (B is the seller of the contract). The forward price is $38, and delivery is on October 10. One month prior to delivery, the forward price for new contracts that call for the delivery of the underlying asset on October 10 is $35. Which party is more likely to default on the contract on September 10?

1.2 Describe how OTC derivatives differ from derivatives traded on public exchanges.

1.3 "Both futures and swaps are equivalent to portfolios of forward contracts." Explain this statement.

1.4 If the price of the underlying asset rises, explain why being long a futures contract would likely be preferred to having a long forward position in that underlying asset, all else equal.

1.5 Explain why notional principal overstates the size of the derivatives market.

1.6 An arbitrageur
   a. tries to profit by trading mispriced assets
   b. tries to manage risk exposure via hedging
   c. tries to manage risk exposure via insurance

d. tries to profit by buying low today and selling high in the future

e. has a view on where the market is heading and tries to profit on those beliefs

1.7 Which of the following statements is true?

a. Futures have more default risk than forwards because the clearinghouse will protect traders of forward contracts.

b. Futures have more default risk than forwards because forward contracts are settled daily (marked to market daily).

c. Futures have more default risk than forwards because forwards are custom-made contracts.

d. Forwards have more default risk than futures because the clearinghouse will protect traders of futures contracts.

e. Forwards have more default risk than futures because futures are custom-made contracts.

CHAPTER 2

Risk and Risk Management

Learning about risk and risk management is an important key to understanding the modern financial landscape. You should be cognizant of the risks and opportunities you face as an investor, as an employee or owner of a business, and as a citizen.

This book deals with the nature of price risk and how you can use derivatives to manage it. A derivative is a contract whose value is derived from the price of some underlying asset. Chapter 1 presented an overview of four well-known derivative contracts that are used to manage risk: forwards, futures, swaps, and options. At the end of Chapter 1, we called your attention to two new professions, financial engineering and risk management.

Financial engineers and risk managers do not just manage a single price risk. Instead, they concern themselves with managing the total risk exposure faced by the firm, known as **enterprise risk exposure**. Managing this total enterprise risk is commonly known as **enterprise risk management**, or **ERM**. **Value at risk (VaR)** is a concept widely used in enterprise risk management. You will learn about VaR in chapter 20, but you will be introduced to some intricate details and uses of individual derivative securities in Chapters 3 through 19.[1]

The purpose of this chapter is to introduce you to the concepts of risk and risk management. As a starting point, recall the basic economic fact that firms utilize inputs to create outputs. If the revenues from the outputs sold are greater than all costs, then profits are earned. Output prices are one element of revenue, and input prices are an important component of total costs. Most firms are not in the business of speculating on the prices of inputs and outputs. Firms prefer knowing what prices will be in the future, so that they will have less uncertainty about the level of their profits. Consider the following simple income statement:

$$\text{Revenues} = \text{Price of output times quantity sold}$$
$$\underline{-\text{Expenses} = \text{Prices of inputs times number of inputs required}}$$
$$\text{Profits}$$

Profit uncertainty is greatly reduced if a firm knows what the prices of its inputs will be and if it can have a guaranteed selling price of its output. Risk cannot be totally avoided, since the firm never knows exactly how much of its output it will be able to sell,[2] nor can it totally control the total cost of all of its inputs (e.g., labor expense, R&D expense, input spoilage, or the expense of raw materials used in undeliverable output). Many risks just cannot be managed. Unusual weather, for example, can affect the amount of goods or services that a firm sells, have an impact on its costs, and even cause catastrophic losses that destroy production capabilities.[3] Another example of a risk that cannot be controlled is competition. If another firm enters a market, existing firms will likely be forced to accept lower selling prices and a lower quantity of goods sold.

If you have had previous finance courses, you have been taught a great deal about risk. You have likely learned the concepts such as default risk, systematic (market) and unsystematic risk, variance, covariance, liquidity risk, and business risk vs financial risk. In this chapter, the following topics will be discussed:

What is risk?

How can risk be measured?

How can risk exposure be determined?

Should firms manage the financial price risks to which they are exposed?

It is certainly important to learn about risk management and derivatives. As you saw in Chapter 1, the use of derivatives has exploded, and by one measure, the size of the market is now over $88 trillion! Improper use of derivatives led to several well-publicized debacles in the 1990s. For example, you may have read about Metalgesellschaft, Procter & Gamble, or Long-Term Capital Management. Some firms and governments have lost billions of dollars through inappropriate trading and the lack of suitable internal controls. Notable recent cases that can be traced to the actions of one individual and the lack of oversight include Orange County (1994), Baring's Bank (1995), Daiwa Bank (1995), and Sumitomo Corp. (1996). A description of the procedures and technologies that can be used to deter inappropriate derivatives usage and subsequent losses is beyond the scope of this textbook. You should well note, however, that implementing and maintaining an effective enterprise risk management strategy is an important, burgeoning area.

Today, corporations, institutions, governments, and individuals routinely use derivatives to manage price risk exposure efficiently and effectively. According to Bodnar, Hayt, and Marston (1998), 83% of large nonfinancial U.S. firms use derivatives. Indeed, failing to use derivatives to deal with price risk is, in itself, dangerous, because it can be argued that firms that fail to manage price risk are simply speculating on prices.

2.1 WHAT IS RISK?

Risk is synonymous with uncertainty. Risk arises because the future is unknown. For example, default risk represents the future possibility that a party will default on a contractual obligation. Regulatory risk refers to the possible future imposition of rules, laws, or regulations that will impede doing business as it is currently done. Somewhat related is accounting risk, which would alter the way in which transactions are accounted for and reported on financial statements. Legal risk is the risk that a contract's terms will prove to be unenforceable, possibly because the instrument was poorly written. Price risk is one component of business risk, and it arises because the prices of goods will fluctuate in unpredictable ways in the future. Two common sources of price risk are foreign exchange rates and interest rates.[4]

What is important to understand is that the future is unpredictable, and the possibility of unexpected defaults in the future, as well as any regulations and price changes, all impact a business and affect future profits and values. Individuals dislike risk. Because they are often willing to pay a price to reduce uncertainty, they are risk-averse. The owners of financial securities, investors, are also risk-averse. Derivative contracts can be used to manage risk. Risk management can take the form of reducing (or even eliminating) price uncertainty via hedging transactions, or purchasing insurance using options to protect against unfavorable future outcomes while allowing participation in future favorable price changes.

Hedging and insuring do not make risk disappear. Instead, they transfer the price risk to those that are more willing and (hopefully) better prepared to accept them. Indeed, the chief economic benefit of derivative contracts is that they provide inexpensive conduits to transfer risk. Buying insurance on your house does not eliminate the risk that your house will burn down. Instead, the insurance contract allocates this risk to an insurance company that is both willing (because it charges you an insurance premium that should be sufficiently high to allow it to earn a profit) and better prepared (because it diversifies its risk exposures and is well capitalized) to deal with the event insured against, should it occur. Similarly, a firm that manages its exposure to the risk that interest rates will rise does not make the threat or the impact of rising interest rates disappear. The consequence of the higher interest rates (a decline in firm value or profits) is still realized. But because it has used derivatives, the firm has effectively transferred the impact to another party.

2.2 HOW IS RISK MEASURED?

This section contains a brief review of the elements of basic probability concepts that should be familiar from statistics and/or finance courses. In this section, we present the building blocks to help you understand other measures of risk that are often incorporated into enterprise risk management. That is, once you understand the basics of measuring risk, you can more readily refine your measure to include, for example, the likelihood of significant price changes.

2.2.1 Random Variables, Probability Distributions, and Variance

Future outcomes are random variables. An individual, firm, or institution facing a random variable is facing risk. In finance, the variance of a random variable is the most frequently used measure of risk.

Think of a random variable as a list of possible outcomes. We do not know which of the outcomes will be realized. If probabilities are attached to this list of possible outcomes, we then have a probability distribution of the random variable. Risk management alters the probability distribution of important random variables such as profits, rates of return, and stockholder's wealth.

Probability distributions may be discrete or continuous. A discrete distribution has a finite list of outcomes, each with its own probability. For example, suppose that the rate of return that will be earned on a common stock investment is a random variable denoted $\tilde{r}$.[5] Then this is a discrete probability distribution:

Outcome	Probability
-0.12	0.10
0	0.15
0.10	0.35
0.20	0.25
0.30	0.15

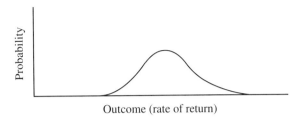

Outcome (rate of return)

Figure 2.1 A continuous probability distribution.

Discrete distributions like this are unrealistic representations of the rates of return on financial assets. Nonetheless, many variables described in this text will be modeled as discrete distributions because they are more easily mathematically handled than continuous probability distributions. A continuous probability distribution has an uncountable number of possible outcomes. For example, Figure 2.1 is a depiction of a continuous probability distribution.

Although rates of return of risky assets are more likely to be continuous random variables, many future prices that we deal with are discrete random variables. These include the prices of commodities such as gold, oil, and wheat, as well as interest rates and the prices of foreign currencies. These random variables are discrete because they are expressed in some minimum unit of account, such as a penny. Other prices, such as stock prices, are constrained by trading rules to be discrete, formerly multiples of 1/8 or 1/16 and now in pennies.

Some assets (such as a pure discount Treasury bill) are riskless, so the rate of return over the asset's life is known with probability 1. Today's prices (spot prices) are known, fixed, and certain. Moreover, there may even be fixed prices quoted today for the delivery of goods in the future; these are called forward prices. But the actual spot price that will exist in the future is a random variable. When we consider a collection of random variables, such as the time series of daily prices during the next year, it is said that we are dealing with a stochastic process.

A probability distribution is characterized by certain measures that are known statistically as **moments**. Given a set of moments (i.e., central tendency, dispersion, skewness), we can create an entire probability distribution. For example, since a normal distribution exhibits no skewness, such a distribution is entirely described once we know its mean and variance.

The first moment, the expected value, is a measure of central tendency. It has the characteristic that if an infinite number of returns were independently drawn from an unchanging probability distribution, then the expected return would be the average value of the random variable.

The expected return of a random variable is a probability-weighted average of the possible outcomes. It is computed by multiplying each outcome by its probability and then adding all the resulting products. For example, the expected return of the discrete random variable just presented (the expected return of the common stock) is computed as follows:

1	2	3
Outcome	**Probability**	**Outcome × Probability:** col. 1 × col. 2
−0.12	0.10	−0.012
0	0.15	0
0.10	0.35	0.035

0.20	0.25	0.05
0.30	0.15	0.045

$$\Sigma = \text{expected return} = 0.118 = 11.8\%$$

It is interesting to note that the expected return is not equal to any of the discrete outcomes that are possible. If $\tilde{r}$ is a discrete random variable, and there are n possible outcomes, then the expected return $E(\tilde{r})$ is

$$E(\tilde{r}) = r_1 \, \text{Pr}(\tilde{r} = r_1) + r_2 \, \text{Pr}(\tilde{r} = r_2) + \cdots + r_n \, \text{Pr}(\tilde{r} = r_n)$$

For this example,

$$E(\tilde{r}) \ = \ (-0.12 \times 0.10) + (0 \times 0.15) + (0.10 \times 0.35) + (0.20 \times 0.25) + (0.30 \times 0.15) = 0.118$$

The short-cut notation for the expected return is

$$E(\tilde{r}) = \sum_{i=1}^{n} r_i \, \text{Pr}(\tilde{r} = r_i)$$

Another widely used measure of central tendency is the median. The median occurs at the value at which there is a 50% chance that the outcome will be below it and a 50% chance that the outcome will lie above it. In the foregoing example, the median lies between 0 and 0.10. This is found by ordering the outcomes from lowest to highest (as they already are), and cumulating the probabilities as we move from the lowest to the highest value, as follows:

Outcome	Probability	Cumulative Probability
−0.12	0.10	0.10
0	0.15	0.25
0.10	0.35	0.60
0.20	0.25	0.85
0.30	0.15	1.00

To find the median, we must find the value at which the cumulative probability equals 0.50. This occurs at an outcome greater than 0 (where the cumulative probability is 0.25) and less than 0.10 (where the cumulative probability is 0.60).

In addition to measures of central tendency, we are interested in measures of dispersion. The greater the dispersion, the less certain we are about what the outcome will be, and the greater the risk.

The simplest measure of dispersion is the range of outcomes. The range is just the difference between the highest and lowest outcomes. In our example, the range is 0.42 [0.30−(−0.12)=0.42].

The range is not an informative measure of dispersion. The range is the same regardless of whether there are just two possible outcomes (0.30 and − 0.12) and the probability of each is 0.50, or many different outcomes and the probability of one of the extreme outcomes is very high and the other extreme outcome is very low. Alternatively, there may be many different outcomes, with the probabilities of each of the two extreme outcomes being very low (say, 0.00001).

The second moment of a probability distribution, and a measure of a random variable's dispersion, is its variance. The definition of variance is "the expected value of the squared deviation from the expected value." While this sounds like something Groucho Marx might say, it is actually quite simple. The calculation of the variance of a random variable can be illustrated as follows.

1	2	3	4	5
Outcome	Probability	Outcome × Probability: col. 1×col. 2	Squared Deviation from the Expected Value	Probability × Squared Deviation: col. 4×col. 2
-0.12	0.10	-0.012	$(-0.12-0.118)^2=0.056644$	0.0056644
0	0.15	0	$(0-0.118)^2=0.013924$	0.0020886
0.10	0.35	0.035	$(0.10-0.118)^2=0.000324$	0.0001134
0.20	0.25	0.05	$(0.20-0.118)^2=0.006724$	0.0016810
0.30	0.15	0.045	$(0.30-0.118)^2=0.033124$	0.0049686
		Σ = expected return = $0.118=11.8\%$		Σ = variance = 0.0145160

We have already discussed the first three columns. Column 4 takes the deviation of each outcome from the expected value and squares it. For example, the first outcome is -0.12. The difference between that outcome and the expected value of 0.118 is 0.238 ($-0.12-0.118$). The square of 0.238 is then 0.056644. This process of finding the squared difference between an outcome and the expected value is repeated for each outcome in column 4.

Whenever you see the word "expected" before another word or set of words, you should immediately think in terms of probability weighting. This is what is done in column 5. Because variance is the expected value of the squared deviation from the expected value, we must attach probability weight to the squared deviations from the expected value. For example, the first squared deviation from the expected value is 0.056644. If we multiply that number by the probability of its occurrence, 0.10, we get the number on the first line of column 5, namely: 0.0056644.

Finally, to complete the computation of variance, add the probability-weighted squared deviations from the expected value, and we find that the variance is 0.0145160.

The units of this return variance is "percentage-squared." The main drawback of variance is that it is difficult to understand the meaning of percent-squared. Thus, standard deviations are often utilized. Standard deviation is the square root of variance. The standard deviation of returns in our example is $\sqrt{0.0145160} = 0.12048 = 12.048\%$.

We can use the following formula to summarize the computational procedures of all these parameters:

$$\text{Var}(\tilde{r}) = \sigma^2(\tilde{r}) = E[r_i - E(\tilde{r})]^2 = \sum_{i=1}^{n} [r_i - E(\tilde{r})]^2 \, \text{Pr}(\tilde{r} = r_i)$$

Expanded, this becomes:

$$\text{Var}(\tilde{r}) = [r_1 - E(\tilde{r})]^2 \, \text{Pr}(\tilde{r} = r_1) + [r_2 - E(\tilde{r})]^2 \, \text{Pr}(\tilde{r} = r_2) + \cdots$$
$$+ [r_n - E(\tilde{r})]^2 \, \text{Pr}(\tilde{r} = r_n)$$

The standard deviation (SD) is the square root of the variance:

$$\text{SD}(\tilde{r}) = \sigma(\tilde{r}) = \sqrt{\text{var}(r)}$$

The greater the variance of a desired variable, such as a rate of return on an asset, the greater its risk. As an outcome becomes more certain, its variance and standard deviation become smaller. Another word that we use interchangeably with variance is volatility. Iomega is said to be a more volatile stock than IBM because the probability distribution from which its rates of return are drawn has a greater variance than IBM's. Because we assume that most individuals are risk-averse, we also assume that most people will pay a premium to reduce variance. Individuals and firms might wish to use derivatives to reduce the variance of the outcomes they face when dealing with prices. Figure 2.2 compares the variance of the profit on a transaction if the price risk is unhedged, to the variance of a transaction's profit if price risk is hedged.[6]

In this book, the standard deviation will often be used to measure risk. This is not to say that standard deviation is the *only* definition of risk. For many individuals and firms, other risk measures are more relevant. For example, many people regard risk as the probability of losing money (the probability of realizing a rate of return less than zero). More generally, they may regard risk as the probability that the rate of return or price is below some critical value a: $\Pr(\tilde{r} < a)$. Others might focus only on the worst possible outcome. The semivariance might be what yet others concentrate on, since only outcomes below the expected value are regarded as being undesirable. The semivariance of a probability distribution is its variance measured only over outcomes that are less than the expected value. If the probability distribution is symmetric, like the normal distribution, then the semivariance and the variance measure risk in identical ways.

The third moment of a probability distribution is its skewness, which arises when the probability distribution is asymmetric.[7] Rather than presenting a formula for skewness, we will illustrate it with a sketch. Figure 2.3a depicts positive skew, and Fig. 2.3b shows negative skew. If the random variable is something desired, such as the rate of return on an asset, then skewness will also be desired, and investors will be willing to pay for positive skew. The purchase of insurance creates a positively skewed outcome, since the downside is truncated at some minimum amount, while the upside still exists.

2.2.2 Measuring Risk Using Past Data

Is the price of oil any more risky than the price of gold? Are short-term interest rates more uncertain (i.e., more volatile) than long-term interest rates?

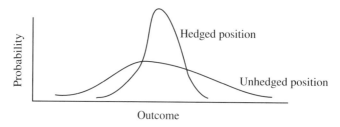

Figure 2.2 The probability distributions for an unhedged and a hedged transaction.

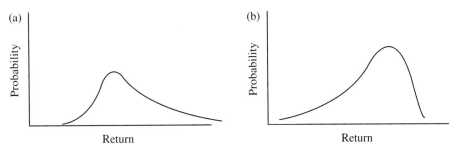

Figure 2.3 (*a*) Positively skewed random variable. (*b*) Negatively skewed random variable.

These questions cannot be precisely answered, although the finance discipline tries. In finance, we like to think that a future price, or a future rate of return, will be drawn out of a probability distribution. The distribution has a variance, and this parameter measures the risk, or uncertainty, regarding that price or rate of return. The greater the variance, the greater the risk. But this distribution is unobservable. Each of us might have a subjective idea of what this distribution is, but no one really knows. In addition, the distribution from which the outcome is drawn may be *time varying* (i.e., changing over time). For example, when interest rates are high and there is a great deal of risk in the stock market, the return on the market might be drawn from a distribution with an expected value of 15% and a standard deviation of 25%. When interest rates are low and stock market risk is low, the market return distribution might have an expected value of 10% and a standard deviation of 20%.

The field of statistics uses historical data to allow us to make inferences about the variance of the distribution from which future outcomes will be drawn. Assuming that past observations were independently drawn from the same (an identically distributed) probability distribution, we can use past data to estimate the mean and variance of the underlying distribution. By "independent" we mean that no outcome was affected by any previous outcomes and will not affect any future outcomes; the occurrence of any outcome does not affect the probability of past and future outcomes. By "identically distributed" we mean that the probability distribution from which the past observations were drawn has remained constant, and it will remain constant in the future. In other words, the expected value and variance have not changed over time.

Prices are *not* independent and identically distributed. The probability distribution from which IBM's historical stock prices were drawn almost certainly looked very different when shares were selling for $50 a piece and when they were selling for $150. It should be obvious, for example, that the means of the two price distributions were different. If today's price is $50, then the mean of the probability distribution from which tomorrow's price is drawn will be around $50. If today's price is $150, then the mean will be around $150. Also, daily prices are not independent. Tomorrow's stock price is very much dependent on today's stock price. Using past *price* data to estimate the variance of the probability distribution of next year's price (a random variable) is not advised.

However, changes in price and rates of return are much more likely to be independent and identically distributed. Thus, past data can be used to estimate the expected value and variance of a security's rate of return distribution. Past data on percentage changes in interest rates can be used to estimate the expected percentage change in interest rates, and the variance of the percentage change in interest rates.

If $\{r_1, r_2, \ldots, r_N\}$ represent N historical observations of the percentage change in some variable of interest, then the expected rate of return can be estimated using the sample mean $\bar{r}$:

$$\bar{r} = \frac{1}{N} \sum_{t=1}^{N} r_t$$

The sample variance is a good estimator of the variance of the distribution from which the percentage changes of the variable were drawn. The sample variance is denoted s^2, and it is computed by means of the following formula[8]:

$$s^2 = \frac{1}{N-1} \sum_{t=1}^{N} (r_t - \bar{r})^2$$

2.2.3 Identifying Risk Exposure

Firms will often hedge individual transactions that induce financial price risk into their business operations. For example, if Merck plans on borrowing €50 million (50 million euros) next year, it is exposed to the risk that euro interest rates will be higher when the company does raise those funds. The intended act of borrowing in the future is a planned individual transaction, and Merck can take steps to protect itself against that risk. Another example of a transaction occurs if Sony has just sold some electronic gear in the United States and will soon receive dollar-denominated receipts; Sony is then exposed to the risk that the value of those dollars, in terms of yen, will be lower in the future. Next year's interest rate for the euro currency, and the future ¥/$ exchange rate, are random variables that in each case will be drawn out of unique probability distributions.

A more advisable tactic is to analyze the firm's overall exposure to economic risks, that is, to measure the enterprise risk exposure. It is quite possible that at the same time one business unit is transacting in such a way that it is becoming exposed to the risk that the dollar price of yen will rise, another business unit is transacting so that it faces the risk that the yen will decline in value. Overall, the entire firm may be hedged. If each business unit separately hedges its exposure, the firm is just creating additional expenses for itself. Instead, a centralized risk management department can determine the firm's overall risk exposure and hedge only the residual risk that exists after such internal hedges have been identified. As another example, many diversified energy companies are internally hedged (partially) against fluctuations in the price of crude oil. If crude oil prices decline, the value of their oil production and reserves is lower. But if oil is also an input to the production of other goods the oil company manufactures, profit margins on these goods might widen if crude oil prices decline.

Besides being aware of all transactions, the overall firm has made and will make in the near future, risk managers must understand that the quantities of inputs the firm needs and outputs it sells may be a function of prices. Changing prices could affect planned capital expenditures, optimal transportation methods and costs, and purchasing, inventory, and distribution decisions. Finally, competitive pressures may also depend on prices, and these will create yet other impacts on profitability and value.

Thus, a firm should carefully assess the nature of its overall risk exposures. This is not an easy task. Even if it concludes that it is exposed, say, to the risk that interest rates will rise, the firm must also assess to what degree it is subjected to this risk. Will a 200-basis-point rise in interest rates cause the value of the firm's stock to decline (by 1%, 5%, …) or cause it to declare bankruptcy? In other words, the extent to which the firm is exposed to a price risk—that is, the set of consequences—is as important as merely determining that a risk exists.

A firm can use various approaches to determine its overall risk exposures. All these approaches try to estimate the relationship between changes in firm value or profits, and changes in prices. The first approach is to estimate previous historical cash flows. These will likely be quarterly figures, and they should be adjusted for any seasonal effects. The firm must decide which currency it should use when determining the amounts of these historical cash flows. Sometimes this is not obvious. For example, Shell Oil is a Dutch company that gets a substantial amount of its crude oil from British North Sea oil fields and sells much of its final product in the United States. Its common stock is listed and actively traded both in the Netherlands and in the United States; it is owned by investors in countries all over the world. Should it compute its cash flows in terms of Dutch guilders, U.S. dollars, or British pounds? The firm must decide the currency in which it wants to maximize profits and value.

Then, the firm can estimate the historical relationship between the changes in these cash flows and changes in the prices of the products to which they have risk exposure. To get a full understanding of the nature of its risk exposure, the firm should perform this analysis both on univariate and on several multivariate bases. For example, Shell may believe that it is exposed to the risk of changing short-term U.S. interest rates, to changing values of the $/£ exchange rate (the symbol £ is used to denote the British pound), and to changing crude oil prices. It will first determine historical quarterly changes in its dollar-denominated cash flows (denoted ΔCF), and quarterly changes in 90-day Eurodollar rates (Δr), the $/£ exchange rate ($\Delta £$), and the dollar price per barrel of crude oil (Δoil). Shell could then estimate the following regression models:

1. Univariate regressions
   a. $\Delta CF_t = a + b(\Delta r_t) + \varepsilon_t$
   b. $\Delta CF_t = a + b(\Delta £_t) + \varepsilon_t$
   c. $\Delta CF_t = a + b(\Delta \text{oil}_t) + \varepsilon_t$

2. Multivariate regressions
   a. $\Delta CF_t = a + b(\Delta r_t) + c(\Delta £_t) + \varepsilon_t$
   b. $\Delta CF_t = a + b(\Delta r_t) + c(\Delta \text{oil}_t) + \varepsilon_t$
   c. $\Delta CF_t = a + b(\Delta £_t) + c(\Delta \text{oil}_t) + \varepsilon_t$
   d. $\Delta CF_t = a + b(\Delta r_t) + c(\Delta £_t) + d(\Delta \text{oil}_t) + \varepsilon_t$

In these models, the regression intercept a is a constant. The regression slope coefficients b, c, and d each estimate the sensitivity of changes in the firm's cash flows to changes in prices. If the firm is truly exposed to the risk that the $/£ exchange rate will rise, then in models 1b, 2a, 2c, and 2d, the slope coefficients for the $\Delta £_t$ variable should be negative. A negative coefficient means that if the $/£ exchange rate rises, cash flows decline.

There are several drawbacks to this approach, starting with its focus on what has happened in the past. Firms change their assets and liabilities, change their product lines, and change where they import from and export to over time. Competition changes over time. All these changes effectively result in time-varying risk exposures, which means that the slope coefficients are not constant. And of course, no matter how accurate the estimation of *past* risk exposure, there is no guarantee that a firm's exposure will remain constant in the future. Next, the firm must be sure that the cash flows it estimates by using past data do not include the impact of any risk management activities it may have undertaken earlier; this may be difficult to determine. Perhaps even more important, the firm must be sure that it is dealing with actual cash flows, not accounting variables, whose creation reflects a great deal of discretionary decision making. Finally, historical cash flows may fluctuate because of factors other than interest rates, exchange rates, and crude oil prices. But because these factors were prominent in quarters during which one or more of the three risk variables changed, the regression models will conclude that cash flows are dependent on those risk variables.

Another similar approach to identifying risk exposure merely substitutes the percentage changes in the firm's stock price (rates of return) for ΔCF in the foregoing regression models. In other words, the firm will determine how investors regard the relationship between equity value and changes in these prices. If investors perceive that the firm is exposed to the risk that the \$/£ exchange rate will increase, then when one is estimating a model in which the stock's rate of return is the dependent variable and the \$/£ exchange rate is the independent variable, the slope coefficient should be negative. While it is useful, this approach hinges on investors' abilities to identify the firm's risk exposures accurately and to incorporate them into security prices.[9]

Finally, if the firm is not confident about the results obtained by using historical data, it can estimate its own model of how its cash flows are determined and use Monte Carlo simulation techniques to simulate the results of the model. Two sets of variables must be estimated. First, the firm must identify how a change in a price will likely affect its cash flows. An increase in interest rates might slow the economy, leading to a reduced level of sales. Also, interest expense will rise. Additionally, creditors might pay off their payables more slowly, and some may even default. Will higher interest rates in this country have a secondary effect on exchange rates and foreign competition and foreign suppliers? All the direct and indirect cash flow impacts of the change in interest rates must be identified and quantified. The second variable that must be identified is the probability distribution from which future interest rates will be drawn. Is it a uniform distribution, with roughly equal probabilities that interest rates will be between 3 and 7%? Or, is it a normal distribution or skewed distribution?

Once the effect of changing prices has been estimated, and a probability distribution for the price hypothesized, Monte Carlo simulation has the researcher randomly draw many, perhaps 10,000 or more, interest rates from the distribution. For each interest rate drawn, there is a predicted impact on the firm's cash flows. Thus, the firm obtains a probability distribution of future cash flows that are dependent on its exposure to the price risk being investigated. The firm can then take steps to modify its exposure if it believes that doing so is beneficial. It can alter its operations, or use derivatives, to manage its risk exposure.

The Monte Carlo approach is good because it is forward looking, and because it disciplines a firm into analyzing the nature of its business risks. The impact of changing prices on *all* the firm's activities can be estimated by using Monte Carlo simulation. But, the Monte Carlo approach suffers from the drawback that the individual setting up the model will often impose personal biases, consciously or unconsciously, on the model. This may ensure that some particular results reflecting these biases will be obtained.

In this section, we have not described every method to measure and manage risk. New methods to measure risk are constantly being introduced. As a result, it is impossible to discuss them all. However, after reading this section, you should have an understanding of the nature and importance of measuring risk.

2.3   SHOULD FIRMS MANAGE RISK?

Many observers would answer this question with a quick "Yes." After all, individuals are assumed to be risk-averse. This means that the firm's managers are risk-averse. Stockholders are risk-averse. And other stakeholders in the firm—employees, customers, suppliers, and so on—are risk-averse. So it would seem to make sense that taking steps to reduce risk would be an act desired by all concerned parties. A decline in the volatility of a firm's profits would appear to result in a lower cost of capital, a greater demand for the firm's shares, and a greater firm value.

On the other hand, some investors may prefer that the firm not hedge, so that they can capture all the profits, should some commodity price, interest rate, or currency price change in a forecasted direction. Suppose you were convinced that gold and oil prices were about to rise and decided to buy the shares of several gold producers and crude oil drilling firms. If you were right about the price increases, you would not be pleased to learn that these firms had hedged their production of gold and oil by selling gold and crude oil futures. What is the obligation of the firm to its stockholders in this case?

One of the most important results in all of finance is that when markets are perfect,[10] financial policy decisions such as the risk management decision do not affect firm value. One way of explaining this result is by asking a question: If stockholders can manage risk to fit their beliefs and level of risk aversion, why should they be willing to pay more for a firm that manages risk? The answer is that they shouldn't. If individuals can hedge, maybe firms should not.

It then follows that if corporate risk management is to increase the value of the firm, the reasons for the success of the venture must lie in market imperfections. In the following subsections, we briefly explain the factors that firms should consider before deciding to manage their exposure to financial price risk. The more applicable these reasons are, the more essential is a plan to manage risk.

2.3.1   Hedging Reduces the Expected Costs of Financial Distress

The value of the firm equals the present value of future expected cash flows that will be received by bondholders and stockholders. At each future date, there is some probability that the firm will default on its contractual debt obligations. In a perfect market, if the firm defaults, the creditors costlessly take control of the firm's assets with no disruptions. But in reality, if the firm defaults, there may be actual direct costs of bankruptcy that the firm will bear. These include additional legal and accounting expenses. In addition, the market may perceive an increasing bankruptcy probability long before the firm actually does declare itself insolvent. We call any additional costs that the firm bears before actual bankruptcy the *costs of financial distress*. In addition to added legal and accounting fees in these future states of financial distress (bankruptcy is the most extreme state of financial distress), there are other costs firms may face:

  a. Customers want a viable firm to stand by its product warranties. If customers believe the firm may not survive in the future, they will not be willing to buy its product.

  b. Suppliers may not be willing to extend trade credit. Instead, they may demand to be paid in full before providing the raw materials necessary to produce the firm's output.

  c. Employees will, all else equal, demand to be paid a premium before they agree to work for a firm in financial distress.

d. Firm management will be distracted by financial distress. Their time will be spent in less productive activities because they will be dealing with tasks that have arisen as a result of the firm's deteriorating financial condition.

e. Investment opportunities may be passed over if the firm is denied access to the capital required to fund them.

f. Losses can be carried back for tax purposes. But once the tax-loss carrybacks have been exhausted, they must be carried forward. This practice decreases firm value because the time value of the tax benefits of negative taxable income makes them more valuable, the sooner they are used. If the firm fails to return to profitability in the future, the tax benefits may be lost forever.

Risk management actions that reduce the variance of the firm's cash flows will reduce the likelihood of its experiencing financial distress, and therefore will reduce expected financial distress costs. Suppose that the firm has $X of future fixed financial obligations, including interest payments, bond principal payments, and lease payments. Failure to meet any of these contractual obligations will result in bankruptcy. Investors have beliefs about what the firm's cash flow distributions will be in future years. The probability that its future cash flow will be below X is directly related to the firm's financial distress costs. As shown in Figure 2.4, hedging reduces the probability that its cash flow will be less than X. Therefore, the firm's expected costs of financial distress will be less and firm value will be greater if it has hedged itself than if it has not. A very effective risk management program might reduce to zero the probability that the firm's cash flows will be less than X.

2.3.2   Hedging Makes It More Likely That Future Attractive Investments Will Be Made by the Firm

Theoretical models have demonstrated that firms may forego positive net present value (NPV) projects when the bondholders will realize most of the investments' benefits, and this is most likely to happen when firms are in financial distress. Firms may even have incentives to accept negative NPV projects that are very high risk, since when the risky project proves to be very profitable, the stockholders will benefit. As an unrealistic but illustrative example, suppose that the firm has $6 of

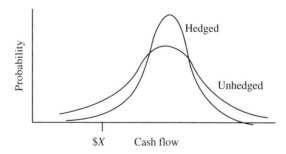

Figure 2.4 Probability distribution of the cash flows for a hedged and an unhedged firm. The firm's costs of financial distress are directly proportional to the probability that cash flow will be less than the firm's fixed financial obligation, which is $X. Pr(unhedged cash flow) <$X is greater than Pr(hedged cash flow) <$X. Thus, expected cash flows to bondholders and stockholders are greater for the hedged firm because of reduced expected costs of financial distress.

bond principal due to be repaid next year. Today, the firm has $3 to invest in one of two projects, which offer the following payoff distributions:

	Payoffs One Year Hence	
Probability	Project A	Project B
0.30	$5	$0
0.39	$5	$0
0.30	$5	$0
0.01	$5	$10

Even though project A is a positive net present value project at any discount rate less than 66.7%, and project B is almost certain to be a negative net present value at any discount rate, a firm whose investment decisions are made for the benefit of the stockholders will adopt project B. Why? Because by accepting project A, the firm would be forced to default no matter what the outcome; the bondholders would reap all the benefits of project A. At least if project B is accepted, there is a 1% chance that the stockholders will benefit, and will continue to control the firm's assets.

This unrealistic example illustrates the nature of the investing decision problem that arises when firms are in financial distress. A firm's stockholders will prefer that management "roll the dice," hoping for a favorable outcome from which they will profit. A firm in financial distress may invest in high risk, lower (and even negative) NPV projects. Bondholders recognize this before the fact and demand to be compensated for such risks. By hedging, these situations become less likely, and therefore the added interest costs of debt, and the possible failure to accept positive NPV projects, are averted.

Another model (Froot, Scharfstein, and Stein, 1993, 1994) that justifies risk management activities is based on the argument that internally generated funds are cheaper than any source of external capital. When future cash flows are unexpectedly low, firms may even be denied access to the capital markets (i.e., the cost of external capital then becomes infinite), and therefore fail to make new investments. By reducing the variance of future cash flows, risk management makes it less likely that the firm will be forced to try to raise costly external capital; that is, it increases the probability that the firm will always have sufficient internally generated cash flow to fund new investments.

2.3.3 It Is Less Costly for the Firm to Hedge Than for Individuals to Hedge

Trading commissions and collateral requirements for using derivatives will likely be less for firms than for individual investors. Indeed, many investors do not have access to many of the risk management tools (e.g., swaps) available to large firms. Many investors are unsophisticated and do not know how to hedge.

2.3.4 Firms May Have Better Information Than Individuals

It is unlikely that any firm, government body, financial institution, or individual can predict future interest rates or currency prices very well. However, when it comes to product prices, some firms may very well have information that is superior to individuals' information. For example, the Hershey Food Corporation probably has better information than most about the future supply of cocoa, and therefore should be skilled at managing this product price risk. Oil companies also have more accurate data about crude oil inventories, production, and demand than parties not involved in energy on a daily basis.

In addition, firms likely have a better conception than individual investors of what their risk exposures to all financial prices (including interest rates and foreign exchange) are. Certainly, they know the risks generated by individual transactions; investors have no access to information about individual firm transactions. For example, suppose a firm's managers know that debt will have to be issued 6 months hence. The firm can hedge against the risk that interest rates will be higher. Individuals will not be privy to the firm's future financing plans.

2.3.5　Nonsystematic Risks Should Be Hedged When Owners Are Not Well Diversified

The finance discipline often dichotomizes risk into a systematic portion and a nonsystematic portion. Investors are compensated (in the form of a higher expected rate of return) for bearing systematic risk. But because rational investors diversify, they are not compensated for bearing nonsystematic risk. For example, an investor can effectively hedge against a decline in the value of the dollar by investing in exporters who benefit from a weaker dollar, that is, those based in the United States. Portfolio diversification is certainly cheaper than having each firm hedge its own risk exposure (ignoring all the other reasons for hedging that are presented in this section). Each investor can use his or her own set of beliefs and degree of risk aversion to make the hedging decision.

However, if a firm is owned by a small group of investors, each of whom has a substantial amount of personal wealth in the form of that company's stock, it might be beneficial for that closely held firm to hedge its risk exposure, even though that risk is nonsystematic (diversifiable).

2.3.6　Hedging Can Increase Debt Capacity

If a firm's risk management activities increase the amount of debt it is able to issue, then it has increased the present value of its interest tax shields and increased firm value. Also, some lenders will lower the interest rate it charges a firm if it has hedged.

2.3.7　Risk Management Can Reduce Taxes

One effect of risk management on taxes has already been mentioned. By reducing the likelihood of future years in which negative taxable income is earned, hedging reduces the probability that a firm will be forced to carry tax losses forward. When tax losses are carried forward, their time value is lost.

But even beyond the lost time value, hedging increases average net income and cash flow because of the tax code. Items that create tax shields are lost if taxable income is too low. For example, interest expense and depreciation expense generate tax shields. The interest tax shield in a year equals $t \times$ int, where t is the firm's marginal tax rate and int is its interest expense. The depreciation tax shield equals $t \times$ dep, where dep is the firm's depreciation expense. By maintaining these tax shields, hedging increases firm value by both increasing average reported net income and actual average cash flow. This is illustrated in Table 2.1.

In Table 2.1, an unhedged firm faces a 50% chance that it will be profitable in any year, and a 50% chance that it will not be profitable. Profitability is measured by earnings before interest,

TABLE 2.1 How Expected Net Income and Expected Net Cash Flow Are Higher When the Firm Is Hedged than When It Is Not Hedged

	Unhedged Scenario		Hedged Scenario	
	Growth	Recession	Growth	Recession
Probability	50%	50%	50%	50%
Gross profit	300	0	150	150
− Depreciation expense	− 80	− 80	− 80	− 80
− Interest expense	−20	−20	−20	−20
Taxable income	200	− 100	50	50
− Taxes (30%)	−60	0	−15	−15
Net income	140	− 100	35	35
Net cash flow	220	− 20	115	115
Expected net income	20		35	
Expected net cash flow	100		115	

depreciation, and taxes (EBIDT). If the firm is profitable, its EBIDT will equal $300. If it is not profitable, its EBIDT will be zero. Profitability is determined by the state of the economy (recession or growth).

By hedging its operations against some price risk, such as energy costs, the firm will lock in its average EBIDT of $150 [($300+$0)/2=$150].

Interest expense and depreciation expense are deducted from EBIDT to compute taxable income. Subtract the taxes due, 30% of taxable income, and we obtain net income. Cash flow in this simple world is defined to equal net income plus depreciation. The example in Table 2.1 shows that average net income and average cash flow are greater when the firm is hedged than when it is not. If the hedged firm's average cash flow is discounted at the same or lower discount rate,[11] then we can conclude that hedging increases the value of the firm. If the market applies the same or higher price–earnings multiple to the hedged firm's average earnings per share, then again we must conclude that hedging increases the value of the firm's common stock.

The source of these conclusions lies in the nature of the tax code. The example presented in Table 2.1 assumes no tax rebates. Note that if the firm was supplied with a $30 tax rebate in the event that taxable income is –$100 (this is the taxable income in the unhedged/recession scenario), expected net income and expected cash flow would be the same regardless of whether the firm is hedged. This would be the case if the tax loss could be carried back.

Another model exists to illustrate how hedging reduces taxes. It rests on the assumption that the tax schedule is convex. A convex tax schedule is one in which the average tax rate increases at an increasing rate as taxable income increases. This is illustrated in Figure 2.5.

The following tax table creates a convex tax schedule:

Taxable Income	Tax Rate
<$100,000	0
$100,000–$200,000	5% on amount>$100,000

$200,000–$300,000	$5,000 + 15\% on amount > $200,000
$300,000–$400,000	$20,000 + 30\% on amount > $300,000
> $400,000	$50,000 + 50\% on amount > $400,000

Table 2.2 illustrates how this convex tax schedule makes hedging valuable by reducing the average taxes the firm must pay. If the firm is unhedged, then in each year there is a 50% chance that its taxable income will either be $150,000 or $450,000. Given the foregoing convex tax schedule, the firm will pay $38,750 per year in taxes on average. But if the firm can hedge so that its taxable income every year is the average of its unhedged yearly taxable income (i.e., $300,000 with certainty), it will pay only $20,000 per year in taxes every year. Thus, when the tax schedule is convex, hedging can reduce the firm's average taxes.

The next question to ask is obvious: Is the U.S. tax schedule (or any other country's) convex? The answer is not so obvious. Merely examining marginal or average tax rates that apply to different levels of taxable income is not sufficient to permit a conclusion because items such as tax loss carryforwards, investment tax credits, and the alternate minimum tax (AMT) provision can induce convexity in tax schedules. The degree of convexity in tax schedules in the United States is subject to debate, and many models suggest that greater convexity exists than is evident by simply viewing average tax rates. Convexity may exist for some firms and not for others.

2.3.8 Risk-Averse Managers Will Prefer to Hedge

Suppose we argue that stockholders should be indifferent to the firm's hedging decision. We might still conclude the firms will hedge because their managers are risk-averse. They have a substantial

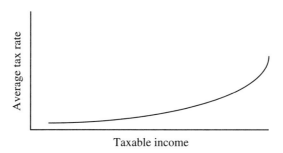

Figure 2.5 A convex tax schedule.

TABLE 2.2 How Hedging Is Valuable When the Tax Schedule Is Convex

Probability	Taxable Income	Taxes
Unhedged		
0.5	$150,000	$2,500
0.5	$450,000	$75,000
	Expected taxes:	$38,750
Hedged		
1	$300,000	$20,000

amount of human capital and wealth invested in their firms. A bad draw from the probability distribution of the firm's operating income might result in a reduction of their pay or in their being fired. In fact, the bad draw might even be due to factors beyond their control. All their prior decisions might have been "correct" given all available information that was available at the time. But totally unpredictable events might subsequently occur that could lead stockholders to replace the firm's management. Some of management's actions might result in lower profits in the short term, but higher profits in the future. It would be unfortunate if managers failed to make these good decisions because of the possible impact of short-term results on their employment.

Thus, all else equal, we can conclude that managers will often prefer to hedge their firm's activities because of their own risk aversion. If a firm's owners are indifferent about the managers' risk management activities, the firm should hedge. Even if the firm's owners don't want the firm to hedge, they should think of any risk management activities that risk-averse managers undertake as a different form of compensation because the owners are bearing excessive amounts of firm-specific risk.

2.3.9 Other Reasons for Using Derivatives

Sections 2.3.1–2.3.8 explained why firms should manage their risk exposures. Now we add some other reasons, not based on risk management, that will enter a firm's decision to use derivatives.

Derivatives can be used to lower interest costs. Later, we will demonstrate that by issuing bonds denominated in a foreign currency and also entering into a swap in which it pays dollars and receives the foreign currency, a firm may have a lower interest expense than would have obtained if it had issued dollar-denominated debt only. A firm that desires fixed-rate debt may find it cheaper to issue floating-rate debt and engage in a swap so that it creates synthetic fixed-rate debt.

Derivatives are useful because they give the firm flexibility. By using derivatives, firms can alter their assets and liabilities, and their revenues and expenses, more quickly and with less cost than is possible by dealing with actual assets and liabilities.

Arbitrage profits can be earned by some firms when they perceive mispricing in different derivative markets.

Finally, some firms and institutions wish to accept some price risks. Another word for this is *speculation*. Derivative contracts are low cost, liquid conduits for price speculation. Unfortunately, some firms have not had adequate controls on some of their employees, who proceeded to incur staggering losses by speculating with derivatives. But many other firms have successfully speculated, and their activities are useful to society in that they are willing and able to bear these risks. Remember that if one firm is bearing these risks, it is quite possible that some other party has shed itself of them.

2.4 WHAT SHOULD BE DONE AFTER RISK EXPOSURES HAVE BEEN IDENTIFIED?

Other decisions remain even after a firm's managers have estimated how and to what extent their company's value is impacted by changing prices.[12]

One important decision that upper management must make is whether the risk management group should be allowed to speculate by selectively hedging the firm's exposures, or whether the goal is to always minimize the firm's risk exposure by maintaining a continuously hedged position.

In the first case, risk management activities will be undertaken only when it is forecast that prices will move in an adverse manner. The firm would then be unhedged when the forecast is that price changes will increase firm value and profits. Most firms selectively hedge their risk exposures (see Dolde, 1993).

Selectively hedging risk exposures is tantamount to speculation. Imagine a selective hedger who is long a cash asset and is always wrong about forecasted price movements. Whenever he believes prices will rise, he maintains an unhedged long position in the cash asset. But prices always subsequently fall. Whenever he believes that the value of his spot position is going to decline, he hedges with the sale of futures contracts. Inevitably, however, prices subsequently rise, and the gains on the cash asset are offset by losses in the futures market. This selective hedger will not have much in the way of assets before long!

A selective hedger should always monitor his performance against two benchmarks: a continuously hedged position and an unhedged position. If markets are efficient, then after accounting for transactions costs and the time needed to analyze market conditions, the selective hedger probably will underperform the continuous hedger, unless the selective hedger has exceptional skills at forecasting future prices.

Brown, Crabb, and Haushalter (2001) analyze the risk management policies of 48 firms from three different industries. They conclude that these firms practice selective hedging, but that few are successful, and any gains are quite small.

Management must be sure to supply sufficient resources to create a knowledgeable and well-trained risk management group. Objectives must be clearly defined. Price data must be supplied. Record-keeping systems must be purchased. Internal controls must be put into place. Performance must be monitored. As part of implementing the risk management plan, guidelines must be established for deciding which tools to use. One method of hedging involves the use of the spot market. These acts, which might be called operational hedges, require that the firm create spot, or physical, assets and liabilities to hedge. For example, many Japanese auto manufacturers built plants in the United States to be able to hedge against the risk of a decline in the yen value of the U.S. dollar. Alternatively, the firm will use the derivative contracts described in Chapter 1.

2.5   ACCOUNTING FOR DERIVATIVES: FAS 133

The rules that define the accounting conventions for derivatives positions are complex. Different rules apply, depending on the purpose of the derivatives. The general practice for traders (speculators) and market makers is to mark all derivatives to market at the end of the accounting period. All profits and losses, regardless of whether they are realized or unrealized, are included in a firm's income statement, if the derivatives are not used for hedging.

On June 15, 1998, the Financial Accounting Standards Board (FASB) issued Financial Accounting Standard No. 133, "Accounting for Derivative Instruments and Hedging Activities" (FAS 133). FAS 133 has applied to all firms that use derivatives for hedging since the accounting period beginning after June 15, 2000. Firms were permitted to adopt the new rule as early as July 1, 1998.

FAS 133 establishes three new classifications of hedges, each with its own accounting treatment. Hedge accounting for derivatives applies only if the hedge meets the definition of one of these three categories. Moreover, procedures must be in place to document and determine the effectiveness of the hedge. The three classifications are as follows.

- **Fair value hedges** exist when the derivatives are used to hedge the risk resulting from changes in the value of an asset, liability, or unrecognized firm commitment (a binding agreement to enter into a transaction with an unrelated party). Both the derivative and the item being hedged are marked to market, and the changes in the value of both are recognized in the firm's net income. If the hedge is effective, the change in the gain (loss) in the value of the derivative will equal the loss (gain) in the value of the item being hedged; then, there will be no net impact on the firm's earnings. A firm that synthetically converts a fixed-rate liability into a variable-rate liability through an interest rate swap is creating a fair value hedge. Another fair value hedge is created when a firm that uses interest rate futures contracts to hedge changes in the value of a fixed-rate debt instrument that is available for sale.

- **Cash flow hedges** are used to hedge forecasted transactions. Firms face risks from changes in the amount of future cash flows that will emerge from recognized assets and liabilities (e.g., interest payments on floating-rate debt or interest income on loans) or forecasted transactions. The key is that the prospective cash flow is uncertain. If the specified criteria for a cash flow hedge are met, an institution can use a derivative to try to "lock in" the amount of a future cash inflow or outflow. Using an interest rate swap to synthetically convert the interest payments on a variable-rate loan to a fixed amount is an example of a cash flow hedge; using a forward rate agreement (FRA) to lock in the interest rate on the forecasted issuance of fixed-rate debt is another. The derivative results must be separated into "effective" and "ineffective" parts. The effective portion of the change in fair value of the derivative is initially recognized in a separate component of equity called "other comprehensive income." Then, in the period during which the forecasted cash flow affects earnings, the effective portion is reclassified as income. The ineffective portion of the hedge is reported in earnings (current income).

- **Foreign currency hedges** protect a firm from the risk resulting from changes in foreign currency values. FAS 133 also defines these as "net investment hedges," which apply to the net investment in a foreign operation. If specified criteria are met, a firm can use derivatives in a foreign currency fair value hedge or cash flow hedge. A firm that uses derivatives to "lock in" the U.S. dollar cost of a foreign currency transaction would be considered to be creating a "foreign currency" hedge. Or, a firm might use a forward contract to hedge the amount of a cash outflow on an anticipated foreign currency–denominated transaction, or purchase a put option to hedge changes in the fair value of a foreign currency–denominated debt security (an asset). The accounting for a foreign currency hedge depends on the transaction, but its treatment will be similar to that of either a fair value hedge or a cash flow hedge.

It is important to recognize that firms are required to establish the effectiveness of derivative hedges. Firms must measure and monitor performance at least quarterly. Knowledge of statistics is essential to accomplish this. Also, derivative hedge transactions must be documented when they first occur. FAS 133 is a very complicated document. Consult an expert before you venture into hedge accounting with derivatives. A website devoted to helping treasurers, risk managers, accountants, and others understand and implement FAS 133 is www.fas133.com/.

It is no secret that neither firms nor investors like earnings volatility. Both prefer steadily increasing earnings that are predictable. The rules that dictate how firms must account for their transactions with derivatives do affect their income statements. These rules affect firms' decisions whether to hedge. If they do hedge, they affect the decision about how to manage risk. It is unfortunate that what should be a rational decision based on economic reality often becomes a poor decision made for cosmetic accounting reasons. In other words, accounting rules affect risk management decisions.

2.6 SUMMARY

This chapter provides an overview of the nature of risk. In this chapter, we focus on the questions of what risk is, how risk is measured, how risk exposure can be determined, and the factors that should induce firms to manage risk.

Risk exists because the future is uncertain. In finance, uncertain future outcomes such as prices and rates of return are called random variables; random variables are characterized by lists of possible outcomes and their associated probabilities. The variance, or standard deviation, of the distribution from which prices or rates of returns are drawn measures the risk of that variable. The greater the variance, the greater the risk or uncertainty about what the outcome will be. In this chapter, we reviewed the computation of the variance of a random variable and explained how historical data can be used to estimate risk.

It is important for a firm to ascertain its risk exposures to different prices. One approach is to estimate the historical relationship between the firm's cash flows, or the rate of return on its common stock, to changes in key commodity prices, interest rates, and prices of currencies. The other method requires the use of Monte Carlo simulation to gain knowledge about how the firm's cash flows will be related to future changes in financial prices.

The key reasons that firms should manage risk are as follows: to reduce the level of expected financial distress costs, to maintain an optimal real investment strategy, to exploit superior information about prices (commodity prices in particular, since no firm should be arrogant enough to believe that its has superior information about future interest rates or foreign exchange rates), to hedge the concentrated investment of the firm's owners in the firm's common stock, to reduce expected taxes, and because management is risk-averse.

FAS 133 has applied to all firms that use derivatives for hedging since June 15, 2000. FAS 133 defines how firms must account for their derivatives transactions that are undertaken to manage risk. These rules result in an impact on earnings. Firms that are concerned about their earnings will let accounting rules affect their risk management decisions.

Further Reading

Some key articles that identify market imperfections that provide risk management incentives are as follows,
    See also Froot, Scharfstein, and Stein (1993, 1994).
Bessembinder, H. 1991. "Forward Contracts and Firm Value: Investment Incentive and Contracting Effects."
    Journal of Financial and Quantitative Analysis, Vol. 26, December, pp. 519–532.
Breeden, Douglas, and S. Viswanathan. 1996. "Why Do Firms Hedge: An Asymmetric Information Model."
    Unpublished working paper.
DeMarzo, Peter, and Darrell Duffie. 1995. "Corporate Incentives for Hedging and Hedge Accounting."
    Review of Financial Studies, Vol. 8, pp. 743–772.

Fite, David, and Paul Pfleiderer. 1995. "Should Firms Use Derivatives to Manage Risk?" In *Risk Management: Problems and Solutions*, William H. Beaver and George Parker, eds. New York: McGraw-Hill.

Gay, Gerald D., and Jouahn Nam. 1998. "The Underinvestment Problem and Corporate Derivatives Use." *Financial Management*, Vol. 27, No. 4, Winter, pp. 53–69.

Lessard, Donald R. 1990. "Global Competition and Corporate Finance in the 1990s." *Journal of Applied Corporate Finance*, Vol. 3, pp. 59–72.

Nance, D.R., Clifford W. Smith, and René Stulz. 1993. "On the Determinants of Corporate Hedging." *Journal of Finance*, Vol. 48, March, pp. 267–284.

Smith, Clifford W., and René Stulz. 1985. "The Determinants of Firms' Hedging Policies." *Journal of Financial and Quantitative Analysis*, Vol. 20, December, pp. 391–405.

Stulz, René. 1984. "Optimal Hedging Policies." *Journal of Financial and Quantitative Analysis*, Vol. 19, June, pp. 127–140.

Stulz, René. 1990. "Managerial Discretion and Optimal Financing Policies." *Journal of Financial Economics*, Vol. 26, pp. 3–28.

Several articles have examined the actual nature of firms' risk management activities. Some recent examples are as follows. See also Bodnar, Hayt, and Marston (1998) and Dolde (1993).

Berkman, Henk, and Michael E. Bradbury. 1996. "Empirical Evidence on the Corporate Use of Derivatives." *Financial Management*, Vol. 25, No. 2, Summer, pp. 5–13.

Bodnar, G. M., G. S. Hayt, R. C. Marston, and C.W. Smithson. 1995. "Wharton Survey of Derivatives Usage by U.S. Non-Financial Firms." *Financial Management*, Vol. 24, Summer, pp. 104–114.

Bodnar, G. M., G. S. Hayt, R. C. Marston, and C. W. Smithson. 1996. "Wharton Survey of Derivatives Usage by U.S. Non-Financial Firms." *Financial Management*, Vol. 25, Winter, pp. 113–133.

Howtan, Shawn D., and Steven B. Perfect. 1998. "Currency and Interest-Rate Derivatives Use in U.S. Firms." *Financial Management*, Vol. 27, No. 4, Winter, pp. 111–121.

Koski, Jennifer Lynch, and Jeffrey Pontiff. 1999. "How Are Derivatives Used? Evidence from the Mutual Fund Industry." *Journal of Finance*, Vol. 54, No. 2, April, pp. 791–816.

Mian, Shehzad L. 1996. "Evidence on Corporate Hedging Policy." *Journal of Financial and Quantitative Analysis*, Vol. 31, September, pp. 419–439.

Nance, Deana, Clifford W. Smith, and Charles W. Smithson. 1993. "On the Determinants of Corporate Hedging." *Journal of Finance*, Vol. 48, March, pp. 267–284.

Phillips, A. L. 1995. "Derivatives Practices and Instruments Survey." *Financial Management*, Summer, pp. 115–125.

Tufano, Peter. 1996. "Who Manages Risk? An Empirical Examination of Risk Management Practices in the Gold Mining Industry." *Journal of Finance*, Vol. 51, No. 4, September, pp. 1097–1138.

References

Bauman, Joseph, Steve Saratore, and William Liddle. 1994. "A Practical Framework for Corporate Exposure Management." *Journal of Applied Corporate Finance*, Vol. 7, No. 3, Fall, pp. 66–72.

Brown, Gregory W., Peter R. Crabb, and David Itaushalter. 2001. "Are Firms Successful at 'Selective' Hedging?" Working Paper. The University of North Carolina at Chapel Hill.

Bodnar, G. M., G. S. Hayt, and R. C. Marston. 1998. "1998 Wharton Survey of Derivatives Usage by U.S. Non-Financial Firms." *Financial Management*, Vol. 27, No. 4, Winter, pp. 70–91.

Dolde, Walter. 1993. "The Trajectory of Corporate Financial Risk Management." *Journal of Applied Corporate Finance*, Vol. 6, Fall, pp. 33–41.

Esty, Ben, Peter Tufano, and Jonathan Headley. 1994. "Banc One Corporation: Asset and Liability Manage-
    ment." *Journal of Applied Corporate Finance*, Vol. 7, No. 3, Fall, pp. 33–65.
Froot, Kenneth A., David S. Scharfstein, and Jeremy C. Stein. 1993. "Risk Management: Coordinating
    Corporate Investment and Financing Policies." *Journal of Finance*, Vol. 48, December, pp.
    1629–1658.
Froot, Kenneth A., David S. Scharfstein, and Jeremy C. Stein. 1994. "A Framework for Risk Management."
    Journal of Applied Corporate Finance, Vol. 7, No. 3, Fall, pp. 22–32.

Notes

[1]There are many websites devoted to financial engineering and enterprise risk management. Any search engine will turn up hundreds. Some good starting points are www.garp.com, the home page of the Global Association of Risk Professionals (GARP), www.margrabe.com/, the online magazine about derivatives, the search engine at www.financewise.com/, and www.erisks.com/, the homepage for Erisk.

[2]Indeed, a change in the output price will likely affect the quantity that a firm sells.

[3]Some companies now sell weather derivatives, which offer payoffs that are contingent on the weather (rainfall amount, temperatre, etc.).

[4]Interest rates are prices, too. An interest rate is the price of current consumption. By consuming today, an individual is foregoing future consumption, since anything spent today cannot be invested to earn interest, thereby providing more (at least in nominal terms) consumption at a later date.

[5]A tilde (~) above a symbol identifies it as a random variable.

[6]Diversification is another method of reducing risk. If the risks possessed by different assets are not correlated, then combining the assets will create a portfolio effect in which variance and standard deviation are reduced.

[7]Note that because it is symmetric, the normal distribution is not skewed.

[8]Frequently, we use another formula for variance, which is known as the maximum likelihood estimator:

$$\frac{1}{N}\sum_{t=1}^{N}(r_t - \bar{r})^2$$

[9]The Postscript to the Banc One Corporation case by Esty, Tufano, and Headley (1994) suggests that corporate managements may have to educate investors about their firms' risk exposures before stock prices begin to reflect those risks.

[10]A perfect capital market is one in which there are no transaction costs (commissions or bid–ask spreads), there are no taxes, there are no costs of financial distress or bankruptcy, individuals cannot affect prices by their trades, and all market participants, including investors and firms, have equal access to information. It is also important to assume that the investment decision has already been determined, and will not be affected by the firm's decision to hedge or not to hedge.

[11]We will not dwell upon the issue of what determines or defines that discount rate, but it could be argued that the discount rate that should be applied to the hedged firm's expected cash flow stream is equal to or lower than the one applied to the unhedged firm's expected cash flows.

[12]See Bauman, Saratore, and Liddle (1994) for a description of a four-step procedure that can establish a corporate risk management framework, including identifying its exposures, formulating management, planning, and policy decisions, implementing policy, and establishing the proper controls and evaluation methods.

PROBLEMS

2.1 What is financial price risk?

2.2 Discuss the factors that induce firms to undertake risk management activities.

2.3 How might a law that changes the tax code to a "flat tax" affect firms' hedging decisions?

2.4 A firm currently sells 1000 gold rings each year. Is it exposed to the risk that gold prices will rise or fall? Compare the nature of its hedging decision (a) if it assumes that demand for its rings is unaffected by changes in the price of gold, and (b) if it believes that demand for its rings is elastic.

2.5 Estimate the expected value, the variance, and the standard deviation for the following random variables.

Price	Probability
$40	0.22
$50	0.58
$60	0.12
$70	0.08

2.6 An energy production firm is trying to decide whether to hedge. It feels that its greatest source of risk exposure lies in whether significant new crude oil discoveries will or will not be made next year. It believes that if none are made, energy prices will rise at a rate of 40%/year for the following two years, and annual earnings before interest, depreciation, and taxes (EBIDT) will be $70 million. But if new discoveries are made, prices will be flat, and EBIDT will be $8 million. The probability that new discoveries will be made is 30%. Interest expense will be $5 million, and depreciation expense will be $12 million. The tax rate is 40%. Compute the firm's expected net income and expected cash flow. Compute the variance of its net income.

Now suppose that if the firm hedges its exposure to changes in crude oil prices, it can reduce the uncertainty about its future EBIDT. Hedging would indicate the belief that if there is no new oil to be discovered, EBIDT will be $55 million; but if there are new discoveries, EBIDT will be $43 million. Compute the firm's expected net income and expected cash flow. Compute the variance of its net income.

2.7 Variance and standard deviation are often criticized as risk measures because they incorporate both downside risk and upside "risk." Discuss this criticism.

2.8 Discuss three ways by which a firm can identify its exposure to different price risks. Identify one good aspect and one drawback for each approach.

2.9 Firms should manage their financial risk exposure for many reasons. Which one of the following is *not* a reason:

   a. To increase the firm's cost of capital

   b. To lower taxes

   c. To reduce the costs of financial distress

   d. To increase debt capacity

   e. To increase the likelihood that the firm will adopt good investment projects in the future

2.10 Central tendency, dispersion, and symmetry can be used to describe a probability distribution. Which of the following alternatives offer correct terms to describe each of these attributes?

Central Tendency	Dispersion	Symmetry
a. mean	median	skewness
b. variance	standard deviation	correlation
c. mean	standard deviation	skewness
d. median	variance	correlation
e. mean	skewness	correlation

2.11   Which one of the following tools can be used to measure or identify a firm's risk exposure to changing interest rates?

    a. Estimating a regression model with the change in interest rates as the dependent variable and the rate of return on the market as the independent variable, as in

$$\Delta(\text{int rate}_t) = a + b\ \Delta\text{RMKT}_t + \varepsilon_t$$

    b. Estimating the firm's beta.

    c. Using Monte Carlo simulation.

    d. Determining the firm's debt capacity.

    e. Determining whether the firm practices selective hedging or continuous hedging.

2.12   There are many reasons for a firm to manage its financial risk exposure. Which of the following is **not** a reason:

    a. Risk management can increase the amount of funds that the firm can borrow.

    b. Risk management can lead a firm to accept good investment projects.

    c. Risk management should be performed by firms when they (the firms) have better information than individuals.

    d. Risk management is beneficial when the firm's owners have a substantial amount of their own wealth invested in the firm.

    e. Risk management can increase taxes when the tax schedule is convex.

A Project

    a. Select a publicly traded firm (preferably a large one), obtain its most recent annual report, and determine whether the firm does business in a foreign country (either as an importer or as an exporter or has foreign-based manufacturing facilities). Also determine whether it has exposure to any commodity prices. Try to predict the direction of the risk exposure (e.g., Eastman Kodak might be exposed to the risk that silver prices will rise because silver is a key input to its products, to the risk that the Japanese yen will decline in value because this would help its Japanese-based competitors export to the United States, and to the risk of rising interest rates because it has a great deal of floating-rate debt outstanding).

    b. Obtain 36 months of the stock's historical rates of return, changes in short-term and/or long-term interest rates, percentage changes in the prices of the foreign currency to which it seems to be most exposed, and percentage changes in the commodity price to which it seems to be most exposed.

    c. Define r_i as the rate of return on the stock, int as the interest rate, fx as the currency to which it is most exposed to risk, comm as the commodity price to which it is most exposed to risk, and r_m as the rate of return on a broad market index such as the S&P 500 or the Wilshire 5000. Estimate the following regression model using the 36 months of historical data:

$$r_i = b_0 + b_1\Delta\,\text{int} + b_2\%\Delta fx$$
$$+ b_3\%\Delta\text{comm} + b_4 r_m + \varepsilon$$

Interpret the meaning of your estimated regression coefficients.

There is no guarantee that your estimated slope coefficients will confirm your predictions, for several reasons. The firm may be managing its risk exposure. Its risk exposures two and three years ago may have differed from last year's level. The magnitude of its risk exposures may be small. Its risk exposures may be systematic (part of market risk) and picked up in the estimated b_4 coefficient. The impact of changing prices may be reflected in the firm's stock price with a delay.

PART 2

FORWARD CONTRACTS AND FUTURES CONTRACTS

CHAPTER 3

Introduction to Forward Contracts

The forward contract is the most basic derivative contract. A forward contract is an agreement to buy or sell something in the future. The agreement is made today to exchange cash for a good or service at a later date. This differs from a spot transaction, which is the usual way of buying or selling something. In a spot transaction, one party pays for a good or service, and immediately receives that good or service.

This chapter first describes the general concepts of forward contracts. Then, greater details are presented concerning two types of forward contract that are prevalent in modern business operations and are used to manage financial price risk: the forward rate agreement (FRA), which is an arrangement to borrow or lend money at a future date at an agreed upon interest rate, and the forward foreign exchange contract, in which a party agrees to buy or sell an amount of a foreign currency at a future date.

3.1 GENERAL CONCEPTS

When a forward contract is created, there must always be two parties: the buyer and the seller. The buyer of a forward contract agrees to buy something in the future. The buyer is also said to have a long position, or be long the forward contract. The seller of a forward contract has the obligation to sell something in the future, and is said to have a short position.

The terms of the contract are agreed upon today, and delivery and payment take place in the future, at what is called either the **delivery date**, the **settlement date**, or the **maturity date** of the contract. The buyer has agreed to take delivery and the seller has agreed to make delivery.

Money rarely changes hands when a forward contract is originated (unless one or both of the parties demands "good faith" money to serve as collateral that backs up the obligations stated in the contract). Payment from the buyer of the forward contract to the seller is generally made only upon the delivery of the good.

Most business transactions are actually forward transactions. A firm might order 10,000 widgets from another firm. The price is agreed upon today. No cash flows occur today. The widgets will be delivered one month hence. Payment is not made until after the widgets have been received. For all practical purposes, this is a forward contract.

The failure of a party to do what has been agreed to, as stated in the contract, is known as default. On the day that a forward contract is originated, both parties face potential **default risk**, the most extreme form of **credit risk**, which describes the future uncertainty concerning the other party's ability and/or willingness to fulfill the terms of the contract.[1] For most everyday forward transactions we enter into, there are no penalties for defaulting. If you fail to show up at a restaurant at which you have made a reservation, it is extremely rare that you will be sued or forced to pay for the meal that you promised to, but did not, consume.[2] Penalties for failing to fulfill the terms of forward contracts vary, however, and in business default is a serious matter that will likely lead to legal action.

We are interested in forward contracts to buy or sell a specific good on a specific future date, at a specific price. This price is called the **forward price**. Thus, a firm may agree today to buy 100,000 barrels (bbl) of oil 6 months hence, at $31/bbl. The forward price is $31/bbl. The forward price will likely differ from the **spot price**, which is today's price for delivery of oil today. There may be many forward prices, one for each possible delivery date. For example, the forward price for delivery 9 months hence may be $32/bbl. Forward prices for most physical commodities will also depend on the delivery location; the forward price for delivering crude oil to a site in Maine will almost certainly be higher than the price for delivery that takes place in Texas.

A fair forward price will result in a forward contract that has no value when it is originated. If the buyer and the seller agree that the forward price is fair, then neither party will have to make a cash payment to the other on the initial agreement date. Even though the spot price of oil is $30/bbl, the parties can agree that $31/bbl is a fair price to pay for oil that will be delivered 6 months hence. The forward buyer will pay the forward seller for the oil on the delivery date. It is important to understand that the equilibrium forward price is a fair price in the sense that the demand for forward contracts equals the supply of forward contracts at that forward price, and the *value* of a forward contract at that fair forward price is zero.

Subsequently, the forward contract will likely become valuable for only one of the two parties. For the party that has a long position, the contract will have a positive value, or become an asset, when the forward price (for delivery on the settlement date of the original contract) rises.

For example, suppose that today is November 26, 2000, and you agree to buy oil 6 months hence, on May 26, 2001, at a price of $30/bbl. The next day (November 27, 2000), $30.20/bbl is the fair price for delivery of oil on May 26, 2001 (note that this is no longer a 6-month forward contract; it is a forward contract for delivery 6 months *less one day* in the future). Your long position is now valuable. You have a contract that entitles you to buy oil at $30/bbl. But new agreements, being originated on November 27, have a forward price of $30.20. Your contract to buy oil at only $30/bbl is "a bargain." It is a valuable asset for you.

It then follows that the forward contract to sell oil at $30/bbl has become a liability for the counterparty to the forward contract. The seller of the forward contract is obligated to deliver oil on May 27, 2001, at only $30/bbl, while new contracts are being created to sell oil at a higher price. *Forward contracts, like all derivatives, are zero-sum games.* Whatever one party gains, the other party must lose. Thus the party that agreed, on November 26, to sell you oil at a price of $30/bbl has, on November 27, a contract with negative value; this party who is short the contract has a liability because the forward price rose.

Table 3.1 summarizes how the parties that are long and short a forward contract profit or suffer losses when forward prices change from the original forward price that was agreed upon in the original contract.

The profits and losses associated with forward contracts are typically realized at delivery. Before delivery, as forward prices for delivery on the settlement date of the original contract fluctuate, each party could experience unrealized gains and losses. For either party, the forward contract may change from being an asset on some dates to being a liability. But the actual profit or loss is realized only on the delivery date.

TABLE 3.1

Position	Profits	Loses
Long a forward contract	Forward prices rise	Forward prices fall
Short a forward contract	Forward prices fall	Forward prices rise

Let us define the following:

Origination date of the forward contract	time 0
Delivery date of the forward contract	time T
Forward price on the origination date of the forward contract	$F(0,T)$
The spot price on the delivery date	$S(T)$

The actual profit or loss for the party that is long the forward contract is then $S(T) - F(0,T)$ per unit of the good under contract. If the spot price on the delivery date is greater than the original forward price, then this is positive, and the long position realizes a profit. If the spot price at delivery is less than the original forward price, the long suffers a loss.

The actual profit or loss for the party that is short the forward contract is the same amount, but the opposite sign: $F(0,T) - S(T)$. Whatever profit the long realizes, the short must lose. If the seller of the forward contact makes a profit because the spot price at delivery is less than the forward price specified on the origination date $[S(T) < F(0,T)]$, the buyer of the forward contract must realize a loss.

In our example of the forward oil contract, $F(0,T) = \$30/\text{bbl}$ for 100,000 bbl of oil. Suppose that at delivery, the spot price of oil is $S(T) = \$28.61/\text{bbl}$. Then, the long realizes a loss of $\$1.39/\text{bbl} \times 100,000 \text{ bbl} = \$139,000$. The long is contractually obligated to buy 100,000 bbl of oil at the originally agreed-upon forward price of $30/bbl. This is higher than the prevailing spot market price of oil on the delivery date. Effectively, the long is forced to overpay for the oil on the delivery date.

The per-barrel profit for the short is $F(0,T) - S(T) = 30 - 28.61 = \$1.39/\text{bbl}$ of oil. The profit arises because the seller earlier contracted to sell the oil at a price that turned out to be higher than the spot market price. Multiply this price difference by the amount of oil specified in the contract, and we obtain the result that the short realizes a profit of $139,000.

Many forward contracts are **cash settled**. This means that no delivery takes place on the settlement date. Instead, the party with the profitable position receives a cash payment from the party with the unprofitable position. The cash payment equals $|F(0,T) - S(T)|$, where the vertical lines are used to denote "absolute value."

Another device for describing how profits and losses occur for long and short forward positions is the profit diagram. The profit diagram for a long forward position is presented in Figure 3.1. The profit diagram for a party that is short a forward contract is shown in Figure 3.2. The profit line for the long position is a positively sloped 45° line. The long's profit increases by a dollar for every dollar that the delivery day spot price exceeds the original forward price, times the number of units of the good that the contract covers. The short's profit is shown as a negatively sloped 45° line. If $S(T)$ is a dollar less than $F(0,T)$, the short's profit is a dollar times the number of units of the good that the contract covers.

Earlier, it was stated that when a forward contract is originated, it has no value. At subsequent times, it will almost surely have positive value for one party and negative value for the other party.

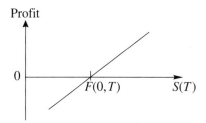

Figure 3.1 Long forward profit diagram: the long profits if the spot price at delivery $S(T)$ exceeds the original forward price, $F(0,T)$.

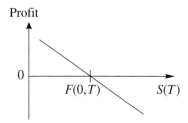

Figure 3.2 Short forward profit diagram: the short profits if the price at delivery $S(T)$ is below the original forward price, $F(0,T)$.

When a forward contract becomes an asset (has positive value) for one party, that party will become concerned about the other party's ability and willingness to fulfill the contract's terms. Many different terms are used to represent the condition of concern: **default risk**, **performance risk**, or **credit risk**. At a point in time, only one party, the one for which the forward contract is an asset, will worry about *current* default risk. If the losing party reneges on its obligation, the winning party will not be able to realize the contract's value.

Thus, if $F(0,T)=30$, and at some later date at time t prior to delivery $(0 < t < T)$, $F(t,T)=31$, the long position has an unrealized profit and will be concerned about whether the party who is short the forward contract will go bankrupt, or just refuse to abide by the terms of the contract at delivery.[3] This fear about current performance is only one sided at time t. The short does not fear that the long will go bankrupt at time t and default on its obligation because the value of the short's position at that time is negative. Given the information about prices that it has as of time t, the short would not mind wiping a liability from its economic balance sheet.

Thus, only one party at one point in time fears that its counterparty will actually default at delivery. Of course, since forward prices change over time, the party exposed to default risk can also change over time. Finally, it should be understood that forward contracts can frequently build up a great deal of asset value for one of the parties (and because they are a zero-sum game, they will therefore become a sizable liability for the counterparty).[4]

Suppose that a party has entered into a forward contract to buy oil and before delivery (time t), it decides that it no longer wants this long position. The ability to quickly buy and sell commodities, securities, and derivative contracts at fair prices is called **liquidity**. Liquidity is a highly desired and valued aspect of any contract and good. The party that is long the forward contract has two ways of ridding itself of the contract. First, it can approach the other party and negotiate its early termination. In this case, the party that has a losing position at time t will have to pay to get out of its obligation. If $F(t,T) > F(0,T)$, then the short will have to pay the long to cancel the forward contract. If $F(t,T) < F(0,T)$, then the long is losing money because the forward price has declined, and he will have to make a payment to the short.

Alternatively, the party who is long the contract, and no longer wants to abide by its terms, can approach a third party and agree to *sell* the good forward, at the fair forward price on day t, $F(t,T)$. Then, this forward selling party has both the obligation to buy the good at time T [at a price of $F(0,T)$], and the obligation to sell the good at time T [at $F(t,T)$]. This new forward contract effectively offsets the original contract. At time T, the long will realize the profit if $F(0,T) < F(t,T)$, because he will buy the good for a lower price than the one he will receive. The long will have to make a payment at delivery if $F(0,T) > F(t,T)$ because the original agreed-upon purchase price is above the price at which he (later) agreed to sell the good.[5]

Businesses around the world transact in forward markets. Forward agreements to buy and sell debt securities issued by most governments of developed nations, such as U.S. Treasury securities, are commonplace. There are well-developed forward markets in many energy products such as crude oil, and precious metals such as gold. Farmers often sell their products before harvesting, to the users of these agricultural products. Forward contracts do not trade on organized exchanges. Instead, firms usually trade with financial institutions that make markets in forward contracts. This market is often called the **OTC market**, or the **over-the-counter market**.

Table 3.2 presents the 10 U.S. bank holding companies with the largest positions in OTC forward contracts, as of December 31, 2000. These 10 banks alone had over 98% of the total notional amount of forward contracts held by all the commercial banks in the United States. Chase Manhattan Corp. has the largest position in forward contracts: almost $3 trillion.

Sections 3.2 and 3.3 describe in great detail two important forward contracts, those for the purchase and sale of interest rates and foreign currencies.

TABLE 3.2 Notional Amount of OTC Forward Contracts Held by Leading U.S. Bank Holding Companies, December 31, 2000 ($ Millions)

Chase Manhattan Bank	$2,813,869
Citibank	$1,848,417
Bank of America	$1,238,559
Morgan Guaranty Trust Co. of New York	$1,084,561
State Street Bank & Trust Co.	$133,895
First Union National Bank	$131,436
Bank One National Association	$104,627
HSBC Bank USA	$90,268
Fleet National Bank	$42,668
Bank of New York	$40,347
Total notional principal of forward contracts for the top 25 holding companies with OTC forward positions	$7,634,246

Source: Website for the Office of the Comptroller of the Currency (www.occ.treas.gov/).

3.2 FORWARD RATE AGREEMENTS

A forward rate agreement (FRA) is a forward contract in which the buyer effectively promises today to borrow an amount of money in the future, at an agreed-upon interest rate. This rate is called the forward rate. The seller of a FRA has the obligation to lend money at the forward interest rate. You should think of the FRA as an agreement for the long to buy an interest rate; if the interest rate rises, the long profits. The long has agreed to borrow money at the original forward rate, and if interest rates subsequently rise, this original forward rate will turn out to be low. Borrowers prefer to borrow at low rates, and thus, the buyer of the FRA "wins" if interest rates rise. The seller of the FRA, like the seller of any forward contract, will realize a profit if the price falls. In this case, the price is the interest rate, so the party who is short a FRA will profit if the spot interest rate at settlement is less than the originally agreed upon forward rate; the short receives a cash payment at maturity when interest rates have declined. The payoffs for FRAs are depicted in Figures 3.3 (for the party that is long the FRA), and 3.4 (for the party that is short the FRA). The symbol for the change in interest rates is Δr.

Because FRAs are cash settled (i.e., money is not actually borrowed or lent at settlement), on the settlement date, the winning party pays the losing party.

Because FRAs have *three* relevant dates, the following special notation is required:

Origination date of the forward contract	time 0
Delivery date of the forward contract (start of the forward period)	time $t1$
The end of the forward period	time $t2$
Forward rate on the origination date of the forward contract	$fr(0,t1,t2)$
The spot rate on the delivery date	$r(t1,t2)$
The length of the loan period	$t2-t1$

More explanation of this notation is needed. At time 0, the buyer of the FRA agrees to borrow money from time $t1$ until time $t2$, at an interest rate of $fr(0,t1,t2)$. The spot interest rate will not be known until time $t1$. The length of time for the forward loan, $t2-t1$, is called the **loan period**.[6] It is the length of time during which money will effectively be borrowed or lent.[7]

Figure 3.5 is a time line that illustrates the difference between the three dates that are important for understanding FRAs: the origination date; the settlement date or delivery date,

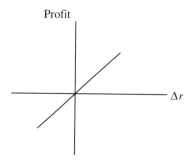

Figure 3.3 The party that is long a FRA profits if interest rates rise (i.e., if Δr is positive).

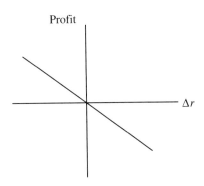

Figure 3.4 The party that has sold a FRA profits if interest rates decline (i.e., Δr is negative).

Figure 3.5 Important dates in a FRA.

which is the start of the forward period; and the end of the forward period. The loan period is the time during which the principal amount is effectively either borrowed or lent.

The interest rate that is covered by the FRA is typically (but definitely not always) a LIBOR[8] rate, and it is specified in the agreement.

While a FRA is originated at time 0, the typical jargon is to refer to it as a $t1 \times t2$ FRA, a $t1$ vs $t2$ FRA, or a $t1$ V. $t2$ FRA, where $t1$ is the starting date of the forward loan and $t2$ is the ending date of the forward period. For example, a 2×5 FRA is an agreement to borrow or lend for a 3-month period, beginning 2 months hence. Verbally, it is stated as "two month against five month," or "2s against 5s." A 1×7 FRA is a 6-month forward rate, beginning 1-month hence and ending 7 months hence; the loan period is 6 months.

Hundreds of banks around the world quote and trade FRAs, and the market is quite liquid. Bid–asked spreads are very narrow: as little as 3 or 4 basis points. Thus, for a 6×12 FRA, a bank might be willing to borrow at a rate of 5.92% for a 6-month period, 6 months hence, and lend at a rate of 5.97%; this is a spread of 5 basis points.

Payment is made on the FRA's settlement day, which is at time $t1$. The payment amount, π, is determined as follows. The spot interest rate at time $t1$ for the loan period specified in the FRA, $r(t1,t2)$, is observed and subtracted from the original forward rate, $fr(0,t1,t2)$. This difference is then "unannualized" to reflect the loan period, and multiplied by the principal amount of the FRA. Then, that amount is discounted, because payment is made in advance (at the start of the loan period), at time $t1$. If we use the following nomenclature:

Principal amount of the FRA $\qquad\qquad\qquad\qquad\qquad\qquad$ P

Number of days in a year (either 360 or 365, as specified in the FRA) $\quad B$

Number of days in the loan period D (=$t2 - t1$, in days)

Fraction of year made up by loan period D/B

Then, the payment amount is:

$$\pi = \left| \frac{P[r(t1, t2) - fr(0, t1, t2)](D/B)}{1 + [r(t1, t2)(D/B)]} \right| \tag{3.1}$$

The numerator of Equation (3.1) is the dollar profit or loss on a loan that was originally contracted at a forward rate of $fr(0,t1,t2)$ when the actual spot rate turns out to be $r(t1,t2)$. Since both these are annual rates, they must be converted to periodic rates by multiplying them by the fraction of the year for the forward loan, D/B. This periodic rate difference is then multiplied by P, the principal amount of the FRA. The denominator of Equation (3.1) is a discounting factor that brings the numerator to a present value amount. The payment is made at time $t1$, the settlement day of the FRA.

Almost always, the number of days in the loan period, D, is the actual number of days between dates $t1$ and $t2$. Thus, a 2×5 FRA may actually have 89, 90, 91, or 92 days in the loan period. The convention for most U.S. dollar FRAs is to define the number of days in a year as $B = 360$. The convention for British pound FRAs is to define $B = 365$. But either definition of a year is possible in either country, since FRAs are custom-made contracts.

If $r(t1,t2)$ exceeds $fr(0,t1,t2)$ then the long position (the buyer of the FRA) receives the amount computed by Equation (3.1). The seller of the FRA (the short) is the loser and must pay the computed amount. The two vertical lines means Equation (3.1) defines the absolute value of the payment amount.

A simple example illustrates how the formula that computes the payment amount works. On September 2, a bank sells a 2×5 FRA with a principal amount of $500 million, at a forward rate of 6%. On the settlement date (2 months hence), spot 3-month LIBOR is 4.8%. A year is defined to be $B = 360$ days. What is the payment that will be made on the settlement day?

First, note that there are 91 days in this particular loan period ($5 - 2 = 3$ months). The payment is made 2 months after the FRA is originated, and the payment amount is computed to be $1,498,485:

$$\left| \frac{(\$500,000,000)(0.048 - 0.06)(91/360)}{1 + [(0.048)(91/360)]} \right| = \$1,498,485$$

Because the 3-month spot rate at time $t1$ is less than the original contracted forward rate of 6%, the bank will *receive* (a profit of) $1,498,485, because it sold the FRA.

The payoff to a FRA is discounted (the denominator discounts the profit) because users of FRAs are interested in hedging the interest expense or income on a loan. The actual interest cash flow on the item being hedged is typically made or received at the *end* of the loan period. For example, a firm may be planning to issue 6-month commercial paper 5 months hence. If interest rates do rise, it will have to pay added interest expense 11 months from today. But the payoff on the 5×11 FRA occurs 5 months from today. To equate any added expense on the commercial paper to the profit from the FRA, the spot 6-month LIBOR prevailing at settlement must be used to discount the FRA's payoff.

TABLE 3.3 A FRA is Analogous to a One-Period Swap

FRA	One-Period Swap
Buyer = long	Pay fixed and receive floating
Seller = short	Receive fixed and pay floating

It is instructive to note now that a FRA is effectively a one-period swap. The buyer of the FRA has agreed to receive a floating interest rate (times the principal amount) and pay a fixed interest rate (times the principal amount). The fixed interest rate in a swap is analogous to the forward rate that is specified in the FRA. If the floating interest rate rises above the contractual fixed rate, the buyer of the FRA receives a net payment on the settlement day. The seller of the FRA has agreed to pay a floating interest rate and receive the fixed interest rate.

Table 3.3 summarizes this analogy.

FRAs exist on all major currencies of the world, including the U.S. dollar, the British pound, euros, and the Japanese yen. Futures contracts also trade on short-term debt instruments denominated in these currencies, and these serve as substitutes for FRAs.

FRAs are used by firms and financial institutions to protect themselves against unexpected changes in interest rates. The parties can use FRAs to lock in a borrowing rate or a lending rate for transactions they will undertake at a future date. By buying a FRA, a party locks in a future borrowing rate. The seller of a FRA locks in the interest rate on a future loan that it will make. Sometimes, FRAs are used to speculate on the future course of interest rates. The next chapter focuses on the usage of FRAs for controlling interest rate risk. Chapter 5 covers the computation of forward interest rates and explains how FRAs are priced.

3.3 FORWARD FOREIGN EXCHANGE CONTRACTS

A foreign currency is a good just like any other good. Given the familiar concept of the dollar price of an apple or the dollar price of a computer, you should have no trouble understanding the concept of the dollar price of a British pound ($/£), which is the number of dollars required to buy a British pound. The dollar price of a Japanese yen ($/¥) specifies how many dollars must be exchanged for one Japanese yen.

But currencies can be priced in terms of any other currency. Thus, it is important to understand that traders can buy British pounds (£), and pay for them with euros (€); in this case, the exchange rate is €/£, which is the number of euros required to buy one pound. And if instead, a trader wants to buy euros, he can pay for them with British pounds; the relevant exchange rate is then £/€. The € price of a £ is the inverse of the £ price of a €. Thus, suppose it costs €1.5 to buy 1£. Then, the price of a euro, expressed in terms of pounds, is £0.6667/€; this is the inverse of 1.5: 0.6667 = 1/1.5.

Frequently, you will read in the financial press that "the dollar strengthened yesterday." This means that the cost of buying dollars rose. However, the headline does not make clear which currency or currencies the dollar strengthened against. Perhaps the dollar rose against the yen, from ¥108/$ to ¥109/$. The dollar may have appreciated against most currencies, but depreciated against others. Nonetheless, a strengthening currency is one that rises in price.

A currency that loses value is said to have weakened, or depreciated in value. The fact that the U.S. dollar strengthened from ¥108 to ¥109 means that the yen must have weakened, relative to the dollar. In this case the yen dropped in value from $0.009259/¥ (1/108=0.009259) to $0.009174/¥ (1/109=0.009174). The yen is less valuable on the second day than on the first; the yen became cheaper, in terms of dollars.

All the foregoing discussion dealt with spot exchange rates. However, firms, governments, and financial institutions often want to contract today to buy or sell foreign currencies in the future. One way of doing this is to transact in the forward foreign exchange market, which is also frequently called the forward exchange market.

A forward foreign exchange contract is an agreement to buy or sell a currency at a later date at a specified price; the specified price is the forward exchange rate. The forward price paid must be expressed in terms of a currency different from the one being bought or sold. In other words, it is not sufficient to discuss the forward price of a euro without asking "in terms of what?" Is it the pound price of a euro (£/€), or the U.S. dollar price of a euro ($/€)?

As with most other forward contracts, there is no payment made when the contract is originated (unless collateral is demanded). On the settlement date, two currencies are exchanged, at the forward exchange rate that was agreed upon at origination. The party that is long the contract profits if the spot exchange rate on the settlement day is greater than the forward exchange rate that was originally set on the origination day. If the party bought Canadian dollars (Can$) forward, and agreed to pay for them with U.S. dollars (U.S.$) at a forward exchange rate of U.S.$0.6845/Can$, then at delivery, this party must pay out U.S. dollars and receive Canadian dollars. If the forward contract specified that Can$3 million was to be bought, then the party receives Can$3 million, and pays U.S.$2,053,500 at delivery.

Put another way, we can define these terms as follows:

Origination date of the forward contract	time 0
Delivery date of the forward contract	time T
Forward exchange rate on the origination date of the forward contract	$F(0,T)$
The spot exchange rate on the delivery date	$S(T)$
Units of foreign currency covered by the contract	N

Both $F(0,T)$ and $S(T)$ are expressed as the price of one currency in terms of another. For example, $F(0,T)$ might be $0.01/¥, which is the price of yen in terms of U.S. dollars. In this case, N refers to the number of yen in the contract. Table 3.4 summarizes the profits and losses realized by the buyer and seller of forward foreign exchange contracts.

TABLE 3.4 Profits and Losses for Forward Exchange Contracts

	Outcomes	
Position	$S(T)<F(0,T)$	$S(T)>F(0,T)$
Long forward exchange contract	Loss = $[F(0,T)-S(T)]N$	Profit = $[S(T)-F(0,T)]N$
Short forward exchange contract	Profit = $[F(0,T)-S(T)]N$	Loss = $[S(T)-F(0,T)]N$

The forward exchange market for short-term transactions is very active and is as liquid as the spot exchange market and the FRA market. Spreads are very narrow for nearby delivery dates; they get wider the more distant the delivery date, reflecting less liquid markets. Some forward exchange contracts are cash settled, and others are settled with the actual exchange of currencies.

A forward foreign exchange contract is equivalent to a pair of zero-coupon bonds. One of the zero-coupon bonds is an asset, and the other is a liability, denominated in a different currency. Figure 3.6 illustrates that at time T, the settlement date, there is an exchange of currencies. In this example, at time 0, the firm agreed to buy 100,000 euros (€100,000) at a forward exchange rate of ¥116/€. This forward transaction had no cash flow associated with it when the contract was originated. At time T, the firm receives €100,000, and pays ¥11.6 million.

Now, compare this forward transaction to a firm that has a zero-coupon German bond on its balance sheet as an asset and a zero-coupon yen-denominated bond on its balance sheet as a liability. The face value of the pure discount German debt instrument is €100,000. The firm also earlier issued a zero-coupon bond denominated in yen, having a face value of ¥11.6 million. Both bonds mature on the same date, at time T. The cash flows resulting from the existence of these two zero-coupon bonds, one an asset and one a liability, are exactly equivalent to the cash flows that will be exchanged at time T because of the forward foreign exchange contract. Thus, a forward contract to buy €100,000 at a forward price of ¥116/€ is equivalent to having a zero-coupon German bond with a face value of €100,000 as an asset and also having a zero-coupon Japanese bond with a face value of ¥11.6 million as a liability.

Let's consider a bit further the equivalency of (a) a forward foreign exchange contract and (b) two zero-coupon bonds (one an asset in one currency, and the other bond as a liability in the other currency). Note that since the values of the cash flows at time T are the same, the cash flows at time 0 must be the same, or else the firm could arbitrage. You know that if the forward rate of ¥116/€ is fair, there is no cash flow for the forward contract at time 0. This means that if the firm did decide to instead issue a zero-coupon bond with a face value of ¥11.6 million, and use the proceeds to buy a zero-coupon bond with a face value of €100,000, then the time 0 prices of the two bonds, when converted to one currency by using the spot exchange rate, must be equal. They must be equal so that there is no residual cash flow at time zero if the firm bought and sold the two zero-coupon bonds, just as there is no cash flow at time zero with the

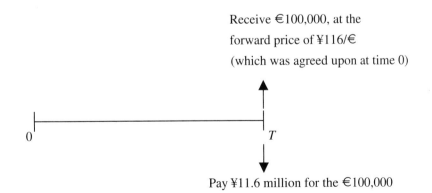

Figure 3.6 Cash flows associated with a forward foreign exchange contract.

forward contract. Put yet another way, the present value of ¥11.6 million must equal the present value of €100,000.

Suppose that the firm could at time 0 buy the zero-coupon German bond maturing at time T for €94,340. Also let the spot exchange rate at time 0 be ¥119.45/€. It must be the case that the firm will receive ¥11,268,913 (€94,340 × ¥119.45/€ = ¥11,268,913) when it issues the zero-coupon bond denominated in yen. If the firm can receive *more* than ¥11,268,913, it should (a) issue the yen-denominated zero coupon bond, (b) take the yen proceeds and convert them to euros at the spot exchange rate, (c) buy the zero-coupon bond denominated in euros, and (d) sell euros forward at the forward price of ¥116/€ (which is equivalent to buying JPY forward at a forward price of €0.00862069/¥, which is the inverse of ¥116/€). This four-step procedure represents arbitrage.

Table 3.5 illustrates the arbitrage process for a firm that can receive ¥11.3 million (which is *more than* ¥11,268,913) when it issues the zero-coupon, yen-denominated bond. Note how the firm has a net cash inflow of €260.21 at time zero, and no cash flow at time one. This illustrates an arbitrage process, which in this case has arisen because the prices violated a relationship that must exist between interest rates, spot exchange rates, and forward exchange rates. You will better understand what the relationship is between spot and forward foreign exchange rates after reading Chapter 5, which covers pricing forward contracts.

Forward foreign exchange contracts are used by firms to lock in the prices they will pay or receive for foreign currencies at future dates. When some firms buy goods abroad, they will have

TABLE 3.5   Illustration of the Arbitrage Process[1]

The situation	Spot exchange rate is ¥119.45/€.
	Forward exchange rate is ¥116/€.
	A zero-coupon German bond can be bought for €94,340; face value is €100,000.
	A zero-coupon, yen-denominated bond can be issued, netting ¥11.3 million; face value is ¥11.6 million.

Time	Transaction	Cash Flow
0	a. Issue a zero-coupon, yen-denominated bond (which then becomes a liability for the firm).	+¥11,300,000
	b. Convert the yen proceeds to euros at the spot exchange rate of €0.0083717/¥ (which is the inverse of ¥119.45).	−¥11,300,000 +€94,600.21
	c. Buy the zero-coupon German bond (which becomes an asset).	−€94,340.00
	d. Sell €100,000 forward at the forward price of ¥116/€.	0
	Net cash flow	+€260.21
1	a. The German bond matures.	+€100,000
	b. Fulfill the terms of the forward contract.	−€100,000 +¥11,600,000
	c. Pay off the owners of the zero-coupon, yen-denominated bond.	−¥11,600,000
	Net cash flow	0

[1]A forward contract is equivalent to a portfolio of zero-coupon bonds, one an asset and one a liability. If the two are **not** equivalent, an arbitrage profit is possible.

to pay for them with the currency the foreign exporter wants, which is typically the exporter's home currency. Other firms that sell goods abroad will often be paid with the foreign currency that was generated when the goods were sold. In general, firms that are involved in foreign trade know that they will have future needs to buy or sell foreign currencies, and forward exchange contracts allow them to manage the risk that the prices of these currencies will change.

Figure 3.7 shows how the *Wall Street Journal* presents spot exchange rates, and also forward exchange rates for some currencies. Note that the U.S. dollar price of each currency is given (in the "U.S. $ equiv." columns), and the foreign currency price of the dollar is also given (in the "currency per U.S. $" columns). Thus, on Friday, it cost $1.4912 to buy one British pound in the spot market. The inverse of 1.4912 is 1/1.4912 = 0.6706, which is the price of the U.S. dollar denominated in British pounds (£0.6706/$).

Forward exchange rates are also presented in Figure 3.7 for the British pound, the Canadian dollar, the French franc, the German mark, the Japanese yen, and the Swiss franc. For example, on Friday, a forward contract to trade British pounds 6 months later (for forward delivery on November 26, 2000) had a forward price of $1.4968/£. (This is above the spot price of $1.4912/£). All the currencies were selling at a forward premium to the dollar; that is, their forward prices were higher than their spot prices.

THE WALL STREET JOURNAL TUESDAY, MAY 30, 2000   C13

CURRENCY TRADING

Friday, May 26, 2000
EXCHANGE RATES

The New York foreign exchange mid-range rates below apply to trading among banks in amounts of $1 million and more, as quoted at 4 p.m. Eastern time by Reuters and other sources. Retail transactions provide fewer units of foreign currency per dollar. Rates for the 11 Euro currency countries are derived from the latest dollar-euro rate using the exchange ratios set 1/1/99.

Country	U.S. $ equiv. Fri	Thu	Currency per U.S. $ Fri	Thu
Argentina (Peso)	1.0007	1.0002	.9993	.9998
Australia (Dollar)	.5741	.5690	1.7419	1.7575
Austria (Schilling)	.06770	.06632	14.771	15.078
Bahrain (Dinar)	2.6525	2.6525	.3770	.3770
Belgium (Franc)	.0231	.0226	43.3041	44.2033
Brazil (Real)	.5444	.5414	1.8370	1.8470
Britain (Pound)	1.4912	1.4720	.6706	.6793
1-month forward	1.4919	1.4727	.6703	.6790
3-months forward	1.4937	1.4746	.6695	.6782
6-months forward	1.4968	1.4781	.6681	.6765
Canada (Dollar)	.6650	.6647	1.5037	1.5045
1-month forward	.6655	.6651	1.5027	1.5035
3-months forward	.6664	.6661	1.5005	1.5013
6-months forward	.6680	.6676	1.4971	1.4979
Chile (Peso)	.001909	.001903	523.95	525.50
China (Renminbi)	.1208	.1208	8.2771	8.2773
Colombia (Peso)	.0004748	.0004729	2106.00	2114.50
Czech. Rep. (Koruna) ...				
Commercial rate	.02559	.02513	39.084	39.791
Denmark (Krone)	.1249	.1224	8.0060	8.1722
Ecuador (Sucre) ...				
Floating rate	.00004000	.00004000	25000.00	25000.00
Finland (Markka)	.1567	.1535	6.3826	6.5152
France (Franc)	.1420	.1391	7.0416	7.1878
1-month forward	.1423	.1394	7.0269	7.1724
3-months forward	.1429	.1400	6.9980	7.1439
6-months forward	.1438	.1409	6.9546	7.0994
Germany (Mark)	.4763	.4666	2.0995	2.1431
1-month forward	.4773	.4676	2.0952	2.1386
3-months forward	.4793	.4695	2.0865	2.1300
6-months forward	.4823	.4724	2.0736	2.1168
Greece (Drachma)	.002769	.002708	361.16	369.33
Hong Kong (Dollar)	.1283	.1283	7.7921	7.7920
Hungary (Forint)	.003584	.003512	278.99	284.76
India (Rupee)	.02255	.02268	44.350	44.100
Indonesia (Rupiah)	.0001174	.0001183	8520.00	8450.00
Ireland (Punt)	1.1829	1.1587	.8454	.8630
Israel (Shekel)	.2404	.2402	4.1593	4.1631
Italy (Lira)	.0004811	.0004713	2078.55	2121.71

Country	U.S. $ equiv. Fri	Thu	Currency per U.S. $ Fri	Thu
Japan (Yen)	.009336	.009313	107.11	107.38
1-month forward	.009389	.009365	106.51	106.78
3-months forward	.009497	.009473	105.30	105.56
6-months forward	.009667	.009643	103.45	103.71
Jordan (Dinar)	1.4075	1.4075	.7105	.7105
Kuwait (Dinar)	3.2510	3.2468	.3076	.3080
Lebanon (Pound)	.0006634	.0006616	1507.50	1511.50
Malaysia (Ringgit)	.2632	.2632	3.8000	3.8000
Malta (Lira)	2.2915	2.2604	.4364	.4424
Mexico (Peso) ...				
Floating rate	.1048	.1051	9.5400	9.5170
Netherland (Guilder)	.4727	.4141	2.3656	2.4148
New Zealand (Dollar)	.4597	.4535	2.1753	2.2051
Norway (Krone)	.1118	.1106	8.9414	9.0388
Pakistan (Rupee)	.01927	.01927	51.900	51.900
Peru (new Sol)	.2836	.2845	3.5255	3.5145
Philippines (Peso)	.02328	.02320	42.950	43.100
Poland (Zloty) (d)	.2220	.2206	4.5053	4.5330
Portugal (Escudo)	.004647	.004552	215.21	219.68
Russia (Ruble) (a)	.03535	.03530	28.285	28.325
Saudi Arabia (Riyal)	.2666	.2666	3.7506	3.7506
Singapore (Dollar)	.5767	.5774	1.7340	1.7319
Slovak Rep. (Koruna)	.02169	.02126	46.106	47.036
South Africa (Rand)	.1405	.1396	7.1178	7.1628
South Korea (Won)	.0008795	.0008851	1137.00	1129.85
Spain (Peseta)	.005599	.005485	178.61	182.32
Sweden (Krona)	.1109	.1096	9.0206	9.1227
Switzerland (Franc)	.5952	.5835	1.6802	1.7137
1-month forward	.5972	.5855	1.6744	1.7079
3-months forward	.6009	.5890	1.6642	1.6979
6-months forward	.6063	.5942	1.6493	1.6829
Taiwan (Dollar)	.03245	.03247	30.815	30.800
Thailand (Baht)	.02552	.02555	39.185	39.145
Turkey (Lira)	.00000162	.00000161	617050.00	619630.00
United Arab (Dirham)	.2723	.2723	3.6729	3.6729
Uruguay (New Peso) ...				
Financial	.08344	.08351	11.985	11.975
Venezuela (Bolivar)	.001463	.001464	683.50	683.00
SDR	1.3122	1.3077	.7621	.7647
Euro	.9316	.9126	1.0734	1.0958

Special Drawing Rights (SDR) are based on exchange rates for the U.S., German, British, French, and Japanese currencies. Source: International Monetary Fund.

a-Russian Central Bank rate. Trading band lowered on 8/17/98. b-Government rate. d-Floating rate; trading bands suspended on 4/11/00. Foreign exchange rates are available from Readers' Reference Service (413) 592-3600.

Figure 3.7 Sample presentation of spot currency rates in *The Wall Street Journal*, (Reprinted with permission of *The Wall Street Journal*, page C15. © May 30, 2000.).

3.4 SUMMARY

A forward contract is an agreement to buy or sell something in the future. If the forward price is fair, then the value of a forward contract on its origination date is zero. Typically, no money changes hands when the contract is originated. If the forward price rises, then the contract takes on a positive value for the long position, which means that it becomes an asset. If the forward price declines, then the long's position takes on a negative value, and a positive value for the party that is short the contract.

Forward rate agreements (FRAs) are forward contracts on interest rates. The party that buys a FRA has effectively agreed to borrow a principal amount at a specified interest rate (the forward rate). If interest rates rise above the forward rate, this party will realize a profit. Sellers of FRAs will profit if interest rates decline below the forward rate that was set when the contract was originated. The party that sells a FRA effectively agrees to lend a principal amount at a fixed interest rate. Because FRAs are cash settled, this party receives a payment that is defined by Equation (3.1).

Forward foreign exchange contracts are agreements to buy or sell a foreign currency on a future date. The forward exchange rate is the price at which the transaction will occur. The forward exchange rate can be above or below the spot exchange rate. The buyer of a forward exchange contract profits if the spot price of the currency on the settlement date is above the forward price that was agreed upon at origination.

Notes

[1]A party may default for any of several reasons. Usually, a party defaults because it lacks the ability to meet the terms of a contract. But a financially sound party has often defaulted because of a loophole in the contract, or because the defaulting party feels that he has been wronged in some way. "Credit risk" is the term often used to describe the possibility that a party may fall into financial distress and therefore fail to perform the terms of the contract.

[2]It is common for hotels to charge you for a guaranteed room if you fail to notify them before a certain time that you will not be arriving. Some rental car firms have begun to charge customers when they reserve a car (a forward agreement) and then default, or fail to appear at the scheduled time.

[3]For example, time 0 might be November 26, 2000, time t might be March 12, 2001, and time T might be May 26, 2001.

[4]In contrast, futures are settled daily, so they do not build up as much asset or liability value for the two parties.

[5]This example should allow the reader to compute what the long would have to pay or receive if he used the first method to offset his obligation (i.e., negotiated with the original counterparty to let him out of the obligations of the original contract). If the forward price has risen, the long should be paid the present value of $F(t,T) - F(0,T)$. If the forward price has declined, the long's position has negative value, and at time t he should pay the present value of $F(0,T) - F(t,T)$.

[6]It is also called the **contract period**.

[7]We use the term "effectively" because no money is actually borrowed or lent in a FRA; the contract is cash settled. The cash settlement amount is the profit (loss) that would have been realized, had money really been borrowed or lent.

[8]For a definition of LIBOR, see note 9, Chapter 1.

PROBLEMS

3.1 On March 2, a firm sells a 3×8 FRA. The contracted forward rate is 5.93%. The principal amount is $80 million. On the settlement date, the following spot Eurodollar rates are observed:

Maturity	Rate
3 months	5.84%
4 months	5.94%
5 months	6.04%
6 months	6.10%
7 months	6.14%
8 months	6.19%

What amount must the firm pay or receive?

3.2 A firm wishes to get out of a forward contract it agreed to 2 months ago. There are still 3 months until delivery. What are the two methods the firm can use to offset (get out of) its obligation?

3.3 Goldfinger, Inc., buys a forward contract for delivery of 5000 oz. of gold eight months hence. The forward price is $340/oz. Three months later, contracts calling for the delivery of gold 5 months hence have a forward price of $331/oz, and contracts calling for the delivery of gold eight months hence have a forward price of $420/oz. Three months after the contract's origination, is this contract an asset or a liability for Goldfinger? Why?

3.4 On June 6, BilboBank buys a 5×11 FRA at a forward rate of 6.25%, on a principal amount of $40 million. On July 6, it wants to offset its obligation. On that day, the following rates are observed:

FRA	Quoted Forward Rate (%)
4×10	6.06
4×11	6.10
5×10	6.03
5×11	6.14

a. Which of the four FRAs would the bank want to sell to offset its obligation? Why?

b. Suppose BilboBank approaches the original counterparty (the party that originally sold the 5×11 FRA on June 6), and essentially asks if it can sell the FRA back. Will BilboBank have to make a payment to the original counterparty or will BilboBank receive a payment? That is, is Bilbobank making a profit on the original FRA on July 6?

c. How much will Bilbobank *likely* pay/ receive for selling the original FRA (see note 5 in this chapter)? Assume that $r(0,4) = r(0,5) = 6\%$ on July 6.

3.5 Let's say that $F(0,T) = \$31/bbl$ and $S(T) = \$32.20/bbl$. The forward contract covers 24,000 barrels of oil. Which party, the one that bought the contract, or the one that sold the contract, made a profit? How much is the profit?

3.6 A market maker quotes 3×5 FRAs, denominated in British pounds (GBP, or £) at 8.1% (bid)–8.18% (asked). You buy a FRA with a principal amount of £60 million. At settlement, the following spot rates are observed:

Maturity	Rate (%)
2 months	9.02
3 months	8.84
4 months	8.78
5 months	8.71

By convention, FRAs denominated in GBP use a 365-day year to compute the settlement amount. When will the payment be made? Will you receive a payment at settlement, or will you have to make a payment? How much will the settlement amount be?

3.7 A firm goes long a forward foreign exchange contract. The contract specifies that the firm agrees to buy £5 million 6 months hence. The forward price is ¥168/£. Six months hence, the spot price is ¥180/£.

   a. What is exchanged on the settlement day?

   b. At settlement, has the firm realized a profit or a loss? What is the amount of that profit or loss?

3.8 A U.S. firm observes that the spot price of Swiss francs is $0.75/SFR. The forward price for delivery 1-year hence is $0.79/SFR. U.S. Treasury strips are riskless pure discount bonds. The price of 1-year strips is 93.9% of face value. What must be the price of a zero-coupon SFR-denominated bond that matures 1-year hence?

3.9 Refer to Figure 3.7.

   a. If a firm agreed to sell 10 million French francs 90 days hence in exchange for U.S. dollars, then how many dollars would it receive?

   b. If the firm instead wanted to receive Swiss francs 90 days hence, use the information in Figure 3.7 to estimate the number of Swiss francs it would receive in exchange for the 10 million French francs.

3.10 Which of the following statements is *false*?

   a. The forward price and the spot price can be different.

   b. Forward contracts are zero-sum games.

   c. Many forward contracts are cash settled.

   d. Most forward contracts trade on organized exchanges.

   e. A forward rate agreement is a type of forward contract.

3.11 Which of the following statements is true?

   a. Going long a forward contract will always be profitable when the spot price of the underlying asset rises.

   b. Going long a forward contract will be profitable when the spot price at delivery is higher than the original forward price.

   c. Going long a forward contract is bearish; such a position will be profitable when prices decline.

   d. Default risk is low on forward contracts because they are guaranteed by the clearinghouse.

   e. A forward contract on foreign exchange is called a FRA.

3.12 What does FRA mean?

   a. Futures rate agreement

   b. Futures risk agreement

   c. Futures rate asset

   d. Forward rate agreement

   e. Forward risk agreement

   f. Forward rate asset

3.13 Suppose that on September 15, 2000, you **sell** €100,000 forward, for delivery on January 15, 2001. On September 15, 2000, the spot price of a € is $0.95 (i.e., the exchange rate is $0.95/€), and the forward price for delivery 4 months later is $0.92/€. Then, on January 15, 2001, the spot price of a € is $0.93, and the forward price for delivery 4 months later (i.e., for delivery on May 15, 2001), is $0.94/€. Did you profit or lose on this forward contract, and how much?

a. Profit of $3000

b. Profit of $2000

c. Profit of $1000

d. Loss of $1000

e. Loss of $2000

f. Loss of $3000

3.14 The buyer of a FRA will profit when

a. Interest rates rise

b. Interest rates decline

c. The price of a foreign currency rises

d. The price of a foreign currency declines

e. Stock prices rise

f. Stock prices decline

CHAPTER 4

Using Forward Contracts to Manage Risk

Firms face price risk in their input markets and their output markets. Price risk exists because the future price of the inputs and outputs are unknown today. Price changes in the input market or output market can adversely affect a firm's bottom line.

Forward contracts are routinely written to help shift price risk on commodities such as crude oil, heating oil, copper, grains, and livestock. However, forward contracts are not limited to commodities. Forward contracts can also help firms protect themselves against adverse changes in interest rates or adverse changes in foreign exchange rates.

Forward contracts provide firms with an efficient means to manage price risk. The main advantage of forward contracts is their flexibility. Forward contracts can be structured for nearly any firm-specific situation that requires protection against adverse price changes. This is a terrific advantage. A disadvantage of a forward contract, however, is that the firm is bound by the terms of the forward contract even when prices move advantageously. Another disadvantage is the risk that the counterparty to a forward contract will default. That is, the counterparty may not live up to the terms of the contract.

In this chapter, we illustrate how forward contracts are used to shift risk. We start by showing how commodity price risk can be managed. Then we demonstrate how forward contracts can be used to manage interest rate risk and foreign exchange risk. Much of the material in this chapter also describes how futures contracts can be used manage risk. Only the discussion of forward rate agreements (FRAs; see Section 4.2) and their use in managing interest rate risk is specific to forward contracts.

4.1 USING FORWARDS TO MANAGE COMMODITY PRICE RISK

4.1.1 Buying Forwards to Hedge Against Price Increases

The user of a raw material faces the risk that the price of that commodity will rise. For example, many industrial firms require crude oil as an input to their production processes. If the price of crude oil rises, then these firms' costs will rise. All else equal, this will lower profits and lower firm value. An elementary income statement is:

$$
\begin{aligned}
\text{Revenues} &= \text{output price} \times \text{units sold} \\
\underline{\text{Costs}} &= \text{input prices} \times \text{input units purchased} \\
\text{Profits}
\end{aligned}
$$

Unless the firm can pass the higher costs on to consumers in the form of higher output prices, its profits will be eroded by higher input (crude oil) prices, and this will cause a drop in firm value. Figure 4.1 illustrates the input price risk faced by a user of a raw material.

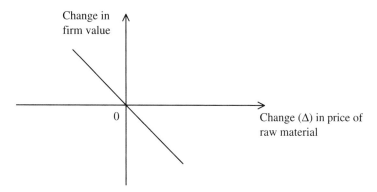

Figure 4.1 An increase in the price of a raw material used by the firm leads to a decline in the value of that firm, all else equal.

A firm facing the risk that the price of one of its inputs will rise can use forward contracts to manage that risk. Buying forward contracts on the raw material will lock in its purchase price. One way to think about using forwards (and futures and swaps) to hedge price risk is that a firm should act to eliminate the price risk in the forward market in the same way that it otherwise would have acted in the spot market. In this case, buying the raw material in the spot market would have eliminated its exposure to the risk that its price would rise. Instead, buying the raw material in the forward market (going long forward contracts) accomplishes the same result; instead of actually buying the raw material today, the firm is committing itself to buy it at a later date. The advantages of buying the forward contract are as follows.

1. There is no cost to taking on a long position in a forward contract; buying the commodity in the spot market requires an initial cash outlay. Because there is an opportunity cost to any cash outlay, it is cheaper to use the forward contract.[1]

2. Buying the good in the spot market will result in storage costs and insurance costs. The firm does not have to incur the expense of storing and insuring the commodity if it buys the forward contract.

3. Should the firm later change its mind about hedging its price risk, or later discover that it has no need for the commodity, it may be easier to offset a long forward position than to find a buyer for a commodity already bought.

4. The amount exposed to default risk in a forward contract is only a fraction of what is at risk in a cash transaction. The principal amount of a forward contract is not at risk; essentially, only the difference between the contracted forward price and the current spot price, times the principal amount, is at risk.

5. The transactions costs (commissions and bid–ask spreads) may be lower in the forward market than in the spot market.

There are also some disadvantages to using forward contracts to manage risk compared with just using the spot market:

1. Two sets of transactions costs may be incurred.

2. The forward market is more or less reserved only for larger organizations.

3. Each party to a forward contract must be concerned about default risk.

4. Unless the asset underlying the forward contract is identical to the item being hedged, the hedge will likely be imperfect.

Figure 4.2 presents the profit diagram for a long forward contract. If the price on the delivery day is greater than the forward price that was agreed upon on the origination day, then the party that is long the forward contract realizes a profit. Suppose a firm is exposed to the risk of an increase in the price of a raw material. This firm then buys a forward contract that constitutes an obligation to buy that raw material in the future. Figure 4.3 show how the exposure to price risk is removed.[2]

4.1.2 Selling Forwards to Hedge Against Price Declines

A producer of a commodity may be exposed to the risk that the price of its output will decline. That is, the firm might be engaged in copper mining, crude oil production, or growing cash crops.

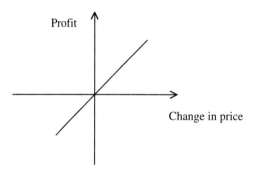

Figure 4.2 Profit diagram for a long forward position. A rise in the price of the good makes a long position in a forward contract profitable.

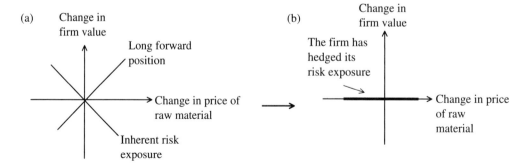

Figure 4.3   A firm that is exposed to the risk that the price of a commodity will rise can manage its risk exposure by buying a forward contract on that commodity (*a*). If the hedge is effective, then all of its risk exposure is removed, as shown in (*b*).

As explained shortly, if the price of the output product declines, and if the product is price inelastic, then the firm's revenues will decline. Figure 4.4 illustrates that when the price of its output declines, the value of a firm declines, all else equal.

An important assumption in the analysis of the effect of a decline in the price of this firm's output is that the demand for its product is price *inelastic*. The "law of demand" states that quantity demanded increases when prices fall. Thus, all else equal, the firm should experience an increase in units sold when the price of its output declines. If the product is price inelastic, then the percentage increase in units sold is less than the percentage fall in its price, so that revenues will decrease. Put another way, when a good exhibits inelastic demand, an $x\%$ decline in its price results in a percentage increase in the quantity demanded that is smaller than $x\%$:

$$\text{Inelastic demand:} \left| \frac{\%\Delta \text{ quantity demanded}}{\%\Delta \text{ price}} \right| < 1$$

For example, if the price of oil rises by 10% and demand for the output of an oil producer declines only 1%, we conclude that the demand for the product is inelastic. If demand for the firm's output good is price inelastic, then all else equal, the decline in price leads to a decline in revenues and a decline in profits:

$$\text{Revenues} = \text{output price} \times \text{quantity sold}$$
$$\frac{- \text{Costs}}{\text{Profits}}$$

In contrast, if demand for a product is price *elastic,* then changes in price will lead to larger changes in the quantity demanded:

$$\text{Elastic demand:} \left| \frac{\%\Delta \text{ quantity demand}}{\%\Delta \text{ price}} \right| > 1$$

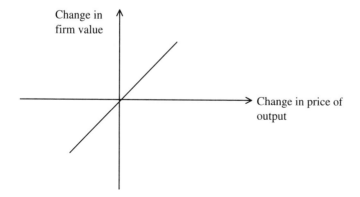

Figure 4.4 When the price of a firm's output declines, its revenues decline (all else equal), and firm value declines.

If demand for firm's product is elastic, it will not be concerned with declining prices because the quantity demanded will increase by such a large amount that its revenues will increase. Figure 4.5 illustrates the difference between elastic demand and inelastic demand.

In general, we should conclude that for an individual firm, demand for its product is price inelastic. Therefore price declines will diminish revenues.[3]

A firm exposed to the risk that the price of a commodity will decline can hedge the risk by selling that good in the spot market today. At times, however, selling the good in the spot market is impossible or not feasible. For example, a wheat farmer who has just planted a crop is exposed to the risk that the price of wheat will decline. Obviously, he cannot sell the wheat in the spot market, since the crop has not been harvested. Instead, the farmer can transact in the forward market in the same way that he would otherwise act in the spot market. That is, he can sell his wheat in the forward market to protect himself. Going short a forward contract, which obligates him to sell the wheat at the contractual forward price, eliminates his exposure to price risk.

Figure 4.6 presents the profit diagram for a firm that is short a forward contract. It shows that a price decline (i.e., the spot price on the delivery day is below the origination day forward price)

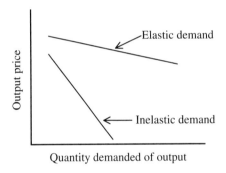

Figure 4.5   When demand is inelastic, a rise in price has only a small impact on the quantity demanded. Elastic demand means that a rise in price leads to a large decline in demand.

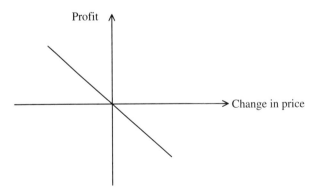

Figure 4.6   Profit diagram for a firm that is short a forward contract. A decline in the price of the good creates a profit for the firm that is short a forward contract.

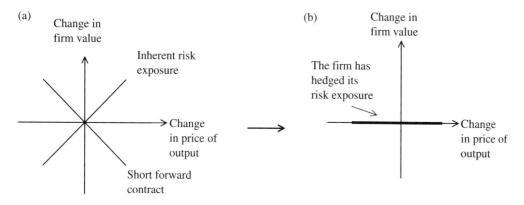

Figure 4.7   A firm that is exposed to the risk that the price of a commodity will fall manages its risk exposure by selling a forward contract on that commodity (*a*). If the hedge is effective, then all of its risk exposure is removed, as shown in (*b*).

leads to profits for a firm that has sold a forward contract. Figure 4.7 combines Figures 4.5 and 4.6 to illustrate that a firm that is exposed to the risk of a price decline can sell a forward contract to hedge its risk exposure.

4.2   USING FORWARDS TO MANAGE INTEREST RATE RISK

Recall that a forward rate agreement (FRA) is a forward contract on an interest rate. That is, if interest rates rise above the forward rate, the buyer of the FRA profits. If the interest rate at maturity is below the forward rate that was originally agreed to in the FRA, then the seller of the FRA realizes a profit. The settlement amount is essentially the present value of the lost/gained interest on the notional principal amount [see Equation (3.1)]. Thus, FRAs can be used to hedge against higher or lower than expected interest expense or revenue. It is important to note that a FRA is used to hedge just *one period* of interest.

4.2.1   Hedging Against an Increase in Interest Rates

A firm that buys a FRA does so to hedge against the risk that interest rates will rise. If interest rates subsequently rise, the hedger will lose money in the spot market and make an offsetting profit with the FRA it bought. For example, a firm that is a borrower at a floating interest rate faces the risk that interest rates will rise; a higher interest rate will lead to an increase in the firm's interest expense, and lower profits, all else equal. When a firm issues a floating-rate debt instrument, it is borrowing at a floating rate, and it loses when interest rates rise.[4] Another firm that plans to issue short-term debt some time in the near future may wish to lock in its interest expense today. Investors who own fixed-rate debt will experience a decline in the value of their assets if interest rates rise. For all these cases, buying a FRA serves to hedge the unwanted effect of higher interest rates.

Figure 4.8 shows the risk exposure of a firm that fears rising interest rates. Figure 4.9 illustrates the profit diagram for a long FRA position. Combining the two creates a hedge.

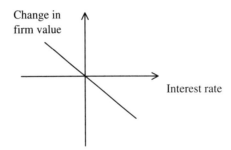

Figure 4.8   Risk exposure of a firm that fears rising interest rates.

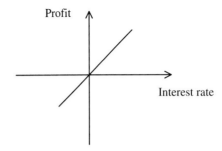

Figure 4.9   Profit diagram for a long FRA position.

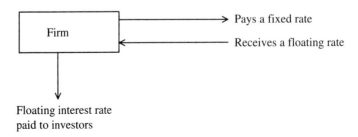

Figure 4.10   A FRA is equivalent to a one-period interest rate swap. It converts a floating-rate expense into a fixed-rate expense for a firm that is exposed to the risk that interest rates rise, such as a firm that has a floating-rate bond outstanding.

Another vehicle for visualizing what entering into a long FRA contract accomplishes in the way of interest rate risk management is shown in Figure 4.10. The firm is paying out a floating interest rate to investors. A long position in a FRA is equivalent to a one-period interest rate swap in which the firm is the fixed-rate payer, and it receives the floating rate. If the formula that establishes both floating rates is the same, then the firm is left with a locked-in fixed rate as a future expense.

Suppose that a firm has borrowed $60 million at a floating rate. The floating rate is reset every 6 months, and 6-month LIBOR at time t establishes the interest payment on the loan at time $t+1$. Thus, the firm knows what its next interest expense will be, 6 months from today. A FRA can be used to hedge one floating-rate interest rate payment, to be made at one future date. To hedge the interest expense it faces a year hence, the firm will buy a 6×12 FRA with a notional principal of $60 million. Suppose the price of the FRA is 8%. Table 4.1 illustrates how the firm has hedged itself.

Note in Table 4.1 that the profit/loss on the FRA is realized six months hence, while the actual interest expense on the loan is paid out 12 months hence. The interest payment to be made six months hence is already known, because LIBOR at time zero determines the interest payment on the floating rate note six months hence.

To be made comparable, and to illustrate the results of the hedge more clearly, we can compound the FRA's profits or losses so that they can be subtracted from or added to the actual interest expense on the floating-rate note. Table 4.2 performs this step. A perfect hedge is not

TABLE 4.1   Hedging Interest Rate Risk with a Long FRA Position: An Example

Six Month LIBOR, Six Months Hence	Interest Expense on the $60 million loan, paid Twelve Months from Today	Profit (+), or Loss (−) on the FRA, realized Six Months from Today[1]
7.0%	(0.070/2) $60 million=$2.10 million	−$291,410.63
7.5%	(0.075/2) $60 million=$2.25 million	−$145,352.34
8.0%	(0.080/2) $60 million=$2.40 million	$ 0
8.5%	(0.085/2) $60 million=$2.55 million	+$144,651.49
9.0%	(0.090/2) $60 million=$2.70 million	+$288,607.19

[1]The figures in this column are computed by means of Equation (3.1); it is assumed that there are 181 days until settlement and the day count method is actual/360. Equation (3.1) is repeated here:

$$\left| \frac{P[r(t1,t2) - fr(0,t1,t2)](D/B)}{1 + [r(t1,t2)(D/B)]} \right|$$

For example, the $291,410.63 loss on the FRA realized when six-month LIBOR is 7% is found by calculating:

$$\left| \frac{\$60,000,000[0.07 - 0.08](181/360)}{1 + [0.07(181/360)]} \right| = \$291,410.63$$

TABLE 4.2   Computing Profits or Losses for a FRA

Six-Month LIBOR, Six Months Hence	Interest Expense, Paid Twelve Months from Today	Compounded Profit (+), or Loss (−) on the FRA[1]	Total Effective Interest Expense
7.0%	$2.10 million	−$301,666.67	$2,401,666.67
7.5%	$2.25 million	−$150,833.33	$2,400,833.33
8.0%	$2.40 million	$ 0	$2,400,000.00
8.5%	$2.55 million	+$150,833.33	$2,399,166.67
9.0%	$2.70 million	+$301,666.67	$2,398,333.33

[1]For example, the compounded loss if LIBOR is 7% is computed as follows:

$$\$291,410.63[1 + 0.07(181/360)] = \$301,666.67$$

achieved (note the figures in the last column) because the FRA uses an actual/360 day count method, while we assumed that the loan uses a 30/360 day count method.

4.2.2 Hedging Against a Decline in Interest Rates

Sellers of FRAs wish to hedge against the risk that interest rates will fall. A decline in interest rates will reduce interest income for a floating-rate lender. But if that lender has sold a FRA, the lender will have hedged, since the drop in interest rates will also result in a profit on the FRA. An investor who owns a portfolio of short-term debt instruments or floating-rate bonds is also exposed to a decline in interest rates. Banks and other financial institutions that have made floating-rate loans, and financed them with fixed-rate sources of capital, also fear declining interest rates; their interest expense is fixed, but their interest income from the loans is variable.

Figure 4.11 illustrates the risk exposure for a firm that fears a decline in interest rates. The decline will lead to lower interest income, hence lower profits and a drop in firm value. Figure 4.12 is the profit diagram for a short FRA position. Selling a FRA will be profitable if interest rates fall below the contracted forward rate; the profits will help offset the decline in the value of a firm that depends on interest income from short-term securities or floating-rate notes. Instead of paying interest expense, this firm will receive interest income. Because the profit or loss on the FRA is reversed when the firm is short the FRA, the firm has greatly reduced the dispersion of interest income.

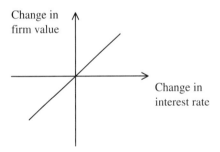

Figure 4.11   Risk exposure of a firm that fears falling interest rates.

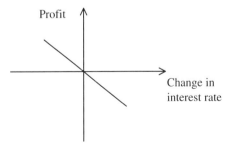

Figure 4.12   Profit diagram for a short FRA position; profits are made if interest rates fall.

4.3   USING FORWARD FOREIGN EXCHANGE CONTRACTS TO MANAGE RISK

Firms that buy and/or sell products in foreign countries are exposed to risks that the prices of foreign currencies will change. Even if a company does not import or export goods, it may be impacted by changing exchange rates if its competitors are either foreign-based exporters or domestic firms that import raw materials. In this section, we discuss the nature of this exposure to exchange rate risk, both from an income statement perspective and from a balance sheet perspective.

Understanding the jargon is important. If the home country is Great Britain, then the price of a foreign currency, say yen (¥), is expressed as £/¥. This is the British pound price of a Japanese yen. If this exchange rate rises, then we say that the yen has risen in value, or that the yen has strengthened (relative to the pound). If the yen becomes more expensive, then it is equivalent to saying that the pound has dropped in value, relative to the yen.

4.3.1   Managing the Risk That the Price of a Foreign Currency Will Rise

Consider a U.S. firm that imports its raw materials and must pay for them in a foreign currency. Assume that this U.S. firm is importing goods from Japan and thus must pay yen for its raw materials, which represents a cost. The U.S. firm wishes to maximize its dollar-denominated profits. A simple income statement is:

$$
\begin{array}{ll}
\text{Revenues} & = \$\text{Revs} \\
\underline{-\text{Costs (in yen)} \times \$/\yen} & \underline{= \$\text{Costs}} \\
\text{Profits (in dollars)} &
\end{array}
$$

The $/¥ exchange rate is what converts the firm's yen-denominated expenses into dollar expenses. This firm is exposed to the risk that the $/¥ exchange rate will rise. If it costs more dollars to buy a yen, then all else equal, this importer's dollar-denominated expenses will rise. Profits will fall and firm value will decline. We are assuming that the firm is unable to pass its increased costs on to the buyers of its products.

Another scenario is based on the balance sheet. A simple balance sheet has the following headings:

Assets   **Owners' Equity Liabilities**

Think of this balance sheet in terms of economic values, not accounting figures. If the market value of a firm's liabilities is subtracted from the market value of its assets, we are left with the market value of the stockholders' equity. The goal of a firm is to maximize the value of the owners' common stock, denominated in its home currency.

Suppose that some of the firm's liabilities are denominated in a foreign currency, and their value (in terms of the firm's local currency) is dependent on the exchange rate. It follows that if the exchange rate rises, the value of the liabilities rise. If all the firm's assets are denominated in the local currency, then assets can equal (liabilities+owners' equity) only if the value of owners' equity declines.

For example, suppose that a firm in France wishes to maximize the value of its common stock in terms of euros. This French firm has some of its liabilities with values that are denominated in terms of yen. The liabilities may be bonds that were issued in Japan, with coupon interest and principal denominated in yen, or perhaps some yen-denominated payables. This French firm has no yen-denominated assets. Using some specific figures, we might have the following balance sheet, in millions of euros, and assuming an initial exchange rate of €0.01 for each yen (€0.01/¥).

Assets	Liabilities and Owners' Equity		
Euro denominated = €145	Euro denominated liabilities = €50		
	Yen denominated liabilities = ¥3000	= €30	
	Owners' equity		= €65
Total assets = €145	Total liabilities and owners' equity		= €145

Now suppose that the exchange rate rises from €0.01/¥ to €0.012/¥. The assets and liabilities that are denominated in euros remain unchanged in value, all else equal. But the euro value of the yen-denominated liabilities rises to €36 million. Because the stockholders' claims are a residual, the value of the firm's common stock must decline to €59 million. The increase in the value of the firm's liabilities is accompanied by a commensurate decline in the euro value of owner's equity.

Thus, we conclude that a firm with substantial liabilities whose values are denominated in terms of a foreign currency is exposed to the risk that the exchange rate (home currency/foreign currency) will rise.

For this reason, many firms try to match their liabilities and assets in terms of currencies. In other words, this firm could hedge itself by selling €30 million of its assets and buying ¥3000 million of yen-denominated assets with the proceeds. By doing this, a rise in the €/¥ exchange rate will increase the value (expressed in euros) of both its assets and its liabilities by the same amount; the value of the firm's common stock will remain unchanged.

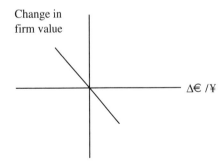

Figure 4.13   A rise in the euro price of a yen will cause a drop in the value of this firm.

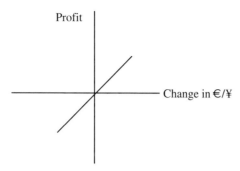

Figure 4.14   Profit diagram for long forward position in yen.

The French firm can also use forward contracts on foreign exchange to manage its risk exposure. Figure 4.13 illustrates the risk exposure of the French firm. Since a rise in the price of the yen causes a decline in the value of its stock, the French firm should buy a forward contract on yen to hedge. Figure 4.14 shows the profit diagram for a long forward position. If the firm depicted in Figure 4.13 buys yen forward, it can be hedged against a rise in the Japanese currency.

4.3.2   Managing the Risk That the Price of a Foreign Currency Will Decline

The exporter of a finished product that is paid in units of a foreign currency is exposed to the risk of a falling exchange rate, where the exchange rate is expressed as home currency/foreign currency. Again, think in terms of a simple income statement. This time consider the example of a Canadian firm that exports its production output to the United States and is paid in U.S. dollars. The firm wishes to maximize its profits in terms of Canadian dollars (Can$):

$$
\begin{array}{ll}
\text{Revenues (U.S.\$)} \times \text{Can\$/U.S.\$} & = \text{Can\$} \\
\underline{-\text{Costs}} & \underline{= \text{Can\$}} \\
\text{Profits} & = \text{Can\$}
\end{array}
$$

The Canadian firm fears that the Can$/U.S.$ exchange rate will decline. If this happens, its revenue stream, denominated in Canadian currency, will decline, and so will its profits. To hedge itself, the Canadian firm should sell U.S. dollars forward. If Can$/U.S.$ falls, the firm's revenues denominated in local currency will decline, but the firm will also realize a profit because it sold U.S. dollars forward.

As before, we can also analyze an exposure to risk in terms of a firm's balance sheet. Suppose that the value of some of a firm's assets is dependent on the exchange rate. It follows that if the exchange rate declines, and if all its liabilities are denominated in the local currency, the lower asset value must be accompanied by a decline in the value of the firm's common stock (denominated in the home currency).

For example, suppose that a firm in France (wishing to maximize the euro-denominated value of its common stock) has some of its assets with a value that is denominated in terms of British pounds. The assets may be British securities (stocks or bonds), or perhaps some undeveloped British real estate, and they are currently worth £30 million. This French firm has no pound-denominated liabilities. Assume an initial exchange rate of €1.5/£, and consider the following simple balance sheet:

Assets (in millions)	Liabilities and Owners' Equity (in millions)	
Euro denominated = €100	Euro-denominated liabilities	= €80
Pound denominated = £30 = €45	Owners' equity	= €65
Total assets = €145	Total liabilities and owners' equity	= €145

Now suppose that the exchange rate declines from €1.5/£ to €1.4/£. The assets and liabilities that are denominated in euros remain unchanged, all else equal. But the euro value of the British assets declines to €42 million. Because the stockholders' claims are a residual, the value of the firm's common stock must decline to €62 million.

Thus, we conclude that a firm with substantial assets whose values are denominated in terms of a foreign currency is exposed to the risk that the exchange rate (home currency/foreign currency) will decline.

This French firm could hedge itself by retiring €45 million of its euro-denominated liabilities and then issuing £30 million of pound-denominated debt. Upon doing this, a decline in the €/£ exchange rate will reduce the value (expressed in euros) of some of its assets *and* its liabilities; the value of the firm's common stock will remain unchanged. Alternatively, the firm could hedge by selling £30 million in the forward market.

As another case, consider a U.S.-based mutual fund that believes not only that some Japanese stocks are undervalued (in terms of their yen prices) but that the $/¥ exchange rate is likely to decline. A fall in the yen would offset the anticipated rise in the price of the Japanese stocks. The mutual fund can hedge its initial investment (but not its profit or loss) in the stocks by selling yen forward.

For example, assume that the spot exchange rate is $0.008696/¥. The mutual fund invests $10 million in the Japanese stocks. Therefore, at the current spot rate, it will invest ¥1.15 billion in Japanese stocks. To hedge its exposure to a decline in the yen, the fund sells ¥1.15 billion forward at the current forward price of $0.009076/¥. This forward contract is for delivery one year hence.

One year hence, the mutual fund is pleased to note that it was correct on both accounts. The value (in yen) of its Japanese stocks rose to ¥1.426 billion (up 24% in yen). But at the same time, the spot exchange rate declined to $0.008475/¥. Thus, the fund also made a profit on the forward contract. Its total dollar-denominated profit is computed as follows:

Sell stocks for ¥1.426 billion.

Exchange yen for dollars at the spot exchange rate: ¥1.426 billion × $0.008475/¥ = $12,085,350

Profit on forward contract: ¥1.15 billion ($0.009076/¥ − $0.008475/¥) = $691,150

Total dollar profit: $12,085,350 + $691,150 − $10,000,000 = $2,776,500

Dollar rate of return = ($12,776,500 − $10,000,000)/$10,000,000 = 27.765%

Had the fund not hedged itself, its dollar profit and dollar rate of return would not have been so impressive because of the decline in the price of yen. Even though the Japanese stocks rose in value by 24%, the fund's profits would have been only 20.85% [($12,085,350−$10,000,000)/ $10,000,000] because the yen dropped in value.

In this example, the fund sold its yen-denominated initial investment forward. It could not sell forward the total amount of yen it subsequently had, one year later, because it did not know how many yen it would have at that time. The value of the Japanese stocks rose, so in this example, the company ended up having more yen to sell. Had the prices of the Japanese stocks declined, it would have had less than ¥1.15 billion to exchange for dollars one year later.

4.4   WHAT QUANTITY SHOULD BE BOUGHT OR SOLD FORWARD?

So far, we have analyzed the direction of a firm's risk exposure and determined whether forward contracts should be bought or sold to reduce the variance of a firm's profits, and/or to reduce the volatility of firm value due to changes in prices. But we have not had much to say about how much should be bought or sold in the forward market to achieve the optimal results.

When an individual transaction is being hedged, it readily follows that the amount to buy or sell forward should equal the amount that underlies that transaction. If a firm will buy 5000 barrels of oil at the end of each of the next four quarters, then it should buy 5000 barrels of oil for forward delivery 3, 6, 9, and 12 months hence. A firm that knows that it will have $30 million in variable-rate debt outstanding for the next 2 years, but wishes to fix its future interest expense will want to buy a strip of FRAs, with delivery dates that correspond to each of the eight future dates on which the interest rate on its debt will be set, and each of which has a principal amount of $30 million.[5] A British firm that has an account receivable in the amount of €30 million will sell that many euros forward, with delivery on or around the date on which it expects to be paid; when it delivers the €30 million to satisfy the terms of the forward contract it will want its counterparty to pay British pounds.

Hedging economic profits (cash flows) or equity value against price risk is more difficult to accomplish. But in Chapter 2 you learned the basic tools that are required to manage risk when a firm has such goals. Suppose that a U.S. exporting firm has decided to hedge the next eight quarterly (2 years) cash flows against foreign exchange price risk; assume that the dollar price of Japanese yen is of concern. The firm must first estimate how its cash flows are related to changes in the $/¥ exchange rate. To do this, it can estimate different regression models with historical data, or use Monte Carlo simulation techniques to evaluate the relationship. Suppose that it estimates that a $0.001 decline in the price of the yen will lead to a decline of $200,000 in quarterly profits (and similarly, quarterly profits will rise at the rate of $200,000 per $0.001 increase in the price of yen). The firm will then want to sell forward a sufficient number of yen to be able to realize a profit of $200,000 on the forward contract for every $0.001 fall in the yen's price. This means that $200,000/($0.001/¥) = ¥200,000,000 should be sold for forward delivery at *each* quarterly delivery date (i.e., eight forward contracts calling for the forward delivery of ¥200 million 3, 6, …, 21, and 24 months hence).[6] This will lock in the forward prices that exist as of "today." Suppose that today's spot price and forward price for delivering yen 9 months hence is $0.0086/¥. Then, 9 months from today, the actual spot price is $0.0080/¥. The firm's operating profits *should* decline by about $120,000. But the firm will realize a profit equal to ¥200,000,000($0.0086/¥ − $0.0080/¥) = $120,000 on the forward contract.[7] Thus, the change in the price of the yen has a reduced impact on total cash flow for the firm that has hedged itself by selling yen forward.

Similar techniques are needed if the firm is managing equity volatility induced by price volatility. The firm must first estimate how equity value is affected by a change in a price of some good. Then, a sufficient quantity of the good must be bought or sold forward to result in a profit in the forward contract equal to the decline in equity value. The firm must also decide what horizon length is of concern.

Chapter 7 presents other aspects concerning the decision of the amount to be bought or sold forward.

4.5 SUMMARY

Forward contracts are used to manage price risk. Each contract, with its own delivery date, is used to manage a single cash flow. Hedgers buy forward contracts to protect themselves against price increases. They sell forward contracts to hedge against price declines. When the spot price at delivery is greater than the forward price, the party that has a long position in the forward contract profits, and the short loses. The party that sells forward contracts realizes a profit when the delivery day price is below the forward price that was agreed upon when the contract was originated.

Products that create revenues for a firm expose it to the risk that output prices will decline, assuming that demand for the firm's product is price inelastic. Inputs are costs, or expenses, and firms fear that the prices of these goods will rise. In both these cases, profits decline.

When a price decline causes a firm's assets to decline in value, then forward contracts should be sold. If a price rise causes a firm's assets to lose value, then forwards should be bought. Price changes will also affect liability values. If a price decline causes liabilities to increase in value, all else equal, the firm's stockholders will see the value of their position be eroded by the price drop and the firm should then sell forward contracts to hedge this risk. If a price rise leads to an increase in a firm's liability values, all else equal, then a long forward position is needed.

FRAs are used to protect firms against interest rate fluctuations. A party will buy a FRA to hedge against interest rate increases. FRAs will be sold when interest rate declines are feared.

Forward foreign exchange contracts are used to manage the risk that is created by changes in exchange rates. For example, suppose the dollar is the home currency, and fx is the foreign currency. Then a U.S.-based exporter that is paid fx for its product faces the risk that the \$/fx rate will decline, because that will lead to decline in its dollar-denominated revenues. Alternatively, a U.S.-based importer that must pay fx for its imports faces the risk that the \$/fx exchange rate will rise. It will take more dollars to buy one unit of fx, creating greater dollar-denominated expenses for the importer.

Another model of analyzing exchange rate risk focuses on the balance sheet. A firm with fx-denominated assets fears a decline in the value of fx. Another firm may have fx-denominated liabilities; it faces the risk that the price of fx will rise. In either case, the value of the stockholders' position declines.

Finally, in the last section of the chapter, we explained that to determine how much of an asset should be bought or sold forward, the firm should estimate how its cash flow or equity value is affected by price changes. Then, the best hedge dictates the buying or selling forward of a sufficient quantity of the asset to result in profits on the forward contract that equal the decline in profits or the decline in the firm's common stock.

References

Luenberger, David G. 1998. *Investment Science*. New York: Oxford University Press.
Wilson, Richard S. 1997. "Domestic Floating-Rate and Adjustable-Rate Debt Securities," in *The Handbook of Fixed Income Securities*, 5th ed, Frank J. Fabozzi, ed. Burr Ridge, IL: Irwin Professional Publishing.

Notes

[1] But the forward price will often reflect some of this advantage, as well as the benefit described in item #2.

[2] For *all* price risk to be removed, it is necessary that (a) the amount of the raw material underlying the forward contract equal the amount it will have to buy in the future to fulfill its production requirements, and (b) the quality of the raw material underlying the forward contract and its delivery location be the same as the quality and delivery location required by the firm in its production process. For example, there are many grades of crude oil, and relative prices can fluctuate. Similarly, the price of crude oil at the physical location of a chemical production plant will likely be different from the price of crude oil at the location at which it is removed from the ground.

[3] We have deliberately ignored another complication. Frequently, a firm's production is negatively correlated with price. Consider a farmer. When his harvest is large, it is likely that the harvests of many farmers are large, and therefore product prices will be lower. In other words, quantity risk naturally serves as a hedge in many cases. See Luenberger (1998, pp. 287–290). We thank Jerald Pinto for directing our attention to this situation.

[4] A floating-rate debt instrument is a security with a coupon or interest rate that periodically changes. The change in the level of interest is typically tied to an index. The index may be a short-term index such as LIBOR, or it may be a long-term index. See Wilson (1997) for a discussion of U.S. floating-rate securities. Floating rate notes are often called FRNs.

[5] If the firm wanted to lock in a fixed interest rate, it would probably prefer to enter into an interest rate swap as the fixed rate payer. Swaps will be introduced in Chapter 11.

[6] A currency swap would accomplish the same goal.

[7] Note two items. First, the firm only *estimated* that its profits would decline by $200,000 if the yen declines by $0.001. The actual change in profits is a random variable. Second, the firm must realize that it is actually hedging against a change in the *forward* price. In other words, profits on the forward exchange contract are realized if the spot price at delivery is less than the original forward price. But changes in operating profits have been estimated as being a function of changes in the spot price of the yen.

PROBLEMS

4.1 What price risk does a gold mining firm typically face? Suppose that demand for gold mining firm A's output is totally independent of the price of gold, while demand for gold mining firm B's output is price inelastic. How will this situation affect how firm A will use forward contracts on gold to protect itself, relative to how firm B will use gold forward contracts?

4.2 A cereal manufacturer buys grains from farmers. What price risk does the cereal manufacturer face? What price risk does the farmer face? How can each party use forward contracts on wheat and corn to manage its price risk?

4.3 Banks and other financial institutions have issued most of the floating-rate debt outstanding in the United States. Why do you think this is so?

4.4 A bank borrows $10 million for 12 months, and lends $10 million for 9 months, both at fixed interest rates. Discuss the interest rate risk that the bank is exposed to. How can it use a FRA to hedge this risk?

4.5 A bank borrows $10 million for 9 months, and lends $10 million for a year, both at fixed interest rates. Discuss the interest rate risk that the bank is exposed to. How can it use a FRA to hedge this risk?

4.6 A firm believes that it will have to borrow money 4 months from today. To what interest rate risk is this firm exposed? If it believes that it will need the funds for 2 months, how can it use a FRA to hedge this risk?

4.7

a. A firm plans on issuing $25 million in 9-month commercial paper. It expects to sell this security 6 months from today. How can it use a FRA to hedge this risk? What is the start and end date of the FRA it should use? That is, should it buy or sell an "N"×"M" FRA? What are the values of "N" and "M"?

b. Suppose that the price of the "N"×"M" FRA is 6%. Prepare a table showing the interest expense on its commercial paper. Assume that the day count method for both the commercial paper and the FRA is 30/360.

Future Relevant Interest Rate	Interest Expense on Issued Commercial Paper	Profit/ Loss on FRA
5%		
5.5%		
6%		
6.5%		
7%		

4.8 A financial institution has a portfolio of floating-rate loans. Its capital structure consists mainly of 5-year CDs and long-term fixed-coupon rate bonds that it sold several years ago. Discuss the interest rate risk that it faces. How can FRAs be used to manage its risk exposure?

4.9

a. A Japanese firm knows that in 4 months it will have 45 million French Francs to deposit in a French bank. It will leave these funds deposited in this interest-earning account (earning FFR-denominated interest) for a period of 8 months, at which time it will need Japanese Yen to pay one of its Japanese suppliers. Discuss the interest rate risk the Japanese firm faces. Discuss the nature of the foreign exchange risk that it faces.

b. Will the Japanese bank want to buy or sell a FRA? Suppose that 4×12 FRAs in France are quoted at 9%. Four months hence, spot 8-month French interest rates are 7.8%. What profit or loss was realized on the FRA?

4.10 A Japanese firm has all its assets in Japan and sells all its products in Japan; all its raw materials are produced domestically, as well. Last year, this firm borrowed money from a U.S. bank. It must pay both interest and principal in U.S. dollars. Discuss the exchange rate risk faced by this firm. How can it use a forward foreign exchange contract to manage this risk?

4.11 A U.S. mutual fund has invested in a portfolio of British stocks. However it does not wish to be exposed to exchange rate risk.

    a. Is the fund exposed to the risk that the $/£ rate will rise or fall?

    b. To hedge, should it buy or sell British pounds forward?

    c. Suppose that the fund invests $16 million in British stocks. The spot exchange rate is $1.68/£. The forward rate for delivery 6 months hence is $1.673/£. Six months later, the stocks are sold for £9 million, and the spot exchange rate is $1.70/£. What final profit or loss would the fund have realized, in terms of dollars, had it originally hedged its initial investment in British stocks? What was its dollar-based *annualized* rate of return? What would have been its dollar-denominated profit and rate of return, had it not hedged?

4.12 A Japanese firm imports U.S. apples and pays for them with dollars. What price risks does it face? How can it use forward contracts to hedge its price risks?

4.13 An insurance company owns a coupon bond that pays interest every November 15 and May 15. The face value of the bond is $45 million, and the coupon rate is 9%. The bond matures on May 15, 2002, and the firm plans on holding the bond until maturity. The insurance company is concerned about the total funds that it will have available on May 15, 2002. Today is October 15, 1997. Discuss how FRAs can be used to manage the insurance company's reinvestment risk (the risk it faces concerning the rates at which the coupons will be able to be reinvested).

4.14 An international portfolio manager located in Germany expects to receive $60 million to invest in German stocks next month. Discuss the price risks the manager faces. How can a forward foreign exchange contract be used to manage the currency risk exposure?

4.15 A firm uses historical data to estimate the following equation:

$$Y = 10 - 4500X$$

where Y = the change in annual cash flows and X = the change in 1-year LIBOR, in basis points. Fully discuss how the firm can use a FRA to manage its risk exposure regarding next year's cash flow, including a discussion of the principal amount of the FRA that should be used.

4.16 The prospectus to an international mutual fund states that the fund may enter into contracts to purchase or sell foreign currencies at a future date.

    a. Under what scenario or situation would it want to buy forward exchange contracts? Under what scenario or situation would it want to sell forward exchange contracts?

    b. The fund prospectus states that "such hedging…does not prevent losses if prices of such securities decline. Furthermore, it precludes the opportunity for gain if the value of the hedged currency should rise." Discuss what these statements mean.

4.17 A Swiss fixed-income mutual fund has invested €50 million in long-term British bonds having a coupon rate of 6%. The current exchange rate is €0.84/£.

a. What interest rate risk does the fund face? Why? How can it use a FRA to manage this risk exposure?

b. What exchange rate risk does it face? Why? How can it use a forward exchange contract to manage this risk exposure?

4.18   A Japanese bank expects to lend €10 million to a Spanish firm. If negotiations are successful, the loan will be made 1-month from today. The terms of the loan have already been established: the Spanish firm is to pay a fixed rate of 5%; the term of the loan will be one year; interest and principal, in euros, will be repaid to the bank 1-year after the loan is made. The Japanese bank is interested in maximizing the yen-denominated wealth of its Japanese stockholders.

a. Clearly discuss the nature of the interest rate risk the Japanese bank faces.

b. Clearly state how the Japanese bank can use forward rate agreements to manage the interest rate risk it faces. Explain how the FRA will reduce the interest rate risk faced by the bank. Be as precise and thorough as you can, given the information provided.

c. Should the bank desire that the contract rate on the FRA be above or below 5%? Why?

d. Clearly discuss the nature of the foreign exchange rate risks the bank will face after the loan is actually made.

e. Given your response in part d, clearly state how the bank can use forward exchange contracts to manage the exchange rate risk it will face after the loan is actually made. Again, be as precise and thorough as you can, given the information provided. Explain how the forward exchange contract will reduce the exchange rate risk faced by the bank.

4.19   Which of the following is true?

a. A firm will sell forward contracts to hedge against the risk that the price (cost) of its raw materials will rise.

b. A firm will sell forward contracts to hedge against the price (cost) of its raw materials falling.

c. A firm will sell forward contracts to hedge against the selling price of its output rising.

d. A firm will sell forward contracts to hedge against the selling price of its output falling.

4.20   A French food manufacturer uses Virginian (U.S.) peanuts as a raw material. It pays dollars for peanuts. This French firm

a. fears an increase in the price of a dollar (an increase in the €/$ exchange rate) and an increase in the price of peanuts

b. fears an increase in the price of a dollar and a decrease in the price of peanuts

c. fears a decrease in the price of a dollar and an increase in the price of peanuts

d. fears a decrease in the price of a dollar and a decrease in the price of peanuts

CHAPTER 5

Determining Forward Prices and Futures Prices

This chapter explains the theory of forward pricing. The forward price of a commodity is the price that is quoted today for delivery of the commodity in the future; the price is contracted today but is paid when the good is delivered in the future. Forward exchange rates exist for the forward purchase or sale of foreign exchange. Forward interest rates are rates that exist for future borrowing and lending opportunities.

All the ideas introduced in this chapter also apply to the pricing of futures contracts. In Chapter 6, we explain why futures prices and forward prices might differ. Since, however, the forces that might cause futures prices to differ from forward prices do not seem to be important, we can fairly safely conclude that they ought to be identical.

In theory, forward prices are determined by the force of arbitrage. In other words, if forward prices are "wrong," then arbitrage opportunities will exist. A fundamental assertion in the theory of finance is that well-functioning markets will not permit arbitrage. When arbitrage opportunities exist, markets are not in equilibrium (i.e., supply does not equal demand), and traders will quickly act to exploit arbitrage profits. (An arbitrage profit is riskless, involving a positive cash inflow at one or more dates, and zero cash flows at all dates. In other words, arbitrage requires no investment and no cash outlay. The arbitrageur generates only cash inflows at one or more dates.)

In the first section of this chapter, we discuss the cost-of-carry model for forward commodity prices. Under perfect markets assumptions, this model should determine one forward price. However, markets are imperfect; in particular, the *convenience yield* must be considered when one is determining the theoretical forward prices of commodities. The convenience yield is a unobservable theoretical construct that arises because there are problems in short selling commodities, and those who own the commodities may be reluctant to sell them. Because of this, it turns out that the cost-of-carry model determines only a maximum forward price that precludes arbitrage. Actual forward prices can be less than the theoretically correct forward price.

In contrast, however, this short selling problem does not exist for financial assets such as foreign currencies and interest rates. Thus, ignoring transaction costs, we will be able to compute one single forward price for these items. Theoretical forward exchange rates are computed in Section 5.2 and theoretical forward interest rates in Section 5.3.

5.1 FORWARD COMMODITY PRICES

5.1.1 The Cost-of-Carry Model

Assume that markets are perfect. This means that there are no transactions costs: no commissions or bid–ask spreads. There are no taxes. Market participants can buy or sell goods without affecting prices. There are no impediments to short selling.[1] Traders who short sell get full use of the proceeds. There is no default risk; each of the two parties to every transaction knows that the counterparty will perform as contractually required. Also assume that all individuals are wealth maximizers. This is equivalent to saying that everyone prefers more wealth to less, or that everyone's marginal utility of wealth is positive. Under these assumptions, the basic forward pricing model is:

$$F = S + CC - CR \qquad (5.1)$$

forward price = spot price + carry costs – carry return

The forward price F is the theoretical price for forward delivery of one unit of the commodity. The spot price S is the current price per unit of the good in the cash market.

Carry costs are best thought of as the additional costs incurred by buying and holding one unit of the commodity. Interest charges on borrowing to buy the good and the opportunity cost of having cash tied up in the asset are the most prominent of the carry costs. They are the only costs that are relevant in forward exchange and forward interest rate determination. Carry costs for physical commodities would also include the costs of insurance, storage, obsolescence, spoilage, and so on. Typically, we assume that all carry costs are paid at delivery.

There is no carry return for commodities. For financial assets, the carry return consists of the future value of the cash inflows that are provided to the holder. For example, dividend payments on stocks (and the interest earned on any dividends received prior to the forward contract's delivery date) would represent the carry return for a forward contract on common stock. Actual or accrued coupon income on bonds (and any interest that can be earned on coupons received) represents carry return for forwards on bonds. The interest that can be earned on a foreign currency is a carry return for forward exchange contracts. CR is the future value of these benefits of owning the cash asset.

An alternative interpretation of the cost-of-carry model is to view the purchase of a forward contract as a substitute for the actual purchase of the underlying asset in the cash market. If the forward price is correct, an investor should be indifferent between the two methods (forward purchase or spot purchase) of buying the asset. Consider the choice between buying 100 oz. of gold, or going long one gold forward contract. Buying the actual commodity requires a cash outlay. Moreover, there is an opportunity cost to that cash outlay: either interest is lost on the dollar amount if the money is withdrawn from an interest-earning asset, or else funds must be borrowed and interest paid on the principal. This makes the long forward position more desirable. To make the two choices equivalent, the forward price must be higher by the amount of interest that is saved by buying forward. Thus $F = S + CC$. When buying spot gold we must also account for any costs of insuring and storing physical gold between today and the delivery date; the forward price must be even higher to reflect those costs. If the cash asset supplies its owner with benefits such as dividends or interest income, then to reflect the benefits of owning the cash asset, the forward price will be lower.

5.1.2 Proof of the Cost-of-Carry Model

As with all proofs of propositions that are based on the absence of arbitrage, the proof of the forward pricing model will first ask what if forward prices are too high (more than what the theoretical pricing model specifies) and then analyze what will happen if forward prices are too low (less that what the model specifies).

Proof: What if $F > S + CC - CR$?

Then $+ F - S - CC + CR > 0$

Next, we will trade so that the cash flows are generated in the directions contained in this inequality. For example, to create a "$-S$", the underlying spot asset must be purchased; "$-S$" is a cash outflow (the minus sign) of S dollars. To create a "$+F$," the forward contract is sold (even-though there is really no cash flow until delivery).

Today, time 0

Sell forward at F_0.   No cash flow. As explained in Chapter 3, buying or selling a
                                          forward contract at its equilibrium price is costless.

Buy deliverable spot asset	$- S_0$
Borrow	$+ S_0$
Cash flow at time 0:	0

On the delivery date, time T

Make delivery to satisfy the terms of the forward contract	$+ F_0$
Pay back loan principal and interest[2]	$- S_0 - CC = - S_0 - \text{int} = - S_0[1 + h(0,T)]$
Receive any carry return[3]	$+ CR$
	$+ F_0 - S_0 - CC + CR > 0$

Thus, if F exceeds $S + CC - CR$, an arbitrage profit can be realized.

The steps one takes to arbitrage if $F > S + CC - CR$ is frequently called a **cash-and-carry arbitrage**. In a cash-and-carry arbitrage, the arbitrageur borrows to buy the spot asset, sells a forward contract, and carries the deliverable asset until the forward delivery date.

The set of trades that an arbitrageur takes to exploit the situation when forward prices are too low, $F < S + CC - CR$, is frequently called a **reverse cash-and-carry arbitrage**. In a reverse cash-and-carry arbitrage, the spot good is sold short, the proceeds of the short sale are lent, and a long position in a forward contract is taken.

Proof: What if $F < S + CC - CR$?

Then $F - S - CC + CR < 0$, or

$- F + S + CC - CR > 0$

Today, time 0

Buy forward at F_0.	0
Sell deliverable spot asset	$+ S_0$
Lend the proceeds from the short sale of the spot asset	$- S_0$
	0

On the delivery date, time T

Take delivery to satisfy the terms of the forward contract, and pay the contractually agreed-upon price	$- F_0$

| Receive loan principal and interest | $+S_0+\text{int}=+S_0+CC=S_0[1+h(0,T)]$ |
| Pay any carry return to the person to whom you sold the asset | |

$$-CR$$
$$\overline{-F_0+S_0+CC-CR>0}$$

In this part of the proof, we assume that the short seller receives full use of the proceeds of the short sale.[4] However, if the forward price is below its theoretical value, any individual who has a long position in the deliverable cash asset could *quasi-arbitrage* by selling it out of her portfolio, thereby receiving the full proceeds from the sale, and then performing all the steps just described. On the delivery date, this individual will be better off than had she continued to hold the cash asset. Thus, the cost-of-carry formula will determine forward prices when short selling is costly as long as some individuals have the deliverable asset in inventory and do not plan to consume it between time 0 and time T.

5.1.3   Examples

5.1.3.1   An Example: No Carry Return

Suppose the spot price of gold is $280/oz., the gold forward price for delivery six months hence is $300/oz., and the yearly interest rate is 10%. The theoretical forward pricing model states that the forward gold price should be $294/oz.:

$$F = S + CC = S[1 + h(0, T)]$$

$$F = 280(1.05) = 294$$

Because $F>S+CC$, borrow to buy an ounce of gold, and sell one overpriced gold forward contract for delivery six months from today:

Today

Sell one forward contract	No cash flow
Buy 1 oz. of gold	-280
Borrow (for six months at 10% annual interest)	$+280$
	0

At delivery, with gold at	$F_T=S_T=270$	$F_T=S_T=300$	$F_T=S_T=330$
Deliver 1 oz. of gold, fulfilling the contract's terms	$+300$	$+300$	$+300$
Pay back loan with interest	-294	-294	-294
	$+6$	$+6$	$+6$

Thus, regardless of the delivery day price of gold, the arbitrage profit is $6 per ounce of gold. Note that the profit is independent of the final spot price of gold on the delivery day.

The FinancialCAD function, aaCDF can be used to compute the forward price of a commodity, as shown in Figure 5.1. The slight difference between the FinancialCAD output forward price of 293.9616439 and the price of 294 we just computed is due to the use of the day count method[5] for unannualizing the annual interest rate of 10%. In this example, the FinancialCAD function uses a periodic rate of $(182/365)(10\%)=4.9863\%$ because it uses an actual/365 day count method.

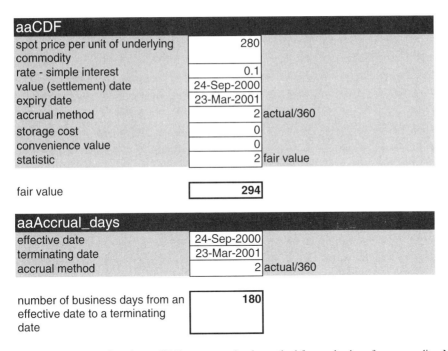

Figure 5.1 FinancialCAD function aaCDF computes the theoretical forward price of a commodity. Note the two dates and the day count method (accrual method).

Figure 5.2 FinancialCAD function aaCDF computes the theoretical forward price of a commodity. Note the two dates and the day count method (accrual method).

In our earlier example, we implicitly used a 30/360 day count method, which produces a six-month interest rate of $h(0, \frac{1}{2}\text{ yr}) = 5\%$.

In contrast, Figure 5.2 solves the same problem, except that the expiry date (delivery date) is March 23, 2001, and the day count method is actual/360. The expiry date is chosen so that delivery occurs 180 days after the contract initiation date; now, delivery takes place a half-year in the future, and $h(0, \frac{1}{2}\,\mathrm{yr}) = 5\%$. Thus, the theoretical forward price is 294. The FinancialCAD function, aaAccrual_days is used to compute the number of days until delivery.

5.1.3.2   An Example: The Underlying Asset has a Carry Return

Suppose that a forward contract on a share of General Mills stock exists. The delivery day is five months hence. Today's stock price is \$36.375. The stock will trade ex-dividend in the amount of \$0.275/share two months hence. The interest rate is 6% for all maturities. Compute the theoretical forward price.

The theoretical price is found by using the cash-and-carry pricing model:

$$F = S + CC - CR$$

$$F = 36.375 + (36.375)(0.06)\left(\frac{5}{12}\right) - (0.275)\left[1 + \frac{(0.06)(3)}{12}\right]$$

$$F = 36.375 + 0.909375 - 0.279125 = 37.00525$$

Note in particular how the **future value** of the dividend is subtracted from $S + CC$. The dividend is paid two months hence. It will earn interest over the subsequent **three** months, until the delivery date. Figure 5.3 shows how the FinancialCAD function aaEqty_fwd solves this problem.

5.1.4   Transactions Costs

If there are transactions costs, there is no single theoretically correct forward price. Instead, the forward price will lie between a lower and upper bound. The cost-of-carry formula becomes:

$$S(\mathrm{bid}) + CC1 - CR - T1 \leq F \leq S(\mathrm{asked}) + CC2 - CR + T2 \tag{5.2}$$

aaEqty_fwd		
value (settlement) date	24-Sep-2000	
expiry date	24-Feb-2001	
accrual method	4	30/360
rate - simple interest	0.06	
cash price of the underlying	36.375	
equity index		
statistic	2	fair value of forward or futures
dividend payment table	t_14	

t_14
dividend payment table

all the dividend dates from the value date to the expiry date	dividend amount
24-Nov-2000	0.275

fair value of forward or futures	37.00525

Figure 5.3 Using aaEqty-fwd to find the theoretical forward price when there is a carry return.

where

$T1$ = transactions costs from the reverse cash-and-carry arbitrage trades of selling the spot good at the bid price, lending the proceeds and buying a forward contract, $T1$ is paid at delivery

$T2$ = transactions costs from the cash-and-carry arbitrage trades of borrowing to buy the spot good at the asked price and selling a forward contract, $T2$ is paid at delivery

$CC1$ = carry costs from the reverse cash-and-carry arbitrage, which should incorporate the arbitrageur's lending rate and, if needed, should be adjusted to reflect the possibility that the short seller will *not* earn the full amount of interest on the proceeds from the short sale

$CC2$ = the carry costs from the cash-and-carry arbitrage trades, which should utilize the arbitrageur's borrowing rate

The lower bound (left-hand side of the inequality) is set by the reverse cash-and-carry arbitrage trades. If the lower bound is violated, buy the cheap forward, sell the spot good, and lend the proceeds.

The upper bound (right-hand side of the inequality) is set by the cash-and-carry arbitrage trades. If the forward price is above the upper bound, sell the overpriced forward, borrow, and buy the spot good.

EXAMPLE 5.1 Consider the example from Section 5.1.3.1 in which the spot price of gold is $280/oz. and the yearly interest rate is 10%. The forward contract calls for the delivery of 100 oz. of gold. Also assume that the total transaction cost of buying or selling 100 oz. of spot gold, and trading one forward contract, is $1/oz. There is no carry return. The range of possible forward prices per ounce of gold that precludes arbitrage is then

$$S + CC1 - T1 \leq F \leq S + CC2 + T2$$
$$280 + 14 - 1 \leq F \leq 280 + 14 + 1$$
$$293 \leq F \leq 295$$

The forward price itself can lie between $293 \leq F \leq \$295$ per ounce, for a forward contract on 100 oz. of gold. Any forward price below $293/oz. will allow reverse cash-and-carry arbitrage. If the forward price is above $295/oz., then cash-and-carry arbitrage is possible.

Alternatively, suppose that the bid price for spot gold is $279.50/oz and that the asked price for spot gold is $280.50/oz. In setting the lower bound, spot gold is sold at the bid price. In setting the upper bound, gold is bought at the asked price. Therefore, the no-arbitrage range of forward prices, in dollars per ounce, is

$$279.50(1.05) - 1 \leq F \leq 280.50(1.05) + 1$$

or,

$$292.475 \leq F \leq 295.525$$

Note that transactions costs widen the no-arbitrage bounds.

Next, suppose that in addition, the individual who is lending *you* the gold to short sell will allow you to use only 60% of the proceeds of the short sale. This means that *your* relevant carry costs (interest earned on the short sale of the spot asset) on the reverse cash-and-carry arbitrage (left-hand side of the inequality) is only [(279.50)(0.6)(0.05)=] $8.385/oz. You can only earn $8.385/oz. if you sell gold short and lend the proceeds that you will receive. The range of no-arbitrage forward prices for *you*, for a contract on 100 oz. of gold, is

$$279.5 + 8.385 - 1 \le F \le 295.525$$

$$286.885 \le F \le 295.525$$

You are at a disadvantage for performing the reverse cash-and-carry arbitrage trades relative to a quasi-arbitrageur who already has the gold in storage and therefore would receive the full proceeds from selling this asset. A quasi-arbitrageur will arbitrage if F falls below 292.475, but *you* cannot arbitrage unless F declines below 286.885/oz.

Example 5.1 illustrates that different individuals will have the ability to arbitrage at different forward prices, depending on their borrowing and lending rates and on the levels of transactions costs they face.

5.1.5 Implied Repo Rates and Implied Reverse Repo Rates

The **implied repo rate** is the rate of return earned on the cash-and-carry trades. In other words, it is the rate of return that a trader earns from buying the deliverable spot asset and simultaneously selling a forward contract.[6] The implied repo rate is effectively a lending rate. The trader buys the spot asset at time 0 for S_0. This requires a cash outflow, just as if money was lent. The sale of the forward contract guarantees a future cash inflow of F at time T. The implied repo rate is the lending rate from performing these trades, from time 0 to time T. It can be found by solving for $h(0,T)$ in the cost-of-carry formula. If there are no carry returns, then

$$F_0 = S_0[1 + h(0, T)]$$

Solving for $h(0,T)$ yields the *unannualized* implied repo rate when carry returns do not exist:

$$\frac{F_0 - S_0}{S_0} \qquad (5.3)$$

This periodic, or unannualized implied repo rate can be annualized by multiplying it by (365/d), where d is the number of days between time 0 and time T. Arbitrageurs will compare the implied repo rate on forward contracts to their own borrowing rate. If they can borrow money at a rate below the implied repo rate (which is a riskless lending rate), then there is a cash-and-carry arbitrage opportunity.

If there are carry returns, the cost-of-carry formula can be used to solve for $h(0,T)$ to compute *IRR*, the unannualized implied repo rate:

$$IRR = \frac{F_0 + CR - S_0}{S_0} \qquad (5.4)$$

EXAMPLE 5.2   You spend $582,500 to buy 10,000 shares of a common stock (at $58.25/share), and you sell a forward contract on these shares at a forward price of $58.50/share. The delivery date is three months hence. The future value of dividends that will be received on the shares during the next three months is $4078; this includes dividends received and the interest that can be earned on those dividends. Thus, the implied repo rate is:

$$\frac{(58.50)(10,000) + 4078 - 582,500}{582,500} = 1.129\%$$

The unannualized implied repo rate is 1.129%. The annualized implied repo rate is 4.517% (0.01129×4). If you can borrow at a rate below 4.517%/year, and face no transactions costs, you can cash-and-carry arbitrage.

The FinancialCAD function aaCDF-repo can be used to compute the annualized implied repo rate for a forward contract on a commodity. See Figure 5.4.

The best borrowing rate available to market participants is the rate that corporations, dealers, institutions, and so on can obtain by engaging in what is called a **repurchase agreement**, or repo. In a repurchase agreement, party A owns some securities. He sells them to party B for a sum of money and agrees to repurchase them at a later date for a somewhat greater sum of money. Thus, A has effectively used the securities as collateral to borrow money from B. The interest rate associated with a repo is called the **repo rate**. Most repos are overnight loans, and sometimes the phrase **overnight repo rate** is used to describe the annualized borrowing rate for individuals who use repurchase agreements for one day. Repos of longer duration are called **term repos**.

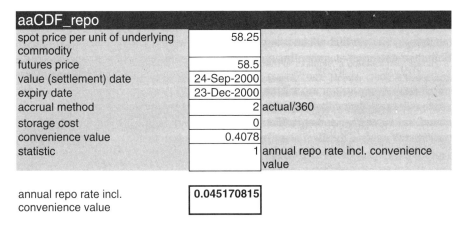

Figure 5.4 The FinancialCAD function aaCDF_repo computes the annualized implied repo rate for a forward contract on a commodity.

EXAMPLE 5.3   Party A owns $1 million face value of Treasury bills that currently have a market value of $950,000. Party A needs cash, and she can raise the needed funds by entering a repurchase agreement. Party A sells the T-bills to party B for $945,000[7] and agrees to repurchase them tomorrow for $945,311. Thus the annualized interest rate on this repurchase agreement is[8]:

$$\frac{F-S}{S} \times \frac{360}{1} = h(0, 1\,\text{day}) \times \frac{360}{1} = \frac{311}{945,000} \times 360 \;(= 0.0003291 \times 360) = 11.848\%$$

Arbitrage is possible if the implied repo rate for a forward contract exceeds actual market repo rates. This is equivalent to saying that the effective lending rate available in the forward market by buying the spot good and selling a forward contract exceeds the arbitrageur's borrowing rate.

The **implied reverse repo rate** is the rate of return earned by selling short the spot good and buying a forward contract. These two transactions are part of the reverse cash-and-carry arbitrage. The implied reverse repo rate is effectively a borrowing rate because the short sale of the spot good will provide a cash inflow, just as would any borrowing transaction. Going long a forward contract locks in a delivery date cash outflow. Arbitrageurs will compare the implied reverse repo rate to their own riskless lending rates. Whenever possible, they will risklessly borrow at the implied reverse repo rate in the forward market and lend at the higher lending rate available to them in the securities or real goods markets.

Summarizing, individuals will engage in cash-and-carry arbitrage if the implied repo rate in a forward contract exceeds the market repo rates. Under these conditions, they will borrow money at the market repo rate, buy the deliverable asset, and sell a forward contract. Individuals will engage in reverse cash-and-carry arbitrage whenever the implied reverse repo rate in a forward contract is less than the riskless lending rate. Recall that a reverse cash-and-carry arbitrage requires the short sale of the underlying asset, the purchase of a forward contract, and the lending of the proceeds of the short sale.

When markets are perfect, the implied repo rate and the implied reverse repo rate are equal. However, if (a) the purchase price of the spot good (the asked price) is greater than its selling price (the bid price), (b) there is a bid–asked spread on the forward contract, and/or (c) there are transactions costs required to do the trades, then the implied repo rate (the lending rate available in the forward market) will be less than the implied reverse repo rate (the borrowing rate available in the forward market). These market imperfections increase the range of forward prices that can exist without permitting arbitrage.

5.1.6   Forward Prices of Commodities: The Convenience Yield

The cost-of-carry model invokes perfect markets assumptions to determine theoretical forward prices. In particular, it is assumed that the commodity can be sold short and that those who own the commodity have no reservations about selling it.

However, for most goods other than financial assets and gold, the cost-of-carry model can be used only to determine an **upper bound**. In other words, for agricultural, energy, and metal forwards, we can say that $F \leq S + CC - CR$. If the forward price is above $S + CC - CR$, one can perform cash-and-carry arbitrage by using borrowed funds to buy the good in the spot market, and selling forward contracts. The carry costs must also account for storing, insuring, and otherwise maintaining the physical commodity.

The model cannot be used to determine the existence of arbitrage opportunities when the cash good must be sold short to arbitrage. The reason for this lies in what makes financial commodities different from all other physical commodities such as agricultural commodities. Financial instruments such as bonds, foreign exchange, and stocks are used for investment purposes. They are not used as part of any production process. Thus if the forward price was too low, no one would be inconvenienced by selling, or selling short, the cash good (the debt instruments, stocks, or foreign exchange) and buying an underpriced forward contract. No one would miss these commodities; they would be replaced on the delivery date of the forward contract. Indeed, individuals who arbitrage would be better off on the delivery date because they had sold these assets short (pure arbitrage) or out of their inventory (quasi-arbitrage).

We call goods that *are* used for production purposes noncarry commodities. The users of noncarry commodities will not always be willing to sell their inventory in the spot market and buy forward contracts to replenish their supplies at a later date. Similarly, potential pure arbitrageurs will not always be able to find supplies of the physical good to borrow and sell short. Producers need to maintain supplies of the goods that are used in their production processes. Cereal manufacturers need wheat and corn in inventory; electrical equipment manufacturers need supplies of copper to manufacture their products. Consequently, the cash prices of these noncarry commodities can even be above the forward price, and it is possible that no one will be willing and able to arbitrage by selling the good in the spot market and buying forward contracts.

The cost-of-carry formula can be modified to account for this situation by defining a new term, **convenience yield** (also sometimes called the convenience return). A commodity's convenience yield is the benefit, in dollars, that a user realizes for carrying inventory of the physical good above his or her immediate near-term needs. An oil refiner receives the convenience yield on crude oil inventories because without it, the refiner cannot produce any finished products.

Financial assets have no convenience return. In contrast, agricultural commodities frequently have a high convenience return because producers face losses if they have none of the commodity in inventory. A commodity's convenience return can be different for different users, and it can vary over time.[9] It will be at its highest when there are spot shortages of the cash good. At these times, spot prices will lie above forward prices.

Thus, for noncarry commodities, the cost-of-carry formula may be presented as follows;

$$F = S + CC - CR - \text{convenience return} \tag{5.5}$$

The problem with this formula is that the convenience return is not easily measured. Some users may have a low convenience return, and they will arbitrage when the forward price lies below $S + CC - CR - their$ convenience return. Other users are indifferent between selling their supplies (or lending them to short sellers) and maintaining their inventory to realize their convenience return. In such cases, the relevant convenience return in Equation 5.5 is the marginal convenience return for that marginal producer. Finally, other producers will have a high convenience return, and they will never wish to sell or lend their supplies of the physical good.

Whenever the cash price of a deliverable commodity is above the forward price, a spot shortage (or temporary excess demand) of the good probably exists, and there is a high marginal convenience return.

5.1.7 Do Forward Prices Equal Expected Future Spot Prices?

5.1.7.1 Financial Assets

The cost-of-carry model determines the theoretical forward prices of financial assets such as interest rates, currencies, and stocks. Under the appropriate assumptions, actual forward prices must equal theoretical forward prices, or else arbitrage opportunities will exist. Expectations of future spot prices are not directly included in the forward prices of these assets. Any expectations of future spot prices are incorporated into the current spot price of the good, and given that spot price, as well as carry costs and carry returns, the forward price is found by the cost-of-carry model.

For example, if all investors expect the stock market to greatly appreciate in value in the near future, then the *spot* prices of stocks will rise to reflect those expectations. No matter how bullish investors are, the forward price of stocks must equal the spot price plus the net carrying costs (interest on the stocks minus the dividends between today and the delivery date).[10] Whether the forward price incorporates the market's expectation of the future spot price of the underlying commodity becomes a matter of semantics. The spot price reflects market expectations, and given the spot price and the cost-of-carry formula, the forward price is determined. The forward price incorporates expectations only because they are reflected in spot prices.

Therefore, the forward price of a financial asset or gold will rarely equal the market's expectation of the future spot price. Suppose that the spot price of gold is $280 and the interest rate is 0%. Then, the forward price must also equal $280, regardless of market expectations about the future spot price of gold.

Recall that market imperfections allow the forward price to lie in a band, or range, of prices without allowing for arbitrage opportunities. In these cases, the forward price will provide more information about market expectations. For example, if the theoretical forward price F is $350 \leq F \leq 352$ and investors are bullish, we would expect to see $F = 352$. If investors are bearish, then F will likely equal 350. Now, forward prices reveal market expectations, and futures prices are theoretically correct.

If F rises above 352, traders will arbitrage by buying the spot good and selling (overvalued) forward contracts. When the spot good is bought, its price will rise; when it is sold forward, the forward price will fall. Eventually, equilibrium will be reestablished, and there will be no opportunities to arbitrage. If F declines below 350, forwards will be bought and the spot good will be sold short.

The situation is different for the forward prices of physical commodities, where the forward price more likely reflects expected supply and expected demand at the delivery date. As such, the forward price does reflect the market's expectation of the future spot price. But it may not equal the expected spot price. There are theories that predict the possible existence of risk premiums in forward prices. A risk premium is defined to be the difference between the forward price and market's expectation of what the spot price will be at delivery. The theories give rise to the concepts of *normal backwardation* and *contango*.[11]

5.1.7.2 Physical Commodities: Normal Backwardation and Contango

In a world of certainty, determining the forward price of any commodity is easy. It will equal the future spot price of the good at delivery, which all investors know with certainty. There is nothing to prevent the spot price from changing in a known, perfectly predictable manner, such that the forward price lies above or below the current spot price. The spot price will fluctuate according to supply and demand conditions. However, all investors know what the spot price will be at every subsequent date, including the delivery date of the forward contract. The spot price that all investors know will exist on the delivery date equals the forward price, and in a world of certainty, the forward price will never change. Buyers and sellers of forward contracts put up no money to assume their positions, and they will realize no subsequent cash flows from any changes in forward prices. Speculators, hedgers, and arbitrageurs have no reason to exist because the spot price at delivery is known with certainty and the forward price is constant.

While the situation is different under conditions of uncertainty, many still believe in the **unbiased expectations hypothesis of forward prices**. According to this theory, the forward price equals the market's expectation of what the spot price will be at delivery:

$$F_t = E_t(\tilde{S}_T)$$

This formulation states that F_t, the forward price at any time t, equals the time t expectation of what the spot price of the commodity will be at delivery (time T). Under this hypothesis, the expected cash flow to any forward position is zero; today's forward price equals the expected forward price on the delivery day. And it should be obvious that the expected forward price for delivery at time T equals the expected spot price on day T.

If the unbiased expectations hypothesis of forward prices is correct, then any forward price is determined because traders have used all the information available to come to the aggregate expectation that on the delivery date, the spot price for the good will be that forward price. In other words, $F_t = E_t(\tilde{S}_T)$.

If speculators are risk neutral, the unbiased expectations theory is likely to explain commodity forward prices. Risk neutrality means that all assets are priced to provide the same riskless rate of return. If any asset was priced to yield an expected return greater than the riskless interest rate, investors would buy it, regardless of the asset's riskiness. Similarly, no investor would ever buy an asset if he thought it would yield a return less than the riskless rate. Forward positions, long and short, can be entered into with no cash outlay. In a risk-neutral world, therefore, the expected cash flow to both longs and shorts must be zero.

Others, however, believe that the forward price is a biased predictor of what the future spot price will be. Keynes (1930) first proposed that forward prices will contain a risk premium. He hypothesized that hedgers tend to sell forward contracts and futures contracts. If hedgers are net short, then it must follow that speculators have more long positions than short positions.[12] But speculators will assume long positions only if they expect to earn a higher return, a risk premium. Therefore, the forward price must be below the spot price that investors expect to prevail at delivery, $F_t < E(\tilde{S}_T)$. The forward price is expected to rise over the life of the contract, to provide a positive expected return to speculators. Risk-averse hedgers are willing to lose a little to shed the price risks they face in an unhedged position.

Keynes called this situation **normal backwardation**. According to the normal backwardation hypothesis, forward prices are below expected future spot prices, and the forward price is expected to rise as the delivery date approaches. The reason for backwardation is that hedgers are usually short forward. A hypothetical price process of a forward contract exhibiting normal backwardation is shown in Figure 5.5.[13]

A **contango** exists whenever the forward price lies above the expected future spot price, $F_t > E_t(\tilde{S}_T)$. Here, the forward price should generally decline as the delivery date nears. This situation arises because for some commodities and at some times, hedgers will be net long forward contracts, and speculators will be net sellers of forward contracts. Speculators must expect to earn a profit if they are to sell forwards. In a contango, forward prices must be expected to fall. A contango is shown in Figure 5.6.

Cootner's (1960) theory about the seasonality of hedging activities can be modified to present a summary statement about the issue of whether forward prices equal expected future spot prices

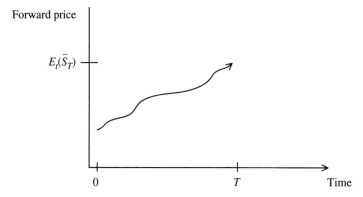

Figure 5.5 Normal backwardation. The forward price will lie below the existing expectation (as of any time t prior to the delivery date, time T) of what the time T (delivery date) spot price will be. The forward price will rise, on average. It is assumed that $E_t(S_T)$ remains unchanged as the delivery date nears.

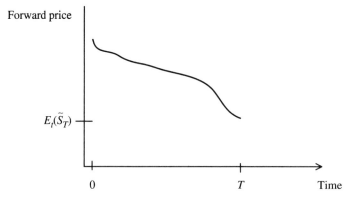

Figure 5.6 Contango. The forward price lies above the existing expectation (as of any time t prior to the delivery date, time T) of what the time T (delivery date) spot price will be. The forward price will fall, on average. It is assumed that $E_t(\tilde{S}_T)$ remains unchanged as the delivery date nears.

for noncarry commodities. Basically his model states that the supply and demand varies over time for short hedges and for long hedges. Any risk premium (the difference between the forward price and the expected spot price on the delivery date) will be a function of the net hedging activity occurring at any moment, and it can change in sign (from backwardation to contango) over the life of the contract.

Thus, if risk-averse hedgers are currently attempting to manage their risk exposures by actively selling forward contracts, the forward price quoted by dealers will decline. This will occur in one of two ways. First, if the dealers are playing the role of speculators, we conclude that they will not be willing to accept the price risk unless there is a risk premium, $F_t < E(\tilde{S}_T)$. Alternatively, the dealers will use other derivatives markets to shed themselves of the price risk they assumed by buying forwards from the hedgers. They will do this by selling futures, or by using options or swaps. But now, *their* hedging activities will suppress prices in those markets, and there will be a resulting secondary impact on forward prices. But either way, we conclude that active short hedging activity will lead to lower forward prices, which are likely to be less than the future spot prices expected by market participants.

It seems naive to believe that hedgers are consistently net short. Users of commodities hedge their planned future purchases of raw materials, too, and they will tend to buy forward contracts in those situations. Thus, like Cootner, we might expect to observe backwardation and contango situations at different times for different commodities. The question of whether forward prices equal expected future spot prices is ultimately an empirical one, and many researchers have examined forward prices for the existence (if any) of a risk premium that would answer whether the unbiased expectations hypothesis holds, or whether backwardation or contango exists.

Kamara (1984, p. 70) summarizes the many studies that test whether forward prices are the unbiased expectation of future spot prices writing about futures markets by stating:

> In sum, although it is widely accepted that futures markets are used by risk-averse hedgers, the evidence suggests that hedgers have been able to purchase the insurance very cheaply. As a result, forward prices on average do not contain a significant risk premium.

5.1.8   Valuing a Forward Contract After Origination

After a forward contract has been originated, forward prices change. In other words, on March 1, you might agree to buy an ounce of gold on October 1, at the forward price of \$320/oz. One month later, on April 1, the forward price for delivery of gold on October 1 might be \$330/oz. The value of your original forward contract (that obligates you to buy gold at \$320/oz.) is merely the present value of the difference between the two forward prices.

Thus, define

$F(0,T)$ = forward price of the original contract, created at time 0, for delivery of the underlying asset at time T

$F(t,T)$ = forward price at time t, for deliver also at time T

$h(t,T)$ = spot interest rate that exists at time t, for borrowing and lending until time t with $h(t,T)$ = $r(T-t)/365$, where r is the annual interest rate for borrowing and lending over $(T-t)$ days.

Then, the value of the original forward contract, at time t, is

$$\frac{F(t,T) - F(0,T)}{1 + h(t,T)}$$

If the forward price has risen $[F(t,T)>F(0,T)]$, the value is positive for the long position (an asset) and negative for the short position (a liability). If the forward price has declined $[F(t,T)<F(0,T)]$, the value is positive for the individual who is short the forward contract and negative for the individual who is long the contract.

5.2 Forward Exchange Rates

5.2.1 The Standard Approach to Deriving the Forward Exchange Rate

The standard cost-of-carry pricing formula, with one small modification, determines foreign exchange forward prices and forward prices. Define:

N = number of units of foreign exchange in one forward contract

T = number of days until delivery

r_d, r_f = annual domestic and foreign interest rates, respectively

$h_d(0,T)$ = domestic unannualized interest rate from today until the delivery date = $(r_d)(T)/365$

$h_f(0,T)$ = foreign unannualized interest rate from today until the delivery date = $(r_f)(T)/365$

When performing the cash-and-carry arbitrage trades, borrow funds to purchase $N/[1+h_f(0,T)]$ units of foreign exchange and sell a forward contract for the delivery of N units. In other words, buy the present value of N units of foreign exchange, where the interest rate used in determining the present value factor is the *foreign* interest rate. Thus, if the cost-of-carry model assumes no carry return,[14] the forward exchange pricing model specifies

$$F = \frac{S}{1+h_f(0,T)}[1+h_d(0,T)] = \frac{S[1+h_d(0,T)]}{1+h_f(0,T)} \tag{5.6}$$

Equation (5.6) is the standard cost-of-carry forward pricing model when there is no carry return, except $S/[1+h_f(0,T)]$ is substituted for S.

When performing cash-and-carry arbitrage,[15] the arbitrageur borrows funds to purchase the present value of N units of foreign exchange and invests those units to earn the foreign riskless interest rate. On the delivery date, the arbitrageur will have N units of the foreign currency to deliver, thereby allowing the requirements of the short forward position to be fulfilled.

Equation (5.6) can be rearranged and reexpressed in terms of annual interest rates as follows:

$$\frac{F}{S} = \frac{[r_d(T/365)]+1}{[r_f(T/365)]+1} = \frac{365+r_dT}{365+r_fT} \tag{5.7}$$

EXAMPLE 5.4 Suppose that the delivery date for forward delivery of euros is 144 days hence. The annualized domestic (U.S.) interest rate is 7% if an individual wishes to borrow or lend for 144 days. The euro interest rate is 4.5%/year. The spot exchange rate is $0.95/€. Determine the theoretical forward price.

Use Equation (5.6) to obtain the solution:

$$F = \frac{S[1 + h_d(0,T)]}{1 + h_f(0,T)} = \frac{0.95[1 + (0.07)(144)/365]}{1 + (0.045)(144)/365} = \frac{0.95(1.027616)}{1.017753} = \$0.9592/€$$

The theoretical forward price is $0.9592/€. By going long one euro forward contract, a trader locks in the purchase price of $0.9592/€. Figure 5.7 shows how FinancialCAD uses the function aaFXfwd to solve the problem. The function aaAccrual_days (also shown in Figure 5.7) is used to verify that there are 144 days between September 24, 1999 and February 15, 2000.

AaFXfwd

FX spot - domestic / foreign	0.95	
Rate – domestic - annual	0.07	
Rate – foreign - annual	0.045	
Value (settlement) date	24-Sep-2000	
Forward delivery or repurchase date	15-Feb-2001	
Accrual method - domestic rate	1	actual/365 (fixed)
Accrual method - foreign rate	1	actual/365 (fixed)
Statistic	2	fair value of forward (domestic /foreign)

fair value of forward (domestic /foreign)	**0.959206418**

AaAccrual_days

Effective date	24-Sep-2000	
Terminating date	15-Feb-2001	
Accrual method	2	actual/360

Number of business days from an effective date to a terminating date	**144**

Figure 5.7 The FinancialCAD function aaFXfwd is used to compute the theoretical forward exchange price. The time from an effective date to a terminating date is found by using a AaAccrual_days.

The FinancialCAD function aaFXfwd_sim allows you to observe how the forward price varies as a function of either the spot rate, the domestic interest rate, or the foreign interest rate. You choose the independent variable on the line titled *x*-axis. The program's output table (Figure 5.8a) was plugged into the Excel Chartwizard to produce a graph (Figure 5.8b).

Now, suppose that the actual 144-day forward price is $0.953/€. Because this price is less than the 144-day theoretical forward price of 0.9592, arbitrageurs will engage in reverse cash-and-carry arbitrage. Assume that *N*=€125,000 An arbitrageur would perform the following series of reverse cash-and-carry trades:

Today

- Borrow 125,000/1.017753=€122,819.58 at the foreign interest rate of 4.5%/year. Sell the €122,819.50 at the spot price of $0.95/€, and receive $116,678.525.
- Lend the proceeds of $116,678.525 for 144 days at the domestic interest rate of 7%/year.
- Go long one forward contract that requires the purchase of €125,000 at the forward price of $0.953/€.

Zero cash flow today

At Delivery (144 days hence)

- Receive the loan proceeds of $116,678.525(1.02762)=$119,901.186.
- Fulfill the requirements of the forward contract: by purchasing €125,000 at the contracted price of $0.953/€. The total purchase price is $119,125.
- Repay the euros borrowed. With interest, the obligation is €125,000.

Cash inflow at delivery=$119,901.186−$119,125=$776.186

Note two points. First, the arbitrage profit of $776.186 is realized with no initial capital outlay. Second, if arbitrage opportunities such as this ever emerged, individuals would sell euros in the spot market and go long forward contracts. The process of arbitrage would lead to a lower spot euro price and a higher forward euro price. Arbitrageurs' trades will correct the initial mispricing.

Data on foreign interest rates can be found at several websites, such as www.bloomberg.com/markets/iyc.html (Bloomberg's site). Charts that depict how foreign interest rates have moved in the past few years can be found at www.yardeni.com/finmkts.html (Ed Yardeni's site). The *Wall Street Journal* gives yields on international government bonds, which are long-term foreign interest rates, in its "Bond Market Data Bank" column; an example is given in Figure 5.9. *Barron's* provides a graph of short-term interest rates for British pounds, euros, and Japanese yen, and a graph of yields for long-term British, German, and Japanese government bonds in its weekly "Current Yield" column; an example is presented in Figure 5.10.

5.2.2   An Alternative Derivation of the Theoretical Forward Price

Assume that you have one dollar to invest for *T* days. You have two ways to invest the money:

Method 1: Invest the dollar in the United States. At the end of the *T* days, you will have $1[1+h_d(0, T)]=1+(r_d T/365)$.

(a)

AaFXfwd_sim		
FX spot - domestic / foreign	0.95	
Rate - domestic - annual	0.07	
Rate - foreign - annual	0.045	
Value (settlement) date	24-Sep-99	
Forward delivery or repurchase date	15-Feb-00	
Accrual method - domestic rate	1	actual/ 365 (fixed)
Accrual method - foreign rate	1	actual/ 365 (fixed)
Statistic	2	fair value of forward (domestic / foreign)
x-axis	1	domestic spot price
Simulation range x-axis	0.01	
Orientation	1	vertical format

Simulation table - aaFXfwd_sim

Items in X axis simulation range	items in Y axis simulation range
0.9405	0.949614353
0.941857143	0.950984648
0.943214286	0.952354943
0.944571429	0.953725238
0.945928571	0.955095533
0.947285714	0.956465828
0.948642857	0.957836123
0.95	0.959206418
0.951357143	0.960576712
0.952714286	0.961947007
0.954071429	0.963317302
0.955428571	0.964687597
0.956785714	0.966057892
0.958142857	0.967428187
0.9595	0.968798482

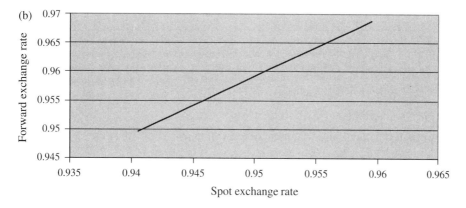

Figure 5.8 (a) The FinancialCAD function aaFXfwd_sim computes a table of theoretical forward exchange prices as a function of either the spot exchange rate, the domestic interest rate, or the foreign interest rate. (b) Forward exchange rate as a function of the spot exchange rate.

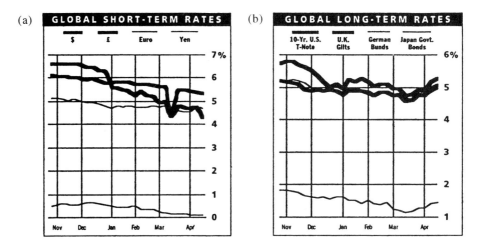

BOND MARKET DATA BANK   6/4/01

INTERNATIONAL GOVERNMENT BONDS

COUPON	MATURITY (Mo. /YR.)	PRICE	CHANGE	YIELD*	COUPON	MATURITY (Mo. /YR.)	PRICE	CHANGE	YIELD
Japan (3 p.m. Tokyo)					**Germany** (5 p.m. London)				
4.50%	06/03	109.03	− 0.01	0.06%	3.25%	02/04	97.23	+ 0.06	4.354%
3.40	06/05	112.50	− 0.03	0.27	5.00	05/05	101.66	− 0.01	4.530
1.30	06/11	100.53	+ 0.04	1.24	5.00	07/11	99.45	+ 0.00	5.069
1.90	03/21	100.07	− 0.22	1.90	5.50	01/31	98.09	+ 0.02	5.683
United Kingdom (5 p.m. London)					**Canada** (3 p.m. Eastern Time)				
7.00%	06/02	101.86	− 0.05	5.080%	6.00%	12/02	101.86	+ 0.04	4.698%
9.50	04/05	114.46	− 0.07	5.312	5.25	09/03	100.55	+ 0.07	4.986
6.25	11/10	108.19	− 0.03	5.146	6.00	06/08	102.05	+ 0.29	5.641
4.25	06/32	88.71	− 0.55	4.968	8.00	06/27	126.97	+ 0.61	5.949

*Equivalent to semi-annual compounded yields to maturity

Figure 5.9 Yields on government bonds from Japan, the United Kingdom, Germany, and Canada. (Reprinted with permission of *The Wall Street Journal*, page C20. © June 4, 2001.)

(a) **GLOBAL SHORT-TERM RATES**   (b) **GLOBAL LONG-TERM RATES**

Figure 5.10 (a) Short-term interest rates for four major currencies. (b) Long-term yields for government bonds of the same countries. (Reprinted with permission from *Barron's*, April 23, 2001, page MW16.)

Method 2:

1. Convert the dollar into fx at the spot exchange rate, S.
2. Invest the $1/S$ units of fx to earn the foreign interest rate of $h_f(0, T)\%$ over T days.
3. Sell a forward contract that obligates you to deliver the $(1/S)[1 + h_f(0, T)]$ units of fx on the delivery date at time T. The forward price is F (expressed as the dollar price of a unit of foreign exchange fx).
4. At time T, your foreign investment will be worth $(1/S)[1 + h_f(0, T)]$ units of fx. Under the terms of the forward contract, each fx unit can be converted to dollars at the exchange rate F. Thus, you will receive $(F/S)[1 + h_f(0, T)]$ dollars.

The two methods are equivalent because they are both riskless lending transactions for T days. Therefore, you should have the same wealth at time T either way you invest. This means that

$$\$1[1+h_d(0,T)] = \$1(F/S)[1+h_f(0,T)]$$

which is the same as Equations (5.6) and (5.7).

If one strategy dominated the other, then investors would invest in the better strategy. For example, if method 1 provided a higher return than method 2, Americans would keep their dollars as dollars, and invest in the United States. Also, foreigners would sell their units of fx for dollars, lend them in the United States, and buy forward contracts on their fx.

5.2.3 The Implied Repo Rate

If the present value (found by using the foreign interest rate) of spot foreign exchange is purchased, and a foreign exchange forward contract is sold, this portfolio creates a long position in a synthetic T-bill. The rate of return earned on this synthetic T-bill is called the implied repo rate. If the implied repo rate exceeds your borrowing rate, cash-and-carry arbitrage is possible.

To find the unannualized implied repo rate, solve Equation (5.6) for $h_d(0,T)$. To compute the annualized implied repo rate when using an actual/365 day count method, solve Equation (5.7) for r_d.

$$\text{unannualized implied repo rate} = h_d(0,T) = \frac{F[1+h_f(0,T)]-S}{S} \tag{5.8}$$

$$\text{annualized implied repo rate} = r_d = \frac{365F - 365S + FTr_f}{TS} \tag{5.9}$$

EXAMPLE 5.5   Assume that you can lend British pounds for three months in Great Britain at the rate of 6%/year. All day count methods are assumed to be 30/360. A long position in a synthetic (U.S.) T-bill is created by purchasing 62,500/[1+(0.06/4)]= £61,576.35 and selling a forward contract requiring the delivery of £62,500 three months hence. At the spot exchange rate of $1.64/£, the purchase of £61,576.35 will cost $100,985.22. The pounds are lent in Great Britain, and a forward contract is sold at the forward price of $1.65/£, which locks in a selling price. Three months later, the £62,500 is delivered, satisfying the terms of the forward contract, and (62,500)(1.65)= $103,125 is received. The implied repo rate is ($103,125−$100,985.22)/$100,985.22= 2.119% over three months, or 8.476%/year. If an individual can borrow in the United States for three months at an annual rate of less than 8.476%, and if transactions costs are ignored, then there is an arbitrage opportunity. Figure 5.11 shows how Financial-CAD would use the function aaFXfwd_repo_d to solve the problem. Note the use of the 30/360 accrual methods for both interest rates.

AaFXfwd_repo_d		
FX spot - domestic / foreign	1.64	
FX forward price - domestic / foreign	1.65	
Rate - foreign - annual	0.06	
Value (settlement) date	24-Sep-99	
Forward delivery or repurchase date	24-Dec-99	
Accrual method - domestic rate	4	30/ 360
Accrual method - foreign rate	4	30/ 360

Domestic repo rate   **0.084756098**

Figure 5.11 FinancialCAD function aaFXfwd_repo_d computes the theoretical domestic repo rate obtained from buying a foreign currency and selling it forward.

In the example just presented, a 30/360 day count method is used, and thus Equation (5.9), the formula for the annualized implied repo rate, must be modified as follows:

$$r_d = \frac{360(1.65) - 360(1.64) + (1.65)(90)(0.06)}{(90)(1.64)} = 0.08476$$

5.3 FORWARD INTEREST RATES

5.3.1 Spot Rates and Forward Rates

A **spot rate** is an interest rate that exists today. If today is denoted time 0, then $r(0, t1)$ is denoted today's spot rate for a debt instrument that matures at time $t1$. Also, r denotes annual interest rates. Thus, $r(0, 3)$ is the spot three-year interest rate, expressed as an annual rate.[16]

To compute a **forward rate**, you need two spot rates for two different annual maturities, $t1$ and $t2$, where $t2 > t1$. Then, the forward rate can be computed by solving for $fr(t1, t2)$ in the following formula:

$$(1 + r(0, t2))^{t2} = [1 + r(0, t1)]^{t1}[1 + fr(t1, t2)]^{t2 - t1} \tag{5.10}$$

In a sense, the forward rate is an interest rate that exists in the future. That is, $fr(t1, t2)$ is the interest rate on a loan beginning at time $t1$ and ending at time $t2$. Note that fr is an annual forward rate. Thus, in Equation (5.10), all times such as $t1$ and $t2$, are expressed in years.

EXAMPLE 5.6   The spot rate for a six-year debt instrument is $r(0, 6) = 12\%$, and the spot rate for a two-year debt instrument is $r(0, 2) = 10\%$. Find the forward rate for a debt instrument that begins two years hence and ends six years hence. That is, find the rate quoted for a 24×72 FRA.

Use Equation (5.10) to solve for the forward rate, $fr(2, 6)$:

$$(1.12)^6 = (1.10)^2[1 + fr(2,6)]^4$$

$$1.9738227 = 1.21[1 + fr(2,6)]^4$$

$$(1.6312584)^{0.25} = [1 + fr(2,6)]$$

$$1.130136 = [1 + fr(2,6)]$$

$$fr(2,6) = 13.0136\%$$

When working with maturities of less than one year, another method of computing forward rates often is more useful. Define $h(0, t2)$ and $h(0, t1)$ as today's unannualized spot interest rates for debt instruments that mature at times $t2$ and $t1$, respectively. Define $fh(t1, t2)$ as the forward unannualized rate for a debt instrument that begins at time $t1$ and ends at time $t2$. Then the following formula can be used to solve for the forward rate:

$$1 + h(0,t2) = [1 + h(0,t1)][1 + fh(t1,t2)] \tag{5.11}$$

Note that in Equation (5.11), there are no exponents. Also, note that the spot and forward rates are *unannualized*.

EXAMPLE 5.7   A $10,000 face value Treasury bill that matures in 34 days is priced at $9907.71, while the price of a T-bill that matures in 55 days is $9836.95. Find the forward rate from day 34 to day 55.

To solve, first, compute the unannualized spot rates. Given $P = 9907.71$, $F = 10,000$, and $T = 1$ period (of 34 days), then $10,000 = 9907.71 (1 + h)$, and $h(0, 34) = 0.9315\%$. By the same logic, the unannualized 55-day spot rate is $h(0, 55) = 1.65753\%$. Equation (5.11) is then used to find the unannualized forward rate, $fh(34, 55)$:

$$1.0165753 = 1.009315[1 + fh(34,55)]$$

$$fh(34,55) = 0.71933\%$$

There are two ways to annualize this rate. If 0.0071933 is multiplied by the number of 21-day periods in a year (there are 21 days from $t1 = 34$ to $t2 = 55$), then the rate is annualized assuming simple interest:

$$0.0071933 \times 365/21 = 12.50256\%$$

Alternatively, the rate of 0.71933% can be compounded to obtain an annualized rate:

$$(1.0071933)^{365/21} - 1 = (1.0071933)^{17.380952} - 1 = 13.26713\%$$

In the case of compounding, interest earns interest every 21 days.

Because the yields on short-term money market instruments are computed in different ways (e.g., different securities use different day count conventions), and because there are different ways to annualize the unannualized yield, it is usually safer and less ambiguous to just deal with prices and unannualized yields, which is what Equation (5.11) does.

Figure 5.12 illustrates how the FinancialCAD function aaFRAi can be used to compute forward rates. It cannot be used to compute rates when they are compounded. Thus, the software cannot be used to compute $fr(2, 6)$ as was done for the four-year interest rate that will exist in two years. The figure presents the solution to the Treasury bill problem when the simple interest approach is used to annualize $fh(34, 55)$. Note that discount factors must be entered, not interest rates. The entry on the line titled "FRA contract rate" is not used when the desired output statistic is the implied forward rate.

The FinancialCAD utility function aaConvertR_DFcrv will convert interest rates to discount factors. The example is shown in Figure 5.13. The October 28, 1999, yield to maturity is computed

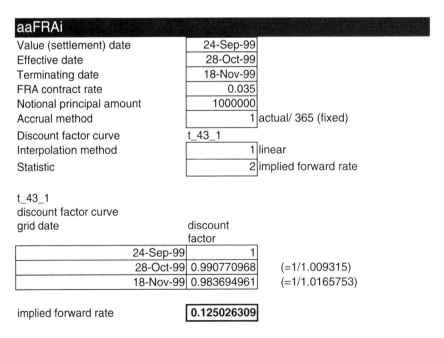

Figure 5.12 FinancialCAD function aaFRAi computes the theoretical forward rate given two spot rates. To use the function, the spot rates must be converted to discount factors.

aaConvertR_DFcrv

value (settlement) date	24-Sep-99	
rate curve	t_48_4	
rate quotation basis	1	annual compounding
accrual method of rate	1	actual/365 (fixed)

t_48_4
holding cost curve

maturity date		yield to maturity
	28-Oct-1999	0.104658291
	18-Nov-1999	0.11527138

discount factor curve - aaConvertR_DFcrv

grid date	discount factor
24-Sep-1999	1
28-Oct-1999	0.990771
18-Nov-1999	0.983695

Figure 5.13 The FinancialCAD function aaConvertR_DFcrv converts interest rates to a set of discount factors.

by $P = 9907.71$, $F = 10,000$, and $T = 34/365 = 0.093150685$ year. Upon entering these values into your calculator, you should find that the yield solution is 10.4658291%. The November 18, 1999, yield is computed by $P = \$9836.95$, $F = 10,000$, and $T = 55/265 = 0.150684932$ year.

One last useful method of obtaining forward yields requires the use of prices. Define the price of a zero-coupon, $1 face value debt instrument that matures at time $t1$ as $P(0, t1)$. Similarly, the price of a pure discount debt instrument that matures to be worth $1 at time $t2$ is $P(0, t2)$. Then, the forward price of a $1 face value debt instrument from time $t1$ to time $t2$, $FP(t1, t2)$, is found by

$$P(0, t2) = P(0, t1)FP(t1, t2) \qquad (5.12)$$

Consider the example in which $r(0, 6) = 12\%$ and $r(0, 2) = 10\%$. We know that $P = F(1 + r(0, t))^{-t}$. Thus, $P(0, 6) = 1(1.12)^{-6} = 0.5066311$, and $P(0, 2) = 1/(1.10)^2 = 0.8264463$. Then, by Equation (5.12), we have

$$0.5066311 = 0.8264463 FP(2, 6)$$

$$FP(2, 6) = 0.6130236$$

Thus, a debt instrument that will be issued two years hence and will be worth $1 six years from today, will sell for $0.6130236 two years from today. The annual rate of return on an investment of $P = \$0.6130236$ that will be worth $F = \$1$ four years later ($T = 4$) is found by solving for the interest rate x in the equation

$$F = P(1 + x)^T$$

$$1 = 0.6130236(1 + x)^4$$

and we find that $x = 13.0136\%$. This is exactly what we earlier found for $fr(2, 6)$.[17]

As another example that uses securities with maturities of less than a year, consider the problem with \$1 face value Treasury bills, where $P(0,34)=0.990771$ and $P(0,55)=0.983695$. Then the forward price, $FP(34,55)$ is:

$$(0.983695) = (0.990771)FP(34,55)$$

$$FP(34,35) = 0.9928581$$

What unannualized rate of return will an investor earn if \$0.9928581 is invested at time 34 and receives \$1 at time 55? The answer is $(F-P)/P=(1-0.9928581)/0.9928581=0.71933\%$. This is exactly what we found earlier for $fh(34, 55)$.

Thus, we have Equations (5.10)–(5.12), given earlier, three equivalent formulas to use when working with spot and forward annualized yields, unannualized yields, and prices:

$$[1+r(0,t2)]^{t2} = [1+r(0,t1)]^{t1}[1+ fr(t1,t2)]^{t2-t1} \tag{5.10}$$

$$1+h(0,t2) = [1+h(0,t1)][1+ fh(t1,t2)] \tag{5.11}$$

$$P(0,t2) = P(0,t1)FP(t1,t2) \tag{5.12}$$

5.3.2 How to Lock in a Forward Rate

Up until now, the forward rate has been just a number that is implicit in the term structure of (spot) interest rates. It turns out that an investor can actually lock in the forward rate as a borrowing rate or a lending rate! First, some assumptions must be made:

There are no transactions costs or bid–asked spreads.

Pure discount debt instruments of \$1 face value trade for any maturity.

These securities can be bought or sold short.

Under these assumptions, any investor can lock in the forward rate as a borrowing rate or a lending rate, from time $t1$ to time $t2$.

Consider the following time line:

```
     |_____|_____|
     0     t1      t2
```

To lock in a borrowing rate from time $t1$ to time $t2$, borrow \$X from time 0 to time $t2$, and lend \$X from time 0 to time $t1$:

```
   <---Lend--------->
   <---------Borrow-------------------->              <---Borrow------>
   |_____|_____|        =       |_____|_____|
   0         t1                  t2               0         t1              t2
```

To lock in a lending rate from time $t1$ to time $t2$, lend $\$X$ from time 0 to time $t2$, and borrow $\$X$ from time 0 to time $t1$:

An investor lends by purchasing debt instruments. An investor borrows by short selling debt instruments.

EXAMPLE 5.8 In Example 5.6 we specified that $r(0,6)=12\%$ and $r(0,2)=10\%$. We then computed the forward rate of $fr(2,6)=13.0136\%$. An investor can lock in 13.0136% as an annual borrowing rate from time 2 to time 6 by borrowing $\$1$ (or $\$X$) for six years at 12%/year and lending $\$1$ (or $\$X$) for two years at 10%/year. The resulting cash flows are as follows:

Time 0

Borrow $\$1$ for six years at 12%/year	$+\$1$
Lend $\$1$ for two years at 10%/year	$-\$1$
Net cash flow	0

Time 2

Get repaid on loan	$+1(1.1)^2=+\$1.21$

Time 6

Repay borrowed funds	$-1(1.12)^6=-\$1.9738227$

The result of both borrowing and lending today is that the investor has locked in a cash inflow at time 2 of $1.21 and a cash outflow at time 6 of $1.9738227. Thus, the investor has borrowed $1.21 for four years at 13.0136%/year. Obviously, by adjusting the value of $\$X$, investors can borrow any amount from time 2 until time 6 at $r(2,6)=$ 13.0136%/year.

EXAMPLE 5.9 We can use the data from Example 5.7 to demonstrate that an investor can lock in a lending rate for a 21-day period, beginning 34 days hence. The unannualized rates are $h(0,34)=0.9315\%$ and $h(0,55)=1.65753\%$. The investor should lend $1 for 55 days and borrow $1 for 34 days. The resulting cash flows are as follows:

Time 0

Borrow $\$1$ for 34 days	$+\$1$
Lend $\$1$ for 55 days	$-\$1$
Net cash flow	0

34 days hence

Repay loan   − 1.009315

55 days hence

Get repaid on loan   + 1.0165753

Thus, suppose a firm knows that 34 days from now, it will receive $750,000 and it knows that 55 days from now, it will have to make a large payment to a supplier. It would like to lock in the prevailing unannualized 21-day forward lending rate of 0.71933% during that time; after compounding, this $fh(34, 55)$ is equal to 13.26713%/year, and the firm believes this is an attractive rate of return.

The firm would borrow $743,078.23 for 34 days, and lend the same amount for 55 days.[18] Then, in 34 days, it would repay its loan with interest, a cash outflow equaling $750,000. Twenty-one days after that, it would receive $755,394.97. The net result is that, at time 0, it has locked in the unannualized forward rate of 0.71933% on a 21-day loan of $750,000 made 34 days hence.

These illustrations of how to lock in forward borrowing and lending rates also provide "proofs" of how forward interest rates are derived using the cost-of-carry model. When we found the forward borrowing rate, what we did was sell short the underlying asset (the six-year debt instrument) and lend the proceeds for the period of the forward contract (two years). When we computed the forward lending rate, we borrowed for the period of the forward contract (34 days) to be able to buy the underlying asset (a debt instrument with 55 days to maturity). Thus, the same cost-of-carry logic used for finding forward exchange rates and forward commodity prices serves also in computing forward interest rates.

5.4   SUMMARY

This chapter derived theoretical forward prices for commodities, foreign currencies (forward exchange rates), and interest rates (forward rates). The standard model for computing theoretical forward prices is the cost-of-carry model, $F = S + CC - CR$. Arbitrage ensures that forward prices conform to this model. If forward prices are too high, traders will borrow, buy the spot good, and sell the overpriced forward contract; this is called cash-and-carry arbitrage. If the forward price is too low, traders will sell the good in the spot market, lend the proceeds, and buy the cheap forward contract; this is called reverse cash-and-carry arbitrage.

The cost-of-carry model works very well for gold and for financial assets such as currencies, debt instruments, and stocks. However, the model sets only an upper pricing level for theoretical forward prices of all physical commodities except gold. What this means is that forward prices of commodities (agricultural goods such as wheat, energy products such as crude oil, etc.) will often be below their theoretical cost-of-carry values. The reason for this is that physical commodities offer a convenience yield. Users of these goods do not wish to sell them, or sell them short, because they need them as part of ongoing production processes.

Forward prices of financial assets, and of gold, do not equal the expected spot prices at delivery. However, forward prices of other physical commodities may equal expected future spot prices; the theory that predicts this is the unbiased expectations hypothesis of forward prices. However if risk-averse hedgers are actively selling forward contracts, the state of prices is called normal backwardation, and forward prices will be below what investors expect to prevail in the future. And if hedgers are actively buying forward, we are said to be in contango, and forward prices lie above expected future spot prices.

Cost-of-carry arbitrage establishes theoretical forward exchange rates. The arbitrageur must buy the present value of the needed units of foreign exchange, discounted at the foreign interest rate. Then, a forward contract is sold. Equation (5.6) is the theoretical forward exchange rate model.

Although the cost-of-carry model was not explicitly used to compute theoretical forward interest rates, the concept is very much present in the derivation of Equations (5.10)–(5.12). This should be apparent by a careful reading of Section 5.3.2.

Theoretically, forward prices and futures prices will be almost identical. In Chapter 6, we explain the differences between forward and futures contracts, and in Section 6.5 of that chapter we address the question of how daily resettlement of futures might create a difference between the prices of the two types of contract.

References

Cootner, Paul H. 1960. "Returns to Speculators: Telser versus Keynes." *Journal of Political Economy*, Vol. 48, No. 4, August, pp. 396–414. Reprinted in A. E. Peck, ed., *Selected Writings on Futures Markets.* Chicago: Chicago Board of Trade, 1977, pp. 41–69.

Teweles, Richard J., Edward S. Bradley and Ted M. Teweles. 1992. *The Stock Market*, 6th ed. New York: John Wiley & Sons.

Kamara, Avraham. 1984. "The Behavior of Futures Prices: A Review of Theory and Evidence." *Financial Analysts Journal*, Vol. 40, No. 4, July–August, pp. 68–75.

Keynes, John Maynard. 1930. *Treatise on Money*, Vol. II, London: Macmillan.

Notes

[1] See Appendix A, at the end of this chapter, for more about short selling.

[2] $h(0, T)$ is the interest rate that applies to the period beginning at time 0 and ending at delivery, time T. If r is the annual interest rate and there are T days until delivery, then we find by using the actual/365 day count method that $h(0, T) = rT/365$. We assume that this interest, and the carry return, are both payable at time T. See Appendix B to this chapter for additional material on different day count methods.

[3] If the carry return cash inflows were received prior to time T, then CR should include the interest that can be earned on those cash flows. In other words, CR is actually the future value of the carry return cash flows. See Appendix C to this chapter for more discussion on computing the future value of the carry return cash flows.

[4] Problems 5.1 and 5.2d ask the student to apply the cost-of-carry formula to situations in which an individual gets to use only a fraction of the proceeds from the short sale.

[5]See Appendix B to this chapter for a discussion of different day count methods.

[6]The purchase of a good and the sale of a forward contract on that good creates what is called a **synthetic Treasury bill**. In a cash-and-carry arbitrage, the synthetic Treasury bill earns a rate of return in excess of spot Treasury bills. Hence, one borrows by selling spot Treasury bills and lends by buying synthetic Treasury bills.

[7]It is not unusual for the loan to be slightly below the securities' market value.

[8]In practice, the day count method for annualizing repo rates is the actual/360 approach.

[9] In addition, storage and carrying costs will also differ across different market participants, and they often change over time.

[10]It is possible that the supply of arbitrage capital is limited or faces competition from other trading strategies. If investors are overwhelmingly bullish, they may perceive greater benefits from buying forwards and futures even when these are overvalued. Similarly, hedgers will buy forward contracts even when their prices are too high, and sell them even when forward prices are below what the cost-of-carry pricing model predicts. If these situations do exist, arbitrage opportunities will also exist and may even persist for extended periods of time.

[11]Note that many of the concepts discussed in this chapter, like normal backwardation and contango, were initially developed in theories of futures pricing. However the theories that lead to these concepts are also applicable for forward prices.

[12]Arbitrageurs were not explicitly considered in Keynes's model.

[13]Many practitioners use the terms backwardation and contango when viewing the term structure of futures prices, vs the spot price. If futures prices are lower, the more distant the delivery date, then these individuals say that the market is in backwardation, or that the futures market is "inverted."

[14]Alternatively, the foreign interest earned by investing the foreign currency can be thought of as a carry return.

[15]When a currency is the underlying asset, this arbitrage is also known as **covered interest rate arbitrage**, and **covered interest parity**.

[16]The spot rates are the yields available on zero-coupon bonds.

[17]Alternatively, enter $PV=-0.6130236$, $FV=1$, $N=4$, and then $CPT\ i=?$ into your financial calculator.

[18]Given that $T=34$ days, and $h(0,34)=0.9315\%$, the present value of $750,000, is $743,078,23.

PROBLEMS

5.1   Assume that you are an individual who gets to use only a fraction, x, of the proceeds from the short sale of the good underlying a forward contract $0 \le x \le 1$. Otherwise, S is the price of the spot good, r is the annual interest rate, and CR is the future value of any carry return. What is the cost-of-carry pricing formula that determines the range (upper bound and lower bound) of prices for which you cannot arbitrage? (Problem 2d provides an application of this model).

5.2

a. Determine the no-arbitrage upper and lower forward price boundaries for a stock that is quoted at $62.50/share (bid) and $63.00 (asked). The stock does not pay any dividends. The delivery date of the forward contract is eight months hence. Your annual lending rate is 6%. Your annual borrowing rate is 7%. Use the FinancialCAD function aaCDF to verify your results (for both boundaries).

b. Suppose that $S=\$62.75$, $r=6\%$, and the stock will pay a $0.40/share dividend next month, and quarterly thereafter (i.e., at $t=1$, $t=4$, and $t=7$). The interest rate is expected to remain constant at 6% for all maturities up to a year in length. Compute the theoretical forward price for the stock. Use aaEqty_fwd to verify your answer.

c. Assume all data from part **b** to be valid. If $F=63$, then compute the implied repo rate for the forward contract. Use aaCDF_repo to verify your answer. How would you arbitrage if $F=63$?

d. Now assume that $S=\$62.75$, $r=6\%$, and there are no dividends, but if you sell the stock short, you will get to use only 70% of the proceeds. Compute the theoretical upper and lower boundaries for the forward price for the stock. These are the relevant price boundaries within which *you* cannot arbitrage.

5.3

a. Spot gold sells for $300/oz. You can risklessly borrow and lend any amount of money at an annual rate of 10%. What is the forward price for a contract that calls for the delivery of 100 oz. of gold 5 months from today? Use FinancialCAD to check your answer.

b. Suppose that $F_0=313$. Explain how you would arbitrage, given the data in part a. Present all the trades you would make today, and the trades that you would make five months hence. Are you performing cash-and-carry arbitrage, or reverse cash-and-carry arbitrage?

c. Given $F_0=313$, compute the implied repo rate for the forward contract. Use FinancialCAD to check your answer.

5.4

a. Spot gold sells for $300/oz. Assume that you can borrow at an annual rate of 10% and risklessly lend any amount of money at an annual rate of 9%. What is the lowest forward price for that contract that will not allow arbitrage for you? What is the highest forward price? The forward contract calls for the delivery of 100 oz. of gold five months from today.

b. Now, in addition to the information in part a, assume that the bid price of gold is $300/oz. and the asked price is $301/oz. Compute the range of gold forward prices (the delivery date is still five months hence) that can exist without permitting you the opportunity to arbitrage. Use FinancialCAD to check your answers.

c. In addition to the data in part b, suppose that you face a $50 commission on the forward contract that is paid upon offsetting your forward position. What are the lowest and highest forward prices that preclude arbitrage, now?

d. Finally, assume that you can short-sell gold, but you will receive only 10% of the proceeds from the short sale; the remainder stays on deposit with the broker. What is the lowest forward price for that contract that will not allow arbitrage for you? What is the highest forward price?

5.5 What is the definition of a risk premium for a forward contract? Define it in terms of net hedging and net speculation concepts (normal backwardation and contango).

5.6 State the differences among the following: repo rate, implied repo rate, and implied reverse repo rate.

5.7 On January 2, 1999, the spot price of West Texas Intermediate crude oil was $12.68/bbl. The crude oil forward prices for July 1999 delivery and January 2000 delivery were $12.57 and $10.43/bbl, respectively. What explains this "inverted market," in which the cash price exceeds the forward price and nearby forward price exceeds forward prices for even more distant delivery dates? What is the likely reason for arbitrageurs' failure to sell spot oil and buy forward contracts? If you expected the spot price of crude oil to be $12/bbl in January 2000, would you believe that the market was exhibiting normal backwardation or contango?

5.8

   a. A stock sells for $125/share. It will trade ex-dividend two months hence, and the dividend amount will be $0.50/share. The interest rate is 5%. Compute the theoretical forward price for delivery four months from today. Use FinancialCAD to check your solution.

   b. If the forward price was $125.40/share, explain how you would arbitrage. What is the implied repo rate of the forward contract? Use FinancialCAD to check your answer.

5.9

   a. Today is March 14. The annual interest rate in Japan is 1%. The annual interest rate in Canada is 5%. The spot price of a Canadian dollar, expressed in terms of Japanese yen, is ¥86.25/Can$. Compute the theoretical forward price for Canadian currency for delivery on June 20 of the same year. Use Financial-CAD to check your answer.

   b. Suppose that the actual forward price is ¥85.25/Can$. How would you arbitrage? Specify all the trades you would make on March 14 and on June 20. Compute the implied repo rate (in terms of Japanese interest rate). Use FinancialCAD to check your answer.

5.10 You have £4 million to invest. If you invest the money in Great Britain for two years, you can earn 5.8%/year. Alternatively, you can invest in France and earn 8%/year. The spot exchange rate is £0.10/FFR. The forward exchange rate for delivery two years hence is £0.098/FFR. Which method of investing do you prefer? Show your results.

5.11 The unannualized spot interest rates for different holding periods are as follows:

Period	Unannualized Interest Rate
1 month $h(0, 1)$	0.01
2 months $h(0, 2)$	0.0205
3 months $h(0, 3)$	0.0305
4 months $h(0, 4)$	0.041
5 months $h(0, 5)$	0.052
6 months $h(0, 6)$	0.063

Compute the unannualized forward rate from month 4 to month 6, $h(4, 6)$. What is the annualized forward rate from month 4 to month 6? Use FinancialCAD to check your answer. Demonstrate how, by trading pure discount spot debt securities today, an investor can borrow $132,000 from month 4 until month 6 at the forward rate you computed.

5.12 If 10-year pure discount bonds are priced to yield 10%/year, and 14-year pure discount bonds are priced to yield 11%/year, at what interest rate can an investor borrow $100,000 from time 10 to time 14? Demonstrate how this can be done, showing the transactions and dollar amounts at all relevant dates.

Assume that all securities are infinitely divisible, that no transactions costs exist, and that investors get full use of the proceeds from short sales.

5.13 An investor wants to invest $10 million in zero-coupon debt instruments maturing 10 years hence. She can invest in the United States and earn a 6.6% annual rate of return. Or, she can convert her $10 million into Japanese yen and buy 10-year, zero-coupon, yen-denominated notes that are currently priced to yield 2.6%. The spot exchange rate is ¥120/$.

   a. At what forward exchange rate (for delivery 10 years hence) will the investor be indifferent between investing in the United States and in Japan? (Equivalently, consider if she chooses not to hedge. Then at what spot exchange rate that will exist 10 years hence will she "break even" in terms of an ex-post rate of return?)

   b. What will be the investor's terminal wealth 10 years hence if she invests in the United States? Show that this equals her terminal dollar wealth if she invests in Japan instead.

5.14 Use current spot interest rate data to compute the forward interest rate for a five-month period commencing four months hence.

5.15 Use current spot interest rate data to compute the forward interest rate for a five-year period commencing four years hence.

5.16 Use current spot interest rate data and spot foreign exchange rate data to compute the theoretical forward price of a Canadian dollar for delivery one year hence.

5.17 On December 30, 1997, an interesting front page *Wall Street Journal* article analyzed why the Indonesian rupiah fell by 50% in value versus the U.S. dollar in the fall and winter of 1997. In discussing why Indonesian

borrowers had borrowed enormous amounts of dollars, the article pointed out that the Indonesian government managed the dollar/rupiah exchange rate so that it declined at a rate of about 4–5% per year. "Indonesian borrowers faced a simple choice. They could borrow rupiah at 18 or 20% and not worry about the exchange rate. Or they could borrow dollars at 9% or 10% a year and then convert the proceeds to rupiah. A year later, they figured, it would take 4% or 5% more rupiah to buy the dollars needed to repay the loan, but the cost was less."

   a. Explain why it was such a "simple choice" for Indonesians to borrow dollars. In particular, focus on the discussion in Section 5.2.2 of this chapter.

   b. Explain what happened to the unhedged Indonesian borrowers of dollars when the dollar rose from about 2300 rupiah in July 1997 to about 5800 rupiah in December 1997.

   c. How could have forward contracts been used to hedge Indonesian borrowers of dollars?

5.18

   a. Today, $S = 48$, where S is the price of the spot asset. If today's one-year interest rate, $r(0,1)$, is 6%, compute the theoretical forward price for delivery one year hence.

   b. Three months later, $S = 42$. The term structure of spot interest rates is as follows:

$$r(0,1/4) = 6\%$$

$$r(0,1/2) = 6.5\%$$

$$r(0,3/4) = 7\%$$

$$r(0,1) = 7.5\%$$

What is the value of the *original* forward contract (described in part a)? For which party is the forward contract an asset, and for which party is it a liability?

5.19   Suppose that on September 15, 1999, you sell €250,000 forward, for delivery on January 15, 2000. On September 15, 1999, the spot price of a euro is $1.05 (i.e., the spot exchange rate is $1.05/€), and the forward price for delivery four months later is $1.02/€.

On October 15, 1999, the following prices are observed:

Spot price	$1.03/€
Forward price for delivery three months hence	$1.04/€
Forward price for delivery four months hence	$1.06/€

Also, on October 15, 1999, the following interest rates are observed (in the United States):

For securities maturing one month later (i.e., on 11/15/99):	4%
For securities maturing three months later (on 1/15/00):	5%
For securities maturing four months later (on 2/15/00):	6%

a. Compute the value of your position as of October 15, 1999. This is equivalent to asking how much is exposed to default risk.

b. Is your position an asset or a liability? Explain why.

c. Are you more likely to want to default, or is your counterparty? Why?

5.20   Compute the forward exchange rate for delivery of euros 13 months hence. The spot exchange rate is ¥113.42/€. The interest rate on 13-month riskless debt instruments in Euroland is 5.25%. The interest rate on 13-month riskless debt instruments in Japan is 0.8%. Use FinancialCAD to check your solution.

5.21   On January 1 (today), a firm sells a 9× 12 FRA. The notional principal is $50 million. The contract rate is 8%. There are 365 days in a year. The following spot interest rates exist today (as shown on the first line of the accompanying table), and subsequently occur in the future (as shown on lines 2–5):

Spot Interest Rates That Occur in the Future

Date	3-Month LIBOR	6-Month LIBOR	9-Month LIBOR
January 1 (today)	7.4%	7.8%	7.9%
April 1	7.5%	8%	8.3%
July 1	8.2%	8.8%	9.1%
October 1	8.6%	9.4%	9.5%
January 1 (next year)	9.2%	9.6%	9.8%

a. If today's 9×12 FRA contract rate of 8% is theoretically correct, compute today's spot 12-month LIBOR. Use FinancialCAD to solve the problem.

b. When will the FRA be settled? (i.e., when will money be exchanged?)

c. Will the firm receive money (a profit) or have to pay money (a loss) on the settlement day? Why?

d. How much will be received or paid at settlement?

5.22   Use the FinancialCAD function aaCDF to compute the theoretical value of a futures contract on gold. The spot price of gold is $295/oz. The delivery day for the futures contract is five months from today. The interest rate is 6%. Assume no storage cost or convenience value. What happens to the theoretical fair value of the futures price if there is a small storage cost of 0.1? Explain why the theoretical futures price changes in that direction when there is a cost for storing the physical commodity.

5.23 Get a recent *Wall Street Journal* and find the column titled "Currency Trading" (its often on the foreign exchange page of Section C). Find and record the spot price of a dollar for Japanese citizens. Also find and record the forward price of a dollar for delivery six months hence. Then use aaFXfwd to compare the theoretical forward price of the dollar to the actual forward price of the dollar. Remember that domestic = Japanese interest rates (you are Japanese, after all), and foreign is U.S. interest rates. Go to www.bloomberg.com. Click on currencies. Click on International Bonds. Record the yield that exists for six-month U.S. treasuries and for 6-month Japanese governments. Use these interest rates in aaFXfwd to compute the fair forward price of a dollar.

5.24 You are a U.S. citizen. The spot exchange rate with Swiss Francs is $0.6495/SFR. The futures price of 1 SFR for delivery six months hence is $0.6624/SFR. The interest rate in Switzerland is 3%. Use aaFXfwd_repo_d to find the repo rate for the futures contract. How does the domestic repo rate you computed compare with the interest rate that exists in the United States for six-month debt instruments?

5.25 Suppose that the spot interest rate for four-month debt instruments is 5%, and the spot interest rate for one-year debt instruments is 6%. First find the unannualized interest rate for a four-month holding period. Use the Financial-CAD function aaFRAi to compute the implied forward rate. Note that the numbers to be entered into the discount factor cells are $1/(1+h)$, where h is the unannualized interest rate.

APPENDIX A Selling Short

It is simple to conceive of a long position in an asset, whether it be a physical or a financial asset. An investor first buys the asset. While he owns it, he has a long, or bullish position. He will sell it at a later date, hopefully at a higher price. Investors always like to buy low and sell high.

A short seller also likes to buy low and sell high. However, short sellers sell the asset first and later buy it back. They hope the price will decline during the time that they are short the asset. They are called "bears."

How can a short seller sell something he doesn't own? His broker borrows the asset from someone else. Thus, suppose A owns 100 shares of XYZ Corp., B wishes to sell 100 shares short, and individual C will buy these 100 shares. B's broker will borrow the shares from A and lend them to B, who then sells these shares to C, who in turn pays investor B for these shares. B hopes that at a subsequent date, XYZ will sell at a lower price. At that time B can buy the shares (at a price lower than the price at which they were sold short). B's broker takes the shares and returns them to A's account. All this is frequently done without A's knowledge, though when A opened his account, he must have consented to allow his shares to be borrowed in this manner.

What if A decided to take possession of the asset, or to sell it? The broker would then have to find another investor who owns the shares of XYZ, and borrow them from that person. It is possible, though unlikely, that no shares of a stock would be available for selling short. It is also possible that B would sell short, and some time after, *all* investors would want their shares; then the loan would be called, forcing B to buy the shares to close his short position. For example, suppose that B sells short and afterward there is a tender offer for the shares of XYZ Corp. In a tender offer, an individual or corporation makes an offer to acquire the existing shares of a company. If enough shares are tendered (including the shares of A, the original owner of the shares that B borrowed), there may be no shares available to be borrowed for short selling, and B will be forced to somehow buy the shares back to "cover" the short position. Another event that would force the short to cover is a proxy fight. Short selling creates more shares owned than the firm originally issued. In our simple example, both A and C own 100 shares. If (a contrived case) the firm has issued only the 100 shares that investor A bought, how can the shares be voted? Both investors A and C own shares, hence own voting rights.

For large corporations and normal voting events, there will be sufficient proxies to satisfy all long positions because many investors do not vote. The brokerage firm will find enough proxies to permit all to vote. But if there is an important vote, and there are no proxies available, the short seller will be squeezed (i.e., forced to buy the stock).

The broker of short seller B will not worry about investor B's ability to buy back the shares she sold short. That is because the proceeds of the short sale must be kept in investor B's account as collateral for the shares he has borrowed.

Moreover, not only does investor B not get to use the proceeds of the short sale, he also must meet margin requirements. Recently this was 50% of the value of the stock. For example, if 100 shares are sold short at $40/share, the short seller must keep the $4000 proceeds in the account as collateral and also deposit another $2000 to meet margin requirements (the $2000 can be in the form of securities, e.g., $2000 worth of another company's stock).

If the stock price starts to rise (to the short seller's dismay), the broker will demand that the short seller deposit more cash or securities.

Dividends offer a complication similar to voting rights. If the firm pays a dividend, who gets it: investor A or investor C? Both get it. The firm pays the dividend to investor C, and also, all short sellers must also pay dividends to the owners of the shares they have borrowed.

Short sales of common stock are subject to an "uptick rule." In the 1920s and earlier, ruthless speculators often sold short stock at prices below the last trade, driving quoted prices down. Shortly thereafter, they would disclose false negative information about the stock, which would cause others to sell their shares, perhaps even creating a selling panic. Then they would close their short positions at a profit.

To eliminate this type of abuse, and also to minimize the price-depressing effects of short selling, the Securities and Exchange Commission outlawed short sales of stock at prices below the last previous trade. An investor can sell short at the same price as the last trade only if the last previous change was an uptick. It is always permissible to sell short a price above the last trade. Thus if the last trade was at $40, you can sell short at $40.10, regardless of the trend in stock prices (assuming that there is a buyer at $40.10). You would be able to short sell at $40 only if the last prior trade was at a price less than $40.

Individuals sell short for many reasons. Bearish investors will sell short, though it is probably wiser to buy a put option. Losses are limited with a put; they are theoretically unlimited with a short sale.[1] Other investors sell short for tax reasons, as part of hedging strategies or for arbitrage purposes.

Note that in many of the valuation models of this book, we will assume that the short seller has full use of the proceeds of a short sale. In some cases, we can relax this assumption, and we will demonstrate the effect of doing so. Also, some large traders are able to negotiate with their brokers, hence can indeed make full use of the proceeds from selling short.

Teweles, Bradley, and Teweles (1992, pp. 162–180) contains a great deal of useful material on short selling.

Reference

Teweles, Richard J., Edward S. Bradley and Ted M. Teweles. 1992. *The Stock Market*, 6th ed. New York: John Wiley & Sons.

Note

[1]Consider an investor who sold short 100 shares of Diana Corp. on May 6, 1996, at a price of $46 per share. After all, the company had reported a loss of $0.18/share in its fiscal year ending March 31, 1995, and a loss of $0.80/share in its fiscal year ending March 31, 1996. But during this time, its stock price actually rose by 700%, from $5 3/4 on August 9, 1995, to $14 1/4 on February 21, 1996, to $46 on May 6, 1996. Obviously, some value-oriented investors might have considered it to be overvalued. Well, less than three weeks later, on May 24, 1996, the stock proceeded to rise to an intraday high of $120/share! Our hypothetical investor who sold short at $46 lost $74/share, or $7400 on the 100 original shares, if he covered his short position at $120! As a postscript, our investor's bearishness on Diana was not totally unwarranted: it plummeted to $39 1/4 on June 26, 1996, and $20 5/8 on August 19, 1996. By June 1997, it had been delisted from the NYSE and was selling for $3.125/share.

APPENDIX B   Day Count Methods

There are several day count methods that are used to compute interest payments over different intervals of time. Thus, if an annual interest rate is quoted, the issue is how to compute interest over holding periods of less than a year.

- **30/360**: Generally assumes that there are 12 months of 30 days each in a year. If a month has 31 days, no interest is earned on the 31st day. Since there are 28 days in February, two extra days of interest are earned on the 28th day; in leap years, one extra day of interest is earned on February 29. One year equals 360 days. In this convention, three months is always one-quarter of a year; six months is always a half-a-year. For example, the period of time between January 28 and July 28 is half a year. Exceptions occur when the last day of the period is on the 31st of the month and the first day of the period is *not* the 30th or 31st. That is, the number of days between January 28 and March 31 is 63 (2 days in January, 30 days in February, and 31 days in March), and there is 0.175 of a year between those two dates (63/360). Oddly, there are also 63 days between January 28 and April 1 (2 days in January, 30 days in both February and March, and 1 day in April). Corporate bonds, municipal bonds, and agency securities generally use the 30/360 day count method when accruing interest.
- **Actual/360**: Count the actual number of days between two dates and divide by 360 to find the fraction of the year. In the United States this is called the "money market basis." Note that there is 1.0138889 year between two dates one year apart in this method (365/360); an annual money market rate of 4% on $100 would produce $4.05556 in interest.
- **Actual/365 (fixed)**: Count the actual number of days between two dates and divide by 365 to find the fraction of the year.

- **Actual/365 (actual)=U.S. government actual/actual=actual/actual**: Count the actual number of days between two dates and divide by 365 to find the fraction of the year in non-leap years. In a leap year, divide by 366. U.S government bonds accrue interest using the actual/actual method.

- **Euro 30E/360**: Always assumes that every month has 30 days and that there are 360 days in a year. No exceptions are made when the last day of the period is on the 31st day of the month. Thus, there are 62 days between January 28 and March 31 (2 days in January, and 30 in both February and March).

APPENDIX C   Computing the Future Value of Carry Return Cash Flows

The theoretical forward price was derived in this chapter to be

$$F = S + CC - CR$$

If today is time 0, a carry return cash flow will be paid at time $t1$, and the delivery date is at time T, then this model may be expressed as follows:

$$F(0, T) = S[1 + h(0, T)] - \text{div}[1 + fh(t1, T)]$$

where

$F(0, T)$=time 0 theoretical forward price for delivery at time T

S=spot price of the underlying asset

$h(0, T)$=unannualized interest rate for the period from today until time T

div=cash flow that is received by the owner of the underlying asset

$fh(t1, T)$=unannualized interest rate that will exist at time $t1$; the cash flow carry return is received at time $t1$, and it will earn this rate of interest until time T

The careful reader might ask how we can derive the theoretical forward price when we don't really know what $fh(t1, T)$ will be. In other words, at time 0, we don't know what amount of interest the cash flow carry return (the dividend) will be able to earn.

The answer comes from Equation (5.11):

$$1 + h(0, T) = [1 + h(0, t1)][1 + fh(t1, T)] \qquad (5.11)$$

Solve Equation (5.11) for $1 + fh(t1, T)$:

$$1 + fh(t1, T) = \frac{1 + h(0, T)}{1 + h(0, t1)}$$

Thus, the theoretical forward pricing equation becomes

$$F = S[1 + h(0,T)] - \text{div}\left[\frac{1 + h(0,T)}{1 + h(0,t1)}\right] = [1 + h(0,T)]\left[S - \frac{\text{div}}{1 + h(0,t1)}\right] = FV[S - PV(\text{div})]$$

where FV is the future value operator and PV is the present value operator; $PV(\text{div})$ is the present value of the carry return cash flow.

This equation is operational at time 0 (today) because both $h(0,t1)$ and $h(0,T)$ are spot interest rates.

CHAPTER 6

Introduction to Futures

In this chapter, we present the essential features of another important derivative security, the futures contract. A considerable amount of terminology and institutional detail surround futures contracts. However, struggling with these details will pay off because these details provide the foundation to understand how futures contracts can be used to manage price risk.

At first, many people think that futures contracts are exactly the same as a forward contract. Although the two instruments are similar, they are not exact substitutes. There are two very important distinctions between these two types of contract. Recall that a disadvantage of a forward contract is that the firm faces the risk of default on the contract by the counterparty. An advantage of a futures contract is that the risk that counterparty default risk is essentially eliminated. However, this benefit comes at a cost. Unlike forward contracts, futures contracts are standardized, which means that they are not as flexible as forward contracts. These distinctions mean that both forward and futures contracts can provide unique risk-shifting benefits.

We begin this chapter with a detailed discussion of the features that distinguish futures contracts from forward contracts. Therefore, a good way to prepare for this chapter is to review Chapter 3, which provides an introduction to forward contracts.

6.1 FUTURES CONTRACTS AND FORWARD CONTRACTS

Speculators use futures to a greater extent than forwards. Speculators buy futures contracts when they believe that the price of the good will rise. Speculators sell futures contracts when they believe that prices will fall. Hedgers also use futures contracts to manage their risk exposure, and arbitrageurs exploit situations when futures prices are sufficiently different from their theoretical values.

For both futures and forward contracts, one party agrees to buy something in the future from a second party; the second party agrees to sell it. The buyer of a contract, who is said to be long the contract, has agreed to buy (take delivery of) the good. The seller is said to be short the contract, and this person has the obligation to sell (deliver) the good at some time in the future. The contract specifies both the quantity and quality of the good, the price, the delivery date or dates, and the delivery location or locations.[1]

Futures and forwards are in zero net supply; for every buyer of a contract, there is a seller. The profits and losses realized in forward and futures contracting represent a zero-sum game; for every dollar one party makes, another party must lose a dollar (ignoring commissions). However, there are several ways in which futures contracts differ from forward contracts.

1. Futures contracts are standardized; only the price is negotiated. All December 2001 gold futures contracts are identical in that the amount of gold (called the **contract size**), quality of gold, delivery date, and place of delivery are specified. In contrast, all elements of forward contracts are negotiated; they are custom-made contracts that can be designed to meet the specific needs of the parties.

2. Futures contracts are usually more liquid than forward contracts, partly because they are standardized. Futures trade on futures exchanges. Refer to Table 1.2 for a list of futures exchanges in the United States. Table 1.4 presents a list of leading international futures exchanges. The party who is long a futures contract can always terminate that obligation by subsequently (but prior to the delivery date) selling a contract for the same good with the same delivery date. Similarly, a short can close that position by later buying the same futures contracts. Each of these actions is called **offsetting** a trade. For example, if you are long a December 2001 gold futures contract, you can close your position by selling a December 2001 gold futures contract. In contrast, with the exception of the FRA market and the forward foreign exchange market, most other forward markets are illiquid.

3. Because forward contracts are agreements between two parties, each party faces the risk that the counterparty will subsequently default. Futures traders need not worry as much about default risk. Once a futures price has been agreed upon and a trade completed, the exchange's clearinghouse becomes the opposite party to both the buyer and the seller.[2] In other words, when party A goes long a futures contract, he buys it from the clearinghouse; when party B goes short a futures contract, she sells it to the clearinghouse. The clearinghouse is always neutral; it is both long and short an identical number of contracts. The number of outstanding contracts is called **open interest**. Because the clearinghouse is a party to every trade, buyers and sellers of futures contracts need be concerned only about the financial integrity of the exchange on which the futures contract trades, *provided their futures commission merchant (FCM) does not fail.*[3] The clearinghouse guarantees all payments of profits as long as its member FCMs are solvent. There have been no futures exchange failures in the United States. Indeed, if a futures exchange ever becomes financially distressed, it has the power to directly assess its members to cover any short-falls, and no U.S. futures exchange has ever had to resort to that move. The requirement that traders post margin and the process of marking to market (both discussed in the next section) protects the exchange by ensuring that the buyers and sellers abide by their contractual obligations.[4]

4. Most futures positions are eventually offset. Only a small percentage, perhaps 1–5%, of a futures contract's open interest ever results in delivery of the good. Indeed, some futures contracts, such as the Chicago Mercantile Exchange's Eurodollar futures contract and stock index futures, are **cash settled**.[5] When this is the case, there are no provisions for delivery of the good; only cash profits and losses are exchanged. In contrast, most forward contracts terminate with delivery of the specified good.

5. Perhaps the most important differences, at least for pricing purposes, are the issues of security deposits (margin) and the timing of cash flows (daily resettlement, or marking to market). No money changes hands initially in a forward contract. Two parties agree on a fair forward price for later delivery, and a cash flow occurs, or a profit or loss is realized, only on the delivery date.[6] At that time, the cash flow (profit) is defined as the difference between the forward price initially agreed upon and the actual spot price of the good on the delivery date.

While profits or losses on forward contracts are realized only on the delivery day, the change in the value of a futures contract results in a cash flow every day. This means that there is less default risk with futures contracts. A forward contract can build up a great deal of value prior to delivery. If the contract becomes a large liability for one of the parties, then that party might seek legal ways (or even illegal ways) to avoid meeting the contract's obligations. In contrast, the daily change in the value of a futures contract must be exchanged, so that if one party (the losing party) defaults, the maximum loss that will be realized is just one day's value change. Thus the incentive to default is greater for forwards than for futures.

Margin requirements and marking to market determine the cash flow consequences of futures contracts. We now discuss these important concepts in turn.

6.2 Margin Requirements for Futures Contracts

When two parties trade a futures contract, the futures exchange requires some good faith money from both, to act as a guarantee that each will abide by the terms of the contract. This money is called **margin**.[7] Each futures exchange is responsible for setting the minimum **initial margin** requirements for all futures contracts that trade there. The initial margin is the amount a trader must initially deposit into his **trading account** (also called a **margin account**) when establishing a position. Many futures exchanges use computer algorithms, the most popular of which is called SPAN (**s**tandard **p**ortfolio **an**alysis of risk), to establish initial margin requirements.[8] The algorithms analyze historical price data to derive what is believed to be a worst-case one-day price movement. An exchange can change the required margin anytime. If price volatility increases, or if the price of the underlying commodity rises substantially, the initial margin required will likely be increased.[9]

It is important to realize that the margin required for trading futures differs from the concept of margin when one is buying common stock or bonds. In the purchase of common stock or bonds, margin is the fraction of the asset's cost that must be financed by the purchaser's own funds. The remainder is borrowed from the purchaser's stock broker. Futures margin, however, is good faith money, or collateral, designed to ensure that the futures trader can pay any losses that may be incurred. Futures margin is not a partial payment for a purchase.

Beyond the initial margin, if the equity in the account falls to, or below, the **maintenance margin** level, additional funds must be deposited to bring the account back up to the initial margin level. Thus, if the initial margin required to trade one gold futures contract is $1000, and the maintenance margin level is $750, then an adverse change of $2.60/oz. will result in a margin call. Because one gold futures contract covers 100 oz. of gold, a decline of $2.60/oz. in the futures price will deplete the equity of a long position by $260. The trader with losses must then deposit sufficient funds to bring the equity in the account back to the initial margin of $1000. The margin that is deposited to meet margin calls is called **variation margin**. A trader who does not promptly meet a margin call will find his position liquidated by the FCM.

Note that once a trader has received a margin call, he must meet that call, even if the price has subsequently moved in his favor. For example, suppose the futures price of gold declines $4/oz. on day t. On day $t+1$, the trader who is long a gold futures contract receives a margin call, regardless of the futures price of gold on day $t+1$. Even if the futures price has risen considerably (by more than $1.50/oz.) since day t's close, the trader must still deposit $400 in variation margin into his account.

FCMs will often set initial and maintenance margin requirements at levels higher than the minimum requirements specified by the exchanges. Margin requirements also differ for different traders, depending on whether the position is part of a spread, a hedge, or a speculative trade. Margin requirements on spreads and hedges are less than those on speculative positions. In a spread, a trader who is long one contract will also be short another related contract. The two contracts may be on the same good, but for different delivery months (called a **calendar spread**, or an **intermonth spread**), or they may be on two similar goods for delivery in the same month (called an **intercommodity spread**, or an **intermarket spread**). In a hedge, the futures trader either owns the good and is short a futures contract or is short the good and long a futures contract. Hedge traders must sign a hedge account agreement declaring that the trades in the account will in fact be hedges as defined by the Commodity Exchange Act of 1936 and as specified by the Commodity Futures Trading Commission (CFTC). Finally, FCMs sometimes set different margin requirements for contracts with the most nearby delivery date and for contracts with delivery in more distant months.

Some sample margin requirements for speculative positions, as required by one discount FCM in July 2000, are shown in Table 6.1. Note that they are always subject to change by either the broker or the exchange. There are different margin requirements for hedgers and for traders who have spread positions (either intracommodity calendar spreads or intermarket spreads). The exchange website on which a futures contract trades will provide its most recent minimum margin requirement.

Initial margin requirements do not have to be met with cash. Instead, Treasury bills can be used to satisfy original margin. Some exchanges and FCMs will also allow a bank letter of credit to meet initial margin requirements. Such a letter from the futures trader's bank guarantees the FCM the trader has sufficient funds to trade and also guarantees that the bank will make up any shortfall, generally by a wire transfer.

TABLE 6.1 Margin Requirements for Selected Futures Contracts: Speculative Positions, July 2000

Commodity	Exchange[1]	Initial Margin	Maintenance Margin
S&P 500	CME	$23,438	$18,750
Nikkei 225	CME	$6,750	$5,000
Japanese yen	CME	$4,212	$3,120
Deutsche mark	CME	$1,249	$925
Mexican peso	CME	$2,500	$2,000
Eurodollar	CME	$675	$500
T-bill	CME	$237	$175
T-bond	CBOT	$2,025	$1,500
10 year T-note	CBOT	$1,350	$1,000
Gold	CMX	$1,350	$1,000
Crude oil	NYM	$3,375	$2,500

Intermarket Spreads	Initial	Maintenance
Deutsche mark vs British pound	$1,485	$1,100
T-bill vs eurodollar	$237	$175
T-bond vs 10-year T-note	$1,080	$800
Crude oil vs heating oil	$1,418	$1,050
S&P 500 vs Value Line (2:5)	$24,250	$19,900

[1]CBOT, Chicago Board of Trade; CME; Chicago Mercantile Exchange; CMX; Commodity Exchange, Inc. (a division of the NYMEX); NYMEX, New York Mercantile Exchange.

Treasury bills and bank letters of credit are the preferred means of meeting initial margin requirements. Cash in a customer's cash account may or may not earn interest (check whether your FCM pays interest on your cash balance in your cash account!). But cash used to meet margin requirements *never* earns interest. Treasury bills and letters of credit allow the trader to earn interest on initial margin, and therefore, they are the preferred means of meeting the initial margin requirement. When securities such as Treasury bills are used to meet the initial margin requirement, all variation margin payments must be made in cash.[10]

6.3   MARKING TO MARKET

All futures traders' positions are **marked to market** daily. The process is also sometimes called **daily resettlement**. What it means is that every day, profits are added to, or losses are deducted from, the equity of a trader's account. In effect, a trader is offsetting his position every day, and realizing each day's profit or loss. The profits and losses are based on changes in the **settlement price**, or closing futures price, for the contract of interest. All profits that increase the margin account balance above the initial margin amount can be withdrawn daily and spent by the trader. Losses deplete the equity in the account, until there is a margin call, at which time variation margin must be deposited to bring the account balance back to the initial margin level.

The process of daily resettlement makes a futures contract equivalent to a time series of one-day forward contracts. Recall that the profit or loss per unit of the underlying asset for a forward contract is $|F(0,T) - S(T)|$, where $F(0,T)$ is the futures price when the contract is originated and $S(T)$ $[= F(T,T)]$ is the spot price on the delivery date. Well, the daily mark-to-market cash flow for a futures contract is $|F(0,T) - F(1,T)|$: that is, the change in the futures price from one day to the next. But for a forward contract calling for delivery one day hence, it is the case that $F(1,T) = S(T) = F(1,1) = S(1)$. Thus, the cash flows arising from a futures contract are the same as if a trader had a forward contract calling for delivery one day hence; every day the forward contract is settled up, profits and losses are realized, and a new one-day forward contract is created. The final sum of the cash flows for the futures contract equals the one-time profit or loss for the forward contract.

Marking to market greatly reduces counterparty default risk. The most a trader has at risk is her one-day profit. There is no buildup of asset value (for one party) and liability value (for the other) as with forward contracts.

The entire daily resettlement process is illustrated with the following example. On November 6, 2001, you sell one gold futures contract for delivery in December 2001. You sell the contract at 10 A.M., when the futures price is $285/oz. The initial margin requirement is $1000, and that sum of money is transferred from your cash account to your margin account. The settlement price at the close on November 6 is $286.40/oz. Your account is marked to market, and your equity at the close is $860. The futures price rose by $1.40/oz, and one contract covers 100 oz of gold; therefore, you have lost $140 on the short position.

On all subsequent days, the account is marked to market. If the futures price falls, your equity rises. If the futures price rises, your equity declines. Maintenance margin calls will have to be met if your account equity falls to a level equal to or below $750. Table 6.2 illustrates the cash flow consequences of marking to market for this example.

On November 7, a further mark-to-market loss (beyond the $140 lost on the day you opened your position) of $240 is realized. This brings your equity in the account down to only $620. A maintenance margin call occurs, and you must deposit $380 to bring your equity in the account

TABLE 6.2 Example of the Mark-to-Market Process[1]

Date	Settlement Price	Initial Cash Balance	Mark-to-Market Cash Flow	Equity	Maintenance Margin Call	Final Cash Balance	Final Equity
11/6	$286.4	$1000	$–140	$860	—	$1000	$860
11/7	$288.8	$1000	$–240	$620	380	$1380	$1000
11/10	$289.0	$1380	$–20	$980	—	$1380	$980
11/11	$288.6	$1380	$40	$1020	—	$1380	$1020
11/12	$290.7	$1380	$–210	$810	—	$1380	$810
11/13	$292.8	$1380	$–210	$600	400	$1780	$1000
11/14	$292.8	$1780	$0	$1000	—	$1780	$1000
11/17	$292.7	$1780	$10	$1010	—	$1780	$1010
11/18	$295.8	$1780	$–310	$700	300	$2080	$1000
11/19	$296.1	$2080	$–30	$970	—	$2080	$970
11/20	$297.1	$2080	$–100	$870	—	$2080	$870
11/21	$296.4	$2080	$70	$940			

[1]*The situation*: at 10 A.M. on November 6, 2001, you sell one December 01 gold futures contract at a futures price of $285/oz. The initial margin requirement is $1000 and the maintenance margin level is $750. It is assumed that all margin calls are met at the end of the trading day that the violation occurs.

back to the initial margin level of $1000. Note that in practice, you would likely receive the margin call just before the market opens on November 10. If you do not pay the $380 in cash, or close your position, your FCM will liquidate the position. Some FCMs will sometimes grant customers a few days to meet a margin call. The same FCMs, under different situations, will allow only a few hours. Note also that it does not matter what happens to the futures price on November 10; you still must meet the maintenance margin call in cash.

At the close of trading on November 11, your equity in the account has risen to $1020. The difference between your equity and the initial margin required is called **excess**. At the close of November 11, your excess is $20. Although some FCMs discourage the practice, you can withdraw excess if it is positive. Doing so is worthwhile because cash in your margin account does not earn interest for you (it will earn interest for your FCM though). By withdrawing the excess and transferring it back to your cash account, you can earn interest on the money.

The daily resettlement process continues, with margin calls at the close of trading on November 13 and again on November 18. Finally, on November 21, you offset your trade by buying one gold futures contract for December 2001 delivery at a futures price of $296.4/oz. The final equity (after the November 21 profit of $70 is accounted for) of $940 is then transferred back to your cash account.

There are at least three ways to compute your loss on this trade; all of them provide the same dollar loss amount. First, since you went short one contract at a futures price of $285/oz, you could offset the trade at a futures price of $296.40. This would mean a loss of $11.40/oz. Since the futures contract covers 100 oz. of gold, your loss on the trade would be $1140.00.

Second, you might add all the cash outflows between your cash account and your margin account. You originally transferred the initial margin of $1000. You also had three margin calls of $380, $400, and $300. Adding, the total amount flowing out is $2080 (which equals the final cash balance in your margin account at the time you offset your trade). If you subsequently transferred your final equity of $940 from your margin account to your cash account, your total loss would be $1140 ($2080 − $940).

Finally, you could just add up the daily mark-to-market cash flow amounts into and out of your margin account. The sum of these cash flows totals −$1140.

It is important to realize that the timing of the cash flows for the futures trade depends on how the initial margin requirement is satisfied and that these cash flow streams differ from those of a forward contract. Figure 6.1a illustrates the timing of these different cash flow streams. For instance, had you sold a forward contract on 100 oz. of gold at a forward price of $285/oz., there would be

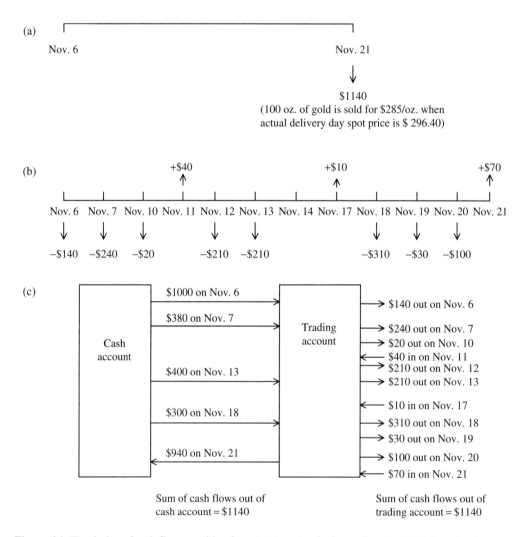

Figure 6.1 The timing of cash flows resulting from (a) the sale of a forward contract, (b) the sale of a futures contract using T-bills or a bank letter of credit for initial margin, and (c) the sale of a futures contract using cash for initial margin (see also Table 6.2).

no cash flow until the agreed upon delivery date (assuming that you did not negotiate good faith money on the initial date of November 6). If the delivery date of the forward contract happened to be November 21, and the spot price of gold on that day happened to be $296.40/oz., then the only cash flow we define is the cash outflow of $1140 on November 21: $F(0,T) - S(T) = 285.00 - 296.40 = -\$11.40/oz.$ The entire loss is realized on November 21, as Figure 6.1a illustrates.

For a futures contract, however, losses are realized gradually over time, depending on how the initial margin requirement was met. Figure 6.1b illustrates the cash flows that would have resulted if you had used a T-bill or a bank letter of credit to satisfy the initial margin requirement on the gold futures contract in the foregoing example. There is no initial cash flow at 10 A.M. on November 8. If both parties pay nothing for the futures contract, it must not be worth anything; in other words, it has a value of zero. Subsequently, the cash flows are the amount by which the value of the contract changes each day. Essentially, then, it is as if the contract is bought back each day at its settlement price and then immediately resold at each day's settlement price. With a T-bill or bank letter of credit in your margin account (earning interest), the mark-to-market cash flows represent variation margin. Thus, at the end of the day on which the contract was sold (November 6) you would have to pay $140 in cash. On November 7 you must pay $240 in cash. On each subsequent day cash will either be debited (losses, or cash outflows) or credited (profits, or cash inflows) to your account. The total cash outflow comes to $1140. After it has been marked to market each day, a futures contract again has zero value; all changes in value are realized daily through the mark to market process.

Figure 6.1c illustrates how cash flows occur if $1000 in cash is used to meet the initial margin requirement. Margin calls take place on November 7, 13, and 18. Either cash will be withdrawn from your cash account or your FCM will quickly notify you to deposit funds into your cash account so that the amount of cash in your trading account can get back to the initial margin requirement amount of $1000.

Like a forward contract, a futures contract has no value on its initiation day. The contract is merely an agreement for one party to buy and the other party to sell something at a later date. On the contract initiation day, presumably both the contract buyer and seller believed that the futures price of $285/oz. was fair. If neither party paid anything for the contract on November 6, it must have been a valueless contract.

But there is a difference between the value of a forward contract and a futures contract on all days subsequent to the day on which it was initiated. For a forward contract, there is no profit or loss on any day except on the delivery date (assuming that it is held until the delivery date). As the price for forward delivery changes, so will the value of a forward contract. There can be a large buildup in the value of a forward contract if the forward price changes considerably from the original forward price. The forward price stays fixed throughout the contract's life. If a newly created forward contract has a forward price that is different from the forward price that was originally negotiated, the original contract will have positive or negative value. The value of a long position will be the negative of the value of a short position.

In contrast, changes in futures prices are settled up daily. Any change in the value of the futures contract is realized by the parties through the daily resettlement process. There is no buildup in the value of a futures contract. The maximum change in value occurs over a one-day interval, just prior to the instant at which it is marked to market. Once a futures contract has been marked to market, its value reverts to zero.

Computing a rate of return on a futures trade is often a problem. On one level of analysis, we can say that the investor has no initial investment. The initial margin is not an investment; it is good faith collateral. The trader can post T-bills or a bank letter of credit to satisfy the requirement. In this case, there is no initial investment, and any rate of return on an initial investment of zero dollars is infinite.

If, instead, the relevant cash flows are the daily mark-to-market cash flows $(-140, -240, -20, \ldots, +70)$ are used to compute the internal rate of return, then again there is no answer, since it is impossible to analyze the internal rate of return for a series of cash inflows and outflows with more than one sign change.[11]

A common solution for computing a holding period rate of return on a futures contract is to consider the initial outlay as the cash outflow required to meet the initial margin. The total profit or loss on the trade is divided by the initial margin cash outflow. This approach suffers from many drawbacks, the most serious of which is that it adds cash flows occurring on different dates (variation margin, or maintenance margin calls). In other words, there is no accounting for the timing of the daily resettlement cash flows. Still, if the initial margin of $1000 in our example was made with cash, we would conclude that the trade resulted in a –114% rate of return. Your initial cash outflow (initial investment) was $1000. If you lost all of that, we would say you lost 100% of your initial investment. But you lost *more than* your initial investment. Thus:

$$\text{rate of return} = \frac{\text{profit or loss}}{\text{initial investment}} = \frac{-1140}{1000} = -114\%$$

Note that this -114% rate of return was achieved during a 15-day holding period. It is *not* annualized.

6.4   BASIS AND CONVERGENCE

Two important concepts in futures trading are basis and convergence.

Basis is usually defined as the spot price (cash price) minus the futures price.[12] There will be a different basis for each delivery month for each contract. In a "normal market," basis will be negative, since futures prices normally exceed spot prices. The reason for this is the theoretical cost-of-carry pricing model, which applies to futures as well as forwards. In an "inverted market," basis will be positive.

Basis will approach zero as the delivery date nears. At the close of trading on the delivery date, basis must equal zero.[13] If the spot price of the deliverable asset at the delivery location on the delivery date does not equal the futures price, there will be an arbitrage opportunity. If the basis was positive on the delivery day, an arbitrageur could buy the futures contract and sell the cash good that is deliverable into the contract.

EXAMPLE 6.1   Suppose that an instant before trading ceases on the delivery date, the spot price of deliverable grade gold at a delivery location is $290/oz. and the futures price of the expiring contract is $289/oz. (basis=+1). Ignoring transactions costs, an arbitrageur could buy the gold futures contract. Then, to satisfy the terms of the contract, he would take delivery of the gold and pay $289/oz. He would then sell the gold in the spot market for $290/oz, realizing the $1/oz. arbitrage profit. A similar arbitrage trade could be done if the basis was negative just before the end of trading.

The process of basis moving toward zero is called **convergence**. Regardless of today's basis, because of the possibility of arbitrage, we know that at the close of trading on the delivery date, the basis will be zero for that contract.

Figure 6.2 illustrates the process of convergence for four commodities during 1996. Note how the basis always declines towards zero as delivery nears.

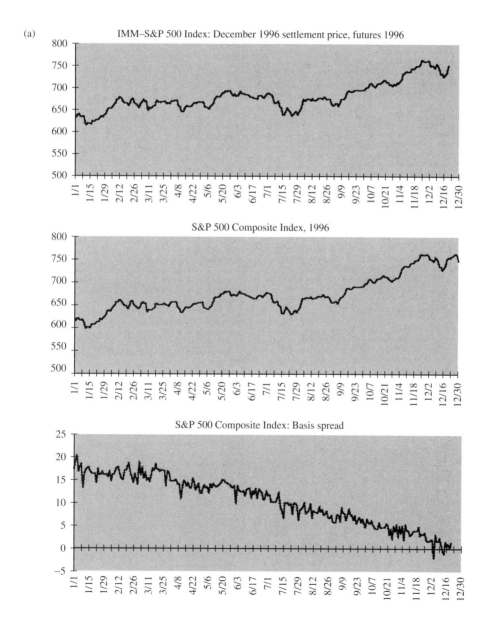

Figure 6.2 Convergence for four commodities during 1996: (a) S&P 500 Index, (b) oil, (c) yen, and (d) Eurodollars.

(b)

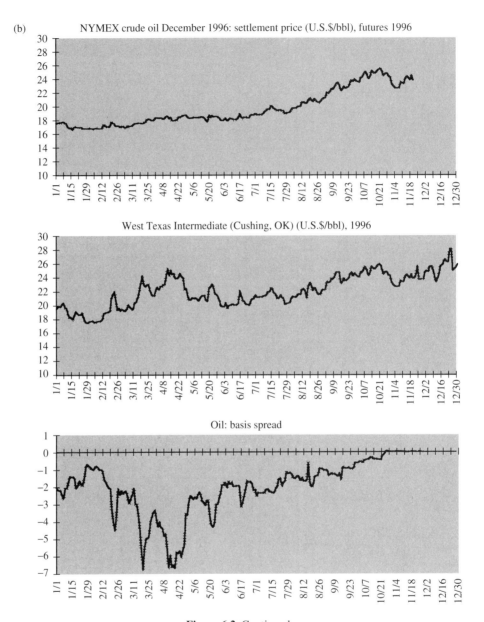

Figure 6.2 Continued.

Regardless of whether the basis is initially positive or negative, and regardless of how the spot price moves, convergence will occur. It is also possible that the basis will fluctuate between being positive and negative as time passes. Convergence will still take place. Figure 6.3 illustrates some different scenarios.

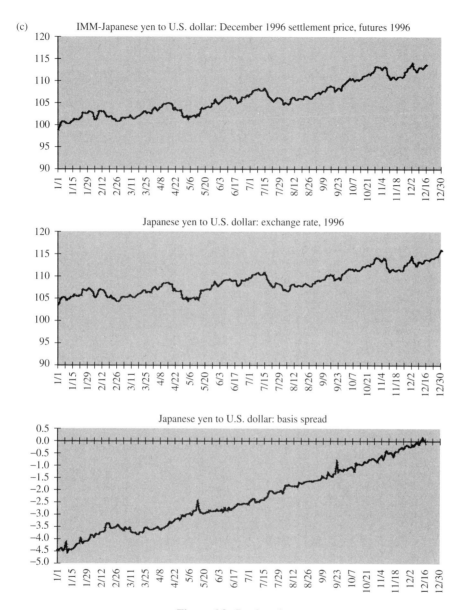

Figure 6.2 Continued.

6.5   SHOULD FUTURES PRICES EQUAL FORWARD PRICES?

You now know about the differences that exist between forward contracts and futures contracts. In Chapter 5, you learned about how theoretical forward prices are computed. You might now wonder whether theoretical forward prices and futures prices are equal. In this section, we study this

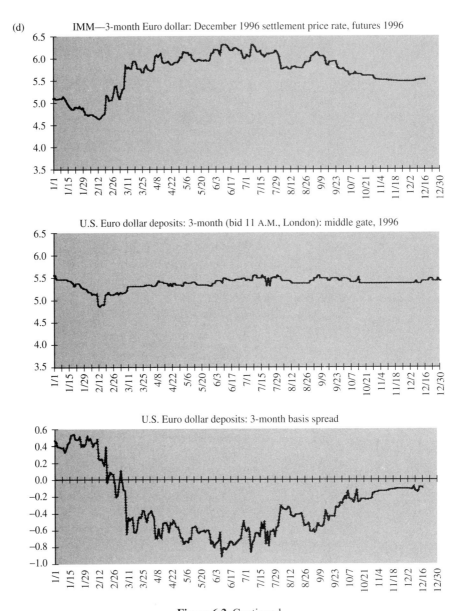

Figure 6.2 Continued.

question. An early study of futures and forward contracts is Black (1976). Cox, Ingersoll, and Ross (1981) is a rigorous further examination of the relationship between futures and forward prices. Many of their results, and other theoretical perspectives, are derived in Richard and Sundaresan (1981) and Jarrow and Oldfield (1981).

Basically, the results are obtained because if tomorrow's interest rate is known today, a futures contract can be transformed into a forward contract. If futures can be transformed into forwards,

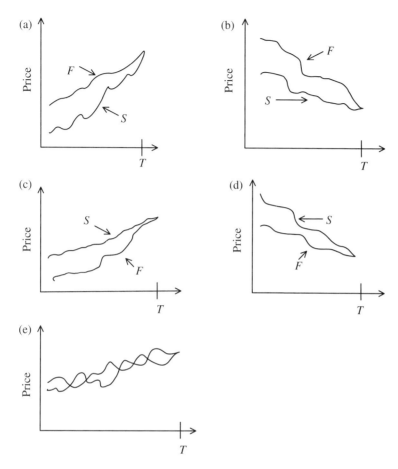

Figure 6.3 Convergence occurs regardless of the basis, and regardless of how the spot price changes over time. (a) Negative basis; spot price rises. (b) Negative basis; spot price declines. (c) Positive basis; spot price rises. (d) Positive basis; spot price declines. (e) Basis alternates between positive and negative.

then we can conclude that futures prices and forward prices will be identical. Note that we are ignoring default risk, transactions costs, taxes, and other market imperfections.

Proposition I. *In a perfect market with nonstochastic (known) interest rates, futures prices equal forward prices.*

We can prove this by example. Today is time 0. Define $r_{t1,\,t2}$ as the interest rate from time $t1$ to time $t2$. For example, assume that you know that at time 1, the three-period interest rate will be $r_{1,4} = 10\%$/period. You also know that the two period interest rate at time 2 will be $r_{2,4} = 9\%$/period. Finally, you know that the one-period interest rate at time 3 will be $r_{3,4} = 8\%$/period. Assume that you satisfy the initial margin requirement to trade a futures contract with a bank letter of credit. Today's futures price for 100 oz. of gold is $300/oz. You do not know what futures prices will be at subsequent times 1, 2, 3, and 4 (the delivery date). You buy $1/(1+r_{1,4})^3 = 0.7513148$ of a futures contract at the time 0 futures price of 400.[14]

Suppose that at time 1, the futures price rises to 310. The mark-to-market cash flow on one futures contract is $1000. Your profit on 0.7513148 futures contract is $751.3148. You invest this profit at the three-period rate of 10% per period. So at time 4, it will have grown to $1000. You also buy enough additional futures contracts to be left with $1/(1+r_{2,4})^2 = 0.84168$ futures contract. In other words, buy 0.0903652 future contracts at the new futures price of 310.

At time 2, the futures price rises to 315. The mark-to-market cash flow on one futures contract is $500. Your profit, however, is $(0.84168 \times 500 =)$ $420.84, because you are long 0.84168 contract. You invest this profit at the two-period rate of 9%/period. At time 4, this will have grown to $500. You also buy enough additional futures to bring your total to $1/(1+r_{3,4}) = 0.9259259$ contract. In other words, buy 0.0842459 additional contract at the futures price of 315.

At time 3, the futures price falls to 290. The mark-to-market cash flow on one futures contract is –$2500. You thus lose $2314.8148 on your long position of 0.9259259 contract. You borrow this amount for one-period at the one-period rate of 8%. At time 4, your debt will equal $2500. You also buy 0.0741741 additional futures contract so that you are now long one contract.

At time 4, owing to convergence, the final futures price equals the $285 spot price of gold. Your mark-to-market cash outflow is $500. Note that you had zero cash flows at times 1, 2, and 3 because all losses were borrowed and all mark-to-market gains were lent. Your cash flow at time 4 equals $+\$1000 + \$500 - \$2500 - \$500 = -\$1500$. But this total cash flow is exactly the same as that of a forward contract, which also has only one cash flow (the total profit or loss at delivery). In other words, had you bought a forward contract at time 0 at a forward price of $300, with the delivery date spot price of gold closing at $285, the value of the long forward contract on the delivery date would have been −$1500.

Since the same analysis can be done with any *known* series of interest rates, and any realization of futures prices (which are stochastic as of time 0), we can conclude that in a perfect market with known interest rates, futures prices must equal forward prices at any date. If they were unequal, an arbitrageur could sell the contract (futures or forward) with the higher price and buy the contract with the lower price. When interest rates are known, a futures contract can be converted into a forward contract by trading in the manner just demonstrated. Basically, to convert a futures into a forward, the trader should always be long or short the present value of a futures contract.

Proposition II. *If interest rates are stochastic, and if corr(ΔF, Δr) > 0, futures prices will exceed forward prices.*[15] *If corr(ΔF, Δr) < 0, futures prices will be less than forward prices.*

If futures prices rise, long positions profit. If corr(ΔF, Δr) > 0, then at the same time interest rates rise, the mark-to-market cash inflows can be reinvested at the higher interest rates. It also follows that if changes in futures prices are positively correlated with interest rates, the losses that long positions experience when futures fall can be borrowed at lower interest rates. These two effects make long futures positions more valuable than long forward positions when corr(ΔF, Δr) > 0. Because of this, investors will bid up futures prices relative to forward prices when there is a positive correlation between futures price changes and interest rate changes.

If, on the other hand, corr(ΔF, Δr) < 0, then an increase in futures prices means that the mark to market profits of a long position will be reinvested at lower interest rates. Furthermore, if futures prices decline, they will tend to do so along with an increase in interest rates. The daily resettlement losses of a long futures position will then have to be borrowed at higher interest rates. Thus, if changes in futures prices are negatively correlated with changes in interest rates, a long futures position is less desirable than a long forward position. To induce investors to buy futures, the futures price will have to be less than the forward price.

EXAMPLE 6.2   This example utilizes the data from the example provided in connection with Proposition I, except if futures prices rise, interest rates and expected interest rates decline. The example demonstrates that because corr(ΔF, Δr) is negative, a long futures position is inferior to a long forward position if both the futures and forward prices are \$400/oz. at time 0.

At time 0, the futures price is \$400. Investors expect that at time 1, the three-period interest rate will be 10%; this is denoted as $E_0(r_{1,4})=0.10$. They also expect that at time 2, the two-period rate will be 9%; $E_0(r_{2,4})=0.09$. Finally, they expect that at time 3, the one-period rate will be 8%; $E_0(r_{3,4})=0.08$. You buy $1/[1+E_0(r_{1,4})]^3=1/(1.1)^3=0.7513148$ futures contract at $F_0=400$.

At time 1, the futures price rises to \$410. Your profit is (\$1000)(0.7513148)= \$751.3148. The spot three-period interest rate is 9%; $r_{1,4}=0.09$. (Note that the increase in the futures price is accompanied by a decline in interest rates.) You lend your \$751.3148 profit for three periods at 9%/period. Investors now expect that the two-period rate at time 2 will be 8%; $E_1(r_{2,4})=0.08$. You buy 0.106024 additional contract at $F_1=410$, putting yourself long $1/[1+E_1(r_{2,4})]^2=1/(1.08)^2=0.8573388$ futures contract. Investors also now expect that the one-period rate at time 3 will be 7%; $E_1(r_{3,4})=0.07$. Both the spot interest rate and all expected rates are thus lower than what investors had originally predicted.

At time 2, the futures price rises to \$415. Your profit is (\$500)(0.8573388)= \$428.6694. The spot two-period interest rate is 7%; $r_{2,4}=0.07$. You lend your \$428.6694 profit for two periods at 7%/period. Investors now expect that the one-period rate at time 3 will be 6%; $E_2(r_{3,4})=0.06$. You buy 0.0860574 additional contract at $F_2=415$, so that you are now long $1/[1+E_2(r_{3,4})]^1=1/1.06=0.9433962$ futures contract. The spot rate and expected rates are even lower than what investors had expected earlier.

At time 3, the futures price falls to \$390. Your loss is (\$2500)(0.9433962)= \$2358.4905. The spot one-period interest rate is 7%; $r_{3,4}=0.07$. You borrow the \$2358.4905 for one-period at 7%/period. You buy 0.0566038 additional contract at $F_3=390$, so that you are now long 1 futures contract. The spot rate is higher than what had been expected at time 2.

At time 4, the futures price falls to \$385. Your loss is \$500. Now repay the money you borrowed at time 3, and get repaid the loans you made at times 1 and 2. The total time 4 cash flow is thus $-\$500-\$2358.4905(1.07)+\$428.6694(1.07)^2+\$751.3148(1.09)^3=-\$1559.8268$.

Because corr(ΔF, Δr)<0, this futures loss is bigger than it would have been if you had gone long a forward contract. The loss for a long forward position is −\$1500 and the loss for the long futures position is −\$1559.8268. Thus, the example illustrates that if investors believe that corr(ΔF, Δr)<0, and the futures price equal the forward price, no one will go long futures. The futures price must be below the forward price if futures price changes and interest rate changes are negatively correlated. If the futures price was equal to the forward price in this example, arbitrageurs would sell futures and buy forwards, and realize an arbitrage profit in time 4. With futures prices and interest rates evolving as they did in the example, the arbitrageurs' profit is \$59.8268.

As usual, the foregoing results apply only in perfect markets. Transactions costs, taxes, liquidity, and contract indivisibilities all work to weaken the stated propositions. The cost-of-carry pricing model is a forward contract pricing model. When it is used to estimate futures prices, we must assume that daily resettlement of futures contracts has no effect on prices. Proposition I demonstrates that if future interest rates are known, then futures prices and forward prices are equal.

If markets are imperfect, but the correlation of futures price changes and changes in interest rates is zero, then futures prices and forward prices should be equal. Marking to market should have no effect on futures prices relative to forward prices. There are some commodities that have both futures and forward markets, and empirical research has concluded that their prices are so close that the effect of daily resettlement appears to be an insignificant institutional matter. We recommend that you always think that theoretically, futures prices and forward prices are equal.

6.6 Futures Contracts, Exchanges, and Regulation

As of January 2001, futures and options contracts traded on 59 different futures exchanges in 29 different countries, including 12 in the United States and 7 in Japan. Each January, *Futures* magazine publishes a Source Book containing a summary overview of the contracts.

Table 6.3 gives the names, addresses, phone numbers, and websites of the major futures exchanges in the United States. Most, if not all, offer many publications describing the contracts

TABLE 6.3 Addresses of Major U.S. Futures Exchanges and Related Agencies and Organizations

1. Chicago Mercantile Exchange
    30 South Wacker Drive
    Chicago, IL 60606
    312-930-1000
    Website: www.cme.com/

The CME has available literally hundreds of publications, films, slides, videos, and so on. The Merc's Education Center offers inexpensive (about $150, on average) courses on futures, futures options, technical analysis, hedging, and even computer courses; you just have to get to Chicago—though many courses are taught in other cities, too.

   The International Monetary Market (IMM) and Index and the International Option Market (IOM) are divisions of the CME.

2. Chicago Board of Trade
    141 West Jackson
    Chicago, IL 60604
    800-THE-CBOT (Publications Department)
    312-435-3500
    Website: www.cbot.com

The CBOT offers an immense amount of literature on futures. Request their publications catalog. The MidAmerica Commodity Exchange (MidAm) is an affiliate of the CBOT, and their phone number is 312-341-3000.

3. New York Board of Trade
    174 Hudson Street, 6th Floor
    New York, NY 10013
    212-625-6669
    Website: www.nybot.com

(Continued)

TABLE 6.3 Continued

The NYBOT is the parent company of the Coffee, Sugar & Cocoa Exchange, Inc. (CSCE) and the New York Cotton Exchange (NYCE). Through its two exchange and their subsidiaries including the New York Futures Exchange (NYFE), FINEX and Citrus Associates, the NYBOT offers a wide variety of agricultural (such as cotton and frozen orange juice) and financial (the U.S. dollar index and the NYSE composite index) products.

4. New York Mercantile Exchange (NYMEX)
   One North End Avenue
   World Financial Center
   New York, NY 10282
   212-299-2000
   Website: www.nymex.com

The NYMEX specializes in energy futures and options on energy futures. The COMEX (Commodity Exchange), which became a subsidiary of the NYMEX in 1994, specializes in precious metals futures and futures options.

5. Kansas City Board of Trade
   4800 Main, Suite 303
   Kansas City, Missouri 64112
   800-821-5228
   816-753-7500
   Website: www.kcbt.com

Futures on wheat, natural gas, and the Value Line Index trade on the KCBOT.

6. Commodity Futures Trading Commission (CFTC)
   Three Lafayette Centre
   1155 21st St. NW.
   Washington, D.C. 20581
   202-418-5498
   202-418-5430 (Division of Trading and Markets)
   202-418-5260 (Division of Economic Analysis)
   Website: www.cftc.gov

7. National Futures Association (NFA)
   200 West Madison St., Suite 1600
   Chicago, IL 60606
   800-621-3570
   312-781-1300
   312-781-1370
   Website: www.nfa.futures.org

8. Futures Industry Association
   2001 Pennsylvania Ave. NW., Suite 600
   Washington, D.C. 20006-1807
   202-466-5460
   Website: www.fiafii.org

The FIA, founded in 1955, is the major trade association for all organizations with an interest in futures markets. It offers publications and courses on futures trading. It also presents Futures and Options Expo every October, in Chicago. In 1988 the FIA established the Futures Industry Institute to provide educational information about the futures, options, and other derivatives markets; its phone number is 202-223-1528.

traded there, as well as other general books, pamphlets, videos, and other educational materials on futures trading. Current minimum margin requirements and recent price information are available at the websites. Before trading futures, you should contact the exchanges that trade the contracts in which you have interest, and obtain any and all information they have to offer.

At the end of Table 6.3 are the addresses of some other agencies and organizations of interest. The CFTC, created on April 21, 1975 pursuant to the Commodity Futures Trading Commission Act of 1974, regulates all futures markets and futures trading in the United States, although it should be noted that the industry is largely self-regulated by the exchanges themselves. CFTC approval is required for all new contracts, contract terms, trading rules, margin requirements and so on. The CFTC enforces the rules that protect futures traders' funds. The CFTC also offers publications on futures trading, many of which are free.

The National Futures Association (NFA) began operations in October 1982. It serves as the futures industry's self-regulatory organization. The NFA has responsibility for any regulation that the CFTC believes should be handled internally by the futures industry itself. For example, the NFA establishes ethical codes for the industry, considers FCM–customer disputes, screens new FCMs and other futures markets participants that deal with the public, and disciplines its members when necessary.[16]

6.7   THE PURPOSES OF FUTURES MARKETS

As Figure 1.2 showed, futures trading has exploded since the early 1980s. An interesting question is: Why do futures contracts exist? Do they serve any useful purpose, or are they merely gambling instruments that have created speculation-based price volatility? Since the stock market crash of 1987, the scandals in the trading pits of the late 1980s, and financial debacles such as those involving Procter & Gamble and Barings in the 1990s, many critics have questioned the raison d'être of futures and have called for their abolition. Indeed, since the first appearance of futures and forward contracts, there have been lengthy periods during which they were banned.

Futures markets exist for several reason:

a. Futures make transactions across time easier. Production, consumption, and inventory decisions can be more optimally made when futures markets exist. They allow individuals to *quickly* create *low cost* agreements to exchange money for goods at future times. Both speculators and hedgers will transact in the futures markets when speed is important. The transactions costs of trading futures are minuscule relative to the dollar amount of the commodity underlying most contracts.

b. Futures allow informed individuals to act on their superior information. In this way, prices will become more efficient. In other words, prices will reflect more information, and therefore resources will be allocated in ways that are closer to optimal.

c. Futures allow individuals to hedge against undesirable (costly) price changes. Producers and users can then do what they do best: produce and use. They should not be in the business of price speculation. Hedgers transfer price risk to speculators. Price volatility and uncertainty are major preconditions for a successful futures contract, attracting both speculators and hedgers.

d. Futures prices contain information. This is called the "price discovery" function of futures. Producers and consumers can get an efficient idea of what the future spot price will be, and what future supply and demand of a good will be, by observing the current futures price. In so doing, they can make better production and storage decisions.

6.8   READING FUTURES PRICES IN *THE WALL STREET JOURNAL*

6.8.1   Commodity Futures

Figure 6.4 is a listing of price data for commodities such as agricultural goods, metals, and energy products. The data come from the July 29, 1999, *Wall Street Journal*, summarizing trading activity on July 28, 1999. Price data for selected financial futures are presented in Section 6.8.2.

The header line of each commodity makes note of the commodity type, the exchange on which the futures contract trades, the quantity of the good underlying one contract, and the units of the price. For example, the first entry gives price data for the corn futures contract that is traded on the Chicago Board of Trade (CBT). One futures contract covers 5000 bushels of corn. The prices are in cents per bushel. A trader can and should contact the exchange for details on the quality of corn that is deliverable, the locations to which the corn must be delivered, and the delivery procedure.

Below each header line are the different delivery months for each contract. For corn, there are futures contracts for delivery in September and December 1999, and March, May, July, September, and December 2000. There may be other delivery months, but volume is insufficient for the *Wall Street Journal* to provide price data. One *very* important question is not answered: What day of the delivery month is the delivery day? Or are there a range of possible delivery dates? Related to these concerns is the absence of a listing for the last day of trading. It is even possible that the individual who is short the contract can initiate delivery in the month before the delivery month. For example, the last trading day for the NYMEX heating oil and unleaded gasoline futures is the last business day in the month preceding the delivery month (August 31, 1999, for the September 1999 contracts); the crude oil contract terminates trading even earlier, in the month preceding delivery (note the natural gas futures for Oct. 2001–June 2002 delivery; it ceased trading on the third business day prior to the 25th calendar day of the month preceding the delivery month, which was July 21, 1999).

Eight items are printed for each delivery month.

1. The **open** is the first price at which a contract traded. The Sept. 1999 corn contract, for instance, opened at 197 cents ($1.97) per bushel. The value of corn underlying this contract of 5000 bushels is therefore $9,850 ($1.97/bu × 5000 bu).

2, 3. The **high** and the **low**, respectively, are the highest and lowest prices at which a contract traded on the preceding day.

4. "**Settle**", the settlement price of 196 cents/bu, determines the mark-to-market cash flow for the day. It is representative of the prices at which contracts traded during a specified closing period, frequently the last minute of trading. If no trades occurred during that closing period, then the exchange selects a representative price that it feels reflects market conditions. That is why more distant contracts frequently all change by the same amount in Figure 6.4 (note the natural gas futures for Oct. 2001–June 2002 delivery).

5. The **change** is the change in settlement prices from the preceding day (Tuesday, July 27, 1999) to the current day (Wednesday, July 28, 1999). Corn for delivery in September 1999 fell by 0.5 cent per bushel, from $196\frac{1}{2}$ to 196 cents per bushel. Tuesday's settlement price can only be inferred, using Wednesday's close of 196, and the change of $\frac{1}{2}$ a cent. The value of corn underlying the contract therefore fell by $25, and all accounts that were short the Sept. 99 corn futures contract were marked to market with a profit of $25.00. Likewise, all long positions were debited (a loss) $25.00.

6, 7. The **lifetime high** and **low**, respectively, are the highest and lowest prices at which each contract has traded, since trading began. The Sept. 99 corn contract first began trading more than

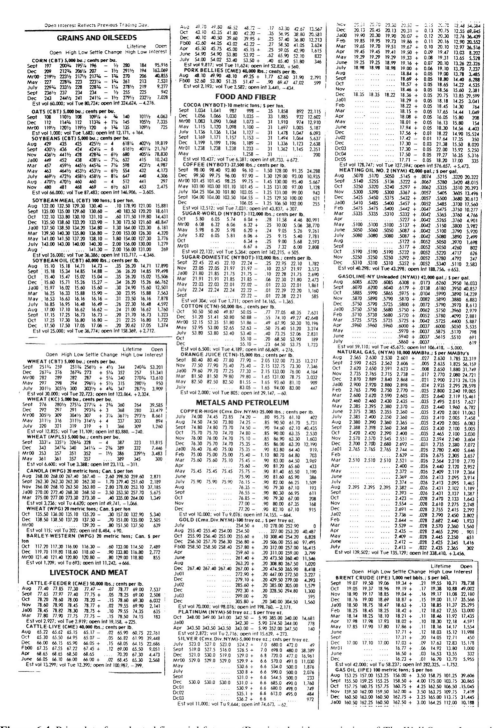

Figure 6.4 Price data for selected financial futures. (Reprinted with permission of *The Wall Street Journal*, © July 29, 1999.)

a year ago, and at one point in its life it traded as high as 280 cents/bu. At another time, a contract traded for as little as 184 cents/bu.

8. The **open interest** is the number of futures contracts outstanding. There are 95,916 Sept. 99 corn contracts outstanding: 95,916 long positions, and 95,916 short positions. Open interest may or may not change when two traders offset their positions in a trade. If you are long one Sept. 99 corn contract, and you sell it to a trader who previously had no position in this contract, then open interest remains unchanged. If, however, you sell it to an individual who was previously short a Sept. 99 corn contract, then open interest declines by one contract.

Below the price information for all the months is the volume on the two most recent trading days; the most recent day is estimated and the preceding day (July 27, 1999) is actual volume. Finally, the total open interest, for all delivery months, is given. There were 4276 fewer corn futures contracts outstanding (for all delivery months) on July 28 than on July 27.

The value of the good underlying the contract can be computed by multiplying the number of units of the good by the price. Because all contracts are marked to market, you can also multiply the contract size by the change in the futures price to determine the cash flow resulting from the day's trading.

EXAMPLE 6.3 If you were long the December 1999 copper contract, then according to Figure 6.4 you realized a mark-to-market loss of $212.50 (+$.0085/lb×its contract size of 25,000 lb). If you were short the October 1999 natural gas contract, your profit was $80 (the futures price fell by $.008/MMBtu×10,000 MMBtu).

6.8.2 Financial Futures

The following is a brief discussion of how to read and interpret *Wall Street Journal* price data for several futures contracts on financial assets and indices, which are shown in Figure 6.5. The data are from the *Wall Street Journal* of January 17, 2001, summarizing transactions made on January 16. Chapters 9 and 10 present more detailed information on Treasury bond, Treasury bill, and Eurodollar futures.

The first set of contracts shown in Figure 6.5 consists of the interest rate futures. The first contract listed is the long-term Treasury bond futures contract, which trades on the Chicago Board of Trade. This contract calls for the delivery of $100,000 face value of long-term (about 20 years to maturity) Treasury bonds. The futures prices are given in "points and 32nds of 100%." Think of this as a percentage of $100,000 of Treasury bonds. For instance, the settlement price for the March 2001 contract was 103-06. This is 103 and 6/32% of $100,000; 6/32 equals 0.1875. The value of the bonds underlying the contract is therefore 1.031875 times $100,000, which is $103,187.50. The value of the bonds underlying the June 2001 Treasury bond futures contract, given its settlement price of 102-30, is $102,937.50 (102 and 30/32 percent of $100,000).[17]

The March and June 2001 Treasury bond futures contracts closed 9/32 (9 ticks) above the previous day's settlement price. In other words, the March contract closed at 102-29 on January 15, 2001, and the June contract closed at 102-21. The bonds underlying the contracts on January 15

Figure 6.5 Financial futures prices for January 16, 2001. (Reprinted with permission of *The Wall Street Journal*, © January 17, 2001.)

were thus worth \$102,906.25 and \$102,656.25 for March and June delivery, respectively. From this, we see that one tick equates to \$31.25 in value (e.g., \$103,187.50 minus \$102,906.25 for the March contract is \$281.25, which is the value of a rise in price of 9 ticks; $9 \times \$31.25 = \$281.25$).

The next contract in the first column of Figure 6.5 is the actively traded Treasury note futures contract, which calls for the delivery of treasury notes with about 6.5–10 years to maturity. Further down are the five-year and two-year Treasury notes contracts. Prices for these three contracts are presented slightly differently than the Treasury bond contract. The (10-year) Treasury notes and the five-year Treasury notes contract actually trade in halves of 32nds, and the two-year Treasury notes contract trades in quarters of 32nds. When prices are given in halves or quarters of 32nds, the *Wall Street Journal* drops the "1" from any price exceeding 100 and adds either a "2" (for $1/4$), a "5" (for $1/2$), or a "7" (for $3/4$) to the last digit of the price. Thus, the closing price for the March Treasury notes contract was actually 104 and 16.5/32, but it is presented as 04-165. Similarly, the closing price of the March two-year Treasury note contract was 101 and 29.25/32, but it is presented as 01-292. The smallest tick size for these three Treasury note contracts is \$15.625. Note that the size of the two-year contract is \$200,000.

Treasury bill futures contracts trade on the Chicago Mercantile Exchange. They call for the future delivery of \$1 million face value of 13-week Treasury bills. In Figure 6.5, the March futures settlement price of 95.10 is actually 100 minus the futures interest rate. In other words, given the futures discount yield of 4.90%, the futures price is then $100 - 4.90 = 95.10$. Each tick represents one basis point, and it equals 0.01, which equals \$25. On the prior trading day, January 15, 2001, the futures price was two ticks higher, or 95.12. Therefore, all shorts profited by \$50, and all longs lost \$50. The discount yield, shown in the next column, is an interest rate that is used for Treasury bills. This futures discount yield is essentially a forward rate, just like you learned about in Chapter 5. The March futures discount yield of 4.90 is a forward three-month rate that exists for delivery on some day in March 2001 (i.e., from some date in March until a day in June 13 weeks later).[18] Buying a March Treasury bill futures contract at a futures price of 95.10 commits you to purchase \$1 million (face value) of three-month Treasury bills in March, at a price that is consistent with a discount yield of 4.90%.

The second most actively traded futures contract in the world (at least during the first 11 months of 2001) is the Eurodollar time deposit futures contract, which trades on the CME. Like the Treasury bill contract, each tick (0.01) equals \$25. Figure 6.5 shows that the February contract rose in price by two ticks, which reflects a two-basis-point decline in the three-month Eurodollar futures interest rate. If a Eurodollar futures price were to fall by *one point*, say, from 94.45 to 93.45, this would reflect a rise in interest rates of 100 ticks, or \$2500. This is equivalent to a rise in the futures yield of Eurodollar time deposits of 100 basis points, from 5.55% to 6.55%. Note the huge open interest of most Eurodollar futures contracts. Also note that the delivery dates stretch out all the way to December 2010, almost 10 years into the future. The December 2010 futures yield of 7.30% is a forward rate that exists for a three-month period beginning in December 2010.

Futures on other Eurocurrencies, such as the Euroyen, the Euribor (for the new currency, the Euro), and the Euroswiss also are actively traded, as are foreign bond futures such as Euro-denominated government bond contracts. You are encouraged to contact the exchange on which the contracts trade to learn the current information concerning any contract you trade.

The next section of contracts shown in Figure 6.5 are currency futures, which require the future exchange of different foreign currencies. For example, the Japanese yen futures contract calls for the delivery of ¥12.5 million. The yen futures prices drop off the first two zeroes, which is why you see

(.00) on the header line for the yen contract in Figure 6.5. The March futures price for one yen is actually $0.008596. Multiply this futures price by ¥12.5 million, and you obtain the value of JPY underlying one futures contract. For March delivery, this equals $107,450 (¥12,500,000× $0.008596/¥).

On January 16, the March yen contract closed $0.000063/¥ higher than its settlement price on January 15. Because **one tick** is the term used to denote the minimum price change that a contract can make, this represents a rise of 63 ticks, from $0.008533/¥ to $0.008596/¥. Alternatively, the value of the yen underlying the contract rose from $106,662.50 to $107,450, or $787.50. Since the rise of 63 ticks increased the value of yen underlying the contract by $787.50, it follows that one tick equals $12.50 ($787.50/63 ticks = $12.50/tick).

The last currency listed is the Euro (€), and the March contract for euros fell by 90 ticks on January 16. One euro futures contract covers €125,000. Therefore, an individual who was long one March euro futures contract lost lost $1125 (90×$12.50). This occurred because the value of the euros underlying the contract fell from $118,987.50 (€125,000×$0.9519/€) to $117,862.50 (€125,000×$0.9429/€).

You should be able to analyze the price data for the other foreign exchange futures contracts by reading the header line concerning the size of the contract (in units of foreign currency), and the price rule (dollars per unit of foreign currency).

In the last section of Figure 6.5 are prices of index futures, most of which are stock index futures. The most popular stock index futures contract, in terms of open interest, is the S&P 500 Index, which trades on the Chicago Mercantile Exchange. The underlying asset of this contract is effectively 250 shares of the S&P 500 Index, which is itself a portfolio of stocks. The value of the stock underlying the contract equals $250 times the futures price. In Figure 6.5, we see that the settlement price for the March 2001 S&P 500 futures contract was 133550 or $1335.50. Therefore, the value of the stock underlying the contract was $333,875 (1335.50×250).

In the "Change" column, the change in the futures price is given. On January 16, 2001, the settlement price of the March S&P contract was 5.20 points above the January 15th settlement price. This means that anyone who was long one S&P 500 futures contract profited by $1300 (5.20×250) as a result of daily resettlement. Short positions lost $1300 per contract. One point equals $250. The value of the stock underlying the March contract on January 16 was $333,875 (1335.50×250). On January 15, the value was $332,575 (1330.30×250). The increase in stock value underlying the March contract, from January 15 to the next trading day of January 16 was $1300 ($333,875 − $332,575, which equals 5.20×250).

Each *tick*, or 0.10 of stock index futures price movement, equals $25 (0.10×250). A tick is the smallest unit by which the price of a S&P 500 futures contract can change. Tick sizes differ for different futures contracts. All stock index futures contracts are cash settled. On the last trading day, the final settlement price is set equal to the spot S&P 500 Index value, which is in units of 0.01. Thus, the size of the last tick for the S&P 500 contract is actually 0.01. Cash settlement means that there is one last mark-to-market cash flow that occurs on the last day of trading, and then the contract ceases to exist. There is no delivery of the underlying asset.

The highest price that the March 2001 S&P 500 contract ever sold for, during the time that it has traded (it has traded for more than a year) was $1642.60. The lowest futures price was $1270.00. At the close of trading on January 16, there were 468,147 contracts for March delivery outstanding (open interest). Below all the price data is the estimated January 16 trading volume of 66,963 contracts, and the actual January 15 trading volume of 72,792 contracts. Finally, the *Wall Street Journal* presents the preliminary (estimated) high, low, and closing values for the *spot*

S&P 500 Index (Id x prl). On January 16, the spot index closed at 1326.65, and this was 7.83 points below its close on January 15.

6.9 LIMITS ON PRICE FLUCTUATIONS

As mentioned earlier, every futures contract has a minimum size for trade-to-trade price changes, called a tick. For example, the tick size for the wool futures contracts that trade on the Sydney Futures Exchange is one Australian cent/kg, or 25 Australian dollars (denoted A$25).

Many futures contracts also have maximum limits on daily price changes, which define the maximum amount by which a price can change in one day. Note that the exchanges will frequently change these limits when they feel it is appropriate or necessary, and the price limit may differ for the most nearby contract from contracts with delivery in more distant months.

The purpose of such price limits is to allow the markets time to digest new information and dampen possible tendencies to overreact. It also may provide an incentive for losers to meet their margin calls (the holder of a losing futures position may meet each of a series of small margin calls, but default on one very large margin call). But the drawback to these daily maximum price change limits is that they also may prevent traders from closing out or opening a desired position. For example, suppose that a revolution in a Middle Eastern country caused the price of oil to rise by $45/bbl. With no price limits, the futures price of crude oil would immediately rise by about $45/bbl. But the daily limit on the NYMEX crude oil futures contract is $15/bbl. Therefore, it would take three trading days during which no trading occurs to reach a price at which futures trades would be made. Today's futures price would immediately rise by $15/bbl (a *limit up* day), and there would be an enormous quantity of buy orders at that price, but no sell orders. The same would happen tomorrow and the next day, for a total of three trading days.

Some believe that without price limits, futures price changes would sometimes be irrational. Daily price limits, in the opinion, serve the useful purpose of allowing markets the time to gather more information, and more accurately assess the implication of the news.[19] (Others believe that no price change can ever be judged to be irrational.)

6.10 ORDERS AND POSITION LIMITS

All orders to trade futures contracts have the following features in common:

Whether the trader wishes to buy or sell

The name of the commodity

The delivery month and year of the contract

The number of contracts

The exchange on which the contract trades (if it trades on multiple exchanges)

Whether it is a market order or a limit order, if the latter, it must include a stated limit price at which the trade should be made

Whether the trade is a day order (if it is not filled by the close of trading, it is canceled) or a good-til-canceled order

If a trader places a **market order** to buy or sell, she will assume a long or short position at the price that is prevailing in the futures **pit** at that time.[20] Upon receiving such an order, a representative of the trader's FCM will go to the pit where that contract trades and try to get the best price possible, based on supply and demand conditions at that moment. There is risk that in a "fast" market, the trade price will be quite different from the one quoted to the customer by the FCM just a minute or two earlier.

Limit orders to buy or sell specify that the trader wishes to trade at the stated price or better. The risk here is that the trade will not be executed. **Market-if-touched** (MIT) orders are like limit orders, except that they become market orders once a trade at the specified price has occurred. For example, an MIT buy order for gold with a specified price of $273.40 becomes a market order as soon as a trade occurs at that price or lower. The trader may get that price, or one above or below it. In a rapidly declining market, the sequence of trades after placing the MIT buy order might be $275, $272.60, $270.80. The trade should be filled at whatever price occurs **after** the trade at $272.60.[21] In this sequence, it should thus be at $270.80.

Stop orders, also known as **stop-loss-orders**, also specify a price. There are two types of stop order: to buy and to sell. A stop order to buy is usually placed by a trader who is currently short the contract and desires to limit his losses should the price start rising.[22] Thus, stop orders to buy are placed at a specified price that is above the current price, and they become market orders when the futures price is at or above the specified stop price. Stop orders to sell are placed at a specified price that is below the current futures price.

In contrast to a stop order to buy, a limit order to buy would specify a limit price *below* the current price. In this case the trader wishes to initiate a long position at a futures price somewhat more favorable (lower) than the current one, or would be satisfied with the profits on an existing short position if the futures price should decline to the specified price.

A **stop limit order** becomes a limit order once the specified price has been reached. Thus, in Example 6.4, if a trade takes place at $300/oz., a stop limit buy order would result in the trader offsetting his short position only at $300/oz. or better (a price less than or equal to $300/oz.). A stop limit order can even specify a stop price different from the limit price. For example, a trader might place a stop limit order to buy back the gold contract, with a stop of $300 and a limit of $297. This means that once there is a trade at $300, the trader will offset his short position, but only at prices between $297/oz. and $300/oz. It is important to note that a trader using stop limit orders has the risk of an order going unfilled in some fast market conditions.

There are many other types of order that can be placed at one exchange or another, and some of these are listed in Table 6.4. Traders should inquire what order types are accepted at exchanges on which contracts of interest trade. For example, MIT orders are accepted at the CME, but not at

---

EXAMPLE 6.4   A trader initially sells a gold futures contract at $290/oz. After that order has been filled, he can place a stop order to buy at $300/oz. to control his losses if it develops that he was wrong in his belief that the price of gold would fall. If a trade takes place at $300/oz., then his order becomes a market order to buy, and he will have his short position offset at the next price, whatever that may be.

TABLE 6.4 Other Types of Futures Orders

1. A **one-cancels-the-other** order consists of two orders placed simultaneously, but as soon as one order is executed, the other is canceled. For example, the current gold futures price for June delivery might be $300/oz. A trader who is long a contract might place the following one-cancels-the other order: "sell one June gold futures contract $305 limit/$295 stop." If the price of gold rises to $305, the long position is offset, profits are taken, and the $295 stop order is canceled. Alternatively, if gold's price declines to $295/oz., the trader cuts his losses and the $305 limit sell order is canceled.

2. A **spread order** specifies two trades that must be filled together. The order can specify a difference in prices, or it can be a market order. For example, a trader who places an order to buy one Eurodollar futures contract and sell one Treasury bill contract might specify a spread price of 85 ticks "to the sell."[1] Suppose that the Eurodollar futures price for September 1999 delivery is 94.53, and the September Treasury bill contract price is 95.33 (see Figure 6.5). Thus the current spread is 80. If the spread widens to 85, the trader wants to speculate that the spread will subsequently narrow. Put another way, he believes that once the spread reaches 85, the Eurodollar futures price will then rise more than the Treasury bill futures price. This is an example of an *intercommodity spread*, or *intermarket spread*. Another type of spread is the *time spread*, or *calendar spread*, in which a trader buys futures on a good for delivery in one month and sells futures on the same good for delivery in another month.

3. A **fill-or-kill order** specifies a limit price, usually close to the current market price, and if the order is not filled (executed) immediately, it is canceled.

4. A **contingent order** places two orders, but only one is entered at the exchange initially. As soon as that order is executed, the second one is entered. Thus, a trader can place an order to sell a crude oil futures contract at 20.60 and, contingent on the execution of that order, buy (offset) the same contract at a limit price of 20.00.

5. A **market-not-held order** is also known as a DRT (disregard tape) order. In this type of order, the trader relies on the skills of the FCM's representative in the pit to decide if and when to fill the order. If the broker in the pit believes he can get the trader a better price in the next few minutes, he will delay executing the order.

6. An **on-the-close** order is one that will be filled during the last minute or so of trading. More common are "limit or market on close" orders, which specify a limit price for the day, but if the order is not executed by the close of trading, it becomes a market order.

[1] If the Treasury bill futures price is above the Eurodollar futures price, and the Treasury bill contract is being sold, the phrase, "to the sell" is used.

the CBOT. Many FCMs can also supply a summary of orders that can be placed at the different exchanges.

There are often limits on the net long and net short positions that any one speculator (or associated group of speculators) can assume in the futures contracts of a given commodity. The Commodity Futures Trading Commission passed the rule that the exchanges impose such position limits after the crisis caused by the Hunt family's attempt to corner the silver market in 1979–1980. The Hunts had a long position in over 18,000 silver futures contracts, and at the same time owned much of the supply of the metal itself. Thus, anyone who was short silver futures contracts would have had trouble finding silver to deliver because the Hunts owned most of it. Position limits, however, do not exist for hedgers.

The position limits themselves differ from commodity to commodity. For example, as of June 2000, the position limits for CME S&P 500 futures and NYMEX light sweet crude oil futures were 20,000 contracts each; for CBOT two-year Treasury notes the position limit was 5000 contracts. There were no position limits for Eurodollar futures or Euro FX currency futures. Often traders with large positions in any one type of contract must provide accountability information on the nature of his position, his trading strategy, and hedging information to the CFTC and/or the exchange. For more discussion on position limits for exchange traded futures and options, see the CFTC's website (www.cftc.gov/opa/backgrounder/opaspeclmts.htm).

6.11   INDIVIDUALS IN THE FUTURES INDUSTRY

In this section, we describe the different types of individual who trade futures, who also play a part in executing trades and determining futures prices.

Besides individuals on the floors of the exchanges, there are usually three broad classes of futures traders: speculators, hedgers, and arbitrageurs.

6.11.1   Speculators

Speculators assume risks, and their goal is to profit from price fluctuations. They may be long or short futures, or they may hold spread positions. Speculators themselves can be subdivided into two subgroups: position traders and day traders.

Position traders enter a position and hold it for several days, weeks, or months. They may use **technical analysis** to develop beliefs about future price movements. Technical traders primarily study price charts to discern trends that they believe will persist. Other position traders employ **fundamental analysis** to form their opinions, using macroeconomic data to develop their predictions about future price movements.[23]

Day traders speculate only about price movements during one trading day. They never go home holding a futures position, and therefore probably sleep better at night. Day trading is costly because prices must be monitored closely throughout the day. Day traders are likely to open and close positions several times during the day, with the goal of making a profit of just a few ticks per trade.

6.11.2   Hedgers

Hedgers initially (before they hedge) are exposed to the risk of a price change. They may initially be long or short a good and would therefore experience losses if prices were to move against them. For example, an oil trading company might purchase a large amount of crude oil to import to the United States. This transaction exposes them to the risk that during the week it takes to transport the oil to the United States, oil prices will fall, and the oil will have to be sold at lower prices. This firm can sell crude oil futures contracts to hedge. If oil prices do decline, the trading company will lose money on the inventory of oil (the spot position) but will make money on the futures contracts that were sold. This is an example of a **short hedge**.

Another company might be short the good, and therefore fearful that prices will rise. This company will enter a **long hedge** by going long futures. For example, a jewelry manufacturer might sign a contract in January 2000 agreeing to deliver gold jewelry to a retailer in September 2000 at a fixed price. The manufacturer does not have the gold in inventory (the gold would have to be insured; the manufacturer may not have sufficient warehouse space, or not enough cash to buy the gold today, etc.) and does not wish to purchase the gold until May 2000, when manufacture of the jewelry requiring that gold is scheduled to begin. The manufacturer is exposed to the risk that gold prices will rise between January and May. If prices rose, it would have to pay more for its raw material. Since the price to be received for the output is already fixed, the manufacturer should hedge by buying gold futures contracts.

The use of futures in risk management will be the subject of Chapter 7.

6.11.3   Arbitrageurs

An arbitrageur profits by observing that a good, or equivalent goods, sells for different prices in two different markets. The cost-of-carry pricing model, covered in Chapter 5 for forward contracts, is the arbitrage mechanism that sets the relationship between spot and futures prices. Sometimes temporary supply and demand disturbances lead to mispricing. When this occurs, arbitrageurs will buy cheap futures and sell the overpriced spot good, or sell overpriced futures and buy the spot good.

6.11.4   Individuals on the Floor of an Exchange

The people who trade on the floor of the exchange can be categorized by their goals and/or functions. Statistics concerning the numbers of individuals who fall into these categories, as of February 2001, can be found at the National Futures Association (NFA) website (www.nfa.futures.org/registration/nfa_membership.html).

Floor traders are exchange members who trade futures contracts in the futures pit. A floor trader who trades solely for his own account is called a **local**. Locals provide liquidity for the market, usually by operating as **scalpers**. A scalper is a very short term trader. Basically, scalpers want to buy futures at the bid and quickly turn around to sell it at the asked.[24] As of September 1998, 1364 floor traders were regulated by the CFTC. Another class of futures markets participants consists of the **floor brokers**, who execute trades for other parties such as FCMs. Floor brokers earn income by charging small fees, perhaps a dollar or two per contract, to the parties for whom they execute trades. There were 9538 floor brokers registered with the CFTC in 1998.

An important regulatory debate emerged in 1989 about floor traders who operate as both locals and floor brokers. Such practice, called **dual trading**, had been abused by some traders. Basically, a floor trader who made two contract purchases in a short period of time at two prices, one for a customer and one for himself, had the "ethical dilemma" of declaring which contract he bought for himself and which he bought for a customer. A 1989 CFTC study concluded that fewer 10% of all floor traders practiced dual trading, and few of the dual traders cheated their customers. However, the study also concluded that, in general, the practice contributed only slightly to the liquidity of futures markets. Dual trading is still permitted today, but there are extensive audit trail procedures and record-keeping systems that monitor the practice and constrain abuse by floor traders.

6.11.5   Other Market Participants

The annual Source Book, published each year in January by the magazine *Futures*, is a good source for some specific names and addresses of the following types of firms and individuals.

We have already mentioned **futures commission merchants**, FCMs, who are the brokers of the futures industry. There are full-service FCMs such as Merrill Lynch and Dean Witter, and discount FCMs such as Lind-Waldock, Jack Carl Futures, and First American Discount Corp. As of February 2001, there were 191 FCMs registered with the CFTC. A list of registered FCMs is available (www.cftc.gov/tm/tmfcm.htm).

Associated persons, APs, are the individuals who work for FCMs in soliciting and accepting orders. Most APs are the futures industry's equivalent to the stock brokerage industry's account executives. In February 2001, there were 47,565 APs registered with the CFTC.

Commodity trading advisers, CTAs, analyze futures markets and give trading advice to anyone who wishes to pay for it. Anyone who makes recommendations to buy or sell futures, develops trading systems, or provides information about commodities must register with the CFTC as a CTA. In February 2001, there were 919 CTAs registered with the CFTC.

Introducing brokers, IBs, are individuals who direct business to FCMs and CTAs but themselves are not APs or CTAs. An IB might solicit orders and take orders, but once received, the orders are passed on to an FCM for execution. Other IBs might pool funds of small investors into a large amount so that they can gain access to a successful CTA who has a large minimum investment requirement. The IB registration category was introduced by the CFTC in 1982. In 2001 there were 1400 IBs registered with the CFTC.

Commodity pool operators, CPOs, are the futures industry's equivalent to mutual funds. They accept money from investors. The monies are pooled and used to trade futures. Many CPOs hire CTAs to make the trading decisions for them, or at least to aid them in making decisions. In 2001 there were 1455 CPOs registered with the CFTC.

Many firms analyze the performance of CTAs and CPOs. Some of the performance data of **Managed Account Reports**, which is one such "CTA tracker," are published monthly in *Futures*. Academic research has been critical of the performance of CPOs (Irwin and Brorsen, 1985; Elton, Gruber, and Rentzler, 1987; Cornew, 1988; Edwards and Ma, 1988; Irwin, Krukemyer and Zulauf, 1993). These studies have found that CPO returns are negative on average: fewer than 50% of them produce positive returns. Moreover, they have very high expenses, and their prior performance is of little value in predicting future performance.

6.12 TAXES AND COMMISSIONS

6.12.1 Taxes

The tax code for hedgers who trade futures differs from the laws that define speculators' tax situations. Hedgers should consult a tax accountant or a tax attorney for advice.

Section 1256 of the IRS code requires that individual speculators mark to market all futures positions for tax purposes on the last trading day of the year. For example, suppose that on November 24, 2000, you sold one gold futures contract for February 2001 delivery at the settlement price of $290/oz. On December 31, 2000, the settlement price for the February 2001 gold contract is $267.40. You offset your position on January 16, 2001 at a futures price of $264.

The tax law requires you to mark to market your position on December 31, 2000, and declare the profit (or loss) for tax purposes. Thus, if capital gains are taxed as ordinary income, your taxable income for 2000 will be $2260 greater than had you not traded the gold futures contract. If you are in the 28% marginal tax bracket, your tax liability will be $632.80 greater. Note that you are realizing this income, eventhough you have not offset your position.

Then, the IRS establishes a new basis[25] for your trade: $267.40. In 2001 you will report a profit of $340 ($26740 – $26400) on the futures trade.

Generally, 40% of the gain or loss is treated as a short-term capital gain or loss, and 60% is treated as a long-term capital gain or loss.

Before 1981, tax straddles were a legal means of deferring taxes. In a tax straddle, a trader would select a volatile futures commodity, buy some contracts for delivery in one month of the following year, and also sell an equal number of contracts for delivery in an adjacent month of that year (a calendar spread). With a volatile commodity, it would then be likely that in late December of the current year, the trader would have a sizable gain on the contracts for one of the months, and a roughly equal loss on the contracts for delivery in the other month. The trader would offset the losing position, thereby realizing a short-term capital loss, which could be used to reduce the tax liability in the existing year. Taxes on the profitable position would be deferred to the next year. The Economic Recovery Tax Act of 1981 ended this means of deferring taxes. Moreover, subsequent tax legislation has since ended the distinction between long-term and short-term capital gains and losses for tax purposes.

See Conlon and Aquilino (1999) for detailed information about the taxation of futures and all other derivatives.

6.12.2 Commissions

Commissions are paid only when futures trades are offset, or end in delivery or final cash settlement. Full-service FCMs charge about $100 to trade one contract (round turn). The per-contract commission declines as more contracts are traded. Some offer discounts for day traders, and some offer discounts to traders who only desire execution, not advice. Discount FCMs might charge between $15 and $40 per contract when the position is closed. Again, the commission per contract can decline with larger trades. In addition, day trader discounts are often offered, and discounts may be available to traders who have access to their own futures price reporting systems. Larger traders such as corporations, banks, and professional trading firms, may pay $10/contract or less. Finally, floor traders on the floor of the exchange pay as little as $1.50/contract to trade.

Sophisticated traders will be willing to pay more in commissions if they feel that they are getting better execution in the pits. An extra few dollars per contract in commissions is a small price to pay if the FCMs representatives can save the customer a tick on a sizable fraction of the trades. Active traders can often get a feel for their FCMs execution abilities after a while.

6.13 SUMMARY

This chapter provided an introduction to futures markets and trading. For novices, futures may seem confusing. Each futures contract has its own set of rules. For this reason, you should initially select just one type of futures contract to learn about before ever trading it.

First, the differences between forward contracts and futures contracts were covered. Perhaps the most important difference for valuation purposes is the margin requirements and daily resettlement (mark-to-market) features of futures. The concepts of basis and convergence were introduced.

Then the different types of futures contract were outlined. Some regulatory issues were discussed. You learned how to read price data presented in the financial press. The different types of order that can be placed were summarized.

The economic rationale for futures trading was briefly discussed. The different individuals who make up the futures markets were categorized. Finally, the chapter provided a brief discussion of taxes and commissions.

The futures exchanges supply a great deal of additional information on futures trading. You might begin by accessing their websites.

References

Anderson, Ronald. 1981. "Comments on 'Margins and Futures Contracts.'" *Journal of Futures Markets*, Vol. 1, No. 2, Summer, pp. 259–264.

Baer, Herbert L., Virginia Grace France, and James T. Moser. 1995. "What Does a Clearinghouse Do?" *Derivatives Quarterly*, Vol. 1, No. 3, Spring, pp. 39–46.

Bates, David, and Roger Craine. 1999. "Valuing the Futures Market Clearinghouse's Default Exposure During the 1987 Crash." *Journal of Money Credit and Banking*, Vol. 31, No. 2, May, pp. 248–272.

Bernanke, Ben S. 1990. "Clearing and Settlement During the Crash." *Review of Financial Studies*, Vol. 3, No. 1, pp. 133–151.

Black, Fischer. 1976. "The Pricing of Commodity Contracts." *Journal of Financial Economics*, Vol. 3, No. 1, January/March, pp. 167–179.

Brennan, Michael J. 1986. "A Theory of Price Limits in Futures Markets." *Journal of Financial Economics*, Vol. 16, No. 2, June, pp. 213–234.

Burghardt, Galen, and Donald L. Kohn. 1981. "Comments on Margins and Futures Contracts." *Journal of Futures Markets*, Vol. 1, No. 2, Summer, pp. 255–257.

Chance, Don M., and Michael L. Hemler. 1993. "The Impact of Delivery Options on Futures Prices: A Survey." *Journal of Futures Markets*, Vol. 13, No. 2, pp. 127–156.

Cita, John, and Donald Lien. 1992. "Constructing Accurate Cash Settlement Indices: The Role of Index Specifications." *Journal of Futures Markets*, Vol. 12, No. 3, pp. 339–360.

Conlon, Steven D., and Vincent M. Aquilino. 1999. *Principles of Financial Derivatives: U.S. and International Taxation*. Boston: Warren, Gorham & Lamont of the RIA Group.

Cornell, Bradford. 1997. "Cash Settlement When the Underlying Securities Are Thinly Traded: A Case Study." *Journal of Futures Markets*, Vol. 17, No. 8, December, pp. 855–871.

Cornew, Ronald W. 1988. "Commodity Pool Operators and Their Pools: Expenses and Profitability." *Journal of Futures Markets*, Vol. 8, No. 5, October, pp. 617–637.

Cox, John C., Jonathan E. Ingersoll Jr., and Stephen A. Ross. 1981. "The Relation Between Forward Prices and Futures Prices." *Journal of Financial Economics*, Vol. 9, No. 4, December, pp. 321–346.

Edwards, Franklin, and Cindy Ma. 1988. "Commodity Pool Performance: Is the Information Contained in Pool Prosepectuses Useful?" *Journal of Futures Markets*, Vol. 8, No. 5, October, pp. 589–616.

Elton, Edwin J., Martin J. Gruber, and Joel Rentzler. 1989. "Professionally Managed, Publicly Traded Commodity Funds." *Journal of Business*, Vol. 60, No. 2, April, pp. 175–200.

Fay, Stephen. 1982. *Beyond Greed*. New York: The Viking Press.

Fink, Robert E., and Robert B. Feduniok. 1988. *Futures Trading: Concepts and Strategies*. New York Institute of Finance.

Fishe, Raymond P. H., and Lawrence C. Goldberg. 1986. "The Effects of Margins on Trading in Futures Markets." *Journal of Futures Markets*, Vol. 6, No. 2, Summer, pp. 261–271.

Fishe, Raymond P. H., Lawrence C. Goldberg, Thomas F. Gosnell, and Sujata Sinha. 1990. "Margin Requirements in Futures Markets: Their Relationship to Price Volatility." *Journal of Futures Markets*, Vol. 10, No. 5, October, pp. 541–554.

Garbade, Kenneth D., and William Silber. 1983. "Cash Settlement of Futures Contracts: An Economic Analysis." *Journal of Futures Markets*, Vol. 3, No. 4, Winter, pp. 451–472.

Goldberg, Lawrence C., and George A. Hachey. 1992. "Price Volatility and Margin Requirements in Foreign Exchange Futures." *Journal of International Money and Finance*, Vol. 11, No. 4, August, pp. 328–339.

Hardouvelis, Gikas A., and Dongcheol Kim. 1995. "Margin Requirements, Price Fluctuations, and Market Participation in Metals Futures." *Journal of Money, Credit and Banking*, Vol. 27, No. 3, August, pp. 659–671.

Hartzmark, Michael L. 1986. "The Effects of Changing Margin Levels on Futures Market Activity, the Composition of Traders in the Market, and Price Performance." *Journal of Business*, Vol. 59, No. 2, Part 2, April, pp. S147–S180.

Hemler, Michael L. 1990. "The Quality Delivery Option in Treasury Bond Futures Contracts." *Journal of Finance*, Vol. 45, No. 5, December, pp. 1565–1586.

Irwin, Scott H., and Wade B. Brorsen. 1985. "Public Futures Funds." *Journal of Futures Markets*, Vol. 5, No. 2, Summer, pp. 149–172.

Irwin, Scott H., Terry R. Krukemyer, and Carl R. Zulauf. 1993. "Investment Performance of Public Commodity Pools: 1979–1990." *Journal of Futures Markets*, Vol. 13, No. 7, pp. 799–820.

Jarrow, Robert A., and George S. Oldfield. 1981. "Forward Contracts and Futures Contracts." *Journal of Financial Economics*, Vol. 9, No. 4, December, pp. 373–382.

Jones, Frank J. 1982. "The Economics of Futures and Options Contracts Based on Cash Settlement." *Journal of Futures Markets*, Vol. 2, No. 1, Spring, pp. 63–82.

Jordan, James V., and George Emir Morgan. 1990. "Default Risk in Futures Markets: The Customer–Broker Relationship." *Journal of Finance*, Vol. 45, No. 3, July, pp. 909–934.

Kahl, Kandice H., Roger D. Rutz, and Jeanne C. Sinquefield. 1985. "The Economics of Performance Margins in Futures Markets." *Journal of Futures Markets*, Vol. 5, No. 1, Spring, pp. 103–112.

Kalavathi, L., and Latha Shanker. 1991. "Margin Requirements and the Demand for Futures Contracts." *Journal of Futures Markets*, Vol. 11, No. 2, April, pp. 213–238.

Kamara, Avraham, and Andrew F. Siegel. 1987. "Optimal Hedging in Futures Markets with Multiple Delivery Specifications." *Journal of Finance*, Vol. 42, No. 4, September, pp. 1007–1021.

Kupiec, Paul H. 1994. "The Performance of S&P 500 Futures Product Margins Under the SPAN Margining System." *Journal of Futures Markets*, Vol. 14, No. 7, pp. 789–811.

Lien Da-Hsiang Donald. 1989a. "Cash Settlement Provisions on Futures Contracts." *Journal of Futures Markets*, Vol. 9, No. 3, pp. 263–270.

Lien, Da-Hsiang Donald. 1989b. "Sampled Data as a Basis of Cash Settlement Price." *Journal of Futures Markets*, Vol. 9, No. 6, pp. 583–588.

Pliska, Stanley R., and Catherine Shalen. 1991. "The Effects of Regulations on Trading Activity and Returns Volatility in Futures Markets." *Journal of Futures Markets*, Vol. 11, No. 2, April, pp. 135–151.

Pring, Martin J. 1991. *Technical Analysis Explained, 3rd ed*. New York: McGraw-Hill.

Richard, Scott F., and Sundaresan, M. 1981. "A Continuous Time Equilibrium Model of Forward Prices and Futures Prices in a Multigood Economy." *Journal of Financial Economics*, Vol. 9, No. 4, December, pp. 347–372.

Sarnoff, Paul, 1980. *The Silver Bulls*. Westport, CT: Arlington House.

Schwager, Jack D. 1995. *Schwager on Futures: Fundamental Analysis*. New York: Wiley.

Silber, William L. 1984. "Marketmaker Behavior in an Auction Market: An Analysis of Scalpers in Futures Markets." *Journal of Finance*, Vol. 39, No. 4, September, pp. 937–954.

Telser, Lester G. 1981. "Margins and Futures Contracts." *Journal of Futures Markets*, Vol. 1, No. 2, Summer, pp. 225–253.

Notes

[1]Many futures contracts have delivery options inherent in them. For example, a contract may specify a range of goods of different quality that can be delivered (Kamara and Siegel, 1987; Hemler, 1990; Chance and Hemler, 1993). Or it may offer several locations to which the goods can be delivered, or several dates on which delivery can be made. It is interesting that the *short* position gets these options. For example, if the futures contract offers a range of delivery dates, the short decides when to make delivery. This differs from American option contracts, in which the owner (the long position) of the option decides when to exercise it.

[2]A clearinghouse is an agency associated with one or more exchanges. Its functions typically include the following: (a) to match, process, register, confirm, settle, reconcile, and/or guarantee trades, (b) to become a party to every trade, so as to (nearly) eliminate credit risk, (c) to operate the mark to market process (collecting and paying variation margin), and (d) to handle the delivery process. A clearinghouse might be a subsidiary of an exchange, or an independent entity. See Bernanke (1990) and Baer, France, and Moser (1995) for further details on the clearing process.

[3]A futures commission merchant (FCM) is the futures industry's equivalent to a stockbroker. The importance of the solvency of a customer's FCM is stressed because a case study and theoretical analysis by Jordan and

Morgan (1990) shows that the clearinghouse in reality guarantees only that its members will be paid. Customers of a failed FCM do bear default risk.

[4]Bates and Craine (1999), however, assess the probability that a major clearinghouse could have failed during the 1987 stock market crash. At that time, there were rumors and fears that a clearinghouse could fail, and the Federal Reserve had to assure markets that the central bank would supply liquidity to the system if needed.

[5]See Jones (1982) and Garbade and Silber (1983) for discussion concerning the economics of cash settlement. Cash settlement is desired when delivery costs are large (e.g., with the S&P 500 Index futures contract), when manipulation is possible by traders who might corner the available supply of the deliverable asset, and/or when the futures price is based on an index. However, Lien (1989a, 1989b) and Cita and Lien (1992) cite several problems with cash settlement, and these are documented in a study of the municipal bond futures contract by Cornell (1997).

[6]As discussed in Chapter 3, the two parties *could* negotiate good faith money, or collateral, to increase the likelihood that each will abide by the terms of the contract, and therefore lower default risk. Each party would then deposit some amount of money, securities, or other assets with a neutral third party.

[7]Recently, it has become more popular to refer to "margin" as "performance bond." Thus, there is an initial performance bond and a maintenance performance bond.

[8]Further discussion on SPAN can be found at the websites of the Chicago Mercantile Exchange (www.cme.com) and the London International Financial Futures and Options Exchange (www.liffe.com). Kupiec (1994) explains why SPAN was developed (in response to the 1987 stock market crash), and how S&P 500 futures margins have been set under SPAN.

[9]For example, in early 1980 the tremendous volatility in silver prices led the COMEX to increase the initial margin requirement to $75,000/contract, equal to about 30% of the value of the silver underlying the contract. In contrast, the initial margin requirement of $2400 in April 1989 was only about 8% of the value of silver in the 5000 oz. contract. For more details on the Hunt brothers' attempt to corner the silver market in 1979–1980, see Paul Sarnoff (1980), Fay (1982), an October 1982 report by the Securities and Exchange Commission, and articles in the *Wall Street Journal* and *Barron's* in early 1980.

[10]Several papers have studied the economic theory behind margin requirements, and their effects on trading. See Anderson (1981), Burghardt and Kohn (1981), Telser (1981), Kahl, Rutz, and Sinquefield (1985), Fishe and Goldberg (1986), Hartzmark (1986), Fishe et al. (1990), Kalavathi and Shanker (1991), Pliska and Shalen (1991), Goldberg and Hachey (1992), and Hardouvelis and Kim (1995). Generally, these papers conclude that margins have served their purpose in protecting the exchanges and FCMs against customer defaults. However, higher margin requirements also decrease market liquidity and increase the cost of hedging. There is disagreement over whether higher margins reduce market volatility.

[11]There are as many rates of return as there are sign changes in the series of cash flows. Some of the rates of return can be negative (or imaginary), and it will not be known which rate is correct, or whether a high or low rate of return will be desired.

[12]Some sources define **basis** as the futures price minus the cash price; therefore, be certain that you and anyone you are conversing with agree on the definition. For example, in talking about index futures, the basis is defined as the futures price minus the cash price. A problem also arises in defining the cash price. Consistency must be maintained for both the quality and location of the spot good. There will be a different basis for each quality and location of the good. For instance, crude oil can have different grades, each with a different price, hence a different basis. Moreover, crude oil of the same grade can sell for different prices at different locations, reflecting relative supply and demand at those places, as well as the transportation costs of moving oil from one place to the other.

[13]Actually, as a result of transactions costs, the basis can be slightly different from zero on the delivery date.

[14]The act of buying the present value of the number of futures contracts is called *tailing*. The difference between 1.0 and the present value of 1.0 is called the tail. In this example, the tail at time 0 equals $1.0 - 0.7513148 = 0.2486852$. This concept will be covered again in the next chapter on hedging with futures contracts.

[15]corr $(\Delta F, \Delta r)$ is the correlation of changes in futures prices with the changes in interest rates. If corr $(\Delta F, \Delta r) > 0$, then when futures prices rise, interest rates will also tend to rise. If corr$(\Delta F, \Delta r) < 0$, then when futures prices rise, interest rates will tend to fall.

[16]See Fink and Feduniak (1988), Chapter 6, and the Chicago Board of Trade's *Commodity Trading Manual* (1994), Chapter 7, for more discussion on regulation of futures trading. The *Journal of Futures Markets* has published some issues with many articles analyzing futures regulation, such as the Summer 1981 and Fall 1984 issues. Also, other issues contain a bibliography listing the latest published research in futures regulation, such as the April 1995 and April 1996 issues.

[17]Computing the value of the bonds underlying the Treasury bond futures contract is actually more complicated than this. See Chapter 9 for more thorough discussion of this complex contract.

[18]Access the CMEs website to find out the exact delivery dates. Contract specifications can be viewed at www.cme.com/clearing/spex/XMLReports/intrRateGroup.htm. Important dates for the T-bill contract can be viewed at www.cme.com/clearing/listings/tbfut.htm.

[19]Brennan (1986) hypothesizes that price limits serve as a substitute for margin requirements by ensuring that losses on futures contracts will be paid. In other words, margin requirements are smaller because of daily price limits.

[20]Most futures trading occurs in pits at the exchanges. A pit is a roughly circular, or polygonal, depression in the floor with steps leading down to a central desk. Traders stand on the steps of the pit facing each other, and shout out and signal (using their hands) trades they wish to make. Other traders can accept any bid or offer, or shout out and signal alternative terms to any proposed trade. This process is called an **open outcry auction**.

[21]The word "should" is used deliberately. Two traders in the pit can agree on a price for a trade. But if *your* representative is not quick, then in a fast market, he may not always get to participate in the next trade after the specified price is touched, or the best possible price.

[22]Stop orders are also used by technical traders trade to initiate new positions based on a series of previous moves. For example, the current futures price of gold might be $276/oz. A technical trader might believe that if it rises above $280/oz. gold will be in a "bullish formation" and will likely go higher. Therefore, he might place a stop-buy order at 280.20. Note that, the specified buy price is above the current futures price.

[23]Several books exist on how to use fundamental and technical analysis when trading futures. See, for example, Pring (1991) and Schwager (1995).

[24]Silber (1984) provides a fascinating study of scalpers' trading activities. Among other results, Silber found that one typical scalper's average holding time of a position was less than 2 minutes and that money was usually lost on a trade if it was held for more than 3 minutes. Also, 48% of the typical scalper's trades were profitable, 22% led to losses, and 30% provided neither. The mean profit per contract was $10.56, but the scalper also traded about 68 round-trip trades per day; this translates to an expected annual profit of about $179,000.

[25]A "new basis" here means a new initial trade price for tax purposes.

PROBLEMS

6.1 Refer to Figure 6.4, and answer the following questions.

  a. What is the value of the gasoline underlying the August gasoline contract?

  b. If you were short one August gasoline contract, what is the mark-to-market

cash flow on the day shown in Figure 6.4?

  c. If you were lucky enough to have bought one October gasoline contract at its lifetime low, and sold it at its lifetime high, what profit would you have realized?

d. If the spot price of gasoline on July 28, 1999, was $0.635/gal, what is the basis of the August futures contract?

e. Is the gasoline futures contract normal or inverted?

f. Why won't firms sell their gasoline on the spot market at $0.635/gal, and buy February futures at the much lower price shown? Isn't this an arbitrage opportunity?

6.2 Suppose you bought one gold futures contract for August delivery at its April 2 settlement price of $279/oz. Assume that both the last trading date and the delivery date are August 27. Assume that your borrowing and lending rates are 8% per year, and that you borrow to meet any mark-to-market cash outflows and lend any mark to market losses.

a. If the gold futures price remains unchanged until August 27, then falls to $250/oz. on that day, what is your profit or loss? (Be sure to *state* whether the result is a profit or loss.)

b. If, instead, the gold futures price falls to $250/oz. on April 3, and stays there until the delivery date, what is your profit or loss?

c. If, instead, the gold futures price rises to $420/oz. on April 3, stays there, and then falls to $250/oz. on August 27, then what is your profit or loss?

d. Given that money has time value, which of the foregoing price scenarios is most attractive: a, b, or c?

6.3 Discuss how futures contracts differ from forward contracts.

6.4 Find the initial and maintenance margin requirements for S&P 500 futures contracts in Table 6.1. Using the March 2001 contract settlement price shown in Figure 6.5, at what futures price will there be a margin call for an individual who goes long one contract?

6.5 If you were short one Canadian dollar futures contract for December delivery, and the *Wall Street Journal* reported the following price information, what would be the mark-to-market cash flow consequences for you?

Month	Open	High	Low	Settle	Change
Dec	.6321	.6340	.6285	.6313	+.0045

6.6 Suppose that you go long one December Treasury bond futures contract at its lowest price for that day, given the following price data. The initial margin requirement is $2700, and the maintenance margin requirement is $2000. At what futures price would you receive a margin call?

Month	Open	High	Low	Settle	Change
Dec	115–02	115–18	114–27	115–03	−7

6.7 Define basis, and compute the (closing) basis for the September S&P 500 futures contract, using the price information in Figure 6.5.

6.8 Suppose you went long one March yen currency futures contract at the settle price shown in Figure 6.5. On the delivery date, the settle price is 0.8500, and delivery takes place. Therefore, to satisfy the terms of the futures contract; must you deliver yen or take delivery of them? How many dollars (the invoice price) will you actually be paid for the yen on the delivery date? What was your mark-to-market profit or loss?

6.9 The crude oil futures contract covers 1000 bbl of oil. One tick is one cent/bbl, and this equals $10/contract. Assume that the initial margin is $3000 and that maintenance margin is $2200. Suppose you buy one crude oil futures contract at 10 A.M, on November 5, when the futures price is $30.45.

The following table contains the subsequent settlement prices:

Day	Settlement Price
11/5	$30.68
11/6	$31.02
11/7	$30.74
11/8	$30.00
11/9	$29.64
11/12	$29.19
11/13	$29.84
11/14	$29.98
11/15	$29.45
11/16	$28.86
11/19	$28.44
11/20	$28.94

You offset your trade on November 20 at 1 P.M when the futures price is 28.81.

a. Prepare a table of daily resettlement cash flows such as in Table 6.2. Be sure to note when maintenance margin calls are received.

b. Suppose instead that you used a bank letter of credit to satisfy the initial margin requirement. What are your variation margin cash flows?

6.10 Explain why the value of a futures contract is zero after it has been marked to market.

6.11 What features make credit risk for a futures contract less than the credit risk contained in a forward contract?

6.12 A corporation plans on borrowing money by issuing bonds next week. Would this firm do a long hedge or a short hedge? Explain your answer.

6.13 Explain what is meant by the following statement: The difference between the initial futures price and the actual cash amount that is paid upon delivery is equal to the sum of the variation margin cash flows.

6.14 A trader notes that the three-month Euroswiss interest rate is 45 basis points higher than three-month Euribor (the interest rate on euros). He investigates, and finds that this had never happened in the preceding five years; usually, Euribor actually exceeds the Euroswiss interest rate. How can the trader use Euroswiss and Euribor futures to speculate that the interest rate anomaly will correct itself? You should refer to actual price data in the financial press to help understand the question.

6.15 Refer to Figure 6.5. Where are three-month interest rates probably the highest: in the United States, the United Kingdom, Japan, the European Union (issuer of euros), or Canada? In which country are they likely the lowest? Why?

6.16 Refer to Figure 6.5. What is the size of one tick (U.S $0.0001/Can. $) for the Canadian dollar futures contract?

6.17 Obtain a recent *Wall Street Journal.* Study the price changes for the preceding day for all the currency futures. For which contract did a short make the greatest mark-to-market profit (or smallest loss)? For which contract did the long make the greatest profit (or smallest loss)?

6.18 Explain how volume can be high, yet open interest can either decline or increase.

6.19 Observe the following price data for feeder cattle:

Delivery Month	Settlement Price
September 2001	$79.50
October	$80.02
November	$81.25

January 2002	$81.62
March	$80.72
April	$80.67

Why wouldn't anyone who owns the actual livestock sell futures for delivery in January 2002 and buy futures for delivery in April 2002? After all, this locks in a selling price in January of $0.8162/lb, and then the "arbitrageur" will have locked in a buying price in April of only $0.8067/lb. The existing livestock can be sold off for a price that is higher than the price that would be paid in April to replenish the inventory.

6.20 Look at a recent *Wall Street Journal*. Record the spot price of crude oil (Nymex crude: it's shown on page C1 every day) and the futures price for delivery six months later. Assume that the delivery day for the futures contract is the first of the month. Assume no convenience value, and use the FinancialCAD function aaCDF_repo to compute the repo rate. Verify your result, using the annualized value of $(F-S)/S = $ implied repo rate.

CHAPTER 7

Risk Management with Futures Contracts

7.1   INTRODUCTION

Because futures are so similar to forwards, most of the concepts that were covered in Chapter 4, Using Forward Contracts to Manage Risk, also apply when one is hedging with futures contracts. Thus, you should review Chapter 4 before reading this chapter. Often, transactions costs, liquidity, accounting rules, and basis risk will determine which contract is preferred.

In this chapter, we will discuss traditional **hedging theory**, which applies to the use of futures to manage price risk. Liquidity risk and basis risk are important considerations when one is comparing futures and forwards for risk management. Also, forward contracts entail greater credit risk, which is the risk that your counterparty will not abide by the terms of the forward contract. In contrast, futures clearing houses and the mark-to-market process essentially eliminate credit risk when futures are used. Using futures to manage price risk also introduces the following risks:

1. Because futures contracts are standardized, the underlying asset, the delivery location, the quantity, and the delivery date may all differ from the asset that is being hedged. This risk is called **basis risk**.

2. If the underlying asset of the futures contract is sufficiently different from the asset being hedged, it is important to determine the degree to which price changes of the two assets are correlated.

3. If the date of the hedging horizon lies beyond the date of the most nearby futures contract, then the choice the correct delivery date must be made. Frequently, hedges must be **rolled forward** by offsetting the position of nearby contracts and entering into a position in contracts with more distant delivery dates.

4. Because futures are marked to market daily, futures hedges must be **tailed**.

In this chapter, these and other aspects of hedging with futures contracts will be discussed.

Futures contracts enable market participants to alter risks they face that are caused by adverse, unexpected price changes. One of the main reasons cited for the existence of futures markets is that they are a low cost, effective way to transfer price risk. It is no accident that interest rate futures markets did not evolve until the 1970s. Before then, unhedged long or short positions in debt instruments were considerably less risky because their prices rarely changed. Figure 7.1 presents interest (discount) rates on three-month Treasury bills since 1950, and Figure 7.2 is a graph depicting yields available on long-term AAA-rated corporate bonds since 1919. Both graphs show that interest rates fluctuated relatively little during the 1940s, 1950s, and early 1960s. When interest rates became volatile in the late 1960s and 1970s, the demand for ways to hedge against this volatility increased, and the interest rate futures market came into existence. The increase in interest rate risk that began in the late 1960s is further illustrated by Figure 7.3, which graphs the volatility (rolling 60-month standard deviation of monthly interest rates) of Treasury bills and AAA-rated corporates since December 1954. Before the late 1960s, the standard deviation of monthly rates was never above 1%. Volatility did not return to those levels until the late 1990s.[1]

Futures contracts are used to manage risk by taking a futures position that is the opposite of the existing or anticipated cash position. In other words, a hedger sells futures against a long position in the cash asset or buys futures against a short position in the cash asset.

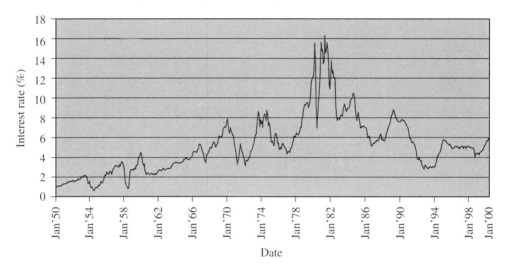

Figure 7.1 Discount rates on newly issued three-month Treasury bills, January 1950–June 2000. (From: www.federalreserve.gov/releases/H15/data.htm.)

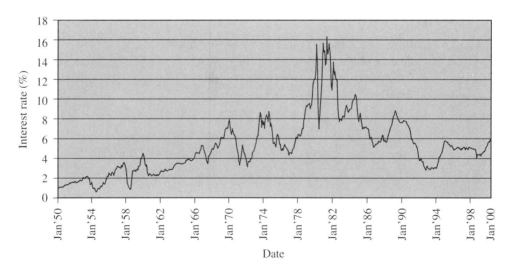

Figure 7.2 Yields to maturity on AAA-rated corporate bonds, January 1919–March 2001. (From: www.federalreserve.gov/releases/H15/data.htm.)

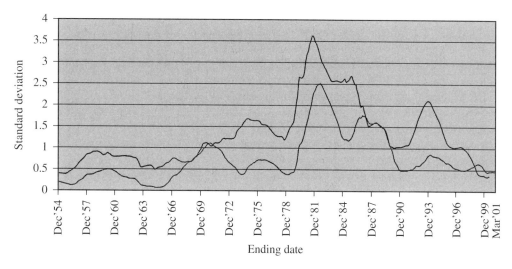

Figure 7.3   Rolling volatility (standard deviation) of three-month discount rates on bills (upper curve) and Treasury AAA-rated corporate bond yields (lower curve), December 1959–March 2001. (From: www.federalreserve.gov/releases/H15/data.htm.)

Futures hedges are often characterized as either long hedges or short hedges. In a **long hedge**, one buys futures contracts. The hedger either is currently short the cash good or has a future commitment to buy the good at the spot price that will exist at a later date (the price is a random variable). In either case, the long hedger faces the risk that prices will rise. Because the long hedger has a long futures position and a short cash position, any subsequent price rise should lead to a profit in the futures market and a loss in the cash market. The hedger must also be aware that prices may fall, in which case a profit will be earned on the spot position, while a loss will be sustained in the futures market. Note that the success of this strategy depends on the linkage between price changes in the two markets; that is, the hedger must be reasonably sure that the changes in the value of his cash position and changes in the futures price will be correlated.

A long hedge might be used by a mutual fund or pension fund money manager who is anticipating the receipt of a large sum of money to invest. The manager expects asset prices to rise between today and the day that the cash will be received. Thus, he should buy futures contracts calling for delivery of an asset (e.g., a stock index or Treasury bond) that is similar to the asset he intends to buy upon receiving the cash. If prices rise, more will have to be paid for the cash assets (a loss in the spot market), but a profit will have been earned on the futures contracts. Long hedges such as this are called **anticipatory hedges**, because they are done in anticipation of a subsequent long position.

In a **short hedge**, futures contracts are sold. Here, the hedger fears that prices will fall, because if they do, losses will be sustained on the spot position. Typically, the short hedger either is currently long the cash good or has a commitment to sell it in the future at an unknown price. With the hedge in place, if prices do indeed decline, losses will occur on the cash position, but profits should be earned on the short futures position.

A firm that is planning on issuing new debt securities (corporate bonds, or commercial paper) in the near future might use a short hedge. It fears that between today and the issuance day, security prices will decline (interest rates will rise). Thus, the firm should sell futures. The asset underlying the futures contracts should be debt instruments that will have price changes correlated with price changes of the securities the firm plans on issuing. Then if security prices do indeed decline, the new securities will have to be sold at a lower price (a loss in the spot market), but the hedger will also realize gains on the short futures position.[2]

The primary motivation of hedging is risk reduction. Because the gains in the futures market offset losses in the cash market, and vice versa, the variability of returns to the hedger is lower than when an unhedged position is held.

Most hedges are **cross hedges**. A cross hedge is one in which the cash asset and the asset underlying the futures contract are not identical. This situation arises when the hedger uses a futures contract with an underlying asset different from the one he is currently long or short. For example, consider a hedger who uses S&P 500 futures contracts to hedge against a decline in the value of his portfolio, which is different from the 500 component stocks in the S&P 500. Or consider an oil refiner who anticipates the purchase of crude oil in the near future. The firm can hedge against possible price increases by going long crude oil futures. This will be a cross hedge if the quality of crude oil the refiner will likely purchase is not the same as the quality of crude oil underlying the futures contract. It will also be considered a cross hedge if the location of the refinery differs from the location at which the crude oil futures contract is being priced, since the price of oil will be different at the two locations. When the price or value of the asset being hedged differs from the price or value of the asset underlying the futures contract, we say that **basis risk** exists.

An investor who uses T-bill futures contracts to hedge against undesired price changes in any debt instrument other than a 90-day T-bill also has a cross hedge. In fact, the only hedging situation that is not a cross hedge with T-bill futures contracts arises when one is anticipating the purchase or sale of 90-day T-bills on the contract's delivery date. If you are currently long $1 million in T-bills that have 90 days to maturity today and hedge with the T-bill futures contract, you are cross hedging, because the futures contract prices 90 day T-bills it *on the delivery date*, not today. Your T-bills may have 90 days to maturity today, but they will have 89 days to maturity tomorrow, 88 days to maturity on the day after that, and still fewer days to maturity on the T-bill futures contract's delivery date. In general, differences in coupon, maturity, or type of debt instrument will create cross hedges when interest rate futures contracts are used.

Because of basis risk, the correlation between the price movements of the futures contract and the cash asset being hedged becomes important. The hedger must be confident that price changes of the spot asset and the futures contract will move together. **Basis** refers to the difference between the price of a cash asset and the futures price[3]:

$$\text{basis} = \text{cash price} - \text{futures price}$$

The relevant cash price differs for different individuals. For a hedger, what is important is the difference between the price of the cash asset that he is long or short (as opposed to the deliverable asset) and the futures price. For example, if a New Jersey refinery is planning to purchase Mexican oil and pay the New Jersey crude oil price, then the basis risk of concern is the difference between the New Jersey crude price and the NYMEX futures price. But the underlying asset of NYMEX crude oil futures contracts is West Texas Intermediate crude oil, priced in Cushing, Oklahoma. For this hedger, the cash asset, defined in terms of the oil's quality and its physical location, differs in quality and location from the crude oil that determines the futures price.

In contrast, when speculators and arbitrageurs discuss basis, they use the price of the deliverable asset underlying the contract. To illustrate, consider the case of the S&P 500 futures contract: a hedger would be concerned with the difference in the value of the stock portfolio being hedged and the futures price of the S&P 500 futures contract. In contrast, an arbitrageur would be concerned with how the futures price deviates from the value-weighted portfolio of 500 stocks that compose the spot S&P 500 index.

Finally, for interest rate futures, basis is sometimes defined as the difference between the forward price and the futures price, or between the forward yield implicit in the today's term structure and the futures yield. The determination of forward interest rates implicit in the spot prices of debt instruments was discussed in Chapter 5. Recall that buying a debt security of one maturity in the spot market and simultaneously selling a debt security of another maturity in the spot market creates a synthetic forward instrument and determines a forward price (and a forward interest rate).

A hedger exchanges price risk for basis risk. To understand this statement, consider an individual who is currently long or short one unit of a cash asset. The current spot price of that asset is S_0. The risk is that the price of the cash asset will change to $\tilde{S}_1$. In other words, the risk faced by an unhedged investor is

$$\tilde{S}_1 - S_0 = \Delta \tilde{S}$$

The hedger should use a futures contract on one unit of an underlying asset that will move in tandem with the cash asset being hedged. Then the risk equals the change in the price of the cash asset minus the change in the futures price:

$$(\tilde{S}_1 - S_0) - (\tilde{F}_1 - F_0)$$

The minus sign used between the two terms in parentheses accounts for the fact that the hedger takes a position in the futures market that is the opposite of the one that exists in the spot market. Rearrange the foregoing statement of risk, we write

$$(\tilde{S}_1 - \tilde{F}_1) - (S_0 - F_0)$$

or

$$\widetilde{\text{basis}}_1 - \text{basis}_0$$

Today's basis, basis_0, is known. The basis at time 1, $\widetilde{\text{basis}}_1$ is generally a random variable.[4] That is, as of time 0, the basis that will exist at time 1 is usually unknown.

An unhedged individual faces price risk: the risk that the price of the cash asset will change. A hedged investor faces basis risk: the risk that the basis will change. Upon combining the definition of basis, $S - F$, and the theoretical cost-of-carry model, $F = S + CC - CR$ we conclude that basis should theoretically equal carry returns minus carry costs. This is also frequently called the *net cost of carry*:

$$\text{basis} = CR - CC$$

Because of convergence, some of the change in basis is predictable. That is, the basis is known to be zero on the delivery date if the cash asset exactly matches the underlying asset of the futures contract.

If the basis is guaranteed to remain unchanged, or if it is perfectly predictable at the end of the hedging horizon, the investor can create a perfect hedge. Since, however, the basis on the day the

EXAMPLE 7.1 Suppose $S = 100$ and $F = 105$. The basis is -5. Because of convergence, the hedger knows that on the delivery date, the basis will be zero.[5] This situation favors the short hedger who is selling the spot good forward at a forward price that exceeds the spot price. If the spot remains unchanged at 100, the futures price will decline. Even if the spot price rises by 10 points to 110, the futures price will rise only 5 points. An aggressive short hedger might sell more than one futures contract to hedge one unit of the spot position, even if the hedge is expected to be of short duration, and even if the risk minimizing hedge ratio calls for only one futures contract to be sold. Further impetus for speculating on the basis occurs when the futures contract is believed to be mispriced. If the hedger in this example, believed that the basis should theoretically be -4 or -3, then the futures price of 105 is too high, and an aggressive hedger would sell more than the theoretical risk minimizing number of futures contracts.

hedge is lifted is rarely known with certainty, perfect futures hedges are rare in practice. To minimize basis risk, price changes of the cash asset and the futures price must be highly correlated. The higher the correlation between the price changes of the cash asset and futures contract, the lower the level of basis risk. As the asset underlying the futures contract becomes more like the cash asset, the correlation between the two approaches 1.0, and basis risk is reduced.

Some aggressive hedgers will "speculate on the basis." A hedger must decide on the number of futures contract to trade with a view to reducing the overall risk exposure as much as possible. If, however, a hedger believes that the basis will change in some predictable way, this hedger may try to profit by trading fewer contracts than would normally be the case, or additional contracts than normal.

7.2 SOME SPECIAL CONSIDERATIONS IN HEDGING WITH FUTURES

The most important decision when one is hedging—whether to go long or short futures—requires proper identification of the direction of risk exposure. Determining the proper number of contracts to trade is also very important and will be discussed in Section 7.3. In addition, the decision to hedge with futures requires both the choice of the proper underlying asset as well as the proper delivery month. Choosing the correct underlying asset or assets can be difficult. Because futures are standardized, a contract that precisely matches the underlying asset being hedged may not be traded on any exchange. For example, Treasury bill, Eurodollar, and/or Treasury note futures might be used to hedge a portfolio of money market instruments and short-term debt securities that has an average time to maturity of one year.

Selecting the delivery month can also require analysis. For example, suppose you are expecting a cash flow on July 20, and futures contracts with delivery dates only in June and September exist. You can (a) use June futures and bear price risk between the delivery date and July 20, (b) use June futures today, offset the June contract just before delivery, and then (in June) use September futures to hedge, or (c) use September futures today and bear the basis risk that exists when you offset the September futures position on July 20.

EXAMPLE 7.2 Suppose that in early May, a firm prepares its cash budget for the remainder of the year and concludes that it will experience a cash shortage of about $5 million into early next year. To cover its cash needs, the firm expects to issue short-term debt securities every three months. In a strip hedge, it would sell futures contracts with different delivery months. For example, today (May 12), it might sell five June, five September, and five December Eurodollar futures contracts. Each group of five futures contracts is offset just prior to its delivery date. On the other hand, a rolling hedge would instead have the firm sell 15 June contracts on May 12. Just before the June delivery date, the hedge is rolled over by offsetting the 15 June contracts, and simultaneously selling 10 September contracts. Just before the September delivery date, the firm offsets the 10 September contracts and sells 5 December contracts.

Sometimes there are several hedging horizon dates. For example, a jeweler might anticipate the purchase of gold every three months over the next year or two. These situations require the risk manager to choose between a strip hedge and a rolling hedge (sometimes called a stacking hedge). A **strip hedge** requires the use of contracts with different delivery dates. A **stacking hedge** requires using contracts with only one delivery date, usually the nearest one. As that delivery date nears, the hedger rolls out of the expiring contracts (they are offset) and moves into contracts with more distant delivery dates.

Deciding whether to use a strip hedge or a rolling hedge will depend on several factors. First, the hedger must consider the liquidity of the nearby contract relative to the liquidity of contracts with more distant delivery dates. Sometimes the hedging horizon lies beyond the latest date of any futures contract, in which case the hedge must be rolled over at least once. The nearby contract will usually be more liquid than contracts with distant delivery dates, and therefore will have a narrower bid–asked spread. Thus, when liquidity is a factor, a rolling hedge is usually appropriate, all else equal.

On the other hand, transactions costs will usually be lower when one is employing a strip hedge. In Example 7.2, the rolling hedge requires trading two times as many futures contracts (30) as the strip hedge. Another factor in deciding between the two methods is relative mispricing: Is the contract with the more distant delivery more or less overpriced than the nearby contract? Finally, the basis risk for a rolling hedge is usually greater than the basis risk existing in a strip hedge.

A more concrete example of the strip hedge/rolling hedge decision will be presented in Chapter 10.

It is important to understand the difference between microhedging and macrohedging. A microhedge is one that protects an individual transaction. The concept of macrohedging requires that the firm examine its *overall* exposure to risk factors. In other words, one division of a company may be exposed to the risk that the $/¥ exchange rate will rise, while another division may be exposed to a declining $/¥ rate. Overall, the firm might be hedged, and there is clearly no need for microhedging. Firms should definitely examine their overall risk exposure before deciding whether hedging is needed.

In addition to these decisions, the hedger must determine the optimal number of futures contracts to trade. The next section discusses this complex decision.

7.3 THE HEDGE RATIO

This section describes two different ways of determining the proper number of futures contracts to buy or sell when one is hedging. Along the way, we will also discuss the factors that dictate the choice of which futures contract to employ as part of the hedge. Note that the process of selecting which futures contract and the number of futures contracts to trade is frequently described as an "art." There is no substitute for gathering as much information as possible and carefully analyzing the data to establish a predicted relationship between the price of the cash good being hedged and a futures price. Naïve use of any one approach without careful thought can lead to costly errors. In both approaches we discuss, the **hedge ratio** is defined to be the ratio between the number of futures contracts (each on one unit of an underlying asset) required to hedge one unit of a cash asset that must be hedged.

For example, if it is determined that 1.2 Treasury note futures contracts are needed to hedge each Treasury note, then the hedge ratio is 1.2. If 0.95 crude oil futures contracts (each on one barrel of crude oil) must be sold to hedge the future production of one barrel of crude, then the hedge ratio is 0.95. Our task is arriving at an approach to determining the hedge ratio.

7.3.1 The Portfolio Approach to a Risk-Minimizing Hedge[6]

Here, we assume that the hedger is interested in risk minimization. Risk is defined to be the variance of portfolio value changes. Price changes are random variables. The current price of the cash asset S_0 and the current price of the futures contract under consideration for hedging purposes F_0 are known. The prices of each at the termination of the hedging horizon, $\tilde{S}_1$ and $\tilde{F}_1$ at time 1, are not known.

Assume that the hedger is long one unit of the cash asset. For ease of interpretation, "one unit" should be defined as the unit of the futures contract (e.g., one barrel of crude oil). Note, however, that the underlying asset of the futures contract may not be exactly the same as the asset being hedged. The current price, or value, of the cash position is S_0. The gain or loss on one unit of the cash position is $1(\tilde{S}_1 - S_0) = 1\Delta\tilde{S}$. The risk of the unhedged position is $\mathrm{var}(1\Delta\tilde{S})$, which equals $1^2\mathrm{var}(\Delta\tilde{S})$, which is the variance of $\Delta\tilde{S}$.[7]

Now, suppose the hedger sells h futures contracts to hedge this position. The gain or loss on the portfolio is

$$1(\tilde{S}_1 - S_0) - h(\tilde{F}_1 - F_0)$$

and the risk of the portfolio is

$$\mathrm{var}[1(\tilde{S}_1 - S_0) - h(\tilde{F}_1 - F_0)]$$
$$= 1^2\,\mathrm{var}(\Delta\tilde{S}) + h^2\,\mathrm{var}(\Delta\tilde{F}) - 2(1)(h)\,\mathrm{cov}(\Delta\tilde{S}, \Delta\tilde{F})$$
$$= \mathrm{var}(\Delta\tilde{S}) + h^2\,\mathrm{var}(\Delta\tilde{F}) - 2h\sigma(\Delta\tilde{S})\sigma(\Delta\tilde{F})\mathrm{corr}(\Delta\tilde{S}, \Delta\tilde{F}) \qquad (7.1)$$

This last result is obtained because $\mathrm{var}(a\tilde{X} - b\tilde{Y}) = a^2\,\mathrm{var}(\tilde{X}) + b^2\,\mathrm{var}(\tilde{Y}) - 2ab\,\mathrm{cov}(\tilde{X}, \tilde{Y})$, where a and b are constants, and $\tilde{X}$ and $\tilde{Y}$ are two random variables. When applying this property of random variables to Equation (7.1), just set $a = 1$ and $b = $h.[8] Finally, also note that:

$$\mathrm{corr}(\Delta\tilde{S}, \Delta\tilde{F}) = \frac{\mathrm{cov}(\Delta\tilde{S}, \Delta\tilde{F})}{\sigma(\Delta\tilde{S})\sigma(\Delta\tilde{F})}$$

To minimize risk, take the first derivative of Equation (7.1) with respect to h:

$$\frac{d[\text{risk}(h)]}{dh} = 0$$

The solution to this equation is

$$h^* = \frac{\text{cov}(\Delta\tilde{S}, \Delta\tilde{F})}{\text{var}(\Delta\tilde{F})} = \frac{\sigma(\Delta\tilde{S})\text{corr}(\Delta\tilde{S}, \Delta\tilde{F})}{\sigma(\Delta\tilde{F})}$$

Now, it is also true that if you ran the following regression model using historical price change data:

$$\Delta S = a + b\Delta F \tag{7.2}$$

the estimated slope coefficient would be[9]

$$b = \frac{\text{cov}(\Delta\tilde{S}, \Delta\tilde{F})}{\text{var}(\Delta\tilde{F})} = h^*$$

In other words, to find the risk-minimizing hedge ratio h^*, you can use historical price data to run a regression like Equation (7.2). The dependent variable is the change in the spot price (or change in the value of the spot position), and the independent variable is the change in the futures price (or change in the value of the deliverable good underlying the futures contract). The resulting estimated slope coefficient defines how many futures contracts to trade, per unit of the spot position, to minimize risk. It is the hedge ratio. The slope coefficient is interpreted as follows:

$$b = \frac{\text{change in the spot price}}{\text{change in the futures price}}$$

If the results of the regression are to be properly applied, you must assume that the historical relationship of price changes will hold reasonably well in the future. If you believe that the past is not an accurate portrayal of the future relationship, you should not use the regression approach; instead, you should use the dollar equivalency method described in the next section.[10]

Figure 7.4 depicts the nature of the regression analysis. Point S is placed at the coordinates $E(\Delta S)$, $\sigma(\Delta S)$ which represent the expected change in the spot price and the standard deviation of the spot price, respectively. The curve illustrates the risk–return combinations of different portfolios of a long position in one unit of the spot good and short positions in futures. In other words, S is a portfolio of 100% in the spot good and no futures (an unhedged long position). As futures are sold, the hedger's position moves down and to the left along the curve. The expected portfolio cash flow decreases, and so does the risk. Eventually, the point noted with an asterisk is reached. At that point, the hedger is long one unit of the cash good and short h^* futures contracts. Risk is minimized. If too many futures are sold, then risk begins to increase, and perhaps even worse, the expected cash flow continues to decline. Eventually, point F is reached; F denotes a situation in which there is no spot position, but futures contracts have been sold. If S is expected to increase in price, then F, which is a *short* position in futures, must be expected to decline in price. Thus, F is below the x axis.

Many hedgers will not wish to minimize risk, nor will they want to be at point S, because it has too much risk. They wish to have a higher expected return than a position like that denoted by the asterisk in Figure 7.4 would provide. Such a hedger has an **indifference curve** U in Figure 7.5, and will want to sell fewer futures contracts than another hedger who is extremely risk averse. An indifference curve shows all risk–return combinations that leave an individual equally satisfied.

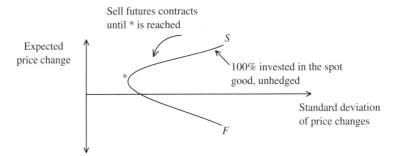

Figure 7.4 How to find the risk-minimizing hedge ratio, as conceptualized by the regression approach. The objective is to find the proper number of futures contracts to sell to reach point *, where the risk of the spot futures porfolio is minimized.

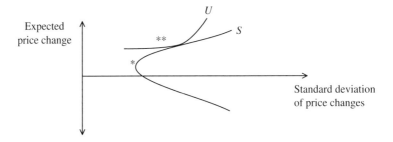

Figure 7.5 Some hedgers may not wish to minimize risk. They will not choose to sell h^* futures contracts to be at point *. For bearing extra risk, they hope to be compensated with additional profit. Given an indifference curve U, such a hedger might sell h^{**} futures contracts and be at point **.

For example, an expected price change of $200 with a standard deviation of $20 might be as desirable as an expected price change of $300 with a standard deviation of $35. The curve, U, depicts the trade-offs for one hypothetical hedger. This hedger will be satisfied (utility will be maximized subject to the opportunities available) at the point denoted by two asterisks (**).

EXAMPLE 7.3 An individual is long 100 oz. of gold. The spot price is $300/oz. The expected monthly price change in the spot price of gold is $4/oz., and the standard deviation of monthly spot price changes is estimated to be $15. The futures price for delivery one year hence is $340/oz.[11] The standard deviation of monthly futures price changes is $18. The correlation of monthly changes in the spot price of gold with monthly changes in the futures price of gold is 0.88. Given these data, Table 7.1 illustrates how a diagram like Figure 7.4 is created, and the risk minimizing number of futures contracts is found.

Figure 7.6 is a graph that illustrates the relationship between expected price changes and the standard deviation of price changes. As futures contracts are initially sold, risk declines, until about 0.7 futures contract has been sold. Beyond 0.7 futures contract sold, risk increases. Thus, the risk-minimizing hedge is found to be $h^* = 0.7$.

TABLE 7.1   Risk and Return as a Function of the Number of Futures Contracts Sold

Number of Futures Contracts Sold (h)	Standard Deviation of Cash Flow Changes[1]	Expected Change in Cash Flow[2]
0	$[(15)^2 + 0 - 0]^{1/2} = 15$	4
0.1	$[(15)^2 + h^2 (18)^2 - 2h(15)(18)(0.88)]^{1/2} = 13.4432$	3.933
0.2	11.9549	3.867
0.3	10.5641	3.8
0.4	9.3145	3.733
0.5	8.2704	3.667
0.6	7.5180	3.6
0.7	7.1498	3.533
0.8	7.2250	3.467
0.9	7.7305	3.4
1.0	8.5907	3.333
1.1	9.7118	3.267
1.2	11.0145	3.2

[1]The standard deviation of the portfolio's cash flows is found by computing the square root of $\text{var}(\Delta \tilde{S}) + h^2 \, \text{var}(\Delta \tilde{F}) - 2h\sigma(\Delta \tilde{S})\sigma(\Delta \tilde{F})\text{corr}(\Delta \tilde{S}, \Delta \tilde{F})$.

[2]The expected monthly change in the portfolio's cash flow is found by the formula $[1 \, E[CF(\text{spot})] - hE[CF(\text{futures})]]$. The individual is long one unit of the spot commodity (100 oz.) and short h futures contracts (each covering 100 oz.). $E[CF(\text{spot})] = \$4/\text{month}$, and $E[CF(\text{futures})] = \$0.667/\text{month}$.

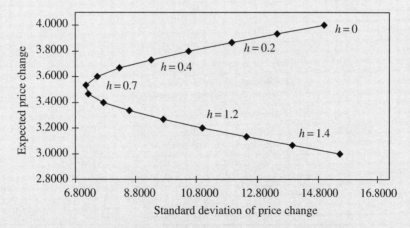

Figure 7.6 Risk and return are a function of the number of futures contracts sold: $h = 0$ denotes an unhedged position; $h^* = 0.7$ is the risk-minimizing number of futures contracts to sell.

If historical data are available, a hedger can regress historical changes in the monthly spot price of gold on historical changes in the monthly futures price of gold to estimate h^*. In other words, estimate the following model:

$$\Delta S = a + b\Delta F \qquad (7.3)$$

where

$\Delta S =$ the monthly change in the spot price of 1 oz. of gold

$\Delta F =$ the monthly change in the futures price of 1 oz. of gold

The estimated slope coefficient $\hat{b}$ equals h^*.

Consider Table 7.2, which contains hypothetical historical price data. A regression of changes in the spot price (ΔS) on changes in the futures price (ΔF) yields the regression coefficients

TABLE 7.2 Hypothetical Historical Price Data for a Commodity

Month[1]	Spot Price	Futures Price Nearby[2]	Futures Price Distant	Changes, Δ In Spot Price, ΔS	Changes, Δ In Futures Price, ΔF
Apr	400	414 Jun	422.2 Sep		
May	410	419.2 Jun	428 Sep	10	5.2
*Jun	406	406.2 Jun	414.3 Sep	−4	−13.0
Jul	388	399.8 Sep	405.4 Dec	−18	−14.5
Aug	394	402.7 Sep	410 Dec	6	2.9
*Sep	377	377.3 Sep	384.8 Dec	−17	−25.4
Oct	397	410.9 Dec	420.7 Mar	20	26.1
Nov	412	418.2 Dec	429 Mar	15	7.3
*Dec	406	405.8 Dec	414 Mar	−6	−12.4
Jan	414	425.5 Mar	434.8 Jun	8	11.5
Feb	412	422.4 Mar	430.8 Jun	−2	−3.1
*Mar	388	387.9 Mar	394.9 Jun	−24	−34.5
Apr	380	391.4 Jun	398.2 Sep	−8	−3.5
May	366	369.9 Jun	375.8 Sep	−14	−21.5
*Jun	371	371.1 Jun	378.5 Sep	5	1.2
Jul	372	378.6 Sep	386.6 Dec	1	0.1
Aug	370	374.9 Sep	382.3 Dec	−2	−3.7
*Sep	366	365.3 Sep	372.7 Dec	−4	−9.6
Oct	379	390.6 Dec	398.8 Mar	13	17.9
Nov	385	396.1 Dec	405.2 Mar	6	5.5

		mean =	−0.78947	−3.34211
$\text{var}(\Delta S) = \dfrac{1}{18} \displaystyle\sum_{j=1}^{19} (\Delta S_j - \overline{\Delta S})^2$		=	142.73099	$\text{var}(\Delta F) = 222.24813$
$\text{std dev}(\Delta S) = [\text{var}(\Delta S)]^{1/2}$		=	11.947008	$\text{std dev}(\Delta F) = 14.90799$

[1]An Asterisk indicates a delivery month for the futures.

[2]The futures price change is that of the nearby contract, except in any month following a delivery month. For example, month 4 (July) is after a delivery month. In that month, ΔF is the change in the futures price of the September contract (399.8 − 414.3 = −14.5). Note that the September contract is the distant futures contract in June, but it becomes the nearby contract in July.

$\hat{a} = 1.7525$ and $\hat{b} = 0.761$. The coefficient of determination R^2 is 0.901. Since we argued earlier that the estimated slope coefficient $\hat{b}$ equals

$$\frac{\text{cov}(\Delta S, \Delta F)}{\text{var}(\Delta F)}$$

and this, in turn, was the definition of h^* for a risk-minimizing hedge, we can conclude from this regression that 0.761 futures contract (each on one unit of the underlying asset) should be sold to hedge one unit of the spot position. If the hedger owned 800 units of the underlying asset, and each futures contract covered 100 units, then 6.088 futures contract should be sold. Problem 7.14 at the end of the chapter asks you to use Excel to run this regression model.

In other words, regressing spot price changes on futures price changes yields h^*, which is the risk-minimizing hedge ratio. When hedging a given quantity of an asset, multiply h^* by the number of units of the spot good per the number of units covered by a futures contract. If 800 units are to be hedged, and one futures contract covers 100 units, then the risk-minimizing number of futures contracts to sell is:

$$\begin{array}{l}\text{number of futures contracts} \\ \text{to trade to have a} \\ \text{risk - minimizing hedge}\end{array} = h^* \times \frac{\text{quantity of the cash asset to be hedged}}{\text{quantity of the asset underlying one futures contract}}$$

$$= 0.761\left(\frac{800}{100}\right) = 6.088$$

Sometimes it is helpful to construct a table like Table 7.3 to conceptualize the hedging process. In Table 7.3, we assume that the futures price subsequently changes exactly as predicted by the regression model of spot price changes on futures price changes. The price change in the spot market is $-\$11.60$. ($388.4 - 400 = -11.60$). Since $\hat{b} = 0.761$, the model predicts that the futures price should have declined by \$15.24. ($-11.60/0.761 = -15.24$). Therefore the futures price on the day the hedge is lifted is predicted to be \$424.76. ($440 - 15.24$).

In the example illustrated in Table 7.3, the hedger realizes a loss in the spot market equal to \$9280. But because the inventory of gold was hedged by selling 6.088 gold futures contracts, there was also a profit of \$9278 in the futures market. This was a perfect hedge (except for some rounding error). When the hedge was initiated ("today"), the risk-minimizing hedge ratio was estimated

TABLE 7.3   A Short Hedge

Cash, or Spot, Market	Futures Market
Today	Today
You own 800 oz. of gold. The spot price of gold is \$400/oz. You fear that the price of gold will decline.	Sell 6.088 gold futures contacts at the futures price of \$440 oz.
T days hence	*T* days hence
The spot price of gold has declined to \$388.40/oz.	Buy 6.088 gold futures contracts at the futures price of \$424.76 oz.
Loss: 800(388.4 − 400) = \$9280	Profit: 6.088(\$44,000 − \$42,476) = \$9278

to be 6.088 contracts. This was based on the historical price data presented earlier, where h^* was estimated to be 0.761. This means that if ΔS was \$11.60/oz. then the *predicted* ΔF was \$15.24/oz. (11.60/0.761), which also turned out to be the *actual* ΔF. The hedge thus turned out to be perfect in the sense that the loss in the spot market equaled the gain in the futures market.

In other cases, the hedge might not have been perfect. The change in the futures price might have been greater or smaller than \$15.24/oz. For example, the futures price on the day that the hedge was lifted might have been \$428/oz. Then, the profit on the futures position would have been only \$7305.60, or (6.088)(\$44,000 − \$42,800). The uncertain basis on the day the hedge is lifted illustrates how basis risk affects hedging effectiveness. Basis risk is the risk that the basis ($\tilde{S}_1 - \tilde{F}_1$) will unexpectedly widen or narrow.

Also be aware that these examples ignore the daily resettlement of the futures contracts. In Section 7.4 we will discuss the concept of "tailing." Tailing attempts to account for the fact that profits or losses on futures are realized daily, while the profit or loss on the spot position is not realized until the end of the hedging horizon.

Again, the hedger *must* be confident that a reliable relationship exists between price changes of the spot asset being hedged and price changes of the futures contract. When one is using historical price data to estimate h^*, the reliability of the relationship is typically measured by R^2, which is the **coefficient of determination**. The coefficient R^2 is the square of the correlation coefficient of the two variables in the regression, and it ranges from a low of 0.0 to a high of 1.0. R^2 measures the percentage of the variability of the dependent variable (ΔS) that can be explained by variability of the independent variable (ΔF). When obtained with historical data, it is an anticipated (ex-ante) measure of hedging effectiveness. The higher the R^2, the more effective the hedge *should* be. We say, "should" because the actual hedge (ex-post) can be better or worse than anticipated. Always be cognizant that historical relationships might not persist into the future. Also note that lower R^2 values imply greater basis risk.

When deciding which of two possible contracts (with different underlying assets) to use to hedge a spot position, a useful approach is to run the historical price change regression model, Equation (7.2) and find the R^2 of each. All else equal, the futures contract with the higher R^2 should be used, since, based on historical data, it has the more reliable relationship with the spot commodity. Figure 7.7 illustrates how two futures contracts can obtain the same slope coefficient in a regression, yet have vastly different values of R^2.

Besides R^2, another important variable to consider when deciding which futures contract to employ for hedging purposes is the liquidity of the contract. If one contract has a higher R^2 but lower liquidity, the hedger must evaluate how much liquidity she is willing to give up to obtain a more reliable hedge. Of course, she must also have confidence that the historical relationship that was so very reliable (high R^2) in the past will persist in the future.

The last factor to consider when deciding which futures contracts to use is the relative under- or overpricing of each contract. When doing a long hedge, buy the contract that is cheaper (the one for which the actual F minus the theoretical F is most negative or least positive). For a short hedge, sell the most overpriced futures contract, all else equal. This is the futures for which $F - (S + CC - CR)$ is most positive or least negative.

It is usually advisable to underhedge as your confidence in the future correlation between ΔS and ΔF declines: that is, as the value of R^2 declines, trade fewer contracts than the number called for by h^*. If R^2 is below some arbitrary value, perhaps 0.5, then it is probably not wise to use that particular futures contract to hedge at all. As illustrated in Figures 7.4 through 7.6, there may be a great cost to overhedging in terms of lower expected returns and higher risk.

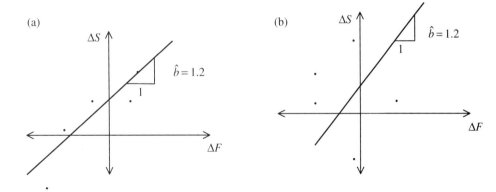

Figure 7.7 The estimated slope coefficient is the same in both regression models: (*a*) a very reliable relationship (i.e., a high R^2) and (*b*) an unreliable relationship (i.e., a very low R^2). Very little of the variation in ΔS is explained by ΔF in (*b*).

In the example developed in connection with Table 7.2 monthly data were used to develop the relationship between spot and futures price changes. An important question to ask is whether monthly data should always be used, or whether other time measurement intervals are adequate or preferred. When one is hedging for only one day, daily price change data should be used in the regression to estimate h^*. Similarly, if the anticipated hedging horizon is only two, three, four, or five days, one should obtain historical spot and futures prices two, three, four, and five days apart, respectively. In other words, for hedging horizons of five days or less, it is recommended that the investor match the anticipated length of the hedge with the interval between historical price data observation points.

Beyond one week, it becomes irrelevant whether weekly, biweekly, or monthly observations are used. But using observations that are *more* than one month apart creates two problems. First, because the estimation error of the slope coefficient (hedge ratio) declines as the number of observations increases, more observations are almost always better than fewer observations. In other words, more observations will increase the accuracy of the estimated slope coefficient in a regression. A more reliable estimate will be obtained from 36 monthly observations than from 12 quarterly observations. Second, if the data go back in time too far, it becomes increasing likely that a different relationship between the spot asset price and the futures price existed at the earlier dates. This also reduces the reliability of the estimated slope coefficient in terms of predicting the future.

On the other hand, observations that are taken only one or a few days apart create another problem that does not exist with weekly or monthly observations. This problem arises from non-synchronous trading and other "noisy influences" that exist for short measurement intervals. The time at which the futures market closes may not coincide with the time the spot price is measured. Observed prices might be customer sales at the bid price or customer purchases at the asked price. These problems create a less accurate measurement for the relationship between spot and futures prices when they are observed daily.

If your hedging horizon is only one or a few days, you must also recognize that you face greater basis risk. In one day, it is possible that the price changes of the spot good and the futures contract will actually be in *opposite* directions. This is less likely to occur if your hedging interval is a week or longer. Usually, this phenomenon will show up in historical price change regressions

[Equation (7.3)] with a lower estimated slope coefficient and a lower R^2. The moral: be cautious when hedging for only one or two days.

7.3.2   Dollar Equivalency

The goal of a hedge is to avoid losses in the cash market resulting from adverse price changes. Therefore, an alternative method of determining how many futures contracts to trade as part of a hedge is to equate the anticipated loss in the cash market if the spot price changes by some amount to the likely gain in the futures market that will occur concurrently with the spot price change. In other words, define the following:

ΔV_S = change in the value of the spot position

ΔV_F = change in the value of one futures contract

h = number of futures contracts

Then the goal of the hedger is to equate:

$$\Delta V_S = h \Delta V_F$$

Sometimes, spot price data are not available to run a regression. At other times, you might suspect that the historical relationship between spot and futures price changes will not exist in the future. Therefore, you might prefer to use a subjective estimate of the relationship between the change in the value of the spot position and the contemporaneous futures price change. In these instances, employ the dollar equivalency approach to finding h^*. The two approaches can serve as checks on each other, increasing the likelihood that the proper number of futures contracts will be being traded.

EXAMPLE 7.4   An oil producer has 100,000 barrels of oil to transport to a refinery. If the spot price changes by some amount, say \$1/bbl, the resulting change in value of the inventory position, ΔV_S, will be \$100,000. The producer estimates that the contemporaneous change in the futures price of crude oil on the New York Mercantile Exchange will be \$1.02, and thus the change in the value of one futures contract will be \$1020 (one futures contract covers 1000 bbl of a specific grade of oil, priced at a specific location). To neutralize the spot market loss of \$100,000 that would occur if the spot price fell by one dollar, sell $h = \Delta V_S/\Delta V_F = 100{,}000/1020 = 98.04$ futures contracts.

Note that the dollar equivalency approach likely produced the same result as the regression approach. Had the producer used historical price data to run the regression model

$$\Delta(\text{spot price of oil}) = a + b\, \Delta(\text{futures price of oil})$$

he might have found $\hat{b} = h^* = 0.9804$ (which says that if the futures price falls by \$1.02/bbl, the spot price should fall by \$1/bbl). Then, multiplying 0.9804 by the number of units of the spot position (100,000) divided by the number of units of oil in one futures contract (1000), we find that, again, the producer should sell 98.04 futures contracts.

As another example, suppose you own a portfolio of corporate bonds and wish to hedge against a rise in interest rates that would cause their value to decline. A regression by means of historical price data might not be desirable for many reasons. For instance, the maturity of the bonds is continuously changing. Consequently, the relationship between spot price changes and futures price changes that existed several years ago will likely not exist today. In addition, some of the bonds may not be publicly traded, which means that no price data are available. Furthermore, the default risk, hence the bond ratings, of some of the bonds might have changed, altering the historical relationship between their price changes and those of Treasury bonds. Finally, the way in which Treasury bond futures prices change as interest rates change is highly dependent on the existing term structure of interest rates.

Therefore, using the dollar equivalency method for determining the appropriate number of futures contracts with which to hedge is sometimes the best alternative. Simply stated, when employing the dollar equivalency approach, the hedger must:

1. Estimate the loss in the spot position that will occur if the spot price changes by some arbitrary amount.

2. Estimate the change in the futures price that will occur if the spot price changes by that arbitrary amount.

3. Compute the change in the value of one futures contract given that change in the futures price.

4. Trade the appropriate number of futures contracts so as to realize a profit in the futures market equal to the spot market loss.

Additional specific examples that employ the dollar equivalency approach will be presented in Chapter 9.

7.4 TAILING THE HEDGE

In the hedging examples just presented, the impact of marking to market cash flows for the futures contracts was ignored. In reality, a long hedger will experience daily resettlement cash outflows on the futures position if futures prices fall. Although these cash flows should be recouped at the termination of the hedge through higher profits on the spot position, there are two consequences of the interim cash outflows.

1. There is an opportunity cost to any daily resettlement cash *outflows*; they must be financed through borrowing, to avoid losing interest by a reduction in the hedger's earning assets. On the other hand, should prices rise, the long hedger will *receive* mark to market cash *inflows*, and these can be reinvested to earn interest. Basically, daily resettlement inflows are desired because they can be reinvested, while daily resettlement outflows are unwanted because they have an opportunity cost.

2. There is a danger that the cash outflows could accumulate to such a point that the hedger's assets become depleted, and will be unable to obtain additional funding. The hedge must then be liquidated prematurely.[12]

The first consequence can be handled by tailing the hedge. In Section 6.5 (see note 14 in particular), we showed how tailing neutralizes the valuation effects of marking to market of futures contracts. If future interest rates are nonstochastic (known), then tailing effectively transforms the futures contract into a forward contract. The same concept exists in hedging. Tailing requires that you trade only the present value of the number of futures contracts found to be optimal using the principles covered in Section 7.3. A tail is particularly crucial when interest rates are high and the hedging horizon is long.

EXAMPLE 7.5 A jewelry manufacturer who has 2000 oz. of gold in inventory fears that prices will fall over the next 60 days. The current spot price of gold is $350/oz. and the futures price for a contract that expires 60 days hence is $359. The hedger knows that the basis of –9 will strengthen toward zero over the hedge period, and this movement of the basis will work in her favor, since she is a short hedger. The spot interest rate is 12%/year. Naively, the manufacturer proceeds to sell 20 futures contracts, each covering 100 oz. of gold, to hedge her inventory. This is an untailed hedge.

If she is wrong, and prices instead rise over the next 60 days, the manufacturer will experience mark-to-market cash outflows on the short futures position. Assume that initial margin is satisfied by using a bank letter of credit. All variation margin cash flow losses must be paid in cash and must be financed by borrowing. Suppose that the futures price remains constant except on the following days:

Day	Days Remaining in Hedge	Futures Price	Additional Margin Required	Interest on Borrowing Variation Margin Until Hedge Termination
3	57	$365	$12,000	$12,000×0.12×57/365 = $224.88
18	42	$370.20	$10,400	$10,400×0.12×42/365 = $143.61
51	9	$377	$13,600	$13,600×0.12×9/365 = $40.24

On the hedge termination date (day 60), the spot price of gold is $372 and the futures price is $372 (convergence). The manufacturer lifts the hedge by offsetting the futures contracts, and, ignoring for now the added interest expense on borrowing to make daily resettlement payments, observes the following results:

	Spot Market	**Futures Market**
day 0	Has 2000 oz. of gold in inventory: spot price = $350	Sells 20 futures contracts at the futures price of $359
day 60	Sells 2000 oz. of gold at new spot price of $372 profit = $44,000	Offsets futures position by buying 20 contracts at $372 each loss = $26,000

The difference between the spot market profit and futures market loss arises because the basis narrowed from –9 on day zero to 0 on day 60. The narrowing in the basis created the net $18,000 profit on the hedge (20 contracts times 9 points times $100/point = $18,000). Recall that the hedger expected the basis to narrow, so this profit may have been entirely expected.

However, the $26,000 loss in the futures market ignores the interest required to finance the mark-to-market cash outflows that occurred. Put another way, the hedger would have lost $26,000 had she originally sold a *forward* contract covering 2000 oz. of gold at a forward price of $359/oz. But because *futures* were sold, we must also account for the interest lost on the interim mark-to-market cash outflows, which totaled

($224.88 + $143.61 + $40.24 =) $408.73. Because futures were sold, and futures prices subsequently rose, these daily resettlement cash outflows must be financed.

By applying a tail to the original hedge ratio of 20 contracts, the hedger can almost completely neutralize the effects of daily resettlement. Assume that the interest rate is constant. A tail is created by reducing the number of contracts initially sold from 20 to the present value of 20. On the initiation day of the hedge, the present value of 20 is

$$\frac{20}{1+0.12(60/365)} = 19.613$$

On every subsequent day, additional (fractions of) futures contracts should be sold, so that the hedger is always short the present value of 20 futures contracts. Thus, one day after the hedge is initiated, the hedger should be short a total of

$$\frac{20}{1+0.12(59/365)} = 19.619$$

contracts.

The *size of the tail* is the difference between 20 and the number of contracts actually sold on any day. As time passes, the size of the tail becomes smaller. By the hedge termination date, there are 20 contracts sold, and the tail is zero. Tailing neutralizes the effect of daily resettlement cash flows by making the interest earned on the investment of mark-to-market cash inflows or paid to finance mark-to-market cash outflows equal to the impact of the hedge ratio reduction. The tail works as follows.

Day	Days Remaining in Hedge	Short Position Contracts Sold	Futures Price	Additional Margin Required	Interest on Borrowing Margin Until Hedge Termination
0	60	19.61311	$359	—	—
3	57	19.63210	$365	($600)(19.6321) = $11,779.26	($11,779.26)(0.12)× (57/365) = $220.74
18	42	19.72760	$370.2	($520)(19.7276) = $10,258.35	($10,258.35)(0.12)× (42/365) = $141.65
51	9	19.94100	$377	($680)(19.9410) = $13,559.88	($13,559.88)(0.12)× (9/365) = $40.12
60	0	20.0	$372	($500)(20.0) = $10,000 (profit)	—

Now, add all the mark-to-market cash flows. There is a net cash outflow of $25,597.49 ($11,779.26 + $10,258.35 + $13,559.88 − $10,000). In addition, the financing charges totaled $402.51 ($220.74 + $141.65 + $40.12). The total loss on the futures position and the financing charges is $26,000 ($25,597.49 + $402.51). The tail has effectively transformed the futures contracts into a forward transaction. Had a forward contract been originally sold, the hedger would have lost $26,000 on the forward contract. By tailing the futures trades, an equal loss is realized on the futures contracts.

The effect of a tail is that the optimal hedge ratio will always be smaller than the one originally computed by means of the hedge ratio models we have discussed. The number of futures contracts to trade is just the *present value* of the risk-minimizing number of futures contracts. Tailing removes the impact of daily resettlement of futures. In Example 7.5, the tail effect is so small that it can likely be ignored (the hedger would have to decide to initially sell either 19 or 20 contracts). But when interest rates are high, and/or it is expected that the hedge will be in effect for a long time, the tail can be significant. Imagine, for example, a one-year hedge when interest rates are 20%/year.

7.5   MANAGING THE FUTURES HEDGE

Hedgers recognize the price risk they face, and they hedge that risk by purchasing or selling the proper number of futures contracts with the appropriate underlying commodity. The hedger first estimates h^*, using either the regression approach or the dollar equivalency approach. This hedge ratio, h^*, should then be multiplied by the number of units of the spot position being hedged relative to the number of units underlying one futures contract. A tail should be applied if necessary. The final task is to monitor, adjust, and evaluate the hedge. Several examples that illustrate the need to monitor environmental conditions are now presented.

The hedger must realize that conditions change over time, and that these changes might warrant altering the hedge, or removing it altogether. For example, risk exposure might change as assets and liabilities change. A jeweler who has hedged his inventory of gold might initially compute some number of futures contracts to sell based on his net gold price risk exposure. If a few days later he unexpectedly liquidates a large portion of his inventory, the number of futures contracts needed to create an effective hedge obviously must be reestimated.

It is also possible that a sophisticated hedger has developed a model that reasonably accurately predicts the future price of the good he has hedged. The signal provided by that model might change, calling for the hedge to be lifted. In fact, most hedgers are selective in nature, rather than continuous. That is, they hedge only when they perceive a substantial risk that adverse price moves are forthcoming.

In another case a bank has initially hedged a loan, but as time passes and the duration of the loan declines, the loan balance may change. Hedges that employ interest rate futures are particularly dynamic and require a great deal of monitoring because the passage of time alters the nature of the asset or liability being hedged.

A hedger's level of risk tolerance might also change over time. On the initiation date of a hedge, it might be felt that business will be strong over the next year, so that risk tolerance is relatively high. Then, at a later date, new information might increase the perceived probability of a business downturn, decreasing the level of risk tolerance, and calling for a more aggressive hedging policy. Similarly, changes in the level of competition a firm faces might dictate changes in its hedging decisions.

Sometimes another futures contract becomes more favorably priced for the hedger. In this case, the initial contract used to hedge should be offset, and the better priced futures employed instead. Additionally, the hedger should always be aware of upcoming delivery dates that will force the hedge to be rolled over. Thus, the hedger should monitor the relative pricing of the nearby and adjacent contracts. With the right information, the rollover trade can be entered as a calendar spread order, thereby reducing commission charges and allowing the hedger to trade when the spread is believed to be favorable.

Finally, all hedges should be evaluated against the hedger's objectives. What was the profit or loss on the futures position, and on the spot position being hedged? If one has been selectively hedging because of an anticipated adverse price change, one must ask whether that expected price change occurred. Do beneficial price changes occur when one is deciding not to hedge? Was the proper hedge ratio used? What was the (ex-post) risk-minimizing hedge ratio, and why was it different from the (ex-ante) h^* that was originally estimated?[13]

Note that many times a loss is realized on the futures position and a gain on the spot position. If you are a selective hedger, and this occurs more than 50% of the time, you should revise your strategy. These results suggest that you are not adept in predicting future spot price changes and/or not skilled at uncovering mispriced futures. You might consider a continuous hedging strategy, or not hedging at all.

7.6 SUMMARY

This chapter provided details specific to hedging decisions using futures contracts. Corporations, banks, institutions, and individuals face price risk; that is, if the price of a good changes, wealth is affected. Futures contracts can be used to manage that risk. By buying futures when a price rise leads to a loss in wealth, and selling futures when price declines are undesired, one can avoid the adverse consequences of price changes.

The hedger should first identify the net exposure to risk. Will a price rise or a price decline hurt? This determines whether futures should be bought or sold. Futures price changes should be highly correlated with price changes of the asset being hedged, and the futures contract should be as liquid as possible. The hedge ratio determines the number of futures contracts that will lead to a risk-minimizing hedge, although some hedgers may not wish to have such a position. The hedge ratio can be estimated using either the regression (portfolio) approach or the dollar equivalency approach. Hedges should be tailed when interest rates are high and/or hedging horizons are long. Finally, hedges should be actively monitored and evaluated.

Chapters 8, 9, and 10 present additional hedging examples dealing with stock index futures and interest rate futures.

References

Cechetti, Stephen G., Robert E. Cumby, and Stephen Figlewski. 1988. "Estimation of the Optimal Futures Hedge." *The Review of Economics and Statistics*, Vol. 70, No. 4, November, pp. 623–630.

Ederington, Louis. 1979. "The Hedging Performance of the New Futures Markets." *Journal of Finance*, Vol. 34, No. 1, March, pp. 157–170.

Johnson, Leland L. 1960. "The Theory of Hedging and Speculation in Commodity Futures." *Review of Economic Studies*, Vol. 27, No. 3, October, pp. 139–151.

Kolb, Robert W., Gerald D. Gay, and William C. Hunter. 1985. "Liquidity Requirements and Financial Futures Hedges." *Review of Research in Futures Markets*, Vol. 4, No. 1, pp. 1–25.

Stein, Jerome L. 1961. "The Simultaneous Determination of Spot and Futures Prices." *American Economic Review*, Vol. 51, No. 5, December, pp. 1012–1025.

Notes

[1]The data are obtained at the Fed's website (www.federalreserve.gov/Releases/H15/data.htm).

[2]The underlying assets of interest rate futures contracts are securities. Thus, an individual who wishes to profit from a rise in interest rates (a decline in debt instrument prices) will *sell* futures. Be cognizant of the difference between this situation and that of a forward rate agreement (FRA), which is a forward contract on an interest rate (*not a security*), so that an individual who uses a FRA to profit from a rise in interest rates will actually *buy* the FRA.

[3]Note that some market participants define basis as the futures price minus the cash price. Moreover, it is common to define basis as $F - S$ for some contracts (in particular financial futures), and $S - F$ for other contracts.

[4]The basis at time 1 is not random if time 1 is the delivery date of the futures contract, the good being hedged is exactly equivalent to the futures' underlying asset, and the hedged good exists at a delivery location of the futures contract. Then, $basis_1 = 0$ because of convergence.

[5]Any time that the basis increases, i.e., it becomes less negative or more positive, it is said to *strengthen*. Basis *weakens* when it becomes less positive or more negative. In this example, basis is expected to strengthen from -5 ("5 under") to zero. Basis (where the spot asset is the asset underlying the futures contract) is guaranteed to be zero on the delivery date (convergence) by the force of arbitrage.

[6]Johnson (1960) and Stein (1961) are widely cited as the seminal works that integrated hedging theory and portfolio theory. Ederington (1979) is the first to apply the model to interest rate hedging.

[7]If $\tilde{X}$ is a random variable and a is a constant, then $\text{var}(a\tilde{X}) = a^2 \text{var}(\tilde{X})$.

[8]Perhaps you have learned some portfolio theory, in which case the following analogy might be useful. Consider an investor who invests $w_1\%$ of his wealth in asset one and $w_2\%$ in asset 2; $w_1 + w_2 = 100\%$. The returns on assets 1 and 2 are random variables denoted $\tilde{R}_1$ and $\tilde{R}_2$. Then the variance of the returns on the portfolio is $\text{var}(w_1\tilde{R}_1 + w_2\tilde{R}_2) = w_1^2 \text{var}(\tilde{R}_1) + w_2^2 \text{var}(\tilde{R}_2) + 2w_1 w_2 \text{cov}(\tilde{R}_1, \tilde{R}_2)$. This is virtually identical to the material presented in the text, except that the hedger is long an asset and *short* a futures contract.

[9]Continuing with the portfolio theory analogy, recall that a stock's beta coefficient is estimated by regressing the stock's returns on the market portfolio's returns:

$$R_i = \alpha + \beta R_m$$

and that the estimated beta, the slope coefficient, is

$$\beta = \frac{\text{cov}(R_i, R_M)}{\text{var}(R_M)} = \frac{\sigma(R_i) corr(R_i, R_M)}{\sigma(R_M)}$$

[10]Cecchetti, Cumby, and Figlewski (1988) cite several problems with using the regression model to estimate a hedge ratio: some hedgers may not want to have a risk-minimizing hedge (cf Figure 7.4 and Figure 7.5), the relationship between ΔS and ΔF will often vary over time; and historical data are frequently not accurate predictors of what is expected to prevail in the future. These authors' method of estimating a hedge ratio, however, is beyond the scope of this text.

[11]Because of convergence, we can calculate the expected monthly futures price change. $S_0 = \$300$. Since $E(\Delta S) = \$4/\text{month}$, then $E(S_T) = \$348$ for $T = 1$ year hence. $F_0 = \$340$. $E(S_T) = E(F_T) = \$348$. Because the futures price is below the expected future spot price, the situation is one of *normal backwardation*. The expected futures price change over the next year is \$8, and the expected monthly futures price change is \$0.667.

[12]Kolb, Gay, and Hunter (1985) examine the nature of this second consequence.

[13]To estimate the ex-post-risk-minimizing hedge ratio, use the *actual* changes in prices during the interval of time that the hedge was in effect to estimate the slope coefficient in the regression model $\Delta S = a + b \Delta F$. The ex-ante h^* was originally estimated at the inception of the hedge from historical data prior to time 0. A change in the relationship between futures price changes and price changes of the asset being hedged might explain much of why a hedge did not perform as expected.

PROBLEMS

7.1 A government securities dealer has a large amount of Treasury bills in inventory. Will he suffer a loss in wealth if T-bill prices rise or fall? Will he suffer a loss in wealth if short-term interest rates rise or fall? If futures are used to manage risk, should he be a long hedger or a short hedger? If he decides to use FRAs instead, will he buy or sell them?

7.2 A U.S. corporation will receive millions of euros from a customer next month. Will the U.S. corporation suffer a loss in wealth if the dollar price of euros (the $/€ exchange rate) rises or falls? Should the firm be a long hedger or a short hedger if futures are used?

7.3 If $\text{basis} = \text{cash} - \text{futures}$, does a short hedger hope that the basis strengthens (increases) or weakens (decreases) during the time that her hedge is in place?

7.4 What are some alternative ways to hedge besides using futures contracts? What are some factors a hedger should use in deciding which mode of hedging to use?

7.5 Choose a long-term government bond, and use a newspaper, such as the *Wall Street Journal*, to obtain about 24 prices on 24 consecutive trading days. Also record the futures prices for the nearby Treasury bond futures contract on those 24 days. Regress the changes of the bond's price on changes of the futures price to obtain $h^* =$ the estimated slope coefficient. The regression model is $\Delta S = a + b\Delta F$.

7.6 You work for a sheet metal producer. The firm plans on purchasing 100,000 lb of tin next month, and you have been requested to hedge the planned transaction using futures contracts. Will you do a long hedge or a short hedge?

There are no tin futures. However, you have regressed changes in the spot price of tin on changes in silver futures prices and in copper futures prices. Define ΔT, ΔS, and ΔC as the change in prices of tin, silver futures ($/oz.) and copper futures ($/lb). Here are your regression results:

$$\Delta T = 0.001 + 0.25\Delta S \quad R^2 = 0.56$$
$$\Delta T = -0.008 + 1.92\Delta C \quad R^2 = 0.72$$

a. Which futures contract appears to be more suitable for your hedging purposes? Why? What other possible information might induce you to switch to the other contract?

b. How many futures contract of the preferable commodity should be used to hedge the planned purchase of 100,000 lb of tin? Note that you must find out how many pounds of copper or ounces of silver underlie each futures contract.

7.7

a. Suppose that you wish to hedge the planned purchase of 20,000 bbl of crude oil. The purchase will take place five months hence. Interest rates are constant at 16%/year. You have estimated the following regression model:

$$\Delta S = 0.003 + 1.109\Delta F$$

where ΔS is the change in the price of the grade of oil that you will be purchasing, and ΔF is the change in the crude oil futures price. Tail your hedge. What is the risk-minimizing number of futures contracts you should trade to hedge your planned purchase? Will you buy or sell the futures?

b. Suppose that when you first instituted the hedge, $S = \$21.40$/bbl and $F = \$19.93$/bbl. During the next five

---

months, the futures price changes as follows:

t	Months Until Hedge Will Be Lifted	F
0	5	$19.93
1	4	$20.04
3	2	$20.95
4	1	$21.09
5	0	$22.35 = F_T$

Do not forget that you have tailed your hedge. What is your final profit or loss on the futures contracts? If $S_T = \$23.82/bbl$ on the hedge-lifting date, what is the final effective purchase price for the 20,000 bbl? In other words, consider both the actual price that you paid for the oil and the profit or loss on the futures contracts. Note that $S_T \neq F_T$ because the grade of oil that you are buying is not the same grade that underlies the futures contract.

c. What was the original basis for your grade of oil? What was the final basis? Suppose that $S_T = \$24.50/bbl$ (instead of the $23.82/bbl that you assumed in part **b**. Now what is the final, effective purchase price for the 20,000 bbl?

d. Discuss why your answers to parts **b** and **c** differed. Be sure to comment on the meaning of "basis risk."

7.8 Your firm plans on issuing 10,000 pure discount (no-coupon) notes with two years to maturity. Each note has a face value of $1000; that is, at maturity, it will be worth $1000. The current yield to maturity on two-year notes like these is 10%/year. You believe that if the Eurodollar futures yield changes by 10 basis points, the change in the required rate of return (yield to maturity) on the notes will be 7 basis points. The mark-to-market cash flow is $25/basis point for Eurodollar futures.

Use the principles of dollar equivalency to compute the proper number of Eurodollar futures contracts to trade in order to hedge the planned issuance of the notes. Will you buy or sell the futures contracts?

7.9 You are a gold producer, and your plans indicate that you will have 10,000 oz. of gold to sell one year from today. The current spot price is $300/oz. The one year interest rate is 12%.

a. Compute the theoretical futures price for delivery one year hence.

b. Suppose that the actual futures price equals the theoretical futures price that you calculated in part **a**. The gold you produce is of the quality that is deliverable into the futures contract. Regressing changes in the spot price of the gold you produce on futures price changes would give a slope coefficient of 1.0. If you did not tail your hedge, how many gold futures contracts would you trade? If you tailed your hedge, how many would you trade? Is this a long hedge or a short hedge?

c. Suppose you did not tail the hedge. You borrow to pay daily resettlement cash outflows, and lend daily resettlement cash inflows. One month after the hedge is put on, the spot price of gold rises to $350/oz. and the futures price rises to $392/oz. Then, during the remaining 11 months of the hedge, the futures price remains constant, and on the hedge-lifting date, $S_T = F_T = \$392/oz$. You sell your gold. After accounting for the impact of interest on the daily resettlement that occurred at $t = $ one month, what was your effective selling price of the gold? In other words, sell your gold, add/subtract futures profits/losses, and account for the interest expense and/or interest income.

d. Now, redo part **c** with the tailed hedge.

7.10   You own 100 oz. of gold. Its spot price today is \$300/oz. You wish to protect your investment against a decline in the price of gold. Therefore, do you buy or sell one gold futures contract? Today's gold futures price for delivery one month hence is \$310/oz. Are these prices an example of a normal or an inverted market? Compute the basis. On the delivery date, what will the basis be? Tomorrow, the gold futures price settles at \$304/oz. After marking to market, what is the value of the gold futures contract? Suppose that two weeks from today, you lift the hedge by offsetting the futures contract and selling the gold. On that date, the spot price of gold is \$285/oz. and the futures price is \$297/oz. Compute the total profit or loss on the hedged position, as we did in Table 7.3.

7.11   A mutual fund prospectus states that the managers use S&P 500 futures "for short-term cash management purposes,… to reallocate the fund's assets among stocks while minimizing transaction costs, maintain cash reserves while simulating full investment, facilitate trading, seek higher investment returns, or simulate full investment when a futures contract is priced more attractively or is otherwise considered more advantageous than the underlying securities." Discuss the benefits to which the prospectus is referring.

7.12   Explain why short hedgers are said to be "long the basis" while long hedgers are said to be "short the basis".

7.13   Explain what is meant by the following statement: Basis equals the net cost of carry.

7.14   Input the price change data shown in Table 7.2 into an Excel spreadsheet. Compute (verify) the mean, variance, and standard deviations of the two time series. Then use Excel's regression tool (tool/data analysis/regression) to regress the change in the spot price on the change in the futures price. Find the y-intercept and slope coefficient of the regression model.

CHAPTER 8

Stock Index Futures

Stock index futures contracts began trading on February 24, 1982, when the Kansas City Board of Trade introduced futures on the Value Line Index. About two months later, the Chicago Mercantile Exchange introduced futures contracts on the S&P 500 Index. By 1986, the S&P 500 futures contract had become the second most actively traded futures contract in the world, with over 19.5 million contracts traded in that year.[1] In May 1982, the NYSE Composite Index futures contract began trading on the New York Futures Exchange. In July 1984, the Chicago Board of Trade, frustrated because Dow Jones & Company went to court to block its attempts to trade futures on the Dow Jones Industrial Average (DJIA), finally gave up and began trading futures contracts on the Major Market Index (MMI). The MMI was very similar to the DJIA. Finally, in June 1997, Dow Jones agreed to allow DJIA options, futures, and options on futures to begin trading. On October 6, 1997, futures on the DJIA began trading on the Chicago Board of Trade.

In their short history of trading, stock index futures contracts have had a great impact on the world's equity markets. Trading in stock index futures has allegedly made the world's stock markets more volatile than ever before. Critics also claim that individual investors have been driven out of the equity markets because institutional traders' actions in both the spot and futures markets cause stock values to gyrate with no links to their fundamental values. Many political figures have called for greater regulation, going so far as to favor an outright ban on stock index futures trading. Fortunately, such extreme measures have been avoided. Stock index futures have become irreplaceable in our modern world of institutional money management. They have revolutionized the art and science of equity portfolio management as practiced by mutual funds, pension plans, endowments, insurance companies, and other money managers.

A futures contract on a stock market index represents the right and obligation to buy or sell a portfolio of stocks characterized by the index. Stock index futures are cash settled. Thus, there is no delivery of the underlying stocks. The contracts are marked to market daily, and the futures price is set equal to the spot index level on the last trading day, leaving one last mark-to-market cash flow.

Figure 6.5 showed only some of the wide range of stock index futures contracts that trade globally, including those on the U.S., Japanese, French, British, German, and Australian stock markets. The most actively traded contract is the S&P 500 futures contract, traded on the CME.

We begin this chapter with a discussion of how different indexes are computed.

8.1 WHAT IS AN INDEX?

An index is, in one sense, just a number that is computed to allow measurement of the value of a portfolio of stocks. Other indexes have been constructed to track the values of securities of other types, such as bonds and futures. Still other indexes track such economic indicators as the consumer price index (CPI) or the index of leading indicators. Note in Figure 6.5 that futures contracts trade on the GSCI (the Goldman Sachs Commodity Index, which is an index of commodity prices), and the U.S. Dollar Index (which is an average value of the dollar).

This section describes three different stock market indexes. When one is constructing a stock market index, three issues are of particular interest: which stocks are in the index, how each stock is weighted, and how the average is computed.

8.1.1   Price-Weighted Indexes: The Dow Jones Average

From 1982 through 1984, the CBOT tried unsuccessfully to trade futures contracts on the Dow Jones Industrial Average (DJIA).[2] As just mentioned, however, Dow, Jones & Company sued to block the efforts of the CBOT, and won in court. It was not until October 1997 that Dow Jones permitted futures trading on the DJIA, which is the most widely followed index by the investing public. The question "How is the market doing?" is usually assumed to refer to the DJIA. Other stock market indices that are computed in the same way as the DJIA, and which have futures and options trading on them include the Nikkei 225 stock index of Japanese stocks.

As of December 2001, the 30 stocks in the DJIA were those in Table 8.1. The DJIA stocks are large corporations. Fourteen of the companies were among the largest 39 companies in the world, according to August 15, 2000, market capitalizations.

The DJIA is computed by adding the prices of the 30 component stocks and dividing the sum by a divisor that is printed in the *Wall Street Journal* every day and is also available in the equity product information area of the CBOT website (www.cbot.com). For example, on April 24, 2001, the divisor for the DJIA was 0.15369402. On September 9, 1999, the divisor was 0.19740463. The divisor is changed when one of two events occurs. Periodically, one of the 30 stocks in the DJIA is removed and replaced by the stock of another company. This will happen when a component stock is taken over by another company or one of the corporations goes bankrupt. For example,

TABLE 8.1   The 30 Stocks in the Dow Jones Industrial Average as of December 2001

Alcoa	Honeywell
American Express	IBM
AT&T	Intel
Boeing	International Paper
Caterpillar	Johnson & Johnson
Citigroup	McDonald's
Coca Cola	Merck
Disney	Microsoft
DuPont	Minnesota Mining & Manufacturing (MMM)
Eastman Kodak	J.P. Morgan Chase
Exxon Mobil	Philip Morris
General Electric	Procter & Gamble
General Motors	SBC Communications
Hewlett Packard	United Technologies
Home Depot	Wal-Mart

Anaconda, long a component of the DJIA, was bought by Atlantic Richfield (ARCO) in 1976. Thus, a new component stock (MMM) was selected to replace Anaconda. At other times, it is decided that the composition of the index stocks is no longer representative of "the market," and Dow Jones deletes one or more stocks, and adds others. This occurred on November 1, 1999, when Home Depot, Intel, Microsoft, and SBC Communications replaced Chevron, Goodyear, Sears Roebuck, and Union Carbide.

The DJIA divisor is also adjusted to reflect stock splits and stock dividends. These events reduce stock prices; without some sort of adjustment in the method of computation, the DJIA would most likely drop sharply every time one of its component stocks split its shares.

The DJIA is called a "price-weighted" index because the impact of each component stock is proportional to its stock price. We now illustrate how a price-weighted average like the DJIA is computed, and how it adjusts for events that affect the divisor. Suppose there were only three stocks in the DJIA. On the first day, the divisor is 2.6, and the prices of the three stocks are:

Stock	Price (Day 1)
A	19 $5/8$
B	27
C	52 $1/2$

The DJIA would be computed to be $(19.625+27+52.5)/2.6=38.125$. At the close of trading on day 1, suppose company A goes bankrupt or is taken over by another firm. Dow Jones decides to replace it with company D, which closed at \$39/share. To maintain continuity of the index, the divisor is changed so that the sum of the three new prices, divided by the new divisor, equals 38.125. The value of the new divisor is found by solving the following equation for X: $(39+27+52.5)/X=38.125$. The new divisor would be $X=3.108197$.

Now, suppose the next day (day 2), the prices of the component stocks are:

Stock	Price (Day 2)
D	39 $1/8$
B	27 $1/2$
C	51 $1/4$

The DJIA would be computed to be $(39.125+27.5+51.25)/3.108197=37.924$. The following day (day 3), suppose stock C splits 3 for 2, and the three component stocks close as follows:

Stock	Price (Day 3)
D	40
B	28 $1/8$
C	34 $1/2$

The index value must be preserved against the effects of the split, and this is accomplished by changing the divisor. Stock C's postsplit price equivalent to the presplit price of \$51.25 is $(51.25/1.5=)$ 34.1667. Thus, the new divisor would become the value of X in the equation $(39.125+27.5+34.16667)/X=37.924$. The new divisor is $X=2.65773$. Stock C's closing price on day 2 has been adjusted to reflect the 3-for-2 split, and then a new divisor is calculated to preserve day 2's index value of 37.924. Now, the DJIA on the ex-split day (day 3) can be computed to be $(40+28.125+34.5)/2.65773=38.614$.

The DJIA is not adjusted to account for regular dividend payments. On some days several component stocks of the DJIA trade ex-dividend. Because each stock will open lower by about the dividend amount, the DJIA will open lower by an amount approximately equal to the sum of the dividends per share divided by the divisor.

To construct a portfolio that is equivalent to the DJIA, an investor must buy an equal number of shares of each of the component stocks. Maintaining the proper underlying portfolio is complicated by the payment of cash dividends and stock distributions. Still, the DJIA is an easy index to replicate, since it has only 30 stocks, each of which is very actively traded.

Because of the weighting and averaging scheme, high-priced stocks carry more weight than low-priced stocks in affecting the movements of price-weighted indexes. If a stock selling for $100/share increases in value by 5%, then the DJIA will increase by 5/divisor points. If a stock selling for $20/share rises in price by 5%, then the DJIA will rise by only 1/divisor point. In other words, any percentage change in price by a high-priced stock will have a greater impact than the same percentage change in price for a low-priced stock.

Futures on the DJIA trade on the Chicago Board of Trade. As shown in Figure 6.5, the value of stock underlying one DJIA futures contract equals $10 times the futures price. One tick is one Dow-point, and this equals $10. Thus, if the DJIA futures price rises one tick, from 10813 to 10814, a trader who is long one contract profits by $10 because the value of the stock underlying the contract rises from $108,130 to $108,140.

8.1.2   Value-Weighted Averages: The S&P 500 Stock Index

Many stock market indexes are value-weighted averages. Most academics would likely argue that a value-weighted index is the best measure for market performance. In the capital asset pricing model (CAPM), a stock's correlation with the market portfolio is the factor that determines its price, and that market portfolio is value weighted.

Besides the NYSE and S&P Indexes, other value-weighted indexes include the Amex Market Value Index, the NASDAQ Composite Index, the Russell 2000 Index, and the Wilshire 5000. The levels of these and yet other indexes are presented daily in the *Wall Street Journal*. While each index is a different portfolio of stocks, the method of computing each index is the same.

To compute the level of a value-weighted index, first find the market value of each of the component stocks on a base day, day 0. The market value of stock i, MV_i, is computed by multiplying the price of stock i, P_i, by the number of shares outstanding of stock i, N_i.

$$\beta_d = w_1 b_1 + w_2 b_2$$

Next, find the total market value of all of the component stocks of the index. That is, sum the market values of all of the component stocks on day 0.

$$MV_0 = MV_{0,1} + MV_{0,2} + MV_{0,3} + \cdots + MV_{0,n}$$

$$MV_0 = \sum_{j=1}^{n} MV_{0,j}$$

Once the total market value of all the n component stocks on day 0 has been found, divide that total market value by an arbitrary divisor to set the initial index value. Call that value I_0. Then, to find the index value on any subsequent day, day t, find the ratio of market values on days t and $t-1$, and multiply the ratio by the earlier day's index value, I_{t-1}.

$$I_t = \frac{MV_t}{MV_{t-1}} \times I_{t-1}$$

EXAMPLE 8.1   Consider the following data on prices and shares outstanding for the four component stocks of an index:

Stock	Shares Outstanding	P_0	P_1	P_2
A	1000	50	52	49
B	1000	10	10	11
C	100	60	60	63
D	100	10	11	12

On the base day, day 0, the total market value of the four component stocks is:

$$MV_0 = (50)(1000) + (10)(1000) + (60)(100) + (10)(100) = 67,000$$

The index developer decides that 100 ought to be the initial index level, so the divisor is set at 670. To compute the index level on day 1, first find and sum the market values of the component stocks:

$$MV_1 = (52)(1000) + (10)(1000) + (60)(100) + (11)(100) = 69100$$

Then multiply the ratio of the two days' total market values by day 0's index value:

$$I_1 = \frac{MV_1}{MV_{01}} \times I_0 = \frac{69,100}{67,000} \times 100 = 103.134$$

The index level on day 2 is found in one of two ways:

$$I_2 = \frac{MV_2}{MV_0} \times I_0 = \frac{67,500}{67,000} \times 100 \quad \text{or} \quad \frac{MV_2}{MV_1} \times I_1 = \frac{67,500}{69,100} \times 103.134 = 100.746$$

Note that even though three of the component stocks rose in price on day 2, the market value index fell. This is because stock A is the largest stock, in terms of market value. Changes in the value of stock A carry the most weight in computing changes in the index level.

As of December 19, 2001, the four largest U.S. firms, as measured by the market values of their equity, were (1) General Electric (GE; market value = $394.3 billion), (2) Microsoft (MSFT; market value = $373.1 billion) (3) Exxon Mobil Corp (Xom; market value = $256.9 billion), and (4) Pfizer (PFE; market value = $255.5 billion). All these stocks are in the S&P 500 and S&P 100 Indexes. Together, just these four stocks made up about 12% of the market value of all of the S&P 500 listed stocks. A 1% change in the price of GE would have a 10 times higher impact on a value-weighted index than a 1% change in the value of DaimlerChrysler, which had a market value of $41.2 billion on December 19, 2001. Some investors attempt (risky) arbitrage by trading portfolios of only 20 to 50 stocks and S&P derivatives. The reasoning is that just 50 stocks might make up 50% of the index and that the correlation of the 50-stock portfolio will therefore correlate very highly with the underlying stock index. However, these investors are bearing a form of basis risk when they rely on such a strategy. The total market value of the component stocks of the S&P 500 together represent about 70% of the market value of all U.S. equities.

Stock splits and stock dividends, in principle, do not affect the market values of companies. Thus, there are no adjustments needed to the method of computing a value-weighted index when one of the component stocks has a stock distribution. Like the DJIA, the computation of these value-weighted indexes is not affected by the payment of regular cash dividends. An investor who replicated a portfolio characterized by a value-weighted index would profit by the percentage change in the index (capital gains) and also by dividends paid. However, dividends would not show up in the index value.

Adjustments occur when the "owner" of the index removes companies from the portfolio, either for arbitrary reasons or because of mergers or bankruptcies. For example, Standard & Poor's periodically revises the stocks that make up the S&P 100 and S&P 500 Indexes to make these listings more representative of the market. Also, when firms make changes in their equity capitalization by issuing or repurchasing stock, adjustments are made.[3]

To form a portfolio of stocks that would replicate a market-value-weighted index, an investor must purchase $x\%$ of the market value of each component stock, where x is some arbitrary constant. For example, one could buy 0.3% of each of stocks A, B, C, and D in Example 8.1. Given their initial market values of $50,000, $10,000, $6000, and $1000, respectively, the investor would invest $150 in stock A, $30 in stock B, $18 in stock C, and $3 in stock D.

Many futures trade on value-weighted indexes. Trading on the CME alone are the S&P 500 futures (the underlying stock is $250 times the index), mini-S&P 500 futures (the underlying stock is only $50 times the index), as well as contracts on the S&P Midcap 400, NASDAQ 100, Russell 2000 indexes, and others. The Midcap 400 is an index of 400 middle-sized firms, while the NASDAQ 100 tracks the performance of the over-the-counter stock market in the United States. The Russell 2000 index is usually used to measure the performance of the asset class known as small cap stocks. The broadest value-weighted index is the Wilshire 5000 index. It consists of every NYSE- and Amex-listed stock, and all actively traded OTC stocks. However, neither options nor futures trade on the Wilshire 5000 index. At times, investors believe that it may be more profitable to concentrate a portfolio in either growth or value stocks. Standard & Poor's Corporation and BARRA, Inc., jointly formed the S&P 500/BARRA Growth and Value Indexes. Each company in the S&P 500 Index is assigned either to the Growth or the Value Index. The indices are designed with about 50% of the S&P 500 capitalization in the Value Index and 50% in the Growth Index.[4]

S&P 500 stock index futures contracts are perhaps the most actively traded stock index futures in the world. The last trading day for this contract is the Thursday before the third Friday of the delivery month, and there are four delivery months, March, June, September, and December. The smallest price change is 0.10 point,[5] which equals $25. Thus, if the S&P 500 futures price falls from 1419.40 to 1419.30, the value of the stock underlying the contract declines from $(1419.40 \times 250 =)$ $354,850 to $(1419.30 \times 250 =)$ $354,825. This one-tick change in the futures price creates a mark to market profit of $25 for an individual who is short one contract.[6]

8.1.3 The Value Line Index

Futures contracts on the Value Line Index trade on the Kansas City Board of Trade. The Value Line Index is an equal-weighted arithmetic average.[7] To compute it, pick any arbitrary index value on the base date, day 0. The index value on any subsequent day, day t, is then:

$$I_t = I_{t-1} \frac{(P_{1,t}/P_{1,t-1}) + (P_{2,t}/P_{2,t-1}) + (P_{3,t}/P_{3,t-1}) + \cdots + (P_{n,t}/P_{n,t-1})}{n}$$

In other words, the index value on day t is the arithmetic average of the price relatives of the n stock, times the preceding day's index value. There are about 1700 stocks in the Value Line Index. They are the stocks followed by the Value Line Investment Service, and include several AMEX and OTC stocks, and even some stocks that trade on Canadian and regional stock exchanges.

To illustrate the calculation of an index like the Value Line Index, consider the data from Example 8.1 of this chapter:

Stock	P_0	P_1	P_2
A	50	52	49
B	10	10	11
C	60	60	63
D	10	11	12

The initial index value on day 0 is arbitrarily set at 50. On day 1, the index is

$$I_1 = \frac{50(52/50 + 10/10 + 60/60 + 11/10)}{4} = \frac{50(4.14)}{4} = 51.75$$

On day 2, the index value is:

$$I_2 = \frac{51.75(49/52 + 11/10 + 63/60 + 12/11)}{4} = \frac{51.75(4.1832)}{4} = 54.1204$$

To replicate an equally weighted arithmetically averaged index like the Value Line, invest an equal number of dollars in each of the component stocks.

EXAMPLE 8.2 The accompanying table gives a 4-day time series for each of three stocks. Compute the index values if they were patterned after (1) a price-weighted arithmetic index (such as the DJIA), (2) a value-weighted arithmetic index (such as the S&P 500), and (3) an equal-weighted arithmetic average (such as the Value Line Index). You can compute the necessary divisors from the index values on day zero. How many shares of each stock would you purchase to replicate each index?

Day	A	B	C	1	2	3
	Stocks			Indexes		
0	10	50	100	10	10	10
1	11	52	99			
2	12	55	95			
3	15	54	98			
4	10	50	95			
Shares outstanding	1000	20	100			

The solution to this problem is as follows. As can be seen from the resulting index values, the method by which an index is created can lead to different pictures of to how the market is performing.

	Stocks			Indexes		
Day	A	B	C	1	2	3
1	11	52	99	10.125	10.4476	10.4333
2	12	55	95	10.125	10.7619	10.8096
3	15	54	98	10.4375	12.3238	11.7586
4	10	50	95	9.6875	9.7619	10.0418

- **DJIA (index 1)**: On day 0, the sum of the prices ΣP_i is 160. The index value is 10, so the divisor is 16. On each subsequent day, add the prices and divide by 16.

- **S&P Indexes (index 2)**: On day 0 the sum of the market values is $(10{,}000 + 1000 + 10{,}000 =)$ 21,000. The index on day 0 is 10, so the divisor is 210. On each subsequent day, multiply:

$$\frac{MV_t}{MV_0} \times I_0$$

That is, divide the market value of all stocks on day t by the market value on day 0 and multiply by the day 0 index value of 10.

- **Value Line Index (index 3)**: Set the day 0 index value to 10. On each subsequent day, find the arithmetic mean of the price relatives and multiply it by the previous day's index. So, on day 1:

$$\frac{11/10 + 52/50 + 99/100}{3} \times 10 = \frac{3.13}{3} \times 10 = 10.4333$$

To replicate the rates of return on index 1, one would purchase an equal number of shares of each of the component stocks. For example, on day 0, buy one share each of stock A, B, and C. This will cost $160. On day 1, the value of the portfolio is $162. The rate of return is $(162 - 160)/160 = 1.25\%$, which equals the rate of return on the index $[(10.125 - 10)/10 = 1.25\%]$.

To replicate index 2, one would invest an amount in each stock that is proportional to its market value. For example on day 0, the market values of stocks A, B, and C are $10,000, $1000, and $10,000, respectively. The total market value is $21,000. Proportionally, the market values of A, B, and C are 0.4761905 $(= 10{,}000/21{,}000)$, 0.047619 $(= 1000/21{,}000)$, and 0.4761905, respectively. If you had $100 to invest, you would invest $47.61905 in stocks A and C, and $4.7619 in stock B. Therefore, on day 0, purchase 4.761905 shares of stock A at $10/share, 0.095238 share of stock B at $50/share, and 0.4761905 share of stock C at $100/share.

To replicate index 3, one would invest the same dollar amount in each of the three stocks. If you had $99 to invest, you would invest $33 in each stock. This means that you would buy 3.333 shares of stock A, 0.66 shares of stock B, and 0.33 shares of stock C.

Note that index 3, the equally weighted arithmetically averaged index (i.e., the Value Line) is the most costly to replicate because every day the dollar amounts invested in each stock must be readjusted so that they are again equal. No such rebalancing is necessary for the other two indexes.

8.2 PRICING STOCK INDEX FUTURES

The fundamental futures and forwards pricing equation, from Chapter 5, is the cost-of-carry model:

$$F = S + CC - CR \qquad (8.1)$$

$$\text{futures price} = \text{spot price} + \text{carry costs} - \text{carry return}$$

For stock index futures contracts, the spot price is the spot index value.[8] The carry cost represents the interest on the value of the stock underlying the cash portfolio; it equals the interest borrowing cost when one is performing cash-and-carry arbitrage and the interest earned on lending the proceeds from selling of stock in the case of reverse cash-and-carry arbitrage. The carry return is found by calculating the future value of the dividends received between today and the delivery date, if the portfolio of stocks underlying the index is owned. In other words, the dividends received are invested to earn interest, from the day they are received until the delivery date.[9] Summarizing, we write

$$F = S + S[h(0,T)] - \Sigma[FV(\text{divs})] \qquad (8.2)$$

where $h(0,T) = rT/365$, where r is the annual interest rate, T is the number of days until the delivery date, and $\Sigma(FV(\text{divs}))$ is the future value of all dividends paid by the component stocks of the index.

Proof

Suppose: $F_0 > S_0 + S_0[h(0,T)] - \Sigma[FV(\text{divs})]$

Then, $F_0 - S_0 - S_0[h(0,T)] + \Sigma[FV(\text{divs})] > 0$

Or: $F_0 - S_0[1 + h(0,T)] + \Sigma[FV(\text{divs})] > 0$

Today

Buy the component stocks of the index in the appropriate weights, so that the index is replicated	$-S_0$
Borrow the foregoing amount for the number of days until the delivery date, at an annual interest rate of $r\%$, which is $h\%$ unannualized	$+S_0$
Sell one futures contract at its current futures price of F_0 (no cash flow results; use a bank letter of credit, or securities, to meet initial margin requirements)	0
Total cash flow	0

On the first ex-dividend date of one or more stocks, t_1

Receive dividends	$+$divs
Lend dividends[10] from t_1 to T	$-$divs
Total cash flow	0

On subsequent ex-dividend dates of component stocks (i.e., on days $t_2, t_3, \ldots, T$)

Receive dividends	$+$ divs
Lend dividends from $t_2, t_3, \ldots, T$ until time T	$-$ divs
Total cash flow	0

On the delivery date

Buy (offset) the futures contract at F_T	$+F_0 - F_T = +F_0 - S_T$
Sell the stocks	$+S_T$
Repay loan and interest	$-S_0 - h(0, T)S_0$
Receive dividends, and interest on	
those dividends	$+\Sigma FV(\text{divs}) = +\text{divs}_{t1}[1 + h(t1, T)]$
	$+\text{divs}_{t2}[1 + h(t2, T)] \cdots + \cdots$
	$+\text{divs}_{T-1}[1 + h(T-1, T)] + \text{divs}_T$
Total cash flow	$+F_0 - S_0 - h(0, T)S_0 + \Sigma FV(\text{divs}) > 0$

Therefore, if market participants observe situations in which $F_0 - S_0[1 + h(0, T)] + \Sigma(FV(\text{divs})) > 0$, they will engage in a cash-and-carry arbitrage. The futures price is "overpriced" in terms of the spot index. Therefore, the cash-and-carry arbitrage calls for buying the spot index (it is relatively cheap), "carrying" it, and selling the futures (it is relatively expensive).

Proof of the other inequality [that arbitrage opportunities exist if $+F_0 - S_0 - h(0, T)S_0 + \Sigma FV(\text{divs}) < 0$] was essentially presented in Chapter 5. You should recall that the set of reverse cash-and-carry trades requires selling stocks, lending the proceeds, and buying futures. To sell stocks requires either selling stock short (in which case we have "pure arbitrage"), or selling stocks already owned (in which case we have "quasi-arbitrage"). In either case, we assume that the arbitrageur will receive full use of the proceeds from the short sale and will not have to post any margin.

If market participants observe situations where $F_0 - S_0(1 + h(0, T)) + \Sigma(FV(\text{divs})) < 0$, they will engage in a reverse cash-and-carry arbitrage. When this occurs, we say that "selling programs have hit the market," and stock prices will almost surely decline. The futures price is "underpriced" in terms of the spot index. Therefore, the reverse cash-and-carry arbitrage calls for buying the futures (it is relatively cheap), selling the spot (it is relatively expensive), and investing the proceeds.

8.2.1 An Illustration of Stock Index Futures Pricing

EXAMPLE 8.3 Consider the D&M3, a value-weighted index of three stocks. Today, at time 0, their prices, shares outstanding, and market values are:

Stock	Price	Shares Outstanding	Market Value
1. Danish Wine Imports	$40	0.25 million	$10 million
2. Maxfu Enterprises, Inc.	$30	0.667 million	$20 million
3. Miss Molly.com	$25	2 million	$50 million

In terms of these market values, the composition of the D&M3 index is $1/8$ of stock 1, $1/4$ of stock 2, and $5/8$ of stock 3.

Suppose the spot index is 1350 and the multiplier of the index is 250. Therefore, there is $337,500 worth of stock underlying the spot index (1350×250). Of this total, $1/8$, or $42,187.5, is stock 1. Stock 2 contributes $1/4$ of the value of the portfolio, $84,375. Finally, $5/8$ of $337,500 is $210,937.50, and this is the value of stock 3 in the aggregate index. Given these values, we can compute the number of shares of each stock that must be bought to replicate the D&M3 index:

Stock	Dollar Value of Stock in 250 Shares of the D&M3	Number of Shares Needed to Replicate 250 Shares of the Index
1	42,187.50	42,187.50/40 = 1,054.6875
2	84,375.00	84,375.00/30 = 2812.50
3	210,937.50	210,937.50/25 = 8437.50

In addition, suppose stock 1 will trade ex-dividend in the amount of $0.80/share 14 days from today. Stock 2 will trade ex-dividend in the amount of $0.50/share 55 days from today. Stock 3 pays no dividends. For simplicity, assume that the dividends will be paid on the ex-dates. The riskless interest rate is 5% per year, and will remain there for all maturities at all dates. Given this information, let us find the theoretical futures price if the futures contact expires in 76 days.

Solution

$$h(0,76) = \frac{rT}{365} = \frac{(0.05)(76)}{365} = 0.01041 = 1.041\%$$

The dividend on stock 1 is received 14 days hence and can be invested for 62 days: $h(14,76) = (0.05)(62)/365 = 0.008493$. The dividend on stock 1 will earn an unannualized interest rate of 0.8493% over 62 days. Similarly, the dividend from stock 2 can be invested for 21 days, at an unannualized rate of $h(55,76) = (0.05)(21)/365 = 0.00288$.

Ignoring transactions costs, the theoretical futures price, per share, for the D&M3 futures contract is:

$$F = [(1350)(250) + (1350)(250)(0.01041)$$
$$-[(1054.6875)(0.80)(1.008493) + (2812.5)(0.50)(1.00288)]]/250$$

$$F = 1355.01$$

If the observed futures price exceeds 1355.01, then arbitrageurs will perform the cash-and-carry arbitrage. They will borrow money to buy the relatively cheap stocks in the D&M3 index and sell the relatively expensive futures contract. If the observed futures price is less than 1355.01, arbitrageurs will reverse these trades. That is, they will sell the stock, invest the proceeds, and buy the futures contract.

8.2.2 Synthetic Stock and Synthetic Treasury Bills

Buying a stock index futures contract and buying Treasury bills (lending) is frequently called a *long synthetic stock position*. If the observed futures price is lower than its theoretical price, an institution will buy stock synthetically by going long stock index futures and buying riskless debt instruments. This will be cheaper than actually buying the shares of stock that make up the index.[11]

Consider an investor who owns $9,523,800 in one-year Treasury bills. The Treasury bills will be worth $10 million one year hence. Suppose the investor has just revised his beliefs about the stock market and wishes to switch his investment into stocks.

He can liquidate his investment in Treasury bills by selling them at the bid price and paying commissions. Then, assuming that he knows which shares of stock he will purchase, he can use the proceeds to buy shares at their asked prices and pay additional commissions.

Since he already owns the Treasury bills, the investor has the opportunity to buy synthetic stock instead. By taking a long position in stock index futures with an underlying value equal to $9,523,800 (based on the spot index), the synthetic stock position is established. Suppose that the S&P 500 futures price is 1375, the spot S&P 500 Index is at 1325, and the futures contract multiplier is 250. Then, 28.7511 futures contracts should be bought [$9,523,800/(1325)(250)]. The total transactions costs are the round-trip commissions on the 28.7511 contracts (which will be bought at the ask price in the pit). These transactions costs will be considerably less than those that would have been incurred by liquidating the Treasury bills and buying shares of stock in many different companies.

Now, suppose that one year hence $S_T = F_T = 1500$. The value of the investor's portfolio is derived from (a) $10 million in maturing Treasury bills and (b) $898,472 in stock index futures profits (125 point gain per contract times $250 profit per point times 28.7511 contracts). Therefore, the total value of the synthetic stock portfolio of long Treasury bills and long stock index futures contracts is $10,898,472. This is a 14.434% gain, given that the investor began the year with $9,523,800.

The 14.434% gain is identical to the return from buying the actual stocks, ignoring transactions costs, and assuming that the initial futures price was theoretically correct. The capital appreciation return on the stocks was 13.208% [(1500−1325)/1325]. However, had the trader purchased stocks, he would have received dividends and interest on those dividends, and this dividend yield component would have been 1.2264%.[12] Thus, the total return is 14.434% (13.208% + 1.2264%). The investor should decide whether to buy actual stock or synthetic stock on the basis of relative transactions costs, ease of execution, and whether the futures price is above or below its theoretical value.

Buying shares of stock that replicate an index and also selling a futures contract on that stock portfolio creates a *synthetic Treasury bill*. The arbitrageur buys the stock and locks in a selling price (ignoring the effects of daily resettlement) by selling a futures contract. Thus, it is effectively a riskless lending transaction, just like the purchase of spot Treasury bills. When performing a cash-and-carry arbitrage, one sells spot Treasury bills (borrows) and buys higher yielding synthetic Treasury bills (lends). The synthetic T-bill is created by buying the spot asset and selling futures contracts on that asset. Note that when observed futures prices are higher than the theoretical futures price, an opportunity exists for arbitrageurs to borrow at a rate lower than the synthetic lending rate. Put yet another way, arbitrageurs buy synthetic T-bills when the implied repo rate exceeds their borrowing rate.

8.2.3   Transactions Costs: Commissions and Bid–Ask Spreads

The existence of transactions costs creates bounds within which stock index futures prices can lie without any arbitrage opportunities:

$$\text{lowest theoretical value} \leq \text{actual futures price } (F) \leq \text{highest theoretical value} \qquad (8.3)$$

If the actual futures price is below the lowest theoretical value, traders will engage in reverse cash-and-carry arbitrage. That is, arbitrageurs will go long the cheap futures contract at its price of F and sell stocks at their *bid* prices. The proceeds would be lent at the appropriate riskless *lending rate*, h_{lend}, which will be less than any available borrowing rates. Because stock is sold short, the arbitrageur must borrow to pay the dividends to the owners of the shares. The borrowing to finance dividends would be done at the arbitrageur's *borrowing rate*. Commissions would also have to be paid. Thus, reverse cash and carry arbitrage establishes the left-hand side of Equation (8.3), which now becomes:

$$S(\text{bid})(1 + h_{\text{lend}}(0, T)) - \sum_{\tau=1}^{T} \text{div}_\tau [1 + h_{\text{borrow}}(\tau, T)] - TC1 \leq F_{\text{obs}} \leq \text{highest theoretical value} \quad (8.4)$$

In this formulation, the future values of all dividends on days after day 0 have been summed and $\tau = 1$ represents tomorrow; $\text{div}_\tau = \text{div}_1$ represents the dividends paid by stocks trading ex-dividend tomorrow, and paying the dividend tomorrow. When $\tau = 2$, div_2 equals the dividend amount of all stocks that trade ex-dividend two days from today. Then $h_{\text{borrow}}(\tau, T) = h_{\text{borrow}}(1, T)$ is the arbitrageur's unannualized borrowing rate from tomorrow ($\tau = 1$) until delivery at time T. When $\tau = 2$, $h_{\text{borrow}}(2, T)$ is the unannualized borrowing rate beginning two days hence ($t = 2$) until time T. The summation performs the same operation on all days $\tau = 1, 2, 3, \ldots, T-1, T$, from tomorrow until the delivery date. Note that the arbitrageur earns no interest on dividends paid on the delivery date itself; that is, $h(T, T) = 0.0$. The term $TC1$ represents all other transactions costs, including commissions for trading stocks and futures contracts, and, in particular, costs that might exist when selling stock short (if pure arbitrage was attempted). Note that $TC1$ is *subtracted* on the left-hand side of the equation, to decrease the lowest possible observed futures price that can exist without allowing any arbitrage opportunities.

If F is above the highest theoretical value, then arbitrageurs will engage in cash and carry arbitrage by selling the overvalued futures contract and buying cheap stock at the *asked* prices. The borrowing to buy the stock would be done at an unannualized interest rate of $h_{\text{borrow}}(0, T)$. All dividends received on day τ would be lent until delivery at the rate $h_{\text{lend}}(\tau, T)$. Commissions and any other transactions costs are denoted $TC2$, and these costs are *added* to the right-hand side of the inequality, to raise the highest possible value of the observed futures price that still precludes arbitrage. Therefore, Equation (8.5) describes the bounds for the theoretical futures price.

$$S(\text{bid})(1 + h_{\text{lend}}(0, T)) - \sum_{\tau=1}^{T} \text{div}_\tau [1 + h_{\text{borrow}}(\tau, T)] - TC1 \leq F_{\text{obs}}$$

$$\leq S(\text{ask})[1 + h_{\text{borrow}}(0, T)] - \sum_{\tau=1}^{T} \text{div}_\tau [1 + h_{\text{lend}}(\tau, T)] + TC2 \qquad (8.5)$$

EXAMPLE 8.4   Consider the information from Example 8.3. Assume that the arbitrageur's borrowing rate is 6.125% per year, and the lending rate is 5.875%/year. Assume that the bid–asked quotes of the stocks are as follows:

Stock	Bid Price	Ask Price
1. Danish Wine Imports	$39.875	$40.125
2. Maxfu Enterprises, Inc.	$29.875	$30.00
3. Miss Molly.com	$25.00	$25.25

Assume that the total transactions costs ($TC1$ and $TC2$) are 0.18% of the value of stock traded plus $12. These costs represent the brokerage commissions needed to trade the stocks and the round-trip futures commission.

Therefore, the number of shares of each stock that must be bought to replicate a long position in the index differs from the number of shares that must be sold to replicate short position:

Stock	Dollar Value of Stock in 250 Shares of the D&M3[13]	Number of Shares Needed to Replicate a Position in 500 Shares of the Index	
		Long	Short
1	$42,187.50	$42,187.50/40.125 = 1051.402	$42,187.50/39.875 = 1057.99
2	$84,375.00	$84,375.00/30 = 2812.500	$84,375.00/29.875 = 2824.268
3	$210,937.50	$210,937.50/25.25 = 8353.96	$210,937.50/25 = 8437.5

The left-hand side of the inequality in Equation (8.5) is the reverse cash-and-carry arbitrage (sell stocks short and lend proceeds). This creates the lower bound for futures prices. Recall that the spot index level is 1350 and the multiplier of the index is 250. Further, recall stock 1 will trade ex-dividend in the amount of $0.80/share 14 days from today and stock 2 will trade ex-dividend in the amount of $0.50/share 55 days from today. Thus, we have for the left-hand side of Equation (8.5):

$$\frac{1}{250}\left\{337{,}500\left[1+\frac{(0.05875)(76)}{365}\right]-\left\{(1057.99)(0.80)\left[1+\frac{(0.06125)(62)}{365}\right]\right.\right.$$

$$+(2824.268)(0.50)\left[1+\frac{(0.06125)(21)}{365}\right]\right\}-[12+(0.0018)(337{,}500)]\right\}$$

$$=\frac{1}{250}\left\{(337{,}500)(1.01223)-[(1057.99)(0.80)(1.01040)\right.$$

$$\left.+(2824.268)(0.50)(1.00352)]-619.50\right\}$$

$$=1354.947=\text{lowest theoretical futures price}$$

The right-hand side of the inequality in Equation (8.5) is created by the cash-and-carry trades. Here, the arbitrageur borrows to buy stock. We have:

$$\frac{1}{250}\left\{337,500\left[1+\frac{(0.06125)(76)}{365}\right]-\left\{(1051.402)(0.80)\left[1+\frac{(0.05875)(62)}{365}\right]\right.\right.$$

$$\left.\left.+(2812.5)(0.50)\left[1+\frac{(0.05875)(21)}{365}\right]\right\}+\left[12+(0.0018)(337,500)\right]\right\}$$

$$=\frac{1}{250}\left\{(337,500)(1.01275)-\left[(1051.402)(0.80)(1.00998)\right.\right.$$

$$\left.\left.+(2812.5)(0.50)(1.00338)\right]+619.50\right\}$$

$$=1360.65=\text{highest theoretical futures price}$$

In sum, the range of futures prices that would preclude arbitrage opportunities is

$$1354.947 < F_{\text{obs}} < 1360.65$$

8.2.4 More on Dividends

This section provides more details on computing the carry return and the future value of dividends, and also discusses the influence of "lumpy dividends" on stock index futures pricing.

The theoretical futures price just derived assumes that the dividend amounts, ex-dividend dates, and payment dates of the component stocks are known. In reality, this knowledge is available only when the delivery date is near, perhaps only a few weeks in the future. For more distant delivery dates, dividend risk increases. Dividends may be unexpectedly increased, reduced, or eliminated altogether, and the ex-dividend dates and payment dates are unknown. When one is using Equation (8.5) to derive the theoretical bounds on stock index futures prices, the future value of dividends are subtracted. Therefore, the smallest future value of the minimum possible dividends should be used on the right-hand side of the inequality to allow computation of the highest possible futures price. The greatest future value of the maximum possible dividends should be subtracted on the left-hand side of the inequality in Equation (8.5) when one is computing the lowest futures price that does not permit arbitrage.

The theoretical futures price is affected by any stock's expected ex-dividend date between tomorrow and the delivery date. The dividend of a stock trading ex-dividend today is unimportant for determining today's futures price because purchasing the stock today does not entitle the buyer to receive that dividend.

On average, dividend payment dates are 25.7 calendar days after the ex-date.[14] The future value of dividends should include interest earned on the dividend from the actual date that the dividend payment is made, until the delivery date. In some cases, the payment date will occur *after* the delivery date of the futures contract, in which case the dividend amount should be discounted from the payment date to the delivery date.

The most serious errors involving dividends arise when there are unexpected dividend omissions and uncertain ex-dividend dates close to the delivery date. Unexpected dividend *increases* are usually small in amount, hence will have only a small impact on the theoretical futures price. The error caused by incorrectly estimating the payment date by a few days will also have only a small effect. However, if a corporation unexpectedly accelerates its ex-div date from one that was expected after the delivery date to one that is before the futures delivery date, there could be a rather substantial effect on the theoretical futures price. The same can be said for a firm that unexpectedly delays its next ex-div date from one that is expected before the delivery date to one that comes after the delivery date. The impact of these errors on the theoretical futures price increases with dividend amounts and increases with the market value of the firm (for value-weighted indexes).

One last important dividend effect must be noted. Stock index futures can sell at a discount to the spot index, even though the annual dividend yield on the index is less than the annual interest rate. This will occur because dividend payments on the component stocks in the index often cluster around certain dates. Rather than existing as a continuous flow, like interest, dividends are "lumpy." If many stocks are going to trade ex-dividend between today and the contract's delivery date, then the periodic dividend yield may exceed the periodic interest rate.

EXAMPLE 8.5 Consider a stock index futures contract on one stock. The current stock price (spot index value) is 100. The delivery date is five days hence. The stock pays dividends quarterly and its annual dividend yield is 2%. The stock will trade ex-dividend, and pay its dividend, two days from today. The annual interest rate is 6%. Compute today's theoretical futures price.

Solution Because the annual dividend yield is 2%, the stock pays a quarterly dividend of \$0.50. Thus, the theoretical futures price equals

$$F = S + CC - CR$$

$$F = 100 + (100)(0.06)(5/365) - [0.50(1 + (0.06)(3/365)] = 99.58$$

This futures price is at a discount to the spot index value of 100. The reason for this is that the dollar dividend amount (the carry return) exceeds the dollar interest amount (the carry cost) during the ensuing five-day period. The concentration of dividend payments in such a short period will cause the stock index futures price to be less than the spot index value.

The theoretical and actual stock index futures price will lie below the spot index value when the future value of dividends prior to delivery exceeds the financing costs. It is not unusual for this to happen at times. Figure 8.1, which illustrates this phenomenon, presents the Dow Jones Industrial Average nearby futures' theoretical and actual basis from October 6, 1997 through September 14, 1999. In Figure 8.1 the continuous line, the theoretical basis (defined as futures minus cash), drops below zero near the expiration of the March 1998 futures contract (DJH8). Further, the actual basis, represented by the dotted curve, was negative on occasion during this period.

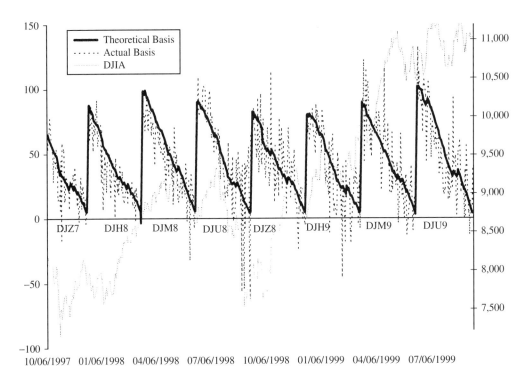

Figure 8.1 CBOT DJIA Nearby futures (dotted curve): theoretical (solid curve), vs actual basis (dashed curve), October 6, 1997–September 14, 1999. *Note*: DJZ7 refers to the December 1997 Dow Jones futures contract. H, M, U, and Z are the symbol codes for the March, June, September and December delivery months, respectively.

8.2.5 Program Trading

Since about 1987, the stock market has rarely made a major move up or down on a given day without stock market analysts attributing the move to "buy programs" or "sell programs."

Program trading is a technique for trading a stock portfolio in one single order. The NYSE defines a program trade as "a wide range of portfolio trading strategies involving the purchase or sale of a basket of 15 stocks or more, and valued at more than $1 million." Program trading may involve stock index arbitrage, option replication strategies, or asset allocation shifts (such as between equities and bonds).[15] Recent growth in program trading has arisen from brokers who offer institutions the ability to trade large portfolios of stocks with low cost and little price impact. In 1999 program trading accounted for approximately 20% of total NYSE volume.

Stock index arbitrage is the exploitation of futures mispricing relative to the stocks' spot values. When futures prices lie outside their no-arbitrage bounds, arbitrageurs will quickly act to realize the (near) riskless profits by buying cheap stock and selling futures, or buying cheap futures and selling stock. Between October 30, 2000, and January 19, 2001, weekly stock index arbitrage as a percentage of total program trading ranged between 6.4 and 18.6%, with an average of 9.4%.

In 1976 the New York Stock Exchange introduced its Designated Order Turnaround (DOT) system, which was improved and renamed SuperDOT in November 1984. SuperDOT is a computerized order-handling system that guarantees that any market order of less than 2100 shares of a stock will be executed within 3 minutes at the prevailing bid price (for a market sell order) or asked price (for a market buy order) at the time the order was entered, or at better prices if possible. Today, the average order through SuperDOT is transmitted, executed, and reported back to the originating firm in 22 seconds. The AMEX and NASDAQ markets now have trading systems similar to DOT.

Originally, DOT was designed to alleviate the traffic around specialists' trading posts by automatically handling the orders of small individual investors. Runners do not have to hand-carry small orders to the specialist. Instead, they are electronically transmitted from order rooms to the specialists' posts.

Little did the designers of DOT realize that their system would be adopted by index arbitrageurs, who now enter orders to buy or sell portfolios of stocks, including the composition of any index-replicating portfolio (1000 shares of IBM, 1267 shares of GM, etc.). Whenever an arbitrage opportunity arises, a trader can literally push a button to submit these orders to buy (at the asked) or sell (at the bid) the entire basket of stocks. On average, the execution of the trade is reported back to the buyer or seller in 22 seconds. At the same time, the arbitrageur will trade the necessary stock index futures contracts. Larger orders (more than 2099 shares of one stock) are handled less efficiently, with trades occurring only after an arbitrageur's human representative carries the order to the specialists' posts. However, Rule 80A of the NYSE denies program traders access to Super-DOT when the DJIA has changed by about 2% or more on one trading day. Moreover Rule 80B of the NYSE halts trading altogether for one hour if the DJIA changes by more than about 10% during one day.[16] These controls are often called "trading curbs."

Even with SuperDOT, there are some risks to index arbitrage. Large orders to trade securities are not guaranteed any price, and prices can change quickly in the few minutes it takes to execute all the desired trades. Arbitrageurs' orders to buy stock may create upward price pressure on those stocks unless there happens to be a contemporaneous flow of sell orders, or the specialist is willing to reduce his inventory of stock. Similarly, program selling will often lead to price declines in the spot stock market. Interest rate risk and dividend risk can transform an ex-ante profitable arbitrage strategy into an ex-post unprofitable set of trades. Arbitrageurs will daily set up minimum and maximum spreads between the spot and the futures that will trigger their trades, and these spreads will be set sufficiently wide to compensate the arbitrageurs for any of these risks.

In practice, if $F > S + CC - CR$, then arbitrageurs' purchases of stock increase stock prices (these are called "buy programs"), and their sales of futures will depress futures prices, until equilibrium is again reached ($F \cong S + CC - CR$), and no arbitrage opportunities exist. The price adjustments should be small and fast. Similarly, if $F < S + CC - CR$, the buying of cheap futures and the sale of expensive stock ("sell programs") should quickly correct the mispricing. Neal (1996) finds that the average gross profit of index arbitrage trades is only about half the size of the bid–ask spread for the S&P 500 Index.

However, critics of program trading say that the quick realignment of prices with only small price changes occurs only in theory. They perceive program trading as frequently being destabilizing and believe that the practice sometimes causes huge price swings that bear no relation to value or new information. There are times that F stays below $S + CC - CR$ even as arbitrageurs buy futures and sell stock, and the periods of mispricing persist, causing the stock market to fall even more.[17]

Empirical studies concerning program trading have conflicting conclusions.[18] Harris, Sofianos, and Shapiro (1994) argue that program trading affects perceived volatility through three sources. The first is that a program buy order will result in the last trades of all the stocks in the program being at their asked prices. Sell programs move all the stocks to their bid quotes. This "bid–ask bounce" can significantly affect intraday volatility. The second reason is that a program trade updates the prices of all the stocks in the program. In other words, index values change when a program trade is filled simply because the old index reflected the last trade, which may have taken place long ago. Finally, program trading may affect perceived real values and/or may create price pressure.

Only the last factor is important in the debate of how program trading affects volatility. Harris, Sofianos, and Shapiro (1994) conclude that program trading occurs only after there have been changes in relevant fundamental information, because the price changes associated with programs appear to be permanent. On average, they find that it takes 10 minutes after a program trade for the cash-futures basis to revert to a theoretically correct value and that prices do not reverse themselves for at least 50 minutes after the trade. They do not believe that futures trading creates volatility. If the market receives new information, investors will trade first where costs are lowest, and that is in the futures market. If stock index futures markets did not exist, investors would use the cash market, at a greater cost.

It is likely that index arbitrage at times has led, and will lead, to greater price volatility. However, if futures prices persist in remaining below the theoretical minimum value, there must be a reason. It is likely that new information has emerged, causing investors to revise downward their expectations about future corporate profits, or to raise their perceptions about the level of equity risk. Such changes in investor expectations will be transmitted to the futures market first because futures trading is inexpensive relative to selling actual shares of stock. Futures are cheaper to trade in terms of brokerage commissions,[19] price pressure (including the bid–asked spread),[20] and execution time. The ability to quickly and inexpensively trade on one's beliefs is an important justification for the existence of futures trading.

The U.S. stock market has changed greatly since the 1960s. In particular, this market has become more institutionalized. Trillions of dollars are now invested in pension funds, mutual funds, and other professional portfolio managers. Much of the money is indexed, meaning that the portfolio manager simply tries to replicate the performance of some index or benchmark portfolio, such as the S&P 500. Portfolio theory teaches that maximizing diversification offers the optimal return per level of risk payoff. When these institutions trade, they want to trade baskets (portfolios) of stocks, and stock index futures are the most efficient means of executing their desired trades. These funds must trade huge sums of money when they make a decision to buy or sell the shares of any given company or companies, and given their size, they often concentrate their investments only in the shares of large, liquid corporations. Stock index futures contracts have become vital trading tools for these portfolio managers. Consider also how futures facilitate institutional risk management, as shown by the hedging examples presented earlier.

The institutionalization of the stock market is a fact. In addition, it is possible that money managers have a "herd instinct." That is, they come to similar conclusions about where the market is headed at about the same time. Therefore, they trade in similar ways. It is quite likely that their concerted buying or selling the stocks alone would create volatility even without futures trading.

It is debatable whether the stock market would be any less volatile if stock index futures were banned. Working (1963) notes that in judging the net social benefit of a futures market, it is not necessary to find that the futures market stabilizes the underlying cash market—it is only necessary to find that futures trading does not destabilize it. Empirical findings concerning this issue are mixed. For example after controlling for macroeconomic influences, Kamara, Miller, and Siegel (1992) find that while *daily* volatility has increased in the postfutures period, *monthly* volatility has not.

8.3 RISK MANAGEMENT WITH STOCK INDEX FUTURES

In this section, we cover several topics concerning risk management with stock index futures. To begin, portfolio managers have reasons for selling parts of a portfolio. These reasons might include (a) a feeling that some stocks no longer offer adequate returns for the risks associated with those stocks, (b) a sense that it is time to turn bearish (or less bullish) on the overall market, or (c) a need to sell to provide cash for clients. Stock index futures provide an efficient means to achieve the objectives for reasons (b) and (c). Stock index futures can be used as surrogates for the purchase of stock when the portfolio manager has received an inflow of cash but has not decided which stocks or market sectors in which to invest; has a growing bullishness about the market; wants to get market exposure in advance of a near-term expected cash inflow; wants an investment that can be quickly liquidated to raise cash, if needed, or is temporarily bearish on the overall market, but believes that his current portfolio of stocks will outperform the market.

Stock index futures contracts offer portfolio managers several ways to manage risk. We begin with a discussion of equity risk, including material on portfolio theory, the capital asset pricing model, and the concepts of market risk versus nonmarket risk.

8.3.1 Equity Risk

The total risk of a stock is usually measured by the variance or standard deviation of its returns distribution. Total risk can be decomposed into two components: market risk (also called nondiversifiable risk and systematic risk) and nonmarket (diversifiable or nonsystematic) risk.

These two components can be described by first estimating the "market model":

$$R_{it} = \alpha_i + \beta_i R_{mt} + e_{it} \tag{8.6}$$

Users of this model assume that the returns of stock i are a linear function of the returns on the market portfolio. The regression coefficients, α_i and β_i in Equation (8.6), are estimated by regressing a historical time series of the returns of stock i on historical returns on the market portfolio. Figure 8.2 depicts this relationship. Each error term e_{it} is the deviation of one return (the tth

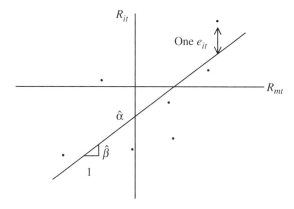

Figure 8.2 Regression of a historical time series of R_{it}, the returns of stock i on R_{mt}, historical returns of a market portfolio.

observation) from its predicted value. In other words,

$$e_{it} = R_{it} - [\hat{\alpha} + \hat{\beta} R_{mt}] \tag{8.7}$$

The term in brackets is the predicted value of R_{it}, given the estimated regression coefficients and a realized value for R_{mt}. The carets above α and β denote that these are the estimated values of the y intercept and the slope coefficient, respectively. The error term is caused by firm i's nonmarket, or nonsystematic, component of risk.

The market model is frequently the starting point for estimating a stock's beta coefficient, β. Beta measures a stock's sensitivity, or better still, a portfolio's sensitivity, to market movements. The greater its beta, the more sensitive a portfolio will be to any market moves. For example, if the stock market rises 3%, a portfolio with a beta of 2.0 will likely rise 6%, while a portfolio with a beta of 0.7 will likely rise only 2.1%. According to the capital asset pricing model (CAPM), investors expect to earn greater returns as beta increases. The CAPM states that

$$E(R_{it}) = R_f + [E(R_{mt}) - R_f]\beta_i \tag{8.8}$$

Beta measures a stock's (or a portfolio's) market risk. This is the risk that cannot be diversified away, and is frequently called nondiversifiable risk or systematic risk. Firm-specific risk, on the other hand, can be eliminated by diversification. Total risk can be separated into two components by taking the variance of both sides of Equation (8.6):

$$\text{var}(R_{it}) = \text{var}(\alpha_i + \beta_i R_{mt} + e_{it})$$

Note that R_{it}, R_{mt}, and e_{it} are random variables, and α_i and β_i are constants. The variance of a constant is zero. Further, the variance of $(a\tilde{X} + \tilde{Y}) = a^2 \text{var}(\tilde{X}) + \text{var}(\tilde{Y}) + 2a\,\text{cov}(\tilde{X}, \tilde{Y})$, where $\tilde{X}$ and $\tilde{Y}$ are random variables and a is a constant. Therefore, we have

$$\text{var}(R_{it}) = \beta_i^2 \text{var}(R_{mt}) + \text{var}(e_{it}) + 2\beta_i \text{cov}(R_{mt}, e_{it})$$

Assume that the covariance of market returns and the error terms is zero. We are left with

$$\text{var}(R_{it}) = \beta_i^2 \text{var}(R_{mt}) + \text{var}(e_{it}) \tag{8.9}$$

which is interpreted as follows:

$$\text{total risk} = \text{market risk} + \text{nonmarket risk}$$

According to the CAPM, investors are compensated only for the level of market risk (β) that they bear. Since nonmarket risk is diversifiable, rational investors will hold well-diversified portfolios that bear no nonmarket risk. Consequently, investors will not earn greater returns for any nonmarket (firm-specific) risk that exists in their portfolios. In fact, the normative prescription of portfolio theory is that rational investors will hold only combinations of the market portfolio of **all** assets which has a beta of 1.0, and riskless assets, which has a beta of 0.0. If they are relatively more risk averse or believe that the prospects for the stock market have declined, investors will lower the beta of their portfolio by shifting a portion of their assets into riskless securities. If they are not very risk averse or if they are bullish about the market, investors will raise their portfolio's beta by borrowing additional capital and investing the borrowed funds in risky securities.

To illustrate, the beta of a portfolio is the weighted average of the betas of the N component securities:

$$\beta_p = \sum_{i=1}^{N} w_i \beta_i = w_1\beta_1 + w_2\beta_2 + \cdots + w_n\beta_n \tag{8.10}$$

where w_i is the fraction of total investment placed into asset i. For a two-asset portfolio, this becomes

$$\beta_p = w_1\beta_1 + w_2\beta_2$$

If asset 1 is the market portfolio (with a beta of 1.0), and asset 2 represents riskless Treasury securities (with a beta of 0.0), then $\beta_p = w_1$. As the fraction of one's total invested wealth (w_1) that is placed into the market portfolio increases, the beta of the portfolio increases. As an investor becomes more bullish, or is willing to hold a riskier portfolio of assets, he should increase w_1. That is, a greater fraction of his wealth should be invested in the market portfolio.

However, stock index futures contracts offer an alternative method of adjusting the beta of a stock portfolio. This is the subject of the next section.

8.3.2 Adjusting the Beta of a Portfolio with Stock Index Futures

Portfolio managers will adjust their portfolio betas to reflect changes in the perceived risk and return offered by the stock market. When they believe that the stock market offers a relatively high expected return for a given level of risk, they will increase the beta of their stock portfolio. When they turn more bearish and/or believe that the risk of the market has increased, they will lower their portfolio's beta.

Section 8.3.1 showed how investors reduce beta by selling part of an equity portfolio and using the proceeds to buy riskless securities. To increase the total portfolio beta, additional investment in the risky equity portfolio is made, and this is financed either by selling riskless securities (which are part of the initial portfolio of stocks and Treasury securities) or by shorting debt instruments (in which case funds are borrowed).

Instead of selling part of an equity portfolio to reduce exposure to market risk, portfolio managers can sell stock index futures contracts. Similarly, instead of buying additional stock to raise the exposure of the portfolio to market risk, a portfolio manager can instead buy stock index futures contracts. The following problem illustrates how this is done.

A portfolio manager owns three stocks[21]:

Stock	Number of Shares Owned	Stock Price	Beta
1	5 million	$8	1.2
2	5 million	$14	0.9
3	5 million	$10	1.1

Assume that the spot S&P 500 Index is at 1,350 and the S&P 500 futures price is 1357. How can this "closet indexer" decrease his portfolio's beta to 0.83 or increase it to 1.66?

Solution   First, it is necessary to compute the beta of the manager's current stock portfolio

Stock	Value of Investment	Fraction of Portfolio, w_i	$w_i\beta_i$
1	$40 million	40/160=0.2500	(0.2500)(1.2)
2	$70 million	70/160=0.4375	(0.4375)(0.9)
3	$50 million	50/160=0.3125	(0.3125)(1.1)
	$160 million	$\Sigma w_i = 1.0$	

The current portfolio beta is:

$$\beta_p = \sum_{i=1}^{3} w_i\beta_i = (0.2500)(1.2) + (0.4375)(0.9) + (0.3125)(1.1) = 1.0375$$

8.3.2.1   Decreasing the Current Beta

To decrease the portfolio beta from 1.0375 to 0.83, the portfolio manager can sell off a portion of the equity portfolio and use the proceeds to buy riskless securities. Define the current portfolio of equities to be asset 1, and the riskless security to be asset 2. The desired portfolio beta is:

$$\beta_d = w_1\beta_1 + w_2\beta_2$$

which can be written as follows:

$$\beta_d = w_1\beta_1 + (1 - w_1)\beta_2$$

Thus,

$$0.83 = w_1(1.0375) + (1 - w_1)0$$

or

$$w_1 = 0.80$$

Therefore, a portfolio consisting of $128 million (0.80×$160 million) invested in our portfolio of three risky equities, and $32 million in Treasury bills ($160 million − $128 million) would create a portfolio with a beta of 0.83.

$$\beta_d = (0.80)(1.0375) + (0.20)(0) = 0.83$$

The portfolio manager can accomplish the same result by selling stock index futures contracts. Recall from Chapter 7 that the proper number of futures contracts to trade in order to hedge is given by

$$\begin{pmatrix} \text{number of futures contracts} \\ \text{to trade in order to have a} \\ \text{risk minimizing hedge} \end{pmatrix} = h^* \frac{\begin{pmatrix} \text{number of units of the} \\ \text{spot position to be hedged} \end{pmatrix}}{\begin{pmatrix} \text{number of units underlying} \\ \text{one futures contract} \end{pmatrix}}$$

The role of h^* in this analysis is played by the beta of the portfolio.[22] If the initial risky asset portfolio beta is used as the estimate of h^*, it should be multiplied by the ratio of the dollar value of the spot position to be hedged to the dollars underlying the spot index:

$$\begin{array}{l}\text{number of futures contracts}\\ \text{to trade to change a portfolio}\\ \text{beta from } \beta_p \text{ to } \beta_d\end{array} = \beta_p \left(\frac{\text{spot price}}{\text{futures price}}\right)\left(\frac{\begin{array}{c}\text{number of dollars in the}\\ \text{spot position to be hedged}\end{array}}{\begin{array}{c}\text{number of dollars}\\ \text{underlying the spot index}\end{array}}\right) \qquad (8.11)$$

The number of dollars of the spot position to be hedged in our example is $32 million, and the number of dollars underlying the spot index is $337,500 ($1350\times$the S&P multiplier of 250). Therefore,

$$\begin{array}{l}\text{number of futures contracts}\\ \text{to trade to change a portfolio}\\ \text{beta from 1.0375 to 0.83}\end{array} = 1.0375\left(\frac{1350}{1357}\right)\left(\frac{\$32,000,000}{337,500}\right)$$

$$=97.8629$$

Instead of selling $32 million of the risky equity portfolio ($\beta=1.0375$), the portfolio beta can be reduced to 0.83 by selling 97.8629 stock index futures contracts. Basically, the portfolio manager is hedging $33.03 million of the portfolio ($250\times1350\times97.8629$). The portfolio manager therefore can achieve the same results by just continuing to own the $160 million stock portfolio and selling 97.8629 futures.

The transaction costs of the two approaches differ greatly. At $12/contract round-trip commission, the sale of 97.86 stock index futures contracts would entail total commissions of about $1174. Alternatively, if the manager sold $32 million of stock, the round-trip commission on trading this amount of stock might be about 0.18% of the value of the stock, or about $57,600. In addition, the stocks would have to be sold at their bid prices, and if the beta adjustment is going to be temporary, the stocks will have to be repurchased later at their asked prices. Thus, there is no question that stock index futures represent a low cost means of adjusting the portfolio's beta to reflect the temporary bearishness of the portfolio manager.

Before concluding that the stock index futures contracts are preferred on the basis of trading costs alone, a manager should examine the futures prices to determine whether they are fairly valued. However it is unlikely that the futures will be mispriced enough to overcome the difference in commissions.

8.3.2.2 Increasing the Current Beta

To raise the current portfolio beta from 1.0375 to 1.66, we first perform the following calculation:

$$\beta_d = w_1\beta_1 + w_2\beta_2$$
$$1.66 = w_1(1.0375) + (1-w_1)0$$
$$w_1 = 1.60$$

This result implies that 160% of the portfolio manager's initial capital of $160 million must be invested in the three-stock portfolio: 160% of $160 million is $256 million. Thus, to accomplish the increase in beta, cash Treasury bills with a market value of $96 million must be sold short. To summarize, the portfolio manager could do the following:

Hold the $160 million current stock portfolio.

Borrow $96 million (short-sell T-bills).

Use the proceeds to buy $96 million worth of additional stock.

Alternatively, instead of buying $96 million of additional stock (with $\beta=1.0375$), the portfolio manager can buy an equivalent amount of stock index futures contracts. The number of futures contracts to buy is determined by using Equation (8.11):

$$\begin{array}{l} \text{number of futures contracts} \\ \text{to trade to change a portfolio} =1.0375\left(\dfrac{1350}{1357}\right)\left(\dfrac{\$96,000,000}{337,500}\right) \\ \text{beta from 1.0375 to 1.66} \end{array}$$

$$=293.59$$

The portfolio manager can buy 293.59 stock index futures contracts to raise the current portfolio beta from 1.0375 to 1.66. That is, the portfolio manager can

Keep the $160 million current stock portfolio.

Go long 293.59 S&P 500 futures contracts.

Let us demonstrate that borrowing $96 million to invest in an equity portfolio with a beta of 1.0375 will provide results equivalent to those from the purchase of 293.59 futures contracts. The spot index level is 1350 and the observed futures price is 1357. Further, suppose the futures contract's delivery date is three months hence and the annual riskless interest rate is 5%. Two assumptions must also be made: (a) the dividend payments received by the holder of the three-stock portfolio are identical to that of the S&P 500, and (b) the observed futures price is theoretically correct.

Now there are sufficient data to estimate the future value of dividends. If the multiplier of the futures contract is 250, then the cost-of-carry formula is

$$F = S[1 + h(0, 0.25 \text{ yr})] - FV(\text{divs})$$

$$(1357)(250) = (1350)(250)(1.0125) - FV(\text{divs})$$

Therefore, the future value of dividends on $337,500 worth of stock equals $2,468.75. On stock worth $96 million, the future value of dividends would be $702,222. This approach implicitly assumes that the dividends from the portfolio are the same as the dividends from the S&P 500. In practice, this would likely not exactly be the case.

Table 8.2 illustrates that the final wealth (0.25 year from today) of an investor who borrows to invest in $96 million of stock (the left-hand side of the table) is (about) the same as it would be if he instead went long 293.59 futures contracts (the right-hand side of the table). The table chooses two arbitrary values for $S_T=F_T$. Discrete dividend payments have caused the results of the two strategies to be slightly different.

TABLE 8.2   Borrowing $96 Million to Buy Stock Provide the Same Results as Going Long 293.59 Futures Contracts

Today	**Today**
Sell $96 million in T-bills (borrow)	Buy 293.59 futures contracts at $F = 1357$
Buy $96 million worth of stock	
0.25 year hence, if $F_T = S_T = 1215$	**0.25 year hence, if $F_T = S_T = 1215$**
The stock market fell by 10%. Since the stock portfolio had a beta of 1.0375, it should have declined by 10.375% to $86,040,000. However, $702,222 was received in dividends. In addition, interest must be repaid on the borrowed funds, and this equals 1.25% of $97.2 million.	The futures position declined 142 points, which is $35,500/contract, or a loss of $10,422,445 on 293.59 contracts.
Loss: $10,457,778	Loss: $10,422,445
0.25 year hence, if $F_T = S_T = 1431$	**0.25 year hence, if $F_T = S_T = 1431$**
The stock market rose by 6%. Since the stock portfolio had a beta of 1.0375, it should have risen by 6.225%, so that it should be worth $101,976,000. Dividends of $702,222 were received. Again, interest on the borrowed funds of $1,215,000 must be paid.	One futures contract rose 74 points, which is $18,500 per contract, and a gain of $5,431,350 for 293.59 contracts.
Profit: $5,478,222	Profit: $5,431,415

We can derive an alternative equation that solves for the number of futures contracts to trade in order to change the beta of a portfolio from β_p to β_d:[23]

$$\begin{matrix} \text{number of futures contracts} \\ \text{to trade to change a portfolio} \\ \text{beta from } \beta_p \text{ to } \beta_d \end{matrix} = (\beta_d - \beta_p) \frac{\begin{matrix} \text{total portfolio value} \\ \text{currently held} \end{matrix}}{\begin{matrix} \text{number of dollars underlying} \\ \text{the futures contract} \end{matrix}} \qquad (8.12)$$

A negative number indicates that futures should be sold to lower the portfolio beta. A positive number means that futures should be bought. Thus, if $\beta_d = 0.83$ and $\beta_1 = 1.0375$, as in the first part of the foregoing example, then

$$\text{number of futures contracts} = (0.83 - 1.0375)\left(\frac{\$160,000,000}{1357 \times 250}\right) = -97.8629$$

If $\beta_d = 1.66$, as in the second part of the example, then

$$\text{number of futures contracts} = (1.66 - 1.0375)\left(\frac{\$160,000,000}{1357 \times 250}\right) = +293.5888$$

A risk-minimizing hedge would set a target beta, β_d, equal to 0.0. A perfect hedge, one that removes all risk, should earn only the riskless rate of return, just as any zero-beta asset should earn.

8.3.3 Stock Picking

Suppose that you are a skilled stock picker but a poor market timer. You are often able to determine that a stock is undervalued but are poor at predicting when the overall market will rise or fall. Stock index futures contracts allow you to sell market risk and keep only the firm-specific risk. As long as your portfolio outperforms the market, after adjusting for market risk, you will earn positive returns. Market-risk-adjusted outperformance is often called "alpha." Thus, stock index futures permit investors to capture the alpha provided by the portfolio manager.

For example, you might believe that energy stocks are undervalued relative to the market. You might consider buying a portfolio of energy stocks, or perhaps a "sector fund," which is a mutual fund that concentrates its investments in one industry. Your analysis leads you to believe that

EXAMPLE 8.6   An equity fund manager owns a portfolio of $20 million in stocks with a portfolio beta of 1.20. She is concerned that the stock market will temporarily decline in the next few days. She does not wish to incur the commission costs and price pressure of selling stocks and then repurchasing them after the anticipated decline. Thus, she decides to use futures contracts to hedge against the expected market decline. Suppose, the S&P 500 Index level is 1275 and the observed futures price is 1280. What is the risk minimizing hedge for this position?

Set the target portfolio beta β_d equal to 0.0. Using Equation (8.12), we conclude that the fund manager should sell 75 futures contracts:

$$\text{number of futures contracts} = (0.0 - 1.20)\left(\frac{\$20,000,000}{1280 \times 250}\right) = -75$$

Suppose the manager is right about the market's movement, and S declines to 1224, which is a 4% drop in the market. The value of her equity portfolio should decline by 4.8% ($1.20 \times 4\%$), if her estimated beta was accurate. This results in a loss in the capital value of her spot position of $960,000.[24]

Now assume that the futures price also declines by 4%, to 1228.80. Note that the original spot index minus futures price basis of -5 ($1275 - 1280$) narrowed to -4.8 ($1224 - 1228.8$). A futures price decline of 51.2 points results in a profit of $12,800 on one futures contract. On a position of 75 short futures contracts, the profit would be $960,000.

The hedge eliminated the effects of the market decline. However the hedge's effectiveness is dependent on the change in the basis. In practice, the basis on the date that the hedge will be lifted is generally indeterminate. The basis on the day the hedge is lifted is known only if the last day of the hedge is the delivery date of the futures contract (convergence).

energy stocks are less risky than the market, and your portfolio of energy stocks has a beta of 0.85. Suppose you invest $7 million in the energy portfolio and wish to hedge against a market decline (because you are not confident about your market-timing ability). Thus, you are willing to profit only from your stock picking ability and are willing to remove the market impact from your portfolio.

If the S&P 500 futures price is 1400, you should sell 17 futures contracts:

$$\text{number of futures contracts} = (0.0 - 0.85)\left(\frac{\$7,000,000}{1400 \times 250}\right) = -17$$

Suppose that the S&P 500 Index declines by 49 points (-3.50%). Further, suppose that cash-futures basis remains constant. Then, the S&P 500 futures price will also decline by 49 points. This leads to a profit of $12,250 on one futures contract and $208,250 on 17 contracts.

Based on its beta of 0.85, the energy portfolio would be expected to decline 2.975%. Any smaller decline represents a positive risk-adjusted performance. Thus, a decline of only 2% on your energy portfolio is a loss of $140,000. Your total profit is $68,250 (a profit of $208,250 on 17 futures contracts and a loss of $140,000 on the equity portfolio). In this example, note that your stock-picking ability leads to profits, despite poor market timing. The key is that your stocks out-performed the market after a risk adjustment; you had positive alpha.

8.3.4   An Anticipatory Hedge

Consider a pension fund manager who anticipates receiving $15 million from the fund sponsor three days from today. He believes that there is a high probability that the stock market will rally during the next three days. Equivalently, consider another portfolio manager who might have received $15 million more than he originally anticipated. While he is bullish about the market, he decides that insufficient analysis has been done to justify to deciding on the specific stocks in which to invest today.

In either case, stock index futures should be bought. Suppose that the fund manager is con-strained to invest in stocks of above average risk, perhaps high growth Internet stocks, with an average beta of 1.6. From Equation (8.12), we find that the initial portfolio beta (β_p) is 0.0 and the desired portfolio beta (β_d) is 1.6. If the S&P 500 futures price is 1500, then both fund managers should buy 64 futures contracts.

$$\text{number of futures contracts} = (1.60 - 0.0)\left(\frac{\$15,000,000}{1500 \times 250}\right) = 64$$

8.3.5   Caveats About Hedging with Stock Index Futures

The stock portfolio risk manager should have confidence in his hedge ratio, which is his portfolio's beta. This means that the market model regression must have a reasonably high coefficient of deter-mination (R^2), **and** the risk manager must believe that the historical relationship will persist in the future. Using the S&P 500 Index futures contract to adjust the beta of a poorly diversified portfolio of perhaps fewer than 10 stocks will likely not provide a high R^2. Individual stock betas are unsta-ble, and a typical stock's market model R^2 will be low, perhaps around 20%. The historical beta of one stock is not a good predictor of its future beta. As more stocks are added to the portfolio, the risk manager will gain confidence that the estimated portfolio beta will persist in the future because errors in estimating one stock's beta will tend to offset errors in another stock's estimated beta.

Similarly, using S&P 500 Index futures to hedge a portfolio of small cap stocks might prove ineffective.[25] The underlying portfolio of the stock index futures contract should be as similar as possible to the portfolio that is being hedged.

In theory, the market model should be used to estimate the betas of the individual stocks (or the portfolio's beta). The percentage change in the futures' price should be the independent variable. In practice, however, beta is more often estimated by using the returns on the spot index as the independent variable. The two methods probably will not provide betas estimates much different from one another. Further, given the estimation errors of beta coefficients, it is unlikely that it matters which is used. Conservatism usually pays, however, and whichever independent variable provides the smaller hedge ratio should probably be used.

You should, however, use the estimate of your portfolio's beta relative to the index of the futures contract that will be used to hedge. If you will use the DJIA futures contract to hedge, then use the returns on the DJIA as the independent variable to estimate betas. If the S&P 500 futures contract is the hedging instrument, then the market return R_{mt} should be the return on the S&P 500 Index.

One should also match the expected hedge duration to the interval used to determine historical returns. That is, if the hedge is to be for one day, daily returns should be used to estimate betas. Use two-day returns if the hedge is expected to be for two days. Beyond one week it does not matter if weekly returns, biweekly returns, or monthly returns are used. You will likely find that betas estimated from daily historical returns are lower than those estimated from returns of longer durations. Also, remember that shorter hedge durations will possess greater basis risk.

Finally, if interest rates are high and/or the expected hedge duration is long, do not forget to tail your hedge.

8.3.6 Using Stock Index Futures to Gain International Equity Exposure

Stock index futures can be used to circumvent dividend withholding taxes, which are levied by a country on foreign investors in its market. Thus, if a European resident bought stocks in the United States and received dividends, the U.S. government would withhold 15% of the dividend amount. The U.S. investor faces the same problem when investing in European equities. Generally, this tax is not recoverable by the investor. Withholding taxes can be avoided if an investor buys stock synthetically by buying stock index futures and lending.

Moreover, there is no currency risk associated with stock index futures on foreign stock markets and this could provide another advantage for using these contracts. For example, if a U.S. investor buys a futures contract on the Nikkei 225 Stock Index, a $25 profit is earned on every 5-point move in the futures price, independent of any changes in the $/¥ exchange rate. In contrast, directly investing in Japanese stocks could prove unprofitable if the stocks rise at the same time that the $/¥ exchange rate declines.

Put another way, define

r_s = rate of return on the foreign stock market, denominated in its own currency

r_{fx} = percentage change *in the price of the foreign currency*

r_{hc} = rate of return denominated in the investor's home currency

The investor will earn $r_{hc} = r_s$ if he invests in stock index futures on the foreign market (and puts up 100% of the dollar value of the stock as margin). Investing in foreign stocks, however, will lead to a gross rate of return of $(1 + r_{hc}) = (1 + r_s)(1 + r_{fx})$. Trading stock index futures on foreign stock indexes allows the trader to separate home currency equity risk from foreign exchange risk.

8.4 SUMMARY

In this chapter, we first described different stock market indexes. The DJIA is a price-weighted index, the S&P 500 is a value-weighted index, and the Value Line is an equally weighted index. Futures on these and other stock market indexes trade in the United States.

We then applied the cost-of-carry formula to determine the theoretical stock index futures price. We found that dividends, the carry return, pose special problems when we are using the formula. The existence of transactions costs creates bounds within which the futures price can lie, without permitting any arbitrage opportunities.

Finally, we studied how stock index futures can be used in risk management. Beta measures a portfolio's level of market sensitivity. Equity risk managers can adjust beta in response to their perception of market risk. They can increase the beta of their portfolios by going long stock index futures. If they become more bearish, portfolio managers can reduce their portfolio betas by selling stock index futures. Stock index futures contracts are well suited for this purpose, because they can be quickly traded with low transactions costs.

Stock index futures also offer advantages for investors who wish to invest in foreign stocks. Dividend withholding taxes can be avoided. Also, futures on foreign stock market indexes have no currency risk associated with them.

References

Eades, Kenneth M., Patrick J. Hess, and E. Han Kim. 1984. "On Interpreting Security Returns During the Ex-Dividend Period." *Journal of Financial Economics*, Vol. 13, No. 1, March, pp. 3–34.

Edwards, Franklin R. 1988. "Futures Trading and Cash Market Volatility: Stock Index and Interest Rate Futures". *Journal of Futures Markets*, Vol. 8, No. 4, August, pp. 421–440.

Grossman, Sanford J. 1988. "An Analysis if the Implications for Stock and Futures Price Volatility of Program Trading and Dynamic Hedging Strategies." *Journal of Business*, Vol. 61, No. 3, July, pp. 275–298.

Harris, Lawrence. 1989. "S&P 500 Cash Stock Price Volatilities." *Journal of Finance*, Vol. 44, No. 5, December, pp. 1155–1176.

Harris, Lawrence, George Sofianos, and James E. Shapiro. 1994. "Program Trading and Intraday Volatility". *Review of Financial Studies*, Vol. 7, pp. 653–686.

Hill, Joanne M., and Frank J. Jones. 1988. "Equity Trading, Program Trading, Portfolio Insurance, Computer Trading, and All That." *Financial Analysts Journal*, Vol. 44, No. 4, July/August, pp. 29–38.

Kamara, Avraham; Thomas W. Miller, Jr., and Andrew F. Siegel. 1992. "The Effect of Futures Trading on the Stability of Standard and Poor 500 Returns." *Journal of Futures Markets*, Vol. 12, pp. 645–658.

Neal, Robert. 1996. "Direct Tests of Index Arbitrage Models." *Journal of Financial and Quantitative Analysis*, Vol. 31, pp. 541–562.

Working, Holbrook. 1963. "Futures Markets Under Renewed Attack." *Food Research Institute Studies*, Vol. 4, pp. 13–24.

Notes

[1]The 1987 stock market crash caused trading in stock index futures to decrease. Volume in the S&P 500 futures contract declined to 19.04 million contracts in 1987, and only 11.4 million contracts in 1988. Similar declines in 1988 volume took place in the other U.S. stock index futures. Since then, U.S. stock index futures trading has exploded; 969.7 million stock index futures contracts and options on stock index futures traded globally in 2000, including 42 million S&P 500 and mini-S&P 500 futures contracts on the CME.

[2]There are other Dow Jones averages besides the DJIA. These include the Dow Jones Transportation Average, the Dow Jones Utilities Average, and the Dow Jones 65-Stock Composite Average.

[3]When it is announced that a stock will be made part of the S&P 500, its price usually increases as index funds scramble to purchase its shares, to be able to replicate the performance of the index.

[4]The CME also trades futures and options on the Nikkei 225 Stock Average. This index is Japan's most widely followed and most frequently quoted equity index. Unlike the other indexes at the CME, however, the Nikkei is price weighted.

[5]On November 2, 1997, the S&P 500 futures contract effectively had a stock split. Prior to that date, the multiplier of the S&P 500 futures contract was 500, and one tick of 0.05 point equaled $25. After that date, the multiplier became 250, and one tick of 0.10 is worth $25.

[6]More information about CME products is available at www.cme.com/clearing.

[7]Before February 1, 1988, the Value Line Index was computed as an equally weighted geometric average. Since then, the Value Line has reported both the geometric and the arithmetic averages. The Philadelphia Stock Exchange's Value Line Index option has been based on the arithmetic average since May 21, 1988.

To compute an equally weighted geometric average, pick any arbitrary index value on the base date, day 0. The index value on any subsequent day, day t, is then:

$$I_t = I_{t-1}[(P_{1,t}/P_{1,t-1})(P_{2,t}/P_{2,t-1})(P_{3,t}/P_{3,t-1}) \cdots (P_{n,t}/P_{n,t-1})]^{1/n}$$

In other words, the index value on day t is the geometric average of the price relatives of the n stocks times the preceding day's index value. See www.valueline.com for more information.

[8]Actually, S equals the spot index value if all stocks traded at the current moment. The reported spot index value is based on the last trade of each component stock. At any moment in time, some component stocks may not have traded for the past several minutes or even hours. In other words, reported spot index values suffer from a lag caused by nonsynchronous trading of their component stocks. The futures price should reflect the fact that some stocks have not traded and that the spot index is "stale."

[9]Only the dividends of stocks that will trade ex-dividend between tomorrow and the delivery date affect F. However, the interest earned on the dividends begins accruing on the payment date. It is possible that some component stocks will trade ex-dividend *before* the delivery date of the futures contract, but the actual payment date will come *after* the delivery date. Dividends like these should be *discounted* back to the delivery date. Also see Appendix C to Chapter 5 for discussion about how to deal with the fact that a trader will not know what amount of interest can be earned in dividends that will be received in the future.

[10]Assume, for simplicity, that the dividend is actually paid on the ex-dividend day. See Section 8.2.4 for more details on the handling of dividends.

[11]Another way to create synthetic stock requires the purchase of a call and the sale of a put, both with the same strike price and time to expiration. See Section 15.9.

[12]The pricing equation is $F = S + hS - \Sigma FV(\text{divs})$. Define d as the effective "future value dividend yield" on the index. In other words, $d = \Sigma FV(\text{divs})/S$. Then $F = S + hS - dS = S(1 + h - d)$. In the example, $F = 1375$, $S = 1325$, and $h = 0.05$. Therefore, $d = 1.2264\%$ for one year.

[13]Based on the last trade of each stock.

[14]This was reported by Eades, Hess, and Kim (1984, p. 11).

[15]See Hill and Jones (1988).

[16]Search for the term "circuit breakers," "80A," or "80B" at the NYSE website (www.nyse.com/search/search.html) to find the most recent information concerning trading collars and circuit breakers.

[17]The persistence of the futures price lying above the theoretical price does not cause as much concern, since it leads to a rising market.

[18]Early studies on the impact of stock index trading include Edwards (1988), Grossman (1988), and Harris (1989).

[19]Consider an institution that pays a commission of $0.03/share when it trades a large block of stock. Thus, if an institution was to buy or sell $30 million of some equities at an average price of $40/share (this was the average stock price of all S&P stocks in 1997), its one-way commission would be $22,500. This is the amount of stock underlying one hundred S&P 500 futures contracts if the index is at 1200. In contrast, the institutional round-trip cost of trading 100 S&P 500 futures contracts might be about $1000.

[20]Consider that the bid–asked spread on a stock index futures contract is typically one tick, or $25. The spread on one stock might be $0.05/share, but the purchase or sale of 100 shares of each of 500 stocks will mean that the $5 spread (per round lot) will be incurred 500 times.

[21]Considerable basis risk would exist if S&P 500 futures were used to manage the risk of a three-stock portfolio. Basis risk here would be defined as variability in the different returns of the three-stock portfolio (S) and the S&P 500 futures contract (F), even after adjusting for the ex-ante risk measure of the portfolio by using its estimated beta. In the market model, regression of the portfolio's historical returns against the historical returns on the market, $R_{pt} = \alpha_p + \beta_p R_{mt} + e_{pt}$, the R^2 will likely be low. In practice, S&P 500 futures would be used to adjust the beta of a much larger portfolio of stocks.

[22]Recall that $h*$ is estimated as $\Delta S/\Delta F$. That is, $h*$ is the slope coefficient in the regression model $\Delta S = a + b\Delta F$. In contrast, β measures the percentage change in S for a given percentage change in F; $\beta = \%\Delta S/\%\Delta F = F\Delta S/S\Delta F$. Thus the *true* relationship between $h*$ and β is obtained by multiplying the beta by S/F, and obtaining $h* = \beta(S/F) = \Delta S/\Delta F$. In general, if S and F are close in value (as they will be when the nearby futures contract is used to hedge), then $h*$ and β will be close in value.

[23]In this formula, the beta of the futures contract is assumed to be 1.00.

[24]Dividends may also be received.

[25]Russell 2000 stock index futures would typically be used to hedge small cap stock portfolios.

PROBLEMS

8.1 Imagine that there is a futures contract on the D&M2. The D&M2 is a value-weighted index of the following two stocks:

Stock	Price/ Share	Shares Outstanding
Dubo Pencil Co.	$40	10 million
Miller Markers	$30	5 million

On November 15, the D&M2 spot index is at 600. The quantity of stock underlying the index is 250 times the index value. There is a futures contract with a delivery date on January 15.

a. If neither stock will trade ex-dividend between November 15 and January 15, what is the theoretical futures price? Assume the annual interest rate is 5%.

b. Suppose instead that Dubo Pencil will trade ex-dividend on December 1 in the amount of $0.50/share and that Miller Markers will trade ex-dividend on January 5 in the amount of $0.20/share. Compute the theoretical futures price.

c. In addition to the ex-div assumptions of part **b**, assume that the borrowing rate is 7% and the lending rate is 6%. Compute the no-arbitrage bounds for the theoretical futures price. That is, what is the lowest theoretical futures price that precludes arbitrage, and what is the highest theoretical futures price that precludes arbitrage?

d. Add to the assumptions of parts **b** and **c** that transactions costs on stock trades are $0.03/share (i.e., it costs 3 cents/share to buy or sell stock) and that the round-trip futures contract commission is $15. Assume that all transactions costs are paid on January 15. Compute the new no-arbitrage bounds for the theoretical futures price.

e. Suppose that the observed futures price is 625. How would you arbitrage, given the conditions in parts **b**, **c**, and **d**? Specifically state what you would do on November 15, December 1, January 5, and January 15. What is your final arbitrage profit?

8.2 Suppose that you are the manager of an indexed equity portfolio that mimics the S&P 500. The value of your portfolio is $100 million, the spot index is at 1333.58, and the futures price for the contract that calls for delivery 84 days hence is 1346.50. The riskless interest rate is 5%/year. You have estimated the dividends that the stocks in which you have invested will pay during the next 88 days, the ex-dates, and the interest that can be earned by investing those dividends. At the end of 84 days, your estimate of the interest, dividends, plus interest on the dividends for your $100 million portfolio comes to $1,420,000. Should you quasi-arbitrage? Assume no transactions costs.

8.3 There are 50 stocks in the Belgian–Czechoslovakian Stock Index (aka the Belch Index). Today (November 13, 2000), 49 of the stocks sell for $5/share and one stock sells for $100/share. All the stocks have one million shares outstanding. The Belch Index is a value-weighted index, and as of today, the spot Belch is at 690.

On December 13, 2000, each of the 49 low-priced stocks will trade ex-dividend in the amount of $0.25/share. On January 2, 2001, the one high-priced stock will trade ex-dividend in the amount of $1/share. Assume that the ex-date and the payment date are the same. The riskless interest rate is 10% per year. There is a futures contract on the Belch. The nearby delivery date is January 15, 2001. Find the theoretical futures price.

8.4 Consider the futures contract on the G&B2, a value-weighted index of two stocks. The delivery date is May 25. Some data on the two component stocks:

Stock	Price	Shares out-stand-ing	Next Ex-divi-dend Date	Dividend amount
Gomuco	30	2 million	April 25	$0.50/ share
Bookuco	40	1 million	June 5	$0.75/ share

Today is April 10, and the spot G&B2 is 110. The contract size of the G&B2 futures contract is 200 times the index value.

a. The interest rate is 7%/year. What is the theoretical futures price?

b. If your borrowing rate is 8% and your lending rate is 6%, then what are the maximum and minimum futures prices that preclude arbitrage? Assume that brokerage costs are zero.

8.5 Suppose that on May 15, 2001, the spot S&P 500 Index is at 1000. The last day of trading the June futures contract is June 16, 2001. The annual interest rate is 7%. Assume that every component stock of the index has the same market value and that every stock sells for $10/share. On May 30, 2001, half the stocks will trade ex-dividend in the amount of $0.50/share, and these stocks will pay their dividends on May 30, too. On June 15, 1998, the other half will trade ex-dividend in the amount of $0.60/share, but these companies will not actually pay their dividends until June 30. Compute the theoretical futures price on May 15.

8.6 In Section 8.3.2.2, we claimed that $256 million in an equity portfolio with a beta of 1.0375 and $96 million in short T-bills (i.e., borrowings) is equivalent to $160 million invested in the equity portfolio with a beta of 1.0375 that is long 293.59 futures contracts.

In addition, the riskless interest rate is 5%/year; the futures' delivery date is 0.25 year from today; $F=1367$ and $S=1350$. Assume that there are no dividends and F is theoretically correct.

Demonstrate that the two portfolios will provide (almost) identical results if the spot index plunges to 1215 on the futures' delivery date.

8.7 Suppose that you are a portfolio manager. Your portfolio consists of $150 million of stock with a beta of 0.94, and $10 million invested in Treasury bills. The spot S&P 500 Index is 1297, and the S&P 500 futures price is 1300.

    a. What is the beta of your portfolio?

    b. If you believe that the probability of a stock market decline has increased, and therefore wish to reduce the beta of your portfolio to 0.60, should you buy or sell stock index futures contracts? How many futures contracts should you trade?

    c. Suppose instead that you wish to reduce the beta of your portfolio to

zero. How many futures contracts should you trade?

d. A zero beta portfolio (as in part **c**) should earn the riskless rate of return. Assume that dividends are zero. Show that if the stock index value is 1100 on the futures delivery date, the realized rates of return on each of the two portfolios are (about) equal:

Portfolio 1

Long $150 million stocks with at beta of 0.94

Long $10 million in T-bills

Short 433.85 S&P 500 stock index futures contracts

Portfolio 2

Long $160 million T-bills

8.8 Today is December 8, 2000. On May 1, 2001, you will finally inherit that $1 million you've been waiting for, and you just can't wait to invest it in four stocks you believe are grossly undervalued. You have already decided on the numbers of shares you will buy of the four stocks. The number of shares you want to buy, the stocks' current prices, and the stocks' betas are as follows:

Stock	Number of Shares to Buy	Price per Share	Beta
Jagger's Daggers	10,000	$10	0.4
Roland Gift's Shrunken Heads	20,000	$10	1.0
World Potty, Inc.	30,000	$10	1.2
Hoodoo Guru Consulting	10,000	$40	1.8

Is the appropriate hedge a long or short hedge? As a hedger, will you buy or sell futures contracts? What other information would you like to have before deciding on which futures contract (S&P 500, S&P Midcap, Russell 2000, NASDAQ 100, etc.) to use to hedge? Hoodoo Guru Consulting has advised you to use the June 2001 S&P 500 futures contract to hedge. How many of the June 2001 S&P 500 futures should you use to hedge if the spot index is 1253.1 and the futures price is 1262.75? Would your answer be different if the interest rate was 5%/year or 50%/year?

8.9

a. The spot stock index is 1300. The stock index futures price is 1315. The borrowing rate is 5%/year, and the lending rate is 4.5%/year. How would you create a synthetic long stock position? How would you create a synthetic long T-bill position?

b. Suppose that the delivery date of the futures contract is 6 months hence and that there are no dividends. You own $10 million of equities, and $10 million of six-month T-bills that are priced to yield 5%/year. Given the information in part **a**, should you sell the stock and buy synthetic stock, or sell the T-bills and go long synthetic T-bills?

c. Suppose that you performed the trades that you recommended in part **b**. Six months later, on the delivery date, the spot stock index is 1500. Are you are better off having made the trades than you would have been if you had maintained your original portfolio?

8.10   On May 1, you have $250,000 to invest. You wish to invest equal amounts in two Japanese stocks: Hitachi, which has a stock price of ¥1389/share, and Fujitsu, which has a stock price of ¥3340/share. The spot exchange rate on May 1 is ¥108/$. On November 1 of the same year, Hitachi's stock price has risen to ¥1500/share, Fujitsu is worth ¥4000/share, and the exchange rate is ¥118/$.

a. How many shares of each stock will you buy?

b. What rate of return did you earn? (Express the rate in terms of the Japanese yen.)

c. What was your rate of return, denominated in U.S. dollars?

d. During the same period, Nikkei Dow futures, which trade on the CBOT, rose from 18,255 to 19,255. Had you bought two Nikkei Dow futures on May 1, what would your dollar profit have been?

8.11

a. Consider stock index futures for delivery one month hence and four months hence. If the term structure of interest rates rises (i.e., the yield curve becomes more steeply sloped) and the spot stock index stays constant, what will **likely** happen to the spread between the one-month and four-month stock index futures contracts? (That is, will the difference between these two futures prices likely increase or decrease?) Explain your answer.

b. Why was the word **likely** used? Is it possible that your prediction will be incorrect? Why?

CHAPTER 9

Treasury Bond and Treasury Note Futures

Because they are useful in a variety of ways to manage risk, futures contracts on U.S. Treasury securities have been immensely successful. For example, during the first 9 months of 2001, the U.S. Treasury bond (T-bond) contract at the CBOT was one of the most actively traded futures contracts in the world, with over 43 million contracts exchanging hands. The five-year and 10-year U.S. Treasury note (T-note) contracts also have been very successful. In fact, since the fall of 1999, open interest in the CBOT's 10-year T-note futures contract has usually surpassed that for its long-term T-bond contract.[1]

Note that while most of the material in this chapter describes the T-bond futures contract, the T-note futures contracts are similar to the T-bond contract. Thus, the T-bond pricing principles and hedging examples are directly applicable to the T-note contracts.

9.1 FEATURES OF THE T-BOND FUTURES CONTRACTS

The T-bond futures contract prices a hypothetical Treasury bond with 20 years to maturity and a 6% coupon. The 6% coupon began with the March 2000 contract. For contracts that expired before March 2000, the assumed coupon was 8%. The hypothetical bond rarely, if ever, exists. Figure 9.1 presents spot price data of Treasury notes and bonds,[2] their bid and asked prices, and their yields to maturity. As shown in Figure 9.1, there are few 6% coupon Treasury bonds that have been issued, but none of them matures in 20 years (i.e., in 2020).

The Chicago Board of Trade futures contract permits the delivery of any U.S. Treasury bonds that, if callable, are not callable for at least 15 years from the first day of the delivery month or, if not callable, have a maturity of at least 15 years from the first day of the delivery month. The seller of the futures contract has the option of choosing which bond to deliver. Hemler (1990) examines this "quality option"[3] for the short. However, the seller cannot deliver a variety of bonds; all the bonds delivered must have the same coupon and maturity date. The asset underlying the T-bond futures contract is $100,000 worth of Treasury bonds, in terms of their face value. Thus, if each T-bond delivered has a $1000 face value, then 100 bonds, all with the same coupon and maturity date, must be delivered.

Any T-note with $6\frac{1}{2}$ to 10 years to maturity or first call (whichever comes first) is deliverable into the 10-year T-note futures contract. The five-year T-note futures contract allows delivery of $100,000 face value of T-notes that had a maturity when they were issued of $5\frac{1}{4}$ years or less, but must have a maturity of more than $4\frac{1}{4}$ years as of the first day of the delivery month.[4] Finally, the two-year T-note futures contract calls for the delivery of $200,000 face value of T-notes that had an original maturity of $5\frac{1}{4}$ years or less and still have a maturity longer than $1\frac{3}{4}$ years on the first

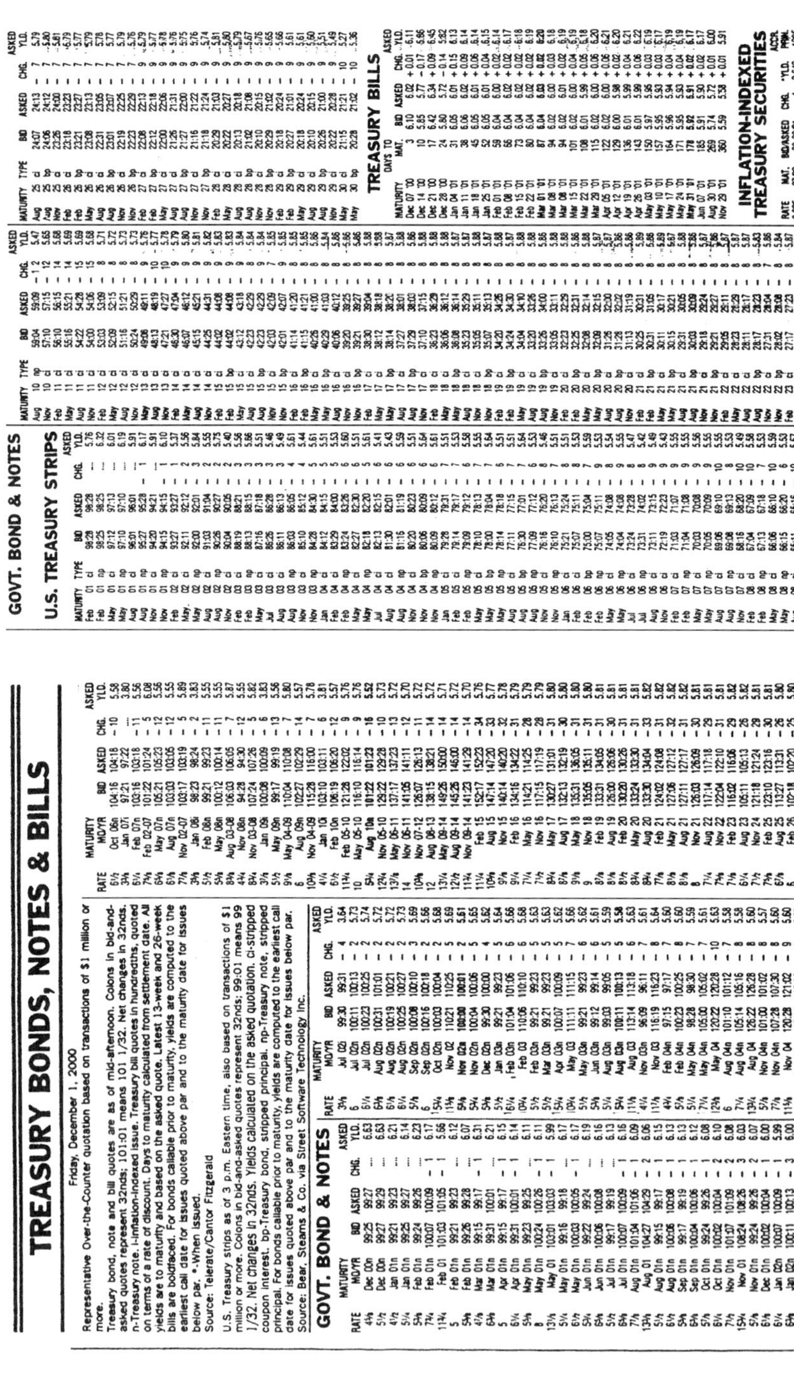

Figure 9.1 Treasury security price data. *Source:* (Reprinted with permission of *The Wall Street Journal*. © December 1, 2000.)

day of the delivery month but less than two years on the last day of the delivery month. Complete contract specifications, including lists of exactly which T-bonds and T-notes are deliverable into each contract, are available under the "market info" header at the CBOT'S website (www.cbot.com).

9.1.1   Reading Spot T-Bond Prices

Before we continue discussing T-bond futures contracts, it is important to understand how to read the price data for the underlying asset: the T-bonds themselves. Figure 9.1 shows the prices of the publicly traded T-bonds and T-notes outstanding as of December 1, 2000. The first column lists the coupon rate, followed by the month and year of maturity. An "n" after the maturity year indicates a T-note.

To the right of the maturity date are columns presenting the bid and asked prices of each T-bond or T-note. These prices are in percent and 32nds of face value. For example, the bid price of the 6 3/8% of Sep 01 T-note is 100 and 4/32% of face value. If the face value of the note is $1000, then the bid price is $1001.25. The asked price of this note is $1001.875. These prices are based on transactions of $1 million or more. In other words, a trader could buy $1 million face value of these notes for about $1,001,875 from a government securities dealer.[5] The prices are quoted flat, that is, without any accrued interest.

The column titled "Chg" is the change in the bid price from the previous day's close, in 32nds. The bid price of the 6 3/8% of Sep 2001 note closed one thirty-second below its closing price on November 30, 2000. Thus, its closing bid price on November 30th was 100:05, or $1,001,562.50 for $1 million face value of these notes. The yield to maturity, based on the asked price, is shown in the last column. The 6 3/8% of Sep 2001 was priced to yield 6.12% on December 1, 2000. The yield to maturity (YTM) is the same concept as an internal rate of return (IRR). It is the interest rate that makes the present value of the remaining cash flows (coupon payments and principal) equal to the bond's gross price. The gross price of a bond equals the quoted price (as seen in the newspaper) plus the accrued interest on the bond.

EXAMPLE 9.1   Compute the yield to maturity of the 6 3/8% of September 2001 T-note shown in Figure 9.1.

Solution   Time 0 is December 1, 2000. Coupons on this note are paid every March 31 and September 30.[6] The ask price is 100:06, or $1001.875 for a $1000 par value bond. The last coupon was paid on September 30, 2000, which is 62 days before December 1, 2000. There are 182 days between the last coupon payment date and the next one on March 31, 2001. Interest accrues on an actual/actual basis. Thus the buyer pays the seller accrued interest equal to:

$$\frac{62}{182} \times \frac{63.75}{2} = \$10.858516 = AI$$

The gross price (principal plus accrued interest) is:

$$P_0 + AI = \$1001.875 + \$10.858516 = \$1012.733516.$$

There are a total of $N=2$ coupon payments remaining. The next coupon will be paid 120 days hence. This is $120/182=0.659341$ of a half-year. Following that, there will be one other semiannual coupon payment of $C/2=\$63.75/2=\$31.875$. The principal will also be repaid when that last coupon is paid. Equate the gross price to the present value of the coupons and principal:

$$1012.7335 = [31.875 + 31.875(\text{PVIFA}, h\%, 1) + 1000(\text{PVIF}, h\%, 1)]$$

$$\times(\text{PVIF}, h\%, 0.6593411)$$

where PVIF is the present value interest factor and PVIFA is the present value interest factor for an annuity. The number in brackets on the right-hand side is the present value of an annuity due, as of the date of the next coupon payment on March 31, 2001. The last present value factor discounts the March 31st present value (the number in brackets) back to December 1, 2000. By trial and error, the semiannual yield to maturity, h, is found to be 3.063%. Annualized using simple interest, we multiply this figure by 2, and conclude the yield to maturity is 6.126%. This confirms the YTM of 6.12% shown in Figure 9.1.

You can use the YIELD function in Microsoft Excel to compute the same answer, by typing the following in a cell:

$$=\text{YIELD}(\text{``12/01/00''}, \text{``9/30/01''}, 0.06375, 100.1875, 100, 2, 1)$$

Alternatively, the FinancialCAD function aaLCB_y can be used to solve for the bond's YTM, as illustrated in Figure 9.2.

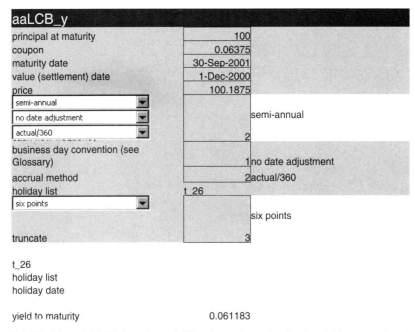

Figure 9.2 The FinancialCAD function aaLCB_y is used to solve for the yield to maturity of a bond.

Some T-bonds are callable. This means that the U.S. government has the option of calling the bonds away from their owners before maturity. If the T-bonds are callable, there are two years presented in the maturity year column; the first number is the year of first call and the second is the year of maturity if the government does not exercise its option. For example, find the "11 3/4% of Nov 09-14" T-bond in Figure 9.1. This bond is first callable in 2009. Otherwise, it matures in 2014. This bond will almost surely be called at the first possible date, given what we know about interest rates as of December 2000. Why?

9.1.2   Reading T-Bond and T-Note Futures Prices

Figure 9.3 shows how price data for interest rate futures contracts are reported in the *Wall Street Journal*. The data summarize trading for December 1, 2000. The CBOT T-bond contract is listed first.[7] Following those price data are the (10-year) T-note, 10-year Agency note, five-year T-note, and two-year T-note futures contracts that trade on the CBOT. What follows describes how to read the CBOT T-bond futures data.

The underlying asset of the T-bond contract is $100,000 (face value) in deliverable T-bonds. The prices are reported in the same way as are spot T-bonds, in "points and 32nds of 100%" of face value. Across each line are the opening price, the high and low prices, and the final settlement price. The column labeled "Change" is the change in the futures price from the previous trading day. Reading down the first column, you can see that delivery dates exist every three months, from December 2000 to September 2001. Delivery months are in March, June, September, and December. For example, in Figure 9.3, the Dec T-bond settle price is 102-02. This equals 102 2/32% of face value, or $102,062.50. The December 2000 futures price was down 17 ticks, or 17/32. This means that on November 30, 2000, the December contract settled at 102-19. A price change of one tick (1/32) will result in a daily resettlement cash flow of $31.25.[8] The life of contract high and low prices follows the price change. In the last column, the open interest, or total number of futures contracts outstanding for each delivery month, is shown. Because the December contract is close to expiration, the open interest peaks for the March contract, and declines as the delivery date becomes more distant.

9.1.3   The Delivery Process for T-Bond and T-Note
Futures Contracts

The delivery process is a three-day sequence of events. The first day is called the **intention day** or **position day**. Even though daily futures trading ends at 2 P.M. Central time,[9] the short has until 8 P.M. Central time on the position day to declare an intention to make delivery (this is called the **wild card option**). The futures settlement price on the position day determines the invoice amount, which is the amount the long must pay the short for the T-bonds. The second day is known as the **notice day**. By 8:30 A.M. on the notice day, the CBOT Clearing Corporation finds the oldest long position and notifies that person that he has been matched to the delivering short. The short has until 2 P.M. on the notice day to decide which bond to deliver. The short then invoices the long. The third day is the **delivery day**. On this day, the short must deliver the T-bonds to the long, and the long pays the short the invoice amount.

It is important to note that the delivery day can be on *any day of the delivery month*. Thus, the first possible position day is two business days *before* the first business day of the delivery month. Traders with short positions in T-bond or T-note futures contracts can announce their intention to deliver as early as two business days before the first trading day of the delivery month. Traders who still have long positions in these expiring contracts at the close of trading on the first position

INTEREST RATE

Treasury Bonds (CBT)-$100,000; pts 32nds of 100%

```
Dec   102-08 102-16 101-27 102-02  —  17 102-27 88-13 126,298
Mr01  102-12 102-16 101-28 102-03  —  18 102-30 88-06 335,468
June  102-02 102-02 101-28 102-01  —  19 102-27 96-21    556
Sept   ...    ...   101-31         —  19 100-19 96-22    160
Est vol 220,000; vol Thu 364,300; open int 462,490, −14,317.
```

Treasury Notes (CBT)-$100,000; pts 32nds of 100%

```
Dec   02-215 102-26 02-125 02-145  — 13.5 02-315 96-075 126,732
Mr01  02-235 103-00 102-17 102-19  — 14.0 03-055 98-04  374,027
June   ...    ...    ...   102-20  — 14.0 102-07 99-11     920
Est vol 254,000; vol Thu 377,071; open int 501,679, −21,877.
```

10 Yr Agency Notes (CBT)-$100,000; pts 32nds of 100%

```
Dec   96-28 97-02 96-22  96-23  — 8.0 97-03 91-17 28,299
Mr01  96-27 97-03 96-225 96-24  — 8.0 97-04 93-25 32,102
Est vol 20,000; vol Thu 42,093; open int 60,401, +4,059.
```

5 Yr Treasury Notes (CBT)-$100,000; pts 32nds of 100%

```
Dec   101-25 01-315 101-23 01-235  — 10.0 02-035 98-13 119,460
Mr01  01-305 102-02 01-245 01-255  — 10.0 102-06 100-11 295,384
Est vol 107,000; vol Thu 193,402; open int 414,844, −9,138.
```

2 Yr Treasury Notes (CBT)-$200,000; pts 32nds of 100%

```
Dec  100-16 00-177 00-157 00-157  — 2.5 10-095 99-12 14,985
Mr01 00-227 00-267 00-225 00-235  — 3.2 00-292 00-075 65,047
Est vol 7,000; vol Thu 26,305; open int 80,032, +1,614.
```

30 Day Federal Funds (CBT)-$5 million; pts of 100%

```
Nov  93.485 93.490 93.485 93.485  .... 93.535 92.900 17,515
Dec  93.54  93.54  93.52  93.53  — .01 93.59 93.11 15,593
Ja01 93.56  93.56  93.54  93.55  — .03 93.61 93.25  8,304
Feb  93.68  93.68  93.65  93.67  — .02 93.75 92.59  8,055
Mar  93.72  93.72  93.70  93.72  — .03 93.75 93.21  2,915
Apr  93.79  93.81  93.79  93.80  — .02 93.83 93.21    764
Est vol 8,100; vol Thu 13,343; open int 53,146, +622.
```

Muni Bond Index (CBT)-$1,000; times Bond Buyer MBI

```
Dec  100-29 101-02 100-12 100-28  — 7 101-06 91-19 15,893
Mr01 100-09 100-17 100-05 100-11  — 7 100-21 98-03  4,166
Est vol 2,600; vol Thu 3,350; open int 20,059, −282.
Index: Close 100-04; Yield 5.81.
```

Treasury Bills (CME)-$1 mil.; pts of 100%

	OPEN	HIGH	LOW	SETTLE	CHANGE	YIELD	CHANGE	OPEN INT.
Dec	94.02	94.02	94.00	94.00	— .01	6.00	+.01	1,174
Mr01	94.15	94.18	94.15	94.16	— .01	5.84	+.01	1,522

Est vol 46; vol Thu 1,615; open int 2,696, +434.

Libor-1 Mo. (CME)-$3,000,000; pts of 100%

```
Dec  93.27 93.28 93.25 93.25 — .01 6.75 +.01 15,851
Ja01 93.49 93.49 93.47 93.48 — .02 6.52 +.02  9,005
Feb  93.58 93.58 93.56 93.58 — .01 6.42 +.01  3,822
Mar   ...   ...   ...  93.64 — .03 6.36 +.03  2,883
Apr   ...   ...   ...  93.70 — .03 6.30 +.03    607
May   ...   ...   ...  93.76 — .03 6.24 +.03    342
June 93.85 93.85 93.85 93.85 — .04 6.15 +.04    558
Est vol 1,924; vol Thu 5,451; open int 33,068, +287.
```

Eurodollar (CME)-$1 Million; pts of 100%

```
Dec  93.33 93.35 93.33 93.35 .... 6.65 ....  482,728
Ja01 93.49 93.51 93.49 93.50 — .01 6.50 +.01  12,968
Feb  93.60 93.60 93.57 93.58 — .02 6.42 +.02   5,896
Mar  93.65 93.68 93.65 93.66 — .03 6.34 +.03 547,572
June 93.82 93.86 93.81 93.82 — .04 6.18 +.04 413,537
Sept 93.91 93.94 93.89 93.90 — .04 6.10 +.04 429,996
Dec  93.84 93.88 93.83 93.84 — .04 6.16 +.04 275,890
Mr02 93.89 93.93 93.88 93.89 — .04 6.11 +.04 227,207
June 93.84 93.87 93.82 93.83 — .04 6.17 +.04 156,075
Sept 93.79 93.82 93.77 93.77 — .04 6.23 +.04 123,908
Dec  93.57 93.71 93.65 93.65 — .04 6.35 +.04  91,581
Mr03 93.69 93.72 93.67 93.68 — .04 6.32 +.04  79,063
June 93.64 93.67 93.62 93.63 — .04 6.37 +.04  62,920
Sept 93.60 93.63 93.58 93.58 — .04 6.42 +.04  58,230
Dec  93.52 93.53 93.48 93.47 — .04 6.53 +.04  42,797
Mr04 93.54 93.55 93.49 93.49 — .04 6.51 +.04  43,460
June 93.50 93.51 93.45 93.45 — .03 6.55 +.03  42,052
Sept 93.42 93.47 93.41 93.40 — .03 6.60 +.03  40,675
Dec  93.32 93.36 93.30 93.30 — .03 6.70 +.03  35,442
Mr05 93.34 93.38 93.32 93.32 — .03 6.68 +.03  29,535
June 93.30 93.34 93.28 93.28 — .03 6.72 +.03  24,881
Sept 93.26 93.30 93.24 93.24 — .03 6.76 +.03  24,422
Dec  93.20 93.21 93.14 93.14 — .03 6.86 +.03  10,746
Mr06 93.22 93.22 93.17 93.17 — .03 6.83 +.03  11,733
June 93.18 93.18 93.13 93.13 — .03 6.87 +.03  10,259
Sept 93.15 93.15 93.10 93.10 — .03 6.90 +.03  10,034
Dec  93.06 93.06 93.01 93.00 — .03 7.00 +.03   6,554
Mr07 93.09 93.09 93.04 93.03 — .03 6.97 +.03   6,391
June  ...   ...   ...  92.99 — .03 7.01 +.03   5,146
Sept  ...   ...   ...  92.96 — .03 7.04 +.03   4,860
Dec   ...   ...   ...  92.87 — .03 7.13 +.03   5,404
Mr08  ...   ...   ...  92.90 — .03 7.10 +.03   4,868
June  ...   ...   ...  92.87 — .03 7.13 +.03   4,682
Sept  ...   ...   ...  92.84 — .03 7.16 +.03   4,197
Dec   ...   ...   ...  92.75 — .03 7.25 +.03   3,369
Mr09  ...   ...   ...  92.78 — .02 7.22 +.02   2,781
June  ...   ...   ...  92.74 — .02 7.26 +.02   2,749
Sept  ...   ...   ...  92.71 — .02 7.29 +.02   2,244
Dec   ...   ...   ...  92.62 — .02 7.38 +.02   1,657
Mr10  ...   ...   ...  92.65 — .02 7.35 +.02   1,511
June  ...   ...   ...  92.62 — .02 7.38 +.02   1,376
Sept  ...   ...   ...  92.59 — .02 7.41 +.02   1,244
Est vol 473,073; vol Thu 878,107; open int 3,352,685, +18,254.
```

Euro-Yen (CME)-Yen 100,000,000; pts of 100%

	OPEN	HIGH	LOW	SETTLE	CHANGE	LIFETIME HIGH	LOW	OPEN INT.
Dec	99.43	99.43	99.43	99.43	— .02	99.68	97.92	14,409
Mr01	99.52	99.52	99.51	99.52	— .02	99.64	98.07	25,337
June	99.54	99.55	99.54	99.55	— .02	99.57	98.20	10,626
Sept	99.50	99.50	99.50	99.50	— .04	99.55	98.05	8,230
Dec	99.40	99.41	99.40	99.41	— .05	99.46	97.89	5,750
Mr02	99.37	99.37	99.37	99.37	— .05	99.44	97.97	3,472
June	....	....	....	99.32	— .04	99.39	97.87	885
Sept	....	....	....	99.21	— .03	99.25	97.84	866

Est vol 3,275; vol Thu 14,205; open int 69,607, −98.

Short Sterling (LIFFE)-£500,000; pts of 100%

```
Dec  93.99 94.00 93.98 93.99 ....  98.80 92.61 153,841
Ja01 94.01 94.01 94.01 94.01 — .01 94.02 93.85   3,017
Mar  94.10 94.15 94.10 94.10 — .02 95.08 92.55 199,080
June 94.18 94.25 94.18 94.20 — .02 95.08 92.49 151,837
Sept 94.22 94.27 94.21 94.22 — .02 95.09 92.41 106,470
Dec  94.18 94.23 94.17 94.18 — .02 95.07 92.31  66,423
Mr02 94.18 94.22 94.17 94.18 — .02 95.13 92.34  69,081
June 94.16 94.19 94.15 94.15 — .02 95.10 92.39  37,218
Sept 94.13 94.14 94.10 94.10 — .02 95.11 92.38  22,225
Dec  94.08 94.08 94.05 94.06 — .01 95.11 92.45  15,796
Mr03 94.04 94.04 94.02 94.02 — .02 94.69 92.49   9,523
June 94.02 94.02 94.02 94.00 — .02 94.05 92.77   8,610
Sept 94.00 94.00 93.98 93.98 — .02 94.04 92.90  11,846
Dec  93.99 93.99 93.99 93.98 — .01 94.03 92.92   1,823
Mr04 93.99 93.99 93.99 93.98 — .01 94.03 93.01   3,234
June  ...   ...   ...  93.98 — .01 93.72 93.04   1,532
Sept  ...   ...   ...  93.98 — .01 93.63 93.35     146
Est vol 72,178 vol Thu 103,781 open int 861,820 +7,252.
```

Long Gilt (LIFFE) (Decimal)-£50,000; pts of 100%

Figure 9.3 Interest rate and futures price data. (Reprinted with permission of *The Wall Street Journal*, © December 1, 2000.)

day must be aware that they might have to take delivery of the securities. The ability to choose the day to make delivery represents a timing option for those traders with short positions. To repeat, the first position day is in the month *preceding* the delivery month.

It is also important to note that the last trading day of the deliverable futures contract is the seventh business day preceding the last business day of the delivery month. Regardless, the short can make delivery on *any* day of the delivery month. This includes the last seven business days of the delivery month, during which there is no futures trading for the now-expired contract. The right of the short to make delivery on any of the last eight days of the delivery month is called the *end-of-the-month option*. The invoice price for delivery during any of the last eight business days is based on the closing settlement futures price on the last trading day. Information about these important dates in the delivery process is available at the CBOT website. Additional information is available in a CBOT booklet, "The Delivery Process in Brief: Treasury Bond and Treasury Note Futures" (EM32-1).

9.1.4 Which T-Bonds Are Deliverable into the T-Bond Futures Contract?

Any Treasury bond that satisfies one of the following criteria as of the first day of the delivery month may be delivered into that delivery month's T-bond futures contract:

If callable, the T-bond must have 15 or more years to first call.

If not callable, the T-bond must have at least 15 years to maturity.

The CBOT lists all T-bonds and T-notes that are deliverable into its T-bond and T-note futures contracts, for different delivery dates. One such list for T-bonds, shown in Figure 9.4, is available on the Internet (www.cbot.com). After accessing the website, follow the successive links to Knowledge Center, Interest Rate Product Information, and US Treasury Bonds/Notes. There, the conversion factors can be downloaded as a spreadsheet. As of November 29, 2000, there were 34 T-bonds deliverable into nearby T-bond futures contracts. As more T-bonds are auctioned by the U.S. Treasury, they will also become deliverable grade securities. By allowing several possible bonds to be delivered, the CBOT creates a large supply of the deliverable asset. This makes it practically impossible for a group of individuals who are long many T-bond futures contracts to "corner the market" by owning so many T-bonds in the cash market that the shorts cannot fulfill their delivery obligation. Figure 9.4 shows that about $442 billion (face value) of T-bonds were eligible for delivery in December 2000. The next section discusses **conversion factors**.

9.1.5 Conversion Factors and Invoice Amounts

Traders with short positions in T-bond or T-note futures contracts can select one of several securities to deliver, should they choose to deliver. They can also make delivery on any day of the delivery month. If they have not offset their short positions by the close of trading on the eighth business day before the end of the delivery month (the day trading ceases), they must make delivery on one of the remaining seven days. The invoice amount, or invoice price, is the amount the short is paid upon delivery of the T-bonds. The invoice amount equals the futures settlement price times a conversion factor plus accrued interest. The conversion factor is the price of the delivered bond ($1 par value) to yield 6%.

	Coupon	Issue Date	Maturity Date	Issuance (billions)	6% Conversion Factors			
					Dec. 2000	Mar. 2001	June 2001	Sep. 2001
1	5 1/4	11/16/98	11/15/28	$10.0	0.8991	0.8996	0.8999	0.9003
2	5 1/4	02/16/99	02/15/29	$10.0	0.8989	0.8991	0.8996	0.8999
3	5 1/2	08/17/98	08/15/28	$10.0	0.9331	0.9332	0.9336	0.9337
4	6	02/15/96	02/15/26	$11.9	1.0000	0.9999	1.0000	0.9999
5	6 1/8	11/17/97	11/15/27	$20.0	1.0164	1.0165	1.0163	1.0164
6	6 1/8	08/16/99	08/15/29	$10.0	1.0170	1.0168	1.0169	1.0167
7	6 1/4	08/16/93	08/15/23	$21.8	1.0306	1.0304	1.0303	1.0300
8**	6 1/4	02/15/00	05/15/30	$15.0	1.0342	1.0342	1.0339	1.0339
9	6 3/8	08/15/97	08/15/27	$9.7	1.0495	1.0491	1.0491	1.0487
10	6 1/2	11/15/96	11/15/26	$10.0	1.0650	1.0649	1.0645	1.0643
11	6 5/8	02/18/97	02/15/27	$10.3	1.0818	1.0813	1.0811	1.0806
12	6 3/4	08/15/96	08/15/26	$9.9	1.0973	1.0968	1.0965	1.0959
13	6 7/8	08/15/95	08/15/25	$10.9	1.1116	1.1109	1.1105	1.1099
14	7 1/8	02/16/93	02/15/23	$16.7	1.1364	1.1355	1.1349	1.1340
15	7 1/4	05/15/86	05/15/16	$18.8	1.1236	1.1225	—	—
16	7 1/4	08/17/92	08/15/22	$9.9	1.1499	1.1489	1.1481	1.1471
17	7 1/2	11/15/86	11/15/16	$18.8	1.1513	1.1500	1.1484	1.1470
18	7 1/2	08/15/94	11/15/24	$10.1	1.1885	1.1877	1.1866	1.1858
19	7 5/8	11/15/92	11/15/22	$8.4	1.1958	1.1949	1.1936	1.1926
20	7 5/8	02/15/95	02/15/25	$10.8	1.2053	1.2042	1.2033	1.2022
21	7 7/8	02/15/91	02/15/21	$10.3	1.2167	1.2151	1.2138	1.2122
22	8	11/15/91	11/15/21	$31.4	1.2354	1.2341	1.2325	1.2311
23	8 1/8	08/15/89	08/15/19	$19.7	1.2355	1.2336	1.2320	1.2300
24	8 1/8	05/15/91	05/15/21	$10.5	1.2470	1.2456	1.2438	1.2423
25	8 1/8	08/15/91	08/15/21	$10.8	1.2488	1.2470	1.2456	1.2438
26	8 1/2	02/15/90	02/15/20	$9.8	1.2812	1.2790	1.2771	1.2749
27	8 3/4	05/15/87	05/15/17	$17.0	1.2828	1.2803	1.2775	1.2750
28	8 3/4	05/15/90	05/15/20	$8.5	1.3113	1.3093	1.3069	1.3048
29	8 3/4	08/15/90	08/15/20	$18.7	1.3136	1.3113	1.3093	1.3069
30	8 7/8	08/15/87	08/15/17	$13.1	1.2985	1.2957	1.2931	1.2902
31	8 7/8	02/15/89	02/15/19	$17.1	1.3138	1.3112	1.3089	1.3062
32	9	11/22/88	11/15/18	$7.7	1.3247	1.3223	1.3195	1.3170
33	9 1/8	05/15/88	05/15/18	$7.6	1.3328	1.3302	1.3272	1.3245
34	9 1/4	02/15/86	02/15/16	$6.8	1.3185	—	—	—
				34	34	33	32	32
				$442.1	$442.1	$435.2	$416.4	$416.4

Figure 9.4 Deliverable Treasury bond conversion factors: all Treasury bonds eligible for delivery into the CBOT Treasury Bond futures contract along with their conversion factors as of Novermber 2000. The most recently auctioned bond eligible for delivery is bond 8, is designated with two asterisks (**).
Source: (Reprinted with permission of the Chicago Board of Trade.)

The purpose of applying a conversion factor is to try to equalize deliverability of all the bonds. In theory, if the term structure of interest rates is flat at a yield of 6%, then with conversion factor adjustments, all bonds will be equally deliverable. If there were no adjustments made, the short would merely choose to deliver the cheapest (lowest priced) bond available, most likely one of the low coupon bonds. For example, the 6% of February 2026 only costs 102 20/32 (see Figure 9.1), and this is much less than the price of 134 22/32 for the 9 1/4% of Feb 2016 T-bond.

Without conversion factors to (partially) equate the incentive to deliver these bonds, the short would clearly buy the 6% of February 2026 bonds and deliver them.

The conversion factor system adjusts the invoice amount when the short decides to make delivery. Thus, a trader who decides to deliver a bond with a low market price, such as the 6% of February 2026, will not be paid as much for it as compared to the amount received for, say, delivering the 9 1/4% of February 2016 T-bond. Specifically, the invoice amount for a deliverable T-bond or T-note is computed as follows:

$$\begin{array}{c}\text{invoice}\\\text{amount}\end{array} = \begin{array}{c}\text{contract}\\\text{size}\end{array} \times \begin{array}{c}\text{futures contract}\\\text{settlement price}\end{array} \times \begin{array}{c}\text{conversion}\\\text{factor}\end{array} + \begin{array}{c}\text{accrued}\\\text{interest}\end{array} \qquad (9.1)$$

The contract size for the T-bond futures contract is $100,000. The settlement price is the futures price on the position day, which is the day that the short declares his intention to make delivery. This price must be expressed as a decimal. That is, a futures price of 102-02 is 1.020625. The conversion factor can be read from a table such as in Figure 9.4, or it can be computed as discussed shortly (see Section 9.1.6). The following formula is used to compute the accrued interest as of the delivery date:

$$\begin{array}{c}\text{accrued}\\\text{interest}\end{array} = \begin{array}{c}\text{semiannual coupon interest}\\\text{on } \$100,000 \text{ face value of the}\\\text{bonds that the short delivers}\end{array} \times \frac{\text{number of days since last coupon}}{\text{number of days in half-year}} \qquad (9.2)$$

9.1.6 Computing the Conversion Factors

The conversion factor (CF) for a deliverable bond roughly equals the price of that bond ($1 face value) if its YTM is 6%. The CBOT makes some approximations in its process of determining actual conversion factors. Here are the steps:

1. Assume it is the first day of the delivery month, and calculate the time to maturity of the bond.

2. Round down this time to maturity to the nearest three-month period. For example, 18 years and 5.5 months becomes 18 years and 3 months. Define this rounded time to maturity as y years and m months.

EXAMPLE 9.2 Suppose that on December 1, 2000, a trader who is short one Dec 00 T-bond futures contract decides to deliver the 9 1/4% of February 2016 T-bonds into his short position.[10] Figure 9.4 shows that the conversion factor of this bond for the Dec 00 contract is 1.3185. Figure 9.3 shows that the final settlement price on December 1, 2000, for the Dec 00 futures contract is 102-02. As of December 1, 2000, there have been 108 days since the last semiannual coupon payment of $4,625 on $100,000 face value of these bonds, paid on August 15, 2000. There are 182 days in the half-year between February 15, 2000, and August 15, 2000. Using Equations (9.1) and (9.2), the trader will be paid the following invoice amount:

$$\text{invoice amount} = (\$100,000)(1.020625)(1.3185) + \$4625\left(\frac{108}{182}\right) = \$137,313.91$$

3. If the rounded time to maturity is $m=0$, then the conversion factor (CF) is the price of the bond if it pays $2y$ semiannual coupons. If $m=6$, then CF is the price if the bond pays $2y+1$ semiannual coupons. In each case, the bond is priced to yield 3% semiannually. Let C equal the annual coupon of a \$1 face value bond. Then:

$$CF = 0.5C\,(\text{PVIFA, }3\%,\ 2y) + 1(\text{PVIF, }3\%,\ 2y)\quad(\text{if }m=0) \tag{9.3a}$$

$$CF = 0.5C\,(\text{PVIFA, }3\%,\ 2y+1) + 1(\text{PVIF, }3\%,\ 2y+1)\quad(\text{if }m=6) \tag{9.3b}$$

4. If m=3 or 9 months, then the CBOT estimates accrued interest to be C/4 (half a semiannual coupon) and assumes that the bond is priced exactly halfway between coupon payments. Under these assumptions, the price of the bond if its semiannual YTM is 3% is found to be:

$$CF = \frac{C/2 + C/2\,(\text{PVIFA, }3\%,\ 2y+1) + 1(\text{PVIF},3\%,\ 2y+1)}{1.03^{0.5}} - \frac{C}{4}\quad(\text{if }m=9) \tag{9.3c}$$

$$CF = \frac{C/2 + C/2\,(\text{PVIFA, }3\%,\ 2y) + 1(\text{PVIF, }3\%,\ 2y)}{1.03^{0.5}} - \frac{C}{4}\quad(\text{if }m=3) \tag{9.3d}$$

The $C/4$ term represents accrued interest. The first $C/2$ in the numerator of the first term on the right-hand side of the equation represents the next coupon, which will be paid three months hence; the numerator itself is that of an annuity due. The denominator of the first term on the right-hand side of the equation discounts the annuity due back three months to time zero.

Table 9.1 illustrates this procedure. Suppose that the bond of interest is the 9% of November 15, 2018. Conversion factors are calculated for different delivery months in 2000 and 2001. The conversion factors are confirmed by observing those presented in Figure 9.4.

9.2 DETERMINING T-BOND AND T-NOTE FUTURES PRICES

As discussed in earlier chapters, the standard futures pricing equation is

$$F = S + CC - CR$$

TABLE 9.1 Sample Calculations of Conversion Factors: The Sample Bond Is the 9% of November 15, 2018

Delivery Date	Time to Maturity[1]	Rounded Time to Maturity	Equation to Compute Conversion Factor
Dec 00	17 years, 11 1/2 months	$y=17, m=9$	(9.3c): $[0.045 + 0.045(\text{PVIFA},3\%,35)$ $+ 1(\text{PVIF},3\%,35)]/1.014889157 - 0.0225 = 1.3247$
Mar 01	17 years, 8 1/2 months	$y=17, m=6$	(9.3b): $0.045(\text{PVIFA},3\%,35) + 1(\text{PVIF},3\%,35) = 1.3223$
Jun 01	17 years, 5 1/2 months	$y=17, m=3$	(9.3d): $[0.045 + 0.045(\text{PVIFA},3\%,34)$ $+ 1(\text{PVIF},3\%,34)]/1.014889157 - 0.0225 = 1.3195$
Sep 01	17 years, 2 1/2 months	$y=17, m=0$	(9.3a): $0.045(\text{PVIFA},3\%,34) + 1(\text{PVIF},3\%,34) = 1.3170$

[1]Amount of time from first day of delivery month until the bond's maturity date which, in this case, is November 15, 2018.

Because the short gets to choose which bond to deliver, the futures price will reflect the spot price (S) of the bond that the market expects the short to select. This is called the *cheapest-to-deliver* (CTD) bond, and is the subject of Section 9.2.1. The carry costs (CC) are the interest charges incurred when an arbitrageur borrows to buy the cheapest-to-deliver T-bond. The carry return (CR) is the accrued interest, actual coupon payments, and interest on the coupons, if any, that a cash-and-carry arbitrageur earns while holding the cheapest-to-deliver T-bonds.

Almost all arbitrage, if it occurs, will be done with cash-and-carry trades. In other words, arbitrageurs will buy the cheapest-to-deliver T-bond and sell the overpriced T-bond futures contracts. Because the short gets to choose which bond to deliver and when to deliver it, performing *reverse* cash-and-carry arbitrage with T-bond futures is almost impossible. Recall that the reverse cash-and-carry strategy involves short selling T-bonds and buying the underpriced futures contracts. However, the bond an arbitrageur short-sells may not be the T-bond the individual who has sold futures decides to deliver. This is a potential problem for the arbitrageur because the short cash position might not be canceled out by the bonds that are delivered into his long futures position. In addition, the arbitrageur does not know which day of the delivery month the short will decide to make delivery.

The shorts' delivery options have value. This means that actual futures price will almost always be below the theoretical futures price computed from the cash-and-carry formula. In other words, the long is compensated for granting the short the delivery options, and the compensation is in the form of a lower futures price.

To understand why $F < S + CC - CR$ because of the shorts' delivery options, first imagine that there are no delivery options. In this case, $F = S + CC - CR$, and a marginal trader would be indifferent between going long or going short the futures contract. Then, suppose that the futures exchange unexpectedly changes the terms of the contract, allowing anyone who is short futures to decide which bond to deliver, and when to deliver it. Clearly, these new terms are advantageous for those who are short futures. At the old futures price of $F = S + CC - CR$, all marginal traders will want to sell futures. This selling will cause futures prices to decline until $F = S + CC - CR - O$, where O is the future value of the delivery options owned by those who are short futures.

Summarizing, futures prices will lie below $S + CC - CR$ because traders who are short futures have valuable delivery options. Because of these delivery options, arbitrage opportunities in the T-bond and T-note futures markets will arise only when futures prices are too high (i.e., when $F > S + CC - CR$). In Sections 9.2.1 and 9.2.2, we describe two approaches for identifying the T-bond most likely to be delivered.

9.2.1 Determining the Cheapest-to-Deliver T-Bond or T-Note: Maximize the Raw Basis

The underlying asset of a T-bond or T-note futures contract is the cheapest-to-deliver (CTD) security. This is because the market knows that if the short does decide to deliver, he will deliver the T-bonds or T-notes that cost the least amount of money (spot price plus accrued interest) and pay the highest amount of money (invoice amount).[11] Thus, *during the delivery month*, the CTD T-bond or T-note is determined by computing the cost and invoice amount (received if that bond is delivered) for each deliverable security. The CTD is the one that maximizes inflows and minimizes outflows for the short.

$$CTD = \max(\text{cash inflows} - \text{cash outflows}) \qquad (9.4a)$$

or,

$$\text{CTD} = \max[\text{invoice amount} - (\text{spot price} + \text{accrued interest})] \quad\quad (9.4b)$$

During every day *of the delivery month*, the quantity [invoice amount − (spot price + accrued interest)] must be negative for all deliverable securities. If it were ever positive for any deliverable T-bond or T-note, an arbitrage profit could be realized by buying that security, selling a futures contract, and immediately declaring the intent to make delivery. The resulting invoice amount cash inflow would be riskless and would exceed the cost of purchasing the T-bond or T-note.

Note that accrued interest appears in both the invoice amount and the total cost of purchasing a bond. Therefore, during the delivery month, the CTD can be computed by using:

$$\text{CTD} = \max[(CF)(F) - S] \quad\quad (9.4c)$$

where CF is a bond's conversion factor, F is the futures price, and S is the spot price (ignoring accrued interest) of a bond. Find the value of $(CF)(F) - S$ for each deliverable T-bond or T-note. The one that is least negative is the CTD security. Be sure to keep F and S in the same face value when using any of the above equations to find the CTD.

The difference between (S) and $(CF)(F)$ is sometimes called a bond's *raw basis*,[12] or if it is adjusted to reflect the contract size of \$100,000, it is called the *loss on delivery*. The CTD T-bond or T-note is the one that minimizes the loss on delivery; this is equivalent to finding the bond with the minimum value of $[S - (CF)(F)]$.

Before the delivery period, we can only estimate which T-bond or T-note will likely be the cheapest to deliver. Therefore, we often say that we are finding *the most likely to be delivered* T-bond or T-note. There are two methods of doing this. The first method is to use Equation (9.4b) or (9.4c) to find the T-bond or T-note that maximizes the difference between expected inflows and outflows. This approach implicitly assumes that today is a possible delivery date. For some bonds, $(CF)(F)$ may exceed (S) prior to the delivery month. Arbitrage will not necessarily be possible, however, because immediate delivery is not possible. Carry costs and carry returns also must be included before declaring an arbitrage profits exists if $(CF)(F)$ exceeds (S) before the delivery period. This method is quick and easy.

The second method is to compute the *implied repo rate* for each deliverable security. The CTD or most likely to be delivered T-bond or T-note is the one with the highest implied repo rate. This is the subject of the next section.

9.2.2 Determining the Cheapest-to-Deliver T-Bond or T-Note: Maximize the Implied Repo Rate

Recall from Chapter 5 that the implied repo rate (IRR) is the rate of return earned by buying the deliverable spot asset and simultaneously selling a futures contract. Selling the futures contract locks in a selling price on the delivery date. The implied repo rate is the rate of return earned on these trades. In other words, the implied repo rate is the rate of return on a synthetic T-bill created by purchasing the spot asset and selling futures.

$$\text{IRR} = \frac{F_0 + CR - S_0}{S_0} \quad\quad (5.4)$$

To compute the implied repo rate for a security that can be delivered into a T-bond or T-note futures contract, first compute the total purchase price of the cash instrument. The total purchase price is the quoted spot price plus accrued interest. This is a cash outflow.

Compute the expected cash inflow on a target delivery date within the delivery month by find-ing the invoice amount based on the current futures price.[13] Another cash inflow is any coupon payment that might be made between the current day and the assumed delivery day, plus any interest that can be earned by investing the coupon.

Annualizing the resulting rate of return from these cash flows results in the implied repo rate. As an example, define the following:

F = futures price

S = asked price for a given deliverable T-bond

CF = conversion factor for the T-bond

AI_0 = accrued interest for the T-bond as of the current date

AI_T = accrued interest for the T-bond as of a target delivery date

T = number of days between today and the assumed target delivery date

C = annual coupon amount, paid t days hence

r = annual interest rate at which the coupon can be invested from day t to day T

If there are no interim coupon payments on the T-bond between today and the target delivery date, the annualized implied repo rate (IRR) is:

$$\text{IRR} = \frac{[(CF)(F) + AI_T] - [S + AI_0]}{S + AI_0} \cdot \frac{365}{T} \tag{9.5a}$$

If there will be a coupon paid between today and the target delivery date, the annualized implied repo rate is calculated by:

$$\text{IRR} = \frac{\{(CF)(F) + AI_T + (C/2)[1 + r(T - t)/365]\} - (S + AI_0)}{S + AI_0} \cdot \frac{365}{T} \tag{9.5b}$$

Note that AI_T in Equation (9.5b) is the interest that accrues on the deliverable bond from the forth-coming coupon payment date (day t) until the delivery date (day T). In Equation (9.5b), the semi-annual coupon earns interest rate at the annual rate of $r\%$, from the day that the coupon is paid (t) until the delivery day (T).

Figure 9.5 is a time line that should clarify the relevant dates involved in computing the implied repo rate when there is an interim coupon.

Since the implied repo rate is the return realizable by creating a synthetic T-bill, it must be less than any possible riskless borrowing rate. If the implied repo rate exceeds a trader's riskless

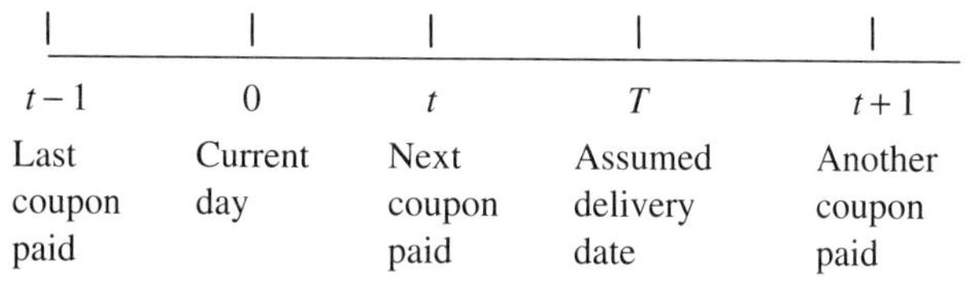

$t-1$	0	t	T	$t+1$
Last coupon paid	Current day	Next coupon paid	Assumed delivery date	Another coupon paid

Figure 9.5 Time line for T-bond futures dates involved in computing the implied repo rate.

borrowing rate, then arbitrage is possible. The cheapest-to-deliver T-bond should have an annualized implied repo rate slightly below the best borrowing rate available. Many T-bonds that are deliverable into the T-bond futures contract will have negative implied repo rates.

It is important to note that as interest rates change and as time passes, the identity of the cheapest-to-deliver T-bond can change.

9.2.3   Determining the Cheapest-to-Deliver T-Bond or T-Note by Using Duration

Participants in the T-bond futures markets often use the durations[14] of deliverable bonds to generate a rule of thumb concerning which bond is the CTD bond. This commonly used rule of thumb is as follows:

1. If yields are above 6%, the CTD bond will be the eligible bond with the highest duration.

2. If yields are below 6%, the CTD bond will be the eligible bond with the lowest duration.

It is important to note that this rule of thumb requires a flat yield curve. Thus, it is not accurate in all situations. However, it is a useful approximation.[15]

9.2.4   An Example of How to Determine the Cheapest-to-Deliver T-Bond

Let us estimate which bond would likely be the cheapest to deliver into the December 2000 T-bond futures contract as of December 1, 2000, using the information in Figures 9.1, 9.3, and 9.4. Table 9.2 illustrates the analysis. The December 2000 futures price on December 1 was 102-02. The delivery date assumed is December 31.

Columns 1 through 4 of Table 9.2 describe each deliverable bond. For example, the first bond is the $8\,7/8\%$ of August 2017. The ask price is obtained from Figure 9.1. Therefore, a price of 132-19 is $132\,^{19}/_{32}\%$ of par value, or \$132.5938 for a \$100 par value T-bond. The column labeled AI_0 is the accrued interest as of December 1, 2000. There are 184 days from August 15, 2000, to February 15, 2001. Because the last coupon was paid 108 days ago, the accrued interest for this \$100 par value bond is $(8.875/2)(108/184)$, or \$2.6046.

Conversion factors are presented in the column following the one with the gross (quoted price plus accrued interest) bond price. The invoice amount is determined from Equation (9.1). The last two columns determine the bonds that are most likely to be delivered. Both methods conclude that one of the first two bonds will likely be delivered.

Depending on whether there is a coupon paid before the assumed delivery date, either equation (9.5a) or (9.5b) is used to compute the implied repo rate (IRR). For example, the IRR for the $8\,7/8\%$ of August 2017 bond is found by using Equation (9.5a) because no coupon is paid on this bond before the assumed delivery date: December 31, 2000, 138 days hence.

$$\frac{(1.2985)(102.0625) + (138/184)(4.4375) - 132.59375 - 2.6046}{132.59375 + 2.6046}\frac{365}{30} \times 100 = 5.92\%$$

The FinCAD function aaBF_repo2 shows that the IRR is 5.92% (Figure 9.6).

If the T-bond with the highest implied repo rate is the T-bond that futures traders are using to estimate theoretical futures prices, then the $8\,7/8\%$ of August 2017 is the CTD because its implied

TABLE 9.2 Determining the Cheapest-to-Deliver Treasury Bond

Coupon Rate	Maturity			Ask Price $100 par[1]	AI_0	Dollar Price ($100 par)	Price+ AI_0	Conv. Factor	Delivery Invoice Price	Eq. (9.4b) Diff.	Implied Repo Rate
	Year	Month	Day								
8.875	2017	8	15	132-19	2.6046	132.5938	135.1984	1.2985	135.1328	−0.0656	5.92
8.500	2020	2	15	130-26	2.4946	130.8125	133.3071	1.2812	133.2570	−0.0500	5.87
8.750	2020	8	15	134-4	2.5679	134.1250	136.6929	1.3136	136.6372	−0.0557	5.85
8.875	2019	2	15	134-5	2.6046	134.1563	136.7609	1.3138	136.6943	−0.0665	5.84
9.250	2016	2	15	134-22	2.7147	134.6875	137.4022	1.3185	137.2841	−0.1181	5.63
8.750	2017	5	15	131-1	0.3846	131.0313	131.4159	1.2828	131.3104	−0.1055	5.59
8.125	2021	8	15	127-17	2.3845	127.5313	129.9158	1.2488	129.8402	−0.0756	5.50
7.875	2021	2	15	124-8	2.3111	124.2500	126.5611	1.2167	126.4906	−0.0706	5.49
8.750	2020	5	15	133-30	0.3846	133.9375	134.3221	1.3113	134.2192	−0.1029	5.49
9.125	2018	5	15	136-5	0.4011	136.1563	136.5573	1.3328	136.4300	−0.1274	5.45
8.125	2019	8	15	126-6	2.3845	126.1875	128.5720	1.2355	128.4827	−0.0893	5.42
7.500	2016	11	15	117-19	0.3297	117.5938	117.9234	1.1513	117.8342	−0.0892	5.35
8.125	2021	5	15	127-12	0.3571	127.3750	127.7321	1.2470	127.6291	−0.1031	5.29
9.000	2018	11	15	135-11	0.3956	135.3438	135.7394	1.3247	135.5978	−0.1416	5.27
7.250	2016	5	15	114-25	0.3187	114.7813	115.0999	1.1236	114.9961	−0.1038	5.11
8.000	2021	11	15	126-9	0.3516	126.2813	126.6329	1.2354	126.4397	−0.1932	4.37
7.250	2022	8	15	117-18	2.1277	117.5625	119.6902	1.1499	119.4894	−0.2008	3.97
7.125	2023	2	15	116-6	2.0910	116.1875	118.2785	1.1364	118.0749	−0.2037	3.88
7.625	2022	11	15	122-10	0.3352	122.3125	122.6477	1.1958	122.3815	−0.2662	3.49
6.250	2023	8	15	105-13	1.8342	105.4063	107.2405	1.0306	107.0199	−0.2206	3.28
7.500	2024	11	15	121-24	0.3297	121.7500	122.0797	1.1885	121.6310	−0.4487	1.59
7.625	2025	2	15	123-16	2.2378	123.5000	125.7378	1.2053	125.2537	−0.4841	1.33
6.875	2025	8	15	113-31	2.0177	113.9688	115.9864	1.1116	115.4703	−0.5161	0.47
6.000	2026	2	15	102-20	1.7609	102.6250	104.3859	1.0000	103.8234	−0.5625	−0.86
6.750	2026	8	15	112-21	1.9810	112.6563	114.6372	1.0973	113.9742	−0.6631	−1.20
6.500	2026	11	15	109-14	0.2857	109.4375	109.7232	1.0650	108.9823	−0.7409	−2.37
6.625	2027	2	15	111-6	1.9443	111.1875	113.1318	1.0818	112.3555	−0.7763	−2.54
6.375	2027	8	15	108-0	1.8709	108.0000	109.8709	1.0495	108.9855	−0.8854	−4.05
6.125	2027	11	15	104-23	0.2692	104.7188	104.9880	1.0164	104.0056	−0.9824	−5.63
5.500	2028	8	15	96-16	1.6141	96.5000	98.1141	0.9331	96.8486	−1.2655	−10.13
5.250	2028	11	15	93-6	0.2308	93.1875	93.4183	0.8991	91.9952	−1.4231	−12.99
5.250	2029	2	15	93-11	1.5408	93.3438	94.8845	0.8989	93.2847	−1.5998	−15.03
6.125	2029	8	15	105-27	1.7976	105.8438	107.6413	1.0170	105.5951	−2.0462	−17.48
6.250	2030	5	15	108-22	0.2747	108.6875	108.9622	1.0342	105.8278	−3.1345	−29.34

[1]Numbers after hyphens are thirty-seconds of a point.

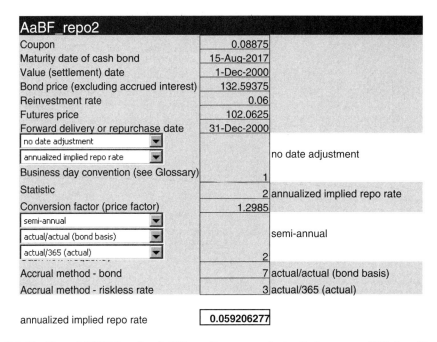

Figure 9.6 The FinancialCAD function AaBF_repo2 computes the implied repo rate, IRR, for a Treasury bond and a T-bond futures contract.

repo rate of 5.92% is higher than any other bond's. The bond with the second highest implied repo rate is the 8 1/2% of February 2020. If Equation (9.4b) is used to estimate the CTD, the 8 1/2% of February 2020 is the CTD bond. Figure 9.4 shows that, in total, these two T-bonds had almost $22 billion face value issued. If there were smaller dollar amounts outstanding, we would have to consider more costly bonds that the marginal investor might have to deliver.

The rule of thumb discussed in Section 9.2.3 helps select the CTD bonds. The 9 1/4% of 2016 has a yield to maturity of 5.79% and a Macaulay duration of 9.21, which is the lowest of the deliverable bonds. By way of comparison, the 8 7/8% of 2016 has a yield to maturity of 5.80% and a Macaulay duration of 9.83. This is the second lowest duration of the deliverable bonds. Duration is the topic of the appendix to this chapter; Section A9.1.2 covers Macaulay duration.

9.2.5 Determining the Theoretical T-Bond Futures Price

Now we have all the ingredients to compute the theoretical futures price. *If we ignore the shorts' delivery options*, inputs into the basic cash-and-carry equation, $F = S + CC - CR$, are as follows:

$F =$ futures price, defined as $(CF)(F)$

$S =$ gross purchase price of the $100 par value CTD bond (which includes accrued interest) is defined as $S + AI_0$

$CC =$ carry costs involved in borrowing to buy the $100 par value CTD bond: $(S + AI_0)(rT/365)$, where r is the annualized borrowing rate of a low cost borrower and T is the number of days until delivery will be made

CR=carry return, consisting of accrued interest on the CTD bond as of the assumed delivery day, any coupons paid between those two days, and the interest that can be earned on any coupons paid

If there are no coupons between the current day, 0, and the assumed delivery day, T, then

$CR = AI_T$ = the accrued interest on the CTD bond as of the delivery date

If there will be a coupon payment on day t between the current day, 0, and the assumed delivery day, T, then the carry return is:

$$CR = \frac{C}{2}\left(1 + \frac{r(T-t)}{365}\right) + AI_T \tag{9.6}$$

The first term on the right-hand side of this expression is the semiannual coupon ($C/2$) that will be paid t days hence, plus interest that can be earned on that coupon amount from day t until day T. The second term on the right-hand side, AI_T, is the accrued interest for the CTD bond from day t to day T. That is, AI_T is the interest accrued from the next coupon payment day, t, until the assumed delivery day, T.

For example, if the 8 7/8% of Aug 2017 bond is the CTD bond, then on December 1, 2000, the theoretical futures price is (ignoring delivery options):

$$(CF)(F) = (S + AI_0)\left(1 + \frac{rT}{365}\right) - AI_T$$
$$F = \frac{1}{CF}\left[(S + AI_0)\left(1 + \frac{rT}{365}\right) - AI_T\right] \tag{9.7}$$

where

$CF=1.2985$

$S=132.5938$

$AI_0=2.6046$

$r=0.06$=approximate annual reinvestment rate for a one-month Eurodollar time deposit

$T=30$=number of days between December 1 and December 31

$AI_T=(8.875/2)(138/184)=3.328125$, because December 31 is 138 days from August 15, 2000, and there are 184 days in the half-year between August 15, 2000, and February 15, 2001

$C=8.875$

Solving for F, the theoretical futures price, we write

$$102.0693 = \frac{1}{1.2985}\left[(132.5938 + 2.6046)\left(1 + \frac{0.06 \times 30}{365}\right) - 3.328125\right]$$

The actual futures price is 102.0625 (see Figure 9.3). Given these data, we might infer that O, the future value of the shorts' delivery options, is worth only about $0.00681 (the difference between the theoretical and actual futures prices) per $100 face value. Here, $O=\$6.81$ for a T-bond futures contract on $100,000 face value of T-bonds. In this case, the very small difference of $6.81 can also be explained by the bid–ask spread.

The FinCAD function aaBFwd will compute the theoretical futures price (Figure 9.7). The theoretical futures price that FinCAD computes (102.0764) differs from the one computed earlier (102.0693) because FinCAD assumes a 360-day year when finding the future value of the gross CTD bond price, and we assumed a 365-day year. That is, FinCAD multiplies $(S+AI_0)$ by $[1+(r)(T)/360]$.

Two last comments are needed. First, if arbitrage opportunities should ever arise, remember that the trades must be tailed to account for the daily resettlement feature of futures contracts. Second, an interesting question to ask is: How will a change in the price of the CTD T-bond affect the futures price, all else equal? We answer that by using Equation (9.7) to take the partial derivative of F with respect to S. Note that $rT/365$ is merely $h(0,T)$, and the result is

$$\frac{\partial F}{\partial S} = \frac{1+h(0,T)}{CF} \qquad (9.8)$$

This says that if the price of the CTD T-bond, S, changes by one point, the futures price, F, will change by an amount equal to $[1+h(0,T)]/CF$. This result will be important when we discuss hedging with T-bond futures.

9.2.6 When Is Delivery Likely to Take Place?

Traders who intend to make delivery of T-bonds will take into account several factors when deciding on which day during the delivery period to make delivery. First, a short might elect to make

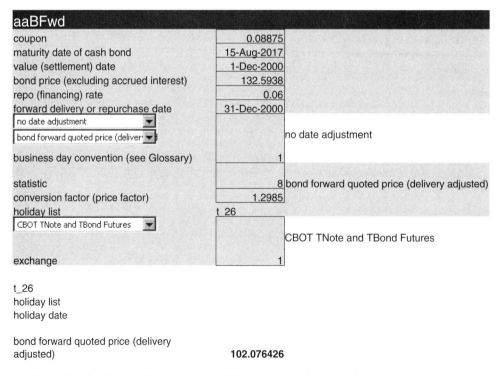

Figure 9.7 The FinancialCAD function aaBFwd computes the theoretical T-bond futures price.

delivery on *any* day simply because he owns deliverable bonds and is planning on selling them, independently of his futures obligation. Tax reasons, liquidity considerations, or portfolio adjustments may necessitate an immediate sale of the bonds. Delivering them to satisfy a short futures obligation might save transactions costs. These unpredictable factors mean that there is a possibility that a short will decide to make delivery on any day during the delivery month, and might not even elect to deliver the CTD T-bond.

The second factor, the short's delivery options, induces a short to generally wait until the last delivery day to make delivery. By making delivery early in the delivery month, a short destroys the value of the quality and timing options that cause actual futures prices to lie below the theoretical prices, computed with the standard cost-of-carry pricing model, $F = S + CC - CR$. The lengthy example presented in Section 9.2.4 showed an actual futures price of 102.0625, slightly below the theoretical futures price of 102.0693. By making delivery early, the short destroys the delivery option value of $6.81. At times, however, the delivery option can be substantially larger, perhaps a few hundred dollars.

It is possible, however, that the short will exercise the delivery option. For instance, a substantial change in interest rates between 2 P.M. and 8 P.M. on any day during the delivery period may induce a trader who is short T-bond or T-note futures to declare the intention to deliver. While the existence of the short's delivery options lowers futures prices and therefore discourages early delivery, there is always a chance that the short will find it advantageous to exercise this "wild card timing option" early.

Finally, in deciding when to make delivery, the short must compare his carry return to his carry cost. If his carry return (the rate at which coupon interest is accruing on the bonds that he intends to deliver) exceeds his carry cost (his short term borrowing rate), he will delay making delivery, all else equal. On the other hand, if there is an inverted yield curve that creates very high short-term borrowing rates, he will more likely deliver early during the delivery month.

In contrast, most commodity futures, such as gold and wheat, have no carry return, so shorts who have the option to choose when to deliver these commodities will typically do so early in the delivery period.

Summarizing, some random factors mean that some deliveries will take place at any time during the delivery month. The short's options will induce delivery late in the month. If the yield curve is upward sloping, then short-term interest rates are less than the carry return (coupons), and delivery will tend to occur late in the delivery period. If the yield curve is downward sloping, some traders may desire to deliver early during the delivery month, all else equal.

9.2.7 The Short's Timing and Quality Options

The trader who is short a T-bond or T-note futures contract has several options that we have already mentioned. This section summarizes these options.

The **quality option** refers to the fact that the short can choose one of several possible bonds to deliver. He will choose the cheapest-to-deliver (CTD) bond. The quality option has value because a trader who is long one particular deliverable T-bond and short futures can at any time sell the T-bond and purchase another T-bond, thus increasing his profits. Sometimes the quality option is called the **switching option** (see Barnhill and Seale, 1988; and Barnhill, 1990).

Another dimension to the quality option is that while the short can announce his intention to make delivery as late as 8 P.M. on the intention day, he has until 2 P.M. on the notice day to decide which bond to deliver. It is possible that the CTD bond will change during this time, thereby providing additional profit to the short. It is also possible that the CTD bond will change during the last seven business days during which there is no trading of the T-bond or T-note futures contracts. This option is called the **end-of-month option**.

We also mentioned two **timing options**. First, the short gets to choose any day within the delivery month to make delivery. Second, the wild card option represents the ability of the short to announce the intention to make delivery as late as 8 P.M., even though the trading day ends at 2 P.M. (both times are Central time).[16]

These options are valuable. Because they exist, the actual futures price will almost always lie below the theoretical futures price that is computed using the standard cost-of-carry pricing model, $F = S + CC - CR$. Equivalently, the implied repo rate of the cheapest-to-deliver bond will almost always be less than any trader's borrowing rate.

The T-bond and T-note futures prices will generally not converge to the spot price because of the end-of-the-month option. Instead, at the close of trading on the eighth-to-last business day of the delivery month, the futures price will be

$$F = \frac{S}{CF} - O \tag{9.9}$$

where O is the combined value of the timing option and the quality options that exist for the remaining seven days of the delivery month; S and CF are the spot price and conversion factor, respectively, of the CTD T-bond. No accrued interest is needed on the last trading day because $AI_0 = AI_T$, and there are no days until delivery.

9.3 USING T-BOND FUTURES TO SHIFT INTEREST RATE RISK

9.3.1 HEDGING FUNDAMENTALS

Once the decision to hedge with T-bond or T-note futures has been made, the hedger must determine whether the cash position will lose value if interest rates rise or if they fall. If an increase in interest rates causes a loss in the spot position, then interest rate futures contracts should be sold. If interest rates subsequently rise, futures prices will fall and profits will be realized on the short futures position. If declining interest rates lead to losses in the spot market, then long positions in T-bond and/or T-note futures should be taken because a decline in interest rates will cause futures prices to rise.

When the hedger has determined whether a short hedge or a long hedge is appropriate, she must decide which contract to trade. That is, should futures contracts on T-bonds, 10-year T-notes, five-year T-notes, or two-year T-notes be traded, or should shorter term futures on T-bills or Eurodollars also be considered? This decision should be made primarily based on the nature (maturity and duration) of the spot position. Changes in the value of the spot position should be highly correlated with changes in the futures price having an underlying asset with the same maturity and duration as the cash asset. For example, if the cash position consists of T-bonds and T-notes with 8–10 years to maturity, then the 10-year T-note futures contract will likely have the least basis risk. Futures on more than one underlying asset may be appropriate when the spot position itself is a portfolio of debt instruments with different maturities. The liquidity and current mispricing (if any) of the different alternative contracts should also be considered.

Finally, the hedger must determine the number of futures contracts that will minimize risk. The dollar equivalency method is best suited for this purpose. A regression model of the form

$\Delta S = a + b \Delta F$ can aid in estimating the hedge ratio, but it suffers from several drawbacks. First, the CTD T-bond may have changed at least once during the period in which historical data were gathered. Thus there is likely to be a distortion in the estimated future relationship between changes in the value of the cash position and futures price changes. Second, when hedging a long position in a bond portfolio, the current maturity and duration of the cash position will differ from what it was during the estimation period. Thus, the current price change of the cash position caused by a change in interest rates, relative to the futures price change, may be different from the predicted one. Finally, there may not be any historical price data for the cash asset if it did not publicly trade in the past.

To use the dollar equivalency method, perform the following steps:

Step 1: Estimate the relationship between yield-to-maturity (YTM) changes on the cash position and YTM changes for the cheapest to deliver T-bond. Sometimes, it will be appropriate to assume a one-to-one relationship. That is, assume that if the YTM on the cash asset rises by 100 basis points,[17] the YTM on the CTD T-bond will also rise by 100 basis points. At other times a regression of the form

$$\Delta r_S = a + b \, \Delta r_{\text{CTD}} \qquad (9.10)$$

will be appropriate. Δr_S is the historical change in the YTM on the spot position, and Δr_{CTD} is the historical change in the YTM of the current CTD T-bond; a and b are regression coefficients that must be estimated. The estimate of the slope coefficient $\hat{b}$ tells us that if the YTM on the CTD T-bond changes by 1 basis point (or 100 basis points), the interest rate on the cash asset will likely change by $\hat{b}$ basis points (or $100\,\hat{b}$ basis points).

Step 2: Compute the change in the value of the CTD T-bond ($100 face value) if its yield changes by 100 basis points. Equation (9.11) can then be used to predict the resulting change in the futures price ($100 face value):

$$\frac{\partial F}{\partial S} = \frac{1 + h(0, T)}{CF} \qquad (9.11)$$

Rearrange Equation (9.11) to find:

$$\Delta F = \left[\frac{1 + h(0, T)}{CF} \right] \Delta S_{\text{CTD}} \qquad (9.12)$$

Equation (9.12) states that the change in the futures price (ΔF) equals the change in the price of the CTD T-bond (ΔS_{CTD}) times $[1 + h(0, T)]/CF$, where CF is the conversion factor of the CTD T-bond. Because the futures contract is on $100,000 face value of T-bonds, the profit/loss on one futures contract, ΔV_F, equals $1000\,\Delta F$. Note that $h(0, T)$ declines to zero as the delivery date nears.

Step 3: Compute the change in the value of the spot position ΔV_S if its YTM changes by $100\,\hat{b}$ basis points [$\hat{b}$ is the estimated slope coefficient from the model of Equation (9.10)].

Step 4: Dollar equivalency requires trading enough futures so that any loss on the spot position equals profits made in the futures market. Trade h futures contracts so that $\Delta V_S = h\,\Delta V_F$.

The sections that follow contain examples of how to use T-bond or T-note futures for purposes of hedging.

9.3.2 Hedging a Long Bond Position: A Short Hedge

Consider a bond portfolio manager who is long $30 million (face value) of the 6 1/8% of November 2027 T-bonds, as of November 15, 2000.[18] Based on the bid price from the November 16, 2000, *Wall Street Journal*, the market value of these T-bonds is 102 $^{30}/_{32}$% of par. Thus the market value is (1.029375)($30 million) = $30,881,250. The manager fears that interest rates are about to rise, and if that happens, the value of his portfolio will decline. To hedge this risk, he decides to sell December 2000 T-bond futures.

The cheapest-to-deliver T-bond is assumed to be the 8 7/8% of August 2017 T-bond. On November 15, 2000, the closing ask price of this bond ($100 face value) was $130.6875. Interest has accrued on this bond from August 15 until November 15, so $AI_0 = (92/184)(8.875/2) = $2.21875. The total price (quoted price plus accrued interest) is $132.90625. The annualized YTM on this T-bond is 5.953%.

Step 1: Assume that if the YTM on the CTD T-bond rises by 100 basis points, that the YTM of the bond being hedged will also rise by 100 basis points. If necessary, the hedger will have to use regression analysis to evaluate how the YTMs of the CTD T-bond (the 8 7/8% of August 2017) and the portfolio bond (the 6 1/8% of November 2027) behave, relative to each other.

Step 2: Compute the price of the CTD T-bond if its YTM rose by 100 basis points, to 6.953%/year, or 3.4765%/half-year. The new price is found by using:

$$P + AI = [C/2 + C/2(\text{PVIFA}, \ h\%, \ N-1) + 100(\text{PVIF}, \ h\%, \ N-1)](\text{PVIF}, \ h\%, \ d)$$
$$= [4.4375 + 4.4375(\text{PVIFA}, \ 3.4765\%, \ 34)$$
$$+ 100(\text{PVIF}, \ 3.4765\%, \ 34)](\text{PVIF}, \ 3.4765\%, \ 76/184)$$
$$= \$121.04455 = (P + AI) = 118.8258 + 2.21875$$

The FinCAD function aaLCB2 computes the fair value without accrued interest (statistic 2) and with accrued interest (statistic 1). On the last line of the spreadsheet output illustrated in Figure 9.8, we add these two values, and find that FinCAD computes the gross price of the bond at the new yield to be 121.0445543, which matches the 121.04455 just computed to five decimal places.

Therefore, if the YTM rises by 100 basis points, the gross price (including accrued interest) of the CTD T-bond will decline by ($132.90625 − $121.04455 =) $11.8617 per $100 face value.

Now, use Equation (9.12) to estimate what the change in the futures price would be if the price of the CTD T-bond fell by $11.8617 per $100 face value. There are 46 days until the target delivery date of December 31, 2000. The short-term interest rate on November 15 is arbitrarily assumed to be 6%/year. Therefore, $h(0, T) = (46/365)(0.06) = 0.0075616$. For the December T-bond futures contract, $CF = 1.2985$ (see Figure 9.4). The predicted change in the futures price is found by using Equation (9.12):

$$\Delta F = \left[\frac{1 + h(0, T)}{CF}\right]\Delta S_{\text{CTD}} = \left(\frac{1.0075616}{1.2985}\right)11.8617 = 9.2040$$

This is $9204 on one futures contract.

Step 3: In step 1, we assume that if the YTM on the CTD T-bond rises by 100 basis points, then the YTM of the bond being hedged will also rise by 100 basis points. On November 15, *The Wall Street Journal* shows the quoted price of the bond being hedged, the 6 1/8% of November 2027 T-bond, as $102.9375 per $100 face value. While *The Wall Street Journal* shows that its

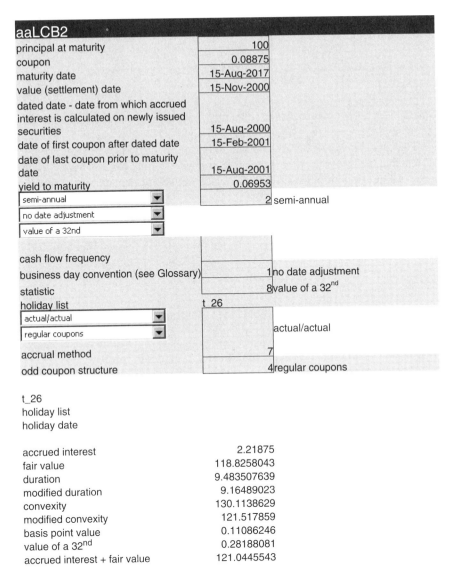

Figure 9.8 The FinancialCAD function aaLCB2 computes the value of a bond, with and without accrued interest.

YTM is 5.91%, the actual YTM is 5.906%. If the yield rises by 100 basis points to 6.906% (3.453% per half-year), the gross price will fall to $90.4994, (Verify this by using a calculator, and the FinCAD function aaLCB2, as we did in step 2 for the CTD bond.) Note that because there is no accrued interest on these bonds on November 15, 2000, the new quoted (flat) price will also be $P = \$90.4994$ per $100 face value. Because the bond portfolio manager has $30 million face value of these bonds, a 100-basis-point rise in bond yields results in a decline in value of $3,731,430 in his portfolio.[19]

Step 4: The dollar equivalency principle leads to the conclusion that

$$h = \frac{\Delta V_S}{\Delta V_F} = \frac{\$3,731,430}{\$9204} = 405.4 \text{ contracts should be sold}$$

As time passes, $h(0,T)$ approaches 0, so that by Equation (9.12), we see that the ΔF resulting from a change in the price of the CTD T-bonds will approach $11.8617/1.2985 = \$9.135$ per $100 face value. Thus, the number of futures contract to be sold will rise to $\$3,731,430/\$9135 = 408.5$. However, note that hedging should be a dynamic process. As time passes and prices change, the entire process we just went through should be repeated frequently, to maintain the risk-minimizing hedge.

Suppose that the bond manager decides to remain short 405 futures contracts until December 15, 2000. Here are the actual results of the hedge, as of two selected subsequent dates. On November 15, 2000, the spot price of the bond being hedged was 102:30 futures price was 100 $15/32$.

Date	Price of 6 $1/8$% of Nov. 2027 Bonds	Profit/Loss from Nov. 15 Until Indicated Date, on $30 Million (Face) of These Bonds	Futures Price	Profit/ Loss on Short 405 Futures Contracts	Hedged Portfolio Profit/ Loss	Accrued Interest on $30 Million of Spot Bonds	h	r
Nov. 15	102-30		100-15					
Dec. 1	104-23	+ $534,375	102-02	− $645,469	−$111,094	$81,216	−0.10%	−2.21%
Dec. 15	108-05	+$1,565,625	104-23	−$1,721,250	−$155,625	$152,280	−0.01%	−0.13%

This was a fairly effective hedge in the sense that the number of futures contacts sold was reasonably accurate. The last two columns show the unannualized rate of return (h) from November 15 until the indicated date, and the annualized rate of return (r). The unannualized rate of return is computed by adding the hedged portfolio gain to the accrued interest on $30 million face value of the spot bond, and dividing by the market value of the spot bond position on November 15 ($\$30,881,250$). Interest accrues at the rate of about $(0.06125/2)(\$30 \text{ million})/181 = \$5076/\text{day}$. A perfect hedge should earn the risk-free rate of return. This hedge earned annualized rates of return of -2.21 and -0.13% if lifted on December 1 and December 15, respectively. In both cases, the short-term risk-free interest rate of about 5.8%, which existed at about that time, exceeded the return on the hedge portfolio.

Remember that basis risk always exists. It is possible that on any lifting date, the futures price and the price of the spot bond could have moved in such a way that profits, or losses, were earned on both positions. Whenever results differ from expectations, the discrepancy should be investigated. Poor results can arise from any of several sources:

1. The CTD T-bond can change over the period that the hedge is in effect, causing the T-bond futures price to track different T-bonds at different times.

2. In step 1 of the hedging analysis, we assumed that if the YTM on the CTD T-bond rises by 100 basis points, the YTM of the bond being hedged will also rise by 100 basis points. This assumption might not be justified. In practice, the hedger should evaluate how the YTM of the CTD T-bond and the YTM of the bond portfolio being hedged are related using regression analysis.

3. All else equal, if *short-term* interest rates decline during the hedging period, it would aid the short hedger, because lower carrying costs will lower futures prices.

4. Miscellaneous other factors might exist. The spot T-bond being hedged and/or the futures contract could be mispriced on any of the relevant dates. Nonsynchronous pricing could affect the reported results (though not actual results). The value of the shorts' delivery options implicit in the futures price could change. For example, if the value of these options is too high on the hedge initiation date, the futures price would be too low on the date the hedger went short. If the value of the delivery options is too low on the hedge lifting date, the futures price would appear to be too high on the date the short futures position is offset.

In this case, the portfolio manager's belief that interest rates would *rise* over the one-month period was incorrect. However, the manager's choice of hedging instrument worked fairly well. Because he held the hedge into the delivery month, he minimized basis risk with the December 2000 futures contract.

9.3.3 Hedging Interest Rate Risk During a GIC Offering Period: A Long Hedge

Insurance companies sell **guaranteed interest contracts** (GIC's) to pension funds. A GIC guarantees a stated rate of return to the pension fund during some stated investment horizon. Frequently, there are several weeks or even months between the day that the GIC is sold and the day that the insurance company actually receives funds from the pension fund. This period is called the *offering period*. During this period, the insurance company will lose money if interest rates decline because bonds must be purchased at a higher price.

An insurance company guarantees a rate of return based on the prevailing rates on the date the GIC is sold. It can guarantee a rate of return because it plans to buy specific bonds with the money it receives from the pension fund.[20] The risk faced by the insurance company during the offering period requires a long hedge. T-bond futures allow the insurance company to lock in the purchase price of a bond.

The *Wall Street Journal* reports GIC rates daily, in its Bond Market Data Bank column. As shown in Table 9.3, a fairly wide range of rates is available for different investment horizons.

TABLE 9.3 Rates on Guaranteed Investment Contracts, July 15, 1999

	1 Year	2 Years	3 Years	4 Years	5 Years
High rate	5.93%	6.40%	6.63%	6.75%	6.76%
Low rate	5.56%	5.96%	6.07%	6.18%	6.28%
Index (an average rate)	5.75%	6.22%	6.40%	6.51%	6.58%
Spread vs Treasuries	+0.77	+0.69	+0.78	+0.80	+0.82

EXAMPLE 9.3 Suppose that on July 15, 1999, an insurance company sells a GIC to a pension fund, guaranteeing a 6.50% annual rate of return over a five-year period. The pension fund finds this rate of return to be attractive because it exceeds the YTM available on five-year T-notes and three-year Treasury strips. In addition, the insurance company will pay all the administrative expenses, management fees, and transactions costs. The insurance company can offer this rate of return because it plans on buying some RJR Nabisco corporate notes. These Baa-rated notes mature on April 15, 2004, and have a coupon of 8 3/4%. On July 15, 1999, these notes sell at a quoted price of 103 1/2 (the gross price is 105.676, which includes accrued interest), and therefore have a YTM of 7.85%. The insurance company believes that the 135-basis-point yield spread is sufficient to pay its costs and leave it with a profit on the GIC it is selling. The insurance company is willing to live with the greater default risk that exists with the RJR Nabisco note.

The pension fund agrees to send $20 million to the insurance company on August 31, 1999. This exposes the insurance company to the risk that bond yields will fall between July 15 and August 31. If that happens, the price of the RJR Nabisco bonds will rise. To hedge against this offering period interest rate risk, the insurance company will construct a long hedge. This is a cross hedge because T-bond futures are being used to hedge against price changes of a corporate bond.

The duration of the RJR 8 3/4% of 2004 is estimated to be 3.92 years. The duration and maturity are roughly similar to those of the 5 1/4% of May 2004 T-note, which is one of two T-notes eligible for delivery against the five-year T-note futures contract. The insurance company assumes the 5 1/4% of May 2004 will be the CTD note for the September 1999 five-year T-note futures contract.

To hedge, the insurance company decides to buy September 1999 T-note futures. To compute how many T-note futures contracts to buy, the company needs the following information:

- P = ask price of the 5 1/4% of May 2004 T-note on July 15 = $98.53125 per $100 par value.
- AI_0 for the T-note = (61/184)(5.25/2) = $0.870245. The gross price of the note is $P + AI_0$ = $99.40195. The YTM of the CTD T-note is 5.60%, and its duration is estimated to be 4.29 years.
- If the YTM on the T-note declines 100 basis points to 4.60%, the gross price (quoted price plus accrued interest) will be 102.782 + 0.870245 = $103.652245.
- Thus, if its YTM falls by 100 basis points, the price of the CTD T-note will rise by $4.250295.

From Equation (9.12), the estimated change in the futures price if the YTM of the CTD T-note fell by 100 basis points is $[1 + h(0, T)](\Delta S_{\text{CTD}})/CF$. Assuming 47 days until the target delivery date, an annual short-term interest rate of 6.00%, and using the CTD's CF of 0.8945, the predicted change in the futures price per $100 face value is

$$\frac{[1 + (0.06 \times 47 / 365)]4.250295}{0.8945} = 4.7883$$

which is $4788.30 per futures contract.

Because this is a cross hedge, the insurance company is unsure of how the YTM of the RJR note will behave relative to the YTM of the current CTD T-note. Therefore, the insurance company runs two regressions:

$$\Delta\text{YTM}_{\text{RJR}} = a_1 + b_1\Delta\text{YTM}_{\text{CTD}}$$

$$\Delta\text{YTM}_{\text{Baa}} = a_2 + b_2\Delta\text{YTM}_{\text{CTD}}$$

The first model regresses historical yield changes of the RJR note on historical yield changes of the CTD T-note. The second model regresses changes in Moody's Baa-rated corporate bond yield index, $\Delta\text{YTM}_{\text{Baa}}$, as the dependent variable. The R^2 values of the two regressions were not statistically different from each other. Being conservative, however, the insurance company chooses to use the lower of the two estimated slope coefficients, $\hat{b}$ = 0.81. Thus, the insurance company estimates that if the YTM of the CTD T-note falls by 100 basis points, the YTM on the RJR note would likely fall by 81 basis points.

The risk to the insurance company of this decline in yields can be calculated as follows. The current YTM of the RJR note is 7.85%. If its YTM fell 81 basis points, the YTM would be 7.04% and its quoted price would be $106.83. Per $100 face value, this is $3.33 higher than the current quoted price of $103.50. The RJR notes pay coupons every April 15 and October 15. On July 15, it has been 91 days since a coupon has been paid. Since there are 183 days between April 15 and October 15, the accrued interest on the RJR notes is

$$\frac{91}{183} \times \frac{8.75}{2} = \$2.175546$$

The insurance company will receive $20 million to purchase RJR notes. Given the current total market value of the RJR note of $105.68 (103.50 + 2.18) per $100 face value, the company could purchase 189,250.57 of these notes, each with a $100 face value. If the price of one $100-face-value RJR note rose by $3.33, the insurance company would have to pay an additional (189,250.57)(3.33) = $630,204.40 to purchase the notes.

To hedge this risk, the dollar equivalency principle requires the establishment of a long position in $\Delta V_S / \Delta V_F$ = $630,204.40/$4788.30 = 131.61 September 1999 five-year T-note futures contracts.

Let's evaluate the performance of the hedge. On August 31, the insurance company received $20 million. On that day, the quote price of the RJR note was $103-00. This is $0.50 per $100 face value lower than it was on July 15. Therefore, if the insurance company buys the 189,250.57 bonds it intended to buy, the price will be $94,625 less than the company had anticipated.

However, the September five-year T-note futures price fell from 109-08 on July 15 to 108-145 on August 31. This is a loss of $796.875 per futures contract. If the insurance company was long 131.61 T-note futures, the futures loss would be $104,876.72. The total loss on both sides of the hedge is $10,251.72 ($94,625 gain on the spot transaction less a $104,876.72 loss in the futures market).

The hedge did not perform quite as well as expected for reasons stemming from the estimated yield change regression model. Recall that the insurance company believed that any yield change on the RJR note would only be 81% as great as the yield change on the CTD T-note. It turned out that the yield on the futures increased by more than anticipated relative to the note being hedged. Obviously, had the insurance company known this in advance, a better hedge would have been devised. This example illustrates how basis risk can be quite high in a cross hedge such as this.

9.4 ADVANCED APPLICATIONS OF T-BOND AND T-NOTE FUTURES CONTRACTS

The examples that follow are based on material presented in "Using Interest Rate Futures in Portfolio Management," published as a Concepts and Applications manuscript by the Chicago Board of Trade.

9.4.1 Changing the Duration of a Portfolio

By buying or selling futures, managers can lengthen or shorten the duration of an individual security or portfolio without disrupting the underlying securities. That is, adding (buying) T-bond or T-note futures to a portfolio increases its interest rate sensitivity, while selling futures decreases the interest rate sensitivity. A portfolio manager will want to increase the duration of her portfolio if she expects interest rates to fall. If she is correct, the value of a bond portfolio will increase more, the greater its duration. Given the price response of a particular futures contract to interest rate changes (the **basis point value**), futures can be bought or sold against the portfolio to replicate the price response of a portfolio with the desired duration.[21]

Hedging decisions are essentially decisions to alter a portfolio's duration. The decision to hedge a portfolio by selling futures lowers the duration of that portfolio. A completely hedged portfolio lowers the duration to the duration of a short-term riskless Treasury bill. The resulting rate of return from a completely hedged portfolio will (theoretically) be the short-term T-bill rate.

The bond portfolio manager will want to change the duration of her existing portfolio to the duration of a target portfolio. This is because if interest rates change by a small amount, say one basis point, the value of her portfolio will change in a predictable way. The following equation [repeated, with discussion, in the chapter appendix: see Equation (9A.7)] can be used to define the change in the value of a bond or a portfolio of bonds if interest rates change by one basis point:

$$dP = -\frac{\text{duration}}{1+r} \times \text{price} \times dr$$

When $dr = 0.0001$ (one basis point), then dP is called the **basis point value** (BPV). If r is defined to be half the bond's annual yield to maturity (YTM), then for a bond portfolio or a single bond, the foregoing equation becomes

$$\text{BPV} = dP = \frac{\text{duration}}{1+\text{YTM}/2} \times \text{market value} \times 0.0001 \qquad (9.13)$$

Instead of using Equation (9.13) for a portfolio of bonds, the portfolio BPV can be calculated by taking the sum of the weighted BPVs for each individual security in the portfolio.[22]

The portfolio manager chooses a target duration so that it will have a particular BPV (i.e., a targeted change in value) if interest rates change by one basis point. Her goal is to choose to buy or sell N_F futures contracts so that [23]

$$\text{BPV (target)} = N_F \, \text{BPV (futures contract)} + \text{BPV (existing portfolio)} \qquad (9.14)$$

EXAMPLE 9.4 As of December 1, 2000, a fixed-income portfolio manager expects a steep decline in bond yields over the next six weeks. Because of his strong beliefs and aggressive management, he decides to more than double the duration of his fixed-income portfolio. The manager wants to profit from his belief that interest rates will decline only over the next six weeks, without disrupting his carefully constructed bond portfolio. Therefore, he decides to buy T-bond futures to increase the duration.

Inputs

Existing portfolio duration	5.7
Target duration	12.0
March T-bond futures price	102-03
Portfolio value	$100,000,000
Portfolio yield to maturity	6.27%

Solution

1. Use Equation (9.13) to find the BPV of the existing portfolio and the target portfolio:

$$\text{BPV(existing)} = \frac{5.7}{1+0.0627/2} \times (\$100,000,000)(0.0001) = \$55,267.36$$

$$\text{BPV(target)} = \frac{12}{1+0.0627/2} \times (\$100,000,000)(0.0001) = \$116,352.35$$

2. Calculate the BPV of the T-bond futures contract. It has a face value of $100,000. You can use the techniques in Section 9.2.4, to determine that the CTD T-bond on December 1 for March futures is the 8.875% of August 2017. On December 1, the conversion factor of this T-bond is 1.2957, its duration is 9.83, and its YTM is 5.80%. Therefore, if interest rates change by one basis point, the value of the CTD T-bond will change by

$$\text{BPV of CTD} = \frac{9.83}{1+0.0580/2} \times \$100,000 \times 0.0001 = \$95.53$$

If the interest rate on six-week Treasury bills is 5%, then $h(0, T) = (0.05)(6)/52 = 0.0058$. Using Equation (9.15), we find

$$\text{BPV of futures:} \quad \frac{\$95.53(1.0058)}{1.2957} = \$74.156$$

3. Determine the number of contracts required to achieve the desired portfolio duration by using equation (9.16):

$$\frac{\$116,352.35 - \$55,267.36}{\$74.156} = 823.736 \text{ contracts}$$

The bond portfolio manager should buy 824 March T-bond futures contracts to increase the portfolio's duration to 12 years.

Thus, the BPV of the existing portfolio, the target portfolio, and the futures contract must be computed. To determine the BPV for either a T-bond or T-note futures contract, the cheapest-to-deliver security must first be identified. The futures price generally tracks the CTD security. The BPV of the futures price can be found by rearranging Equation (9.8):

$$\frac{\partial F}{\partial S} = \left(\frac{1 + h(0,T)}{CF} \right) \tag{9.8}$$

$$\text{BPV(futures)} = \partial F = \left(\frac{1 + h(0,T)}{CF} \right) \partial S = \left(\frac{1 + h(0,T)}{CF} \right) \text{BPV(CTD)} \tag{9.15}$$

This might be interpreted as saying that the present value of the BPV of the futures contract, BPV(futures)/$[1 + h(0,T)]$, is the BPV of the cheapest-to-deliver instrument divided by the CTD's conversion factor. Rearrange Equation (9.14) to solve for the appropriate number of futures contracts needed to change the duration of an existing portfolio to a target duration:

$$N_F = [\text{BPV (target)} - \text{BPV (existing portfolio)}]/\text{BPV (futures)} \tag{9.16}$$

9.4.2 Synthetic Instruments

Portfolio managers can use debt instrument futures such as T-bond and T-note futures to create what are called synthetic instruments. Consider the following diagram:

A synthetic instrument with a maturity of T years can be created by purchasing a short-term security that matures at time t and also going long T-bond or T-note futures. Alternatively, by purchasing a long-term Treasury bond in the cash market and selling Treasury bond futures, a synthetic short-term instrument that matures at time t is created. Creating a synthetic instrument in this way is just a variant of the technique for changing the duration of a portfolio.

Synthetic instruments are created primarily to take advantage of a mispriced futures contract, or to profit from a predicted shift in the yield curve. Example 9.5 illustrates how a synthetic five-year instrument will outperform a cash five-year T-note if expectations are realized.

9.4.3 Asset Allocation

Asset allocation strategies refer to decisions to switch the amounts invested in different broadly defined sectors. For example, a portfolio manager might want to switch from stocks to bonds, or from stocks and bonds to cash (T-bills). The growth in size and liquidity of the stock and debt instrument futures markets facilitates asset allocation decisions. Futures permit faster executions at lower cost (brokerage fees and market impact). In addition, it is much easier to sell futures than to sell short underlying assets.

EXAMPLE 9.5   On December 1, 2000, a fixed-income manager receives a $20 million cash inflow and wants to buy the 5 $\frac{7}{8}$% Treasury note maturing on November 15, 2005. The manager expects a shift of the yield curve in the next month such that long-term bonds will outperform five-year notes. The portfolio manager can either buy five-year T-notes in the spot market, or he can create a synthetic five-year instrument by purchasing one-year T-notes and also going long the appropriate number of T-bond futures contracts to match the duration of the five-year note. If his expectations prove true, the synthetic five-year security will outperform the actual five-year security. In the tabulation that follows, note the predicted T-bond futures prices in the last column.[24]

Inputs	T	Predictions, at Time $T+30$
T-Bond futures price	102-03	105-30
1-Year T-note yield	6.00%	6.00%
5-Year T-note yield	5.54%	5.50%
15-Year T-bond yield	5.80%	5.50%
1-Year T-note price	100-04	100-04
5-Year T-note price	101-14	101-19
15-Year T-bond price	132-19	136-18
1-Year T-note duration	0.994	
5-Year T-note duration	4.365	

To calculate the number of futures contracts to buy in order to match the five-year T-note duration:

1. Use Equation (9.13) to estimate the BPV of the one-year T-note:

$$\frac{0.994}{1+0.06/2}(\$20,000,000)(0.0001) = \$1930.10$$

This is the estimated change in the value of a $20 million portfolio of one-year T-notes if the YTM changes by one basis point.

2. Compute the BPV of the target five-year T-note:

$$\frac{4.365}{1+0.0554/2}(\$20,000,000)(0.0001) = \$8494.70$$

3. From Example 9.4, we know the BPV of the T-bond futures contract is $74.16. Thus, the number of futures contracts required to achieve the desired portfolio duration is:

$$\frac{\$8,494.70 - \$1,930.10}{\$74.16} = 88.519 \text{ contracts}$$

Assuming that the manager goes long 88 T-bond futures contracts on December 1, 2000, and that the predictions concerning the time $T+30$ shape of the yield curve are correct, here is a comparison of the results of the two strategies:

	T	Rate of return	$T+30$
Purchase Actual T-Notes			
Value of 5-year T-notes ($5\,^7/_8\%$ of November 2005)	$20,000,000		$20,030,807
Accrued interest on T-notes	$51,934		$149,309
Days of accrued interest	16		46
Annualized return		7.78%	
Synthetic T-Notes			
Value of 1-year T-notes ($6\,^1/_8\%$ of December 2001)	$20,000,000		$20,000,000
Accrued interest	$565,642		$53,846
Days of accrued interest	169		16
Coupon received			$612,500
Futures gain			$338,250
Annualized return		25.97%	

The synthetic five-year instrument (which incorporates long T-bond futures) outperformed the actual cash five-year note because the yield curve changed according to the portfolio manager's expectations.

To reduce the amount allocated to equities and at the same time increase bond market exposure, a portfolio manager would sell stock index futures and go long T-bond futures. If a portfolio manager wants to quickly reallocate her investment from bonds to stocks, she will go long stock index futures and sell T-bond futures. Example 9.6 shows how this is done. The number of futures contracts chosen is intended to maintain the duration of the current cash bond portfolio. Obviously, it is also possible to increase or decrease the duration of the fixed-income component by buying or selling additional futures contracts, respectively.

In this example, the manager avoided short-term losses of $6.12 million by using futures to reallocate her portfolio mix. If she wishes to make this reallocation permanent, she must then gradually sell off the desired stocks (and at those times offset her short stock index futures position). The proceeds from the sale of the stocks would be used to buy debt instruments, at which time the manager would offset pieces of her long T-bond futures position. If this is only a short-term portfolio adjustment, the manager would hold the futures positions only until she decides the time is right to restore the original asset allocation.

EXAMPLE 9.6 Asset Allocation   On December 1, 2000, a portfolio manager fears a short-term equity decline. The manager has a $500 million portfolio, 80% of which is invested in a broadly diversified portfolio of stocks, and 20% of which is in five-year T-notes. Because of her short-term bearishness regarding the stock market, the manager wishes to reduce equity exposure to 60% and increase bond holdings to 40%. If only cash market trades are undertaken, the manager would make this change by selling $100 million of stock and purchasing $100 of five-year T-notes. The costs (commissions, bid–ask spreads, and market impact) would be significant if spot market trades were made. In addition, since this is only a temporary move, all the costs would have to be borne twice. It is much more efficient to accomplish this asset allocation shift with the use of stock index futures and T-bond futures.[25]

Inputs

Bond portfolio duration	4.365
Bond portfolio yield	5.54%
BPV of T-bond futures	$74.16
Stock index futures price	1,340.00
Stock portfolio beta	1.0
Stock index futures market value	$335,000 ($= 1340 \times 250$)
Current equity value (80%)	$400,000,000
Current T-note value (20%)	$100,000,000

The BPV of the-target T-note is:

$$\frac{4.365}{1+0.0554/2}(\$100,000,000)(0.0001) = \$42,473.48$$

In Example 9.4, we found the BPV of the CTD T-bond underlying the March T-bond futures contract to be $74.16. Therefore to maintain the portfolio's duration, the following number of T-bond futures must be bought:

$$\frac{\$42,473.48}{\$74.16} = 572.73, \text{ or } 573 \text{ contracts}$$

Assuming that the index futures have a beta of one, the number of stock index futures to sell, using relative market values is given by

$$\frac{\$100,000,000}{\$335,000} = 298.507, \text{ or } 299 \text{ contracts}$$

The results of the asset reallocation decision are (using prices on January 3, 2001):

	December 1, 2000	No Reallocation: January 3, 2001	With Reallocation: January 3, 2001
Equity value	$400,000,000	$385,000,000	$385,000,000
T-note value	$100,000,000	$103,000,000	$103,000,000
March S & P 500 futures	1340.00		1290.00
March T-bond futures	102-03		106-08
S&P futures gain			$3,737,500
T-bond futures gain			$2,381,531
Net dollar decline in portfolio		($12,000,000)	($5,880,969)
Percentage decline in portfolio		–2.4%	–1.2%

9.4.4   The NOB, FOB, FITE, and MOB Spreads

In addition to taking outright positions in T-bond or T-note futures contracts in hopes of profiting from their interest rate expectations, speculators can also take advantage of anticipated movements in the yield curve. Several spread trades to accomplish this have become quite popular. These include the NOB (**n**ote **o**ver **b**ond) the FOB (**f**ive-year note **o**ver **b**ond), and the FITE (**fi**ve-year note over **te**n-year note).

Traders initiate the NOB, FOB, and FITE spreads when they believe a shift in the term structure is likely. If the yield curve is expected to steepen, traders will sell T-bonds and buy T-notes. If the yield curve is expected to become flat or inverted, traders will go long T-bonds and go short T-notes. Before trading the NOB, FOB, or FITE, however, careful analysis of each contract's CTD security and duration is required. Only after proper analysis can traders calculate the changes in futures prices that should result from projected yield changes.

The NOB, FOB, and FITE spreads can also be used to exploit anticipated parallel shifts in the yield curve. If all YTMs will rise by the same amount, T-bond prices will decline more than T-note prices. If an upward parallel shift is anticipated, the trader will sell T-bond futures and buy T-note futures. If the yield curve is expected to shift downward in a parallel fashion, traders will go long T-bond futures and sell T-note futures.

Traders perform the MOB (**m**unicipal **o**ver **b**ond) spread when they believe that the YTMs offered by high quality municipal bonds ("munis") will change relative to the YTMs of T-bonds. Low risk muni-bond YTMs are almost always below T-bond YTMs because the interest earned on munis is exempt from federal income tax. There is a municipal bond futures contract that trades on the CBOT. This futures contract is based on the **Bond Buyer** Municipal Bond Index. When traders believe that municipal bond prices will outperform T-bond prices, they will buy the muni contact and sell T-bond futures. This trade will be done when the spread is expected to widen (e.g., when muni-bond YTMs will fall more than T-bond YTMs). Traders will go short the muni futures contract and go long the T-bond contract when they expect T-bond prices to outperform the prices of municipal bonds. Again, however, careful analysis of the profits and losses that will occur if YTMs change in the predicted manner is necessary before a MOB spread is undertaken. See Arak et al. (1987) for more on the MOB spread.

9.5   SUMMARY

Futures contracts on T-bonds and T-notes are probably the most complex futures contracts that trade. After reading this chapter you likely agree. They are also among the most successful financial innovations in history of financial markets. They are indispensable to bond portfolio managers, to financial risk managers of financial institutions and other corporations, to government securities dealers, and to countless other individuals and firms.

This chapter began with a description of T-bonds and T-notes. In particular, we learned how to read their prices in the financial press and how to compute their yields to maturity (YTMs).

Then we learned how to read futures prices for T-bond and T-note contracts. The delivery process for T-bond and T-note futures is a three-day process. The short gets to choose which bond to deliver and when to deliver it. The short also has a wild card option, which allows him to declare his intent to deliver as late as 8 P.M., but he may use the 2 P.M. futures settle price to determine the invoice amount. In addition, the short has until the next day to decide exactly which bonds or notes he will deliver.

To make the eligible deliverable securities roughly equally desirable to deliver, the CBOT uses a system of conversion factors (CFs) to apply when computing the invoice amount. The CF system is not perfect. As a result, some securities will be cheaper to deliver than others. A bond that is relatively cheap to deliver will cost relatively little, and the short receives relatively more in terms of the invoice amount.

We applied the cost-of-carry pricing formula to compute theoretical T-bond or T-note futures prices. However, the model depends critically on predicting the security most likely to be cheapest to deliver. Also, the actual futures price will almost always be below the price of the standard cost-of-carry model because of the shorts' delivery options. This means that the implied repo rate will almost always be below any trader's borrowing rate. When doing any cash and carry arbitrage, the present value of CF futures (a tail) should be sold for every $100,000 face value of CTD T-bonds or T-notes purchased.

Section 9.3 focused on hedging and risk management applications of T-bond and T-note futures. The dollar equivalency approach is the best method for determining the proper number of futures contracts to trade. We illustrated a short hedge that preserves the value of a bond portfolio. We demonstrated how a long hedge can protect a life insurance company against the risk that the price of bond that it plans to purchase will rise.

Finally, we presented three advanced applications using T-bond and T-note futures. First, we showed how these instruments can be used to adjust the duration of a bond portfolio. This is a valuable tool to use when changes in interest rates are expected. The final two applications dealt with creating a synthetic T-note and with changing a portfolio's asset allocation between stock and bonds.

References

Arak, Marcelle, Philip Fischer, Laurie Goodman, and Raj Daryanani. 1987. "The Municipal–Treasury Futures Spread." *Journal of Futures Markets*, Vol. 7, No. 4, August, pp. 355–372.

Barnhill, Theodore M. 1990. "Quality Option Profits, Switching Option Profits, and Variation Margin Costs: An Evaluation of Their Size and Impact on Treasury Bond Futures Prices." *Journal of Financial and Quantitative Analysis*, Vol. 25, No. 1, March, pp. 65–86.

Barnhill, Theodore M., and William E. Seale. 1988. "Optimal Exercise of the Switching Option in Treasury Bond Arbitrages." *Journal of Futures Markets*, Vol. 8, No. 5, October, pp. 517–532.

Hemler, Michael L. 1990. "The Quality Delivery Option in Treasury Bond Futures Contracts," *Journal of Finance*, Vol. 45, No. 5, pp. 1565–1586.

Jones, Robert A. 1985. "Conversion Factor Risk in Treasury Bond Futures: Comment." *Journal of Futures Markets*, Vol. 5, No. 1, pp. 115–120.

Kilcollin, Thomas E. 1982. "Difference Systems in Financial Futures Markets." *Journal of Finance,* Vol. 37, No. 5, December, pp. 1183–1197.

Livingston, Miles. 1984. "The Cheapest Deliverable Bond for the CBT Treasury Bond Futures Contract." *Journal of Futures Markets*, Vol. 4, No. 2, pp. 161–172.

Livingston, Miles. 1987. "The Effect of Coupon Level on Treasury Bond Futures Delivery." *Journal of Futures Markets*, Vol. 7, No. 3, pp. 303–310.

Meisner, James F., and John W. Labuszewski. 1984. "Treasury Bond Futures Delivery Bias," *Journal of Futures Markets*, Vol. 4, No. 4, pp. 569–577.

Notes

[1]On October 31, 2001, the Treasury Department announced that it was suspending issuance of the 30-year bond. However, the press release left open the possibility that 30-year borrowing might again be necessary later in the decade. Given this possibility, and the fact that there were still $360 billion in outstanding Treasury bonds that satisfied delivery conditions for the CBOT Treasury bond futures contract, it appears that the contract will likely survive in the forseeable future.

[2]When issued, a Treasury note has 1 to 10 years to maturity. Treasury bonds can have any time to maturity when issued, some as long as 30 years. All Treasury bonds mature on the 15th of the maturity month. Treasury notes may mature in the middle or at the end of the maturity month. For all practical purposes, there are no real differences between T-bonds and T-notes other than their initial times to maturity when they were issued.

[3]Other commodity contracts also allow the seller a quality option. For example, the wheat futures contract traded on the Chicago Board of Trade allows 11 different qualities of wheat to be delivered to satisfy a short position. The delivery options for T-bond futures will be more thoroughly discussed later in this chapter.

[4]These terms became efffective January 1, 2000.

[5]Government securities dealers bear risk of price changes because they have considerable capital tied up in long T-bond positions or will require capital to cover short positions in T-bonds. T-bond futures markets are of extreme importance to these dealers for hedging purposes. In fact, the U.S. government has in the past postponed its scheduled debt auction when the CBOT planned to close early (e.g., for Christmas). Without the futures market, dealers are unable to hedge and therefore would likely submit lower bids.

[6]Semiannual coupons paid on U.S. government Treasury bonds, and five- and 10-year Treasury notes (when they were first issued) are always paid on the 15th of the appropriate month. Newly issued two-year Treasury notes pay interest on the last day of the appropriate month.

[7]A smaller contract, on $50,000 of deliverable bonds, trades on the MidAmerica Commodity Exchange (MCE).

[8]The 10-year and five-year T-note futures contracts are quoted in points ($1000) and half of $1/32$ point. For example, in Figure 9.3, the high price of the December five-year T-note contract is shown to be 01-315. This is 101 and 31.5/32, or $101,984,375. A tick is half of $1/32$, or $15.625. The two-year T-note contract's size is $200,000 face value in two-year T-notes, and it is quoted in points and one quarter of a thirty second of a point. For example, quoted high and low prices for the December contract of 00-177 and 00-157 equal 100 and 17.75/32 and 100 and 15.75/32, respectively. One tick is one quarter of $1/32$, or $15.625, when applied to the $200,000 two-year T-note contract (which is twice the size of the five-year T-note, 10-year T-note, and T-bond contracts).

[9]The 2 P.M. settlement price establishes daily resettlement cash flows for the T-bond futures contract, even though there are afternoon and overnight trading sessions for T-bonds.

[10]As already discussed, the delivery process for T-bond and T-note futures contracts takes three days, and the short can declare the intention to make delivery as early as two business days before the first business day of the delivery month.

[11]It is possible that other T-bonds could be delivered for one of several reasons. A short might be planning to sell some bonds as part of a portfolio adjustment. It might be cheaper, after transactions costs, to deliver the bonds the short is planning to sell, rather than buy other bonds, deliver them, and also sell the original bonds as part of the portfolio adjustment. Tax considerations might also induce a short to deliver a bond that is not necessarily the cheapest to deliver. Finally, the CTD T-bond might be in short supply (recall that Figure 9.4 presented the amount outstanding for each deliverable security), forcing some shorts to deliver a more expensive bond. In the latter case, the market will likely reflect the shortage in a higher futures price. Obviously, those who are fortunate to be long the CTD bond that is in short supply will benefit.

[12]Recall that basis equals the spot price minus the futures price. For T-bond and T-note futures contracts, the raw basis equals the spot price of the cash security (ignoring accrued interest) minus the adjusted futures price, $[(CF)(F)]$.

[13]The implied repo rate will likely differ depending on which day is chosen as the target delivery date. The factors that influence a trader's choice of a delivery date are discussed shortly. When the yield curve is normal (i.e., upward sloping), the target delivery date is typically the last trading day.

[14]The appendix to this chapter discusses the concept of duration.

[15]Kilcollin (1982), Livingston (1984, 1987), Meisner and Labuszewski (1984), and Jones (1985) discuss this issue in detail.

[16]The CBOT now has evening trading for several of its contracts, including T-bond futures. A trading day begins with the evening session and ends with the settlement price at 2 P.M. on the next day.

[17]In most of the analysis, we assume a 100-basis-point change as a benchmark. However *any* basis point change (basis point, 10 basis points, etc.) can be used. When value changes resulting from a 1-basis-point change in the YTM are analyzed, the method is frequently called the **basis point value** (BPV) method.

[18]More frequently, a portfolio of bonds will be hedged, not a single bond. To compute the change in total value of the portfolio if interest rates change, the analysis that follows can be applied to each of the bonds in the portfolio.

[19]Note that the percentage gross price decline of the CTD T-bond is 8.92%, while the percentage gross (and flat) price decline of the spot bond is 12.08% (i.e., its price volatility is 33% greater). This follows from the fact that a bond's price volatility increases with its duration. The duration of the bond being hedged (13.71) is 39% greater than that of the CTD bond (9.83).

[20]The insurance company would plan to buy a bond portfolio with a duration equal to the investment horizon of the GIC. It would then be immunized against a change in interest rates (though not necessarily against default by the bonds' issuers). As time passed, it would want to remain immunized by keeping the duration of the portfolio equal to the time remaining to the GIC. Futures can be used to adjust a bond portfolio's duration.

[21]Note that the price changes of a portfolio of cash bonds and futures may differ from the price changes of a portfolio consisting only of cash securities with the same duration. Nonparallel changes in the yield curve can have

different effects on the two portfolios because the futures contracts can either underperform or outperform cash securities of similar duration, depending on the nature of the yield curve change.

[22]Taking the sum of the weighted BPV of each security is the more precise method.

[23]We assume that the CTD bond and the bond portfolio will both experience a one basis point change in yield. The portfolio manager may want to estimate the expected relationship between yield changes in the CTD security and the bond portfolio using regression analysis.

[24]This predicted T-bond futures price is derived from estimating the price of the CTD T-bond if its yield declines to 5.5% one month hence. Use Equation (9.7) or the FinCAD function aaBFwd.

[25]Certainly, T-note futures could be used instead of T-bond futures.

PROBLEMS

9.1 Compute, by hand, the yield to maturity of the 12% of May 2005 T-bond, as of December 1, 2000. Assume semi-annual coupons. Check your answer in Figure 9.1, and use FinCAD to compute the bond's YTM.

9.2 How does a bond's flat price differ from its gross price?

9.3 A trader buys the September 1999 T-bond futures contract at 116-28 and simultaneously sells the December 1999 contract at 116-12. Does this trader hope that **short-term** interest rates will rise or fall? Why? Suppose that two weeks later the trader offsets these trades when the September contract is at 115-19 and the December contract is at 115-01. What is the profit or loss on this calendar spread?

9.4 In Table 9.2, which bond is the worst possible choice for the short to deliver? Why?

9.5 A trader who is short the December 2000 T-bond futures contract decides to deliver the 9 1/4% of February 2016 T-bonds on December 7, 2000. Assume that the T-bond futures price is 102-02. How much will the short be paid for delivering these securities? That is, compute the invoice amount. Assuming these T-bonds are not the CTD, why might the short elect to deliver these T-bonds?

9.6 As of November 29, 2000, compute the conversion factor for the 7 1/8% of February 2023 T-bond, for delivery into each of the four contracts (four delivery dates) of December 2000 and March, June, and September 2001.

9.7

a. Assume that the 9 1/8% of May 15, 2018, is the cheapest-to-deliver T-bond into the June 2001 T-bond futures contract. The price of this T-bond on April 20, 2001, is 135-15. Assume that you can borrow and lend for any period of time less than one year at an annual rate of 5%. Assume that the target delivery date for the June 2001 contract is June 20, 2001. Compute the theoretical June 2001 T-bond futures price on April 20, 2001, assuming that there are no delivery options.

b. Who has the delivery options: the long or the short? Briefly describe these delivery options. Because of these options, will the actual T-bond futures price be above or below the theoretical price you just computed? Explain.

c. If the actual futures price on April 20, 2001, for the June 2001 contract is 100-16, compute the implied repo rate for the CTD T-bond.

9.8 If you are a speculator and you are short one March 2001 T-bond futures contract, what are your beliefs concerning interest rates? Suppose you sold one March 2001 T-bond futures contract at its lowest price on December 1, 2000 (see data in Figure 9.3), and deposited the initial margin requirement of $3500 in cash. At the end of trading on December 1, your account will be marked to market. What is the dollar amount of this marking to market cash flow? Is it a profit or a loss for you? Assume the maintenance margin for T-bond futures is $2000. At what March 2001 T-bond futures price will you receive a margin call?

9.9 Suppose that it is November 9, 1990. Assume that the cheapest-to-deliver T-bond is the 8 $^1/8$% of August 15, 2019, and that the quoted price of this bond (not including accrued interest) is 95-10. The target delivery date for the December T-bond futures contract is December 20, 1990. Assume that investors can borrow and lend at an annual rate of 7.75%. Compute the theoretical futures price, assuming no delivery options. If the actual price is 92-17, compute the implied repo rate for the CTD T-bond.

9.10 Which of the following three bonds was likely to be the cheapest to deliver into the March 1997 T-bond futures contract as of January 13, 1997? Use two methods to find the CTD T-bond. The futures price is 110-13.

Bond	Conversion Factor	Quoted Price on January 13, 1997
6% of Feb 2026	0.7782	88:19
8% of Nov 2021	1.0000	112:00
9% of Nov 2018	1.1019	122:24

9.11 Usually, the T-bond futures prices display inversion. In other words, as the time until delivery increases, futures prices decline. Why is it incorrect to infer from this that investors

believe that future spot prices of T-bonds will decline as time passes? What is the real reason for the inversion?

9.12

a. Suppose that today is April 10, 1989. A firm plans on issuing $50 million in 20-year corporate bonds on May 25. It will trade June T-bond futures to hedge. Should the firm buy or sell futures to hedge? Why?

b. Assume that the cheapest-to-deliver T-bond is the 7 $^1/2$% of November 15, 2016, T-bond, which has a conversion factor of 0.9447, for delivery into the June contract. Its quoted price is 84:25. Verify that the conversion factor is correct. Compute the YTM of this CTD T-bond.

c. Assume that the target delivery date is June 20. The short-term interest rate is 8%. Compute the theoretical futures price using the cost-of-carry model. Explain the likely sources for the difference between the actual futures price of 88-06 and the theoretical price.

d. If the firm issued the bonds today, it could sell them at par with a 10.25% coupon, paid semiannually. Assume that interest rates on the firm's bonds and those on T-bonds move in a one-for-one fashion. How many futures contracts should it trade to hedge the planned sale of corporate debt?

e. Suppose instead that the firm estimated the following regression model:

$$\Delta r_S = -0.001 + 0.91 \Delta r_{CTD}$$

where r_S is the YTM on bonds of similar risk and maturity as the issuing firm's bonds. How many futures contracts should be used to hedge now?

9.13 Today is April 10, 1989. A pension fund manager plans to buy $60 million of the 12% of August 15, 2008-13 T-bond on April 30, 1989. Today's quoted price for that T-bond is 124. Use any information in Problem 9.12 and compute the number of futures contracts the pension fund manager should trade to hedge her planned purchase.

9.14 In Example 9.3 of Section 9.3.3, the insurance company estimated that if the YTM on the CTD T-note fell by 100 basis points, the YTM on the Baa-rated note would fall by only 81 basis points. The result was that 131 futures were bought. Rework the problem, assuming that if the YTM on the CTD T-note falls by 100 basis points, the YTM on the Baa-rated note bond also falls by 100 basis points. How many futures should be bought? Given the price data that subsequently evolved on August 31, 1999, with the Baa-rated note price of 103-00, and futures price of 108-145, what is the result of the hedge?

9.15

a. A portfolio manager owns $10 million (market value) of a Treasury bond that has a YTM of 10.70% and a duration of 8.513 years. Does he face the risk of increasing or decreasing interest rates? To hedge this risk, should he buy or sell T-bond futures?

b. Suppose that the price of the CTD T-bond is 79-16. Its conversion factor is 1.2440. Its YTM is 10.96%. The duration of the futures contract is 9.170 years. Assume that any YTM change of the spot bond will equal the YTM of the CTD bond. Also assume that the short-term periodic interest rate from today until the delivery date of the T-bond futures contract is 1% (a constant). Compute the number of futures contracts to trade that will completely

immunize the long position in the cash T-bond (i.e., that will change the duration of the spot position from 8.513 to zero).

c. If YTMs rise by 10 basis points, what loss will the portfolio manager experience on his spot position? What will be the change in the value of the CTD T-bond? What will be the profit on the futures position that immunized the one-bond portfolio against interest rate risk?

9.16 Here is the balance sheet for the Bank Of the Guatemalan United States (BOGUS):

Assets	Liabilities
$12 million cash	$10 million (market value) of 1 year CDs, priced to yield 8%

Owners' Equity

$2 million

a. Suppose the bank has two investments in which to invest its cash: 91-day T-bills that currently yield 7% and/or 30-year bonds with a coupon rate of 12%, selling at $990 per $1000 par value bond with a yield of 12.13%. Compute the duration of the 30-year bond, assuming semiannual coupons, the next of which is six months hence. What amount should the bank invest in each security to immunize itself against a shift in interest rates? Assume that the percentage change in interest rates is the same for all types of debt instruments.

b. Suppose the bank instead decides to invest all $12 million in the 30-year bonds, and use T-bond futures for June delivery to immunize. The cheapest-to-deliver T-bond is the 11 1/4% of February 15, 2015. Its conversion factor is 1.3513 for delivery into the

June futures contract, and its quoted price is 122:13. The duration of the T-bond futures contract is 9.75 years. Assume that the percentage change in interest rates is the same for all types of debt instrument. Should futures contracts be bought or sold in order to immunize? How many should be traded?

9.17 A mutual fund manager is expecting a cash inflow of $50 million in three months. Today is December 1, 2000. He plans to invest the funds in the August 2020 ci (coupon interest) U.S. Treasury strips.

    a. Should the mutual fund manager be concerned about rising prices or falling prices? Why?

    b. Should he buy or sell Treasury bond futures a hedge until the funds are available for investment?

    c. Use the price data in Figures 9.1, 9.3, and 9.4 to estimate how many March T-bond futures contracts he should trade. Assume that the CTD T-bond is the 9 1/8% of May 2018.

9.18 A bond portfolio manager owns $100 million (market value) of high-rated corporate bonds. The duration of this portfolio is 11.3 years, and the average yield of the portfolio is 7%.

    a. Should the portfolio manager be concerned about rising or falling yields? Why?

    b. Should he buy or sell T-bond futures to hedge against this adverse change in yields? Why?

    c. Suppose that on the date in question, the 8 3/4% of May 2017 T-bond is the cheapest-to-deliver bond. Its conversion factor is 1.0709. The T-bond futures price is 112. Short-term interest rates are 6.1%. The bond portfolio manager estimates the following regression equation:

$$\Delta YTM(port) = -0.002 + 1.035 \Delta YTM(CTD)$$

    where $\Delta YTM(port)$ = changes in the yield of the corporate bond portfolio and $\Delta YTM(CTD)$ = changes in the yield of the CTD T-bond.

    Estimate the number of T-bond futures contracts to trade to hedge the bond portfolio.

    d. What risks exist that might make this a less than perfect hedge?

9.19 In Figure 9.4, some bonds, such as the 9 1/4% of February 15, 2016 bond, have no conversion factors for some delivery months. Explain this.

APPENDIX   Duration and Convexity

A 9.1   DURATION

Before a market participant begins to use T-bond or T-note futures to shift interest rate risk, it is important to understand how interest rate movements affect the prices of T-bonds or T-notes. The bond pricing formula shows that an interest rate change will affect the price of the bond through the bond's maturity and the bond's coupon rate. For a given change in interest rates, the change in bond prices will be *greater* the *longer* the bond's maturity and the *lower* its coupon rate, all else equal.

The *duration* of a bond is a useful summary measure of its price sensitivity to interest rate changes. Duration incorporates both the maturity effect and the coupon effect into a single number that measures the price sensitivity to interest rate changes. Duration is useful because it can be used to match price sensitivities between a spot bond position and a futures market position.

The price of a high duration bond is more sensitive to interest rate changes than is the price of a low duration bond. Bonds with relatively low coupons and long maturities have high durations. Bonds with relatively high coupons and short maturities have short durations.

A 9.1.1 Relation Between a T-Bond's Market Price and Its Yield to Maturity

Like the value of any financial asset, the value of a bond equals the present value of the cash flows investors expect to receive. Assuming a low probability that the U.S. government will default on a coupon or principal payment, the relationship between a T-bond's yield to maturity and its market price (per $\$F$ face value) is

$$P = \sum_{t=1}^{N} \frac{C}{(1+r)^t} + \frac{F}{(1+r)^N} \tag{A 9.1}$$

$$= \text{present value of coupon annuity} + \text{present value of face value}$$

In Equation (A9.1), C is the periodic coupon payment, N is the number of remaining periodic coupon payments, and r is the annualized yield to maturity divided by the number of payment periods in a year.[1] In the case of semiannual bond payments, then, $r = \text{YTM}/2$.

A 9.1.2 Macaulay Duration

A bond's duration is a weighted average of the times that cash flows are received.[2] Thus, if a bond will produce three cash flows, one, two, and three periods hence, its duration is a weighted average of the timing of those cash flows. The weight to be applied to each of those times is the fractional contribution of the present value of the cash flow to the bond's total value. The bond's total value equals the present value of all of the cash flows.

To be strictly accurate, each cash flow should be discounted by its own interest rate. These discount rates can be estimated by observing the current term structure of interest rates. Here, however, we will make an approximation that is often used in practice. We simply assume that one discount rate applies to all cash flows. This assumption is strictly valid if the yield curve is flat. Otherwise, we are only approximating the bond's duration. Given this assumption, the duration measure is calculated as follows:

$$D = \frac{1}{P} \times \sum_{t=1}^{N} \frac{t W_t}{(1+r)^t} \tag{A 9.2}$$

where D is the duration of the bond, P is the current price of the bond, N is the number of payment periods remaining, t is the period counter, W_t represents the bond payment in period t, and r is the bond's yield to maturity divided by the number of payment periods in a year. With semiannual coupon payments, r is the semiannual YTM, which is half the annual YTM.

How does the bond's price change as yields change? The intuitive appeal of duration can be seen by taking the derivative of Equation (A 9.1) with respect to r.

$$\frac{dP}{dr} = -\sum_{t=1}^{N} \frac{tC}{(1+r)^{t+1}} - \frac{NF}{(1+r)^{N+1}} \qquad (A\ 9.3)$$

By combining the cash flows received in the Nth period, we get

$$\frac{dP}{dr} = -\sum_{t=1}^{N} \frac{tW_t}{(1+r)^{t+1}} \qquad (A\ 9.4)$$

Multiplying both sides by $1+r$, dividing by P_t, and rearranging, we have:

$$\frac{1}{P} \times \sum_{t=1}^{N} \frac{tW_t}{(1+r)^t} = D = -\frac{(1+r)dP/P}{dr} \qquad (A\ 9.5)$$

By rearranging Equation (A 9.5), we derive a very important attribute of duration:

$$\frac{dP}{P} = -D\frac{dr}{1+r}$$

Recognizing that dP/P = the percentage change in price, and $dr/(1+r)$ is the percentage change in $1+r$, we conclude that

$$D = -\left(1 + \frac{YTM}{2}\right)\left(\frac{\text{percentage change in price}}{\text{change in semi-annual YTM}}\right) \qquad (A\ 9.7)$$

Because calculus was used to derive Equation (A9.5), it works best for small changes in yields. It does show, however, that the duration of a bond is a summary figure for the price volatility of a bond for a given change in bond yields. Because the percentage change in price is $\partial P/P$, Equation (A 9.6) can be restated in terms of the effect of a change in the semiannual YTM (i.e., ∂r), on the change in price:

$$\partial P = -\frac{\text{duration}}{1+r} \times \text{price} \times dr \qquad (A\ 9.7)$$

That is, if the semiannual YTM falls by 0.0001, Equation (A 9.7) gives the increase in the bond's price. This effect is sometimes known as the **basis point value** (BPV) of the bond. Another duration measure, known as modified duration, appears in Equation (A 9.8). That is,

$$\text{modified duration} = -\frac{\text{duration}}{1+r} \qquad (A\ 9.8)$$

Several FinCAD functions will compute duration (and convexity, which is described next), including aaBond_p, aaBond_y, aaBond2_p, and aaBond2_y.

yield

Figure 9 A.1 A bond's price is negatively related to its yield. The relationship is convex.

A 9.2   CONVEXITY

The relationship between changes in a bond's yield and its resulting price changes is not linear. The typical price–yield relationship is convex. As the yield rises, the bond price declines, but the decline is smaller as the yield increases. This is illustrated in Figure A 9.1.

For a large change in yield, it is necessary to account for this nonlinear relationship. The change in the bond's price, correcting for the convex relationship between price and yield is:

$$\Delta P = -\frac{\text{duration}}{1+r} \times \text{price} \times \Delta r + \left[\frac{1}{2} \times \text{price} \times \text{convexity} \times (\Delta r)^2 \right] \qquad \text{(A 9.9)}$$

where

$$\text{convexity} = \frac{1}{P(1+r)^2} \left[\sum_{t=1}^{T} \frac{t(t+1)W_t}{(1+r)^t} \right] \qquad \text{(A 9.10)}$$

Convexity has two important facets. First, the greater the convexity of a bond, the less accurate duration will be as a measure of bond price volatility. As a calculus concept, duration is a tangency to a curve. But the more "bowed" the price–yield relationship, the less accurate will be the measurement for any discrete change in yield. Second, investors desire more convexity to less, all else equal. To see why, consider two bonds with equal prices and yields. Then, for any decrease in bond yields, the value of the bond with greater convexity will increase more. For increases in bond yields, the value of the bond with more convexity will decline less. Thus, in well-functioning markets, market prices of bonds will reflect convexity. The higher the convexity, the higher the price, all else equal.

The CBOT offers a series of *Concepts and Applications* papers. EM34-1 is titled "Understanding Duration and Convexity." To obtain this paper, call 800-THE-CBOT, or access their Internet site (www.cbot.com).

Notes

[1] Note that it is not necessary for the discount rates to be the same at each future time t. It is possible that $r_j \neq r_k$ for two different dates, j and k. Almost always, the coupon payments are all the same, so that $C_t = C$ for all t.

[2] The concept of duration is usually attributed to F. R. Macaulay. *Some Theoretical Problems Suggested by the Movements of Interest Rates, Bond Yields, and Stock Prices in the United States Since 1856*. New York: Columbia University Press, 1938.

CHAPTER 10

Treasury Bill and Eurodollar Futures

This chapter covers the pricing and hedging applications of short-term interest rate futures contracts, with a particular focus on Eurodollar and Treasury bill futures. Chapters 3, 4, and 5 contain important background material concerning forward contracts (FRAs), how they are used to hedge, and how they are priced. Because FRAs are very similar to Eurodollar and T-bill futures, you should review these three chapters before reading this chapter.

Here, we study institutional details of short-term interest rate futures, including unique features concerning their pricing and their use in risk management. In general, arbitrage ensures that forward interest rates computed from spot interest rates equal futures interest rates. Futures contracts are resettled daily, but most market participants agree that this fact has little or no impact on price differences between futures prices and the forward prices. Trading frictions such as transactions costs (bid–ask spreads and commissions) and restrictions on short-selling debt instruments will create a range of futures prices that can exist without any arbitrage opportunities. The additional costs associated with short selling a spot instrument, which is required when one is performing reverse cash-and-carry arbitrage, can be built into any theoretical futures pricing model.

To begin, we will look at the spot market for Treasury bills.

10.1   THE SPOT TREASURY BILL MARKET

A Treasury bill is a pure discount debt instrument sold by the U.S. government. At maturity, the owner of a T-bill receives its face value, which is usually $10,000, although other denominations as high as $1 million are also issued. Maturities as of the issue date are either three months, six months or one year.[1] Three-month T-bills are auctioned every Monday (except on holidays and on days of unexpected acts of nature).[2] T-bills are usually quoted on a discount yield basis. For example, Figure 10.1 is a reprint of price data on T-bills from *The Wall Street Journal*. The columns labeled "Bid" and "Asked" are discount yields. The discount yield, *DY*, is defined as follows:

$$DY = \frac{F-P}{F}\frac{360}{t} \tag{10.1}$$

where F represents the face value, P is the price, and t is the days to maturity.

There are two problems with selecting the discount yield to serve as a rate of return measure. First, a periodic rate of return is computed as $(F-P)/P$, not $(F-P)/F$. Second, the discount yield annualizes this expression incorrectly by using a 360-day year, not a 365-day year. Both these conventions cause the discount yield to be smaller than the true rate of return.

TREASURY BONDS, NOTES & BILLS

Wednesday, July 28, 1999

Representative Over-the-Counter quotations based on transactions of $1 million or more.

Treasury bond, note and bill quotes are as of mid-afternoon. Colons in bid-and-asked quotes represent 32nds; 101:01 means 101 1/32. Net changes in 32nds. n-Treasury note. Treasury bill quotes in hundredths, quoted on terms of a rate of discount. Days to maturity calculated from settlement date. All yields are to maturity and based on the asked quote. Latest 13-week and 26-week bills are boldfaced. For bonds callable prior to maturity, yields are computed to the earliest call date for issues quoted above par and to the maturity date for issues below par. *-When issued.

Source: Dow Jones/Cantor Fitzgerald.

U.S. Treasury strips as of 3 p.m. Eastern time, also based on transactions of $1 million or more. Colons in bid-and-asked quotes represent 32nds; 99:01 means 99 1/32. Net changes in 32nds. Yields calculated on the asked quotation. ci-stripped coupon interest. bp-Treasury bond, stripped principal. np-Treasury note, stripped principal. For bonds callable prior to maturity, yields are computed to the earliest call date for issues quoted above par and to the maturity date for issues below par.

Source: Bear, Stearns & Co. via Street Software Technology Inc.

TREASURY BILLS

Maturity	Days to Mat.	Bid	Asked	Chg.	Ask Yld.
Aug 05 '99	7	4.54	4.46	−0.16	4.53
Aug 12 '99	14	4.55	4.47	+0.02	4.54
Aug 19 '99	21	4.54	4.46	....	4.53
Aug 26 '99	28	4.50	4.42	+0.01	4.50
Sep 02 '99	35	4.53	4.49	+0.04	4.57
Sep 09 '99	42	4.56	4.52	+0.04	4.61
Sep 16 '99	49	4.55	4.51	+0.03	4.60
Sep 23 '99	56	4.53	4.49	+0.05	4.58
Sep 30 '99	63	4.48	4.46	+0.03	4.56
Oct 07 '99	70	4.53	4.51	+0.03	4.61
Oct 14 '99	77	4.59	4.57	+0.02	4.68
Oct 21 '99	84	4.59	4.57	+0.03	4.68
Oct 28 '99	**91**	**4.58**	**4.57**	....	**4.69**
Nov 04 '99	98	4.60	4.58	+0.03	4.70
Nov 12 '99	106	4.61	4.59	+0.02	4.72
Nov 18 '99	112	4.60	4.58	+0.01	4.71
Nov 26 '99	120	4.60	4.58	+0.01	4.72
Dec 02 '99	126	4.61	4.59	+0.02	4.73
Dec 09 '99	133	4.62	4.60	....	4.74
Dec 16 '99	140	4.61	4.59	....	4.74
Dec 23 '99	147	4.62	4.60	+0.01	4.75
Dec 30 '99	154	4.62	4.60	+0.03	4.76
Jan 06 '00	161	4.59	4.57	+0.04	4.73
Jan 13 '00	168	4.59	4.57	+0.03	4.73
Jan 20 '00	175	4.61	4.59	+0.07	4.76
Jan 27 '00	**182**	**4.58**	**4.57**	....	**4.74**
Feb 03 '00	189	4.57	4.55	+0.05	4.72
Mar 02 '00	217	4.62	4.60	+0.04	4.78
Mar 30 '00	245	4.61	4.59	+0.03	4.77
Apr 27 '00	273	4.63	4.61	+0.02	4.81
May 25 '00	301	4.68	4.66	+0.02	4.87
Jun 22 '00	329	4.73	4.71	+0.02	4.94
Jul 20 '00	357	4.78	4.77	+0.02	5.01

INFLATION-INDEXED TREASURY SECURITIES

Rate	Mat.	Bid/Asked	Chg.	*Yld.	Accr. Prin.
3.625	07/02	99-00/01	....	3.963	1038
3.375	01/07	95-27/28	−01	4.015	1049
3.625	01/08	97-04/05	−01	4.020	1029
3.875	01/09	98-25/26	−01	4.019	1013
3.625	04/28	93-22/23	....	3.992	1028
3.875	04/29	97-30/31	+04	3.990	1011

*-Yld. to maturity on accrued principal.

Figure 10.1 Treasury bill price data as shown in the *Wall Street Journal*'s daily listing of quotations on Treasury bonds, notes, and bills. *Source*: (Reprinted with permission from *The Wall Street Journal*. © July 29, 1999.)

To determine the price of a T-bill, given its discount yield, Equation (10.1) is rearranged as follows:

$$P = F\left[1 - \frac{(DY)(t)}{360}\right] \tag{10.2}$$

Note that there are both bid and asked discount yields in Figure 10.1, which reports prices for July 28, 1999. Most secondary market transactions of Treasury securities settle on "the next day." Because July 28 was a Wednesday, trades settled on Thursday, July 29, 1999. The invoice price is computed by using the number of days between the settlement date and the maturity date. Thus on July 28, 1999, a government securities dealer would have been willing to sell a $10,000 face value T-bill that matures on September 30 (63 days after the transaction's settlement date) for $9921.95, because Figure 10.1 shows that the ask discount yield is 4.46%:

$$P = \$10,000\left[1 - \frac{(0.0446)(63)}{360}\right] = \$9921.95$$

The FinCAD function aaDS confirms this result (Figure 10.2).

Dealers would have bought the same bill for $9921.60. One can verify this using the bid discount yield of 4.48%. As noted at the top of each day's "Treasury Bonds, Notes & Bills" column in The *Wall Street Journal,* these quotes are based on transactions of $1 million or more. The bid–asked spread on $1 million (face value) of these T-bills is only $35. Such a narrow bid–ask spread is typical for T-bills.

There is another yield, the bond equivalent yield, that restates T-bill yields on the same basis as yields that are computed for Treasury notes and Treasury bonds.[3]

To compute the bond equivalent yield (BEY), given a T-bill price, use the following:

$$BEY = \frac{F-P}{P}\frac{365}{t} \qquad (10.3)$$

To compute the BEY from a T-bill's discount yield, substitute Equation (10.2) into (10.3) to obtain

$$BEY = \frac{(365)(DY)}{360-(t)(DY)} \qquad (10.4)$$

The bond equivalent yields are presented in Figure 10.1 in the column headed "ask Yld."[4] They are based on the asked discount yields. Thus for the September 30, 1999, T-bill,

$$BEY = \frac{(365)(0.0446)}{360-(63)(0.0446)} = 0.04557$$

which is rounded to 4.56% in the *Wall Street Journal.*

Equations (10.3) and (10.4) apply only if the T-bill matures in six months or less. To compute the BEY on a T-bill with a maturity of more than 182 days, use the following formula:

$$BEY = \frac{-2t/365 + 2\{(t/365)^2 - [(2t-365)/365)](P-1)/P\}^{1/2}}{((2t-365)/365)} \qquad (10.5)$$

where $t =$ days to maturity and $P =$ the price for a $1 face value T-bill.

aaDS		
principal at maturity	100	
maturity date	30-Sep-99	
value (settlement) date	28-Jul-99	
discount rate	0.0446	
accrual method	2	actual/ 360
statistic	1	fair value
fair value	99.2195	

Figure 10.2 FinancialCAD function aaDS computes the price of a Treasury bill, given a discount yield.

EXAMPLE 10.1   Use the information in Figure 10.1 to compute the BEY for the May 25, 2000, T-bill. First, use Equation (10.2) and the asked discount yield to compute the price of the $1 face value T-bill:

$$P = 1 \left[1 - \frac{(0.0466)(301)}{360} \right] = \$0.961037$$

Then, use the price of $P = 0.961037$ and the days to maturity of $t = 301$ in Equation (10.5) to compute the BEY:

$$BEY = \frac{-\dfrac{(2)(301)}{365} + 2 \left[\left(\dfrac{301}{365} \right)^2 - \left(\dfrac{(2)(301) - 365}{365} \right) \left(\dfrac{0.961037 - 1}{0.961037} \right) \right]^{1/2}}{\dfrac{(2)(301) - 365}{365}}$$

$$BEY = \frac{-1.649315 + 2 [0.68006 - (0.649315)(-0.04054266)]^{1/2}}{0.649315} = 0.048696 = 4.87\%$$

In reality, an investor who purchases any pure discount debt instrument can be certain of only one yield, or rate of return. That return is the unannualized rate of return earned during the holding period from time 0 to time t:

$$h(0, t) = \frac{F - P}{P} \tag{10.6}$$

An investor who buys the $10,000 face value T-bill with 63 days to maturity for $9921.95 (the asked price) will earn 0.786640% over the 63-day holding period:

$$h(0, 62) = \frac{10,000 - 9921.95}{9921.95} = 0.00786640$$

There are two ways of annualizing this periodic rate of return. Using simple interest (as for the bond equivalent yield if $t \leq 182$ days), the annualized rate is:

$$(0.00786640)(365/63) = 0.045575 = 4.60\%$$

Alternatively, it may be assumed that interest is compounded over each 63-day interval in a year. In this case, $1 + h(0, 63)$ is raised to the number of 63-day periods in a year to compute the "effective annual rate of return":

$$(1.00786640)^{365/63} - 1 = (1.00786640)^{5.79365} - 1 = 4.64\%$$

10.2   T-BILL FUTURES CONTRACTS

The underlying asset of a T-bill futures contract is specified as three-month (13-week) U.S. T-bills having a face value at maturity of $1 million.[5] The delivery dates are in March, June, September, and December, and the two nearest serial months. Thus, there are contracts trading for six delivery dates, including the next three months. The last trading day is at 12:00 noon (Chicago time) on the day of the 91-day T-bill auction in the week of the third Wednesday of the contract month. The T-bill futures contract is cash-settled.

Table 10.1 presents T-bill futures price data for July 28, 1999. Price data for many interest rate futures contracts are available at the CME website (www.cme.com/market/quote.html).

The futures "prices" in Table 10.1 are actually IMM Index levels:

$$\text{IMM Index} = 100 - DY \tag{10.7}$$

In Equation (10.7), DY is the discount yield for the futures contract. Thus, the September 1999 futures settlement price of 95.345 corresponds to a discount yield of 4.655%. This is effectively a forward rate, in the sense of the forward rates we discussed in Chapter 3 through 5. A trader who buys the September 1999 T-bill futures contract at a futures price of 95.345 has agreed to buy $1 million (face value) of 13-week T-bills on the delivery date, at a price that is consistent with a discount yield of 4.655%. This trader has agreed to a forward lending situation, in as much as buying T-bills represents lending money to the U.S. government. A trader who sells this contract has agreed to deliver, or sell, $1 million (face value) of 13-week T-bills at a price consistent with a discount yield of 4.655%.

TABLE 10.1   U.S. Treasury Bills: Settlement Prices as of 07:00 P.M., July 28, 1999.

Mth/ Year	Open	Daily High	Daily Low	Last	Sett	PT CHGE	EST VOL	Prior Day Sett	Prior Day Vol	Prior Day Int
Sep99	95.33	95.345	95.32	95.345	95.345	UNCH	82	95.345	134	872
Dec99	95.18	95.24	95.18	95.19A	95.19	−3	17	95.22	0	29
Total							99		134	901

Source: Reprinted with permission from Chicago Mercantile Exchange, Inc.

The "A" in the price of the December 1999 contract in Table 10.1 refers to an ask quote (if there were a "B," this would refer to a bid quote.) T-bill futures trade in half-tick sizes of 0.005, valued at \$12.50/half-tick. Thus, the December 1999 contract declined three ticks, from 95.22 to 95.19, on July 28, 1999. A trader who was short one contract earned a mark-to-market profit of \$75.

Now, unfortunately, we must introduce a bit of ambiguity. The underlying asset for the T-bill futures contract is a \$1 million face value T-bill that will have 91 days to maturity on the delivery date. However, a fictitious 90-day T-bill is used to compute changes in value caused by futures price changes. This is how we can properly interpret the \$12.50 per half-tick (which is one-half of a basis point in discount yield). Thus, given the discount yield of 4.655%, the value of the fictitious 90-day T-bill underlying the futures contract is [from Equation (10.2)]:

$$P = \$1,000,000\left[1 - \frac{(0.04655)(90)}{360}\right] = \$988,362.50$$

If the discount yield changes by one basis point (one one-hundredth of a percent; i.e., to either 4.645 or 4.665%), then the IMM index will change by one tick (0.01), and the value of 90-day T-bills will change by \$25. From Equation (10.2) we write

$$P = \$1,000,000\left[1 - \frac{(0.04645)(90)}{360}\right] = \$988,387.50$$

All T-bill futures positions are marked to market by using one half-tick = one half-basis point = \$12.50. Thus for every half-tick (0.005) that the futures price rises, a long position profits by \$12.50 and a short position loses \$12.50. Anyone who has not closed his position before the close of trading on the last trading day (usually a Wednesday) will see his position marked to market one last time, at noon. The final settlement price will be equal to 100 minus the average discount rate at the Treasury's third 91-day T-bill auction of the contract month.

10.3   THE EURODOLLAR CASH MARKET

Dollars deposited into foreign banks are called Eurodollars. These funds are called Eurodollars because the practice of depositing dollars into foreign banks began in Europe. However now, the foreign bank can be anywhere in the world, not only in Europe. Depositors of Eurodollars can be, for example, a foreign or domestic corporation, individual, bank, or government. Today, dollar-denominated deposits, worth trillions of dollars, exist in banks all around the world. Eurodollar time deposits have fixed terms ranging from overnight to several years. However, most are for short terms of less than one year.

Yields on Eurodollar time deposits are always greater than those on T-bills, and they usually exceed the yields available on other U.S. money market instruments such as domestic negotiable certificates of deposit and commercial paper. T-bill yields are the lowest of all money market yields because they have no default risk (as long as the U.S. government exists). Eurodollar yields are higher for several reasons. First, foreign banks can offer higher yields because they operate under less regulation, such as reserve requirements and deposit insurance costs, than domestic banks. Second, U.S. investors demand higher yields because they are moving their capital abroad, where there may be risk that the foreign government will interfere with the movement of funds, as well as default risk. Finally, although the U.S. government, namely, the Federal Reserve

System, has rescued several large domestic banks, it is not clear that foreign governments will do the same.

The benchmark interest rate that foreign banks pay on Eurodollar time deposits made by other banks is usually the London Inter-Bank Offer Rate, or LIBOR. Typically, in the Eurodollar spot market, a borrower and a lender agree on the principal amount and an annual rate on day t. On settlement day, generally day $t + 2$, the borrower receives the principal. At loan maturity, the borrower pays back the principal and interest, calculated on an actual/360 basis.

LIBOR is an **add-on yield**. Define

F = future value

P = present value

t = time to maturity

Then,

$$F = P\left[1 + \left(\text{LIBOR}\,\frac{t}{360}\right)\right] \tag{10.8}$$

Rearranging Equation (10.8), we define the add-on yield, AOY, as follows:

$$\text{AOY} = \text{LIBOR} = \frac{F - P}{P}\,\frac{360}{t} \tag{10.9}$$

10.4 EURODOLLAR FUTURES CONTRACTS

Eurodollar futures began trading on the Chicago Mercantile Exchange on September 9, 1981.[6] Eurodollar futures quickly surpassed T-bill futures in popularity in 1984 and have dominated trading ever since. In 2001 the average daily volume for CME Eurodollar futures was 730,220 contracts, dwarfing the 123 T-Bill futures contracts that were traded during an average day. At least two factors help explain the great success of the Eurodollar futures contract. First, the size of the spot Eurodollar market is enormous, estimated to be in the trillions of dollars. Second, buyers and sellers of other money market instruments that possess a default risk premium find that Eurodollar futures yields are more highly correlated with yields on their spot securities than T-bill yields. That is, Eurodollar futures are more effective at hedging a firm's or a financial institution's interest expense than T-bill futures.

Eurodollar futures prices are quoted in terms of the IMM Index:

$$\text{IMM Index} = 100 - \text{LIBOR} \tag{10.10}$$

For Eurodollar futures, LIBOR is the futures interest rate. If the IMM Index is at 94.19, then the futures LIBOR is 5.81%. The CME Eurodollar futures contract is cash settled. On the last trading day, which is usually the second business day in London before the third Wednesday of the delivery month, all open positions are marked to market for the last time.[7] The final settlement price is 100 minus the British Bankers' Association interest settlement rate for three-month Eurodollar interbank time deposits, rounded to the nearest 1/10000th of a percentage point. Decimal fractions ending in a "five" are rounded up (e.g., an average rate of $5\,^{21}/_{32}\%$ would be rounded up to 5.6563, in which case the final settlement IMM Index would be 94.3437).

The underlying asset of the Eurodollar futures contract is a three-month Eurodollar time deposit with a principal value of $1 million. From Equation (10.8), the interest on this time deposit is:

$$\text{interest at maturity} = \text{principal} \times \text{futures LIBOR rate} \times \frac{90}{360} \qquad (10.11)$$

If the futures LIBOR rate is 5.81%, interest at maturity is

$$\$14,525 = 1,000,000 \times 0.0581 \times \frac{90}{360}$$

If the futures LIBOR rate rises by one basis point to 5.82%, the interest at maturity increases by $25 to $14,550. Futures traders keep track of these basis point moves using ticks. As shown in Equation (10.10), if the futures LIBOR rate increases by one basis point, the IMM Index falls one "tick."[8] So, each basis point change in the futures LIBOR rate results in a $25 cash flow. If the futures LIBOR rate increases by 100 basis points, a trader who is short one Eurodollar futures contract is credited with a $2500 cash inflow. Eurodollar futures trade in half-ticks, worth $12.50 per half-tick. The expiring month contract trades in quarter-ticks, worth $6.25 each.

Table 10.2 presents July 28, 1999, Eurodollar futures price data from the CME website (www.cme.com). Eurodollar futures trade on the International Monetary Market (a division of the CME) and on the London International Financial Futures Exchange (LIFFE). At the CME, Eurodollar futures products trade simultaneously via the GLOBEX electronic trading system and via open outcry on the trading floor. At the CME, delivery dates for the IMM contract extend 10 years into the future. In December 2001 the most distant contract had a delivery date in December 2011.

10.4.1   Theoretical Pricing of Eurodollar Futures Contracts

The concepts presented in Section 5.3 can be used to calculate theoretical Eurodollar futures prices. In a market free from arbitrage, the theoretical futures price will reflect the forward interest rate implied in the existing term structure of interest rates. Recall the unannualized term structure model of Equation (5.11):

$$1 + h(0, t2) = [1 + h(0, t1)][1 + fh(t1, t2)] \qquad (10.12)$$

In Equation (10.12), $h(0, t)$ is a spot unannualized interest rate over the time period beginning today and ending at time t. The unannualized forward interest rate beginning at time $t1$, and ending at time $t2$, is $fh(t1, t2)$.

If time T is the last day of trading the Eurodollar futures contract, then the Eurodollar futures yield is an interest rate from day T to day $T+90$, and Equation (10.12) can be rewritten as follows:

$$[1 + h(0, T + 90)] = [1 + h(0, T)][1 + fh(T, T + 90)] \qquad (10.13)$$

or, assuming a 360-day year and immediate settlement of Eurodollar time deposits, the fundamental no-arbitrage equation for the forward rate implied by Eurodollar futures is

$$1 + [r(0, T + 90)]\frac{T + 90}{360} = \left\{ 1 + [r(0, T)]\frac{T}{360} \right\} \left\{ 1 + [fr(T, T + 90)]\frac{90}{360} \right\} \qquad (10.14)$$

TABLE 10.2 Eurodollar Settlement Prices as of 07:00 P.M., July 28, 1999

Mth/ Strike	Open	High	Daily Low	Last	SETT	PT CHGE	EST Vol	Prior SETT	Vol	INT
AUG99	94.625	94.63	94.6225	94.6225	94.625	UNCH	1220	94.625	1831	26787
SEP99	94.55	94.565B	94.545	94.555	94.555	0.5	36K	94.55	28122	563750
OCT99	94.29	94.29	94.28	94.28	94.285	−3	328	94.315	737	4825
NOV99	—	—	94.24A	94.24A	94.255	−0.5	0	94.26	80	672
DEC99	94.19	94.205	94.175	94.19	94.19	−1.5	33K	94.205	31195	455706
JAN00	94.305	94.315B	94.3	94.315B	94.315	0.5	493	94.31		605
MAR00	94.17	94.19	94.155	94.19	94.185	1	66K	94.175	50721	422021
JUN00	93.935	93.96B	93.92	93.95	93.95	1	26K	93.94	31597	259147
SEP00	93.745	93.77	93.735	93.77	93.765	1.5	14K	93.75	18007	207067
DEC00	93.51	93.545	93.51	93.54	93.535	1.5	9860	93.52	8869	163452
MAR01	93.52	93.555	93.515	93.55	93.55	2	9068	93.53	7213	126127
JUN01	93.465	93.49	93.46	93.49	93.49	2	6087	93.47	6653	106486
SEP01	93.45	93.47	93.44	93.47	93.465	2	4613	93.445	4714	84048
DEC01	93.36	93.38	93.36	93.375	93.375	2.5	2904	93.35	3790	76259
MAR02	93.37	93.4	93.365	93.4	93.4	3	2796	93.37	4291	70868
JUN02	93.36	93.37	93.35	93.365	93.36	3	2494	93.33	3403	54284
SEP02	93.335	93.345	93.32A	93.33	93.33	3	2072	93.3	1962	49058
DEC02	93.23	93.255	93.23	93.245	93.24	3.5	1797	93.205	4470	54452
MAR03	93.23	93.265B	93.23	93.26A	93.255	3.5	1932	93.22	1794	49993
JUN03	93.185	93.22B	93.185	93.215A	93.215	4	1622	93.175	1432	38001
SEP03	93.16	93.195B	93.155	93.185A	93.185	4	2203	93.145	1687	42692
DEC03	93.09	93.1	93.08A	93.085	93.085	4	1808	93.045	3138	28449
MAR04	93.1	93.11B	93.095	93.095A	93.095	4	1818	93.055	1646	26231
JUN04	93.01	93.06B	93.01	93.045A	93.045	4	2003	93.005	1385	15919
SEP04	93	93.025B	92.97A	93.01	93.015	4	651	92.975	187	10663
DEC04	92.905	92.94	92.875A	92.915	92.92	4	709	92.88	763	11917
MAR05	92.91	92.935B	92.88A	92.92	92.925	4	631	92.885	178	10016
JUN05	92.865	92.89B	92.835A	92.875	92.88	4	626	92.84	149	9283
SEP05	—	92.85B	92.795A	92.84A	92.84	4	365	92.8	164	7210
DEC05	—	92.76B	92.705A	92.75A	92.75	4	365	92.71	169	4385
MAR06	92.765	92.765	92.71A	92.755A	92.755	4	423	92.715	264	4735
JUN06	—	92.72B	92.665A	92.71A	92.71	4	390	92.67	178	3461
SEP06	—	92.68B	92.625A	92.67A	92.67	4	138	92.63	56	3162
DEC06	—	92.59B	92.535A	92.58A	92.58	4	138	92.54	56	3188
MAR07	—	92.595B	92.54A	92.585A	92.585	4	138	92.545	56	3320
JUN07	—	92.555B	92.50A	92.545A	92.54	3.5	138	92.505	56	2684
SEP07	—	92.515B	92.46A	92.505A	92.5	3.5	138	92.465	56	2551
DEC07	—	92.425B	92.37A	92.415A	92.41	3.5	138	92.375	56	4362
MAR08	—	92.425B	92.37A	92.415A	92.41	3.5	138	92.375	56	2913
JUN08	—	92.385B	92.33A	92.375A	92.37	3.5	138	92.335	56	3565

(continued)

MONEY RATES

Wednesday, July 28, 1999

The key U. S. and foreign annual interest rates below are a guide to general levels but don't always represent actual transactions.

PRIME RATE: 8.00% (effective 07/01/99). The base rate on corporate loans posted by at least 75% of the nation's 30 largest banks.

DISCOUNT RATE: 4.50% (effective 11/18/98). The charge on loans to depository institutions by the Federal Reserve Banks.

FEDERAL FUNDS: 5 1/8 % high, 4 1/2 % low, 4 3/4 % near closing bid, 5% offered. Reserves traded among commercial banks for overnight use in amounts of $1 million or more. Source: Prebon Yamane(U.S.A) Inc. FOMC fed funds target rate 5% effective 6/30/99.

CALL MONEY: 6.75% (effective 07/01/99). The charge on loans to brokers on stock exchange collateral. Source: Telerate.

COMMERCIAL PAPER: placed directly by General Electric Capital Corp.: 5.08% 30 to 36 days; 5.11% 37 to 52 days; 5.09% 53 to 73 days; 5.15% 74 to 114 days; 5.12% 115 to 135 days; 5.45% 179 to 230 days; 5.40% 231 to 270 days.

EURO COMMERCIAL PAPER: placed directly by General Electric Capital Corp.: 2.57% 30 days; 2.60% two months; 2.63% three months; 2.64% four months; 2.59% five months; 2.88% six months.

DEALER COMMERCIAL PAPER: High-grade unsecured notes sold through dealers by major corporations: 5.09% 30 days; 5.12% 60 days; 5.17% 90 days.

CERTIFICATES OF DEPOSIT: 4.83% one month; 4.79% two months; 4.92% three months; 5.11% six months; 5.32% one year. Average of top rates paid by major New York banks on primary new issues of negotiable C.D.s, usually on amounts of $1 million and more. The minimum unit is $100,000. Typical rates in the secondary maket 5.15% one month; 5.26% three months; 5.62% six months.

BANKERS ACCEPTANCES: 5.10% 30 days; 5.13% 60 days; 5.16% 90 days; 5.22% 120 days; 5.24% 150 days; 5.48% 180 days. Offered rates of negotiable, bank-backed business credit instruments typically financing an import order.

LONDON LATE EURODOLLARS: 5 3/16% - 5 1/16% one month; 5 1/4 % - 5 1/8 % two months; 5 5/16% - 5 3/16% three months; 5 3/8 % - 5 1/4 % four months; 5 7/16% - 5 5/16% five months; 5 21/32% - 5 17/32% six months.

LONDON INTERBANK OFFERED RATES (LIBOR): 5.1800% one month; 5.3125% three months; 5.64375% six months; 5.81625% one year. British Banker's Association average of interbank offered rates for dollar deposits in the London market based on quotations at 16 major banks. Effective rate for contracts entered into two days from date appearing at top of this column.

EURO LIBOR: 2.62875% one month; 2.68063% three months; 2.94125% six months; 3.09125% one year. British Banker's Association average of interbank offered rates for euro deposits in the London market based on quotations at 16 major banks. Effective rate for contracts entered into two days from date appearing at top of this column.

EURO INTERBANK OFFERED RATES (EURIBOR): 2.630% one month; 2.685% three months; 2.944% six months; 3.095% one year. European Banking Federation-sponsored rate among 57 Euro zone banks.

FOREIGN PRIME RATES: Canada 6.25%; Germany 2.50%; Japan 1.375%; Switerland 2.875%; Britain 5.00%. These rate indications aren't directly comparable; lending practices vary widely by location.

TREASURY BILLS: Results of the Monday, July 26, 1999, auction of short-term U.S. government bills, sold at a discount from face value in units of $1,000 to $1 million: 4.535% 13 weeks; 4.520% 26 weeks.

OVERNIGHT REPURCHASE RATE: 4.96%. Dealer financing rate for overnight sale and repurchase of Treasury securities. Source: Telerate.

FEDERAL HOME LOAN MORTGAGE CORP. (Freddie Mac): Posted yields on 30-year mortgage commitments. Delivery within 30 days 7.81%, 60 days 7.86%, standard conventional fixed-rate mortgages: 5.625%, 2% rate capped one-year adjustable rate mortgages. Source: Telerate.

FEDERAL NATIONAL MORTGAGE ASSOCIATION (Fannie Mae): Posted yields on 30 year mortgage commitments (priced at par) for delivery within 30 days 7.77%, 60 days 7.83%, standard conventional fixed-rate mortgages; 6.55%,6/2 rate capped one-year adjustable rate mortgages. Source: Telerate.

MERRILL LYNCH READY ASSETS TRUST: . Annualized average rate of return after expenses for the past 30 days; not a forecast of future returns.

CONSUMER PRICE INDEX: June, 166.2, up 2.0% from a year ago. Bureau of Labor Statistics.

Figure 10.3 Eurodollar price data as shown in The *Wall Street Journal. Source:* (Reprinted with permission of *The Wall Street Journal.* © July 29, 1999.)

TABLE 10.2 Continued

Mth/ Strike	Open	High	Daily Low	Last	SETT	PT CHGE	EST Vol	SETT	Prior Vol	INT
SEP08	92.35	92.35	92.29A	92.335A	92.33	3.5	158	92.295	102	3050
DEC08	—	92.255B	92.20A	92.245A	92.24	3.5	138	92.205	96	2571
MAR09	—	92.255B	92.20A	92.245A	92.24	3.5	138	92.205	96	2163
JUN09	—	92.215B	92.16A	92.205A	92.2	3.5	138	92.165	97	1934
Total							EST VOL		VOL	OPEN
Total							238903		221628	3024032

Source: Reprinted with permission from Chicago Mercantile Exchange Inc.

where $fr(T, T+90)$ is the theoretical annualized LIBOR futures rate (expressed as a decimal) and T is the number of days until delivery. Finally, because IMM Index $= I = 100[1 - fr(T, T+90)]$, Equation (10.14) can be solved for the theoretical, no-arbitrage IMM Index for Eurodollar futures prices[9]:

$$I = \frac{36,000 + (500)(T)(r(0,T)) - (400)(T + 90)[r(0, T + 90)]}{360 + (T)[r(0,T)]} \tag{10.15}$$

Figure 10.3 is the "Money Rates" column from the *Wall Street Journal* on July 28, 1999. This is one public source for spot data on Eurodollar rates. Market professionals obtain data from services such as Bloomberg, Reuters, or Telerate. The spot LIBOR data presented in the *Wall Street Journal* are incomplete for estimating theoretical Eurodollar futures prices. Approximations must be made.

10.4.2 Arbitrage Pricing of Eurodollar Futures Contracts

10.4.2.1 Cash-and-Carry Arbitrage Trades

In Example 10.2 on page 280 we find that an arbitrage opportunity existed for the September Eurodollar futures contract. Given that $r(0, 47) = 5.2175\%$, and $r(0, 137) = 5.4855\%$, we computed a theoretical $fr(47, 137)$ of 5.5874%, hence a theoretical futures price of $(100 - 5.5874 =)$ 94.4126. This theoretical futures price was below the actual futures price of 94.555; the interest rate implied by this futures price is 5.445%. Thus, an arbitrageur would want to borrow at the futures interest rate of 5.445% (sell the overpriced futures contract) and lend at the theoretical forward rate of 5.5874%. Recall from Chapter 5 that you can use spot debt instruments to establish this forward lending rate by lending in the spot market for 137 days and borrowing in the spot market for 47 days:

```
    <----Borrow----->
    <---------------Lend--------------->        =              <-----Lend------->
    |_____|_____|                 |_____|_____|
    0               47                 137                 0             47             137
```

EXAMPLE 10.2a Estimating Theoretical Eurodollar Futures Prices   The September 1999 Eurodollar futures contract expired on September 13, 1999. Thus, on July 28, 1999, there were $T = 47$ days to the final settlement day, and $T + 90 = 137$. From Figure 10.3, we can estimate that the spot LIBOR rate, $r(0, T) = r(0, 47) = 5.2175\%$. This linear interpolation estimate uses the one-month spot rate of 5.18% and the three-month spot rate of 5.3125%. Similarly, by using the three-month spot rate and the six-month spot rate of 5.64375%, we can use linear interpolation to estimate another spot LIBOR rate, $r(0, T + 90) = r(0, 137) = 5.4855\%$. We can use Equation (10.15) to estimate the theoretical futures price:

$$94.4126 = \frac{36,000 + (500)(47)(0.052175) - (400)(137)(0.054855)}{360 + (47)(0.052175)}$$

The actual futures settlement price for the September 1999 Eurodollar futures contract on July 28, 1999, was 94.555, which is about 14 ticks higher than the theoretical futures price.[10] Because the observed futures price is greater than the theoretical futures price, potential arbitrage will require the cash-and-carry trades: borrow for T days, invest in a $(T + 90)$-day Eurodollar time deposit, and sell the overpriced futures contract with a delivery date T days hence. Assuming zero transactions costs, these trades will yield an arbitrage profit of $356.00 per futures contract; this is simply the difference between the observed futures price and the theoretical futures price multiplied by $25/tick.

EXAMPLE 10.2b   The March 2000 Eurodollar futures contract expired on March 13, 2000. Thus on July 28, 1999, there were $T = 229$ days to the final settlement day, and $T + 90 = 319$. We can use a linear interpolation between the six-month LIBOR of 5.64375% and the one-year LIBOR rate of 5.81625% to estimate the spot LIBOR rate, $r(0, T)$, is $r(0, 229) = 5.7000\%$. Similarly, we can estimate another spot LIBOR rate, $r(0, T + 90)$, as $r(0, 319) = 5.777\%$. Again, we can use Equation (10.15) to estimate the theoretical futures price:

$$94.23607 = \frac{36,000 + (500)(229)(0.05700) - (400)(319)(0.05777)}{360 + (229)(0.05700)}$$

Note that the actual futures settlement price for the March 2000 Eurodollar futures contract on July 28, 1999 was 94.185, about 5 ticks lower than the theoretical price. Because observed futures prices are less than theoretical futures prices, arbitrageurs will do the reverse cash-and-carry trades: sell the $(T + 90)$-day Eurodollar time deposit, lend the proceeds for T days, and buy cheap futures with a delivery T days hence.[11] Assuming zero transactions costs, these trades will yield an arbitrage profit of $127.67 per futures contract; this is simply the difference between the observed futures price and the theoretical futures price multiplied by $25/tick.

Summarizing, arbitrage requires the sale of the September Eurodollar futures, borrowing for 47 days at 5.2175%, and lending for 137 days for 5.4855%. The actual trades are as follows:

- *On July 28*: Go short a September futures contract at 94.555. This establishes an unannualized 90-day forward borrowing rate of 1.36125% (5.445%/4 = 1.36125%), from September 13 until December 12. September 13 is the delivery day of the futures contract, 47 days hence. An investment of $1 million in a 90-day Eurodollar time deposit on September 13 will have grown to $1,013,612.50 on December 12.

- *On July 28*: The spot annual lending rate for the next 137 days is $r(0,137) = 5.4855\%$. Solving Equation (10.8) for P provides the amount that must be invested today so that 137 days hence, you will have $1,013,612.50:

$$F = P\left[1 + \left(LIBOR \times \frac{t}{360}\right)\right]$$ (10.8)

$$P = \frac{F}{1 + r(0,137)137/360}$$

$$\frac{(1,000,000)(1.0136125)}{1 + [0.054855 \times (137/360)]} = \$992,885.64$$

Thus, $992,885.64 should be lent for 137 days.

- *On July 28*: The 47-day borrowing rate is 5.2175%. Borrow $992,885.64 at this rate for 47 days (i.e., to September 13). The net result for all three of these transactions on July 28 is a zero cash flow.

- *On September 13*: Borrow $1 million for 90 days at the borrowing rate established (locked in) by the short position in the futures contract ($fh = 1.36125\%$).

- *On September 13*: Repay the original 47-day loan:

$$992,885.64\left[1 + \left(0.052175 \times \frac{47}{360}\right)\right] = \$999,648.91$$

The net cash flow on September 13 is therefore $+\$1,000,000 - \$999,648.91$, which results in a cash inflow of $351.09.

- *On December 12*: Receive $1,013,612.50 from the original 137-day investment.

- *On December 12*: Pay $1,013,612.50 on the 90-day loan.

Summarizing the cash flows from these transactions:

Date	Cash In	Cash Out
July 28	$992,885.64	$992,885.64
September 13	$1,000,000.00	$999,648.91
December 12	$1,013,612.50	$1,013,612.50

The net cash inflow of $351.09 on September 13 is the arbitrage profit. Note that if this amount was to be reinvested at the theoretical $fr(47,137)$ of 5.5874% [which equals $fh(47,137)=$ 1.39685%], then the future value of this profit is $356. This exactly equals the difference between the actual Eurodollar futures price (94.555) and the theoretical futures price (94.4126), times $25.

These cash-and-carry trades are equivalent to purchasing a 47-day $1 million face value investment for $992,885.64 on July 28. The implied repo rate on this "synthetic" investment is:

$$\frac{1,000,000 - 992,885.64}{992,885.64} = 0.7165\%$$

for 47 days. Annualized on a 360-day year, this is 5.488%. The arbitrageur must compare this implied repo rate to his effective *borrowing* rate to determine whether there is a cash-and-carry arbitrage. Since his borrowing rate [here, $r(0,47)=5.1275\%$] is less than the implied repo rate (5.488%), then the arbitrageur makes money by borrowing at the lower rate and synthetically lending at the higher rate.

10.4.2.2 Reverse Cash-and-Carry Arbitrage Trades

To profit from the December Eurodollar futures mispricing in Example 10.2b, an arbitrageur will want to use spot debt instruments to borrow forward, from March 13 until June 12. This is done by borrowing for 319 days and lending the same amount for 229 days:

```
      <------Lend------>
      <---------------Borrow--------------->    =                    <----Borrow----->
      |               |                    |           |            |               |
      0              229                  319          0           229             319
```

At the same time, the arbitrageur will lend in the Eurodollar futures market by buying a Eurodollar futures contract for March delivery. The Eurodollar futures price is too low.

- *On July 28*: Go long a March 2000 futures contract at 94.185. This establishes a 90-day forward lending rate of $fh(229,319)=1.45375\%$ ($=5.815\%/4$) starting on the futures expiration date (March 13, 2000).

- *On July 28*: The estimated 319-day borrowing rate is 5.777%. Borrow

$$\frac{(1,000,000)(1.0145375)}{1+[0.05777(319/360)]} = \$965,131.79$$

- *On July 28*: The estimated 229-day lending rate is 5.7000%. Lend $965,131.79 at this rate until the March Eurodollar futures contract expires (i.e., on March 13). The net cash flow on July 28 is zero.

- *On March 13*: Receive

$$\$965,131.79 \times [1+0.05700(229/360)] = \$1,000,125.86$$

from the 229-day investment.

- *On March 13*: Lend $1 million for 90 days at the lending rate established by the long position in the futures contract (1.45375%). The net cash inflow from the two events is +$125.86.

- *On June 12, 2000*: Repay the original 319-day loan:

$$\$965,131.79 \times [1+.05777(319/360)] = \$1,014,537.50$$

- *On June 12, 2000*: Receive:

$$\$1,000,000 \times [1+.05815(90/360)] = \$1,014,537.50$$

from the 90-day investment that began on March 13.
Summarizing the cash flows from these transactions:

Date	Cash In	Cash Out
July 28	$965,131.79	$965,131.79
March 13	$1,000,125.86	$1,000,000.00
June 12	$1,014,537.50	$1,014,537.50

Excess cash inflow on March 13 = $125.86

(before transactions costs)

Recall that the theoretical futures price (IMM Index) was 94.23607. This implies a theoretical forward interest rate of $(100-94.23607=fr(229,319)=)$ 5.76393%. This in turn equals an unannualized forward rate of $fh(229,319)=1.441\%$ (=5.76393%/4). If the $125.86 is invested at this theoretical forward rate, then the arbitrage profit is $125.86 (1.01441) = $127.67. This equals the difference between the theoretical futures price (94.23607) and the actual futures price (94.185), times $25.

The reverse cash-and-carry trades are equivalent to selling (borrowing) a 229-day $1 million face value investment for $965,131.79 on July 28. The implied repo rate[12] on this "synthetic" investment is:

$$\frac{1,000,000 - 965,131.79}{965,131.79} = 3.6128\%$$

for 229 days. Annualized on a 360-day year, this is 5.6795%. The arbitrageur must compare this implied repo rate to his *lending* rate to determine whether there is a reverse cash-and-carry arbitrage. If his lending rate is higher than this implied repo rate of 5.6795%, then the arbitrageur makes money by synthetically borrowing at the low implied repo rate and lending at the higher lending rate.

10.5   TWO USEFUL APPLICATIONS OF EURODOLLAR FUTURES CONTRACTS

In this section, we reexamine the examples in Section 10.4 to show how an individual, institution, or firm can exploit mispricing in the short-term interest rate futures market. In the first case, we show how Eurodollar futures can be used to shorten the maturity of an investment from $T+90$ days to T days. In the second case, we show how Eurodollar futures can be used to lengthen the maturity of an existing Eurodollar time deposit that matures T days hence. These examples essentially illustrate how to realize the highest rate of return on an investment with the desired time to maturity. Note, however, that when you use Eurodollar futures to change the maturity of an existing investment, you must be aware of basis risk, which may prevent the yield spread between Eurodollar rates and the interest rate of your investment from remaining constant.

10.5.1   Shortening the Maturity of a Eurodollar Time Deposit

In Example 10.3, Eurodollar futures contracts are used to shorten an investment that matures $T+90$ days hence. Suppose a firm has a large sum of money to invest for the next T days. Further suppose that the delivery dates for Eurodollar futures contracts are $T-90$ days, T days, and $T+90$ days hence. The firm can invest its funds in one of three ways:

1. Deposit the funds into a Eurodollar time deposit for T days.
2. Deposit the funds into a Eurodollar time deposit with $T+90$ days to maturity and also go short a Eurodollar futures contract with a delivery date T days hence. Here, the firm is lending money for $T+90$ days and, by selling the Eurodollar futures contract, has agreed to borrow money from day T until day $T+90$. Its net position is that it has lent money for the next T days—just as in strategy 1.
3. Deposit the funds into a Eurodollar time deposit for $T-90$ days, and go long Eurodollar futures contracts with a delivery date $T-90$ days hence. Here, the firm is lending money for $T-90$ days and, by its long position in the Eurodollar futures contract, has agreed to lend

EXAMPLE 10.3   On July 28, 1999, the treasurer of a company has \$75 million in cash to invest for the next 47 days. The treasurer knows that 47-day spot LIBOR rate is 5.2175%. The treasurer also observes that the September 1999 Eurodollar futures contract price is 94.555. Using Equation (10.14) and a 137-day rate of 5.4855%, the treasurer estimates the theoretical futures price to be 94.413. The actual futures price of 94.555 is too high. Thus, the treasurer knows that the firm can earn a higher rate of return using strategy 2 instead of strategy 1. If the treasurer invests the \$75 million in a 47-day Eurodollar time deposit, the firm will have

$$F = \$75,000,000 \ [1+(0.052175(47/360))]$$
$$F = \$75,510,880$$

in 47 days. However, if the treasurer creates a synthetic 47-day instrument by investing the \$75 million in a 137-day Eurodollar time deposit and going short 75 September 1999 Eurodollar futures contracts, the firm will have

$$F = \$75,000,000 \times \frac{1+[0.054855(137/360)]}{1+[0.054450(90/360)]}$$
$$F = \$75,537,400$$

in 47 days, which is \$26,520 more. Note that the short position in the September futures contract implies a 90-day forward borrowing rate of 5.445%. Here, the treasurer has used the Eurodollar futures market to shorten a 137-day investment to the desired 47 days.

money from day $T-90$ to day T. Its net position is that it will be lending money for the next T days. Strategies 2 and 3 are known as "synthetic" T-day Eurodollar time deposits.

Method 1 is the optimal strategy when Eurodollar futures prices are near their theoretical values. Method 2 will provide a higher rate of return when futures interest rates are too low: that is, when Eurodollar futures prices are above their theoretical values. Method 3 is preferred when futures interest rates are too high: that is, when Eurodollar futures prices are below their theoretical values.

10.5.2 Lengthening the Maturity of a Eurodollar Time Deposit

Suppose a firm has a large sum of money to invest for the next $T+90$ days. Further suppose that there are Eurodollar futures contracts with delivery dates T days and $T+90$ days hence. The firm can invest its funds in one of three ways:

1. Deposit the funds into a Eurodollar time deposit for $T+90$ days.
2. Deposit the funds into a Eurodollar time deposit with T days to maturity and also go long a Eurodollar futures contract with delivery in T days. This is known as a "synthetic" $(T+90)$-day Eurodollar time deposit.

EXAMPLE 10.4   On July 28, 1999, the treasurer of a company has $50 million in cash to invest for the next 319 days. The treasurer knows that the 319-day LIBOR spot rate is 5.777%. The treasurer also sees that the March 2000 futures contract price is 94.185. Using Equation (10.14) and a 229-day rate of 5.70%, the treasurer estimates the theoretical March 2000 futures price to be 94.236. But the actual futures price is 94.185, which is too low. Thus, the treasurer knows that the firm can earn a higher rate of return using the foregoing strategy 2 instead of strategy 1. If the treasurer invests the $50 million in a 319-day Eurodollar time deposit, the firm will have

$$F = \$50,000,000 \ [1 + 0.05777 \times (319 \, / \, 360)]$$

$$F = \$52,559,532$$

in 319 days. However, if the treasurer creates a synthetic 319-day instrument by investing the $50 million in a 229-day Eurodollar time deposit and going long 50 March 2000 Eurodollar futures contracts, the firm will have

$$F = \$50,000,000 \ \{1 + [0.05700(229/360)]\} \ \{1 + [0.05815(90/360)]\}$$

$$F = \$52,566,147$$

in 319 days, which is $6615 more. Note that the long position in the March futures contract implies a 90-day lending rate of 5.815%. In this case, the treasurer has used the Eurodollar futures market to lengthen a 229-day investment to the desired 319-day investment horizon.

3. Deposit the funds into a Eurodollar time deposit with $T + 180$ days to maturity and go short a Eurodollar futures contract with delivery date $T + 90$ days hence.

Method 1 is preferred when Eurodollar futures prices are near their theoretical values. Method 2 will provide a higher rate of return when futures interest rates are too high: that is, when Eurodollar futures prices are below their theoretical values. Method 3 is preferred when futures interest rates are too low: that is, when Eurodollar futures prices are above their theoretical values. Method 2 is used in Example 10.4 to lengthen the maturity of an investment.

Before using Eurodollar futures to change the maturity of a time deposit, a treasurer must consider a few risks. First, the firm must remember that interest is lost on mark-to-market cash outflows, should there be losses on the futures position. Such losses, however, will likely not be significant. Second, the transactions costs on any futures-related strategy will exceed those on a spot investment in Eurodollar time deposits. Finally, there is the risk that the interest rate that determines the price of its time deposit $T + 90$ days hence will not exactly equal the final settlement LIBOR for the futures contract.

Still, even with these risks, a good cash manager should at least consider using Eurodollar futures contracts for enhancing returns. By selling overpriced futures contracts, cash managers can shorten the maturity of a longer term investment to a shorter desired time to maturity. Or, cash managers can buy underpriced futures contracts to lengthen the maturity of a short-term investment to a desired longer term investment. In both cases, cash managers can take advantage of mispricings in the Eurodollar futures markets to earn a higher rate of return.

10.6   HEDGING WITH SHORT-TERM INTEREST RATE FUTURES

When deciding whether to use T-bill futures (or perhaps two-year T-note futures) or Eurodollar futures, the hedger should consider the following:

- Eurodollar futures are more liquid than T-bill futures.

- Eurodollar futures prices are based on a money market instrument that has a default risk premium. If the spot instrument also has a default risk premium, Eurodollar futures probably should be used because Eurodollar yields will likely correlate better with those on the spot instrument than will T-bill yields. If a position in T-bills is being hedged, T-bill futures probably should be used to hedge.

- Mispricing should be considered. If, for example, the T-bill futures contract is overpriced, and the Eurodollar contract is underpriced, and the hedge calls for the sale of futures, then T-bills might be used (all else equal). Further, the hedger might consider the spread between T-bills futures yields and Eurodollar futures yields. This spread is called the **TED spread** (the "T" stands for Treasury bill, and the "ED" stands for Eurodollar). If the TED spread is very narrow (perhaps vs its historical values), then there is a very small risk premium in Eurodollars and, all else equal, Eurodollar futures should be sold if a short hedge is called for and T-bill futures should be bought if the trades are part of a long hedge. The hedger is effectively speculating that the risk premium will return to a more normal value by the day the hedge is lifted.

- The hedger should regress changes in the yields of the spot instrument being hedged [Δr(spot)] on changes in (a) the futures yields of T-bill futures and (b) the futures yields of

Eurodollar futures, to determine which has the higher R^2, and is therefore more likely to provide the better hedging vehicle, all else equal. It is imperative that changes in the value of the spot position, or anticipated spot position, be highly correlated with changes in the futures price.

Summarizing, if an individual holds a spot position that will experience losses if short-term interest rates rise (prices of debt instruments fall), then this short hedger will sell short-term interest rate futures contracts. An increase in interest rates will then lead to losses in the spot position, but profits in the futures market. If an individual holds a cash position that will experience losses when short-term interest rates fall, this long hedger will buy short-term interest rate futures contracts. Thus, the hedger must first identify whether higher or lower interest rates are feared. Then she must choose the proper futures contract to trade (both the underlying asset and the maturity month). Finally, the "proper" number of futures contracts to be bought or sold (the hedge ratio) must be determined.

10.6.1 Short Hedge Situations

1. A manager of a portfolio consisting of short-term debt securities fears that a rise in short-term interest rates will cause the value of the portfolio to decline.
2. A bank makes a one-year fixed-rate loan and funds it with 90-day negotiable CDs. After 90 days, the bank will have to return to the credit market to borrow for another 90 days. It fears interest rates will be higher at that date.
3. A bank plans to issue CDs, or a corporation plans to sell commercial paper (or take out any short term loan) in the near future.
4. An individual buys a house, but the bank will not guarantee the mortgage rate until the loan has been approved, which will be in six weeks. The loan rate is tied to a short-term Treasury security index.
5. An institution plans on selling a part of its investment portfolio of money market investments to meet an upcoming cash requirement.
6. A government securities dealer who is carrying an inventory of T-bills fears that a rise in interest rates will lower its value.
7. A firm has an existing variable-rate loan, and next week the interest rate will be reset.

10.6.2 Long Hedge Situations

1. A bank or firm wishes to purchase six-month CDs as an investment, but either the supply of these securities is temporarily insufficient or the bank or firm temporarily lacks the cash needed to make the purchase.
2. A portfolio manager knows that $X million will be received at the end of this month for investment in short-term securities. Current yields are very attractive, and the manager fears interest rates will fall between today and the day that the funds will be received.
3. A bank makes a variable-rate loan that is financed with a longer term CD.

10.6.3 The Hedge Ratio

As discussed in Chapter 7, the principle behind the hedge ratio is dollar equivalency. A good hedge is one in which dollar losses in the spot market are made up with gains in the futures market.

Define the following terms:

ΔV_S = change in value of the spot position or anticipated spot position if interest rates change by one basis point

ΔV_F = cash flow generated by the change in the futures price of one futures contract if interest rates change by one basis point

The principle of dollar equivalency dictates trading h futures contracts so that

$$\Delta V_S = h\Delta V_F, \tag{10.16}$$

given a change in short-term interest rates. This formulation assumes that the interest rate on the spot instrument and the futures interest rate are perfectly positively correlated. However, it is possible that changes in interest rates of the cash instrument being hedged do not correlate perfectly with changes in the futures rates of the chosen futures contract (i.e., T-bills, Eurodollars, etc.). Then the hedger might wish to first run a regression using data on historical interest rate changes:

$$\Delta r_S = a + b\Delta r_F \tag{10.17}$$

where

Δr_S = historical changes in interest rates of the cash instrument

Δr_F = historical changes in the futures interest rate[13]

a, b = regression coefficients

Suppose your regression result is that the estimated slope coefficient is $\hat{b} = 0.8$. This means that changes in the interest rate of the cash security average only 80% of the change in the futures interest rate. The hedger still wishes to equate losses in one market to gains in the other market, but she will wisely account for the relationship between yield changes in the spot and futures markets. Thus, redefine the terms:

ΔV_S = change in value of the spot position *if interest rates change by $\hat{b}$ basis points*

ΔV_F = cash flow generated by the change in the futures price of one futures contract *if interest rates change by one basis point*

Again, use Equation (10.16) to solve for h, the proper number of futures contracts to trade for a risk-minimizing hedge. If $\hat{b} = 0.8$, then fewer futures will be used to hedge in comparison to a situation in which $\hat{b} = 1$. Since interest rates on the cash instrument will not be as volatile as interest rates on the futures contract (vs situations in which $\hat{b} > 1.0$), fewer futures are required.

When hedging for just one day, the Δr_S and Δr_F used in the regression model of Equation (10.17) should be daily changes in interest rates. One-week hedges should use weekly changes. Hedges that may last for longer than two weeks can safely use biweekly or monthly data.

10.6.4   Using T-Bill Futures to Protect the Value of a Portfolio

A corporate treasurer has the firm's surplus cash ($10 million) invested in short-term pure discount T-bills with a maturity of six months. He fears that short-term rates will rise sharply during the next week and wishes to hedge against this interest rate risk. Currently, the six-month T-bill discount yield is 4.52%.

TABLE 10.3 Weekly Discount Yields for T-Bill Hedging Example

Week	Discount Yields 6-month T-bill, r_S	T-bill Futures, $r_F{}^1$	Δr_S	Δr_F
1	0.0390	0.0357		
2	0.0374	0.0355	−0.0016	−0.0002
3	0.0410	0.0382	0.0036	0.0027
4	0.0418	0.0393	0.0008	0.0011
5	0.0400	0.0376	−0.0018	−0.0017
6	0.0398	0.0378	−0.0002	0.0002
7	0.0395	0.0377	−0.0003	−0.0001
8	0.0424	0.0404	0.0029	0.0027
9	0.0445	0.0437	0.0021	0.0033
10	0.0423	0.0405	−0.0022	−0.0032
11	0.0432	0.0408	0.0009	0.0003
12	0.0452	0.0444	0.0020	0.0036
		Mean	0.000564	0.000791
		SD	0.001962	0.002146

Regression result: $\Delta r_S = -0.009568 + 0.808501\,\Delta r_F$, $R^2 = 0.955$
$(t = 14.55)$

---

[1]T-bill futures discount yield = 100 − IMM Index%.

Weekly discount yield data on six-month spot T-bills and T-bill futures yields are gathered. The data are given in Table 10.3.[14]

Based on the information in Table 10.3, if the futures discount yield rises 100 basis points, the six-month spot discount yield will rise 81 basis points. This makes sense to the treasurer because he has learned that longer term rates are usually less volatile than short-term rates.

If the six-month spot rate rises 81 basis points, the value of the firm's portfolio will decline by an estimated $41,908. This is computed by using Equation (10.2). The market value of the firm's portfolio is currently $10 million, given the prevailing discount yield of 4.52%. Use Equation (10.2) to solve for the face value F of the securities:

$$\$10,000,000 = F\left[1 - \frac{(0.0452)(182)}{360}\right]$$

$$F = \$10,233,855$$

If the discount yield rises 81 basis points, to 5.33%, then the value of the portfolio declines to $9,958,092:

$$P = \$10,233,855\left[1 - \frac{(0.0533)(182)}{360}\right] = \$9,958,092$$

Thus, if spot interest rates instantaneously rise 81 basis points, the portfolio declines $41,908 in value from $10,000,000 to $9,958,092. Therefore, $\Delta V_S = -\$41,908$.

To achieve dollar equivalency, the treasurer needs to sell enough futures contracts to profit by the same amount, $41,908. He decides not to tail the hedge, as discussed in Chapter 6, because of the small number of futures contracts needed.

If six-month rates rise 81 basis points, the futures discount yield, currently at 4.44%, is expected to rise 100 basis points to 5.44%. At $25 per tick, an increase of 100 basis points means that one short futures contract will profit by $2500. This means that 16.76 contracts must be sold to realize a profit of $41,908 in the futures market. In other words, $\Delta V_S = -\$41,908$ if the discount yield on the spot instrument rises 81 basis points. Therefore, $\Delta V_F = +\$2500$ if the discount yield on T-bill futures rises 100 basis points. Therefore, by Equation (10.16), $h = 16.76$ futures contracts.

If the T-bill futures contract was overpriced (relative to its theoretical value), the treasurer could be more aggressive, and sell 17 contracts. Similarly, he must examine his (subjective) probability distribution for future interest rates. What is the probability that interest rates will rise? The less certain he is of a rise in interest rates, the fewer contracts should be sold. Finally, if the probability of an 81-basis-point increase in spot six-month rates is high, what are the consequences of losing $41,908 in the cash market? If these would be disastrous, the treasurer should most certainly hedge.

Once the hedge has been put on, the treasurer must monitor the hedge, adjusting it as time and conditions change. For example, suppose that interest rates haven't changed two weeks later, but the treasurer still fears they will rise. He will have to adjust the hedge to account for the decline in the maturity of the portfolio. Two adjustments must be made. First, the spot instrument data in Table 10.3 and the dependent variable in the regression model, should be $5\,^1/_2$-month T-bills, not six-month T-bills. This will provide a new $\hat{b}$. Second, the treasurer must compute the value decline of his $5\,^1/_2$-month T-bills if $5\,^1/_2$-month spot interest rates rise by $\hat{b}\,(100)$ basis points. This will differ from the value decline of six-month T-bills. With 168 days to maturity, a face value of $10,233,855, and the same discount yield of 4.52%, the market value of the spot T-bills is $10,017,989. If the spot discount yield on $5\,^1/_2$-month T-bills rose by 81 basis points to 5.33%, the market value would decline to $9,979,305. This is only a $38,684 decline in value. Therefore, two weeks later, the short hedge will require only $h = \Delta V_S / \Delta V_F = 38684/2500 = 15.47$ contracts.

As time passes, fewer futures contracts will be required to maintain the hedged position of this portfolio. There is a simple reason for this: pure discount instruments are being hedged. As such, the duration of the securities equals their maturity. Percentage changes in bond values are directly proportional to duration, as shown in the appendix to Chapter 9. Thus, as the duration of the spot instrument declines, the change in value caused by a given change in yield declines. In the foregoing example, by the time the maturity of the spot instrument is down to three months, the duration of the futures contract is the same as the duration of the spot instrument, and the changes in value of the two are equal. Then, only 10 futures contracts are needed for the hedge, versus 17.18 when the hedge was initiated. In other words, the hedge ratio declines as time passes.

10.6.5 Using Eurodollar Futures to Lock in a Single-Period Borrowing Rate

In the arbitrage pricing section, arbitrageurs knew that they could borrow and lend at known rates in the *future* by using futures contracts *today*. This section presents an example wherein a market participant locks in a future borrowing rate.

On July 28, 1999, a bank plans to make a 90-day loan for $50 million beginning on September 13, 1999. The bank will fund the loan by borrowing in the Eurodollar spot market on September 13. The 90-day loan agreement calls for a fixed rate of 7%. As shown in Figure 10.3, the current spot three-month Eurodollar rate is 5.3125%. However, this rate does not matter to the bank because the bank will not be borrowing at the *current* spot three-month rate. The bank will be borrowing in the spot market *47 days hence*. Thus, on July 28, the lending rate is known, but the interest rate at which the bank will be borrowing on September 13 is unknown.

The bank fears that when it comes time to borrow the funds in the Eurodollar spot market, interest rates will be higher. Such a situation calls for a short hedge using Eurodollar futures contracts.

As shown in Table 10.2, the closing price for September Eurodollar futures is 94.555.[15] By shorting 50 Eurodollar futures contracts on July 28, 1999, the bank can lock in a 90-day borrowing rate of 5.445%. Note that in this example transactions costs are assumed to be zero.

Case I. Spot 90-Day LIBOR on September 13 is 5.445%.

From Equation (10.11), the bank's interest expense is

$$\$680,625 = 50,000,000 \times 0.05445 \times \frac{90}{360}$$

Because September 13 is the settlement date for the Eurodollar futures contract, the futures price will equal the spot price. Thus, there is no profit or loss on the futures contracts because the bank went short at 94.555.

Case II. Spot 90-Day LIBOR on September 13 is 5.845%.

Here, the bank's actual interest expense is $730,625. This is higher than "anticipated" because interest rates rose above the original futures interest rate:

$$\$730,625 = 50,000,000 \times 0.05845 \times \frac{90}{360}$$

Because interest rates are higher, the bank profits from its short futures position. To calculate the futures profit on the 50 contracts, one must recall that each full-point move in the IMM Index (i.e., 100 basis points) represents $2500 for one futures contract. The delivery day futures price is $100 - 5.845 = 94.155$. Thus,

$$(94.555 - 94.155)2500 \times 50 = \$50,000$$

Again, the net interest expense for the bank is $730,625 - $50,000 = $680,625$.

Case III. Spot 90-Day LIBOR on September 13 is 5.045%.

The bank's actual interest expense is only $630,625:

$$\$630,625 = 50,000,000 \times 0.05045 \times \frac{90}{360}$$

However, because interest rates are lower, the bank loses on its short futures position. The delivery day futures price is $100 - 5.045 = 94.955$. The futures loss is:

$$(94.555 - 94.955)2500 \times 50 = -\$50,000$$

The net interest expense for the bank equals the interest expense with the 5.045% rate, plus the loss on the futures position. It is the same as cases I and II: $\$630,625 + \$50,000 = \$680,625$.

It is important to note that the bank has removed basis risk from the transactions described in Cases I–III because the loan commenced on the futures' expiration date. This example set shows that no matter what the spot rate is in 47 days, the bank can protect itself from higher rates. Note that part of the cost of this protection is the foregone opportunity to make more money if rates fall.

10.6.6   Using Eurodollar Futures to Lock in a Multiperiod Borrowing Rate

10.6.6.1   A Strip Hedge

Now suppose that on July 28, 1999, the bank plans to make a one-year fixed-rate loan for $50 million beginning on September 13, 1999. The fixed rate will be 7.50%. The bank plans to fund the loan by borrowing in the spot Eurodollar market. In 47 days, the bank could borrow at the one-year spot rate, or the bank could borrow quarterly in the spot market. If the bank chooses to borrow at the one-year spot rate, it might hedge by selling about 250 two-year Treasury note futures contracts for delivery in September 1999. Each two-year Treasury note futures contract has as its underlying asset $200,000 (face value) in Treasury notes with about two years to maturity.

Instead, to borrow quarterly, the bank would likely use a portfolio of 90-day Eurodollar futures contracts to hedge this borrowing cost, and it has two basic choices in the way it could hedge against increases in quarterly borrowing rates. These are a **strip hedge** and a **stack hedge** (frequently called a **rolling hedge**). To execute a strip hedge, the bank would sell 200 Eurodollar futures contracts: 50 in each of *four different* delivery months. To execute a stack hedge, the bank would initially sell 200 futures contracts in *one* delivery month. We will begin with an example of a strip hedge.

Since the bank will borrow $50 million in September and every 90 days three times thereafter, the bank initiates a strip hedge by selling 50 Eurodollar futures contracts in each of four delivery months: September, December, March, and June. The short positions in these 200 futures contracts are *all* entered on July 28. Thus, a strip hedge can be thought of as a portfolio of single-period hedges. In the strip hedge we shall consider, the hedger has hedged borrowing costs for four successive quarters. Table 10.4 contains data for the strip hedge example. In this example, the firm faces a new loan rate at the start of each of four successive 90-day loan periods.[16] As an example of how to read the table, "S 50 @94.555" means go short 50 contracts at a futures price of 94.555, and "L 50 @94.35" means go long 50 contracts at a futures price of 94.35.

In this strip hedge example, the effective borrowing rate for each quarter is the implied futures rate at the time the hedge is placed. This is just as it is in the one-period case given earlier. Thus, one can see that a strip hedge is a portfolio of one-period hedges. We are assuming that spot LIBOR = futures LIBOR on each date that the firm goes to the capital market to actually borrow

TABLE 10.4 Strip Hedge Using Eurodollar Futures[1]

Date	Spot 3-Month LIBOR	September 1999	December 1999	March 2000	June 2000
7/28/1999	5.3125%	S 50 @ 94.555	S 50 @ 94.19	S 50 @ 94.185	S 50@ 93.95
9/13/1999	5.65%	L 50 @ 94.35			
12/13/1999	5.85%		L 50 @ 94.15		
3/13/2000	6.00%			L 50 @ 94.00	
6/19/2000	5.90%				L 50 @ 94.10
Futures LIBOR rate (on 7/28/99)		**5.445%**	**5.81%**	**5.815%**	**6.05%**
Gain (Loss) in Eurodollar future:		$25,625	$5,000	$23,125	($18,750)[2]

[1]Rates and prices known as of July 28 appear in italics.

[2]The $18,750 loss occurs because the June 2000 futures price rose from 93.95 to 94.10. This is a loss of 15 ticks. Each tick is worth $25, and the bank sold 50 futures contracts: 15 ticks × $25/tick × 50 contracts = −$18,750.

Quarter	Firm's Borrowing Rate	Quarterly Interest Expense	Gain (Loss) on Futures Positions	Net Interest Expense	Effective Borrowing Rate
Sep 99–Dec 99	5.650%	706,250[3]	25,625	680,625	**5.445%**
Dec 99–Mar 00	5.850%	731,250	5,000	726,250	**5.810%**
Mar 00–Jun 00	6.000%	750,000	23,125	726,875	**5.815%**
Jun 00–Sep 00	5.900%	737,500	(18,750)	756,250	**6.050%**
				Average:	**5.78%**

[3]$50 million × 0.0565 × 90/360 = $706,250.

$50 million for another three months. You can see this by noting that the four diagonal futures prices (L 50 @ 94.XX) equal 100-spot LIBOR on those four dates. This can be assured only if the firm borrows on each of the futures contracts' delivery days.

10.6.6.2 A Stack Hedge

To execute a **stack hedge** (frequently called a **rolling hedge**), the hedger would sell 200 September 1999 futures contracts on July 28, 1999. The 200 contracts are being sold because the firm needs the protection provided by 50 futures contracts for each of four quarters. If the firm only sold 50 September futures contracts, it would be hedging only the first quarter's borrowings. Thus, the firm "stacks" the hedges for subsequent quarters in one nearby delivery date. In this example, this is the September futures contract. Because the Eurodollar futures contract is cash settled, the firm will hold the 200 September futures contracts through expiration on September 13, 1999.[17] On that date, the firm will offset (repurchase) its 200 September futures contracts and sell 150 December futures contracts; the firm will then be short these 150 December futures through their expiration on December 13, 1999. On December 13, the firm will offset (buy back)

Table 10.5 Stack Hedge Using Eurodollar Futures[1]

Date	Spot LIBOR	September 1999	December 1999	March 2000	June 2000
7/28/1999	*5.3125%*	*S200@94.555*			
9/13/1999	5.65%	L200@94.350	S150@93.985		
12/13/1999	5.85%		L150@94.150	S100@94.145	
3/13/2000	6.00%			L100@94.000	S50@93.765
6/19/2000	5.90%				L50@94.100
Futures LIBOR rate		**5.445%**	**6.015%**	**5.855%**	**6.235%**
		(on 7/28/99)	(on 9/13/99)	(on 12/13/99)	(on 3/13/00)
Gain (Loss) in ED future:		$102,500	($61,875)	$36,250[2]	($41,875)

[1]Rates and prices known as of July 28 appear in italics.

[2]The $36,250 gain occurs because the futures price, fell from 94.145 to 94. This is a profit of 14.5 ticks, worth $25/tick. The bank was short 100 futures contracts, and 14.5 ticks × $25/tick × 100 contracts = $36,250.

Quarter	Firm's Borrowing Rate	Quarterly Interest Expense	Gain (Loss) on Futures Positions	Net Interest Expense	Effective Borrowing Rate
Sep 99–Dec 99	5.650%[3]	706,250[4]	25,625	680,625	**5.445%**[5]
Dec 99–Mar 00	5.850%	731,250	(20,625)	726,250	**5.810%**
From Sep/Dec			25,625		
Mar 00–Jun 00	6.000%	750,000	18,125	726,875	**5.815%**
From Sep/Dec			25,625		
From Dec/Mar			(20,625)		
Jun 00–Sep 00	5.900%	737,500	(41,875)	756,250	**6.050%**
From Sep/Dec			25,625		
From Dec/Mar			(20,625)		
From Mar/Jun			18,125		
				Average	**5.78%**

[3]The futures price on 9/13/99 is 94.35; 100 − 94.35 = 5.65.

[4](0.0565/4)$50,000,000 = $706,250.

[5](680,625/50,000,000)4 = 5.445%.

its 150 December contracts and sell 100 March 2000 contracts. This process continues for the March and June futures—allowing the firm to hedge its quarterly borrowing rate for one year.

Table 10.5 contains data for a stack hedge example. Note that the only difference between the Tables 10.4 and 10.5 is in the futures prices at the time of the hedge placement. That is, the futures prices at the time the hedge is lifted are the same. Of course, this implies that the spot LIBOR at the expiration of the futures contracts is the same in both examples.

To calculate the effective borrowing rate in the stack hedge (shown in the lower half of Table 10.5), gains and losses from previous quarters' futures trading must be allocated to the current quarter. For example, one-fourth of the $102,500 gain from the Eurodollar futures hedge in place during the Sep 99–Dec 99 quarter must be allocated to the Dec 99–Mar 00 quarter. The net interest expense during this quarter will reflect a $25,625 Eurodollar futures gain from the previous quarter as well as a $20,625 Eurodollar futures loss in the current quarter (one third of $61,875).

Upon careful examination of the information presented in Tables 10.4 and 10.5, one will note something peculiar. Both hedges resulted in an average effective borrowing rate of 5.78%! This is not a fluke; there is an explanation for this coincidence. Note that in Table 10.4, the September futures rate is 0.1325% above the spot LIBOR on July 28. Also on July 28, the December futures rate is 0.365% higher than the September futures rate; the March futures rate is 0.005% higher than the December futures rate, and the June futures rate is 0.235% higher than the March futures rate.

Now, note that in Table 10.5, on July 28 the September futures rate is also 0.1325% higher than the spot LIBOR rate. Further, in Table 10.5, note that on September 13, 1999, the December futures rate is 0.365% higher than the spot LIBOR rate. On December 13, 1999, the March futures rate is 0.005% higher than the spot LIBOR rate, and on March 13, 2000, the June futures rate is 0.235% higher than the spot LIBOR rate.

Movements in the futures yield curve determine the relative effectiveness of a stack hedge versus a strip hedge. When the futures term structure shifts in this parallel fashion, a strip hedge or a stack hedge will result in the same effective borrowing rate. Other changes in the futures term structure will favor one hedge over the other.

10.6.7 Choosing Between a Strip Hedge and a Stack Hedge

For most futures contracts, the advantage of the stack hedge is that the hedger is always trading the most liquid futures contract. From Table 10.2, one can see that in almost all cases the volume (liquidity) for Eurodollar futures exceeded 1000 contracts until the year 2004—over 20 expirations later. However, from Table 10.1, one can see that the volume for T-bill futures is concentrated in the most near-term delivery. Thus, hedgers can use either a strip or a stack hedge in the Eurodollar futures markets. But, when they are dealing with T-bill futures, they are forced to use a stack hedge.

Stack hedges offer hedger the opportunity to take advantage of relative mispricings when they are switching the delivery months. That is, if a hedger sees a mispricing between two futures contracts, it is possible to roll the hedge into (sell) the relatively higher priced futures contract. Stack hedges, however, will result in higher transactions costs (commissions).

The relative performance of stack hedges vs strip hedges will depend on the movement of the yield curve, which, of course, is unknown on the day the hedge in implemented. Table 10.6 presents an example in which the futures term structure slopes subsequently upward. That is, note that in Table 10.6, on July 28, the September futures rate is 0.1325% higher than the spot LIBOR rate. However, note that on September 13, 1999, the December futures rate is 0.23% higher than the spot LIBOR rate. On December 13, 1999, the March futures rate is 0.33% higher than the spot LIBOR rate, and on March 13, 2000, the June futures rate is 0.43% higher than the spot LIBOR rate. As a result, the average effective borrowing rate for the stack hedge in this case is 5.89%. Under these conditions, the firm would have been better off (in terms of interest costs) with a strip hedge instead of a stack hedge. However, if the futures term structure slopes subsequently downward, a stack hedge would outperform a strip hedge.

TABLE 10.6 A Stack Hedge Using Eurodollar Futures with a Futures Term Structure Slope That Subsequently Increases[1]

Date	Spot LIBOR	September 1999	December 1999	March 2000	June 2000
7/28/1999	5.3125%	S200@94.555			
9/13/1999	5.65%	L200@94.35	S150@94.12		
12/13/1999	5.85%		L150@94.15	S100@93.82	
3/13/2000	6.00%			L100@94.00	S50@93.57
6/19/2000	5.90%				L50@94.10
Futures LIBOR rate		**5.445%**	**5.88%**	**6.18%**	**6.43%**
Premium (Discount) to spot LIBOR at hedge		0.1325%	0.230%	0.330%	0.430%
		(5.445 − 5.3125)	(5.88 − 5.65%)	(6.18% − 5.85%)	(6.43% − 6%)
Gain (Loss) in ED futures		$102,500	($11,250)	($45,000)	($66,250)

Quarter	Firm's Borrowing Rate	Quarterly Interest Expense	Gain (Loss) on Futures Positions	Net Interest Expense	Effective Borrowing Rate
Sep 99–Dec 99	5.650%	706,250	25,625	680,625	**5.445%**
Dec 99–Mar 00	5.850%	731,250	(3,750)	709,375	**5.675%**
From Sep/Dec			25,625		
Mar 00–Jun 00	6.000%	750,000	(22,500)	750,625	**6.005%**
From Sep/Dec			25,625		
From Dec/Mar			(3,750)		
Jun 00–Sep 00	5.900%	737,500	(66,250)	804,375	**6.435%**
From Sep/Dec			25,625		
From Dec/Mar			(3,750)		
From Mar/Jun			(22,500)		
				Average	**5.89%**

[1]Rates and prices known as of July 28 appear in italics.

10.7 EURODOLLAR BUNDLES AND PACKS

10.7.1 BUNDLES

Introduced in September 1994, Eurodollar bundles are a convenient way to trade a strip of Eurodollar futures contracts. A Eurodollar bundle is the *simultaneous* sale or purchase of one contract, which consists of a series of consecutive Eurodollar futures contracts. Trading in bundles can help hedge LIBOR-based floating rates. Potential users include investment bankers carrying inventories of floating-rate notes and corporations planning to issue floating-rate debt. The commercial bank in the example in Section 10.6.6.1 might have used bundles to help hedge its loan agreement. Bundles are a convenient way to construct a Eurodollar strip position because all contracts are entered concurrently. That is, by not being obliged to construct the strip contract by contract, the trader eliminates execution risk.

Generally, the first contract in any bundle is the first quarterly contract in the Eurodollar strip (i.e., from the March, June, September, December quarterly cycle). The last contract in any bundle depends on the bundle's maturity. At the Chicago Mercantile Exchange, trading in bundles covers 1, 2, 3, 5, 7, and 10 years to maturity. For example, on March 31, 2001, the three-year bundle consisted of the first 12 quarterly contracts having delivery dates in June 2001, September 2001, ... , and a terminal (12th) contract in March 2004.[18]

10.7.2 Packs

Packs are the simultaneous purchase or sale of an equally weighted, consecutive series of four Eurodollar futures. Packs offer another way of executing a strip trade. With a pack, the trader has all four contract months executed at once—lowering execution risk.

Generally, there are nine packs trading. Packs are designated by a color code that corresponds to their position on the Eurodollar futures yield curve. These color codes help market participants identify particular years in the strip. The first pack is designated "Red" and represents the fifth through eighth Eurodollar futures contract (the second Eurodollar futures year). Subsequent years are represented by the following color codes, respectively: green (the third Eurodollar futures year), blue, gold, purple, orange, pink, silver, and copper.

Bundles and packs are simply execution conventions. There is no effective difference between a position in a bundle or pack, or a position established by trading contracts individually.

You can learn more about bundles and packs by accessing www.cme.com/products/interest_rate/products_interestrate_ed_bundles.cfm and www.cme.com/products/interest_rate/products_interestrates_ed_packs.cfm.

10.8 SUMMARY

In this chapter, we covered the pricing and hedging applications of short-term interest rate futures contracts, with a particular focus on Eurodollar and Treasury bill futures. We began with a discussion of the spot Treasury bill market and how to read T-bill prices in the *Wall Street Journal*. Then, we discussed the T-bill futures market.

A presentation of the spot Eurodollar market in Section 10.3 preceded our treatment of Eurodollar futures markets. In Section 10.4.1 we showed how to calculate the theoretical value of a Eurodollar futures contract. In the two sections that followed, we constructed the cash-and-carry and reverse cash-and-carry arbitrage trades that align Eurodollar futures prices and LIBOR rates. This discussion continued in Section 10.5, where we demonstrated how market participants can take advantage of mispricings in the Eurodollar futures market to realize the highest rate of return on an investment with the desired time to maturity.

Following a general discussion of hedging with short-term interest rate futures, we presented an example of how a hedger could use the T-bill futures market to hedge against a decline in the value of a portfolio. Then, we presented examples of how to use Eurodollar futures contracts to lock in both one-period and multiperiod borrowing rates. We concluded with a brief discussion of Eurodollar bundles and packs—two useful ways of initiating hedges with Eurodollar futures contracts.

In the Eurodollar hedging examples presented in this chapter, the hedger was able to obtain a known borrowing rate over four subsequent quarters. For example, by using a strip hedge (as shown in Table 10.4), the firm was able to lock in known borrowing rates of 5.445, 5.81, 5.815, and 6.05%. Suppose, however, that the hedger wants to have a known and constant borrowing rate over the life of the loan. Further suppose that the firm does not want to trade Eurodollar futures directly. The firm can accomplish these goals by entering a financial transaction known as a swap. The market for swaps has been one of the fastest growing areas of derivatives and account for the explosive growth in Eurodollar futures contracts. The next three chapters of this text discuss swaps, swap pricing, and using swaps to manage risk.

Reference

Stigum, Marcia. 1990. *The Money Market*, 3rd ed. Burr Ridge, IL: Irwin Professional Publishing.

Notes

[1]In July 2001, the U.S. Treasury commenced weekly auctions of 28-day Treasury bills.

[2]The actual process of government issuance of T-bills, and how investors purchase them is described in Stigum (1990).

[3]See Stigum (1990, pp. 67–70) for more on the bond equivalent yield.

[4]Several of the bond equivalent yields in Figure 10.1 are off by 1 basis point. This occurs because the discount yields are rounded to the nearest whole basis point.

[5]The T-bill contract changed in October 1997 and became a cash-settled contract. Before then, there was physical delivery of $1 million (face value) of 91-day T-bills, and the contract traded in whole-tick sizes of $0.01 = 25.

[6]This is about four years after the inception of T-bill futures contract on January 6, 1976.

[7]Holidays will result in different rules for determining the last trading day.

[8]Several of the contracts with nearby delivery dates will trade in half-ticks, or one-half of a basis point, worth $12.50.

[9]Problem 10.3 at the end of this chapter asks the student to derive Equation (10.15). Note that if borrowing or lending with Eurodollar time deposits involves a two-day settlement (which is common), the interest on the 90-day Eurodollar time deposit will be paid or received on date $T + 92$.

[10]Note that transactions costs were ignored in the computation of this theoretical futures price. Bid and ask LIBOR rates and other transactions costs can be used to determine the bounds within which the Eurodollar futures price can lie without permitting arbitrage. In addition, the existence of different borrowing and lending rates can be incorporated.

[11]Selling $(T + 90)$-day Eurodollar time deposits represents borrowing money for $T + 90$ days at the Eurodollar time deposit interest rate.

[12]Often, when the underlying asset is sold and a futures contract is purchased, the rate of return is called the *implied reverse repo rate*. The implied reverse repo rate is a borrowing rate. The short sale of the underlying asset provides a cash inflow, and the long futures position locks in a cash outflow.

[13]Be consistent in using discount yields, add-on yields, or bond equivalent yields.

[14]More than 12 weeks of data should be gathered. One year (52 data points) would probably be optimal.

[15]For ease of presentation, the loan begins on the expiration date of the September futures contract, September 13, 1999. Loans beginning on any other date will mean that the hedge possesses some basis risk.

[16]In this example (as well as those presented in Tables 10.5 and 10.6), interest expenses are calculated assuming a 90-day period. The actual days between dates are as follows:

From	To	Days
9/13/1999	12/13/1999	91
12/13/1999	3/13/2000	91
3/13/2000	6/19/2000	98
6/19/2000	9/12/2000	85

[17]In practice, a firm might roll over the maturing contract (September) into the next delivery date (December) prior to expiration.

[18]In addition, a five-year "forward" bundle trades at the CME. This bundle covers years 5 through 10 of the Eurodollar strip. Therefore, on March 31, 2001, the "forward" bundle began with the 21st contract in the strip (June 2006) and ended with the 40th contract (December 2011).

PROBLEMS

10.1 Suppose you pay $9259 for a $10,000 face value T-bill that has 265 days to maturity.

   a. Compute the periodic (unannualized) rate of return you will earn during the 265-day holding period.

   b. Use simple interest to annualize the answer you found in part a.

   c. Use compound interest to annualize the answer you found in part a.

   d. Compute the discount yield for this T-bill.

   e. Briefly explain why the rate of return you found in part c exceeds the one you computed in part b, which in turn exceeds the discount yield you computed in part **d**.

10.2 Today's date is June 15, 1999. The delivery date for September 1999 T-bill futures contracts is September 13, 1999 (90 days from today). The deliverable T-bill matures on December 13, 1999 (181 days from today). Suppose the discount yield of the December 13 spot T-bill is 4.83%. The discount yield of the September 13 spot T-bill is 4.58%.

   a. Compute the prices of the spot T-bills.

   b. Use spot T-bills to compute the implied forward price for a 91-day T-bill that will exist 90 days from today.

   c. The IMM Index for the September T-bill futures contract is 95.13. Compute the value of 91-day T-bills underlying the contract.

10.3 Derive Equation (10.15) from Equation (10.14).

10.4 A firm can borrow $1million from the bank for 110 days at an annual rate of 6.5%. Alternatively, it can borrow $1million at the bank for 20 days at an annual rate of 6.25% and sell one Eurodollar futures contract at a futures price of 93.70. The futures contract's delivery date is 20 days hence. At the end of 20 days, the firm can borrow from the bank for 90 additional days at LIBOR plus 50 basis points. Which method should the firm use to borrow? Analyze the problem, first assuming that spot LIBOR is 6.68%/year 20 days hence, and then assuming that spot LIBOR is 5.92%/year 20 days hence. Assume that all interest rates are computed on the basis of a 360-day year.

10.5   Suppose today is November 23, 2000. Spot LIBOR rates are as follows:

Maturity	Rate
$t \leq 1$ month	$7\,^7/_8\%$
1 month $< t \leq 3$ months	$8\,^1/_8\%$
3 months $< t \leq 6$ months	8%
6 months $< t \leq 1$ year	$7\,^{15}/_{16}\%$
1 year $< t \leq 1\,^1/_2$ year	$7\,^7/_8\%$

The delivery dates for Eurodollar futures contracts are December 17, 2000, March 18, 2001, June 17, 2001, and September 16, 2001. Compute the theoretical Eurodollar futures prices for December, March, June, and September deliveries.

10.6   You have graduated with your finance degree and are now a high-powered horse trader and commodity futures arbitrageur. Suppose you are on the phone with a hapless trainee at Dix, Oort, Radger, Karen, and Shelton (DORKS). The trainee quotes you a Eurodollar futures price of 94.34, seven-day LIBOR of 5.00%, and 97-day LIBOR of 5.50%. You know that the futures contract expires in seven days and that your transactions costs are negligible. When you ask whether these quotes are firm, the trainee says yes. You decide to teach this loser a lesson. "Buy 50 futures," you order. What other trades do you make to complete the arbitrage? How much money do you make on this arbitrage?

10.7   The phone rings. It is the trainee from DORKS. "I have made a terrible mistake," he moans. "Please let me off the hook. I thought you asked for a quote on the futures contract that expires in 97 days, not seven days. That futures quote was for a futures contract that expires in 97 days. Also, a 97-day LIBOR rate is 5.00% and a 187-day LIBOR rate is 5.50%. Please, please, let's bust that previous trade." You're thinking, "What a whiner." You ask "Are your price quotes firm this time?" "Yes

sir!" exclaims the trainee. "Okay," you say, "Bust the previous trade and now ... sell 150 futures!" What other trades do you make to complete the arbitrage? How much money do you make on this arbitrage?

10.8   A firm intends to issue $20 million (face value) in 30-day commercial paper 15 days from today. The spot rate (add-on yield) on 30-day commercial paper is currently 7%. The 90-day Eurodollar futures price, for contracts calling for delivery 29 days hence, is currently 92.30. The firm has regressed changes in the spot 30-day commercial paper interest rate on changes in futures discount yields. The estimated slope coefficient is 1.20.

    a. Should the firm buy or sell futures contracts to hedge?

    b. How many Eurodollar futures contracts should it trade to hedge?

10.9   A firm takes out a one-year loan for $20 million on November 19. Spot LIBOR on November 19 is 6%. The firm must pay 100 basis points over spot LIBOR, so that the initial interest rate is 7%, and this determines its initial interest payment of $550,000. However, this interest rate is fixed for the first three months only. The firm's subsequent interest payments will be whatever spot LIBOR is on February 19, May 19, and August 19, plus 100 basis points. On November 19, the following Eurodollar futures prices are observed:

Delivery Month	Futures Price (IMM Index)
December	94.22
March (next year)	94.25
June	94.07
September	93.86

    a. If the firm believes that futures prices incorporate market expectations, what interest rates might it expect to pay on

February 19, May 19, and August 19? State any assumptions you make in answering this. Compute the firm's expected total interest expense for the $20 million loan.

b. What trades should the firm make to hedge by means of a strip hedge? What trades should the firm make in order to hedge by using a rolling hedge? Suppose that ultimately, the following spot LIBOR's and futures prices are observed:

	Spot	Futures Prices		
Date	**LIBOR**	**Mar.**	**June**	**Sept.**
Feb. 19	6.00%	94.02	94.00	93.82
May 19	7.06%		92.90	92.62
Aug. 19	7.94%			91.92

What interest expense would the firm have actually paid if it did not hedge? What interest expense would it have paid if it used a strip hedge? What interest expense would it have paid if it used a rolling hedge and did all its trades on the three dates as tabulated?

10.10 Today is November 26, 2000. A corporate treasurer has noted that his firm has borrowed $25 million (face value) from a bank, and the loan is due to be repaid on December 17, 2000. The bank has told the company that it is willing to extend the loan, to March 17, 2001, at a rate equal to whatever LIBOR is on December 17, plus 100 basis points. Currently, futures prices are as follows:

Delivery Date	Futures Price
December 17, 2000	91.98
March 18, 2001	92.47
June 17, 2001	92.56
September 16, 2001	92.53

a. Should the firm hedge by buying or selling futures? Which delivery month (or months) should the firm use? How many futures contracts should it trade?

b. Suppose that on December 17, 2000, the actual three month spot LIBOR is 7.81%. If the firm did not hedge, what would be its interest expense on the new bank loan? If the firm did hedge, what would be its interest expense, after considering profits/losses on the futures contracts? What is the firm's annualized interest rate on the hedged borrowing transaction? How does it compare to the November 26 futures price?

c. Suppose instead that the firm desires to extend the loan for a year, until December 17, 2001. The new loan will be a fixed-rate, one-year loan. How many futures contracts should the firm trade on November 26 in order to hedge? Will all the futures contracts be for the same delivery month? Why or why not?

d. Suppose the firm wants to extend the loan for a year. The new loan will be a variable-rate loan, with interest rates reset quarterly. How many futures contracts should the firm trade on November 26? What factors dictate the delivery month, or months, that the firm should use?

10.11 Suppose a hedger places a stack hedge as in Table 10.5 (i.e., in terms of the number of contracts traded). However, suppose that when the hedger places the stack hedge the following futures prices are obtained:

Date	Futures Contract	Futures Price
7/28/1999	September 1999	94.555
9/13/1999	December 1999	94.320

12/13/1999   March 2000   94.220

3/13/2000   June 2000   94.170

a. Suppose the futures prices at the time of the hedge rollover are the same as they are in Table 10.5. Calculate the futures contract gain or loss.

b. Calculate the firm's net interest expense for each quarter.

c. Calculate the firm's effective loan rate for each quarter.

d. Calculate the average effective loan rate. Was this hedge more or less effective than the strip hedge presented in Table 10.4? Explain.

e. What do you notice about the futures premium (or discount) to the spot LIBOR at the time the hedge is placed?

10.12 Suppose a hedger places a stack hedge as in Table 10.5 (i.e., in terms of the number of contracts traded). However, suppose that when the hedger places the stack hedge the following futures prices are obtained:

Date	Futures Contract	Futures Price
7/28/1999	September 1999	94.555
9/13/1999	December 1999	94.320
12/13/1999	March 2000	94.220
3/13/2000	June 2000	94.170

a. Suppose the futures prices at the time of the hedge rollover are the same as they are in Table 10.5. Calculate the futures contract gain or loss.

b. Calculate the firm's net interest expense for each quarter.

c. Calculate the firm's effective loan rate for each quarter.

d. Calculate the average effective loan rate. Was this hedge more or less effective than the strip hedge presented in Table 10.4? Explain.

e. What do you notice about the futures premium (or discount) to the spot LIBOR at the time the hedge is placed?

PART 3

SWAPS

CHAPTER 11

An Introduction to Swaps

Swaps are contractual agreements between two parties to exchange cash flows. The cash flows that are swapped may be determined on the basis of interest rates, exchange rates, or the prices of indexes (such as stock indexes) or commodities. To determine the dollar amounts that will be exchanged these prices are applied to a base amount, called the **notional principal** of the swap. The two parties that agree to exchange the cash flows are called the **counterparties** of the swap. One of the counterparties will typically be a swap dealer (market maker); it is rare for two firms to negotiate the terms of a swap contract by themselves.

In this chapter, the basic features of different types of swaps are described. The **plain vanilla**, fixed-for-floating interest rate swap is covered first, in Section 11.1. A plain vanilla swap is a standard swap with no unusual features. Other interest rate swap structures are briefly covered. Currency swaps are discussed in Section 11.2, and commodity swaps in Section 11.3. Finally, the issue of credit risk in swaps is considered.

11.1 INTEREST RATE SWAPS

The fixed-for-floating fixed–floating interest rate swap is the most basic form of a swap, in which one of the parties agrees to pay (to the other counterparty) a fixed amount of money on specific dates. The fixed payments are expressed as a percentage of the swap's notional principal. For example, 8% of $20 million would create an annual payment of $1.6 million; if semiannual payments are required, the fixed amount would be $800,000 every six months. The notional principal of the swap is not exchanged; it serves only as the basis for calculating the swap payments. The percentage is the fixed interest rate, and it is multiplied by the notional principal to compute the fixed payment. The same party, who is called the fixed-rate payer, also receives a floating, or variable, amount of money on each of the specified dates. The amount to be received is also computed by multiplying a randomly fluctuating interest rate by the swap's notional principal. This floating payment is determined by a floating interest rate that changes over time, such as three-month LIBOR. If this interest rate rises, the fixed-rate payer will receive a greater floating amount of money. If the floating interest rate declines, the fixed-rate payer will receive a smaller floating amount. In practice, the amount received at each date is offset, or netted out, against the amount paid. Thus, if on one particular date, the fixed-rate payer is supposed to pay $1,600,000, and also receive $1,200,000, the net payment made is $400,000 ($1,600,000 − $1,200,000 = $400,000 outflow). When the counterparties' obligations are netted in this manner, the payment ($400,000) is called a **difference check**.

An important characteristic of most interest rate swaps is that the floating interest rate (e.g., LIBOR) that determines the floating-rate payment is set *one period before the payment date*. This means that the net payment to be made on any date is actually known one period earlier.[1] It follows that the first net payment, which will be made one period after the swap's origination date, is known on the origination date.

11.1.1   An Example of a Plain Vanilla Fixed-for-Floating Interest Rate Swap

Party A pays the fixed interest rate (and receives the floating rate). Counterparty B receives the fixed payment (and pays the floating rate). The notional principal is $40 million. The fixed rate is 7%. The fixed rate day count method is **the 30/360 day basis**.[2] The floating rate is six-month LIBOR, which is also determined on a 30/360 day basis. The swap's **origination date** is July 20, 1999, and the **termination date** is July 20, 2002. The first payment date is January 20, 2000. Semiannual payments will then be made on each July 20 and January 20, up to and including the termination date.

Assume the actual six-month LIBOR that exists on the origination date, and the six-month LIBOR that subsequently exists on all future relevant dates is as follows (of course, on the origination date only the first floating LIBOR is known).

Date	Six-Month LIBOR
July 20, 1999 (origination date)	6.5%
January 20, 2000	7.0%
July 20, 2000	7.3%
January 20, 2001	7.7%
July 20, 2001	7.0%
January 20, 2002	6.2%
July 20, 2002 (termination date)	5.9%

On each payment date, party A, the fixed-rate payer, must pay half of the fixed rate (half of 7%) times the notional principal of $40 million:

$$(0.07/2)(\$40 \text{ million}) = \$1.4 \text{ million}$$

Half of 7%, or 3.5%, is used to compute the fixed-rate payment because payment dates occur every six months, or half a year. If fixed payments were made annually, the fixed amount would be 7% of $40 million, or $2.8 million. If fixed payments were made quarterly, the fixed payment amount would be $(0.07/4)(\$40 \text{ million})$, or $700,000. Thus, a 7% interest rate becomes a 3.5% semiannual rate, or a 1.75% quarterly rate, as appropriate.

In a typical swap, LIBOR at time $t-1$ will determine the floating payment six months later, at time t. Six-month LIBOR on July 20, 1999 determines the first floating-rate payment made on January 20, 2000 by party B to counterparty A. Thus, the floating-rate payment amount on January 20, 2000 is

$$(0.065/2)(\$40 \text{ million}) = \$1,300,000$$

TABLE 11.1   Cash Flows Resulting from the Swap[1]

Date	Six-Month LIBOR	Fixed Payment	Floating Payment	Net Cash Flow
July 20, 1999	6.5%			
January 20, 2000	7.0%	$1,400,000	$1,300,000	−$100,000
July 20, 2000	7.3%	$1,400,000	$1,400,000	$0
January 20, 2001	7.7%	$1,400,000	$1,460,000	+$ 60,000
July 20, 2001	7.0%	$1,400,000	$1,540,000	+$140,000
January 20, 2002	6.2%	$1,400,000	$1,400,000	$0
July 20, 2002	5.9%	$1,400,000	$1,240,000	−$160,000

[1]Note how the floating payment at time t is determined by the interest rate at time $t-1$. The net cash flows are the difference between the fixed and floating payments. A negative net cash flow means that the fixed-rate payer is making a cash payment to the receive–fixed counterparty.

The cash flows that are exchanged are presented in Table 11.1. Party A is the fixed-rate payer, who pays $1,400,000 on each of the payment dates and receives the amounts in the "Floating Payment" column on each payment date. The cash flows are netted, so that only the amounts in the column labeled "Net Cash Flow" are exchanged. The amounts in the last column are denoted as "–" or "+" from the fixed-rate payer's viewpoint. Thus, party A will pay (a "–" sign) $100,000 on January 20, 2000, and receive (a "+" sign) $60,000 on January 20, 2001.

Note again that the LIBOR that exists at time $t-1$ determines the floating cash flow at time t. Therefore, net cash flows are always known six months in advance. On July 20, 2000, six-month LIBOR is 7.3%. This locks in the floating payment that will be made six months later, on January 20, 2001. The floating payment on January 20, 2001 will be (0.073/2)($40,000,000) = $1,460,000.[3]

The cash flows arising from the swap may be depicted through the use of a cash flow diagram as shown in Figure 11.1. The arrows pointing up represent the cash inflows for the fixed-rate payer; they are the floating payments. The arrows pointing down represent the fixed payments of $1,400,000 made every six months by the fixed-rate payer (party A).

11.1.2   Generalizing the Plain Vanilla Fixed–Floating Interest Rate Swap

We can generalize the structure of a plain vanilla fixed-for-floating interest rate swap as follows. Define:

NP = notional principal

h_f = unannualized fixed rate

$\tilde{h}_t$ = variable (floating) unannualized rate, such as LIBOR, that exists at time t

The term "unannualized" refers to the practice of converting an annual interest rate to a partial-year rate. If there are t days between payments, and if there are 365 days in a year then

$h = (r)(t/365)$. The tilde ($\sim$) that is placed above the floating interest rate means that on the origination date, the floating rate is unknown (it is a random variable characterized by a probability distribution) on all dates beyond time 0. Then, the fixed-rate payer must pay $(h_f)(NP)$ at each payment date and will receive ($\tilde{h}_t$)(NP) at payment date $t+1$. Figure 11.2 illustrates the cash flow structure for a three-year standard fixed–floating interest rate swap with semi-annual payments.

Note in Figure 11.2 that the first "floating" payment is not a random variable. The time 0 floating interest rate determines the time 1 floating cash flow. The floating payments occurring beyond time 1 are unknown as of the swap's origination date. Each net payment is always known one period before the exchange of cash flows.

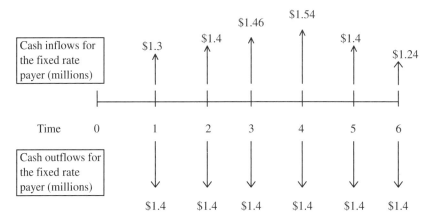

Figure 11.1 Cash flow diagram for the swap example. The cash flows are netted against each other to produce one payment from the losing party to the winning party.

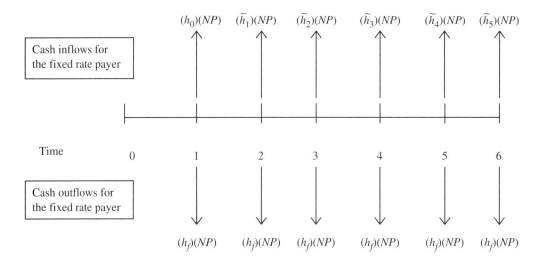

Figure 11.2 Cash flow diagram for a plain vanilla interest rate swap.

11.1.3   Characterizing a Fixed–Floating Interest Rate Swap as a Portfolio of FRAs

A fixed–floating interest rate swap contract may be more easily understood by realizing that it is virtually equivalent to a portfolio of forward contracts, each of which has a different settlement (termination) date, and each of which has the same forward rate. Thus, instead of entering into a fixed–floating swap as the receive-fixed party (this is the party that pays the floating rate and receives the fixed rate), a firm or institution could instead sell a portfolio of forward rate agreements. In a swap, if the floating interest rate is below the fixed rate, the receive-fixed party will benefit, because the floating cash flow amounts paid are less than the fixed rate payments received; the difference check will be paid by the pay-fixed party to the receive-fixed counterparty at each settlement date. Similarly, at each settlement date of a FRA, if the spot interest rate is below the contract rate (interest rates have declined), the seller of the FRA will receive a payment from the party that bought the FRA.

Table 11.2 summarizes the analogy between a fixed–floating interest rate swap and a portfolio of forwards.

For example, consider the swap described in Section 11.1.1. The last column of Table 11.1 shows the cash flows for the pay-fixed party, so the cash flows for the receive-fixed counterparty will just be the negative of those shown. Instead, the receive-fixed counterparty could have sold a strip of five FRAs: a 6×12 FRA, a 12×18 FRA, an 18×24 FRA, a 24×30 FRA, and a 30×36 FRA. Recall that an $N \times M$ FRA covers an interest rate for the period beginning at month N and ending at month M. The contract period is $(M - N)$ months. The first cash flow of the swap, on January 20, 2000, does not require a FRA because that payment is predetermined on the swap's origination date. The receive-fixed party knows that $100,000 will be received on January 20, 2000.

Recall that Equation (3.1) is used to determine the settlement cash flow of a standard FRA:

$$\pi = \left| \frac{P[r(t1,t2) - fr(0,t1,t2)](D/B)}{1 + [r(t1,t2)(D/B)]} \right| \qquad (3.1)$$

settlement amount $= [P \times (\text{difference between settlement rate and contract forward rate})$

$\times \text{contract period}]/[1 + (\text{settlement rate} \times \text{contract period})]$

The contract period in this formula is a fraction of a year. It converts the annualized rates $[r(t1, t2)$ and $fr(0, t1, t2)]$ into unannualized rates.

To establish equivalency between the strip of FRAs and the swap, each of the five FRAs should have the same contract rate of 7%, and the length of each contract period is six months (which is 0.5 year when the 30/360 day count method is used). The January 20, 2000, settlement cash flow comes from the 6×12 FRA with a notional principal of $40 million. On January 20, 2000,

TABLE 11.2   An Interest Rate Swap Is Analogous to a Strip of FRAs

Swap Party	FRA Party	Receives Settlement Payments
Pay-fixed	Buy a portfolio of FRAs	If interest rates rise
Receive-fixed	Sell a portfolio of FRAs	If interest rates decline

six-month LIBOR is 7.0%. The settlement amount is therefore $0 (both the settlement rate and the contract forward rate are 7.0%, so the difference between them is 0.00). Note that this is the same net cash flow for the swap *six months later, on July 20, 2000.*

On July 20, 2000, six-month LIBOR is 7.3%. Therefore, the settlement amount paid by the seller of the FRA is:

$$\frac{(\$40,000,000)(0.073 - 0.07)0.5}{1 + (0.073)(0.5)} = \$57,887.12$$

This settlement amount, $57,887.12, is the present value of $60,000.[4] Note that undiscounted amount of $60,000 is the cash flow paid by the receive-fixed counterparty of the *swap six months later, on January 20, 2001.*

Table 11.3 summarizes the cash flows arising from the swap (from the receive-fixed party's view), and from a party who sells a series of five FRAs, each with the same contract rate of 7%.

The lines are drawn in Table 11.3 connecting the swap net cash flows to the corresponding FRA settlement payments. The differences between the cash flows from the two contracts arise from their different standard settlement features. A typical FRA uses the spot floating rate on the settlement date to determine the cash flow, which is discounted. A typical swap uses the time $t-1$ spot floating rate to determine the time t cash flow, and it is not discounted. However, recall that the parties to over-the-counter derivatives contracts can negotiate terms. An arrears reset swap (see note 1 in this chapter) is more similar to a portfolio of FRAs because it uses the time t spot floating rate (rather than the time $t-1$ spot rate) to determine the floating-rate payment. FRAs that do not have the cash flows discounted can also be negotiated, although these would be defined as being "nonstandard" contracts. The other important difference between a strip of FRAs and a swap is that each of the FRAs will have a unique contract rate, while the fixed rate of a swap is applied to each of its cash flows. Basically, the swap's fixed rate is an "average" of the different contract rates of the strip of FRAs. We will cover swap pricing in Chapter 13.

What is important to know is that the cash flows arising from a swap and a portfolio of forwards differ only because of their different settlement conventions. Conceptually, they are equivalent.

TABLE 11.3 Summary of Cash Flows Arising from the Swap and from the Sale of Five FRAs[1]

Date	Six-Month LIBOR	Swap Net Cash Flow	FRA Settlement Payment	FRA
July 20, 1999	6.5%			
January 20, 2000	7.0%	+$100,000	$0	6 × 12
July 20, 2000	7.3%	$0	−$ 57,887.12	12 × 18
January 20, 2001	7.7%	−$ 60,000	−$134,809.82	18 × 24
July 20, 2001	7.0%	−$140,000	$0	24 X 30
January 20, 2002	6.2%	$0	+$155,189.14	30 × 36
July 20, 2002	5.9%	+$160,000		

[1]The interest rate at time t determines a swap's cash flow paid at time $t+1$. But in a FRA, the time t interest rate determines the discounted cash flow at time t.

In general, a firm should use a FRA when it is managing a single-period interest rate risk (a FRA is essentially a single-period swap). A swap will be preferred when the interest rate risk exists at several periodic (quarterly, semiannually, etc.) future points in time.

There are other elements that make a swap different from a portfolio of FRAs, and these should be considered when one is deciding which contract to use. The credit risk arising from dealing with a counterparty is relevant. The liquidity of the two contracts must be analyzed. It is also important to compare the quoted prices to the contracts' theoretical prices, so that the cheaper contracts are bought (or the higher priced contracts are sold). In theory, after the settlement differences, default risk, and liquidity have been accounted for, the values of the swap and the portfolio of FRAs should be identical, but this does not mean that the actual prices (by different dealers, in particular) will be the same. Relative supply and demand in different markets in the short-run can create price differentials. The principles of pricing swaps are covered in Chapter 13.

Finally, firms should carefully examine the accounting treatment of swaps vs FRAs, any regulatory considerations that might permit one but not the other (e.g., some firms and institutions are prohibited from using futures and options, but not swaps), and whether the tax treatments of the two derivatives would differ.

11.1.4   Characterizing a Fixed–Floating Interest Rate Swap as a Coupon-Bearing Asset Plus a Coupon-Bearing Liability

Engaging in a fixed-for-floating interest rate swap is tantamount to creating a new asset, funded with a new liability. The pay-fixed party to the swap has effectively issued a coupon bond (a liability). In both a swap and a coupon bond, a fixed amount must be paid periodically (almost always every six months in the case of the corporate bond). The only difference is that the firm still owes the principal when it issues a bond, while the notional principal is not owed in an interest rate swap.

The pay-fixed party to the swap has also effectively purchased a floating-rate bond (an asset), where the interest received changes every period. Again, you should remember that the pay-fixed swap party does not receive the notional principal payment at the swap's termination, whereas the owner of a floating rate bond does receive principal when the bond matures.

Another difference exists regarding the accounting treatment of the transactions. The financial assets will appear on a firm's balance sheet. As of late 1996, swaps were considered to be off–balance-sheet financial instruments; thus, you would not see swaps on either the asset side or the liability side of a firm's balance sheet.

11.1.5   Quoting Prices of Plain Vanilla, Fixed–Floating Interest Rate Swaps

As the swap market developed, many conventions evolved that facilitated the quoting of prices. For each floating rate (three-month LIBOR, six-month LIBOR, etc.), the price of a fixed–floating interest rate swap is quoted for different maturities. Standard maturities are 2, 3, 5, 7, and 10 years. Another name for the maturity of a swap is its **tenor**. Thus, for three-month LIBOR, a set of prices will exist, depending on whether the swap tenor will be two years, three years, etc. A different set of prices will be quoted for two-year, three-year, etc. swaps, when the floating rate is six-month LIBOR. When a firm desires a swap tenor that is not quoted, its spread is interpolated from the two maturities that are quoted and then added to the yield of a Treasury instrument with a maturity equal to the desired tenor.

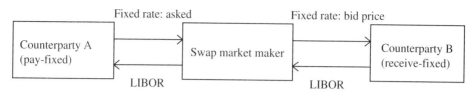

Figure 11.3 The swap dealer receives the fixed asked price and pays the fixed bid price.

Market makers quote prices in terms of the fixed rate. Essentially, the floating rate is either bought or sold, and the price paid is the fixed rate. When prices change, the change will appear as a change in the quoted fixed rate.

Most typically, swap rates are quoted as a spread, or margin, over the Treasury note rate with the same time to maturity as the swap's tenor.[5] Thus, if the yield to maturity for a five-year Treasury note is 6.60%, a swap market maker might quote the swap spread as 27/24 over 6.60%. This means that the pay-fixed party must pay a fixed interest rate of 6.87% (27 basis points above 6.60%) and will receive LIBOR. A firm that wishes to be the receive-fixed counterparty will receive a fixed interest rate of 6.84% (24 basis points above 6.60%) and pay LIBOR. The swap market maker earns the bid–asked spread of three basis points as a profit. Under typical market conventions, the 27-basis-point swap spread quote is the offer price, or asked price. The quote of 24 basis points is the bid swap price. Figure 11.3 illustrates the nature of these quotes.

Dealers will quote wider spread quotes (e.g., 30/20) for less creditworthy counterparties. The wider spreads serve as risk premiums that compensate the dealer for bearing credit (default) risk. Thus, the dealer will both pay a lower fixed rate (when acting as the pay-fixed party), and receive a higher fixed rate (when acting as the receive-fixed party) when dealing with riskier counterparties. When swap dealers are dealing with counterparties they feel are more likely to default, they may also require collateral (equivalent to initial margin for a futures contract), ask for a letter of credit, require the counterparty to pay for swap insurance, or demand that the swap be marked to market.

The floating rate is said to be quoted **flat**, with no margin above any floating rate index.

About 75% of all U.S. dollar based interest rate swaps are based on LIBOR. Other U.S. floating rates that are swapped and quoted, include commercial paper rates, the Fed funds rate, the prime rate, and Treasury bill rates. Still other fixed–floating interest rate swaps are based on foreign interest rates such as sterling LIBOR (for British pounds), yen LIBOR, and Euribor (the Euro Interbank Offered Rate) for euros.[6] In plain vanilla fixed–floating interest rate swaps, each of these floating rates is swapped against the respective fixed rates in the same currency. Many other swap structures exist, including swaps in which a fixed rate in one currency is exchanged for a floating rate denominated in a different currency.

11.1.6   Other Interest Rate Swap Structures

Many other interest rate swaps exist, other than plain vanilla fixed–floating interest rate swaps. In this section, just a few of the more common ones are discussed.

Ignoring the bid–asked spread, fairly priced **at-market** swaps have no value when they are originated.[7] In an **off-market swap** (also called an **off-market coupon swap**), the fixed rate is "away" from the market. For example, a swap dealer may be quoting a price of 30 basis points over the seven-year Treasury rate of 7.04% for a swap with a tenor of seven years. However, a firm might not want to pay 7.34% fixed; it may want to pay only 6.5%, and still receive LIBOR. In this case, an initial payment from the firm to the dealer will have to be negotiated. The payment reflects the value of only paying 6.5% fixed, when the current market price is 7.34%. Another firm might wish to pay 8% fixed. In this case, the dealer will make an initial payment to the firm.

Firms will desire off-market swaps to hedge an existing interest rate risk precisely. For example, a mutual fund that owns an 8% coupon bond and expects interest rates to rise might wish to convert this bond into a floating-rate bond. Even though current swap quotes are below 8%, it might want to pay a fixed rate of 8%.

Another firm may wish to unwind a swap entered into earlier in which it was receiving a fixed interest rate of 6.5%. It will then wish to pay a fixed rate of only 6.5% at a time when an at-market swap might require that this firm pay a fixed rate of 7.34%. By entering into this off-market swap, the firm will effectively offset its old swap. Note that the off-market swap should have a tenor equal to the remaining time to maturity of its old swap. In both swaps, the same LIBOR serves as the floating rate.

In some swaps, the notional principal will change according to a predetermined schedule; these are called **amortizing swaps**.[8] In an **index-amortizing swap**, the rate at which the notional principal declines is based on some interest rate index that changes randomly over time. For example, if LIBOR declines to some level, the notional principal may drop to 75% of its original level. Index-amortizing swaps are used in mortgage finance to deal with prepayment risk. When interest rates decline, homeowners will typically increase their prepayments of mortgages. When mortgages are paid off early, the principal underlying a mortgage-backed security will decline. Index-amortizing swaps can be used to hedge this prepayment risk faced by the owners of mortgage backed securities.

A **basis swap** is one in which both interest rates float. For example, three-month LIBOR might be exchanged for the five-year Treasury rate, or the prime rate might be exchanged for the three-month commercial paper rate. At each settlement date, both floating rates are observed, and when multiplied by the swap's notional principal, the two cash flows are determined. Instead of one rate being held constant, as the fixed rate is in a fixed–floating swap, both rates randomly change as time passes. These are also called **floating–floating swaps**. When one or both of the floating rates is a long-term rate, the basis swap may be called a **yield curve swap**. Basis swaps allow speculators to bet on a forecasted shift in the yield curve. Another use arises if a firm has a floating-rate liability; the basis swap allows it to change the index rate that determines its floating-rate payments from one rate to another.

A firm may wish to execute a swap contract today but not begin exchanging payments until a date in the distant future. This is called a **forward swap**. Alternatively, another firm may want to have the option to enter into a swap at some future date, only if interest rates have changed to its benefit; such options on swaps are called **swaptions**. A swaption may give the firm the right but not the obligation to enter into a swap as a fixed-rate payer any time in the future, up to some stated date, or it may give the firm the right to enter into a swap as a receive-fixed party. **Callable swaps** give the pay-fixed party the right to exit an existing swap contract, and **putable swaps** give the receive-fixed party the right to exit an existing swap.

11.2 CURRENCY SWAPS

In a currency swap, two different currencies are periodically exchanged. One important difference between interest rate swaps (which are in one currency) and currency swaps (which are in two different currencies) is that in the latter, the principal amounts are *typically* exchanged, both on the origination date and at maturity, based on the *initial* spot exchange rate.[9]

Exchanging the principal amounts at the swap's origination at the prevailing spot exchange rate has no valuation consequences. Suppose that the exchange rate is ¥104/$. If two parties agree to exchange ¥104 million for $1 million, the exchange is of no value for either party. Because of this, we can conclude that a currency swap is equivalent to a firm issuing a coupon bond in one currency (a liability) and buying a coupon bond (with an equal value to its liability) in the other currency.

There are actually four types of basic currency swaps:

1. Fixed (in one currency) for fixed (in the other currency)
2. Fixed for floating
3. Floating for fixed
4. Floating for floating

11.2.1   An Example of a Fixed–Fixed Currency Swap

Define P_1 and P_2 as the initial principal amounts in currencies 1 and 2, respectively (e.g., $P_1 = $10 million, $P_2 = $¥1040 million). Also define r_1 and r_2 as the fixed interest rates in currencies 1 and 2, respectively (e.g., $r_1 = 5\%$, $r_2 = 1\%$). Note that r_2 is the interest rate earned on Japanese yen. The swap terminates three years hence. Payments are semiannual, on a 30/360 day count basis. The first payment is six months hence, and the last is on the termination date.

Currency swaps have three stages to their cash flow exchanges. First, at origination, party A gives $10 million to counterparty B, and receives ¥1040 million from counterparty B. In the second stage, periodic payments are swapped. In the third and last stage, party A returns ¥1040 million to B, and B gives $10 million back to party A.

Note that typically, the spot exchange rate on the swap's commencement date determines the amounts exchanged *both* initially (stage 1) and at maturity (stage 3). In this example, the spot exchange rate at origination is ¥104/$ (which equals $0.009615/¥). In the second stage, there are periodic exchanges of currencies. Party A gives to B ¥5.2 million every six months, because $(0.01/2)($¥1040 million$) = $¥5.2 million. Counterparty B gives $250,000 to party A, because $(0.05/2)($10 million$) = $250,000. Figure 11.4 illustrates the three stages to this fixed–fixed currency swap.

11.2.2   An Example of a Fixed–Floating Currency Swap

In this swap, which has a tenor of three years, $P_1 = $¥2080 million, and r_1 is a fixed rate of 1% in yen; $P_2 = $20 million, and r_2 is a floating rate of six-month LIBOR, denominated in dollars. Settlement dates are every six months, beginning six months hence. On the origination date, six-month LIBOR is 5.5%. At subsequent dates, six-month LIBOR is tabulated as follows:

Time	6-Month LIBOR
0.5	5.25%
1.0	5.5%
1.5	6%
2.0	6.2%
2.5	6.44%

On the origination date, the fixed-rate payer pays $20 million to the fixed-rate receiver. The fixed-rate receiver pays ¥2080 million to the fixed-rate payer.

The stage 2 cash flows occur every six months. Table 11.4 shows the actual cash flows that are exchanged on all settlement dates of the swap. As with an interest rate swap, the floating rate at time $t-1$ determines the floating rate payment at time t. For example, because six-month LIBOR on the origination date is 5.5%, the dollar cash flow six months later is $(0.055/2)(\$20$ million) $=\$550,000$. On the termination date (time 3.0 in Table 11.4), the time 2.5 LIBOR of 6.44% determines periodic payment of $644,000 [(0.0644/2)(\$20,000,000)=\$644,000]$. In addition, the principal amounts are again swapped at maturity. The pay-fixed party gives ¥2080 million to counterparty B; B gives $20 million back to party A.

Figure 11.5 is a cash flow diagram that illustrates the cash inflows and outflows from the viewpoint of party A (the pay-fixed party, who is paying fixed in yen, and receiving floating dollar periodic payments).

Note again that the time $t-1$ floating rate is used to determine the floating cash flow at time t. Also note that the termination date cash flows include the original principal amounts. These are

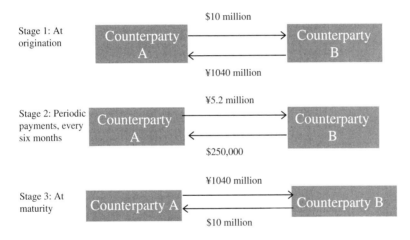

Figure 11.4 The three stages of a fixed–fixed currency swap.

TABLE 11.4   Payments That Arise as Part of a Fixed–Floating Currency Swap

Time	6-Month LIBOR	Fixed Rate Payment	Floating Rate Payment
0	5.5%	$20 million	¥2080 million
0.5	5.25%	¥10.4 million	$550,000
1.0	5.5%	¥10.4 million	$525,000
1.5	6%	¥10.4 million	$550,000
2.0	6.2%	¥10.4 million	$600,000
2.5	6.44%	¥10.4 million	$620,000
3.0		¥10.4 million	$644,000
		+¥2080 million	+$20 million

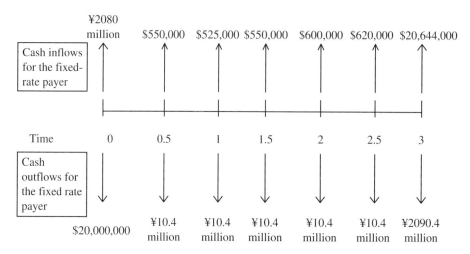

Figure 11.5 Cash flows arising from a fixed-for-floating currency swap.

typical of plain vanilla fixed–floating currency swaps, but other structures can be negotiated, including those in which only the initial principal amounts are swapped (but not at maturity), or no principal amounts are swapped. And, as with in-arrears interest rate swaps, a firm can request that the time t floating interest rate establish the floating cash flow at time t.

11.2.3   Other Currency Swap Structures

In a standard currency swap, principal amounts are exchanged at the swap's origination and at maturity. When principal amounts are not exchanged either at origination or at maturity, a fixed-fixed currency swap is called a **coupon-only swap**, or an **annuity swap**.

In Section 11.1.6, off-market, amortizing, and forward swaps, and swaptions were discussed in relation to interest rate swaps. These variations exist for currency swaps, too. When the current floating interest rate (or interest rates) is used to establish current settlement amounts, the swap is called an in-arrears swap, and this form exists for both interest rates and currency swaps, as well.

Differential swaps are more commonly called **diff swaps**. A diff swap is a floating–floating currency swap, except both floating rates are applied to the notional principal of *just one of the currencies*, and *the swapped payments are in that single currency*. Diff swaps allow a firm that is engaging in a currency swap to eliminate currency risk exposure. Because only one currency is involved, the notional principal is not exchanged, and the exchanged cash flows are netted, so only one difference check is paid from one party to the other.

For example, a firm may wish to make semiannual payments based on six-month yen LIBOR, receive six-month U.S. dollar LIBOR, and have both the payments and receipts denominated in dollars. Because current Japanese interest rates are below U.S. interest rates, the firm will have to pay yen LIBOR plus a spread. Assume the spread is 400 basis points.[10] At each settlement date, both yen LIBOR and U.S. dollar LIBOR are observed, and these are netted to determine the net payment or receipt, in dollars. The swap's tenor is two years, payments are semiannual, and the day count method is 30/360. Assume that rates are determined as in an in-arrears swap, so that the two time t floating interest rates determine the time t cash flows. The notional principal of the swap is $10 million.

Six months hence, six-month U.S. LIBOR is 5.6% and six-month yen LIBOR is 1.2%. The firm is required to pay $[((0.012+0.04)/2)(\$10,000,000)]=\$260,000$. The firm will receive $280,000, or $(0.056/2)(\$10,000,000)$. The difference check received is $20,000.

11.3 COMMODITY SWAPS

Commodity swaps are contracts in which the counterparties agree to exchange cash flows that are determined on the basis of commodity prices. They are equivalent to a strip of forward contracts on a commodity, each of which has a different maturity date, and the same forward price. The most typical underlying commodities are crude oil and other energy-related products. To a much lesser extent, some commodity swaps exist using precious metals such as gold and silver, other metals such as copper, and some agricultural products such as wheat. Most commodity swaps are fixed-for-floating swaps based on one commodity product.[11] One party agrees to pay a fixed price for a notional principal of the commodity, at a set of future dates. The other counterparty agrees to pay a floating price. The notional principal of the commodity is not exchanged. Commodity swaps require that the quantity and quality of the commodity, as it is priced at a specific location, be defined.

For example, consider a commodity swap involving a notional principal of 100,000 barrels of crude oil. One party agrees to make fixed semiannual payments at a fixed price of $21/bbl, and receive floating payments. Payments are in dollars (they could be in any currency).

On the first settlement date, if the spot price of crude oil is $20.46/bbl, the pay-fixed party must pay $(\$21/bbl)(100,000 \text{ bbl})=\$2,100,000$. The pay-fixed party also receives $(\$20.46/bbl)$ $(100,000 \text{ bbl})=\$2,046,000$. The net payment made (a cash outflow for the pay-fixed party) is then $54,000.

Commodity swaps allow producers and users of different commodities to fix the prices they will receive or must pay for the commodities on each of several dates in the future.

11.4 EQUITY INDEX SWAPS

In equity index swaps, frequently called **equity swaps**, the counterparties pay and receive cash flows based on the rates of return of a stock market index (against either a fixed or floating interest rate), or two stock market indexes. In some equity swaps, the notional principal of stock may be a narrowly defined index (such as a major oil company stock index), or just an institution's portfolio. A party may wish to pay the return on its stock portfolio and receive LIBOR, and it will engage in this swap instead of actually selling the stocks in its portfolio.

It is interesting to note that the return on a stock index could be negative. If this happens, the party that receives the return on the stock index will actually receive a negative return; that is, this party will have to *pay* the negative stock index return *and* also pay the interest rate.

Equity index swaps have become popular for several reasons. They allow institutions to gain exposure to stock markets in countries where the governments have created high entry costs. They let equity money managers quickly execute asset allocation decisions at low cost. They can be used to customize exchange rate exposure, since the payments may be made in any desired currencies. Equity index swaps also allow securities dealers who finance their portfolios with borrowed funds (at LIBOR) to hedge against unexpected changes in the value of their portfolios.

Finally, equity index swaps have been used to circumvent tax laws in some cases. Suppose you own a stock portfolio that has appreciated in value. You have now turned bearish and wish to sell your portfolio, but if you do, you will have to pay a great deal in capital gains taxes. Instead, you can engage in an equity swap and agree to pay the rate of return on your portfolio and receive LIBOR. However, changes in the tax laws effective in 1997 have reportedly reduced the advantages swapping your portfolio's returns to avoid taxes.

11.5 CREDIT RISK IN SWAPS AND CREDIT SWAPS

A basic definition of credit risk is the risk that one of the parties to a transaction will default, and fail to abide by the contractual obligations in the contract. The most simple form of credit risk occurs when the issuer of a bond fails to make the coupon payments or fails to repay the bond's principal. The maximum amount exposed to a bond's credit risk is its market value (the present value of its remaining coupon payments and its principal).

When at-market swaps are first originated, the initial amount at risk should one of the parties default is zero. As will be seen in Chapter 13, swaps are priced to be zero net present value transactions for both parties, except for a (typically) small profit for the swap dealer, created by the bid–asked spread.

However, after its origination, the swap will likely become a valuable asset for one of the parties, which means that it will assume a negative value (become a liability) for the other counterparty. When the swap becomes a liability for one of the parties, the other (the party for whom it has become an asset) will face credit, or default, risk.[12] Default risk is the exposure to the possibility that the other (losing) party will default, and not make its future expected net payments. In other words, the present value of the expected payments to be made by the party likely to default exceeds the present value of its expected receipts. When the swap is originated, it is impossible to know who will subsequently face the credit risk.

Firms will default on swaps when they fall into financial distress and cannot fulfill the terms of a swap. However, swap dealers are not very concerned with a customer's financial situation if the swap is an asset for the counterparty and a liability for the swap dealer. In other words, the credit risk faced by a swap dealer depends both on the financial condition of its customer and how interest rates or foreign exchange rates have changed since the swap's origination. Changes in financial prices create positive swap value for only one party and negative swap value for the other. Generally, a swap dealer will be concerned about the other party defaulting only when the swap is an asset for itself.

Consider a plain vanilla interest rate swap with a tenor of three years. When it was originated, party A agreed to pay 8% fixed, and to receive six-month LIBOR. Suppose that six months after origination, the price of a swap with a tenor of $2^{1}/2$ years is 7.2% (in exchange for six-month LIBOR). This swap has now become a liability for party A and an asset for the swap dealer. The swap dealer faces default risk because the decline in the price has created an incentive for party A to default. If it could walk away from its original swap contract and enter into a new one, A could save 80 basis points per year, for $2^{1}/2$ years, as applied to the swap's notional principal. If party A is facing financial difficulties, the market will recognize the greater default risk, and the value of the swap for the dealer is less.

This example illustrates one method of assessing the amount of a swap that is really at risk. Recall that prices of interest rate swaps are quoted as a fixed rate. It is the floating rate that is bought or sold in an interest rate swap. Thus, credit risk can be measured by comparing the price of the old swap to the price of a replacement swap. If the prices differ, the swap is an asset for one party and a liability for the other. The party for whom the swap now has a negative value has the incentive to default. The party for whom the swap now has positive value faces the default risk.

In comparison to a plain vanilla interest rate swap or to currency swaps in which there is no exchange of principal at maturity, there is greater potential default risk with a currency swap that requires a final exchange of principal. The increased default risk arises because the contractual obligation to exchange the (relatively) large principal amounts will likely create a greater buildup in value if exchange rates change during the life of the swap.

For example, in the fixed–floating currency swap in Section 11.2.2, the fixed-rate payer is obligated to exchange ¥2080 million and receive $20 million at the maturity of the swap. This implies that the exchange rate at the swap's origination was ¥104/$. If the yen price of a dollar declines, the fixed-rate payer will have a greater incentive to default. Under the terms of the swap, he must pay ¥104/$. If the exchange rate declines to, say, ¥85/$, the pay-fixed party has a large liability, and an incentive to default on his contractual obligations.[13]

Swap dealers will use different approaches to manage the credit risk they face. As discussed in Section 11.1.5, swap dealers will price the credit and default risk they perceive by quoting wider spreads when they quote prices to prospective customers. Some institutions are willing to assume the credit risk that exists in completed swap contracts. Some institutions will insure swap contract performance for a fee. **Credit enhancements** refer to swap terms that are designed to compensate swap dealers for the risk that a counterparty will experience credit deterioration, hence greater default risk. Swap dealers may demand collateral, a letter of credit, and/or that the swap be marked to market. Less creditworthy parties to a swap must also face the possibility that a financially strong swap dealer will falter. This happened to customers of Enron (which was a swap dealer) in 2001.

Finally, note that the terms of swap contracts do not allow a party to default only on the swaps that have become liabilities. **Netting agreements** have become standard. Netting means that if a party defaults on a swap that has become a liability, the swap dealer does not have to make payments on any swaps that have become positive value assets for that defaulting party. Netting agreements mean that swap dealers can use portfolio approaches for measuring the default risk they face with any one counterparty.

Credit derivatives represent an innovative approach to managing credit risk. Credit derivatives are derivative contracts with payoffs that are determined by some credit event. Thus, a credit derivative may pay off if a party (a firm, sovereign government, etc.) experiences a bond rating decline, if some asset experiences a price decline because of increased credit risk, or if the party misses a scheduled payment (defaults) on a financial contract. There are swaps, forwards, and options with payoffs that are determined by credit events. All are custom-made OTC contracts.

The **credit swap** is a common credit derivative. The buyer of a credit swap is the party that pays a fixed payment each period (an annuity) to the counterparty. The buyer receives nothing at each date as long as the credit event has not occurred. If the credit event occurs, the buyer receives a contractually specified dollar amount. For example, a bank doing a great deal of business with Riscorp might be concerned about the impact on itself if Riscorp's credit quality declines. This bank might buy a credit swap. In the credit swap, it agrees to pay basis points of the notional principal amount to the swap dealer. The swap dealer will make a payment to the bank only if Riscorp is downgraded by Moody's or an other rating agency (the credit event).

A **total return swap** is also a credit derivative. As an example of a total return swap, consider a mutual fund that owns some bonds of the BBB Corporation. The mutual fund is required to hold only investment grade bonds, and it wishes to hedge against any possible further credit deterioration in the BBB Corp.[14] The swap dealer agrees to pay a fixed or floating interest rate to the mutual fund. In turn, the mutual fund agrees to pay the periodic rate of return on the bonds to the dealer. The periodic rate of return consists of both capital gains/losses and the income yield:

$$\text{periodic rate of return} = \frac{P_t - P_{t-1} + C}{P_{t-1}}$$

where P_t is the security price at the end of the period, P_{t-1} is its price at the beginning of the period, and C is the interest paid during the period.

If BBB Corp. experiences a decline in its credit quality, then its bond prices will decline and the periodic rate of return will be low or negative. In this way, the mutual fund is compensated for the credit risk it faces.

Credit derivatives such as credit swaps permit intermediaries to strip out credit risk from a financial instrument. Thus, investors can customize financial products and retain the amount of credit risk they desire. An expert bond manager who wishes to manage her portfolio based on her interest rate forecasts can do so without worrying about changes in the bonds' default risk premia.

The credit swap market grew rapidly from zero in the 1990s. By the first quarter of 2001, the Office of the Comptroller of the Currency estimated that the notional principal of *credit derivatives* was $426 billion (www.occ.treas.gov/deriv/deriv.htm). *RISK,* a publication devoted to financial risk management, claimed that early in 2001, the notional value of outstanding credit derivatives transactions was close to $1 trillion.[15]

The International Swaps and Derivatives Association (ISDA) has published credit swap documentation, which can be downloaded (www.isda.org/). A website devoted to credit derivatives is www.margrabe.com/CreditDerivatives.html. ISDA is a global trade association made up of over 450 members, including 208 "primary members" (the swap dealers) and 120 "subscriber members" (the corporate, sovereign, and supranational end users of swaps); many dealers are also end users. The remaining members, called "associate members," consist of software, accounting, consulting, and legal firms that are active in the OTC derivatives market.

We will return to the topic of credit derivatives again in Chapter 20.

11.6 SUMMARY

This chapter provides a broad overview of the nature of common swaps of several types. A swap contract is an agreement between two counterparties to exchange cash flows. The amounts exchanged depend on interest rates (interest rate swaps), foreign exchange rates (currency swaps), the prices of commodities (commodity swaps), or the level of stock indexes (equity index swaps).

A swap contract creates an asset and a liability for each party. A swap will involve the contractual promise to make payments (a liability) and to receive payments (an asset). A swap is also equivalent to a portfolio of forward contracts, each with a different maturity date.

The notional principal of interest rate swaps is not exchanged at origination or at maturity. However, the principal of currency swaps is usually exchanged both at origination and at maturity. In a currency swap, the values of the amounts swapped are as a rule equal at origination because they are based on the initial spot exchange rate. At maturity, the same amounts, based on the *initial* exchange rate, are again exchanged. Typically, the rate observed at the start of a period determines the floating rate cash flow that will be exchanged at the end of the period.

Credit risk refers to the decline in the value of a swap or other derivative if there is a decline in the credit quality of one of the parties to the derivative. Ultimately, the concern is that the increasingly risky party will default on its obligations. Default risk is a function of both the credit-worthiness of a party and the fact that interest rates or exchange rates have changed since the swap's origination date so that the swap is now a liability for that party. Credit derivatives are used to manage credit risk and default risk. In a credit swap, the buyer receives a periodic cash inflow only if there has been some triggering credit event.

Reference

Patel, Navroz. 2001. "Credit Derivatives: Vanilla Volumes Challenged." *RISK*, Vol. 14, No. 2, February, pp. 32–34.

Notes

[1] In some swaps, the floating-rate payment is based on the floating rate that exists two days before the payment date. These are called **arrears reset swaps, arrears swaps, reset swaps, or in-arrears swaps**.

[2] In practice, several different methods are used to calculate partial year cash flows, and they are described in Appendix B to Chapter 5. The 30/360-day basis essentially assumes there are 12 months in a year, each of which has 30 days. An 8% interest rate becomes a 2% quarterly rate, or a 4% semiannual rate. A few exceptions exist, but they are unimportant for the purposes of this text.

[3] The example is simplified by assuming a 30/360 basis for computing the floating-rate payment. In practice, this is not typical. See note 2.

[4] Note that the numerator of the settlement amount equation is $60,000. This is a future amount, to be received six months hence. The denominator converts the $60,000 to be received six months hence into a present value of $57,887.12.

[5] Several Treasury notes may exist with similar maturities about equal to the swap's tenor, each of which has a different coupon rate. On the swap's origination date, it is specified exactly which of these notes' yields the quoted spread will be applied against.

[6] To learn more about Euribor, access www.euribor.org.

[7] This will be illustrated when swap valuation principles are discussed in Chapter 12.

[8] In an **index-accreting swap**, the notional principal *increases* at one or more times before the swap's maturity date.

[9] The term "typically" is used because, as with all OTC derivative contracts, anything is negotiable.

[10] This spread, in part, reflects the difference in interest rates for Treasury securities of the same maturity as the swap. For example, two-year riskless Japanese interest rate might be 2%, and the two-year riskless U.S. interest rate might be 6%; hence the example incorporates a 400-basis-point spread.

[11] In some commodity swaps, two commodities serve as the notional principals. The fixed price applied to the notional principal of one commodity is exchanged for the floating price applied to the notional principal of a different commodity. Floating–floating commodity swaps, with two different commodities also exist (these are basis swaps). Also, some commodity swaps may compute the average floating price during the period as the floating price for the swap (this is similar in concept to an Asian option, in which the payoff is based on the average price of the underlying asset during a defined period of time, rather than its expiration day price).

[12]Credit risk refers to the risk that the deterioration in the creditworthiness of a party will reduce the probability that the more risky party will make future payments. This reduces the value of the swap for the more creditworthy party. Default risk is the risk that a payment will not be paid.

[13]Changes in the floating interest rate also affect the incentive to default. In the example of Section 11.2.2, a decline in U.S. interest rates will add to the pay-fixed party's incentive to default, since he is paying yen fixed and receiving floating dollars. The decline in the interest rate at which the floating dollars are received can be invested to further reduce the asset value of the swap for the pay-fixed party.

[14]Note that in this example, the mutual fund will be paid off if BBB's creditworthiness declines or if there is an increase in the market's aversion to default risk. The latter will affect all corporate bonds exposed to nontrivial default risk, even if there is no real change in the credit quality of a specific bond issuer.

[15]See Patel (2001).

PROBLEMS

11.1 In an arrears reset swap, the floating payment is based on LIBOR on the payment date. In a normal fixed–floating swap, the floating payment is based on LIBOR one full period before the actual payment date. Suppose that you are a receive-fixed party, and you believe that the floating interest rate will decline. The swap dealer is quoting you the same fixed rate for both types of swap. All else equal, would you prefer to enter into an arrears reset swap or a normal swap? why?

11.2 Consider a three-year plain vanilla fixed–floating interest rate swap. The notional principal is $20 million. The swap fixed rate is 6%. The floating rate is six-month LIBOR. The payment dates are every six months, beginning six months hence. On the origination date, six-month LIBOR is 5.5%. The day count basis for both the fixed rate and the floating rate is 30/360. On subsequent dates, the six-month. LIBOR is:

Time	6-Month LIBOR
0.5	5.25%
1.0	5.5%
1.5	6%
2.0	6.2%
2.5	5.44%

Compute the cash flows that are exchanged between the two counterparties.

11.3 Suppose the fixed rate payer in Problem 11.2 buys a 12×18 FRA with $NP = 20 million, and a contract rate of 6% (buying a FRA is an agreement to buy LIBOR). What is the settlement day cash flow? Note that Problem 11.2 presents the subsequent six-month LIBORs. Assume a 30/360 day count method. Why does your answer differ from the time 1.5 cash flow you computed for the swap in Problem 11.2?

11.4 You observe a market maker quoting a bid price of 6.8% to firm A on a fixed–floating interest rate swap and a bid price of 7.0% on the same swap to firm B. Suppose you also observe that the asked quotes are greater than the bid quotes for each counterparty. Is the market maker going to become the pay-fixed or receive-fixed counterparty in these swaps? Why? Which firm, A or B, is financially weaker? Why?

11.5 If interest rates decline after a fixed–floating interest rate swap has been originated, who benefits, the pay-fixed counterparty or the receive-fixed counterparty? Equivalently, for which of the two counterparties does the swap contract have positive value after the interest rate decline? After the interest rate decline, who has the greater probability of defaulting?

11.6 What changes do swap dealers make to swap contracts when dealing with counterparties that are perceived to be likely to default?

11.7 On a fixed–floating interest rate swap, a dealer quotes a swap spread price of 35/32. What does this mean?

11.8 A firm observes that 10-year Treasury yields are at 7.1%, and two-year Treasury notes are yielding 7.0%. It believes that the 10-basis-point spread is very narrow and will likely widen in the near future. What kind of swap can the firm enter into speculate on these beliefs?

11.9 A firm wants to enter into a two-year fixed–fixed yen–deutschemark (DEM) currency swap. The spot exchange rate is ¥77/DEM. The principal amount is 20 million DEM. The swap dealer is quoting fixed rates on this type of swap of 2% in yen and 5% in DEM. Payments are quarterly, on a 30/360 day count basis. The firm wants to pay fixed DEM and receive fixed yen. What are the cash flows that will be exchanged if the firm agrees to the swap?

11.10 A firm wants to enter into a two-year currency swap. The firm wishes to pay a fixed rate of 6% in euros and receive floating sterling (British pounds). The euro payments will be semiannual, and the pound payments will be quarterly, both on a 30/360 day count basis. The principal amounts are £40 million and €70 million. Today, three-month sterling LIBOR (the floating rate) is 5%. Subsequent realizations of three-month sterling LIBOR are as follows:

Time	3-Month Sterling LIBOR
0.25	5.25%
0.50	6%
0.75	6.3%
1.0	6.85%

1.25	6.5%
1.50	6.2%
1.75	6%
2.0	6.3%

What are the cash flows that the firm will pay and receive, at each date?

11.11 A firm enters into a diff swap in which it agrees to pay interest in euros based on three-month dollar LIBOR and receive interest in euros based on three-month Euribor. The notional principal is €200 million. A margin of 50 basis points will be added to three-month Euribor. Payments are quarterly. The rates that determine the first payment are 6% (Euribor) and 5.65% (U.S. dollar LIBOR). The initial exchange rate is $0.70/€. What is the amount of the first difference check? Why is a margin of 50 basis points added to Euribor?

11.12 A gold mining firm and a gold user wish to enter into a commodity swap, with a swap dealer as an intermediary. The gold producer wants to fix the price it will receive for the gold it will mine over the next three years. The gold user wants to fix the price it will have to pay for the gold it needs for the next three years. The notional principal is 10,000 oz. of gold. The fixed price is $420/oz. Settlement is semiannual, based on the average price of gold during the past six months. Subsequent spot gold prices are as follows:

Time	Average Gold Price During Past Period
0.5	$405
1.0	$430
1.5	$468
2.0	$502
2.5	$448
3.0	$400

Determine the cash flows for the gold producer.

11.13 When will a firm exercise its swaption that gives it the right to enter into a swap as a fixed rate payer: when interest rates have risen, or when they have declined? When will a firm exercise the option in its puttable swap to exit an existing swap in which it is the fixed-rate receiver: when interest rates have risen, or when they have declined?

11.14 (a) What is a credit derivative? (b) How might a credit swap be used by a mutual fund that invests in bonds that are rated below investment grade?

11.15 In words, explain and interpret the "plain vanilla" interest rate swap diagram in Figure P11.15. Party A is the pay-fixed party. The price of the swap is 8%. The floating rate for the swap is LIBOR. LIBOR on the swap initiation day is 6%. LIBOR six months later will be 7% (Fed Chairman Alan Greenspan has told you this). Swap payments are made semi-annually. The notional principal of the swap is $35 million.

As part of your answer, you should (a) explain how the swap works, (b) label the arrows that define the swap, (c) compute the first net payment (be sure to state which party pays what amount), (d) explain why party A is entering into this swap, and (e) explain anything else you believe is relevant for this question, given the information provided.

11.16 A firm is part of a "plain vanilla", typical, fixed–fixed currency swap. It is paying

yen at a fixed rate of 2% and receiving dollars at a fixed rate of 6%. For this firm, the swap is essentially equivalent to (select either **a** or **b**)

a. having a yen-denominated asset and a dollar-denominated liability

b. having a dollar-denominated asset and a yen-denominated liability

11.17 In addition to what you were told in Problem 11.16, you know that the principal amount of the swap is $30 million, and the spot exchange rate on the day the swap was initiated was ¥105/$. Alan Greenspan has told you that he guarantees that on the swap's termination day, the spot exchange rate will be ¥110/$. There are two years remaining to the swap, and there will be an exchange of principal amounts on the swap's termination date. Payments are made semiannually. Therefore, which of the following is true about the firm's last swap payment (on the swap's termination day):

a. The firm will pay ¥288,571.

b. The firm will pay ¥300,000.

c. The firm will pay ¥30,300,000.

d. The firm will pay ¥31,500,000.

e. The firm will pay ¥3,181,500,000.

f. The firm will pay ¥3,333,000,000.

g. The firm will have to pay both yen and $30 million dollars on the termination day.

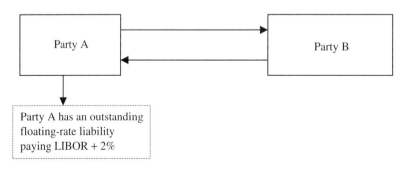

Figure P11.15

CHAPTER 12

Using Swaps to Manage Risk

Swaps are an efficient vehicle for firms to manage the composition of many assets and liabilities. Because the value of an asset or liability is the present value of cash flows that are attributed to that asset or liability, it becomes apparent that swaps also let firms manage revenues and expenses. Swaps are preferred to forwards and futures under the following circumstances:

a. When the cash flow stream is periodic, or regularly occurring. A single risk exposure is better hedged using forwards or futures.

b. When the cash amounts are equal and occur at regular (e.g., quarterly) intervals.

c. When the user wishes to manage the entire stream of cash flows in the same way. In contrast, forwards and futures allow the risk manager to hedge a portion of some cash flows, leave others unhedged, and to hedge others completely.

In this chapter, the focus is on using swaps to manage the risk to the firm caused by an unexpected financial price change. However, swaps can be used to create value for a firm. Using interest rate swaps to reduce borrowing costs is one example of how a swap can create value for a firm.

12.1 USING INTEREST RATE SWAPS

12.1.1 Swapping to Lower Borrowing Costs

Frequently, the default risk premium on issued debt instruments is greater in the long-term, fixed-rate bond market than it is in the floating-rate debt market. That is, there is a quality differential between fixed and floating borrowing. In the early days of swaps, market participants attributed the quality differential to the relatively risky, low-rated firm having a **comparative advantage** in the floating-rate market.[1]

Suppose a quality differential exists between fixed and floating borrowing. Consider the following example. The BBB Company, rated BBB by Standard & Poor's, has the opportunity to borrow either at a fixed rate of 8% or at a floating rate of LIBOR + 75 basis points.[2] AA Corporation, which is rated AA by Standard & Poor's, can borrow either in the long-term fixed-coupon debt market at 7% or at a floating interest rate of LIBOR + 25 basis points.

The AA Corp. has an absolute advantage in both markets because it faces lower interest rates in both markets. But AA has a comparative, or relative, advantage in the fixed-rate market because it can borrow there at 100 basis points below BBB Co. In contrast, BBB has a comparative advantage in the floating-rate market because it must pay only 50 basis points more than AA in the floating-rate market. In the fixed-rate market, BBB must pay 100 basis points more than AA. The term "quality differential" describes the differences in credit risk spreads that the two firms face in the two different markets (the fixed market and the floating-rate market).

Assume that neither firm wants to actually borrow funds in the market in which it enjoys its comparative advantage. In other words, BBB wants fixed-rate debt, and AA wants floating-rate debt.

A plain vanilla fixed-for-floating interest rate swap can benefit both firms when such a comparative advantage exists. First, each party should borrow in the market in which it has a comparative advantage. Then, the two parties can engage in an interest rate swap. The result will be that each firm will have effectively borrowed in the market in which it wants to borrow and will have done so at a lower cost than would have been possible without the swap.

Thus, AA goes to the long-term fixed-rate bond market and issues $100 million in seven-year fixed-rate debt with a coupon of 7%. BBB borrows the same amount in the floating-rate debt market for seven years at a rate of six-month LIBOR + 75 basis points. Payments for both firms will be semiannual.

Then, the two firms enter into a plain vanilla fixed-for-floating interest rate swap with a tenor of seven years. AA becomes the receive-fixed party in the swap. BBB is the pay-fixed party. AA agrees to pay a floating rate of LIBOR, and receive a fixed rate of 7%. Counterparty BBB agrees to pay a fixed rate of 7%, and receive a floating rate of LIBOR. The entire transaction is illustrated in Figure 12.1.[3] To summarize:

AA Corp.

Pays 7% to the capital market	-7%
Receives 7% fixed in the swap	$+7\%$
Pays LIBOR in the swap	$-\text{LIBOR}$
Net	$-\text{LIBOR (floating)}$

If AA Corp. had issued a floating-rate bond directly to the capital market, it would have had to pay LIBOR + 25 basis points. Therefore, AA has saved 25 basis points by issuing **synthetic floating-rate debt** with the aid of the swap. That is, by issuing fixed-rate debt and then swapping cash flows, AA creates **synthetic floating-rate debt**.

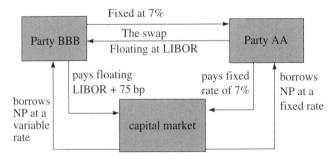

Figure 12.1 How swaps can lower the borrowing costs for both counterparties. After the swap, party BBB has borrowed at a fixed rate of 7.75%, and party AA has borrowed at a floating rate equal to LIBOR. By swapping, each party has saved 25 basis points (bp) in comparison to the situation in which each issues in its desired market (which is *not* the market in which it has a comparative advantage).

BBB Company

Pays LIBOR + 75 bp to the capital market	− LIBOR − 75 bp
Pays 7% fixed in the swap	− 7%
Receives LIBOR in the swap	+ LIBOR
Net	− 7.75% (fixed)

If BBB had issued a fixed-rate bond directly in the spot debt market, it would have had to pay 8%, so BBB has saved 25 basis points by issuing **synthetic fixed-rate debt** with the aid of the swap.

The gains derivable from these swaps that lower borrowing costs have diminished in recent years, but judging from surveys on derivatives usage, the gains still exist.[4]

It is important to note that these swaps are contracted with swap dealers. That is, firms do not arrange swaps themselves as in the foregoing example. Thus, in reality, each party will not save 25 basis points. Firm AA might receive 6.97% fixed and pay LIBOR. Firm BBB might pay 7.03% and receive LIBOR. The counterparty to each firm would be a swap dealer. The swap dealer would be neutral regarding LIBOR but earn a profit of 6 basis points (7.03% − 6.97%) per year on the notional principal of the swap. Thus, in this example, each firm would only save 22 basis points because of the swap.

Put another way, there is a total benefit of 50 basis points to be carved up between AA, BBB, and the intermediary (the swap dealer). To compute the number of total number of basis points that can be saved, subtract the rate differential in the floating-rate market from the rate differential in the fixed-rate market:

Rate differential in the fixed-rate market	8% − 7% = 100 basis points
Rate differential in the floating-rate market	(LIBOR + 75 bp) − (LIBOR + 25 bp) = 50 basis points
Number of basis points to be saved	50 basis points

Frequently, however, after the expenses, the fees, and the swap dealer's bid–asked spread have been accounted for, the comparative advantage will be too small for any net benefit to be realized by the two counterparties.

It is important to note that these firms could have also used a strip of futures or a strip of FRAs to achieve essentially the same result as the swap. However, the advantages of the swap market over the futures market (in particular) are many. For example:

1. There are no six-month LIBOR futures contracts. Two three-month Eurodollar futures contracts with adjacent delivery dates would have to be traded to effectively create a six-month LIBOR contract.

2. One swap transaction will cover the firms for seven years.

3. If each firm needs $100 million, the transaction costs of using futures would be high. Each three-month LIBOR contract covers $1 million. Thus, 100 contracts would cover a $100 million bond issue over a single three-month period; 200 contracts would be needed for a six-month period. This means that over the seven-year tenor, 2800 contracts would have to be traded by each firm.

4. AA, being a high quality firm, could negotiate an advantage to itself, namely, that its swap not be marked to market. BBB is riskier, so it may have to offer collateral to the swap

dealer, or the swap dealer may demand that the swap be marked to market. Both firms would be marked to market if futures were used.

5. Eurodollar futures contracts expire quarterly. Basis risk would exist unless a bond payment date coincided with the futures expiration date.

The primary difference of a swap versus a strip of FRAs is that each FRA will have a different price. The benefits that can be realized from lower borrowing costs should be about equal for the strip of FRAs and for the swap. In general, a FRA is used to hedge the borrowing or lending rate for a single period, while a swap is used to hedge a series of periodic cash flows. However, the costs of engaging in each transaction, and the prices of the contracts, should be carefully analyzed to decide which hedging vehicle is better.

12.1.2 Swapping to Hedge Against the Risk of Rising Interest Rates

Swaps are valuable hedging tools because they allow a firm with a sizable floating-rate debt to hedge, or protect, itself against the risk of rising interest rates. If interest rates do rise, a firm with floating-rate debt will experience higher floating interest rates. Because interest paid is an expense item on an income statement, net income declines if interest expense rises, all else equal. A greater percentage of the firm's operating income will flow to the floating-rate bondholders, leaving less for the stockholders. Thus, firms with floating-rate debt are exposed to the risk of rising interest rates.

Bodnar, Hayt, and Marston (1998) report that 96% of firms in their survey at least sometimes swap from floating rates to fixed rates, whereas only 60% of firms swap from fixed to floating (obviously, many firms do both). These result could be attributed to the very low level of interest rates that existed at the time of the survey, in 1998; firms would want to lock in those low rates by transforming their floating-rate debt to fixed-rate debt via the swap market.

Entering into a fixed-for-floating interest rate swap as the pay-fixed party permits a firm to transform existing floating-rate debt into synthetic fixed-rate debt. That is, the firm can lock in a fixed rate for the remaining life of the bond.

Before the swap, the firm has floating-rate debt. As Figure 12.2 illustrates, after the swap, the firm has altered the nature of this liability and is now in the position of having a fixed-rate liability.

Consider the following example of transforming a floating-rate asset into a fixed-rate asset. Suppose a Japanese bank has outstanding a considerable amount of three-month certificates of deposits (CDs), and these CDs are repriced at a new interest rate every three months. The bank

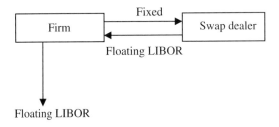

Figure 12.2 A swap changes a floating-rate liability into a synthetic fixed-rate liability, and hedges the firm against rising interest rates.

fears that interest rates will rise, and it would like to lock in its funding costs for a longer period of time. Interest on these CDs is paid at the maturity of the CD, and the interest rate is set when the customer buys the CD. The Japanese bank would like to have a greater amount of fixed rate debt. It can enter into a fixed-for-floating interest rate swap in which it is the pay-fixed party.

Suppose that on the CDs, the bank pays interest at the rate of yen LIBOR + 25 basis points. The desired swap tenor is three years, with quarterly payments. The swap dealer quotes a fixed rate of 2% in exchange for yen LIBOR. The notional principal amount is ¥3 billion.

This transaction locks in a fixed rate 2.25% for three years, as illustrated in Figure 12.3.

Table 12.1 shows that regardless of what happens to interest rates in the future, the Japanese bank will pay a fixed rate of 2.25%. The column heads show three different interest rate levels (in terms of three-month yen LIBOR) that occur at time t. Below that are the interest paid at time $t+1$ on ¥3 billion in CDs, and the swap cash flows on a notional principal of ¥3 billion.

12.1.2.1 Forward Swaps

A **forward swap** can be used to protect against a rise in interest rates in the future. A forward swap is a forward contract that obligates the firm to enter into a swap some time in the future.

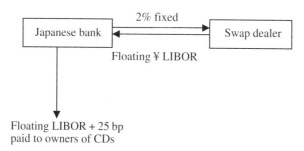

Figure 12.3 The Japanese bank is the pay-fixed party in this swap. It uses the swap to hedge against rising interest rates.

TABLE 12.1 A Swap in Which the Pay-Fixed Party Has Locked in a Fixed Rate of 2.25% Regardless of the Floating Rate

Payment	Three-Month Yen LIBOR at Time t		
	1.82%	2%	2.05%
CD interest paid at time $t+1$	−15,525,000[1]	−16,875,000	−17,250,000
Swap cash flow payment at time $t+1$	−15,000,000[2]	−15,000,000	−15,000,000
Swap cash flow receipt at time $t+1$	+13,650,000[3]	+15,000,000	+15,375,000
Net payment	−16,875,000[4]	−16,875,000	−16,875,000

[1] 1.82% + 25 bp = 0.0207. The quarterly payment is then (0.0207/4)(¥3 billion) = ¥15,525,000.

[2] Fixed swap payment of 2%. The quarterly payment is then (0.02/4)(¥3 billion) = ¥15 million.

[3] Floating swap payment is LIBOR. The quarterly payment is then (0.0182/4)(¥3 billion) = ¥13,650,000.

[4] A quarterly payment of ¥16,875,000 is an annual interest rate of 2.25%: (¥16,875,000 × 4)/¥3 billion = 2.25%.

Usually, the initial payments that will be exchanged in forward swaps commence one year or more after such an agreement has been originated.

Several scenarios would dictate the use of a forward swap to manage risk exposure:

a. To hedge against an anticipated rise in interest rates next year, a firm would enter into a forward swap as a fixed-rate payer. If interest rates do rise, the floating-rate payments the firm will receive will be greater than its fixed payments.

b. A firm wants to have a floating-rate liability next year. However, because it will likely have a comparative advantage in issuing fixed-rate debt, it instead plans on issuing long-term fixed-rate debt next year. This firm can enter into a forward swap as the receive-fixed party. One year hence, it will issue fixed-rate debt; at that time, the swap's obligations will commence, and the firm that wanted floating-rate liability at that time will indeed have synthetic floating-rate debt. This example would apply if the firm expected interest rates to fall next year.

c. Finally, consider a firm that already has floating-rate debt outstanding and anticipates that rates will stay low for about a year before beginning to rise. It should enter into a forward swap as the pay-fixed party.

Note that elements of speculation are associated with the foregoing scenarios. The firm in example **c** has outstanding floating-rate debt and is exposed to the risk of rising interest rates. To hedge, it should lock in its interest rate expense today, and the way to do that is to enter into a swap that begins today, not a year from today. Entering into a forward swap results in continued exposure to rising interest rate risk for the next year. Of course, the forward swap strategy will work only if the firm's beliefs about interest rates during the next year are correct.

Bodnar, Hayt, and Marston (1998) report that 66% of the firms in their sample timed their interest rate hedges based on their view of what interest rates would do (rise or fall) in the future. In other words, they practiced selective hedging.

12.1.3   Swapping to Hedge Against the Risk of Falling Interest Rates

Consider the case of a mutual fund manager who just added some rather unique corporate notes to his fixed-income portfolio. Suppose a recent sharp run-up in interest rates made these corporate notes particularly attractive to the fund manager, who paid slightly under par for the notes. However, the fund manager now fears a reversal in interest rates. Of course, this would ruin the attractive return the notes currently offer because of an interesting feature of these corporate notes. The coupon notes in question have a face value of $750 million and a variable coupon, currently at 8%. Starting today and every six months hereafter for five years, the variable coupon rate is set equal to the spot 10-year U.S. Treasury note rate plus 150 basis points.

The fund manager decides to enter an interest rate swap wherein he is the receive-fixed party. A swap dealer has agreed to pay the fund manager a fixed rate of 7.96% for each of the 10 remaining coupon payments in exchange for the variable coupon payment with the notional value set to $750 million. Given the series of subsequent spot U.S. T-note rates listed in Table 12.2, we can compute the resulting cash flows.

TABLE 12.2 Computing Cash Flows That Would Result from Various T-Note Rates

Time	Spot U.S. 10-Year T-Note Rate	Payment to Swap Dealer	Receipt from Swap Dealer	Net Cash In flow (Outflow)
Now	6.50%	$0	$0	$0
Months later				
6	6.25%	$30,000,000[1]	$29,850,000[2]	$(150,000)
12	6.00%	$29,062,500	$29,850,000	$787,500
18	6.25%	$28,125,000	$29,850,000	$1,725,000
24	6.35%	$29,062,500	$29,850,000	$787,500
30	6.75%	$29,437,500	$29,850,000	$412,500
36	7.00%	$30,937,500	$29,850,000	$(1,087,500)
42	7.25%	$31,875,000	$29,850,000	$(2,025,000)
48	7.00%	$32,812,500	$29,850,000	$(2,962,500)
54	6.95%	$31,875,000	$29,850,000	$(2,025,000)
60		$31,687,500	$29,850,000	$(1,837,500)

[1] $[(0.065 + 0.015)/2]\$750,000,000 = \$30,000,000.$

[2] $[0.0796/2]\$750,000,000 = \$29,850,000.$

In this example, the fund manager was able to hedge the risk of a decrease in interest rates over the short run. However, because interest rates rose during the later years of the swap, the fund manager would have lost money in this period (assuming nothing else was done to manage the portfolio after once the swap had been entered).

Consider another example in which an investments company can invest only in assets with maturities less than a year. The existing yield curve is sharply upward sloping, and two-year debt instruments are yielding a great deal more than one-year securities. Moreover, the company believes that interest rates are about to decline.

This investments company can synthetically extend the maturity of investments by engaging in a swap as the receive-fixed party. It can agree to pay the one-year floating interest rate (perhaps the Treasury rate) and receive the existing, fixed, two-year interest rate. No physical securities need to be traded, and the investments company still owns only securities with maturities less than one year.

12.1.4   Swaps, Gap Analysis, and Duration

Financial institutions, such as banks, utilize the tools of **gap analysis** and **duration** to analyze their exposure to interest rate risk:

$$\text{gap} = \text{rate} - \text{sensitive assets} - \text{rate sensitive liabilities}$$

An asset or liability is "rate sensitive" when it will be repriced during a defined period. The defined period is called the **gapping period**. For example, if a bank owns a debt instrument with a maturity of five months, or has lent money to a client and the loan is due to be repaid in five months, the face value of that security or loan would be a rate-sensitive asset for any gapping period greater than five months. The security will have to be replaced, probably with a higher or lower interest rate, in five months. If a bank has issued a three-month CD, it is a rate-sensitive liability for any gapping period greater than three months.[5]

If gap is positive, the bank has more rate-sensitive assets than liabilities (for the relevant gapping period). This means that if interest rates decline, more assets will be repriced at lower rates, reducing net income. If gap is negative, the bank faces the risk of rising interest rates because more liabilities will be repriced at higher rates, increasing interest expense.

Financial institutions (and other firms, too) also estimate the duration of their assets and liabilities. One definition of duration (dur) is:

$$\text{dur} = -\frac{\%\Delta\text{value}}{\%\Delta(1+r)} = -\frac{(V_1 - V_0)/V_0}{(r_1 - r_0)/(1+r_0)}$$

where

V_0 = today's value (of an asset or liability) at an initial interest rate of r_0,

V_1 = the value at a new interest rate of r_1.

Rearranged, this is

$$\%\Delta\text{value} = -\text{dur} \times \%\Delta(1+r)$$

If the duration of a financial institution's assets exceeds the duration of its liabilities, a rise in interest rates will cause the value of its assets to decline more than the resulting decline in the value of its liabilities. Then, the value of owner's equity must decline. Figure 12.4 uses a simple balance sheet to depict this situation.

If the duration of the institution's liabilities is greater than the duration of its assets, the owners face the risk of declining interest rates. Should rates decline, the increase in the value of the liabilities will exceed the increase in the value of the assets. This also means that the value of owner's equity will decline. To summarize, if:

duration assets > duration liabilities
&/or
negative gap
} risk is that interest rates will rise.

duration assets < duration liabilities
&/or
positive gap
} risk is that interest rates will fall.

A financial institution can use swaps to hedge against the risk of changing interest rates when the duration of its assets differs from the duration of its liabilities and/or the financial institution has a positive or negative gap.

If the institution is exposed to the risk of rising interest rates, it should be the pay-fixed party in a swap. If interest rates subsequently rise, the floating rate that it receives will rise. Thus, the

Assets   **Liabilities**

Long duration   => if r rises,   Short duration   => if r rises, V declines
                 V declines a lot   by a smaller amount

Owner's Equity

∴the value of owners equity must decline,
since equity = assets − liabilities

Figure 12.4 If the duration of a firm's asset exceeds the duration of its liabilities, the firm is exposed to the risk that interest rates will rise. A balance sheet approach illustrates this concept.

swap benefits will offset its other exposures to rising interest rate risk. An institution that is exposed to the risk of falling interest rates should be the receive-fixed party in a swap.

12.2   USING CURRENCY SWAPS

12.2.1   Swapping to Lower Borrowing Costs in a Foreign Country

Multinational firms borrow funds in many different currencies to finance their international oper-ations. A typical multinational will have a comparative advantage in borrowing in some countries, and not in others. Comparative advantages will arise when a firm that is very well known in one country is not well known in another. It may then face relatively lower borrowing costs in the country in which it is well known. Oddly enough, a multinational may also face relatively lower borrowing costs in a country in which it had never before floated a bond issue. That country's investors may be eager to realize the diversification benefits of buying bonds, issued in their own country's currency, sold by a large foreign firm. Should that country's economy sour, its domestic firms may experience higher default rates. But at the same time, the foreign company may con-tinue to prosper and pay its debts. Thus, to realize the benefits of diversification, it is beneficial to buy bonds issued in your home country's currency, but issued by a wide range of issuers, includ-ing domestic firms, foreign firms, and governments.

A firm or government that has a comparative advantage in issuing bonds in currency A, but needs funds denominated in currency B, can exploit this situation as follows. First, debt is issued in currency A, and then a currency swap is entered in which currency A is received and currency B is paid. As a result, a lower borrowing cost in currency B may be realized than if it had directly issued bonds denominated in currency B.

As an example, suppose that Phyllis Morris is a large U.S.-based multinational that has never before issued bonds denominated in Swedish krona (SEK). Swedish investors are eager to buy SEK-denominated bonds issued by this highly rated U.S. company. But, Phyllis Morris needs British pounds (GBP). If Phyllis Morris issues bonds in Great Britain, denominated in GBP, it will have to pay 9%. If Phyllis Morris floats a bond issue in Sweden, denominated in SEK, it will face an interest of 10%. The company approaches a swap dealer and requests a quote on a fixed-for-fixed currency swap in which Phyllis Morris will receive SEK at a fixed rate of 10%. The swap dealer quotes a price of 8.7% fixed in terms of GBP.

Figure 12.5 shows that if Phyllis Morris issues the SEK-denominated debt, which is the currency in which it has a comparative advantage but is also the currency it does not want, and also engages in the fixed-for-fixed currency swap, it will end up with synthetic GBP debt and realize a savings of 30 basis points. Recall that there are three stages to a typical currency swap. The principal amounts, denominated in two different currencies, are exchanged both at origination and at maturity. The amounts that are swapped are equal in value at origination, since they are linked by the exchange rate at origination. In this example, the spot exchange rate at origination is SEK13.91/£. Phyllis Morris wishes to borrow £15 million, so the face value of its bond issue will be SEK208.65 million. At both origination (Figure 12.5a) and maturity (Figure 12.5c), £15 million will be exchanged for SEK208.65 million.

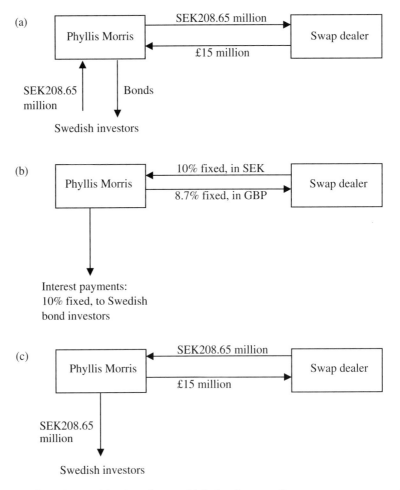

Figure 12.5 Cash flows (a) at origination of swap, (b) during the swap (interest payments are exchanged), and (c) at maturity of swap.

12.2.2   Swapping to Hedge Against the Risk of a Decline in a Revenue Stream

Consider U.S. Apple, a U.S.-based firm that exports apples and sells them for yen in Japan. An abbreviated form of its income statement is:

$$\text{Revenues} = P \, Q$$

$$-\,\text{Expenses}$$

$$\overline{\text{Operating income}}$$

where P is the price the firm receives for the apples it sells in Japan (¥), Q is the quantity of apples it sells in Japan, and expenses are in U.S. dollars.

   The goal of U.S. Apple is maximize its dollar profits—typical for a U.S.-based firm. U.S. Apple is exposed to the risk that the $/¥ exchange rate will fall. If the $/¥ declines, the dollar value of the firm's yen revenues will be less, and its dollar profits will be less.

   U.S. Apple can use a fixed-for-fixed currency swap to hedge its risk exposure. It can estimate its yen-denominated revenues for the next several years, and agree to pay fixed yen and receive fixed U.S. dollars in each of the next several years.

   U.S. Apple will still be exposed to the risk of fluctuation in the quantity of apples it sells in Japan. The number of apples it can sell in Japan will vary as its crop size (in the United States) varies, as the selling price of apples grown and sold in Japan varies, as the prices of other competing fruits in Japan varies, as import/export laws change, and as tastes change in Japan.

12.2.3   Swapping to Hedge Against the Risk of an Increase in Cost

Chocoswiss is a Swiss manufacturer of liqueur-filled chocolates. It must import all its liqueurs from France, and it pays for the liqueurs in euros. However, it sells its product in Switzerland only. Chocoswiss want to maximize its profits, which are denominated in Swiss francs (SFR). An abbreviated version of Chocoswiss' income statement is:

$$\text{Revenues (in SFR)}$$

$$-\,\text{Expenses (a significant portion is in euros)}$$

$$\overline{\text{Operating income}}$$

   Chocoswiss faces the risk that the SFR/€ will rise. If the SFR/€ rate rises, then the SFR cost of its imports will rise. As costs rise (denominated in SFR), SFR-denominated profits for Chocoswiss will decline. To hedge its currency risk exposure, Chocswiss can use a fixed-for-fixed currency swap in which it pays SFR and receives euros. There is no need to exchange principal amounts.

12.2.4   Swapping to Hedge Against the Risk of a Decline in the Value of an Asset

Suppose a U.S. company has a three-year £50 million investment (an asset) that yields 7% annually (in GBP) and pays interest twice per year. The current exchange rate is $1.60/£. The U.S. corporate treasurer thinks that the dollar will strengthen against the pound sterling. Equivalently, this means that the dollar value of the GBP will decline (the $/£ exchange rate will decline), which means that the dollar value of any GBP-denominated assets will decline.

If the treasurer is correct, each future interest inflow of £1,750,000 will purchase less than $2,800,000. For example, if the exchange rate is $1.50/£, the interest payment of £1,750,000 will purchase only $2,625,000. However, because the current three-year interest rate in the United States is 7.40%, the treasurer does not want to swap each subsequent interest payment of £1,750,000 for only $2,800,000. Not only will the decline in the value of the GBP mean that the value of the interest rates will be less, but the dollar value of the U.S. firm's investment will decline, too.

The treasurer finds a swap dealer willing to swap interest payments each six months of £1,750,000 for $2,940,000 over the next three years. In addition, there will be a final swap of £50 million for $80 million. Under this swap, the U.S. company has transformed its three-year £50 million investment that yields 7% into a three-year $80 million investment that yields 7.35%.

As another example, consider a Japanese company that owns some real estate in the United States; that is, the Japanese company has a dollar-denominated asset. If the ¥/$ exchange rate declines, the value of this asset, in yen, will decline. To hedge, the Japanese company can buy yen futures or forwards. Alternatively, the Japanese company can enter into a swap, paying dollars and receiving yen.

12.2.5 Swapping to Hedge Against the Risk of a Rise in the Value of Liability

If the value of a firm's liability rises and its asset values remain unchanged, it follows that the value of the firm's stock must decline. This must be the case because assets = liabilities + owners' equity.

Suppose a U.S. company has a two-year debt (a liability) of €100,000,000 at 7.7% annually and interest is paid quarterly. The current exchange rate is €0.9720/$. The U.S. corporate treasurer's staff is predicting that the dollar will weaken against the euro (i.e., the €/$ exchange rate will fall). This is equivalent to predicting that the $/€ rate will rise. If the dollar price of the euro rises, then the dollar-denominated value of this firm's liability will rise.

If the staff is correct, each future interest payment of €1,925,000 will cost more than $1,980,453. For example, if the exchange rate changes to €0.9400/$, the interest payment of €1,925,000 will cost the firm $2,047,872.

The treasurer finds a swap dealer willing to swap quarterly cash flows of €1,925,000 for $2,004,750 over the next two years. In addition, there will be a final swap of €100,000,000 for $102,880,658. Under this swap, the U.S. company has transformed its two-year 7.7% debt for €100,000,000 into a 2-year $102,880,658 debt with an interest rate of 7.79%.

12.3 USING COMMODITY SWAPS

A commodity swap can be used to fix the price of any physical commodity over a time period. Commodity swaps can be arranged through a swap deal for commodities such as aluminum, copper, silver, gold, crude oil, heating oil, or any other desired commodity.

In a commodity swap, the fixed-price payer makes periodic fixed payments for a notional quantity of the specified commodity; this locks in the purchase price for the commodity. The floating-price payer makes periodic payments for a notional quantity based (usually) on an average of the spot price over some time period. The notional quantity of the asset is not exchanged between the counterparties to the commodity swap. Instead, each party makes or takes delivery of the commodity through the spot market.

To demonstrate how a commodity swap can be used, consider the following. Suppose a small airline wishes to fix the price it pays for its monthly use of 50,000 gallons of jet fuel. The airline chooses a three-year tenor. At the same time, a small oil refiner wishes to fix a three-year price it receives for its monthly production of 100,000 gallons of heating oil (which is often used to price jet fuel). Note that it is not necessary for these two parties to arrange a direct swap: each can use a swap dealer. The terms of the swap call for a monthly floating payment based on the average of the daily 4 P.M. spot price for heating oil (diesel fuel) at a specified location.

Suppose the current spot price for heating oil/jet fuel is $0.74 per gallon and assume a $0.04 swap spread. Then, each month for the duration of the swap, the airline's obligation is to pay the swap dealer $0.76 per gallon of jet fuel and the refiner has the obligation to sell heating oil to the swap dealer for $0.72 per gallon. In turn, the swap dealer has the obligation to pay the airline the average floating payment and refiner has the obligation to pay the swap dealer the average floating payment. The net effect of these obligations is that the airline pays a fixed price of $0.76 per gallon for jet fuel over the next three years and the refiner receives $0.72 per gallon for heating oil over the next three years.

The swap dealer faces a risk here in that the notional amounts are not equal. The swap dealer would either have to find an appropriate counterparty for the extra 50,000 gallons or hedge this risk in the heating oil futures market.

12.4 USING EQUITY SWAPS

In an equity swap, the fixed-price payer makes periodic fixed interest payments on a notional principal. The floating-price payer makes periodic payments that are determined by the total return on a given stock index. By agreement, the total return could exclude dividends. The notional principal is not exchanged between the counterparties to the equity swap. Note that the equity index used is negotiable as well. Therefore, it could be a broad-based index like the S&P 500, the Nasdaq 100, or the Russell 2000. Or, it could be a foreign index like the Nikkei in Japan, the DAX in Germany, or the CAC in France. The equity index could even be a specific sector, like a bank index, a biotech index, or a pharmaceutical index, or a specific diversified portfolio of stocks.

For example, suppose a manager of an equity portfolio want to reduce his downside risk exposure from the collection of semiconductor stocks in his portfolio. This fund manager has a long-term bullish outlook on the semiconductor sector but feels that the sector could suffer some losses over the next year. Further, suppose the returns on the $25 million worth of semiconductor stocks in the fund manager's portfolio have a correlation coefficient of about 0.95 with the semiconductor index constructed by the Philadelphia Stock Exchange.[6]

Instead of selling the stocks in the portfolio (and paying the capital gains tax), and instead of using options on the Semiconductor Index (SOX), the fund manager decides to enter into an equity swap with a 12-month tenor. Under the terms of the swap agreement, the fund manager agrees to receive a fixed payment of 8% and pay the swap dealer the capital gain return on the semiconductor index (i.e., the dividends paid by any component stocks of the index are excluded). Payments are made quarterly and the notional principal is set at $25 million.

Using an equity swap, the fund manager has transformed the semiconductor portion of his portfolio into a quasi-riskless asset that yields 8% for one year. Note that the transformation will not be entirely riskless unless the returns on the actual equity portfolio equal the SOX index returns times the notional principal.

Further note that because the return on the semiconductor index could be positive or negative, the floating-rate payer (i.e., the fund manager) could make a payment or receive a payment from the swap dealer. For example, suppose the quarterly returns on the semiconductor index are 5.75, 16.75, −3.00, and 14.50%. Further, assume the actual portfolio returns equal the semiconductor index returns and that the beginning dollar value of the actual portfolio equals the notional principal. Then,

Quarter	(Payment to) Receipt from Swap Dealer	Receipt from Swap Dealer	Net Payment
First	($1,437,500)	$500,000	($937,500)
Second	($4,187,500)	$500,000	($3,687,500)
Third	$750,000	$500,000	$1,250,000
Fourth	($3,625,000)	$500,000	($3,125,000)
	($8,500,000)	$2,000,000	($6,500,000)

Ignoring the time value of money effects, if the gains on the actual portfolio holdings during the year equal $8,500,000, the portfolio manager has effectively turned his semiconductor stocks into a riskless asset yielding 8%. Of course, if the gains on the actual portfolio are not equal to the payments to the swap dealer, the portfolio manager's returns will not equal 8%.

12.5   USING INDEX SWAPS

A pension plan owns a great deal of real estate. It wants to reduce its exposure to real estate because it forecasts rising interest rates and declining rental income, which will depress real estate values. It feels that having 20% of its portfolio in real estate represents too much exposure to this asset class. On the other hand, it does not want to sell the real estate now, because it would generate a huge amount of capital gains, and it does not want to pay capital gains taxes now; it would rather defer those taxes for a few years. Also, real estate is an illiquid asset class that often cannot be sold quickly without price concessions.

This pension plan can use an index swap to manage its risk. It can enter into a swap in which it pays the swap dealer the rate of return on a real estate value index[7] and receives LIBOR.

If the pension plan expects to sell off some of its properties over time, as conditions permit, it can estimate this timetable and let the notional principal of the index swap decline as the index swap approaches maturity. This is an example of an amortizing swap, but note that the pension plan faces the risk that its real estate will be sold at a rate that is faster or slower than anticipated.

As another example, consider a mutual fund based in Great Britain that would like to invest in the U.S. stock market. However, if it directly buys U.S. equities, it will have to pay a 15% withholding tax on all dividends it receives (U.S. investors in British stocks have to pay corresponding 15% tax). The British mutual fund can use an equity index swap to circumvent this tax. It can agree to swap payments and receive the returns on a U.S. stock index. It might agree to make payments based on returns on a British stock index if it would otherwise fund its U.S. investment by selling British stocks. It might agree to make payments based on GBP LIBOR if it otherwise funds its U.S. investments by either selling British bonds or borrowing GBP. It might instead agree to make payments based on U.S. dollar LIBOR if it thought that U.S. interest rates were going to fall, if it would otherwise have funded its U.S. equity investment by borrowing in the United States, or if it had U.S. debt securities it was planning on selling.

12.6   USING DIFF SWAPS

Diff swaps allow a firm to eliminate currency risk exposure when engaging in a currency swap. Recall from Chapter 11 that a differential swap, commonly called a diff swap, is a floating–floating currency swap. However in a diff swap, both floating rates are applied to the notional principal of just one currency, and the swapped payments are only in that currency. Because only one currency is involved, the notional principal is not exchanged, and the exchanged cash flows are netted, so only the difference check is paid from one party to the other.

For example, a firm may wish to make quarterly payments based on three-month Euribor, and receive three-month U.S. dollar LIBOR. Because three-month Euribor rates are less than three-month U.S. dollar LIBOR rates, the firm will have to pay a spread. Suppose this spread is 200 basis points. Further, suppose the firm wants to have both the payments and the receipts denominated in dollars. The swap's tenor is two years, payments are quarterly, and the day count method is 30/360. Assume that rates are determined as in an in-arrears swap. That is, the time t floating interest rates determine the time t cash flows. The notional principal of the swap is $150 million.

At each settlement date, both Euribor and U.S. dollar LIBOR rates are observed, and these two rates are netted to determine the net payment or receipt, in dollars. Suppose we observe the following sequence of interest rates over the next two years:

Quarter	Euribor Rate	Firm Pays	LIBOR Rate	Firm Receives	Net Flow
1	4.77%	$2,538,750	7.16%	$2,685,000	$146,250
2	4.95%	$2,606,250	7.26%	$2,722,500	$116,250
3	5.11%	$2,666,250	7.32%	$2,745,000	$78,750
4	5.30%	$2,737,500	7.38%	$2,767,500	$30,000
5	5.36%	$2,760,000	7.35%	$2,756,250	($3,750)
6	5.46%	$2,797,500	7.36%	$2,760,000	($37,500)
7	5.54%	$2,827,500	7.37%	$2,763,750	($63,750)
8	5.66%	$2,872,500	7.43%	$2,786,250	($86,250)

At the first payment date, three-months from now, the three-month U.S. LIBOR is 7.16% and the three-month Euribor is 4.77%. The firm is required to pay

$$\frac{0.0477 + 0.0200}{4} \times \$150,000,000 = \$2,538,750$$

However, the firm will receive

$$\frac{0.0716}{4} \times \$150,000,000 = \$2,685,000$$

Thus, the firm will receive the first difference check, for $146,250.

12.7 SUMMARY

In this chapter, we have presented various examples of how firms can use swaps to manage risk. It is important to remember that swaps are negotiable. That is, the terms of a swap can be tailored to the needs and desires of the counterparties.

A firm can use interest rate swaps to lower borrowing costs, protect itself from an increase in future interest rates, or protect itself from a decrease in future interest rates. Floating-rate assets (liabilities) can be transformed into fixed-rate assets (liabilities). A firm can use currency swaps to decrease borrowing costs in a foreign country. In addition, a firm can use currency swaps to protect itself when a change in the price of a currency will decrease the (home-currency-denominated) value of a revenue stream, increase a cost, decrease the value of an asset, or increase in the value of a liability.

In this chapter, we also provided examples of using commodity swaps, equity swaps, index swaps, and diff swaps.

References

Bodnar, Gordon M., Gregory S. Hayt, and Richard C. Marston. 1998. "1998 Wharton Survey of Financial Risk Management by US Non-Financial Firms." *Financial Management*, Vol. 27, No. 4, Winter, pp. 70–91.
Smithson, Charles W. 1999. *Managing Financial Risk*. New York: McGraw-Hill.
Smithson, Charles W., Clifford W. Smith, Jr., and D. Sykes Wilford. 1995. *Managing Financial Risk*. Chicago: Irwin Professional Publishing.

Notes

[1] The growth of the swap market suggests that there is a tremendous economic benefit of these derivatives. Smithson (1999) summarizes several explanations for the quality spread. These include comparative advantage, risk shifting, differential cash flow packages, informational asymmetries, and tax and regulatory arbitrage.

[2] It is assumed that the BBB Company can lock in this floating rate (LIBOR + 75 basis points) for the entire tenor of the swap and its floating-rate bond issue.

[3] Recall from Chapter 11 that it is customary for LIBOR to be bought or sold flat in a swap. The fixed rate is the price paid or received for LIBOR.

[4] Smithson, Smith, and Wilford (1995) cite a 1993 survey by *Treasury* magazine that reports that 64% of the responding firms use derivatives to reduce funding costs.

[5] Gap analysis can be treacherous when the issuer of a security has the option to call the security for early prepayment. The question of when the asset or liability will be repriced becomes a random variable that depends on the level of interest rates or other factors.

[6] The Semiconductor Index is a price-weighted index that was created by the Philadelphia Stock Exchange. Options on the SOX Index began trading on September 4, 1994. As of May 9, 2001, the 16 stocks in the index were Altera

Corp. (ALTR), Applied Materials, Inc. (AMAT), Advanced Micro Devices (AMD), Intel Corporation (INTC), KLA-Tencor Corp. (KLAC), Linear Technology Group (LLTC), Lattice Semiconductor (LSCC), LSI Logic Corp. (LSI), Motorola, Inc. (MOT), Micron Technology, Inc. (MU), National Semiconductor (NSM), Novellus Systems, Inc. (NVLS), Rambus, Inc. (RMBS), Teradyne, Inc. (TER), Texas Instruments, Inc. (TXN), and Xilinx, Inc. (XLNX). For more information on the SOX, see the website of the Philadelphia Stock Exchange (www.phlx.com).

[7]There are several real estate value indexes. See, for example, the National Council of Real Estate Investment Fiduciaries website (www.ncreif.com).

PROBLEMS

12.1 Popsico has a great deal of floating-rate debt outstanding. Currently, the yield curve is upward sloping. Popsico believes that for the next year interest rates will remain low and the yield curve will remain upward sloping. Beyond a year, Popsico fears that short-term interest rates will begin to rise sharply. What can Popsico do both to take advantage of the current low short-term rates and to hedge against the risk that short-term rates will begin to rise in a year or two?

12.2 Electronic Business Machines (EBM) needs to borrow $20 million immediately. It can borrow for three years at a fixed rate of 7.5% or at a floating rate of LIBOR + 40 basis points. Plain vanilla fixed-for-floating three-year swaps are priced at 7.3% fixed, in exchange for floating LIBOR. If EBM believes that interest rates are about to rise sharply, what should it do? If EBM believes that interest rates are about to decline sharply, what should it do?

12.3 Atlantis-Morris Seats is a chair manufacturer that is too small to borrow in the long-term fixed-rate debt market. All its borrowed funds have been obtained by borrowing from banks, which change the rates they charge depending on market conditions. Explain how this firm can use the swaps market to obtain fixed-rate funds.

12.4 The Goo-Goo Doll Manufacturing Company is a major toy maker. Eight years ago, it borrowed $30 million for 10 years at a fixed rate of 10%. Today, dealers are quoting fixed-for-floating interest rate swaps as follows:

Swap Tenor	Yield on Treasury Securities	Swap Spreads (Basis Points)	
		Bid	Ask
1 year	4.8%	20	24
2 year	5.3%	25	29
3 year	5.7%	27	32
⋮	⋮	⋮	⋮
8 years	6.4%	31	36
10 years	6.5%	33	38

If the Goo-Goo Doll Company prefers to have floating-rate debt for the next two years, how can it use the swap market to accomplish this? If the firm believes that interest rates are going to rise about 200 basis points over the next year, should it use a swap to convert its fixed-rate debt to synthetic floating-rate debt?

12.5 Why do swap dealers exist? Why don't firms just swap with themselves?

12.6 A firm enters into a typical plain vanilla, fixed–fixed currency swap. It is paying yen at a fixed rate and receiving dollars at a fixed rate. This firm likely entered into this swap because

    a. It had a comparative advantage borrowing in yen, or faced the risk that a rising ¥/$ exchange rate would hurt profits.

    b. It had a comparative advantage borrowing in yen, or faced the risk that a falling ¥/$ exchange rate would hurt profits.

    c. It had a comparative advantage borrowing in dollars, or faced the risk that a rising ¥/$ exchange rate would hurt profits.

    d. It had a comparative advantage borrowing in dollars, or faced the risk that a falling ¥/$ exchange rate would hurt profits.

12.7   Suppose that you are a U.S. citizen concerned about personal U.S. dollar-denominated wealth and you own a large portfolio of Canadian utility stocks that are paying quarterly dividends, denominated in Canadian dollars. Do you face the risk that the Canadian dollar will get stronger or weaker? Why? To hedge, you have decided to engage in a swap with no initial and no terminating exchange of principal. Will you be the party that is buying U.S. dollars or selling U.S. dollars?

CHAPTER 13

Pricing and Valuing Swaps

Determining the theoretical price of a swap is quite simple. In Chapter 11, you learned that a swap is equivalent to an asset and a liability and that an at-market swap has zero value (ignoring the impact of the bid–ask spread) when it is originated. This means that to determine the fixed price for a swap, a firm should find the present value of the swap's payments and the swap's receipts. The price that equates the two present values results in a zero net value for the two parties. Then the swap dealer, to make a profit in her service as a market maker, can adjust the price to quote a bid–ask spread. Thus, valuing swap cash flows involves no more work than valuing two sets of cash flows.[1]

After its origination, the swap can be valued by comparing the new present value of the remaining cash payments to the new present value of the remaining cash receipts. *Current* interest rates and exchange rates must be used to compute these two present values. The remaining *fixed* cash flows are the same as they were when the swap was originated, although they will be discounted at new, current rates. The remaining expected *floating* cash flows will likely be different, and they too will be discounted at new current rates. Remember that a swap is a **zero sum game**, so that if the swap has a positive value for one party, it must have the same negative value for the counterparty.

Another way to value swaps after origination is to compare the price of the old swap with the current price for a swap with a tenor equal to the remaining time to maturity of the old swap. Then, one compares the present value of the old swap's fixed cash flows with the present value of the fixed cash flows for a new swap. This shortcut is valid because the same LIBOR serves as the floating rate in both cases.

If valuation is properly done, the value of the swap will be the same regardless of which approach is used. The differences between the two approaches will become apparent when an example is worked out, later in the chapter.

This chapter begins with an example of the method that prices and values plain vanilla fixed–floating interest rate swaps.

13.1 PRICING AND VALUING PLAIN VANILLA FIXED–FLOATING INTEREST RATE SWAPS

In a fixed–floating interest rate swap, one party agrees to make a series of fixed payments and receive a series of floating, or variable, payments. Thus, the goal of swap pricing is to determine the fixed interest rate that makes the present value of the fixed payments equal to the present value of the floating receipts. At its origination, the theoretically correct swap price will create a swap with zero value (unless it is an off-market swap).

Finding the present value of the fixed payments is a straightforward problem of finding the present value of an annuity because the fixed payments are known as soon as the swap price is set. However, only the first floating cash flow is known because, in a typical fixed–floating interest rate swap, the floating rate at origination establishes the first cash flow. Because the remaining floating cash flows are unknown, the floating cash flows must either be estimated or, more accurately, set equal to the cash flows the swap dealer will face if the swap is hedged. For example, a swap dealer who will *receive* a series of floating cash flow may be able to use forward rate agreements (FRAs) to *pay* the same floating cash flows. In this case, the swap dealer has hedged the floating cash flows. If interest rates decline, the swap dealer will receive less from the floating-rate swap payments but will also have to pay out less on the FRAs. Because he is hedged, he can use the FRA prices as the floating interest rates.

13.1.1   An Example of Fixed–Floating Interest Rate Swap Pricing

Recall that the spot yield curve is used to determine theoretical futures prices and FRA prices. Thus, it should be apparent that swap dealers can use FRAs, futures prices, and spot zero coupon interest rates to determine swap prices. An example illustrates the steps needed to determine swap prices:

Define

$r(0, t) =$ spot interest rate for a zero coupon bond maturing at time t

$fr(t1, t2) =$ forward interest rate from time $t1$ until time $t2$

Suppose the spot term structure is $r(0,1) = 5\%$, $r(0,2) = 6\%$, $r(0,3) = 7.5\%$. From these spot rates on pure discount debt instruments, the one year forward rate, one-year hence, can be computed to be $fr(1,2) = 7.01\%$:

$$(1.06)^2 = (1.05)[1 + fr(1,2)]$$

$$fr(1,2) = 0.070095$$

The one-year forward rate, two years hence, is $fr(2,3) = 10.56\%$:

$$(1.075)^3 = (1.06)^2[1 + fr(2,3)]$$

$$fr(2,3) = 0.10564$$

Now consider a three-year swap. The floating rate is one-year LIBOR. Settlement payments are made yearly. What is the fair fixed rate of the swap (i.e., the swap price)?

For conceptual ease only, it is sufficient to assume that the pure expectations theory of the term structure of interest rates is correct. Thus, forward rates equal expected future spot rates, and forward rates can be used to compute expected floating cash flows.[2]

Arbitrarily, suppose the swap's notional principal is $100. Thus, the expected floating cash flows are as follows:

$$CF_1 = 0.05 \times 100 = 5$$

$$CF_2 = 0.070095 \times 100 = 7.0095$$

$$CF_3 = 0.10564 \times 100 = 10.5640$$

Next, value these floating cash flows at the appropriate discount rates, the spot zero coupon interest rates:

$$\frac{5}{1.05} + \frac{7.0095}{1.06^2} + \frac{10.5640}{1.075^3} = 19.50394$$

Since the value of an at-market swap at its origination is zero, the value of the floating payments must equal the value of the fixed payments. Therefore, the fixed-rate payments must satisfy the following:

$$19.50394 = \frac{A}{1.05} + \frac{A}{1.06^2} + \frac{A}{1.075^3} = A\left(\frac{1}{1.05} + \frac{1}{1.06^2} + \frac{1}{1.075^3}\right)$$

$$2.647338A = 19.50394$$

$$A = 7.36738$$

This means that if a swap dealer agrees to make fixed payments of 7.3674% of the notional principal amount, and receive floating payments, the values of the two cash flow streams are equal.[3]

To make a profit, the swap market maker might quote prices of 7.34% to a fixed-rate receiver and 7.39% to a fixed-rate payer. Recall from Chapter 11 that interest rate swaps are typically quoted as a spread over the yield to maturity of Treasury securities. Thus, if the yield on the most recently issued three-year Treasury note is 7.05%, the quoted swap spreads might be 29/34. The 29 is the bid quote, and this means that a firm that wishes to be the receive-fixed counterparty will receive 29 basis points over 7.05%, which is 7.34%. If the firm wishes to be the pay-fixed counterparty, it will have to pay 34 basis points over 7.05%, which is 7.39%.

The steps in pricing an at-market swap can be summarized as follows:

1. Find the present value of the floating-rate cash flows. Use the forward rates to determine the floating amounts to be exchanged and the spot rates on zero-coupon bonds as the appropriate discount rates.

2. Find the fixed rate that makes the present value of the fixed payments equal to the figure computed in step 1. The fixed rate determines the fixed amounts to be exchanged, and the spot rates are used on zero-coupon bonds as the appropriate discount rates.

13.1.2 A Shortcut to Pricing At-Market Fixed–Floating Interest Rate Swaps at Origination

It is important to understand the pricing model presented in Section 13.1.1. Later, we will see that it is needed to value off-market swaps and to value a swap after its origination date. However, there is a shortcut to pricing at-market fixed for floating interest rate swaps.

The key to understanding why this shortcut works is as follows. The value of a floating rate bond is approximately equal to its face value, because the next cash flow is always repriced to reflect the level of current interest rates.[4]

This last point can be more easily understood by using a simple example. Consider a two-year floating-rate bond that will pay annual interest. The dollar floating coupon amount paid one year hence is based on today's one-year rate. The amount paid two years hence is calculated based on the one-year rate one year hence, which is currently unknown. For conceptual ease, assume that the one-year spot rate that will actually exist one year hence is expected to equal today's one-year forward rate, for delivery one year hence. In other words, the pure expectations theory of the term structure is appropriate. Let $r(0,1)=5\%$, and $fr(1,2)=8\%$. The face value of the bond is \$100. The value of this bond is

$$\frac{5}{1.05} + \frac{108}{(1.05)(1.08)} = 100$$

If interest rates change so that, say, $r(0,1)=6\%$ and $fr(1,2)=7.5\%$, the value of the bond is still \$100:

$$\frac{6}{1.06} + \frac{107.5}{(1.06)(1.075)} = 100$$

Thus, we have shown that the value of a floating rate bond will always be very close to its par value. Because of this, the swap pricing problem is reduced to finding the fixed payment that makes the value of a fixed-coupon bond equal to its par value. The discount rates are the spot rates on zero-coupon bonds.

Returning to the example in Section 13.1.1, the problem is to solve for the value of the unknown, A, that makes the value of the fixed cash flows on an ordinary fixed coupon bond equal to 100:

$$100 = \frac{A}{1.05} + \frac{A}{1.06^2} + \frac{A}{1.075^3} + \frac{100}{1.075^3}$$

$$100 = A\left(\frac{1}{1.05} + \frac{1}{1.06^2} + \frac{1}{1.075^3}\right) + 80.4961$$

$$19.5039 = 2.647338A$$

$$A = 7.36736$$

The example concludes that the fixed rate that should be quoted for the swap is 7.3674%. Except for some minor rounding errors, this is exactly what we computed before.

The FinancialCAD function aaParSwap can be used to price a plain vanilla interest rate swap.[5] Figure 13.1 illustrates how this is done.

13.1.3   Valuing an Interest Rate Swap After Origination

Interest rates will almost certainly change after the swap's initiation. As interest rates change, the swap value changes. This section explains how to value a swap after swap initiation. The valuation method is the same as the one used in Section 13.1.1. That is, we can either find the present value of the swap's remaining payments and receipts or find the present value of the fixed payments on a newly originated swap, and compare them to the present value of the fixed payments on the old swap. Both methods yield the same result.

Valuing swaps after they have been originated is important for many related reasons. First, firms wish to know their current financial position. Even if a swap is an off–balance sheet transaction, firms will want to know the true value of all their assets and liabilities, even those that are off–balance sheet items. Second, firms wish to know the default risk they face. If a swap has become

AaParSwap

Settlement date	24-Sep-2000	
Terminating date	24-Sep-2003	
effective date	24-Sep-2000	
date of first coupon after dated date		
date of last coupon prior to maturity date		
cash flow frequency	1	Annual
accrual method for coupons	1	actual/365 (fixed)
accrual method for accrued interest	1	actual/365 (fixed)
holiday list	t_26	
business day convention (see Glossary)	1	no date adjustment
interpolation method	1	Linear
discount factor curve	t_43_1	

t_26
holiday list
holiday date

1-Jan-1995

t_43_1
discount factor curve

grid date	Discount factor	
24-Sep-2000	1	
24-Sep-2001	0.952380952	=1/1.05
24-Sep-2002	0.88999644	=1/(1.06)^2
24-Sep-2003	0.80496057	=1/(1.075)^3

par swap rate

0.073673794

Figure 13.1 The FinancialCAD function aaParSwap solves for the fixed rate of a plain vanilla, fixed-for-floating, interest rate swap. The key is to enter the proper discount factors.

a net asset for them, they will become more concerned about the ability of the counterparty to make its payments. Third, many swaps are marked to market. This requires valuing swaps after they have been originated.

As in the last example, the spot term structure is $r(0, 1)=5\%$, $r(0, 2)=6\%$, $r(0, 3)=7.5\%$. Now, the problem is extended by letting the four-year spot interest rate, $r(0, 4)$, equal 8%. In the last example, we computed $fr(1, 2)=7.0095\%$ and $fr(2, 3)=10.5640\%$. The one-year forward rate, for delivery three years hence, is $fr(3, 4)=9.5140\%$:

$$1.08^4 = 1.075^3[1 + fr(3, 4)]$$

$$fr(3, 4) = 0.095140$$

The swap's notional principal is \$30 million and payments are annual. The price of a four-year plain vanilla fixed–floating interest rate swap is 7.8339%, computed by using the shortcut method in Section 13.1.2 as follows:

$$100 = \frac{A}{1.05} + \frac{A}{1.06^2} + \frac{A}{1.075^3} + \frac{A}{1.08^4} + \frac{100}{1.08^4}$$

$$100 = A\left(\frac{1}{1.05} + \frac{1}{1.06^2} + \frac{1}{1.075^3} + \frac{1}{1.08^4}\right) + 73.503$$

$$26.497 = 3.38237A$$

$$A = 7.83386$$

The swap dealer quotes a price 7.83% in exchange for one-year LIBOR. There is no bid–asked spread. The dollar amount of each fixed payment is $(0.0783)(\$30,000,000) = \$2,349,000$. Now suppose that one year after origination, the term structure has changed, and $r(0, 1) = 4.5\%$, $r(0, 2) = 5\%$, and $r(0, 3) = 5.5\%$. What is the value of the swap for the pay-fixed counterparty? This is answered in two ways.

13.1.3.1   Valuing an Interest Rate Swap After Origination: Method 1

In the first method, find the present value of the remaining fixed cash payments and the present value of the remaining expected floating receipts. Both these are discounted at current spot interest rates to find the present value. The difference between these two present values is the value of the swap.

The annual fixed payments are: $(0.0783)(\$30,000,000) = \$2,349,000$. The present value is $6,378,900:

$$\frac{2,349,000}{1.045} + \frac{2,349,000}{1.05^2} + \frac{2,349,000}{1.055^3} = \$6,378,900$$

The present value of the expected remaining floating payments is computed as follows. First, it is necessary to find the forward rates that will exist one year after the swap's origination:

$$1.05^2 = 1.045[1 + r(1,2)]$$

$$fr(1,2) = 0.055024$$

$$1.055^3 = 1.05^2[1 + r(2,3)]$$

$$fr(2,3) = 0.065072$$

Therefore, the present value of the expected floating receipts is[6]:

$$\frac{(0.045)(\$30,000,000)}{1.045} + \frac{(0.055024)(\$30,000,00)}{1.05^2} + \frac{(0.065072)(\$30,000,000)}{1.055^3} = \$4,451,604$$

Because the present value of the fixed payments is $6,378,900, and the present value of the floating receipts is only $4,451,604, the swap, which now has a negative value of $1,927,296 has become a liability for the pay-fixed party. Of course, the swap is a positive value asset for the receive-fixed counterparty.

13.1.3.2 Valuing an Interest Rate Swap After Origination: Method 2

In the second method, we find what swap dealers are now quoting (one year after the swap's origination) as a fixed rate to be swapped for one-year LIBOR. This new swap should have a tenor of only three years. The difference between the original swap's fixed payments and a new swap's fixed payments equals the original swap's value.

Using the shortcut method to value an at-market swap, we find that the new price is 5.464258%:

$$100 = \frac{A}{1.045} + \frac{A}{1.05^2} + \frac{A}{1.055^3} + \frac{100}{1.055^3}$$

$$100 = A\left(\frac{1}{1.045} + \frac{1}{1.05^2} + \frac{1}{1.055^3}\right) + 85.1614$$

$$14.8386 = 2.7156A$$

$$A = 5.464258$$

This means that given the notional principal of $30 million, the fixed payments on a new swap would be $(0.05464258)(\$30,000,000) = \$1,639,277$. The difference between the old swap's fixed payments and the new swap's fixed payments is $\$2,349,000 - \$1,639,277 = \$709,723$ per year. The present value of the difference in fixed cash flows, given the new discount rates is $1,927,310:

$$\frac{\$709,723}{1.045} + \frac{\$709,723}{1.05^2} + \frac{\$709,723}{1.055^3} = \$1,927,310$$

Except for some rounding errors, this is the same number we computed by using method 1 (Section 13.1.3.1). Thus, if this swap were marked to market after one year, the pay-fixed party would have to pay $1,927,310 to the receive-fixed counterparty. If the pay-fixed party approached a swap dealer and asked to get out of the swap contract early, the swap dealer would agree for a payment of $1,927,310.

Note that if spot interest rates were $r(0,1) = 4.5\%$, $r(0,2) = 5.0\%$, and $r(0,3) = 5.5\%$, and if a firm approached a swap dealer requesting to be the pay-fixed party in an off-market swap with a price of 7.83%, the swap dealer would pay the firm $1,927,310. This up-front payment would be compensation for the firm because it has asked to pay 7.83% fixed, when the market price is only 5.464258%.

The FinancialCAD function aaSwpi provides the same answer for valuing an existing swap after time has passed and the term structure of interest rates has changed, as in the example we just covered. Figure 13.2 shows the solution.

13.1.4 Using FRAs and Futures to Price Swaps

Theoretical forward interest rates are derived from spot interest rates for pure discount bonds. Futures interest rates are theoretically equal to forward interest rates, except for the impact of marking futures contracts to market daily, which could have a small impact on theoretical futures prices. Thus, the prices of FRAs, as well as futures interest rates and spot interest rates, can all be used to price swaps.

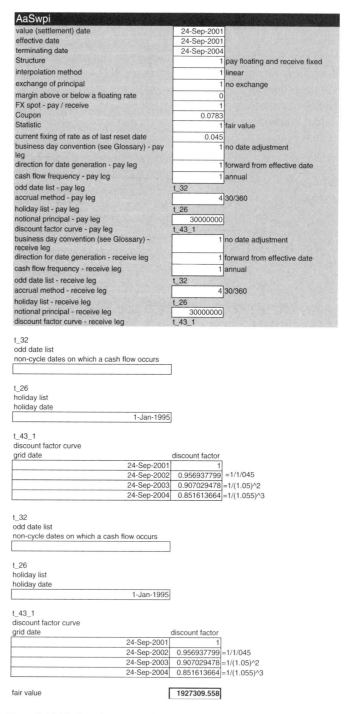

AaSwpi

value (settlement) date	24-Sep-2001
effective date	24-Sep-2001
terminating date	24-Sep-2004
Structure	1 pay floating and receive fixed
interpolation method	1 linear
exchange of principal	1 no exchange
margin above or below a floating rate	0
FX spot - pay / receive	1
Coupon	0.0783
Statistic	1 fair value
current fixing of rate as of last reset date	0.045
business day convention (see Glossary) - pay leg	1 no date adjustment
direction for date generation - pay leg	1 forward from effective date
cash flow frequency - pay leg	1 annual
odd date list - pay leg	t_32
accrual method - pay leg	4 30/360
holiday list - pay leg	t_26
notional principal - pay leg	30000000
discount factor curve - pay leg	t_43_1
business day convention (see Glossary) - receive leg	1 no date adjustment
direction for date generation - receive leg	1 forward from effective date
cash flow frequency - receive leg	1 annual
odd date list - receive leg	t_32
accrual method - receive leg	4 30/360
holiday list - receive leg	t_26
notional principal - receive leg	30000000
discount factor curve - receive leg	t_43_1

t_32
odd date list
non-cycle dates on which a cash flow occurs

t_26
holiday list
holiday date

1-Jan-1995

t_43_1
discount factor curve

grid date	discount factor	
24-Sep-2001	1	
24-Sep-2002	0.956937799	=1/1/045
24-Sep-2003	0.907029478	=1/(1.05)^2
24-Sep-2004	0.851613664	=1/(1.055)^3

t_32
odd date list
non-cycle dates on which a cash flow occurs

t_26
holiday list
holiday date

1-Jan-1995

t_43_1
discount factor curve

grid date	discount factor	
24-Sep-2001	1	
24-Sep-2002	0.956937799	=1/1/045
24-Sep-2003	0.907029478	=1/(1.05)^2
24-Sep-2004	0.851613664	=1/(1.055)^3

fair value	1927309.558

Figure 13.2 The FinancialCAD function, aaSwpi, solves for the value of a swap after it has been originated, and interest rates have changed.

In practice, swap dealers will hedge their floating cash flows. They will hedge them by using either FRAs or futures, depending on factors such as relative prices and liquidity. Another relevant factor is that Eurodollar futures have specific delivery dates, and they will likely not coincide with the dates on which the swap cash flows will be exchanged. Swap dealers who are planning to use these contracts to hedge a swap's floating cash payment or receipt will price their swaps from FRA prices or futures prices.

EXAMPLE 13.1 Pricing A Forward Swap Using a Strip of Eurodollar Futures Contracts   A forward swap is one that is executed today, but the cash flows begin at a future date (beyond what you expect in a plain vanilla swap). Forward swaps are also often called **forward start swaps**. They are equivalent to two partially offsetting swaps, both of which begin today, but one is longer than the other. Thus, a two-year payer swap and a five-year receiver swap together create a three-year receiver swap that begins two years hence.

A swap is equivalent to a strip of futures contracts. Often, the price of a swap is obtained by using the prices of futures contracts. Here, we show how Eurodollar futures prices can be used to determine the theoretical price of a forward, fixed-for-floating interest rate swap.

For our example, consider the following. On July 28, 1999, suppose a firm has committed to borrow $50 million with a floating interest rate, for two years, beginning in September. The firm now wishes it had borrowed at a fixed rate. The firm approaches a swap dealer to get a price for a fixed-for-floating swap, expressing the desire to be the pay-fixed party.

Under the current conditions of the loan, the interest rate is set quarterly to the prevailing spot three-month LIBOR rate. In addition, the date on which the floating interest rate is set coincides with the settlement dates of Eurodollar futures contracts. Assume for simplicity that the interest expense is calculated by using a 30/360 day count method. Also assume that the first interest expense payment will be made three months after the loan begins (i.e., in December 1999).

Based on the Eurodollar futures settlement prices from Table 10.2, the swap dealer can generate the following information:

Contract in Strip?	Month/ Strike	Euro dollars Futures Settlement	Yield Settle	Unannualized Forward Rate	Discount Factor	Inverse of Discount Factor
No	Aug 1999	94.625	5.375	—	—	—
Yes	Sep 1999	94.555	5.445	0.013613	1.013613	0.986570
No	Oct 1999	94.285	5.715	—	—	—
No	Nov 1999	94.255	5.745	—	—	—
Yes	Dec 1999	94.190	5.810	0.014525	1.028335	0.972446

No	Jan 2000	94.315	5.685	—	—	—
Yes	Mar 2000	94.185	5.815	0.014538	1.043285	0.958511
Yes	June 2000	93.950	6.050	0.015125	1.059064	0.944230
Yes	Sept 2000	93.765	6.235	0.015588	1.075572	0.929737
Yes	Dec 2000	93.535	6.465	0.016163	1.092956	0.914950
Yes	Mar 2001	93.550	6.450	0.016125	1.110580	0.900430
Yes	June 2001	93.490	6.510	0.016275	1.128655	0.886010

Note that the quarterly payments of the swap determine which futures contracts should be in the strip that is equivalent to the swap. The September Eurodollar futures contract is linked to the three-month interest rate that will exist beginning in September, and this is the same interest rate that determines the first cash flow of the swap, in December.

Each unannualized forward rate is calculated as follows:

$$\text{unannualized forward rate}_i = \left(\frac{\text{yield settle}_i}{100}\right)\left(\frac{90}{360}\right)$$

and the discount factors are calculated by compounding the unannualized forward rates. For example, the entry for the March 2000 discount factor is given by

March 2000 discount factor $= 1.013613 \times 1.014525 \times 1.014538 = 1.043285$ and the inverse discount factor column is simply

$$\text{inverse}_i = \frac{1}{\text{discount factor}_i}$$

For example, the inverse of the March 2000 discount factor is $1/1.043285 = 0.958511$. In addition, the swap dealer can calculate the floating payments as follows:

$$\text{floating payment}_i = \text{unannualized forward rate}_i \times \$50,000,000$$

For example, the last floating payment of \$813,750 is computed using $0.016275 \times \$50,000,000 = \$813,750$. The floating payments are then discounted using the discount factors. These discounted floating payments are the present value (as of September 1999) of the floating payments:

$$\text{discounted floating payment}_i = \frac{\text{floating payment}_i}{\text{discount factor}_i}$$

With these formulas, the swap dealer can generate the following additional information:

Borrowing Period Starting	Floating Payment	Discount Factor	Discounted Floating Payment
Sept 1999	\$680,625	1.013613	\$671,484 (=\$680,625/1.013613)
Dec 1999	\$726,250	1.028335	\$706,239
Mar 2000	\$726,875	1.043285	\$696,718
June 2000	\$756,250	1.059064	\$714,074

Sept 2000	$779,375	1.075572	$724,614
Dec 2000	$808,125	1.092956	$739,394
Mar 2001	$806,250	1.110580	$725,972
June 2001	$813,750	1.128655	$720,991 (=$813,750/1.128655)
Total			$5,699,486

The swap dealer can now calculate the fixed payment each 90 days that would have the same present value as the floating payments. That is, solve the following equation for F:

$$F\left(\sum_i \frac{1}{\text{discount factor}_i}\right) = F\left(\sum_i \text{inverse}_i\right) = \$5,699,486$$

$$F(7.492884) = \$5,699,486$$

$$F = \$760,653$$

The fixed rate is then given by:

$$\text{fixed rate} = \left(\frac{\text{fixed payment}}{\text{notional value}}\right)\left(\frac{360}{90}\right)$$

$$\text{fixed rate} = \left(\frac{\$760,653}{\$50,000,000}\right)4$$

$$\text{fixed rate} = 6.08522\%$$

Note that the swap dealer could approximate an unannualized fixed rate with an IRR calculation. In this calculation, the notional value is the cash outlay beginning at the loan's initiation in September. Beginning in December, each quarterly floating payment and the notional value are subsequent cash inflows:

$$0 = -\$50,000,000 + \left(\sum_i \frac{\text{floating payment}_i}{(1 + F_{\text{IRR}})^i}\right) + \frac{\$50,000,000}{(1 + F_{\text{IRR}})^8}$$

$$F_{\text{IRR}} = 1.5214\%$$

$$F \approx 1.5214\% \times 4 \approx 6.0856\%$$

This IRR approach is a shortcut in the estimation of the theoretical swap price, using futures prices. The shortcut solution of 6.0856% is not much different from the more precise rate of 6.08522%, which we computed earlier. You are asked to use excel to compute the IRR solution in end-of-chapter Problem 13.14.

In this example, because the firm wants to pay a fixed rate, the swap dealer might quote a price of, say, 6.12%. Note that the firm itself has the opportunity to use Eurodollar futures contracts to"lock in" all the interest rate payments. If it does so, then each interest rate payment will be known, but the amount will be different at each date. If the firm does not want to go to the trouble of hedging the interest rate payments, and/or if the firm wants to have a known and constant interest rate payment, the firm will enter into the swap.

13.2   PRICING A CURRENCY SWAP

In a plain vanilla currency swap, the principal amounts, expressed in terms of two different currencies, are exchanged at origination at the prevailing spot exchange rate. Thus, this initial swap of principal amounts has no pricing or valuation consequences. If the current exchange rate is $1.61/£, then swapping $25,000,000 for £15,527,950 is currently a valueless transaction from the viewpoint of both parties to the swap.

Pricing a currency swap involves the same principles as pricing an interest rate swap. The present value of the payments must equal the present value of the receipts, so that an at-market swap has a value of zero at origination. If the principal amounts are again exchanged at the swap's termination (as they typically are), these amounts must be included in the valuation process. The present values can be expressed in either currency, and the link between the two present values is the exchange rate at origination. Either payment can be fixed or floating. A currency swap is equivalent to a firm selling, or issuing, a bond denominated in one currency and buying a bond in a different currency. When converted at the spot exchange rate, the values of the asset and the liability are equal.

13.2.1   An Example of Pricing a Fixed–Fixed Currency Swap

Consider the following swap:

Maturity	Three years
Principal	$25 million
Currency	deutschemarks
Fixed dollar rate	8%
Fixed deutschemark rate	To be determined
Payment dates	Every six months
Day count method	30/360

It is also necessary to know that the spot exchange rate is $0.70/DEM and that spot interest rates on zero-coupon debt instruments in each country are as follows:

Years to Maturity	United States	Germany
0.5	0.045	0.060
1.0	0.055	0.062
1.5	0.062	0.060
2.0	0.065	0.058
2.5	0.067	0.058
3.0	0.068	0.058

Now, the problem is to solve for the fixed rate, denominated in deutschemarks, that makes the value of the payments (in dollars) equal to the value of the receipts (in DEM), when valued at the current spot exchange rate of $0.70/DEM.

To proceed, note that the present value of the fixed dollar payments is $25,915,014. This is computed by discounting the six semiannual payments of $1 million each (at the spot U.S. interest rates) and also by discounting the principal value of $25 million to be swapped three years hence (at the termination of the swap). The semiannual payment is $1 million because the fixed U.S. dollar swap rate is 8%, payments are made semiannually, and the day count method is 30/360. Therefore, the semiannual interest rate is 4%, and 4% of $25 million is $1 million.

$$\frac{\$1,000,000}{1.045^{0.5}} + \frac{\$1,000,000}{1.055} + \frac{\$1,000,000}{1.062^{1.5}} + \frac{\$1,000,000}{1.065^2} + \frac{\$1,000,000}{1.067^{2.5}}$$

$$+ \frac{\$26,000,000}{1.068^3} = \$25,915,014$$

Now, it is necessary to solve for the unknown, fixed German interest rate that determines the fixed periodic DEM cash flows that will be swapped. The principal amount, expressed in DEM, is based on the origination date exchange rate of $0.7/DEM:

$$\$25,000,000 \, (DEM / \$0.7) = DEM35,714,286$$

Thus, DEM35,714,286 will be exchanged for $25 million both at origination and at termination. The exchange at origination has no impact. The exchange at termination must be included in the pricing problem. The present value of the fixed DEM cash flows, when converted back to dollars, is[7]:

$$\left[\begin{array}{l} \frac{x(DEM35,714,286)}{1.06^{0.5}} + \frac{x(DEM35,714,286)}{1.062} + \frac{x(DEM35,714,286)}{1.06^{1.5}} + \\[2mm] \frac{x(DEM35,714,286)}{1.058^2} + \frac{x(DEM35,714,286)}{1.058^{2.5}} + \frac{x(DEM35,714,286)}{1.058^3} + \\[2mm] \frac{DEM35,714,286}{1.058^3} \end{array} \right] \times \frac{\$0.7}{DEM}$$

Note that at time 3, *both* a payment of $x(DEM35,714,286)$ *and* the principal amount (DEM35,714,286) are exchanged and discounted back three periods at the three-year rate of 5.8%. The term in the square brackets [ ] is the present value of the DEM cash flows, denominated in deutschemarks. The last term, $0.7/DEM converts this DEM value into dollars at the origination date spot exchange rate. The foregoing equation must equal the present value of the dollar cash flows. Setting them equal results in the solution for the unknown, fixed German interest rate that determines the fixed periodic DEM cash flows that will be swapped (i.e., x):

$$(DEM194,124,972x + DEM30,156,780)\$0.7/DEM = \$25,915,014$$

$$DEM35,887,480x = DEM4,805,268$$

$$x = 0.035362$$

Thus, the fixed German interest rate is 3.5362%. This is the unannualized, half-year rate that equates the present value of the fixed dollar cash flows to the present value of the fixed DEM cash flows. The fixed DEM rate, expressed as an annual percentage, is then 7.0724%.

FinCAD can be used to find the same solution, but only in a roundabout way that utilizes Excel's goal seek tool.

13.2.2   Pricing a Fixed–Floating Currency Swap

To price a fixed-to-floating currency swap, find the fixed rate that makes the present value of the fixed cash flows equal to the present value of the floating cash flows. Because the floating cash flows are unknown, however, they are typically estimated by theoretical forward prices. Alternatively, and almost equivalently, they will be the forward prices or futures prices that swap dealers will have to pay or receive when they use forward foreign exchange contracts or futures contracts to hedge *their* risk exposures.

For example, consider a fixed–floating currency swap with the following structure:

Maturity	Three years
Principal	$25 million
Floating currency	Deutschemarks
Fixed dollar rate	To be determined
Payment dates	Every six months
Day count method	30/360

The spot exchange rate is $0.70/DEM, and spot interest rates on zero-coupon debt instruments in each country are as follows:

	Spot Interest Rates, r	
Years to Maturity, T	U.S., r_{US}	Germany, r_G
0.5	0.045	0.060
1.0	0.055	0.062
1.5	0.062	0.060
2.0	0.065	0.058
2.5	0.067	0.058
3.0	0.068	0.058

The goal is to solve for the fixed U.S. dollar interest rate that makes this at-market swap valueless from the viewpoint of both swap parties. First, we must solve for the theoretical forward exchange rates that exist, given the spot exchange rate and the term structures prevailing in each country. These theoretical forward prices are computed by using Equation (13.1) (which was originally introduced in Chapter 5):

$$F = S\left[\frac{1+r_{US}}{1+r_G}\right]^T \tag{13.1}$$

where F and S are expressed as $/DEM, and $S=0.70$.

Although they are not necessary to solve the problem, we can use the theoretical forward foreign exchange formula and the interest rates presented here to compute this set of forward exchange rates:

Years to Maturity	Forward Rate ($/DEM)
0.5	0.69503
1.0	0.69539
1.5	0.70198
2.0	0.70929
2.5	0.71498
3.0	0.72004

These values are the theoretical forward prices and futures prices. If a swap dealer is the pay-fixed party, he will receive floating DEM payments. He faces the risk that the dollar value of these future unknown DEM payments will decline. To hedge these risky DEM cash inflows, he can sell a strip of DEM forward contracts or sell a strip of DEM futures contracts. By selling DEM forward, the swap dealer locks in the selling price of the DEM cash flows.

To solve the swap pricing problem, forward German interest rates must be computed. These are found using Equation (13.2) (also introduced in Chapter 5):

$$[1+r(0,t2)]^{t2} = [1+r(0,t1)]^{t1} \times [1+fr(t1,t2)]^{t2-t1} \tag{13.2}$$

Given the spot German interest rates, the annualized forward rates and the unannualized forward rates for semiannual compounding are:

$r(0.0, 0.5)$	0.06000	0.02956
$fr(0.5, 1.0)$	0.06400	0.03151
$fr(1.0, 1.5)$	0.05601	0.02762
$fr(1.5, 2.0)$	0.05202	0.02568
$fr(2.0, 2.5)$	0.05800	0.02859
$fr(2.5, 3.0)$	0.05800	0.02859

Each $fr(t1, t2)$ is a six-month forward interest rate for the period beginning at time $t1$ and ending at time $t2$. Today is represented as time 0. As an illustration of how the formula works, we will use Equation (13.2) to compute $fr(1.5, 2.0)$, the six-month forward rate that begins 18 months hence:

$$1.058^2 = 1.06^{1.5}[1+fr(1.5,2.0)]^{0.5}$$

$$1.119364 = 1.091337[1+fr(1.5,2.0)]^{0.5}$$

$$1.025682 = [1+fr(1.5,2.0)]^{0.5}$$

$$1.05202 = [1+fr(1.5,2.0)]$$

$$0.05202 = fr(1.5,2.0)$$

To obtain the semiannual forward rate from the annualized forward rate, use

$$fr_{semi}(t1,t2) = [(1+fr(t1,t2))^{1/2} - 1]$$
$$= [(1+0.05202)^{1/2} - 1]$$
$$= 0.02568$$

If these semiannual forward German interest rates represent expected future six-month German spot interest rates, then they can be used to compute the estimated floating DEM swap cash flows.[8] Then, the present value, in DEM, of the expected floating cash flows is:

$$\frac{(0.02956)(DEM35,714,286)}{1.060^{0.5}} + \frac{(0.03151)(DEM35,714,286)}{1.062} + \frac{(0.02762)(DEM35,714,286)}{1.060^{1.5}}$$
$$+ \frac{(0.02568)(DEM35,714,286)}{1.058^2} + \frac{(0.02859)(DEM35,714,286)}{1.058^{2.5}}$$
$$+ \frac{(0.02859)(DEM35,714,286)}{1.058^3} + \frac{DEM35,714,286}{1.058^3}$$
$$= DEM35,714,286$$

There are four important points here: (1) the floating cash flow at any time is determined by the unannualized interest rate one period earlier; (2) the forward rates determine the expected DEM floating cash flows; (3) the expected DEM floating cash flows are discounted by using spot German interest rates; and (4) the principal of DEM35,714,286 is exchanged at maturity.

Note also that the present value of the expected floating cash flows just computed, DEM35, 714, 286, is the principal value of the swap ($25,000,000/($0.70/DEM)). This is no coincidence. Recall from Section 13.1.2. that the shortcut method of pricing an at-market fixed-for-floating interest rate swap at origination requires the assumption that the present value of floating cash flows will approximately equal the principal value of the swap.

We can conclude that it is important to know and understand why and how to compute the present value of the floating payments. In particular, it is important to be able to know and understand how to value an off-market swap, where, say, a party wishes to pay or receive floating LIBOR plus or minus a margin. Also, it is important for valuing swaps after origination. However, for pricing an at-market fixed–floating currency swap, we can assume that the value of the floating cash flows is equal to the principal value.

Because DEM35,714,286 equals $25 million, the problem now is to compute the fixed U.S. interest rate that makes the present value of the fixed payments equal $25 million. Let this fixed U.S. semiannual rate equal x. The appropriate pricing equation is then

$$\frac{x(\$25,000,000)}{1.045^{0.5}} + \frac{x(\$25,000,000)}{1.055} + \frac{x(25,000,000)}{1.062^{1.5}} + \frac{x(\$25,000,000)}{1.065^2} + \frac{x(\$25,000,000)}{1.067^{2.5}}$$
$$+ \frac{x(\$25,000,000)}{1.068^3} + \frac{\$25,000,000}{1.068^3} = \$25,000,000$$

$$x(24,455,799) + x(23,696,682) + x(22,843,005) + x(22,041,482) + x(21,258,321)$$
$$+ x(20,522,310) + 20,522,310 = \$25,000,000$$

$$x(\$134,817,600) = \$4,477,690$$

$$x = 0.0332$$

Annualizing the semiannual rate of 3.32%, the fixed U.S. rate is 6.64%. If the swap dealer pays the fixed U.S. cash flows, he will offer to pay a rate somewhat below 6.64%, and receive floating DEM. If the swap dealer is the receive-fixed party, he will require a rate slightly above 6.64%, and pay floating DEM.

The FinancialCAD function aaSwp_cpn provides the same answer for valuing this fixed for floating currency swap, as shown in Figure 13.3. The discount rates are computed using $1/[1 + r(0,y)]^y$, where y is the number of years until maturity, assuming a 30/360 day count method.

13.2.3 Valuing a Fixed–Floating Currency Swap After Origination

Suppose that at origination, a fixed–floating currency swap in which fixed U.S. dollars are swapped for floating DEM is priced at 6.64% (fixed U.S. interest rate). The swap tenor is three years, the principal amount is $25 million, payments are semiannual, and the spot exchange rate is $0.70/DEM. This is the swap described in Section 13.2.2.

One year after this swap was originated, *two-year* fixed US $ for floating DEM swaps are being quoted at 7.78% (fixed U.S. interest rate). Also, one year after the swap's origination, spot U.S. interest rates are as follows:

Years to Maturity	Interest Rate
0.50	8.25%
1.00	8.20%
1.50	8.00%
2.00	7.90%

How much is the swap worth for the pay-fixed party (one year after origination)?

Recall from Section 13.1.3 that there are two methods for valuing an interest rate swap after origination. Here, however, there are insufficient data to use the first method to value this currency swap, because German interest data, which are needed to value the remaining floating DEM cash flows, have not been provided. However, there are sufficient data to value the swap by means of the second approach. We will compute the present value of the remaining fixed U.S. dollar payments of the existing swap and compare them to the present value of fixed U.S. dollar payments on a newly originated swap. The value of the swap is the difference between the two. That is, compare the present values of the following two sets of cash flows. The first series of cash flows is the present value of the remaining payments on the old swap:

$$\frac{(0.0664/2)(\$25,000,000)}{1.0825^{0.5}} + \frac{(0.0664/2)(\$25,000,000)}{1.082} + \frac{(0.0664/2)(\$25,000,000)}{1.080^{1.5}}$$
$$+ \frac{(0.0664/2)(\$25,000,000)}{1.079^2} + \frac{\$25,000,000}{1.079^2}$$
$$= \text{present value of remaining payments on existing swap}$$

$$\$797,745 + \$767,098 + \$739,507 + \$712,911 + \$21,473,217 = \$24,490,478$$

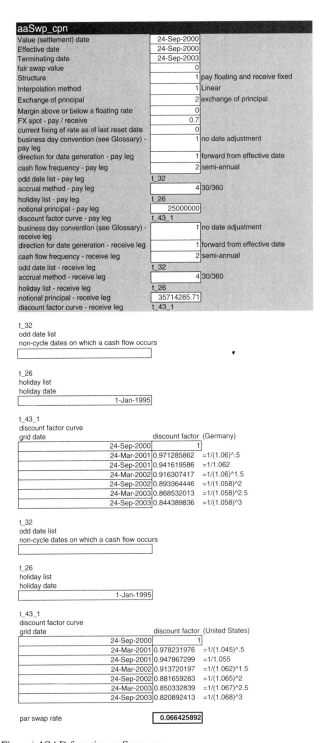

Figure 13.3 The FinancialCAD function aaSwp_cpn.

The second series of cash flows is the present value of the fixed U.S. dollar payments for a new swap:

$$\frac{(0.0778/2)(\$25,000,000)}{1.0825^{0.5}} + \frac{(0.0778/2)(\$25,000,000)}{1.082} + \frac{(0.0778/2)(\$25,000,000)}{1.08^{1.5}}$$

$$\frac{(0.0778/2)(\$25,000,000)}{1.079^2} + \frac{\$25,000,000}{1.079^2}$$

= present value of fixed U.S. dollar payments on a new swap

$$\$934,707 + \$898,799 + \$866,471 + \$835,308 + \$21,473,217 = \$25,008,502$$

Thus, the value of the swap for the pay-fixed party is $518,024. The pay-fixed party of the existing swap is fortunate to be paying cash flows with a present value of only $24,490,478, when new swaps would require the payment totaling $25,008,502.

The FinancialCAD function, aaFixlg_cfx, can solve this problem. It can be used to solve for the present value of the remaining payments on the old swap, and then used to solve for the present value of payments on a newly originated swap. The last line of the spreadsheets in Figure 13.4 shows the present value of the payments that remain to be made on the old swap. You should use aaFixlg_cfx to verify that the present value of the payments on a new swap is $25,008,502. (*Hint:* Just change the coupon from 0.0664 to 0.0778.) The value of the swap ($518,024) is the difference between the two present values.

13.2.4 Pricing a Diff Swap

Recall from Chapter 11 that a diff swap is a currency swap in which all payments and receipts are made in one currency. In other words, the notional principal is expressed in one currency. Payments are determined by applying one floating interest rate in one country to that notional principal. Receipts are determined by applying a different floating interest rate from a different country to that same notional principal. If the interest rates in the two countries are different (which they almost certainly will be), a margin is added to one of the two rates. The pricing problem is to determine that margin.

For example, suppose a firm wishes to pay U.S. dollar six-month LIBOR and receive the British pound sterling six-month interest rate, and have both payments denominated in pounds sterling on a notional principal of £100 million. The swap's tenor is two years, and payments are semiannual. Current spot interest rates on zero-coupon debt instruments are as follows:

Years to Maturity	U.S.	Britain
0.5	6.00%	7.00%
1.0	6.60%	7.00%
1.5	6.95%	6.85%
2.0	7.10%	6.75%

The interest data are sufficient to determine forward rates. Define $fr(t1,t2)$ as the six-month forward rate for the period beginning at time $t1$, and ending at time $t2$. Equation (13.2) is used to determine the forward rates:

$$[1 + r(0,t2)]^{t2} = [1 + r(0,t1)]^{t1}[1 + fr(t1,t2)]^{t2-t1}$$

aaFixlg_cfx		
Settlement date	24-Sep-2001	
Terminating date	24-Sep-2003	
effective date	24-Sep-2001	
date of first coupon after dated date		
date of last coupon prior to maturity date		
Coupon	0.0664	
Principal	25000000	
cash flow frequency	2	Semi-annual
accrual method for coupons	4	30/360
accrual method for accrued interest	4	30/360
holiday list	t_26	
business day convention (see Glossary)	1	no date adjustment
exchange of principal	3	at maturity
trade position	1	Long
Interpolation method	1	Linear
discount factor curve	t_43_1	
output table selection	1	Eight column extended cashflow table (incl date,cpn,npa,total,pvcpn,pvnpa,pvtot,acc)

T_26
holiday list
holiday date

1-Jan-1995

T_43_1
discount factor curve

grid date	discount factor
24-Sep-2001	1
24-Mar-2002	0.961138663
24-Sep-2002	0.924214418
24-Mar-2003	0.890972638
24-Sep-2003	0.858928693

extended cashflow table - aaFixlg_cfx

Date	cash flow amount	Notional principal amount	total cash flow	present value cash flow	present value of the notional amount	total present value of cashflows
24-Mar-2002	830000	0	830000	797745.1	0	797745.1
24-Sep-2002	830000	0	830000	767098	0	767098
24-Mar-2003	830000	0	830000	739507.3	0	739507.3
24-Sep-2003	830000	25000000	25830000	712910.8	21473217	22186128
						24490478

Figure 13.4 Using the FinancialCAD function aaFixlg_cfx to value a fixed–floating currency swap after origination.

Thus, the **unannualized** forward rates are:

	U.S.	Britain
$fr(0, 0.5)$	0.029563	0.034408043
$fr(0.5, 1.0)$	0.035390729	0.034408043
$fr(1.0, 1.5)$	0.037561811	0.03223365
$fr(1.5, 2.0)$	0.037069253	0.0317488

Swap dealers will be able to hedge the floating payments by using forward rates, which are the theoretical prices for FRAs. It may be convenient to think that these rates are the expected future spot rates, which will therefore determine the future expected floating payments. However, recall that these forward rates are the expected future spot rates only if the pure expectations theory of the term structure is valid.

Our problem here is to find a margin to add to (or subtract from) the six-month U.S. LIBOR so that the payments, made in pounds sterling, equal the receipts, also made in that currrency. Define x as the margin added to U.S. LIBOR. Also, recall that the time t interest rate typically determines the cash flow at time $t+1$. The present value of the pounds sterling payments (based on U.S. LIBOR) is:

$$\frac{(0.029563+x)(\pounds100,000,000)}{1.0700^{0.5}} + \frac{(0.035390729+x)(\pounds100,000,000)}{1.0700^{1.0}}$$
$$+ \frac{(0.037561811+x)(\pounds100,000,000)}{1.0685^{1.5}} + \frac{(0.037069253+x)(\pounds100,000,000)}{1.0675^{2}} = PV$$

Expanding:

$$2,857,673 + 96,673,649x + 3,307,545 + 93,457,944x + 3,400,829 + 90,539,525x$$
$$+3,252,955 + 87,753,457x = \text{present value of the } \pounds \text{ payments based on U.S. LIBOR}$$

Collecting terms:

$$368,424,575x + 12,819,002 = \text{present value of the } \pounds \text{ payments based on U.S. LIBOR}$$

Note that the payments are made in pounds and that the discount rates are the spot British interest rates. However, the payments are made on the basis of U.S. LIBOR plus a margin. Half the U.S forward rates is used because payments are made semiannually.

The (expected) cash flow receipts are determined on the basis of forward British rates. Half of the forward British rates is applied to the notional principal amount. The present value of the pound sterling receipts is:

$$\frac{(0.034408043)(\pounds100,00,000)}{1.07^{0.5}} + \frac{(0.034408043)(\pounds100,000,000)}{1.07^{1.0}} + \frac{(0.03223365)(\pounds100,000,000)}{1.0685^{1.5}}$$
$$+ \frac{(0.0317488)(\pounds100,000,000)}{1.0675^{2}} = \pounds12,252,236$$

To solve for the unknown margin, x, set present value of the pound payments based on the U.S. LIBOR equal to the present value of the pound receipts:

$$368,424,575x + 12,819,002 = 12,252,236$$

$$x = -0.00153835$$

Thus, 15 basis points will be subtracted from the semiannual U.S. LIBOR. That is, negative 15 basis points is the (semiannual) price of the swap. Each period, the U.S. LIBOR is observed. Then, to determine the pound payment amount at the next payment date, take half the observed interest rate and subtract 15 basis points. The pound cash flow received at time t is determined by taking half the observed British interest rate at time $t-1$.

13.3   PRICING A COMMODITY SWAP

Commodity swaps are priced in the same way as interest rate and currency swaps. Again, the key is to equate the present values of the payments and the receipts. One type of commodity swap is the fixed–floating commodity swap. One party agrees to pay a fixed price at regular intervals for a commodity and the counterparty agrees to pay a floating price. Generally, the notional principal is not exchanged. Rather, the two payments are netted. A commodity swap is equivalent to a strip of forward contracts, each of which has the same forward price. The pricing problem is to solve for that fixed price.

For example, let us find the fixed price for the following fixed-for-floating oil price swap. Suppose the tenor is 12 months with settlement occurring every three months, beginning three months from today. The floating price on each settlement date is the spot price of West Texas Intermediate (WTI), which is a well-known type of crude oil. The problem is to find the fixed price of the swap.

If WTI futures or forward prices are readily available, this is not difficult. Assume that WTI futures prices and spot interest rates are as follows.

Months Until Delivery	WTI Futures Price ($/bbl)	Spot Interest Rate
3	$21.55	4.2%
6	$20.04	4.8%
9	$19.18	5.1%
12	$18.40	5.2%

The swap dealer will use futures contracts to hedge the floating cash flows, so that he can use the futures prices to find the present value of the floating cash flows:

$$\frac{21.55}{1.042^{0.25}} + \frac{20.04}{1.048^{0.5}} + \frac{19.18}{1.051^{0.75}} + \frac{18.40}{1.052} = \$76.87$$

The present value of the fixed cash flows, where x represents the fixed price of the swap, is:

$$\frac{x}{1.042^{0.25}} + \frac{x}{1.048^{0.5}} + \frac{x}{1.051^{0.75}} + \frac{x}{1.052} = x\left(\frac{1}{1.042^{0.25}} + \frac{1}{1.048^{0.5}} + \frac{1}{1.051^{0.75}} + \frac{1}{1.052}\right)$$
$$= 3.88055x$$

By equating the present values of the fixed and floating cash flows, we find that the solution for x is:

$$76.87 = 3.88055x$$

$$x = \$19.81/bbl$$

Thus, the fixed price of the oil swap is $19.81/bbl. If the swap dealer is paying fixed, he will quote a price a few cents below $19.81/bbl. If the swap dealer is receiving fixed, he will quote a price a few cents above $19.81/bbl.

If forward contracts or futures contracts do not exist on exactly the same commodity underlying the swap, the dealer will use the most similar available commodity to price the swap. In these cases, however, the dealer will most likely widen the bid–asked spread around the theoretical swap price to adjust for risk.

The FinancialCAD function aaSwpcd_bmrk can be used to solve for the theoretical price of a commodity swap, as shown in Figure 13.5.

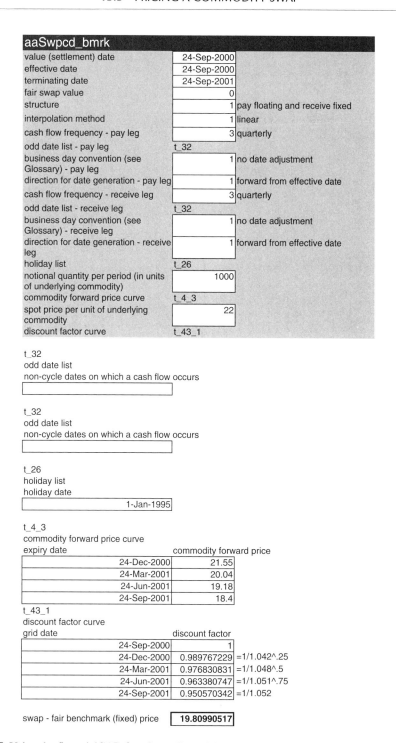

Figure 13.5 Using the financialCAD function aaSwpcd_bmrk to solve for the theoretical price of a commodity swap.

13.4   SUMMARY

Pricing swaps is a matter of equating the present value of the payments to the present value of the receipts. Usually, the floating payments are "known" in the sense that the swap dealer will use forward prices or futures prices in their valuation. Then, the pricing problem is usually to solve for the fixed price that makes the present value of the fixed cash flows equal to the present value of the floating cash flows. The discount factors are the yields on zero coupon debt instruments.

Notes

[1]This chapter will ignore the different settlement conventions of forward contracts (covered in Chapter 3) and swaps (covered in Chapter 11).

[2]The assumption that the pure expectations theory is correct is not necessary. Recall from Chapter 5 that market participants can lock in forward rates as their actual future borrowing or lending rates by trading zero-coupon bonds in the spot market. In other words, a swap dealer can make the forward rates be equal to the actual future spot rates they will face as borrowers or lenders, and the "expected" cash flows used in the example can be locked in as actual cash flows.

[3]Although the swap dealer does not know what the future floating payments will be, they can be hedged by engaging in FRAs, which will then effectively fix the floating rates. Similarly, the future floating rates can be locked in by trading spot bonds. Theoretical forward rates for a 12×24 FRA and a 24×36 FRA are 7.0095 and 10.5640%, respectively.

[4]The value of a floating-rate coupon bond may not always exactly equal its par value for three reasons. First, if the issuer becomes more risky (more likely to default) after issuing the bond, the bond will sell at a discount to provide a default risk premium. Second, typically, there will be a lag between the time at which the next floating coupon amount is determined and when it is paid. Third, the rate that determines the coupon payments may not equal the rate used for discounting.

[5]The FinancialCAD function aaSwp_cpn can also be used to price this swap, and to price swaps when there are payments at times less than a year apart (e.g., semiannually or quarterly). However it takes an unusual approach to computing the floating payments (which are based on the forward rates implied in the current term structure). Normally, we would divide the implied forward rates by 2 or 4 to compute semiannual or quarterly cash flows. However, aaSwp_cpn instead solves for the semiannual rate, which if compounded, would give the annual forward rates, and uses them to determine the floating payments (Use the function aaFlleg_cfs to determine floating payments, and you would conclude that they are computed in this way.) The student should solve Problem 13.1 at the end of chapter to learn the processes.

[6]The first payment is determined by the existing one-year LIBOR, at time zero. Each subsequent payment is determined by the interest rate that exists at the start of the period.

[7]The astute reader will recognize that DEM35,714,286 $\times$ \$0.7/DEM = \$25,000,000. Thus the problem is actually to solve for x in the following equation:

$$x\left[\frac{\$25\text{mm}}{(1.06)^{0.5}} + \frac{\$25\text{mm}}{1.062} + \frac{\$25\text{mm}}{(1.06)^{1.5}} + \frac{\$25\text{mm}}{(1.058)^2} + \frac{\$25\text{mm}}{(1.058)^{2.5}} + \frac{\$25\text{mm}}{(1.058)^3}\right] + \frac{\$25\text{mm}}{(1.058)^3} = \$25,915,014$$

[8]However, the assumption that these are *expected* cash flows is not necessary. See note 2 in this chapter.

PROBLEMS

13.1 The spot term structure is $r(0, 1/2) = 4.8\%$ (this is the spot six-month interest rate), $r(0, 1) = 5.3\%$, $r(0, 1 1/2) = 5.7\%$, $r(0, 2) = 6\%$. Compute the price of a plain vanilla fixed–floating interest rate swap with a tenor of two years. Payments are semiannual, beginning six months hence. Use FinancialCAD to solve the problem.

13.2 The spot term structure on August 3, 2000, is

> One-year rate $= 9.5\%$
>
> Two-year rate $= 9\%$
>
> Three-year rate $= 8.75\%$
>
> Four-year rate $= 8.6\%$

a. Find the price of a four-year swap with a notional principal of $25 million. The floating rate is one-year LIBOR. Payments are annual.

b. Suppose that one year after the swap in part (a) was originated, the spot term structure has changed to

> One-year rate $= 6\%$
>
> Two-year rate $= 7.3\%$
>
> Three-year rate $= 7.8\%$
>
> Four-year rate $= 8.1\%$

What is the value of the swap for the receive-fixed counterparty?

13.3 The spot term structure is $r(0, 1/4) = 7.2\%$, $r(0, 1/2) = 8\%$, $r(0, 3/4) = 7.8\%$, $r(0, 1) = 7.7\%$, $r(0, 1 1/4) = 7.6\%$, $r(0, 1 1/2) = r(0, 1 3/4) = r(0, 2) = 7.5\%$. A firm approaches a swap dealer and requests that an off-market swap be priced in which the firm is the pay-fixed counterparty. The firm wishes to pay 6.5% fixed. Assume a national principal of $25,000,000. What payment will the swap dealer request?

Who will make the payment, the firm or the swap dealer? Why?

13.4 A firm enters into a plain vanilla fixed–floating interest rate swap with a swap dealer. Here are the terms:

Notional principal	$50 million
Fixed rate paid by firm	8%
Floating rate received by firm	Six-month LIBOR
Tenor	Three years
First payment	Six months after origination
Subsequent payment dates	Every six months, up to and including the termination date
Day count method	30/360

The terms of the swap require that it be marked to market every year. One year after the swap's origination (immediately after the second payment), otherwise equivalent new swaps with a tenor of two years are priced with a fixed rate of 7%. How much will the mark-to-market cash payment be? Who will pay this amount? Use the FinancialCAD function aaSwpi to solve this problem; note that your answer obtained through FinancialCAD will differ from your hand-calculated solution as a result of the process discussed in note 5. Assume the spot rates one year after the swap's originations are: $r(0, 0.5) = 6\%$; $r(0, 1) = 6.30\%$; $r(0, 1.5) = 6.90\%$, $r(0, 2) = 7.10\%$.

13.5 Consider the plain vanilla swap in Section 13.1. Suppose that two years after the swap was originated, the pay-fixed party must mark the swap to market. The remaining tenor of the swap is only two years. At that date (two years after origination), the term structure of interest rates is $r(0,1)=7.5\%$, $r(0,2)=7\%$, and $r(0,3)=6.8\%$. What is the value of the swap for the pay-fixed party? Also use Financial-CAD to solve this problem.

13.6 Rework out the currency swap pricing problem in Section 13.2.1 assuming that the principal amounts are **not** exchanged at the swap's maturity.

13.7 A firm wishes to enter into a fixed–fixed currency swap. The principal amount is $60 million, and the firm wishes to receive a fixed rate of 7.5% in U.S. dollars. The firm will pay Japanese yen. Suppose the spot exchange rate is ¥98/$. The swap tenor is two years, and payments will be quarterly. Principal amounts will be swapped at origination and at termination. Spot interest rates on zero coupon debt instruments in the U.S. are as follows:

Years to Maturity	Interest Rate
0.25	5.25%
0.50	6.00%
0.75	6.60%
1.00	7.00%
1.25	7.25%
1.50	7.40%
1.75	7.50%
2.00	7.55%

Forward rates in Japan, defined as $fr(t1,t2)$, where the forward period begins at time $t1$ and ends at time $t2$ are as follows:

$$fr(0,0.25)=0.80\%$$
$$fr(0.25,0.50)=0.88\%$$
$$fr(0.50,0.75)=1.0\%$$
$$fr(0.75,1.00)=1.2\%$$
$$fr(1.00,1.25)=1.29\%$$
$$fr(1.25,1.50)=1.35\%$$
$$fr(1.50,1.75)=1.42\%$$
$$fr(1.75,2.00)=1.45\%$$

Compute the fixed Japanese interest rate for the swap.

13.8 Use the data in Problem 13.7 to find the fixed U.S. interest rate that prices a fixed–floating currency swap. Fixed U.S. dollars will be swapped for floating yen.

13.9 Given the price determined in the diff swap in Section 13.2.4., suppose that six months after the swap was originated, six-month U.S. LIBOR is 6.2% and six-month British LIBOR is 7.9%. What is difference check amount? Who will pay it and who will receive it?

13.10 A firm wishes to pay quarterly yen LIBOR and receive quarterly U.S. dollar LIBOR, and have both payments denominated in U.S. dollars on a notional principal of $60 million. This diff swap's tenor is two years, and payments are quarterly. Current spot interest rates on zero coupon debt instruments are as follows:

Years to Maturity	U.S.	Japan
0.25	4.5%	1.0%
0.5	5.0%	1.2%
0.75	5.4%	1.6%
1	5.8%	1.8%
1.25	5.9%	2.0%
1.5	6.0%	2.3%
1.75	6.1%	2.5%
2	6.2%	2.7%

Determine the price of this swap.

13.11 Find the fixed price for a fixed-for-floating gold price swap. Settlement will be every six months, beginning four months from today. The tenor will be 22 months. The floating payment will be based on the spot price of gold on each settlement date. Today's gold futures prices are:

Delivery_months hence	gold futures price
4	409.20
10	415.10

16	420.40
22	425.80

Spot interest rates for zero coupon bonds are $r(0, t)$, where t is the number of months until the bond matures are $r(0, 0.33)=4\%$, $r(0, 0.83)=$ 4.2%, $r(0, 1.33)=4.5\%$, $r(0, 1.83)=4.7\%$. Find the price (the fixed price) of the swap. Also use FinancialCAD to check your solution.

13.12 A mutual fund owns a portfolio of German stocks. It wishes to enter into an equity index swap in which it agrees to pay the rate of return on the DAX index (the DAX is a German stock index), plus or minus a margin, and receive German 3-month LIBOR. The tenor will be one year, and payments will be quarterly, beginning 3 months hence. A payment at time t will be made on the basis of the actual rate of return on the stock index during the period ending at time t, and the interest rate at time t. The notional principal is €80 million. The day count method for the interest rate is 30/360. The swap dealer observes the following futures prices:

Delivery months hence	DAX futures	German LIBOR futures
3	2560	7.0%
6	2598	6.9%
9	2633	6.8%
12	2660	6.6%

At origination, the DAX index is at 2,540, and spot 3-month German LIBOR is 7.1%. Compute the proper margin that the swap dealer will add or subtract to the DAX index. Why would the mutual fund wish to engage in this swap? Why would the dealer?

13.13 A firm has a floating-rate liability. At time t, it pays whatever six-month LIBOR was at the start of the period. The liability matures in two years, and interest payments are made every six months. The firm believes that interest rates are about to rise.

a. How can the firm use a swap to hedge against the risk that interest rates will rise?

b. How can the firm use a strip of FRAs to hedge against the risk that interest rates will rise? If the 6×12 FRA is quoted by a dealer at 7.3/7.4, which rate is appropriate for the firm?

c. Which should be used, the swap or the strip of FRAs? Suppose that spot six-month LIBOR is 7%. The swap dealer will receive 8% or pay 7.9% against six-month LIBOR. FRAs are quoted as follows:

6×12	7.3/7.4
12×18	8.1/8.22
18×24	8.42/8.54

Should the firm use the swap or the FRA?

13.14 In Section 13.1.4, the IRR for a series of uneven cash flows is reported as 1.5214%. Use Excel to compute this IRR. The present value in June 1999 is $50 million. The cash flows are as follows:

Borrowing Period Starting	Floating Payment
Sept 1999	$680,625
Dec 1999	$726,250
Mar 2000	$726,875
June 2000	$756,250
Sept 2000	$779,375
Dec 2000	$808,125
Mar 2001	$806,250
June 2001	$813,750

13.15 On April 28, 2000, a firm wants to use Eurodollar futures prices to compute the theoretical price of a plain vanilla interest rate swap. The tenor of the swap is three years, and payments will be made quarterly. The first payment will be made in September 2000. The notional principal of the swap is $60 million.

Here are the Eurodollar futures prices that existed on April 28, 2000:

Expiration Month	Futures Price (IMM Index)
May 2000	93.39
June	93.25
July	93.15
August	93.04
September	92.96
December	92.75
March 2001	92.71
June	92.67
September	92.65
December	92.62
March 2002	92.69
June	92.70
September	92.71
December	92.66
March 2003	92.60

Find the theoretical price of the swap.

PART 4

OPTIONS

CHAPTER 14

Introduction to Options

To this point, we have presented three classes of risk management instruments: forward contracts, futures contracts, and swaps (which can be viewed as a portfolio of forward contracts). These three classes of risk management instruments share two important features. First, both parties to these contracts, (i.e., the *long* and the *short*) are initially bound by the terms of the contract. Second, there is no cash payment required by one party from the other at the initiation of the contract.

In this chapter, we introduce a new class of risk management instruments known as options. There are a number of new terms, concepts, and institutional details associated with options. From a risk management standpoint, a mastery of these fundamental definitions and ideas provides a basis for understanding how options can be used to manage risk.

Perhaps the most fundamental option concept is that option contracts separate rights from obligations. That is, the *long* has rights, whereas the *short* has obligations. As a consequence of this separation, the long must pay the short a dollar amount at the initiation of the option contract. This dollar amount, called either the option price, the option premium, or the option value, is the subject of Chapters 17 and 18.

Depending on the nature of the rights and obligations in the option contract, options are classified into two categories known as call options or put options. We begin the study of options by examining the features of call options.

14.1 CALL OPTIONS

A call option is a contract that gives its owner the right, but not the obligation, to buy something at a specified price on or before a specified date. The "something" that can be bought with the option is called the **underlying asset**. In this book, the price of the underlying asset will be usually denoted as an S. Much of the description of options in this text will involve options on 100 shares of a specific firm's stock. For example, if you buy one call option on IBM today, you have the right to purchase 100 shares of IBM's common stock at a specified price, any time between today and a prespecified date.

The fact that the call owner does not have the obligation to exercise the option means that he has limited liability. Should the price of the underlying asset fall, he can just walk away from the call contract without ever having had to acquire the underlying asset.

The specified price is called the **exercise price**, the **strike price**, or the **striking price**, and in this text, it will be denoted K (in other books and articles it may be denoted X, or in some cases, E).

The **expiration date** of an option, or the time to expiration, will be denoted T in this text. The expiration date of U.S. exchange listed options on 100 shares of common stock is the Saturday immediately following the third Friday of the expiration month. The last trading day is the third Friday of the expiration month. Some **index options**[1] expire on other dates, and **futures options**[2] expire on a wide range of dates. Finally, **OTC options**,[3] which are custom-made contracts that do not trade on any exchanges, and **flex options**,[4] which are custom-made contracts used by institutional traders, may expire on any day. Investors in options should always ascertain the expiration dates of contracts they are trading.

The general option definition just given applies to **American-style** options. The owner of an American option can exercise it *on or before* the expiration date. The owner of a **European-style** option can exercise it only on the expiration date. The geographic designation, however, is largely irrelevant. Most options that are actively traded in the world (including in Europe) are American-style options. Because American options give the owner an additional timing option (the right, but not the obligation, to exercise early), they cannot be worth less than otherwise equivalent European options. Note, however, that the holder of any traded option can sell the option at any time before expiration.

Most likely, when you think of an option, you think of a call option on 100 shares of an underlying stock. However, other actively traded options exist on stock market indices, futures contracts, foreign exchange, and debt instruments. The OTC interest rate option market is tremendous. Options on other assets can also be created. Companies acquire options to buy other companies. Real estate developers purchase options to buy land. A professional sports figure might negotiate a contract that gives his team an option to utilize his services in the last year of the contract at a specified salary; if the team decides not to exercise the option, it pays the ballplayer a small amount, thereby freeing him to offer his skills to any other team. A **warranty** is an option to return the good to the manufacturer of the item or the store in which it was purchased.

A call option's price, frequently referred to as the option **premium**, will be denoted C. Frequently, time subscripts will be necessary for S, the underlying asset, and for C. The subscript 0 will be used in reference to "today." Thus, C_0 is today's call price, and S_0 is today's stock price. Two other time subscripts often used are T for the option's expiration date, and t for some general date between today and expiration.

Option contracts are created when a buyer and a seller (the seller is frequently referred to as the option **writer**) agree on a price. The buyer pays the premium to the seller. If the call owner can exercise the call, thereby calling away the underlying asset, the call writer must deliver it. In other words, the writer of a call has the obligation to sell the underlying asset to the call owner at the strike price, should the owner decide to exercise. The call writer then receives $\$K$ in exchange for the underlying asset.

The call writer might not own the underlying asset. In this case, the arrangement is referred to as a **naked call**. If the owner of a call exercises his option and if the exercise is assigned to a naked writer, the naked writer must buy the underlying asset at its prevailing market price, which will then allow him to sell the asset at the strike price to the exerciser of the call. When an individual writes a naked call, brokers will want a guarantee that the capital is available to buy the underlying asset if necessary. Margin requirements exist as a form of collateral to ensure that the writer of a naked option can fulfill the terms of the contract. The term **covered call** is applied when the underlying asset is owned when the call is sold.

Call buyers hope that the price of the underlying asset will increase in value. An investor profits if, say, he owns a call to buy 100 shares of IBM at a strike price of $120 per share and IBM rises from $120/share to $125/share soon after the purchase of the call. All else equal, an option to buy IBM at $120 is certainly more valuable when IBM is selling for $125 than when it sells for $120. Thus, all else equal, the call option increases in value as the price of IBM rises. The writer of the naked call hopes IBM shares will tumble or, at the very least, will not exceed their price level at the time the option was written, for under these circumstances the writer profits.

On any day, option owners may take one of three actions regarding their positions:

a. Do nothing.

b. Close out the position in the options market. Thus, one who owns a publicly traded option (i.e., is long the option) can sell it at the market price. Someone who has previously written an option can buy it back. A nontraded option can be effectively offset when its owner sells an option with terms equivalent to the one he owns.

c. The owner of an American option can exercise it. In this case, the call seller must deliver the underlying asset. The exerciser of the call then pays the strike price to an investor who earlier wrote the call, and was assigned the exercise.

If the call owner has done nothing by the close of trading on the call's expiration day, one of two things will happen

a. If the price of the underlying asset is less than the strike price, the call expires worthless. For example, if $K = 40$, and the expiration day stock price is $S_T = 37$, the call owner will not exercise the call; because if he did, he would have to pay $K = \$40$ to acquire the asset, but the asset price in the spot market is only $37/share. In this case, $C_T = 0$ and option exercise is irrational.

b. If the price of the underlying asset exceeds the strike price, then ignoring such "market imperfections" as transactions costs and taxes, the call owner would be irrational not to exercise. After all, the call owner has the right to pay K to buy something that is worth more than K. If the call owner has not closed the position or exercised it by the last trading day, his brokerage house may exercise the option for him. An investor must sign an "option agreement" before beginning to trade options, and such contracts normally spell out what the brokerage house will do if an investor fails to exercise an option when it would be rational to do so ($S_T > K$ for a call). Note that some brokerage houses demand that option owners provide notification that they intend to exercise **before** the close of trading on the last trading day.

14.2 PUT OPTIONS

The owner of an American put option has the right, but not the obligation, to sell something at a specified strike price, on or before a specified expiration date. A European put can be exercised only on its expiration date. As with call options, however, owners of traded put options can sell them before expiration.

The seller of a put has the obligation to take delivery of the underlying asset, should the put owner decide to exercise his option. The put seller must then pay K for the underlying asset. When a put contract is created, the put buyer pays the put premium to the put seller. If the price of the underlying asset rises above the strike price, and stays there, the put expires worthless. The put seller gets to keep the premium as a profit, and the put buyer suffers a loss.

Buying puts is a bearish strategy.[5] That is, put buyers believe that the price of the underlying asset will fall. The price of the underlying asset must fall below the strike price for the put to have value at expiration. Selling puts is a bullish strategy. Put sellers believe that the price of the underlying asset will be above the strike price at expiration.

14.3   IN THE MONEY, AT THE MONEY, OUT OF THE MONEY

At any time t, an option may be **in the money**, **at the money** or **out of the money**. A call is said to be in the money if the current stock price is greater than the strike price. A call is at the money when the stock price equals the strike price, and out of the money when the stock price is less than the strike price. If $S_t \gg K$ (the stock price is "much" higher than the strike price), the call is deep in the money, or way in the money. If $S_t \ll K$, the call is deep out of the money. If the stock price is close to K, the appropriate jargon is that it is near the money, at the money, just out of the money, or just in the money. The terms are reversed for puts. Thus, if the stock price is below the strike price, the put is in the money. If $S_t > K$, the put is out of the money.

Table 14.1 summarizes these terms.

14.4   INTRINSIC VALUE AND TIME VALUE

At all times before expiration, any option premium can be split into two parts: **intrinsic value** (sometimes called parity value) and **time value** (sometimes called premium over parity). The intrinsic value of a call is the amount the option is in the money, if it is in the money. If the call is at or out of the money, its intrinsic value is zero. Thus,

$$\text{intrinsic value of a call} = \begin{cases} S_t - K & \text{if } S_t > K \\ 0 & \text{if } S_t < K \end{cases}$$

Another way of denoting this is:

$$\text{intrinsic value of a call} = \max[0, S_t - K]$$

which is read: "The intrinsic value of a call is the greater of 0 or $S_t - K$."

The time value of a call is the difference between its premium and its intrinsic value. Therefore, a call that is out of the money or at the money has only time value. Usually, the maximum time value exists when the call (or put, for that matter) is at the money. A call that is in the money may or may not have time value. It will have no time value if $C_t = S_t - K$. An in-the-money call will have time value if $C_t > S_t - K$. The longer the time to expiration, the greater a call's time value, all

TABLE 14.1 In the Money, Out of the Money, and At the Money

	Calls	Puts
In the money	$S_t > K$	$S_t < K$
Out of the money	$S_t < K$	$S_t > K$
At the money	$S_t \cong K$	$S_t \cong K$

else equal.[6] At expiration, a call will have no time value and will sell for either 0 (if $S_T < K$), or $S_T - K$ (if it finishes in the money, in which case $S_T > K$).

Before expiration, the time value of a call is:

$$\text{time value of a call} = C_t - \left\{ \max\left[0,\ S_t - K\right] \right\}$$

Similar concepts exist for puts:

$$\text{intrinsic value of a put} = \begin{cases} K - S_t & \text{if } S_t < K \\ 0 & \text{if } S_t > K \end{cases}$$

That is, the intrinsic value of a put can be stated as $\max[0,\ K - S_t]$. The premium for a put consists only of time value if it is out of the money or at the money. If the put is in the money, it may or may not have time value:

$$\text{time value of a put} = P_t - \left\{ \max\left[0, K - S_t\right] \right\}$$

14.5 PAYOUT PROTECTION

Few, if any, traded options are protected against regular cash dividend distributions. Thus, suppose a stock trades ex-dividend.[7] The value of the stock should fall by about the amount of the dividend.[8] It is logical that the stock's value should fall by the ex-dividend amount. Consider this: on the day before the ex-date, the stock price should equal the per share value of all the firm's assets, after debt claims have been paid. On the ex-date, the firm's assets have changed: they have been reduced in value by the amount of the cash dividend. Thus a stock's price should fall by the ex-dividend amount on the ex-dividend day.[9]

Option contract terms are not affected by dividend payments or by announcements that the firm will make a future payment. This is what is meant by payout *un*protected. But, the stock price will nonetheless likely fall on the ex-date. Knowing that the firm will trade ex-dividend in the near future (before the option's expiration date) has the effect of making calls less valuable, and puts more valuable. Owning a call is a price appreciation strategy, and ex-dividend days usually result in price declines. However, owners of puts want the prices of the underlying assets to decline, and ex-dividend days therefore make puts more valuable, all else equal.

Listed option contract terms are, however, adjusted for stock distributions such as stock dividends and stock splits.[10] For a stock split that maintains round, hundred-share lots (e.g., a 2-for-1 or 3-for-1 split), the calls split, too. For example, suppose you own a call on a stock currently selling for $60/share; the strike price is $50. Now assume the stock splits 2 for 1. The stock price will fall to about $30, and you will own 2 calls with $25 strike prices. Each call will cover 100 shares of the post-split stock.

Option contract terms are adjusted in other ways when there are odd-sized splits (e.g., 3 for 2), or stock dividends (e.g., a 10% stock dividend). Most frequently, the strike price is adjusted, as are the number of shares underlying the contract. For example, consider the call with a $50 strike price. Now assume the stock has a 10% stock dividend. The call contract's terms will be adjusted to reduce the strike price by 10% to $45, and the contract will cover 110 shares of stock.

When a firm is merged into an existing firm, is taken over by another firm, or spins off a subsidiary firm, option terms will again be adjusted.

14.6   PRICING AT EXPIRATION

In our discussion of pricing at expiration, we will assume that there are no transactions costs of any kind. In other words, investors can buy and/or sell stock and options at a single price (there are no bid–ask spreads or price pressure caused by the trade), with no commissions, and they can do so instantaneously. Furthermore, we assume that investors can trade as many options as they want at the quoted price. In reality, markets are not like this, though the conditions are approached for some market participants.

14.6.1   Call Values at Expiration

If the stock price at expiration is less than or equal to the strike price, the call has finished out of the money and is worthless. This means that if $S_T \leq K$, then $C_T = 0$. No one would be willing to buy an option to buy something today at a (strike) price that exceeds the (market) price. If an out-of-the-money call did sell for a positive price at expiration (or one second prior to expiration), an investor could earn an arbitrage profit by selling it, and receiving the premium (a cash inflow). Then, assuming the option is not exercised (and no rational person should ever exercise out-of-the money options), the call writer keeps the premium. If a call owner irrationally exercised the out-of-the-money call, the call writer would buy the underlying asset for S_T and deliver it for K; since $S_T \leq K$, the call writer would receive yet another cash inflow. In other words, if $C_T > 0$ when $S_T \leq K$ an investor could have a positive cash flow by writing the call and a nonnegative cash flow an instant later. This is arbitrage, which should not exist in well-functioning markets.

If the option finishes in the money, it will be worth its intrinsic value. For a call,

$$C_T = \begin{cases} S_T - K & \text{if } S_T > K \\ 0 & \text{if } S_T \leq K \end{cases}$$

That is, $C_T = \max [0, S_T - K]$, which says that C_T is the greater of 0 and $S_T - K$.

We can prove that an in-the-money call must sell for exactly $S_T - K$ at expiration. In the remainder of this book, several proofs of propositions will be made. The method of proof will almost always be the same. First we will ask: "What if the proposition is violated?" If it is violated, we can create an inequality in the form $A > 0$. The trades implied by A will then be made, leading to a cash inflow. An "arbitrage table" will then be constructed to demonstrate that there is a cash inflow on at least one date, and positive or zero cash flows at all other dates.

So, suppose $C_T < S_T - K$?

Then, $C_T - S_T + K < 0$.

This means that $-C_T + S_T - K > 0$. Note that this is an inequality in the form $A > 0$, where $-C_T + S_T - K$ is expression A. Table 14.2a presents an arbitrage table that proves the proposition.

TABLE 14.2a   Arbitrage Table for $-C_T + S_T - K > 0$

Transaction Today	Cash Flow
Buy call	$-C_T$
Exercise call to acquire stock	$-K$
Sell stock	$+S_T$
	>0

EXAMPLE 14.1   Suppose that a call with a strike price of $K=40$ is selling for $C_T=$ 3 3/4 at expiration, when the stock is selling for $S_T=44$. To arbitrage, an individual could buy the call on 100 shares of stock for $375. Then he will exercise the call, and acquire the 100 shares of stock for $4000. Finally, he will sell the shares in the spot market for $4400. The arbitrage profit is $25.

EXAMPLE 14.2   Suppose that $C_T=4\,1/8$ when $S_T=44$ and $K=40$. An arbitrageur can sell the call on 100 shares of the stock, thereby receiving $412.50, and buy the stock for $4400. When the in-the-money call is exercised, he delivers the shares and receives $4000. The arbitrage profit is $12.50.

You can see that the strategy of purchasing a call, exercising it immediately to acquire the stock, and then selling the stock generates a positive cash flow at no risk. This is an example of arbitrage.

To finish the proof that $C_T=S_T-K$ if $S_T>K$, ask:

What if $C_T>S_T-K$?

Then, $C_T-S_T+K>0$.

Table 14.2b summarizes the arbitrage transactions that an investor can undertake to exploit this mispricing.

TABLE 14.2b   Arbitrage Table for $C_T-S_T+K>0$

Transaction Today	Cash Flow
Sell call	$+C_T$
Buy stock	$-S_T$
Deliver stock (if exercised, as it should be, if it is in the money)	$+K$
	>0

Example 14.2 illustrates how an arbitrage profit can be realized if $C_T>S_T-K$.

The pricing of a call at expiration can be summarized in a simple diagram. The value of a call at expiration is a function only of the price of the stock on that date, relative to the strike price. Figure 14.1 shows that if $S_T<K$, the call has finished out of the money and is worthless. This is the horizontal line segment at $C_T=0$, to the left of K. If the stock price at expiration exceeds the strike price, the call is worth the difference between the two, or $C_T=S_T-K$. This is shown as the diagonal line that rises from $S_T=K$ at a 45° angle.

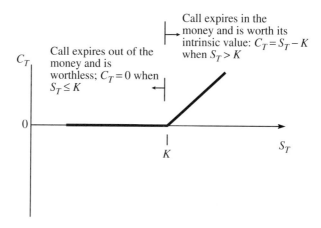

Figure 14.1 Call value at expiration.

14.6.2   Put Values at Expiration

If the put finishes out of the money, the put is worthless because $S_T > K$. To prove this, ask: What would an investor do if $S_T > K$ and $P_T > 0$? He would sell the put just before expiration, and receive the premium. This is a cash inflow. A rational put owner would never exercise an out-of-the-money put. To do so would mean selling something to a put writer for $\$K$ when it could have been sold for a higher price in the market for $\$S_T$. Even if an irrational owner did exercise, the investor who sold the out-of-the-money put at expiration would profit even more, because he would pay $\$K$ for the asset and immediately resell it for the higher price, $\$S_T$.

A put that finishes in the money must sell for $K - S_T$. To prove this, first ask:

What if $P_T > K - S_T$?
Then, $P_T - K + S_T > 0$.

Table 14.3a is the arbitrage table that shows the steps that would provide an arbitrage profit.

Suppose $P_T < K - S_T$?
Then, $P_T - K + S_T < 0$, or $-P_T + K - S_T > 0$.

Table 14.3b presents the arbitrage table for the situation in which $P_T < K - S_T$ exists.

Figure 14.2 depicts the expiration day pricing of puts. If $S_T > K$, the put finishes out of the money and is worth zero. If the stock price closes below $\$K$ per share, the put has an intrinsic value of

TABLE 14.3a   Arbitrage Table for $P_T - K + S_T > 0$

Transaction Today	Cash Flow
Sell put	$+P_T$
The put will be exercised, acquire stock	$-K$
Sell stock	$+S_T$
	>0

TABLE 14.3b Arbitrage Table for $P_T - K + S_T < 0$

Transaction Today	Cash Flow
Buy put	$-P_T$
Buy stock	$-S_T$
Exercise put	$+K$
	>0

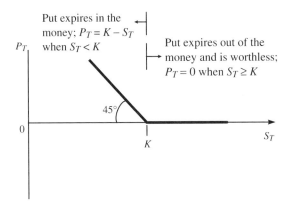

Figure 14.2 Put value at expiration.

$P_T = K - S_T$, and this is shown as the diagonal line with a slope of -1 that originates on the x axis at K. The highest value a put can attain occurs if $S_T = 0$, in which case the put is worth $\$K$ at expiration. Summarizing, we write

$$P_T = \begin{cases} K - S_T & \text{if } S_T < K \\ 0 & \text{if } S_T \geq K \end{cases}$$

Stated another way, P_T is the greater of 0 and $K - S_T$, or $P_T = \max[0, K - S_T]$.

14.7 A BRIEF LOOK AT OPTION PRICING BEFORE EXPIRATION

14.7.1 Calls

Before expiration, calls will *usually* sell for at least their intrinsic value.[11] That is, before expiration, calls may or may not have time value. Each curve in Figure 14.3a illustrates how C_t is a function of S_t for different times to expiration. A call that has several months until expiration might sell according to curve a in Figure 14.3a. Given the strike price that is indicated K, and any stock price at a time $t1$ months prior to maturity, S_{t1}, curve a shows how a typical call would be valued as a function of the stock price. As time passes, so that there are $t2$ months until maturity, with $t2 < t1$, the pricing curve gradually moves to a position depicted as curve b. As more time passes, the pricing curve moves toward curve c. At expiration, curve c is the pricing curve, the same as depicted in Figure 14.1.

Consider Figure 14.3b. In this example, the call has a strike of 40, and curve *a* prices a call with four months to maturity. If the stock price at that date is 35, the call might sell for $2.50 ($250 for a call on 100 shares). If the stock price suddenly jumped to $40 per share, the call might sell for $5 (all else equal). If the underlying stock sold for $45/share, the call might be worth $8.375. As time passes, the value of the call will decline, all else equal. Thus, if curve *b* is for one month to maturity, the call might be worth only $0.50, $2.375, and $6 at stock prices of $35, $40, and $45, respectively. Options are frequently termed "decaying," or "wasting" assets because they lose value as time passes, all else equal.[12]

Thus, we have alluded to three variables that contribute to a call's value prior to its expiration date: the stock price, the strike price, and the time to expiration (S_t, K, and T, respectively). There are at least three other variables that affect call values. They are the variance of the stock's distribution of returns (volatility), the interest rate, and the dividend amounts on any ex-dividend dates between the current date and the expiration date.[13]

The next step is to develop some intuition about whether call values should increase or decrease in the event of a change in any of these six variables, all else equal. Eventually a model will be introduced that will provide us with a theoretical value of an option: the Black–Scholes

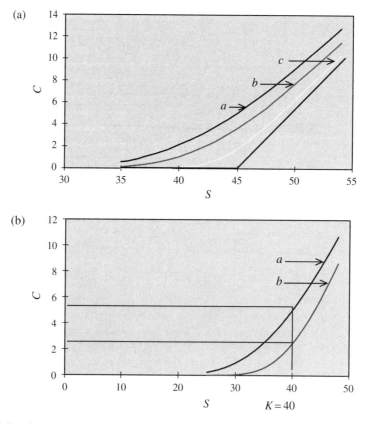

Figure 14.3 Call option values are a function of the stock price and the time to expiration. The call depicted by curve *a* has the longest time to expiration. Curve *c* has no time to expiration. In Figure 14.3b, The at-the-money call decays in value from $5 to $2.375 as three months pass.

option pricing model. This model is a tool that can more precisely predict how option values will change, given a small change in any one of the parameters of the model, and holding all other parameters equal. Those familiar with differential calculus will recognize that we are referring to "partial derivatives."

Based on earlier discussion, we predict that a European call's value will be higher when:

a. The strike price K is lower.

b. The stock price S is higher.

c. The time to expiration T is longer (assuming no dividends).

Statement *a* is intuitive because an investor would like to pay as little as possible for the underlying asset, should he exercise the call. Statement **b** is true because the higher the stock price, the more valuable the right to acquire it at a fixed price, K. Finally, statement **c** ought to be intuitive: Would you rather have the right to acquire something during the next month or during the next year? A call option with a longer life provides more time to realize the favorable outcomes that lead to profits for the call owner.

For the other three important determinants of call values, we predict that a call's value will be higher when:

d. The volatility σ of the underlying asset is higher.

e. The level of interest rates r is higher.

f. The dollar dividends to be paid on ex-dividend dates prior to expiration are smaller.

Mathematically, these relations are denoted as follows for European call options:

$$\frac{\partial C}{\partial K} < 0, \quad \frac{\partial C}{\partial S} > 0, \quad \frac{\partial C}{\partial T} > 0, \quad \frac{\partial C}{\partial \sigma} > 0, \quad \frac{\partial C}{\partial r} > 0, \quad \text{and} \quad \frac{\partial C}{\partial \text{div}} < 0$$

The partial derivative notation denotes how a call's value changes when one of its determinants changes by a small amount, all else equal. For example the notation $\partial C/\partial S > 0$ means that when the price of a stock rises a small amount, the value of a call on the stock is predicted to rise, with all else (K, T, σ, r, div) held unchanged. These partial derivatives are widely used by options traders, and some have been named. For example $\partial C/\partial S$ is a call's **delta**, and $\partial C/\partial T$ is a call's **theta**.

We understand intuitively that calls increase in value when the volatility of the underlying asset increases because if the variance of possible future stock prices increases, the call owner will likely benefit if the stock happens to increase by a large amount. It is true that if the variance increases, there is also a greater probability of a price decline. But call owners do not care how much the call is out of the money at expiration. The call is worthless at expiration if S_T is just one-eighth of a point below K, or 8 points or more below K. Call owners profit from the wider range of expiration day stock prices above K, but do not lose from the wider range of possible stock price declines below K. Hence, calls are worth more when the variance of returns for the underlying asset is greater.

Concerning the increase in call values as interest rates rise, consider the purchase of a call as a substitute for actually buying the underlying asset. We will soon see that calls will always sell for less than the underlying asset itself. Thus an investor can buy the stock, or buy a call for a fraction of the stock's price and invest the remainder in riskless interest-bearing assets (e.g., Treasury bills). The higher the level of interest rates, the more the latter alternative will be preferred, since more can be earned on the investment in T-bills. Thus, calls are worth more as interest rates rise, all else equal.

There is another intuitive explanation for the sign of $\partial C/\partial r$ that will become clearer when the binomial option pricing model and the Black–Scholes option pricing model are discussed. We will see that under certain assumptions, if an investor buys a fraction X $(0 \leq X \leq 1)$ of a share of stock and sells 1 call, he will have created a riskless position that will earn the riskless rate of return. This portfolio will provide the same payoff no matter what comes to pass at the next date. All else equal, if interest rates rise, a higher riskless rate of return must be earned on the portfolio. This can occur only with a higher call price, which will lower the initial investment in the stock plus written call portfolio. Thus, if interest rates rise, call values must rise.

Finally, we have already discussed how stock prices fall on ex-dividend days. Thus, the greater the dividend amounts on ex-days prior to the expiration day of the call, the less calls will be worth.

14.7.2   Puts

The pricing of puts prior to expiration might follow the process depicted in Figure 14.4.[14] Curve a shows put values for a range of stock prices when there is a great deal of time until expiration. Curve b is for a shorter times to expiration, and d illustrates expiration day pricing of puts. The situation represented by curve d corresponds to Figure 14.2. The slope of each curve ranges from almost 0 at the far right (deep out-of-the-money puts) to -1.0 at the far left (deep-in-the-money puts).

It should be intuitive that put values increase as the strike price increases, and as the price of the underlying asset declines. Puts are more valuable the more cheaply the owner can purchase the underlying stock, and also put the shares to someone at a higher strike price.

The influence of time passage on put prices, all else equal, is not so intuitive, though. If there is more time to expiration, then there is a greater range of possible stock prices that can exist at expiration.[15] This works to increase put values. However, the purchase of a put is also a substitute for selling the stock. If an investor sells the stock today, the proceeds are received today. If, instead, a put is purchased, the proceeds from the stock sale are not received until the put has been exercised, possibly as late as the expiration date. All else equal, an investor would rather have the proceeds today than at the later expiration date. The longer the time to expiration, the less valuable is the receipt of the proceeds from the put's exercise. In other words, the present value of $\$K$ is

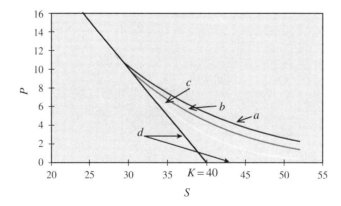

Figure 14.4 Put pricing prior to expiration. Curve a is for a put with a long time to expiration. The time to expiration for put option b is shorter than that of a. The option of curve d has no time to expiration.

less, the longer the time to expiration. Thus, the value of the put is less, when viewed as a substitute for selling the stock today. In sum, these two competing influences (the greater range of possible stock prices vs the delayed receipt of the K proceeds) make for an indeterminate prediction for how puts change in value as time passes.[16]

Greater volatility of the underlying asset increases the value of a put. A greater range of future stock prices increases the chance of high payoffs. The effect becomes less important, however, as the price of the underlying asset declines. At very low stock prices, there is not much range for further price declines. Thus, the impact of volatility on put prices declines as the price of the underlying asset declines.

The same argument about the timing of the receipt of K applies to the prediction that as interest rates rise, put values decline, all else equal. The purchase of a put is a substitute for the sale of the stock. An investor gets the proceeds from the cash sale of the stock immediately but must wait to receive the K until exercising the put. At high interest rates, an investor would rather sell the stock today to be able to get the use of the proceeds today, rather than wait to get the strike price at expiration; holding onto in-the-money puts thus becomes less attractive at high interest rates.

Finally, because stock prices decline on ex-dividend days, and put owners profit from such stock declines, the greater the dividend amounts on ex-days prior to expiration, the higher are put values.

In the partial derivative notation, for European put options we have:

$$\frac{\partial P}{\partial K} > 0, \quad \frac{\partial P}{\partial S} < 0, \quad \frac{\partial P}{\partial T} \begin{smallmatrix}>\\<\end{smallmatrix} 0, \quad \frac{\partial P}{\partial \sigma} > 0, \quad \frac{\partial P}{\partial r} < 0, \quad \text{and} \quad \frac{\partial P}{\partial \text{div}} > 0$$

The partial derivative $\partial P/\partial S$ is a put's delta, and $\partial P/\partial T$ is called its theta. We cannot predict how European put values will change as time passes, all else equal. Therefore, the sign of theta for European puts is indeterminate $((\partial P/\partial T)(>/<)0)$. However, American put values cannot rise in value as time passes. Thus, for American puts, $\partial P/\partial T \geq 0$.

14.8   STOCK OPTIONS MARKETS

Listed stock options on stocks may trade on one or more of five exchanges: the Chicago Board Options Exchange (CBOE), the American Stock Exchange (AMEX), the Philadelphia Stock Exchange, the Pacific Stock Exchange, and the New York Stock Exchange. To be approved for option trading, a stock must meet specific requirements. As of 1997, the firm-specific factors that determined eligibility for trading as an underlying security to an option included:

- At least 7 million shares in the public's hands.
- At least 2000 stock owners.
- At least 2.4 million shares traded in the last 12 months.
- A closing stock price of at least $7.50/share on a majority of trading days during the last three months.
- The company must be in compliance with the rules for making timely reports as required by the Securities and Exchange Act of 1934.
- The company must not have defaulted on any interest payments, sinking fund payments, preferred stock dividends, or lease payments during the past 12 months.

An exchange can decide to discontinue trading in an option for failing to meet a set of requirements similar to the foregoing, or for any other reason, in which case trading will continue in existing options, but no new expiration dates will be introduced. If a company's stock ceases to trade—because of a merger, for example—trading in its options will cease.

The addresses of the major U.S. options exchanges are given in Table 14.4. The exchanges usually offer (free or for a small charge) books, pamphlets, courses, and videos on options and options trading. If you have never traded options before and are thinking about starting, you should contact the exchanges for the information they offer.

14.8.1 Strike Prices for Listed Stock Options

Each exchange selects option strike prices on a particular underlying stock. Typically, strikes just above and below the current market price of the stock are opened for trading. If the stock price moves above the highest strike price, the exchange will open a new series of options for all expiration months with a strike just above the previously existing highest strike. The same holds for movements below the lowest strike. For example, suppose a stock is selling for $42/share. The exchange will open for trading options with 40 and 45 strikes. If the stock were to decline below $40/share, options with a 35 strike would likely open for trading. Most strike prices are $5 apart, though low-priced stocks that sell for less than $25/share and stocks with little price volatility may have strikes just $2.50 apart, and high-priced stocks that sell for more than $200/share will have strikes $10 apart.

TABLE 14.4 Major U.S. Options Exchanges

1. Chicago Board Options Exchange
   400 South LaSalle Street
   Chicago, IL 60605
   800-OPTIONS
   www.cboe.com

2. New York Stock Exchange
   Options and Index Products
   20 Broad Street
   New York, NY 10005
   800-692-6973
   www.nyse.com

3. American Stock Exchange
   86 Trinity Place
   New York, NY 10006
   800-THE-AMEX
   www.amex.com

4. Pacific Stock Exchange
   301 Pine Street
   San Francisco, CA 94104
   415-393-4000
   800-TALK-PSE (recorded messages)
   www.pacificex.com

5. Philadelphia Stock Exchange
   1900 Market Street
   Philadelphia, PA 19103
   800-THE-PHLX
   www.phlx.com

14.8.2 Expiration Dates for Listed Stock Options

Each listed stock option falls into one of three cycles that determines what expiration months are available for trading. Basically, expiration dates exist for the most nearby two months, plus two more distant months, depending on which of the three "cycles" (January, February, or March) a stock falls into. Table 14.5 illustrates how the cycles work. For example, consider the February cycle. From the Monday after the third Friday in December until the third Friday in January,

TABLE 14.5 The Expiration Months Are Available for Trading. Each Traded Option Falls into One of These Three Cycles

I. January Cycle

From the Monday After the Third Friday in	Until the Third Friday in	Available Months			
January	February	Feb	*Mar*	Apr	Jul
February	March	Mar	Apr	Jul	Oct
March	April	Apr	*May*	Jul	Oct
April	May	May	*Jun*	Jul	Oct
May	June	Jun	Jul	Oct	*Jan*
June	July	Jul	*Aug*	Oct	Jan
July	August	Aug	*Sep*	Oct	Jan
August	September	Sep	Oct	Jan	*Apr*
September	October	Oct	*Nov*	Jan	Apr
October	November	Nov	*Dec*	Jan	Apr
November	December	Dec	Jan	Apr	*Jul*
December	January	Jan	*Feb*	Apr	Jul

II. February Cycle

From the Monday After the Third Friday in	Until the Third Friday in	Available Months			
January	February	Feb	*Mar*	May	Aug
February	March	Mar	*Apr*	May	Aug
March	April	Apr	May	Aug	*Nov*
April	May	May	*Jun*	Aug	Nov
May	June	Jun	*Jul*	Aug	Nov
June	July	Jul	Aug	Nov	*Feb*
July	August	Aug	*Sep*	Nov	Feb
August	September	Sep	*Oct*	Nov	Feb
September	October	Oct	Nov	Feb	*May*
October	November	Nov	*Dec*	Feb	May
November	December	Dec	*Jan*	Feb	May
December	January	Jan	Feb	May	*Aug*

TABLE 14.5   Continued

III. March Cycle

From the Monday After the Third Friday in	Until the Third Friday in	Available Months			
January	February	Feb	Mar	Jun	*Sep*
February	March	Mar	*Apr*	Jun	Sep
March	April	Apr	*May*	Jun	Sep
April	May	May	Jun	Sep	*Dec*
May	June	Jun	*Jul*	Sep	Dec
June	July	Jul	*Aug*	Sep	Dec
July	August	Aug	Sep	Dec	*Mar*
August	September	Sep	*Oct*	Dec	Mar
September	October	Oct	*Nov*	Dec	Mar
October	November	Nov	Dec	Mar	*Jun*
November	December	Dec	*Jan*	Mar	Jun
December	January	Jan	*Feb*	Mar	Jun

a stock in the February cycle had options expiring in January, February, May, and August. The August options were introduced on the Monday after the third Friday in December, which is why *Aug* is in bold italic type. On the third Friday of January, the options expiring in January cease trading. On the Monday following the third Friday of January, options that expire in March are introduced, so from that date until the third Friday in February, options expiring in February, March, May, and August trade.

The system provides that each stock has options trading that expire in the two nearby months, and also in two more distant months. The maximum expiration date possible is always eight months away.[17] Generally, the greatest liquidity is in the two nearby months.

14.8.3   Market Makers

If you wished to buy or sell an option in a world without market makers, you would have to wait for another party to contact you about taking the opposite position. This could take a long time, and might involve a lot of effort on your part.

Each exchange, however, has one or more market makers who must always stand ready to trade by quoting a bid price and an ask price. Whenever you wish to sell, you can be sure there will be a price at which a market maker is willing to buy the option (the bid price). Whenever you wish to buy options, the market maker will quote an ask price (i.e., the price at which he will sell them to you). The Chicago Board Options Exchange and the Pacific Stock Exchange have competing market makers. The American, Philadelphia, and New York Stock Exchanges use a specialist system of market making. The specialist is given the franchise of market making at these exchanges, though other competition exists for specialists.

Market makers quote bid and ask prices. The **bid** is the price at which the market maker is willing to buy the option. The **ask** is the price at which he will sell the option. The ask price always exceeds the bid price. The minimum spread between the bid and asked quotes is $0.05 for options selling for less than $3 and $0.10 for options trading for more than $3. Actively traded options will have spreads at these minima. If the option is thinly traded, i.e., low volume, the bid–ask spread will be wider. Market makers are expected to maintain fair and orderly markets. To do so, they are expected to keep bid–ask spreads narrow. The individual exchanges specify maximum spreads for options. For example, as of December 2001, the maximum quote spreads for CBOE options were: $0.25 if the option's bid quote was priced at $1.99 or less, $0.40 if the option was priced between $2.00 and $4.99, $0.50 if the option was priced between $5.00 and $9.99, $0.80 for options selling between $10.00 and $19.99, and $1 ($100 for an option on 100 shares of stock) if the last trade of the option equaled or exceeded $20. These guidelines are not binding in any way, though other exchange members grade market makers on their abilities and ethics. Those who perform poorly can be penalized. The guidelines are not applicable to the series of options with the longest time to expiration, and they do not apply if the price of the underlying asset is rapidly changing (this is termed a "fast market") or if market conditions are "unusual."

Market orders are orders placed by investors who wish to trade immediately. Thus, if an investor places a market order to buy an option, he will usually pay the ask price. An investor placing a market order to sell an option will usually receive the bid price.

The bid–ask spread is the cost of immediacy for investors who want to trade quickly. The market maker, who "makes a market" by always being available to trade, generally earns profits by buying at the bid price and selling at the ask price. Investors themselves compete against market makers when they place **limit orders**, which are orders to buy or sell at a specified price. If the existing spread is 3 bid to 3.40 asked, an investor can place a limit order to sell between the spread, say at a price of 3.30. If no trader on the floor wishes to buy the option at that price at that time, the order is entered into a book of unfilled limit orders, and the prevailing bid–ask spread becomes 3 to 3.30 (the investor's order to sell). The investor's order has supplied competition, and the spread has been narrowed.

14.8.4   The Role of the Options Clearing Corporation

Options are created when a buyer and a seller agree on a price. Once a trade has been made, however, the Options Clearing Corporation (OCC) steps in and becomes a party to both sides of the trade. In other words, the option buyer purchases the option from the OCC, and the seller sells the option to the OCC. In this way, each investor is free from the worry that the other party will default on the contractual obligations. Each option investor simply looks to the OCC. The OCC itself is an agency consisting of brokerage firms called "clearing members." To guarantee the performance of all trades, the OCC has capital contributed by clearing members. If existing capital were to prove insufficient, the OCC could draw additional funds from its members, thus ensuring the integrity of the options markets.

When an option holder exercises an option, the broker contacts the OCC. Before the opening of trading on the next business day, the OCC will randomly assign the exercise to a clearing member that has a customer who is short that option. Then, the clearing firm either randomly assigns the exercise to one of its customers or assigns the option on a "first-in, first-out" basis.[18] All brokerage firms are required to inform customers which method is used. An investor should realize that an option assignment notice might arrive several days after assignment. Thus, option traders with short option positions that might be assigned should stay in contact with their brokers.

14.9 READING OPTIONS PRICES IN THE FINANCIAL PRESS

Figure 14.5 presents stock options' price data from the *Wall Street Journal* of May 10, 2001. Note that these are options on 100 shares of individual stocks. These options expire on the Saturday following the third Friday of the expiration month.

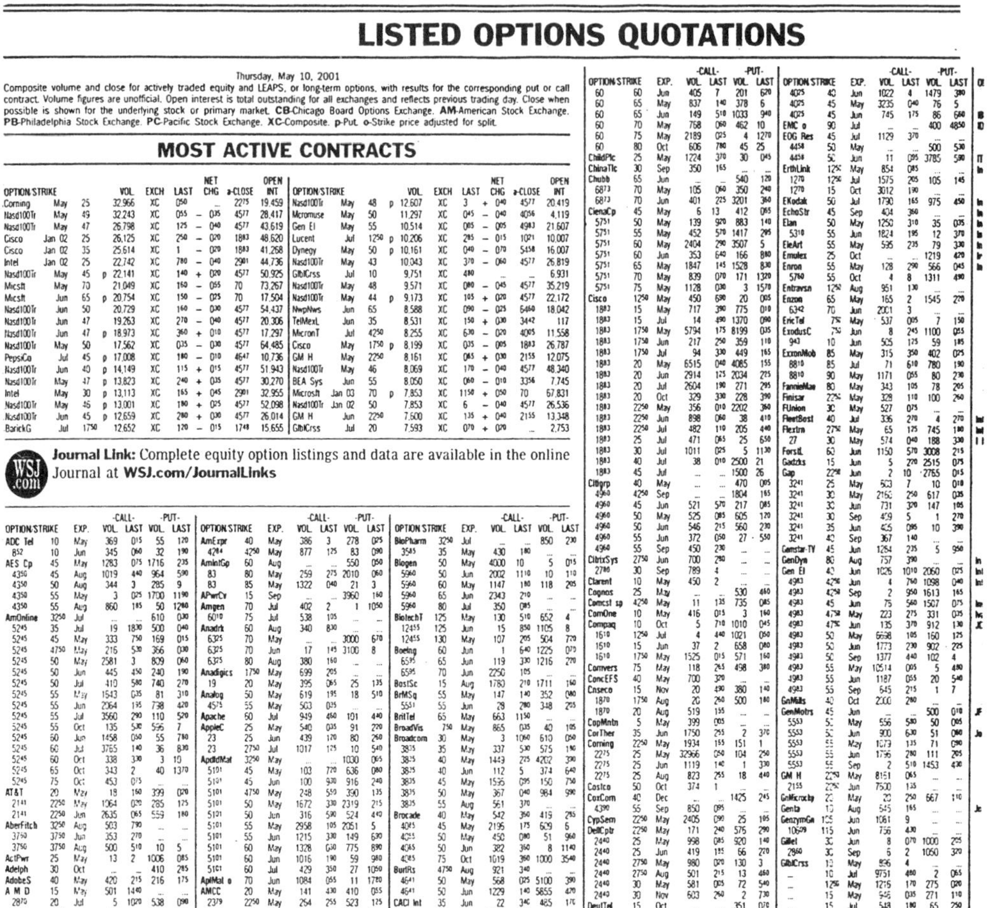

Figure 14.5 Some listed option quotations as presented in *The Wall Street Journal*. *Source:* (Reprinted with permission from *The Wall Street Journal*. © May 10, 2001.)

The first column gives the name of the company and its closing stock price. If options data for only one strike price are presented, no closing stock price is listed. For example, locate the entries for ActPwr and Apache. Note that the stock prices on this option page might not equal the prices given on the pages with the closing stock prices. This is because closing stock prices are "composite closing prices." After trading in equities in New York ceases, there may be additional trades on other exchanges such as the Pacific Stock Exchange, trades handled by "over-the-counter" market makers such as large brokerage houses, or on one of several new aftermarket electronic markets. The stock prices given on the options page are the closing prices on each stock's primary exchange (usually the NYSE).

The next column presents the strike prices. For Cisco Systems (Cisco), data on options with nine different strikes are presented: 12.50, 15, 17.50, 20, 22.50, 25, 30, 40, and 45. Following the strike column is a column containing the expiration month. Then, there are two columns with the volume and last trade price for calls, and two columns with volume and last trade price for puts. For example, July 20 calls on Cisco last traded at 1.90 (that is $190 on a call option covering 100 shares of Cisco), and 2604 of these calls traded on May 10, 2001. July 20 puts on Cisco last traded at 2.95, and 271 of these puts traded on May 10.

The *Wall Street Journal* provides data only for the most actively traded options. Data on all option prices can be obtained from a stockbroker, or from Internet sites such as www.cboe.com.

The exchanges introduce only "around the money" options when a new expiration month begins. Thus, at some time in the recent past, Cisco's common stock price was as low as about 14 (so that the 12.50 strikes were introduced) and as high as 41 (so that the 45 strikes commenced trading). The constitution of each exchange provides the guidelines for the procedure of introducing new option strike prices and expiration dates. The constitutions are available from the Commerce Clearing House in Chicago, or by visiting the websites of the options exchanges (e.g., www.cboe.com).

Two comments must be made about the "reliability" of the prices in Figure 14.5. The first involves the problem of nonsynchronous trading. The option prices shown are those of the last trade. However, we do not know the time of that trade. It may have been at any time between 8:30 A.M. and 3:02 P.M. (Central Standard Time), which are the times during which CBOE options on individual equities trade (index options on the CBOE trade until 3:15 P.M. Central Standard Time). Note that, from Figure 14.5, we do not know the price of the underlying stock at the time of the last option trade. We only know the closing stock price. Since most stocks are more actively traded than their options, it is likely that most option prices reflect information that existed earlier in the day than when the stock last traded.

The second problem concerns bid–ask spreads. We do not know whether any given price in Figure 14.5 was that of an investor's market buy order at the asked price or an investor's market sell order at the bid price, or a price within the bid–ask spread. Of course, owing to nonsynchronous trading, the actual bid–ask spread at the close of trading might be considerably different from the bid–ask spread that existed at the time of the last trade.

14.10   TRANSACTION COSTS

There are two primary types of transaction cost. One is termed **market impact**. Market impact consists of the bid–ask spread and price pressure. Placing market orders to buy a security will usually be filled at the ask price, while market orders to sell will be done at the bid price. The spread represents the cost of immediacy (the price an investor pays for an immediate trade). An investor can *try* to overcome this cost by placing a limit order, but at the risk of not having the order filled. The bid and asked prices quoted by market makers are good only for specified numbers of options. Price pressure occurs when an investor tries to trade a large number of options. For large trades, higher purchase prices and/or lower sale prices can result.

The other important transaction cost is the broker's commission. There is a range of commissions for options, much of which is determined by whether an investor deals with a discount broker or a full-service broker. In addition, trades entered electronically over the Internet usually have lower commissions than trades that involve a broker or phone representative. The options commission schedules of two discount brokers are shown in Tables 14.6 and 14.7. Even though both call themselves discounters, you can see that there is a substantial difference in their rates for inactive traders. The minimum commission on any options trade done through broker A and broker B is $25 and $36, respectively. But broker B's commissions for active traders are very competitive with those of A.

Full-service brokers such as Merrill Lynch and Morgan Stanley usually charge more than discount brokers. However, the investor receives personalized service for the higher commissions. An account executive is assigned to each investor and will discuss specific stock or option recommendations (which, generally speaking, are probably no better than any stocks or options you could randomly pick). In addition, a full-service broker will be able to provide more information about the security, planned and potential trades, and general market conditions. A good account executive will be able to minimize your trading costs after assessing your needs by determining your

TABLE 14.6 Price Schedule for Discount Broker A

Market order up to and including 30 contracts	$15 + $1.50 per contract
Market order over 30 contracts	$15 + $1.75 per contract
Limit orders	$15 + $1.75 per contract
All broker-assisted option orders	$25 + $1.75 per contract
Minimum commission: $25.00	

TABLE 14.7 Price Schedule for Discount Broker B

Transaction Amount	Commission Rate
$0–$2500	$28.75 + 1.60% of principal
$2501–$10,000	$48.75 + .80% of principal
>$10,000	$98.75 + .30% of principal

Minimum: $34.25 plus $1.75 per contract (a minimum of $36, but not to exceed maximum charge).

Maximum: $36 per contract for the first two contracts, plus $4 per contract thereafter; or half the principal amount (whichever is less).

There is a 25% discount to the amounts above for electronically placed orders.

Accounts that trade stocks, bonds, or options 36 or more times in a rolling 12-month period face a minimum commission of $27, or the following:

Trades electronically placed	$20 + $1.75 per contract
Trades placed via a phone representative	$35 + $1.75 per contract

level of risk aversion and your need for current income versus your need to invest for retirement. A good broker will call you when important news has been released. He or she may warn you about the likelihood of being assigned an option in the near future, or about the advisability of exercising or selling a given option. Full-service brokers may also offer a wider range of products than discounters. Unfortunately, many full-service account executives also make their living from your trading costs, which can cause a conflict of interest. In contrast, discounters such as broker A are little more than order intermediaries. Deep-discount brokers will give you some price information, take orders, and pass them on to their floor representatives at the appropriate exchanges.

14.11 MARGIN

The practice of borrowing money from a broker to buy securities is known as "buying on margin." Investors can buy most securities on margin. If the Federal Reserve Board sets the initial margin requirement at $x\%$, then an investor must put up at least $x\%$ of the purchase price in cash and can borrow at most $(1-x)\%$ from the broker. Currently, the initial margin on stock purchases is 50%.

An investor must have at least $2000 to open a margin account. Thus, with **initial margin** at 50%, an investor can buy as much as $4000 worth of stock with that money (ignoring brokerage fees).

Exchanges and brokers also set **maintenance margin** requirements, which become effective after the securities have been purchased. The maintenance margin requirement fixes the point at which the investor receives a margin call. If the value of the collateral for the loan has declined, a **margin call** commands the investor to deposit additional cash or securities into the account. That is, suppose the maintenance margin requirement is $z\%$. Then, if an investor's equity position falls to $z\%$ of the current market value of the account, the investor must place additional cash and/or securities into the account to increase the account balance to the initial margin level.

Buying on margin allows an investor to create leverage. That is, if an investment does well, higher rates of return will be earned. In Example 14.3, if the stock price increases to $60/share,

EXAMPLE 14.3 Suppose that the initial margin requirement is 60%, and the maintenance margin requirement is 25%. An investor can buy $10,000 worth of stock with $6000 of his own money and borrow $4000 from his broker. Assume the purchase is for 200 shares of a stock selling for $50/share, and ignore all commissions. Suppose the stock price declines to $26.625/share, so that the total value of the stock in the account is $5325. The investor's equity in the account is reduced to $1325. That is, if the investor sold the 200 shares, he would receive $1325 after repaying his loan. Thus, the investor's margin now is only ($1325/$5325=) 24.88%. The investor would have to deposit additional cash and/or securities to increase the account balance. If the investor does not act quickly, the broker will sell shares to ensure repayment of the margin loan. Note that for simplicity in this example, the interest on the loan has been ignored. The effect of accrued interest is that the investor would have received the margin call at a stock price higher than $26.625.

which is a 20% increase in price, the investor earns a 33.33% rate of return on the $6000 investment (again ignoring commissions and the repayment of interest). However, leverage is a double-edged sword. If the margin requirement is 60%, then any $x\%$ decline in the stock's price will result in a loss of $x/0.6\%$. If the stock in Example 14.3 declined 20% to $40/share, an investor who purchased the stock on margin will have lost 33.33% on his $6000 investment.

Option purchases are already levered positions. As such, the Federal Reserve's Regulation T states that all options purchases must be for cash only. Investors cannot borrow from brokers to purchase options. At times, however, investors must post margin to maintain an option position—for example, when an investor sells an option but does not have a position in the underlying shares. This practice is known as "selling naked options."

The sale of naked options is risky. Losses are theoretically unlimited on written naked calls, and a writer of naked puts is obligated to pay the strike price (K) for the purchase of the stock, should a put owner exercise it. Brokers, the exchanges, and the Fed want assurance that writers of naked option will fulfill their obligations. Consequently, there are rather substantial margin requirements on written naked positions. Indeed, some brokers will not handle requests to write naked options at all, and others demand that clients have substantial equity in their accounts before allowing them to trade in this way.

At the CBOE, the initial margin required to write a naked call option on common stock was, as of 2001 (it is always subject to change):

$$\max\{C + 0.1S, \ C + 0.2S - (\max[0, K - S])\}$$

where C is the call premium, S is the price of 100 shares of the underlying stock, K is the strike price, and $\max[0, K - S]$ represents the amount, if any, by which the call is out of the money.

This formula says that the required margin is either (a) the market value of the call plus 10% of the market value of the stock or (b) the market value of the call plus 20% of the market value of the stock minus any out-of-the-money amount. The required margin is the greater of (a) and (b).

EXAMPLE 14.4   Suppose an investor writes one naked June 17.50 Cisco put for $1.10, when the stock is selling for $18.83/share (see price data in Figure 14.5). The margin required is:

$$\max\{110 + 0.1(1883), \ 110 + 0.2(1883) - 133\}$$

$$\max\{298.3, 353.6\} = \$353.60$$

While this might seem small relative to the funds involved in a trade of 100 shares of Cisco stock ($1883), keep in mind that this put has no intrinsic value. If price of Cisco remains above the put's strike price, the option will expire worthless. Even if a put is in the money, and the writer of a naked put is assigned the option, the writer can always then sell the assigned stock immediately,[19] and the realized loss will be only the put's intrinsic value. From the exchange's viewpoint, the margin amount protects the exchange from the risk that the put writer will default when assigned the stock. The amount at risk is only the put's intrinsic value.

Similarly, the CBOE initial margin requirement for writing naked puts on common stock is:

$$\max\{P+0.1S,\; P+0.2S-(\max[0,S-K])\}$$

where P is the put premium, S is the price of 100 shares of the underlying stock, K is the strike price, and $\max[0,S-K]$ represents the amount, if any, by which the put is out of the money.

Writers of naked options can use cash to satisfy the margin requirement, or they can use securities. However, the required market value of the securities differs, depending on the nature of the collateral. That is, the market value of Treasury securities or common stock used to meet initial margin requirements will almost certainly be greater than the \$353.60 in cash that is required to write the Cisco put of Example 14.4.[20]

In one commonly used strategy, the **covered call**, an investor owns the stock, and sells a call. In this situation, margin is required on the stock position, but there is no margin required for the short call position. Indeed, the call premium received from the sale of the call can be used to reduce the margin required on the stock.

If the call is in the money, then the investor can borrow (i.e., by buying on margin) only 50% of the strike price, plus the premium received from the written call. In example 14.5, if $S=50$, $K=45$ and $C=6\,^{1}/_{2}$, the investor can borrow as much as $(0.5\times\$4500+\$650=)$ \$2900. This maximum borrowing amount is fixed as long as the call remains in the money.

Margin requirements can become quite complex when more complex strategies, such as those discussed in the next chapter, are used. Investors should consult their brokers to learn the rules for margin requirements if any of these strategies are used.

14.12 TAXES

What follows describes some of the basic tax rules for option positions. Most option profits are taxed as ordinary income. Therefore, depending on the option trader's income, the marginal tax rate on option profits is 15, 28, 31, 36, or 39.8%. Tax laws frequently change, however, and they can be quite complex for some types of transaction. Thus, an option trader should consult a recent tax guide, a tax accountant, or a tax attorney before doing his taxes.

Rule 1. Open and then close (at a subsequent date) a position of options on common stock. When the position is closed, there is a capital gain or a capital loss. The option trader must pay taxes on any gain (less commissions) at his marginal tax rate in the year the position is closed.

Total capital losses of less than \$3000 in one year will lower your taxable income for that year. In Example 14.6, if you sold the put for \$300 in November 1999, and offset that trade by buying the put for \$425 in January 2000, there would be a net capital loss after commissions of

---

EXAMPLE 14.5 An investor buys 100 shares of a \$50 stock on margin and writes an at-the-money or out-of-the money call for \$212.50. Ignoring commissions, and assuming that the initial margin requirement is 50%, the investor is required to deposit $(0.5\times \$5000-\$212.50=)$ \$2287.50 to meet the initial margin requirement on the position.

($125 + $42 =) $167. Taxable income would be reduced by this amount. If your marginal tax rate is 28%, then your 2000 tax obligation would be reduced by $46.76 (0.28 × $167).

Total capital losses exceeding $3000 in one year can in some cases be carried back for three years, if they can be applied to gains made on the same types of security during those years. Otherwise, capital losses above $3000 must be carried forward to future years.

Rule 2. Open and close a position on index options or futures options. If the trades both occur during the same year, the loss or gain is taxed as just described. If the position is carried from one year to the next, the investor must "mark to market" on the last trading day of the year. Index options and futures options are referred to as "Section 1256 contracts," which means that they must be "marked to market" at the end of the year for tax purposes. Example 14.7 illustrates this rule.

Rule 3. Open a long position and then exercise your option. Alternatively, you may open a short position and later be assigned the option. The basis of the position taken in the underlying security is adjusted by the original option premium. Taxes are deferred until disposal of the underlying asset. Example 14.8 illustrates this rule.

EXAMPLE 14.6   You sell a naked put for $300 in November 2001 and offset the trade by buying the same put for $75 in January 2002. There is a capital gain of $225. Total commission on the two trades is $42, so the net capital gain is $183. If your marginal tax rate is 28%, then $51.24 is the tax due on the gain. This tax is payable on your 2002 tax return.

EXAMPLE 14.7   You buy an S&P 500 Index option call for $6.10 in December 2001. At the close of the last trading day of 2001, the call closes at 5. You realize a loss of $110 for tax purposes in 2001 [(5 − 6.10)100]. Your basis for the call purchase now becomes 5. If you subsequently sell the call for $6 in January 2002, you have a taxable profit of $100 in 2002.

EXAMPLE 14.8   You buy a call on 100 shares of stock for $300. You subsequently exercise the call and buy the stock for the aggregate strike price of $5000. For tax purposes, your purchase price of the stock is $5300 (plus all commissions). Tax effects are realized only when the stock is later sold. This can make for an effective tax strategy. Suppose you buy a December call in August. The stock price rises sharply between August and early December. If you sell the call in the first three weeks in December, you will realize a large taxable gain in the current year. Instead, you may wish to exercise the call and hold the acquired stock until January. By selling the stock in January, you will have postponed the taxes on the gain for a year. Of course, you will also bear price risk, since the price of the stock can change during December.

After reading Example 14.8, you might be asking, "Why not buy a put or sell a deep-in-the-money call (after exercising the original call) to lock in the gain, and then wait until the next year to offset all the positions?" This would remove much of the price risk that exists between the exercise date and the January selling date. However, this may or may not be allowable. Rather than discuss all the possible ways one can postpone paying taxes on gains and hasten the tax inflows because of losses, you are urged to investigate before you act.[21]

14.13   INDEX OPTIONS

Index options began trading in the United States on March 11, 1983. The first index option was the CBOE 100, which was later renamed the S&P 100. It is now also frequently called the OEX, which is its ticker symbol. By the end of 1983, options on different index traded not only on the CBOE but on the American, Philadelphia, and New York Stock Exchanges. Figure 14.6 shows how price data on index options are presented in the *Wall Street Journal*. Other index options currently exist, however there is insufficient volume for the financial press to provide price data.

The index option with the largest open interest is on the S&P 500 Index. Its ticker symbol, and common name, is SPX. Listed options on portfolios of stocks concentrated in certain sectors such as banking stocks, drug stocks, and Internet stocks, have been introduced, and trading information on some of these are also shown in Figure 14.6. The NYSE once tried to develop interest in an option on a portfolio of the NYSE stocks with the highest "beta"[22]. Every quarter, the NYSE ranked all listed stocks by their relative volatility (beta) and grouped the highest of them into a portfolio called the beta index. Thus, investors who wished to speculate by trading options on the riskiest stocks on the NYSE could do so. The option could also be expected to serve the hedging needs of certain investors holding portfolios of risky stocks. However, the option on the beta index was not a success and trading ceased at the end of 1987. In 1991 the CBOE introduced OEX LEAPS (**l**ong-term **e**quity **a**nticipation **s**ecurities), and SPX LEAPS. These instruments have times to expiration as long as three years. The strike prices and index values of these index LEAPS equal one-tenth of the levels of the S&P 100 and S&P 500 indexes. For example, if the S&P 500 Index is at 1300, the S&P 500 LEAP Index equals 130.0. Strike prices would be around 125, 130, and 135.

Index options offer investors an efficient way to speculate on the future direction of the stock market. Some investors possess better timing skills than stock selection skills. They may be correct in predicting when the stock market will rise but tend to buy stocks (or options on individual stocks) that underperform the market. Index options also offer a low cost way to effectively buy the market today when a large cash inflow, not currently available, is nevertheless anticipated. Index options can be used to hedge an existing portfolio against a systematic decline in equity values. Note that there are a few differences between index options and individual equity options, and they are discussed in the sections that follow.

14.13.1   Index Options Are Cash Settled

Listed index options do not permit the delivery of the underlying asset. It would be quite difficult and costly to accumulate each of several hundred stocks in their proper weights to make or take delivery. Instead, when index options are exercised, they are settled by a cash payment. The cash amount exchanged when a call is exercised equals the index value minus the strike price, times 100.

INDEX OPTIONS TRADING

Thursday, May 10, 2001

Volume, last, net change and open interest for all contracts. Volume figures are unofficial. Open interest reflects previous trading day. p-Put c-Call

RANGES FOR UNDERLYING INDEXES

Thursday, May 10, 2001

	High	Low	Close	Net Chg	From 12/31	% Chg
DJ Indus (DJX)	109.79	108.69	109.10	+ 0.43	+ 1.23	+ 1.1
DJ Trans (DTX)	290.88	286.53	289.98	+ 3.41	− 4.68	− 1.6
DJ Util (DUX)	384.89	381.27	383.52	− 0.22	− 28.64	− 6.9
S&P 100 (OEX)	658.85	651.10	651.42	− 0.72	− 35.03	− 5.1
S&P 500 -A.M.(SPX)	1268.14	1254.56	1255.18	− 0.36	− 65.10	− 4.9
CB-Tech (TXX)	651.14	627.68	627.75	− 8.83	− 55.37	− 8.1
CB-Mexico (MEX)	84.74	83.94	84.30	+ 0.32	− 2.95	− 3.4
CB-Lps Mex (VEX)	8.47	8.39	8.43	+ 0.03	− 0.29	− 3.3
MS Multintl (NFT)	748.16	739.48	739.68	− 2.90	− 34.51	− 4.5
GSTI Comp (GTC)	253.19	244.62	244.63	− 3.33	− 38.94	− 13.7
Nasdaq 100 (NDX)	1926.95	1838.02	1838.32	− 38.55	− 503.38	− 21.5
NYSE (NYA)	641.90	636.29	637.99	+ 1.70	− 18.88	− 2.9
Russell 2000 (RUT)	494.33	490.16	490.58	+ 0.42	+ 7.05	+ 1.5
Lps S&P 100 (OEX)	131.77	130.22	130.28	− 0.15	− 7.01	− 5.1
Lps S&P 500 (SPX)	126.81	125.46	125.52	− 0.03	− 6.51	− 4.9
Volatility (VIX)	27.57	26.71	27.24	− 0.58	− 2.99	− 9.9
S&P Midcap (MID)	516.48	511.22	511.82	+ 0.60	− 4.94	− 1.0
Major Mkt (XMI)	1082.61	1073.50	1075.15	+ 1.65	− 2.41	− 0.2
Eurotop 100 (EUR)	334.00	332.05	333.50	+ 1.75	− 19.75	− 5.6
HK Fltg (HKO)	262.19	262.19	262.19	+ 0.22	− 33.33	− 11.3
IW Internet (IIX)	211.91	202.79	203.04	− 3.00	− 76.56	− 27.4
AM-Mexico (MXY)	101.09	99.23	100.35	+ 1.08	+ 9.42	+ 10.4
Instbu'l -A.M.(XII)	693.18	684.89	685.13	− 1.43	− 51.18	− 7.0
Japan (JPN)			148.16	− 0.47	+ 3.74	+ 2.6
MS Cyclical (CYC)	552.36	544.07	551.53	+ 7.46	+ 40.35	+ 7.9
MS Consumr (CMR)	559.18	555.09	558.53	+ 3.44	− 55.38	− 9.0
MS Hi Tech (MSH)	615.26	590.46	590.58	− 11.44	− 77.64	− 11.6
MS Internet (MOX)	21.87	20.97	21.00	− 0.21	− 7.79	− 27.1
Pharma (DRG)	401.04	395.05	396.67	− 2.50	− 50.71	− 11.3
Biotech (BTK)	574.00	548.38	549.79	− 15.83	− 84.53	− 13.3
Gold/Silver (XAU)	59.99	58.14	59.50	+ 0.33	+ 8.09	+ 15.7
Utility (UTY)	371.52	368.30	370.84	+ 0.02	− 22.42	− 5.7
Value Line (VLE)	1240.51	1229.32	1231.60	+ 2.28	+ 106.83	+ 9.5
Bank (BKX)	887.85	878.50	881.62	+ 4.26	− 19.80	− 2.2
Semicond (SOX)	648.36	618.93	619.04	+ 0.20	− 42.43	− 7.4
Street.com (DOT)	277.92	267.22	267.69	− 1.73	− 32.94	− 11.0
Oil Service (OSX)	125.38	122.88	123.57	− 1.30	− 1.21	− 1.0
PSE Tech (PSE)	780.73	755.94	756.00	− 6.30	− 58.43	− 7.2

[The remainder of this page consists of dense columns of index options trading price data — reprinted from The Wall Street Journal — under the headings CHICAGO, AMERICAN, and individual index listings (DJ INDUS AVG (DJX), DJ TRANP AVG (DTX), DJ UTIL AVG (DUX), GC TECH COMPOSITE (GTC), NASDAQ-MINI (MXNI), NASDAQ-100 (NDX), S & P 100 (OEX), RUSSELL 2000 (RUT), S & P 500 (SPX), INTERNET (IIX), JAPAN INDEX (JPN), MAJOR MARKET (XMI), MORGAN STANLEY (MOX), MS CYCLICAL (CYC), MS HI TECH 35 (MSH), etc.), each with columns STRIKE, VOL., LAST, NET CHG., and OPEN INT.]

Figure 14.6 Some index options trading prices from *The Wall Street Journal. Source:* (Reprinted with permission of *The Wall Street Journal.* © May 10, 2001.)

If an index option is exercised before its expiration day, the index value used for cash settlement is the closing value on the day it is exercised. If the index option finishes in the money on its expiration day, the index value for final cash settlement is determined and used to define the cash flow from the option writer to the owner.

For example, if an SPX call with a strike of 1350 expires, and the closing spot SPX index is at 1352.40, the owner of each call receives $240 from the writer of each call.

Note that over time exchanges have changed the method of computing the final settlement value. For example, the CBOE has changed the final settlement for the SPX from closing prices to opening prices. Exchanges have also settled options on days other than the third Friday of the month and have used multipliers other than 100. Thus, as with all derivatives, investors should always be aware of the current contractual terms.

Investors who exercise their American-style index options early should do so as late in the day as possible. The cash settlement is based on the *closing* index value on the early exercise day. The early exerciser faces risk that the index will change in value between the time he instructs his broker to exercise the option and the close. It is even possible that an irrational early exerciser will have to *pay* the option writer. For example, the owner of an S&P 100 put with a strike price of 735 might exercise his option at 10 A.M. when the S&P 100 Index is at 733, expecting to be paid $200. However, if the S&P 100 Index closed at 736, the put owner would actually have to pay $100 to the person who is assigned the option!

Adding to the risks of exercising listed index options is the institutional fact that many brokers have specific cutoff times for customers who wish to exercise their options. For example, a broker might demand that any customer who exercises an option do so before noon.

14.13.2 Timing Risks

The writers of listed options will typically not learn that they have been assigned options until the day *after* the actual assignment day that determines the required cash flow. The writers' stockbrokers will be informed before trading commences on the day after the assignment. A competent stockbroker will then immediately inform his customers. However, not all brokers are so conscientious. Also, a writer who cannot receive the phone call will not learn of the assignment until after trading has commenced on the day after assignment. This creates some unique risks for index option writers.

For example, consider an investor who owns a highly diversified portfolio of stocks similar to those in the S&P 100 Index and writes an OEX call. The purpose of this strategy is to try to write a covered call. Suppose that the investor is assigned the call and is therefore liable for a cash payment to the exerciser. At best, the investor will not be informed of the assignment until just before the market opens on the day after his assignment cash flow liability has been established. But by then, the hedge position (long stock and short call) is no longer in effect because the investor is only long stock. Should the stocks open lower, the investor will have to sell the stocks at prices lower than the cash settlement reflected.

The writer of a covered call on a specific stock faces no such risk. Should he be assigned, he will merely deliver the stock he owns. Here, the option writer does not care if the stock's value has changed.

Similar timing risks face investors who use some of the strategies described in the next chapter. In a spread, for example, the investor buys one option and sells another option with a different strike price. With options on individual stocks, if the written option is assigned, an investor can merely exercise the long position to satisfy the settlement obligation. With index options, if the index value moves adversely between the time the option is exercised and the time the investor learns of the assignment, losses might accumulate.

14.14 FOREIGN EXCHANGE OPTIONS

Foreign exchange (FX) options have traded on the Philadelphia Stock Exchange (PHLX) since 1982. Exchanges outside the United States also list FX options. Calls on foreign exchange give the owner the right to buy the stated amount of foreign exchange at the strike price. The strike price is itself an exchange rate. Foreign exchange puts give the owner the right to sell FX at the strike price. The exchange traded currency options market is quite illiquid; the OTC currency options market is geared toward institutions and is more active. To become more competitive, the PHLX has introduced customized currency options; you can read more about these innovative contracts at the exchange's website (www.phlx.com/products/currency.html). The prices (premiums) of the contracts that trade on the PHLX are presented in the *Wall Street Journal's* "Currency Trading" section. An example of the price data is shown in Figure 14.7.

Six types of spot FX trade on the PHLX: Australian dollars, British pounds, Canadian dollars, Japanese yen, Swiss francs, and euros. Each of these are options on the $/FX exchange rate. Customized options on "cross-rate" FX options also trade on the PHLX. Finally, note that both European and American FX options trade on the PHLX. European FX options, which have been traded on the PHLX only since August 1987, are specifically noted in the *Wall Street Journal* reprint in Figure 14.7. If there is no designation, the price data are for American options. Two expiration dates are offered: midmonth and end of month. Besides its customized options, the PHLX has also been quite innovative by offering long-term options with expirations two years in the future and options that expire on a weekly basis (which are useful for hedging weekend currency risk exposure). Additional information on PHLX FX options is available at its website (www.phlx.com).

Figure 14.7 shows only data for options with sufficient volume to be reported in the *Wall Street Journal.* Observe the euro options in Figure 14.7. The underlying asset is €62,500. On May 15, 2001, the spot price of a euro was $0.8815/€. Two strikes are reported for European-style calls expiring in May: 88 and 90. The 88 strike is for 88 cents/euro ($0.88/€). The May 88 call closed at 0.47 cent per euro. Multiply that by the €62,500 underlying the FX call, and the price per option is $293.75. At expiration, the payoff of the May 88 call is:

$$C_T = 0 \qquad\qquad \text{if } S_T \leq \$0.88/\text{€}$$
$$C_T = \text{€}62,500(S_T - \$0.88/\text{€}) \quad \text{if } S_T > \$0.88/\text{€}$$

where S_T is the expiration day exchange rate, expressed as $/€. The May 88 call is in the money and has an intrinsic value of 0.15, or ($0.0015/€)×€62,500=$93.75. The remainder of the call premium is time value.

Besides these listed FX options, there is a huge OTC market for customized currency options. The decision maker should consider such factors as liquidity, flexibility in designing the contract to most precisely meet needs, transactions costs, relative pricing, and advice and/or any other business relationship that may be gained by dealing with the OTC dealer. In addition, the decision maker must weigh the risk that the Options Clearing Corporation will default versus the risk that the OTC option dealer will default. Both are probably small, but ratings agencies such as Standard & Poors can provide guidance.

CURRENCY TRADING

EXCHANGE RATES

Tuesday, May 15, 2001

The New York foreign exchange mid-range rates below apply to trading among banks in amounts of $1 million and more, as quoted at 4 p.m. Eastern time by Reuters and other sources. Retail transactions provide fewer units of foreign currency per dollar. Rates for the 12 Euro currency countries are derived from the latest dollar-euro rate using the exchange ratios set 1/1/99.

Country	U.S. $ EQUIV. Tue	U.S. $ EQUIV. Mon	CURRENCY PER U.S. $ Tue	CURRENCY PER U.S. $ Mon
Argentina (Peso)	1.0003	1.0004	.9997	.9996
Australia (Dollar)	.5216	.5198	1.9170	1.9240
Austria (Schilling)	.06386	.06353	15.659	15.740
Bahrain (Dinar)	2.6525	2.6525	.3770	.3770
Belgium (Franc)	.0218	.0217	45.9060	46.1423
Brazil (Real)	.4274	.4322	2.3395	2.3140
Britain (Pound)	1.4241	1.4201	.7022	.7042
1-month forward	1.4227	1.4187	.7029	.7049
3-months forward	1.4201	1.4163	.7042	.7061
6-months forward	1.4164	1.4130	.7060	.7077
Canada (Dollar)	.6466	.6447	1.5465	1.5510
1-month forward	.6464	.6445	1.5471	1.5516
3-months forward	.6460	.6441	1.5480	1.5525
6-months forward	.6455	.6437	1.5492	1.5536
Chile (Peso)	.001650	.001654	605.95	604.45
China (Renminbi)	.1208	.1208	8.2769	8.2771
Colombia (Peso)	.0004206	.0004207	2377.50	2376.75
Czech. Rep. (Koruna)				
Commercial rate	.02552	.02542	39.182	39.332
Denmark (Krone)	.1177	.1172	8.4930	8.5346
Ecuador (US Dollar)-e	1.0000	1.0000	1.0000	1.0000
Finland (Markka)	.1478	.1470	6.7661	6.8009
France (Franc)	.1340	.1333	7.4647	7.5031
1-month forward	.1339	.1332	7.4681	7.5082
3-months forward	.1338	.1331	7.4753	7.5120
6-months forward	.1336	.1330	7.4829	7.5170
Germany (Mark)	.4493	.4470	2.2257	2.2372
1-month forward	.4491	.4468	2.2267	2.2381
3-months forward	.4487	.4465	2.2288	2.2398
6-months forward	.4482	.4462	2.2311	2.2413
Greece (Drachma)	.002579	.002566	387.77	389.76
Hong Kong (Dollar)	.1282	.1282	7.7999	7.7998
Hungary (Forint)	.003406	.003400	293.62	294.10
India (Rupee)	.02128	.02119	47.000	47.190
Indonesia (Rupiah)	.0000874	.0000877	11445	11400
Ireland (Punt)	1.1158	1.1101	.8962	.9008
Israel (Shekel)	.2411	.2410	4.1480	4.1500
Italy (Lira)	.0004538	.0004515	2203.44	2214.78

Country	U.S. $ EQUIV. Tue	U.S. $ EQUIV. Mon	CURRENCY PER U.S. $ Tue	CURRENCY PER U.S. $ Mon
Japan (Yen)	.008098	.008114	123.48	123.24
1-month forward	.008127	.008144	123.04	122.78
3-months forward	.008180	.008197	122.25	121.99
6-months forward	.008261	.008281	121.05	120.77
Jordan (Dinar)	1.4069	1.4069	.7108	.7108
Kuwait (Dinar)	3.2478	3.2520	.3079	.3075
Lebanon (Pound)	.0006604	.0006604	1514.25	1514.25
Malaysia (Ringgit)-b	.2632	.2632	3.8001	3.8000
Malta (Lira)	2.2002	2.1930	.4545	.4560
Mexico (Peso)				
Floating rate	.1088	.1092	9.1890	9.1550
Netherlands (Guilder)	.3988	.3967	2.5078	2.5207
New Zealand (Dollar)	.4191	.4205	2.3861	2.3781
Norway (Krone)	.1095	.1092	9.1329	9.1583
Pakistan (Rupee)	.01623	.01627	61.600	61.450
Peru (new Sol)	.2779	.2776	3.5980	3.6025
Philippines (Peso)	.01992	.01988	50.200	50.300
Poland (Zloty)-d	.2497	.2491	4.0050	4.0150
Portugal (Escudo)	.004383	.004361	228.14	229.32
Russia (Ruble)-a	.03443	.03442	29.043	29.053
Saudi Arabia (Riyal)	.2666	.2666	3.7506	3.7506
Singapore (Dollar)	.5498	.5493	1.8190	1.8205
Slovak Rep. (Koruna)	.02036	.02026	49.121	49.352
South Africa (Rand)	.1252	.1256	7.9850	7.9625
South Korea (Won)	.0007673	.0007708	1303.35	1297.30
Spain (Peseta)	.005281	.005254	189.34	190.32
Sweden (Krona)	.0975	.0971	10.2611	10.2970
Switzerland (Franc)	.5734	.5710	1.7439	1.7513
1-month forward	.5739	.5715	1.7426	1.7498
3-months forward	.5747	.5724	1.7400	1.7470
6-months forward	.5761	.5740	1.7358	1.7421
Taiwan (Dollar)	.03040	.03041	32.900	32.880
Thailand (Baht)	.02197	.02196	45.525	45.535
Turkey (Lira)-f	.00000087	.00000087	1145000	1155000
United Arab (Dirham)	.2723	.2723	3.6730	3.6730
Uruguay (New Peso)				
Financial	.07648	.07663	13.075	13.050
Venezuela (Bolivar)	.001400	.001400	714.25	714.13
SDR	1.2602	1.2599	.7935	.7937
Euro	.8788	.8743	1.1379	1.1438

Special Drawing Rights (SDR) are based on exchange rates for the U.S., German, British, French, and Japanese currencies. Source: International Monetary Fund.
a-Russian Central Bank rate. b-Government rate. d-Floating rate; trading band suspended on 4/11/00. e-Adopted U.S. dollar as of 9/11/00. f-Floating rate, eff. Feb. 22.

PHILADELPHIA EXCHANGE OPTIONS

	CALLS VOL. LAST	PUT VOL. LAST		CALLS VOL. LAST	PUT VOL. LAST		CALLS VOL. LAST	PUT VOL. LAST
ADlr		54.26	81 Jun	— —	2 0.86	Euro		88.15
50,000 Australian Dollar EOM-European.			81 Jul	— —	40 1.12	62,500 Euro-cents per unit.		
52 May	6 0.30	— —	81 Sep	— —	15 1.50	88 Jun	1 1.37	— —
CDlr		66.48	83 Sep	1 1.55	— —	90 Sep	4 1.54	— —
50,000 Canadian Dollars-cents per unit.			Euro		88.15	92 Jun	1 0.15	— —
65 Sep	— —	100 1.08	62,500 Euro-European style			92 Sep	1 1.00	— —
JYen		92.53	88 May	5 0.47	— —	SFranc		57.83
6,250,000 J.Yen-100ths of a cent per unit.			90 May	8 0.15	— —	62,500 Swiss Francs-cents per unit.		
79 Sep	— —	2 0.92	Euro		88.15	59 Jun	8 0.19	— —
80 Sep	— —	6 1.18	62,500 Euro-European style.			Call Vol. 46	Open Int. 12,803	
			94 Sep	10 0.63	— —	Put Vol. 166	Open Int. 19,561	

KEY CURRENCY CROSS RATES

Late New York Trading Tuesday, May 15, 2001

	Dollar	Euro	Pound	SFranc	Guilder	Peso	Yen	Lira	D-Mark	FFranc	CdnDlr
Canada	1.5465	1.3591	2.2024	0.8868	.61668	.16830	.01252	.00070	.69484	.20718	....
France	7.4647	6.5600	10.6305	4.2805	2.9766	.81235	.06045	.00339	3.3539	....	4.8268
Germany	2.2257	1.9559	3.1696	1.2763	.88751	.24221	.01802	.00101	....	.29816	1.4392
Italy	2203.4	1936.4	3137.9	1263.5	878.63	239.79	17.844	....	989.99	295.18	1424.8
Japan	123.48	108.51	175.85	70.807	49.238	13.438	....	.05604	55.479	16.542	79.845
Mexico	9.1890	8.0753	13.086	5.2692	3.6642	....	.07442	.00417	4.1286	1.2310	5.9418
Netherlands	2.5078	2.2039	3.5714	1.4380	....	.27291	.02031	.00114	1.1267	.33595	1.6216
Switzerland	1.7439	1.5325	2.4835	....	.69539	.18978	.01412	.00079	.78353	.23362	1.1276
U.K.	.70220	.6171	....	.4027	.28001	.07642	.00569	.00032	.31550	.09407	.45406
Euro	1.13790	....	1.6205	.65251	.45375	.12383	.00922	.00052	.51126	.15244	.73580
U.S.	....	.8788	1.4241	.57343	.39876	.10883	.00810	.00045	.44930	.13396	.64662

Source: Reuters

Figure 14.7 Currency option prices from *The Wall Street Journal*. *Source:* (Reprinted with permission of *The Wall Street Journal*, p. C16. © May 16, 2001.)

14.15 FUTURES OPTIONS

A call futures option gives the owner the right, but not the obligation, to assume a long position in an underlying futures contract. As in other options, the buyer of a futures call option pays a premium to the futures call option seller (writer). The writer of a futures call has the obligation to deliver a futures contract to the futures call owner, should the futures call owner decide to exercise the option. If the writer had written a naked futures option, upon exercise he will have a short position in a futures contract. If the option were written as part of a covered write, the writer will just deliver the futures contract he owns. That is, the call owner will effectively assume the long futures position at the strike price of the futures option. Upon exercise of a futures call, the positions are marked to market. Thus, whereas the exerciser of an "ordinary" call must pay $\$K$ to acquire the asset, the exerciser of a futures call is actually paid the option's intrinsic value, $F-K$, to go long a futures contract. Note that F is the futures settlement price on the exercise day.

The owner of a put option on a futures contract has the right to go short a futures contract at the strike price. The writer of a futures put must accept a long position in a futures contract, should he ever be assigned an exercise. Again, all positions are marked to market once the owner has exercised his put.

Futures options trade on many different exchanges, with underlying assets consisting of virtually every successful futures contract. The *Wall Street Journal* presents their prices in a table named "Futures Options Prices." Figure 14.8 illustrates how such futures options price data are presented.

Different conventions exist for interpreting futures options price data. Therefore, before you ever trade futures options, be sure to learn how to read the data. Let's look at some examples.

EXAMPLE 14.9 On November 4, 2001, a trader buys a call option on a December 2001 S&P 500 futures contract. The call costs $8925, has a strike price of 1370, and expires on the Saturday following the third Friday of December (but the last trading day is actually the preceding Thursday). On that day, the December futures price is 1362.64. By buying this out-of-the-money call, the trader has the right to go long a December futures contract at a futures price of 1370. He will not want to exercise his call unless the futures price of the December contract rises above 1370. However, he can sell the futures call at any time.

Suppose that before expiration, the December S&P 500 futures price rises to 1425.00 and the futures call premium rises to $14,000. The trader can sell his futures call for $14,000, or he can exercise it. If he does the latter, he will then assume a long position in one December S&P 500 futures contract at a futures price of 1370. Since the futures settlement price for the contract on the day he exercises is 1425.00, his long position is marked to market, and he receives a cash inflow of $(250)(1425-1370)=\$13,750$. On subsequent days, his long futures position is marked to market until he offsets his futures position (or the last trading day is reached). Recall that S&P 500 futures are cash settled. Note that the trader receives more money by selling the futures call option than by exercising it.

If the trader does exercise his futures call, a writer is assigned the exercise. If the individual who is assigned is a naked writer, he must assume a short position in a March S&P 500 futures contract at a price of 1370. Because his position is immediately marked to market, he also has a cash outflow of $13,750. If the individual who is assigned the futures call is a covered writer, he will deliver his futures contract at a futures price of 1370. He also will pay $13,750. However, if he originally went long that contract at a futures price below 1425, he has realized some daily resettlement cash inflows on his long futures position.

Figure 14.8 Some futures options prices from *The Wall Street Journal*. (Reprinted with permission of *The Wall Street Journal*, p. C18. © May 16, 2001.)

In Figure 14.8 the June 113 call on a Dow Jones Industrial Average futures contract has its premium listed as 21.40. However, note that at the heading says "$100 times premium." This means that the dollar cost of this futures call is ($100)(21.40)=$2140. This option no intrinsic value because the June futures settlement price on May 16, 2001 was 11,252 while the strike price of this call is 11,300. If the futures price subsequently rises above 11,300, then the call will be in the money. Note that the futures price for the June DJIA futures contract does not appear in Figure 14.8. It could be found in *The Wall Street Journal* for that day, however, in data like that shown in Figure 6.5. Note also that the underlying asset of the July DJIA futures options is a September DJIA futures contract. This illustrates an important fact that all users of futures options should investigate: many futures options have expiration dates in months that are not the same as the delivery months for the futures contracts that underlie them.

The June 101 put on a T-bond futures contract has a premium of 1-45. According to the header line of the table, this is 1 $45/64$% of $100,000. Thus, the dollar cost of this put is $1,703.125. This put consists of 1 $18/32$ (101 − 99 $14/32$) of intrinsic value and $9/64$ (1 $45/64$ − 1 $18/32$) of time value, because the June T-bond futures settlement price was 99 − 14 (99 $14/32$: whereas T-bond option prices are quoted in 64ths, T-bond futures prices are quoted in 32nds) on that day. This put is in the money. The T-note futures option prices are read in the same way as T-bond futures options.

For the foreign exchange futures options on Japanese yen, Canadian dollars, British pounds, and Swiss francs, the premiums listed are presented as cents per unit of foreign exchange. That is, to compute the price of the futures option *in cents*, take the listed price and multiply it by the number of units of foreign exchange in a futures contract. Divide that figure by 100 to get the price in dollars. For example, the June 1450 British pound futures call has a listed premium of 0.40, or 0.40 cent per pound. In dollars, this is ($0.0040/£)(£62,500)=$250. This call is out of the money because the June British pound futures settlement price was $1.4294/£ on that day. Note that the June British Pound futures settlement price does not appear in Figure 14.8. It would have appeared, however, in *The Wall Street Journal* in data like that shown in Figure 6.5.

The Japanese yen futures options are a little different. Look at the header line of the table. It states that the prices are in "cents per 100 yen." This is actually the same convention that is used for yen futures price data, where the header line reads "$ per yen (.00)." The June 8200 put price is 1.24. The dollar price of this put is ($0.0124/100 yen)(¥12,500,000)=$1550.

The last trading day of futures options differs from contract to contract, and it can differ for a given contract, depending on whether the option expires in the futures' delivery month or in a non-delivery month. Always contact the exchange on which a futures option (or futures contract) trades for current contract specifications, since these can change at any time.

Futures options were illegal in the United States for long periods of time in the past. They were blamed for creating excessive volatility, and a subsequent collapse in grain prices, in July 1933. Because of that, the Commodity Exchange Act of 1936 made trading in options on "regulated commodities" illegal. However many commodities, such as metals, were not regulated. In the late 1960s and early 1970s options on spot gold and silver were sold to some investors. In addition, other firms bought commodity options in London (they were legal there) and sold them to American investors.

New scandals emerged as many investors found that they had grossly overpaid for these options. Some investment firms sold options they did not own, and when investors tried selling them or exercising them, the firms declared bankruptcy. The CFTC proceeded to ban trading in virtually all commodity options (options on individual stocks were legal, however) and futures options in June 1978. After considerable research, the CFTC rescinded its ban in 1982 and allowed futures options to trade on futures exchanges. The new futures options were regulated to minimize the likelihood of fraud and scandals.

14.16   OTHER OPTIONS

There are two broad classifications of "other options." The first consists of the set of options on various other underlying assets. For example, there is the huge OTC market for customized interest rate options (and options on debt instruments). When interest rate options are used to manage floating interest rate risk, they are called *caps* and *floors*, because they create a cap (a maximum) interest rate that will be paid in the future, or a floor (a minimum) on the interest rate that will be received. A cap is actually a call option on an interest rate, or a series of call options with future periodic expiration dates (such as quarterly or semiannually). A floor is actually a put option, or a series of puts, on an interest rate. Caps and floors are discussed in Chapter 19. Options on debt instrument are covered in Chapter 20.

Another interesting underlying asset is a swap. A **swaption** gives the owner the right to enter into a swap as either the fixed-rate payer or the fixed-rate receiver. Furthermore, since a swap is nothing but a portfolio of forward contracts, each having a different settlement date, a swaption is actually an option on this portfolio of forwards. In Chapter 20, we discuss swaptions. Related derivatives are the *callable swap*, which is a swap with the option giving the pay-fixed party the right but not the obligation to exit the contract, and the *puttable swap*, which is a swap that permits the receive-fixed party to terminate the contract. Be careful when using this terminology; be sure that both you and your counterparty understand the contract's terms in the same way.

The second broad classification of "other options" consists of *exotic* options, which are options that have unusual payoff mechanisms. In Chapter 20, we discuss several exotic options. Exotic options are generally classified into two groups: *path-dependent options*, which are options with pay offs that depend on the price path of the underlying asset before expiration, and *free-range options*, whose value is not path dependent.

Financial engineers are providing an endless stream of options that help manage risk. Interested readers should refer to Chapter 20, and also seek out other information on path-dependent and free-range exotics.[23]

14.17   SUMMARY

This chapter is an introduction to options and options markets. An American call option gives the owner the right, but not the obligation, to buy the underlying asset at the strike price on or before the expiration day. The writer of a call has the obligation to sell the underlying asset, should he be assigned the exercise. An American put option gives the owner the right but not the obligation to sell the underlying asset at the strike price on or before the expiration date. The put writer is obligated to buy the put if he is assigned the exercise. European options can be exercised only on the expiration day.

The intrinsic value of an option is the greater of zero or its in-the-money amount. Time value equals the option's price minus its intrinsic value. At expiration, an option is worth only its intrinsic value. If option prices on the expiration day are not exactly $C_T = \max[0, S_T - K]$ and $P_T = \max[0, K - S_T]$, there will be arbitrage opportunities. Before expiration, options will almost always have some time value. The exceptions are deep in-the-money European options.

European call values C are higher for lower strike prices K, higher prices of the underlying asset S, longer times to expiration T (assuming no dividends), higher volatility of the underlying asset σ, higher interest rates r, and lower dividends prior to expiration. Put values P are higher if the strike price is higher, the price of the underlying asset is lower, the volatility of the underlying asset is higher, interest rates are lower, and dividends are higher. American puts cannot rise in value as time passes, all else equal, but it cannot be predicted how the value of a European put will change as its expiration day nears (all else equal).

Several features of options markets were described. Market makers at options exchanges quote bid prices, at which individuals can sell options, and asked prices, at which investors can buy options. The asked price always exceeds the bid price. Investors will typically either place market orders or limit orders to trade options. Market orders are likely filled at the current bid (if it is being sold by the individual) or the current asked (if the option is being purchased by the individual). Those who place market orders demand immediacy. In contrast, those who place limit orders are supplying liquidity, but they face the possibility that their orders to buy or sell options at a specific price will not be filled. The Options Clearing Corporation guarantees that the terms of all listed options will be fulfilled.

Finally, this chapter explained how to read prices in the financial press, and it briefly covered the topics of margin requirements, transaction costs, and taxes.

References

Fama, Eugene F., and Merton H. Miller. 1972. *The Theory of Finance*. Hinsdale, Ill: Dryden Press.
Hull, John C. 2000. *Options, Futures, and Other Derivatives, 4th ed.* Upper Saddle River, NJ: Prentice Hall.
Konishi, Atsuo, and Ravi Dattatreya, ed. 1996. *The Handbook of Derivative Instruments*, 2nd ed. Chicago, Irwin Professional Publishing.
Wilmott, Paul. 1998. *Derivatives*. West Sussex, England: John Wiley & Sons, Ltd.

Notes

[1] An index option is an option on a portfolio of stocks, such as the S&P 500, the S&P 100, or the Dow Jones Industrial Average.

[2] A futures option is an option on a futures contract.

[3] An OTC (over-the-counter) option is a custom-made option that does not trade on an organized exchange.

[4] Flex options were created by options exchanges in the United States to gain market share of the institutional option market. Institutions desired contracts that were custom made according to expiration date, strike price, and European vs American style. Flex options can be designed in these ways, and they trade on option exchanges.

[5] When a person who owns the underlying asset buys a put, he is purchasing insurance. If the value of the asset declines below the strike price, he will exercise his put and receive $\$K$. He has insured against the possibility that the value of his underlying asset will fall below K. The price of the purchased put is the cost of insurance.

[6]This statement may not be true with respect to European calls on stocks that will pay dividends some time between the current day and the expiration day. It is always true for American calls, and for European calls on non-dividend-paying stocks.

[7]There are rules that define exactly who is entitled to distributions of cash and/or stock made by a firm. On a stock's ex-dividend day, the stock trades without the dividend. Thus an investor who buys a stock on its ex-dividend day is *not* entitled to receive that distribution. Prior to the ex-date, a stock is said to trade cum-dividend or with-dividend.

[8]We say "should" because in reality, stocks, on average, seem to fall by somewhat less than the dividend amount.

[9]This simple view of the world holds under specific assumptions. For example, it holds in a world of perfect capital markets and no taxes. Capital markets are said to be "perfect" when (a) there are no transactions costs; (b) securities are infinitely divisible, so that investors can buy fractions of securities; (c) information is costlessly available to everybody; and (d) investors are price takers, which means that their trades do not affect prices. See Chapter 3 of Fama and Miller (1972).

[10]In a stock split or stock dividend, a firm distributes x new shares for every old share an investor owns. For example, in a 2-for-1 split, an investor receives 2 new shares for every old share, thus doubling the number of shares owned. However, the price of the stock will fall by about 50%. Thus, an investor might own 100 old shares of a stock selling at $60/share before a split. On the ex-split date, he will own 200 new shares of a stock that will likely sell at $30/share. Stock dividends are usually smaller distributions than stock splits (e.g., a 5% stock dividend), and the two events are handled somewhat differently for accounting purposes.

[11]The exception to this statement is a European call on a stock that will trade ex-dividend prior to the expiration date. If the dividend amount is large, the call could be worth less than its current intrinsic value.

[12]There is an exception to this statement. In-the-money European puts can actually rise in value as time passes, all else equal. This phenomenon will be discussed in Chapter 15.

[13]Other variables that may play a role in option valuation include the skewness of the stock's distribution of returns, the probability that the stock will jump in value (a discontinuity in price), uncertainty about the future movements in interest rates, taxes, investors' risk aversion and/or beliefs (expectations) about future stock price movements, transactions costs, margin requirements for the options and for the underlying asset, and market microstructure (e.g., the level of competition among market makers, trading volume, and market-maker positions in the options).

[14]This diagram is a more accurate picture of American put pricing than of European put pricing. In-the-money European puts can sell for less than their intrinsic value and can also rise in value as time passes, a phenomenon that will be discussed in Chapter 16.

[15]Consider the range of possible stock prices for a typical $50/share stock tomorrow; you might believe the range is $49–$51. However, the dispersion of possible stock prices one week from today will likely be wider, perhaps $45–$50. One year from now, the stock might sell anywhere between $20 and $100. Thus, the longer the time horizon, the greater the dispersion of possible stock prices.

[16]The discussion in the text about the indeterminate relation between put values and time to expiration applies only to European puts. All else equal, American puts will never rise in value as time passes. If the second argument about the timing of the receipt of the sales proceeds becomes important, the holder of an American put would be well advised to exercise it early. Also, note that the first effect concerning the range of stock prices dominates when the put is out of the money. The second argument becomes increasingly important as the stock price falls, and the put becomes deeper in the money.

[17]In October 1990 the CBOE and AMEX initiated trading in options with times to expiration of up to 30 months. These options are called LEAPS (**long-term equity anticipation securities**).

[18]In other words, the customer of the clearing firm that wrote the option at the earliest date is assigned.

[19]There is some timing risk here. The option writer who is assigned an exercise may not learn of it for a day or two. During that time the stock price may change.

[20]If an investor writes a naked **index option**, the formulas for margin are slightly different. Instead of using 20% of the market value of the underlying stock, use 15% of the market value of the stock underlying the index.

[21] The CBOE publishes a useful booklet titled "Taxes and Investing: A Guide for the Individual Investor," which can be downloaded at the exchange's website (www.cboe.com/resources/tax.htm).

[22] A security's beta is its relative volatility compared to the market. If a stock tends to rise (fall) $x\%$ when the market rises (falls) $x\%$, then it has a beta of 1.0. A stock that tends to rise (fall) by 1 $1/2\%$ when the market rises (falls) by 1% has a beta of 1.5. Beta is usually estimated by regressing the stock's returns on the market (the market model):

$$R_{it} = a_i + b_i R_{mt} + e_{it},$$

where

R_{it} = return on security i during period t
R_{mt} = return on the market during period t
a_i, b_i = regression coefficients; b_i is the estimate of security i's beta
e_{it} = a random error term

[23] See, for example, Konishi and Dattatreya (1996, Chapter 41), Wilmott (1998), or Hull (2000, Chapter 18).

PROBLEMS

14.1   There are six basic derivative positions:

1. Long forward
2. Short forward
3. Long call
4. Short (written) call
5. Long put
6. Short (written) put

Figure P14.1 shows the six profit diagrams for the six positions. In each diagram, the profit is on the y-axis (the vertical axis) and the expiration day price of the underlying asset is on the x-axis. Match each diagram (a–f) with the appropriate position listed above.

14.2   Which is worth more: a deep in-the-money call or a deep out-of-the-money call?

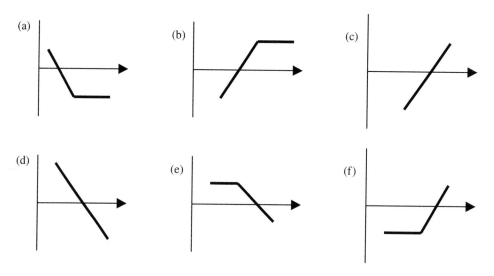

Figure P14.1.

14.3 Explain why ex-dividend days will make calls less valuable and puts more valuable, all else equal.

14.4 Suppose you owned a call, and after the close of trading, the company announces that its next dividend will be considerably greater than you, or any one else, expected. The next ex-dividend date falls prior to your call's expiration date. Will your call open higher or lower the next day?

14.5 Refer to the America Online (AmOnline) option price data in Figure 14.5.

    a. Are the calls with a strike price of 55 in the money or out of the money? Why?

    b. Are the puts with a strike price of 55 in the money or out of the money? Why?

    c. What is the intrinsic value of the July 50 calls? What is the time value of the July 55 calls?

    d. What is the intrinsic value of the July 50 puts? What is the time value of the July 55 puts?

    e. Suppose you bought one July 55 call at the price shown, and at the close of trading of the expiration day, America Online closed at $57/share? What would be your profit or loss? What would be your holding period rate of return? What would be your annualized rate of return?

    f. Suppose you wrote one July 50 naked put at the price shown, and at the close of trading of the expiration day, America Online closed at $43. What would be your profit or loss? Under what conditions would the owner of a July 50 put exercise the put at expiration?

14.6 How is it possible for the value of a call to rise from one day to the next if the stock price remains unchanged on those two days?

14.7 An option is quoted at "2.70 bid–3 asked." What are the potential benefits and costs of placing a limit order to buy the option at 2.70 versus placing a market order to buy?

14.8 Suppose that at expiration, a stock is quoted at "44.10 bid–44.20 asked." A put option with a strike price of 45 is quoted at "0.90 bid–1.00 asked." Demonstrate whether an arbitrage opportunity does or does not exist. Suppose that the put is quoted at "0.60 bid–0.70 asked." Demonstrate whether an arbitrage opportunity does or does not exist.

14.9 What are the six fundamental determinants of option values? Predict how call values change (increase or decrease) as each of the six parameters decreases, all else equal. Predict how put values change as each of the six parameters decreases all else equal.

14.10 Refer to Figure 14.5. What would be the required margin for writing a naked Cisco July 25 put? Why would an individual want to write this naked put? In general, compare the benefits, risks, and costs to these two strategies: writing a naked put versus buying a call.

14.11 Which is worth more: an American option or a European option? Why?

14.12 In Figure 14.5, refer to the AmOnline and ApdldMat calls with a strike price of 50 that expire in June. Discuss the possible reasons that the ApdldMat calls sell for more than the AmOnline calls.

14.13 Refer to the Broadcom options in Figure 14.5. Use the information to infer whether Broadcom common stock has been generally rising or falling over the past several months.

14.14 Explain why an increase in volatility increases the range of both good and bad outcomes for a stock, yet it unambiguously increases the value of both put and call options.

14.15 What makes index options different from ordinary options on individual equities?

14.16 Refer to Figure 14.8 to answer the following questions.

    a. What is the call premium for the June 8100 call on a Japanese yen futures contract? What is the underlying asset of this futures option?

    b. The yen futures price for the contract deliverable into the June futures options was $0.008126/¥. In dollars, what are the intrinsic value and the time value of the June 8100 futures call? What are the intrinsic value and the time value of the June 8200 futures call? What are the intrinsic value and the time value of the July 8050 and July 8300 puts on yen futures?

    c. If a yen futures option premium is $187.50, what price would you see in the presentation of futures options price data, as in Figure 14.8?

14.17 Which of the following correctly describes the situation of the writer of a call option?

    a. has the right to sell the underlying asset at the strike price.

    b. has the right to buy the underlying asset at the strike price.

    c. has the obligation to sell the underlying asset at the strike price if the call owner exercises.

    d. has the obligation to buy the underlying asset at the strike price if the call owner exercises.

    e. has both the right and the obligation to sell the underlying asset at the strike price.

    f. has both the right and the obligation to buy the underlying asset at the strike price.

14.18 The stock price is 37. A put with a strike price of 35 has a premium of 3. Which of the following is true?

    a. The intrinsic value is 2 and the time value is 1.

    b. The intrinsic value is 3 and the time value is 1.

    c. The intrinsic value is 5 and the time value is 1.

    d. The intrinsic value is 0 and the time value is 3.

    e. The intrinsic value is 2 and the time value is 3.

    f. The intrinsic value is 5 and the time value is 3.

14.19 Which of the following offers an investor the chance to make an unlimited profit if the underlying asset rises in price, but with limited losses if the underlying asset declines in price (i.e., the position requires only a small initial investment, which is the most that an investor can lose)?

    a. Going long a forward contract.

    b. Buying a call.

    c. Buying a put.

    d. Writing a call.

    e. Writing a put.

CHAPTER 15

Option Strategies and Profit Diagrams

A **profit diagram** depicts the profits and losses from an option investment strategy as a function of the price of the underlying asset at expiration. Profits and losses are on the y axis, and a range of expiration date (time T) prices of the underlying asset are on the x axis. These diagrams are sometimes called payoff patterns or payoff profiles.

The payoff pattern to a long position in an asset is linear. For example, if you own one share of stock and its prices rises by a dollar, your profit is a dollar. In contrast, options offer nonlinear payoff patterns. If you own a call option on one share of stock then, at expiration, your profit rises by one dollar for every one-dollar increase in the stock price *only if the option is in the money*. If the option is out of the money, your profit is fixed (constant) for any expiration day price of the underlying asset; that is, you have lost the initial premium you paid for the option, and this is independent of how much the option finishes out of the money. Thus, a long call offers two piecewise linear payoff segments. Even more unusual payoff patterns are created when several different options are used, perhaps combined with the underlying asset. Some of these strategies have colorful names: spreads, straddles, strips, straps, butterflies, and condors, for example. This chapter presents many different option strategies and their profit diagrams.

In most of this chapter, we assume there are only two relevant dates for the purchase and/or sale of the assets involved: the initial date (time 0) and the expiration date (time T). Nothing, however, prevents an investor from closing out positions early. We also ignore the possibility that the options will be exercised early. Dividends, commissions, and margin requirements are not explicitly dealt with, but can easily be incorporated into one's preparation of profit diagrams. Remember, too, that because of nonsynchronous trading and bid–asked spreads, prices in the financial press may not reflect prices at which an investor can buy or sell the options. Finally, our discussion focuses on nominal dollar cash flows. This means that the timing of cash flows is ignored—we will simply add dollar cash flows that occur at two dates. Although this is a common practice in preparing profit diagrams, in concept, it is sacrilegious. We all know that a dollar inflow at time 0 is more valuable than a dollar received later.

Profit diagrams can provide additional valuable information if they are prepared on a rate-of-return basis, and also if they are prepared showing profits and losses that result when positions are closed at dates earlier than expiration. These two types of diagram will be illustrated at the end of the chapter.

Table 15.1 contains the notation that will be used in this chapter.

15.1 Profit Diagrams for Long Stock and Short Stock

The easiest way to illustrate a profit diagram is to begin with the two basic positions in the underlying asset. An investor can buy the asset today for S_0 and sell it at a future date at an unknown

TABLE 15.1 Notation

Variables	Subscripts
S = stock price	0 = today (strategy initiation date)
K = strike price	T = expiration date
C = call premium	H = high strike price
P = put premium	L = low strike price
T = time to expiration	

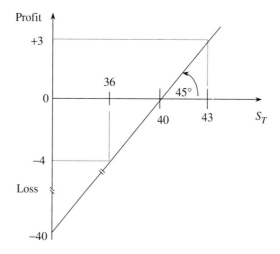

Figure 15.1   Long stock.

price $\tilde{S}_T$. Once purchased, the investor is said to be "long" the asset. In this chapter, we will assume that the underlying asset is 100 shares of common stock, but it could as easily be 100 ounces of gold, $1 million of Treasury bills, 6.25 million Japanese yen, a futures contract, or an office building.

The profit diagram for a long position in stock is shown in Figure 15.1: the stock is purchased at S_0 = $40/share. If, at a later date, the stock is sold at a price of S_T = $43/share, the investor will earn a profit of $3/share. Similarly, if the stock is later sold for $36/share, a loss of $4/share will be realized. The maximum loss (the y-axis intercept) is $40/share, which occurs if S_T falls to $0. Note that the profit diagram is a straight line that passes through the $40 point on the x axis, creating a 45° angle; thus, if the stock is later sold for $40 (the purchase price), a $0 profit results. It is clear from the diagram that a stock purchase is a bullish strategy because profits will be realized from price appreciation.

Investors can also sell stock short. The profit diagram for a short sale of stock is presented in Figure 15.2. In this type of trade, an investor sells the stock today and later repurchases it. However, the investor does not initially own the stock that is sold. Rather, the stock is borrowed from someone else. When the stock that was sold is later repurchased, it is returned to the original owner. Selling short is a bearish strategy because profits accrue when the underlying asset price declines.[1]

Observe Figure 15.2 and assume that the stock is sold short at S_0 = $50/share. If the stock is later purchased at the same price, there is no profit or loss. If the stock declines in price, profits are made. The profit is $1 per share for every dollar decline in price. If the stock price falls to zero, the maximum profit of $+\$S_0$ will be earned; if $S_0 = 50$, then the maximum profit is $50. If the stock price declines to $46, the short seller's profit is $4/share. For smaller stock price declines, the profit is $S_0 - S_T$, where S_T is the purchase price at time T. If the stock price rises, however, the investor loses. The potential loss is theoretically infinite. While infinite losses have never been observed, short selling can lead to losses many times over the original stock price.

Summarizing, the profit diagrams for stock-only positions are seen to be straight lines that pass through the original transaction price with zero profit. The line for the long stock position has a slope of $+1$, while that for the short stock position has a slope of -1. Option positions create many other payoff patterns.

15.2   LONG CALLS

Figure 15.3 shows the profit diagram for the purchaser of a call option. Here, the strike price is $50/share and the call premium is $3/share. If, at expiration, the stock price is $50 or lower, the option expires worthless. The call buyer will lose the premium paid of $3/share ($300 for a call on 100 shares). If the stock price closes on the expiration date at 53, the call buyer breaks even. He initially paid $3 for the call, and at expiration, the call is worth $3 [Recall that at expiration, a call is worth $C_T = \max(0, S_T - K)$.] At any stock price above $53, the call buyer will realize a profit. For every $1 increase in the stock price, the call is worth $1 more. Thus, the diagonal portion of the line in Figure 15.3 has a slope of $+1$.

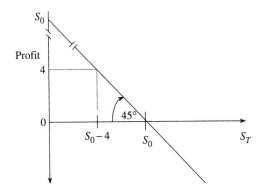

Figure 15.2   Short stock.

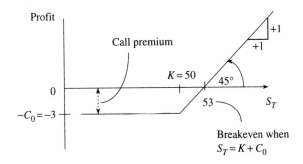

Figure 15.3   Long call.

It is clear from Figure 15.3 that buying a call is a bullish strategy with respect to the underlying asset. If the stock price remains unchanged (or declines), the buyer of an at-the-money call or an out-of-the-money call will lose 100% of his initial investment. If the call buyer is to profit, the expiration day price of the underlying asset must rise above the strike price to cover the initial price paid for the call. The buyer of an out-of-the-money call will profit only if the stock price rises by more than the call premium *plus* the amount by which the call is originally out of the money. For example, if $K=50$, $S_0=46$, and $C_0=2$, the stock price must rise by \$6 at time T for the call buyer to break even. Brokerage commissions on the purchase and the sale of the option add to the amount the stock must rise to merely break even.

15.3 WRITING A NAKED CALL

Figure 15.4 depicts the profit diagram for the writer of a naked call. The writer of a naked call does not own the underlying security.

Figure 15.4 is a general example of a profit diagram because algebraic symbols are used instead of specific numerical values. The strike price is K. The original call premium received by the seller is C_0. If the stock price at expiration S_T is at or below K, the option expires worthless and the call writer keeps the premium. Thus, there is a horizontal line with a profit of $+C_0$ for all $S_T \leq K$ in Figure 15.4. If $S_T > K$, the call will have value at expiration, and the call writer will have to buy back the call for the amount $C_T = S_T - K$. Thus, for every dollar the stock price rises above K, the call writer loses a dollar, and the diagonal portion of the line has a slope of -1. The break-even point (\$0 profit) occurs when $S_T = K + C_0$. In this case $C_0 = C_T$.

Writing a naked call is a bearish strategy.[2] If the stock remains unchanged or declines, the writer of an at-the-money or out-of-the-money naked call will keep the premium and the interest earned on the premium over the time she was short the call. However, the writer should also be aware of potentially substantial margin requirements on naked option positions. The call writer must also be aware that there are substantial risks if one is wrong about the future price movement of the stock. Observe in Figure 15.4 that losses are potentially unlimited as the stock price rises.

Call writers can write at-the-money calls, out-of-the-money calls, or in-the-money calls. When writing out-of-the-money calls, one will still keep the premium if the stock rises in price somewhat or remains unchanged. The risk of being assigned an exercise is less, but the out-of-the-money call premium will be smaller than the premium of an at-the-money call, so the potential

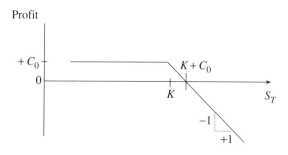

Figure 15.4 Writing a naked call.

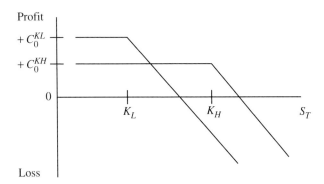

Figure 15.5   The trade-offs associated with writing calls with different strike prices. If a call with a high strike K_H is written (perhaps an out-of-the-money call), a smaller premium, C_0^{KH}, is received, but there is a larger range of expiration day prices of the underlying asset for which the call writer gets to keep that premium as profit. In contrast, writing a call with a lower strike price K_L provides a larger premium of C_0^{KL}, for the call writer; however there is a greater probability that this call will finish in the money and therefore create a loss for the call writer.

profit is smaller. This concept is illustrated in Figure 15.5. Here, a call writer may write an at-the-money call for a premium of C_0^{KL} at a strike price of $S_0 = K_L$. Alternatively, an out-of-the-money call may be written with a higher strike price of K_H. A smaller premium (C_0^{KH}) is received, but there is a greater probability that the call writer will keep that premium.

15.4   LONG PUTS

Figure 15.6 illustrates the long put profit diagram. If $S_T > K$, the put closes out of the money at expiration, and the put buyer will lose the price initially paid for the put, P_0. If the stock price at expiration is less than the exercise price, the put will have value at time T. Recall that $P_T = 0$ if $S_T \geq K$, and $P_T = K - S_T$ if $S_T < K$. If S_T is $1 below K, the put is worth $1 at expiration. The put buyer will break even (zero profit) if S_T equals $K - P_0$. The maximum profit is earned if $S_T = 0$. The put will then be worth K at expiration, and the profit equals $K - P_0$.

Buying a put is a bearish strategy. If an at-the-money put is bought and the stock price remains unchanged (or rises), the investor loses 100% of the initial investment. The benefit to this strategy is that the put buyer can lose only the initial premium paid. Contrast this to the short seller of the stock, who is exposed to theoretically unlimited losses (see Figure 15.2). In addition, a considerable amount of margin funds may be required in selling stock short, while a put purchase requires an outlay consisting of only the cost of the put (plus commissions).

15.5   WRITING A NAKED PUT

Suppose that an instant before the close of the market on May 10, 2001, an investor writes a naked put option on Applied Materials (ApdldMat in Figure 14.5). More specifically, the put is the June

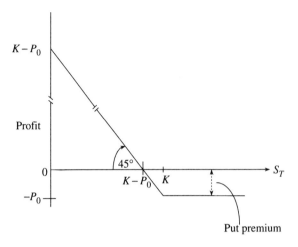

Figure 15.6 Long put.

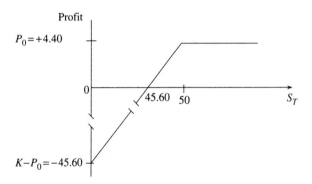

Figure 15.7 Writing a naked put.

50 put, and the premium received is 4.40 ($440 for a put on 100 shares). The profit diagram for the written put position shown in Figure 15.7 uses some numbers from the *Wall Street Journal* reprint shown earlier (Figure 14.5). If AMAT (the ticker symbol for Applied Materials) closes at a price of $50 or higher on the third Friday in June, the put will expire worthless. In this case, the put writer keeps the $4.40 per share. Therefore, Figure 15.7 shows a $4.40 profit for all $S_T > 50$. If, however, AMAT closes at $45.60 at expiration, the put writer breaks even ($S_T = K - P_0$). At lower prices, the put writer loses $1 for every dollar that AMAT's stock price falls. If AMAT's stock were to fall to zero in June (the probability of this happening is extremely small, to say the least), the maximum loss of $K - P_0 = \$45.60$ would be realized. This is shown at the y-axis intercept.

Writing a naked put is a bullish position with respect to the underlying stock, and the writer must be prepared to accept ownership of the shares, should the put owner decide to exercise.[3] In the foregoing example, the risk of early exercise on May 10 (the day of the prices shown in Figure 14.5) is zero, because AMAT's stock price is $51.01. Because $S_0 > K$, the put is out of the money. But, should AMAT fall below $50/share, the possibility of early exercise could increase because the put moves in the money. If AMAT is below 50 at expiration, the put owner will most certainly exercise the option.[4]

The name **cash-secured written put** is given to the strategy in which the investor writes a naked put and invests the strike price amount in riskless securities. Usually, an out-of-the-money put is used. Thus, if AMAT is at $51.01/share, writing a naked put with a strike price of 50 is a substitute for a limit order to buy AMAT at 50. There are, however, some differences:

a. Once AMAT has fallen to a price of 50, the limit buy order will be executed at that price or lower. In contrast, the put writer may observe AMAT's price temporarily fall below 50; but if the put owner elects not to exercise, the put writer will not get to purchase the stock. If the stock then proceeds to rise, the put writer may never be assigned an early exercise and will regret not having placed a limit order to purchase the stock.

b. Suppose that an imbalance of too many sell orders results in the temporary suspension in trading in AMAT's stock. Perhaps AMAT's earnings were disappointing, or the firm unexpectedly lost a lawsuit. AMAT's price could conceivably reopen for trading at, say, $30/share, when the last trade on the previous day was at $51.01/share. Had a limit order to buy at $50 been placed, the investor would have had the pleasure of knowing that his purchase price would be $30. The naked put writer, however, would have been forced to pay $50/share.

Keep in mind that the put writer is paid $4.40 (see Figure 14.5) for the June 50 put to assume these risks over the upcoming five weeks (until the expiration day).

Many other payoff patterns can be created with various long and/or short positions in calls, puts, and/or the underlying asset. Several of these will now be illustrated, and several others are outlined later in this chapter. Note, however, that one popular strategy called the horizontal spread, also known as a time spread, cannot be covered until we have learned how to value options.[5]

15.6   COVERED CALL WRITING

A covered call is an example of a "hedge position," where an option provides some compensation for the risk that the price of the underlying asset will decline. When writing a covered call, the investor buys (or already owns) 100 shares of stock and writes a call. The purpose of the strategy is to generate income from the proceeds of the written call. However, we will see that the covered call writer is effectively selling some of the upside potential of the stock in exchange for the premium.

The easiest way to prepare a profit diagram for a covered call, or for any complicated strategy, is to first prepare a profit table. This is done in two steps:

a. Calculate the initial inflow or outflow.

b. Calculate the expiration values of the assets involved, given several potential expiration day stock prices around the relevant strike prices of all options that are used in the strategy.

For example, refer again to Figure 14.5, and suppose that an investor buys 100 shares of Cisco for $18.83/share and writes 1 July 20 call option for $1.90 per call on one share. Initially:

Buy 100 shares of Cisco	− 18.83 per share	Cash out:	− $1883.00
Write 1 July 20 call	+1.90 per share	Cash in:	$190.00
Initial cash flow at time 0, CF_0	− 16.93 per share	Net cash out:	− $1693.00

Next, consider a range of possible prices of the underlying asset on the expiration day, T. Then, compute the cash flows by reversing all open positions at time T:

Price of Cisco, S_T	Sell Cisco	Buy (offset) July 20 Call for $C_T = \max[0, S_T - K]$	Time T Cash Flows, CF_T	Profit/Loss $CF_0 + CF_T$
14	+14	0	14	−2.93
15	+15	0	15	−1.93
16	+16	0	16	−0.93
17	+17	0	17	+0.07
18	+18	0	18	+1.07
19	+19	0	19	+2.07
20	+20	0	20	+3.07
21	+21	−1	20	+3.07
22	+22	−2	20	+3.07
23	+23	−3	20	+3.07

At any expiration day price at or below 20, the call expires worthless. The investor sells the shares for whatever closing price occurs for Cisco on the expiration date, S_T. At any price above 20, the call finishes in the money, so that the covered call writer will have to repurchase the option for $S_T - K$. However, the covered call writer will also be able to sell Cisco at the higher price.[6] The result is that for every dollar increase in Cisco's stock, the investor profits by $1 because of the long position in the stock, but loses $1 because the call was written. In the last column in the foregoing tabulation, we add the time T cash flow, CF_T, to the initial cash outflow of $CF_0 = -16.93$ per share. This determines the profit or loss from the strategy.

Actually, because all these profit diagrams produce straight lines that may be "kinked" at the strike prices, we need only consider time T prices around the strike price. In this example, we only had to prepare a table for $19 \leq S_T \leq 21$. For prices below 19 and above 21, we can extrapolate when preparing the profit diagram. An important point to remember is that in expiration date profit diagrams, kinks occur only at exercise prices. In this example, a kink occurs only at $K = 20$.

The profit diagram for a covered call on Cisco, using the July 20 call, is shown in Figure 15.8. The zero-profit (breakeven) point occurs when $S_T = \$16.93$. At that closing price at expiration, the loss on the stock ($16.93 - 18.83$) equals the proceeds from the written call (1.90).

An alternative method of preparing profit diagrams is to consider only the basic positions and then vertically add them.[7] This approach is shown in Figure 15.9, where we see that at prices of 20

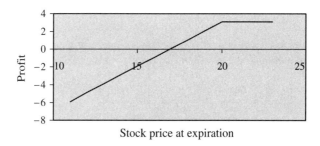

Stock price at expiration

Figure 15.8 Writing a covered call. In this covered call strategy, $S_0 = \$18.83$, $C_0 = \$1.90$, and $K = \$20$. The maximum profit of $3.07 is realized when $S_T \geq \$20$. The break-even point (zero profit) is at $S_T = \$16.93$.

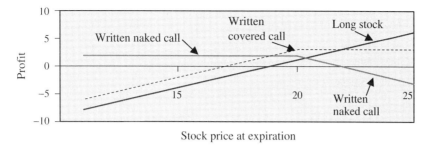

Figure 15.9 Alternative approach to preparing a profit diagram for a covered call.

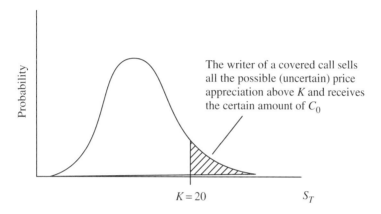

Figure 15.10 Writing a covered call.

and above, there are two 45° lines, one with a +1 slope (long stock) and one with a −1 slope (short call). Adding these creates the horizontal-line portion of the covered call shown with a profit of +3.07 when $S_T \geq 20$ in Figure 15.9. As we move below 20, the investor loses on the long stock position but gets to keep the call premium. Thus, we add a constant amount (slope=0), the call premium, to the long stock position, and the result is the diagonal line in Figure 15.9, with a slope of +1, when $S_T < 20$.

In effect, the writer of covered call sells off all (risky) price appreciation potential above K in return for a riskless cash inflow, the call premium. This is illustrated in Figure 15.10.

Often, a writer of a covered call believes the stock is attractively priced and offers some upside potential for price appreciation. Thus, the chosen strike price will usually lie above the current stock price; that is, out-of-the-money calls are generally written. If the price rises, the writer of a covered call will capture some of that price increase (up to the exercise price), as well as keep the call premium. If the investor is wrong, and the stock declines, the losses are tempered somewhat by the call premium that is kept.

However, keep in mind that if the stock price rises sharply, the writer of a covered call will regret having written the call. Any price appreciation above K has been sold. Also, if the stock price falls sharply, the writer will regret having bought the stock. If, for example, Cisco were to plummet to $10/share between the date the call was written and the third Friday in July, the investor with a covered call position still loses a substantial sum.

Covered call writing on stocks that pay high dividends can be an attractive cash management tool for corporations. Usually, corporations pay taxes on only 30% of the dividends they receive from their ownership in the shares of other firms. Corporations can buy the shares before an ex-dividend date and write the calls. On the expiration date, the positions are reversed.[8]

Comparison reveals that Figures 15.7 and 15.8 are almost identical. Actually, a written naked put is the same as a covered call position, except for a scale factor. In Chapter 16, we will see that put–call parity on European options with no dividends explains why the positions are equivalent and that the scale factor is the present value of K.[9]

Finally, there is no need to write only one call against the 100 shares of stock. **Variable-ratio hedges** allow the selling of any number of options against the 100 shares the investor owns, and each of these strategies leads to a different profit diagram. Indeed, an investor can write an appropriate number of calls per 100 shares of stock to maintain a riskless hedge (the position yields the risk-free rate of interest) for small movements in the underlying stock. This idea will be covered in Chapters 17 and 18, and it has great significance for the derivation of the Black–Scholes option pricing model, which is discussed in Chapter 18. Other variable-ratio hedges might involve the purchase of puts as protection against price declines in the underlying long stock position, or "reverse" hedges where stock is sold short and either calls are bought or puts written. Examples of these strategies are posed as problems at the end of this chapter.

15.7 VERTICAL SPREADS

Vertical spreads are also called money spreads or price spreads. The use of the term "vertical" arose because of the format in which option price data formerly were presented in the financial press: different strikes were listed vertically. In a vertical spread, an option with one strike price is bought, and another option with a different strike price (but the same time to expiration)[10] is sold. One can create a bullish vertical spread with puts or with calls. Similarly, a bearish vertical spread can be created with puts or with calls.

15.7.1 Bullish Vertical Spread with Calls

You are surfing www.cboe.com and see a Jan 80 Home Depot call selling for $3.75. Suppose you felt there was a high probability that Home Depot shares would sell for at least $80 by the third Friday in January. If you purchased the Jan 80 call and the stock closed right at $80 on the expiration date, you would lose your $3.75 call premium. You also see a Jan 75 call selling for 5, so if you bought this call, and if $S_T = 80$, you would still not profit. (the initial cost of the call is $500, and the call would be worth $S_T - K = \$500$ at expiration, so the profit is zero).

A bullish vertical spread lowers your initial outlay to only $125, and at any $S_T \geq 80$, your proceeds at expiration would be $500. This is a 300% return on your initial investment. An investor buys this vertical spread by buying a call with the lower exercise price, $K_L = 75$, and selling a call with a higher exercise price, $K_H = 80$. In our example:

Buy 1 Jan 75 Home Depot call	−5
Sell 1 Jan 80 Home Depot call	+3.75
Initial cash flow at time 0	$-1.25 = CF_0$

The expiration day profit table is then as follows:

S_T	Time T		Cash Flow, CF_T	Profit/Loss $CF_0 + CF_T$
	Sell Jan 75 Call	Buy Jan 80 Call		
74	0	0	0	−1.25
75	0	0	0	−1.25
76	+1	0	+1	−1.25
77	+2	0	+2	+0.75
78	+3	0	+3	+1.75
79	+4	0	+4	+2.75
80	+5	0	+5	+3.75
81	+6	−1	+5	+3.75
82	+7	−2	+5	+3.75

At all prices ≤75, both calls expire worthless. At all prices ≥80, the cash inflow at expiration, CF_T, is $500. Figure 15.11 is the profit/loss diagram for this example of a bullish vertical spread using calls.

You might try drawing profit/loss diagrams for a bullish Home Depot call spread using the January 70 and January 80 calls. The premium for the Jan 70 call is 7.40. Then, compare the resulting diagram and Figure 15.11 to another diagram generated by buying the January 70 call and selling the January 75 call.

15.7.2 Bullish Vertical Spread with Puts

In a bullish vertical spread with puts, the investor writes a put option having a high exercise price K_H and buys a put with a low exercise price K_L. Consider the Jan 75 and 80 puts on Home Depot. Initially, suppose:

Write 1 Jan 80 Home Depot put	+13
Buy 1 Jan 75 Home Depot put	−10.8
Initial cash inflow	+2.2 = CF_0

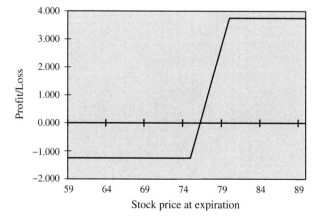

Figure 15.11 Bullish vertical spread with calls: $K_H = 80$, $C_H = 3\ 3/4$, $K_L = 75$, $C_L = 5$. The low strike call is bought, and the high strike call is sold.

Then, at expiration, we have:

	Time T			
S_T	**Buy Jan 80 Put**	**Sell Jan 75 Put**	CF_T	**Profit/Loss, CF_0+CF_T**
74	−6	+1	−5	−2.8
75	−5	0	−5	−2.8
76	−4	0	−4	−1.8
77	−3	0	−3	−0.8
78	−2	0	−2	+0.2
79	−1	0	−1	+1.2
80	0	0	0	+2.2
81	0	0	0	+2.2

In this table, CF_T is the expiration day cash flow generated by the repurchase of the Jan 80 put and the resale of the Jan 75 put; these offset the original trades. The total profit, shown in the last column, is depicted in Figure 15.12.

Note that this bullish spread with puts has an added element of risk if the written put is in the money. Thus there is risk that the written in-the-money put can be exercised early by its owner. However, should the investor's expectations turn out to be correct, both puts will expire worthless, there will be no exercise, and transactions costs will be saved.

In contrast, for the bullish spread with calls, the calls currently have no risk of early exercise; but should Home Depot's stock price rise above 80, the investor will have to pay commissions on the resale and repurchase of the two calls. If Home Depot were to trade ex-dividend between the day the strategy is executed and the expiration day of the options, and if Home Depot were selling for more than $80/share just prior to that day, the investor would bear the risk that the written call would be exercised.[11] Thus, there are benefits and risks to each bullish strategy.

15.7.3 Bearish Vertical Spread with Calls

Bearish vertical spreads with calls are created by the sale of a call with a low exercise price K_L and the purchase of a call with a high exercise price K_H. For example, suppose E*Trade.com option prices allow the following:

Write 1 E*Trade Dec 30 call	+3.4
Buy 1 E*Trade Dec 35 call	−1.3
Initial cash inflow	+2.1 = CF_0

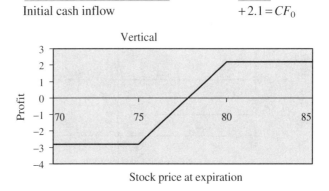

Figure 15.12 Bullish vertical spread with puts: buy the $K=75$ put and sell the $K=80$ put.

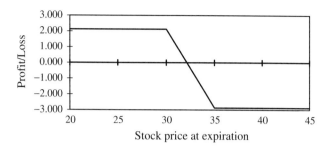

Figure 15.13 Bearish vertical spread with calls: the $K_L=30$ call is sold and the $K_H=35$ call is bought.

Continuing with the profit table, at time T, we find the following:

S_T	Buy Dec 30 Call	Sell Dec 35 Call	Time T Cash Flow CF_T	Profit/Loss $CF_0 + CF_T$
29	0	0	0	+2.1
30	0	0	0	+2.1
31	−1	0	−1	+1.1
32	−2	0	−2	+0.1
33	−3	0	−3	−0.9
34	−4	0	−4	−1.9
35	−5	0	−5	−2.9
36	−6	+1	−5	−2.9
37	−7	+2	−5	−2.9

Figure 15.13 shows the profit diagram for this bearish vertical spread using the E*Trade calls.

15.7.4   Bearish Vertical Spread with Puts

To create a bearish vertical spread with puts, a put with a high exercise price, K_H, is bought and a put with a low strike price, K_L, is written. This results in an initial cash outflow of $P(K_H)-P(K_L)$, because the put with the high strike price costs more than the proceeds generated from writing a put with a low strike price. If both puts finish in the money, they will be worth K_H-S_T and K_L-S_T, respectively, and the cash inflow at time T equals K_H-K_L. The total profit (CF_0+CF_T) will be $(K_H-K_L)-[P(K_H)-P(K_L)]$. If both puts finish out of the money, there is no cash flow at time T, and the total loss equals the initial cash outflow, $P(K_H)-P(K_L)$. The final profit diagram looks like Figure 15.14.

The reader is urged to work out an example of a bearish vertical spread with puts using price data from Figure 14.5, or recent option prices from the *Wall Street Journal* or Internet sources (such as www.cboe.com).

15.7.5   Other Thoughts on Vertical Spreads

Some simple logic might make the spread terminology easier to remember.

- Whenever you experience an initial cash outlay with puts (e.g., you buy a put spread by purchasing an expensive put and selling a cheap put), you must be bearish. Just recall that if you bought a put (a cash outflow), you must be bearish.

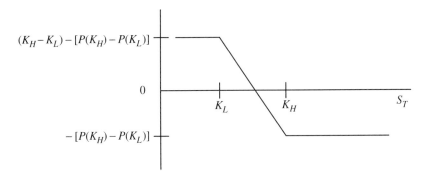

Figure 15.14 Bearish vertical spread with puts.

- If you were to buy a call spread, you experience a cash outlay at time 0. In this case (just as when you buy any call), you must be bullish. To buy a bullish call spread, you buy an expensive (low K) call and sell a cheaper (high K) call.

- The seller of a call is bearish, and an initial cash inflow is received. When you sell a call spread you are bearish. Selling a vertical spread with calls entails a cash inflow at time 0. This means you must sell an expensive call and buy a cheaper call to set up a bear spread with calls and generate a cash inflow.

- Finally, consider the seller of a put spread. There is a cash inflow at time 0. A naked put seller also has a cash inflow at time 0 and is bullish. Thus, the seller of a put spread must be bullish. To sell a put spread, realize a cash inflow at time 0 by selling an expensive put and buying a cheaper put.

There are several situations that would lead an investor to use vertical spreads. First, a vertical spread should be placed if an investor believes that the stock price will move only to the strike price that generates the maximum profit. For example, either of the two bullish spreads involving Home Depot should be used if an investor believes the stock will rise only to $80 or a little higher. An investor who is very bullish should just buy the calls.

A bullish investor who buys a call might always consider the sale of an out-of-the-money call to recapture a small part of the premium paid for the low strike call. Sometimes this can be done shortly after initially entering into a long call position, particularly if the stock moves in the investor's favor. This is called "legging" into a position, and in this case the investor is legging into a bullish spread with calls. For example, one might buy the Jan 70 Home Depot calls for 7.40. A few days later, if Home Depot has risen from 68.75 to, say, 74, perhaps the Jan 75 calls might have a bid quote of 7. The investor can then "leg" into the bullish vertical spread by writing the Jan 75 calls. The net investment is then only $0.40 (the Jan 70 calls were bought for 7.40 and the Jan 75 calls were sold for 7). If Home Depot rises to 75 or higher at the expiration day the maximum time T, cash inflow of 5 will be realized.

Another argument for using vertical spreads applies to a writer of naked options, who can effectively buy insurance against large losses by buying out of the money options. For example, an investor who believes that Home Depot's stock price will rise might write the Jan 70 put to generate, and hopefully keep, its premium of, say, $700. The risk is that large losses are possible if Home Depot shares fall in price. If Home Depot Stock fell to zero, the writer of the Jan 70 put faces a loss of $6300 ($7000 – $700). The purchase of the Jan 60 put represents insurance that would limit the loss to $300 plus the cost of the Jan 60 put ($700 – $1000 – cost of Jan 60 put).

The primary reason for avoiding vertical spreads, and indeed all the more complex strategies considered in this chapter, is that they double the commissions paid. Indeed, many have accused brokerage houses of pushing these strategies on their clients to generate additional commissions. Investors who use strategies such as spreads should deal with discount brokers, who charge just a few dollars per contract.

Finally, note that all the vertical spreads we examined were 1:1 (i.e., one option was bought and one was sold). Different payoff patterns are created by varying this ratio. Problems at the end of the chapter will allow you to create and examine these diagrams. Sometimes these strategies can be used to exploit mispriced options.

15.8 STRADDLES AND STRANGLES

Straddles and strangles are examples of "combinations," which are positions involving both puts and calls. Traders buy a straddle or strangle when they expect the underlying asset to be volatile but do not have any beliefs about whether the price will rise or fall. That is, the trader believes it will *either* rise *or* fall considerably.

A straddle is *purchased* by *buying* a put and a call on the same stock, with each option having the same exercise price and the same time to expiration. For example, from Figure 14.8, we see that one could initially buy a June 5700 call and a June 5700 put on a Swiss franc futures contract. The price of the call is $0.0105/SF, which is $1312.50 because the underlying asset is SF125,000. The price of the put is $0.0031/SF, which is $387.50. Thus, the total initial cash outflow for buying the put and the call is $CF_0 = -\$1700$.

In the following tabulations S_T is the expiration day price of a June Swiss franc futures contract, in terms of $/SF. In addition, C_T and P_T are the expiration day values of the call and the put, respectively, when the underlying asset is SF125,000; $CF_T = C_T + P_T$. The last column adds the initial day cost of the straddle (−$1700) to the expiration day cash flow.

S_T	C_T	P_T	CF_T	$CF_0 + CF_T$
0.53	0	5000	5000	3300
0.535	0	4375	4375	2675
0.54	0	3750	3750	2050
0.545	0	3125	3125	1425
0.55	0	2500	2500	800
0.555	0	1875	1875	175
0.56	0	1250	1250	−450
0.565	0	625	625	−1075
0.57	0	0	0	−1700
0.575	625	0	625	−1075
0.58	1250	0	1250	−450
0.585	1875	0	1875	175
0.59	2500	0	2500	800

0.595	3125	0	3125	1425
0.6	3750	0	3750	2050
0.605	4375	0	4375	2675
0.61	5000	0	5000	3300

At even lower or higher prices, the straddle buyer makes greater profits. The profit diagram for the straddle buyer is shown in Figure 15.15.

A long **strangle** strategy involves the purchase of a put and a call at *two different* exercise prices. This allows an investor to position the strategy according to his beliefs and it can lower the initial cost of the strategy relative to purchasing an at-the-money straddle. For example, suppose the current futures price of a June SF futures contract is $0.5774/SF, and an investor believes that the Swiss franc is more likely to move sharply lower than it is to increase in price. Then, purchasing the June 5800 futures call (for a premium of $0.0053/SF; see Figure 14.8) and the June 5700 futures put (for a premium of $0.0031/SF) would allow speculation on these beliefs. The initial cost of this strategy is $CF_0 = -\$1050$. The profit diagram of this strangle is present in Figure 15.16. You should prepare the profit table and compare it to Figure 15.16.

Figure 15.16 shows that the initial cost of the strangle strategy, which is also the maximum loss if both options expire worthless, is $1050. This is less than the initial cost of buying a straddle. In addition, the strangle buyer makes a greater profit (or smaller loss) if $S_T < \$0.575/SF$. If the strangle buyer instead thought there was a greater probability that the Swiss franc would move higher rather than decline, he might buy the June 5700 call and buy the June 5650 put. Such a strategy shifts the strangle diagram in Figure 15.16 to the left. Problem 15.9 at the end of the chapter asks you to verify this by preparing a profit table and drawing a profit diagram.

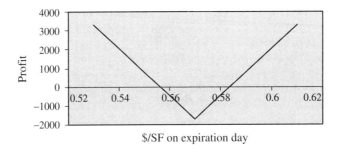
Figure 15.15 Buying a straddle.

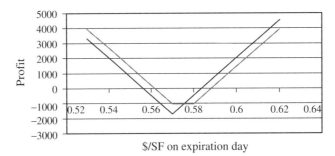
Figure 15.16 Long strangle vs long straddle.

The straddle or strangle *writer* profits from price stability. In selling a straddle, a put and a call with the same exercise price are sold. For example, see Figure 14.5, and consider the written straddle using the Cisco October 20 options:

Sell 1 Cisco October 20 call	+3.30
Sell 1 Cisco October 20 put	+3.90
Initial cash flow, CF_0	+7.20

At expiration, we have the following:

	At Time T			
S_T	Buy Jan 20 Call	Buy Jan 20 Put	Cash Flow CF_T	$CF_0 + CF_T$
17	0	−3	−3	+4.20
18	0	−2	−2	+5.20
19	0	−1	−1	+6.20
20	0	0	0	+7.20
21	−1	0	−1	+6.20
22	−2	0	−2	+5.20
23	−3	0	−3	+4.20

In this example, losses are realized if Cisco falls below 12.80 or rises above 27.20. The profit diagram is shown in Figure 15.17.

There are two sources of substantial risk in writing a straddle. First, unless Cisco is exactly at 20 on and just before the option's expiration day, there will always be some risk of early exercise because one of the options will always be in the money. In Chapter 16, we will learn that an in-the-money put may always be exercised early. Furthermore, while an in-the-money call *should* be exercised early only immediately before an ex-dividend day, some investors might wish to exercise a few days before the ex-date, and others might exercise a few days before the expiration date even in the absence of dividends. For example, tax considerations might motivate early exercise of an in-the-money call. Second, there is risk of significant losses if Cisco rises or falls sharply. At $S_T = 50$, for example, the total loss is $2280. The potential losses should Cisco rise in price are theoretically unlimited.

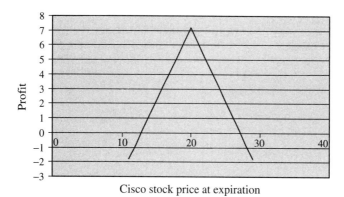

Figure 15.17 Written straddle.

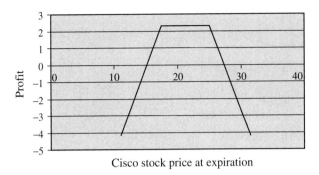

Figure 15.18 Written strangle.

Selling a strangle, however, removes part of the early exercise risk. An investor who expects Cisco to trade in a price range of $17.50–$25/share could sell the July 17.50 Cisco put and sell the July 25 call. Figure 15.18 shows the profit diagram of this written strangle.

Again, an investor need not trade only one put and one call. Different profit strategies can be tailored to an investor's beliefs by varying the ratio of puts to calls, thereby creating different profit diagrams. Some of these combinations are given in the end-of-chapter problem set.

15.9 SYNTHETIC FORWARD

Buying a call and simultaneously writing a put with the same strike price and time to expiration creates a "synthetic" long forward position in the underlying asset. For example, observe the right-most column of Figure 14.6. Suppose a trader buys the May 1250 SPX call and writes the May 1250 SPX put.

Buy 1 SPX 1250 call	− 19.90
Sell 1 SPX 1250 put	+ 12.50
	$CF_0 = -7.40$

Thus, this strategy costs $740 to initiate. At expiration, both option positions are offset:

S_T	Sell 1 SPX May 1250 Call	Buy 1 SPX May 1250 Put	Time T Cash Flow, CF_T	Profit/Loss $CF_0 + CF_T$
1247	0	−3	−3	− 10.4
1248	0	−2	−2	− 9.4
1249	0	−1	−1	− 8.4
1250	0	0	0	− 7.4
1251	+1	0	+1	− 6.4
1252	+2	0	+2	− 5.4
1253	+3	0	+3	− 4.4
1254	+4	0	+4	− 3.4
1255	+5	0	+5	− 2.4
1256	+6	0	+6	− 1.4

1257	+7	0	+7	−0.4
1258	+8	0	+8	+0.6
1259	+9	0	+9	+1.6

The profit diagram is shown in Figure 15.19.

Note that Figure 15.19 is similar to the long stock position shown in Figure 15.1. However, there are some differences between actually buying the underlying asset (SPX) and taking the long synthetic forward position. First, consider that one must invest $125,518 to effectively buy 100 shares of the S&P 500 (the spot SPX was at 1255.18 on May 10, 2001), but only $740 to assume the long synthetic forward position. Clearly, the return on investment will be higher for the synthetic forward. Second, while the breakeven price is $1255.18 if the underlying spot asset is purchased, the breakeven price is $1257.40 for the synthetic forward (the strike price plus the cost of the position). This synthetic forward price of $1257.40 should theoretically equal the cost-of-carry pricing model price ($F=S+$ carry costs − future value of dividends); see Chapter 5. Finally, be aware that selling the May 1250 put will entail a substantial initial margin requirement.

Symmetrically, writing a call and buying a put creates a synthetic *short* forward position in the underlying asset. Using the same May 1250 SPX options, this strategy generates a cash inflow of $740 at initiation:

Sell 1 SPX 1250 call	+19.90
Buy 1 SPX 1250 put	−12.50
	$CF_0 = +7.40$

At expiration, both option positions are offset:

S_T	Buy 1 SPX May 1250 Call	Sell 1 SPX May 1250 Put	Time T Cash Flow, CF_T	Profit/Loss $CF_0 + CF_T$
1247	0	+3	+3	+10.4
1248	0	+2	+2	+9.4
1249	0	+1	+1	+8.4
1250	0	0	0	+7.4
1251	−1	0	−1	+6.4
1252	−2	0	−2	+5.4

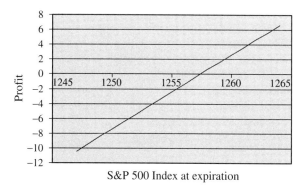

Figure 15.19 Synthetic long forward position in the SPX.

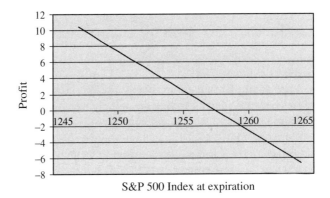

Figure 15.20 Synthetic short forward position in the SPX.

1253	−3	0	−3	+4.4
1254	−4	0	−4	+3.4
1255	−5	0	−5	+2.4
1256	−6	0	−6	+1.4
1257	−7	0	−7	+0.4
1258	−8	0	−8	−0.6
1259	−9	0	−9	−1.6

The profit diagram from this synthetic short forward strategy is shown in Figure 15.20. Note that the trader is effectively short at a price of \$1257.40 (the strike price plus the premium generated at initiation).

15.10 OTHER STRATEGIES

By now you should be able to draw any profit diagram for any strategy. For example, consider a put ratio spread. A put ratio spread consists of one long put with a relatively high strike price (K_H), and selling two, three, or more puts with a relatively low strike price (K_L). Let's use the SPX price data in Figure 14.6 to construct a put ratio spread profit table and profit diagram for June put options (they are in the right-most column of Figure 14.6). Initially, we buy one June 1325 put and sell three June 1300 puts. Thus, $K_H = 1325$ and $K_L = 1300$. The time 0 cash flows are as follows:

Buy 1 June 1325 put	−74.50
Sell 3 June 1300 puts	+166.50 (each of these has a premium of 55.50)

$$CF_0 = +92.00$$

The time T cash flows, and the total profit/loss, are as follows:

S_T	Sell 1 1325 Put	Buy 3 1300 Puts	CF_T	$CF_0 + CF_T$
1200	125	−300	−175	−83
1205	120	−285	−165	−73
1210	115	−270	−155	−63

1215	110	−255	−145	−53
1220	105	−240	−135	−43
1225	100	−225	−125	−33
1230	95	−210	−115	−23
1235	90	−195	−105	−13
1240	85	−180	−95	−3
1245	80	−165	−85	7
1250	75	−150	−75	17
1255	70	−135	−65	27
1260	65	−120	−55	37
1265	60	−105	−45	47
1270	55	−90	−35	57
1275	50	−75	−25	67
1280	45	−60	−15	77
1285	40	−45	−5	87
1290	35	−30	5	97
1295	30	−15	15	107
1300	25	0	25	117
1305	20	0	20	112
1310	15	0	15	107
1315	10	0	10	102
1320	5	0	5	97
1325	0	0	0	92
1330	0	0	0	92
1335	0	0	0	92
1340	0	0	0	92
1345	0	0	0	92
1350	0	0	0	92

The resulting profit diagram is shown in Figure 15.21.

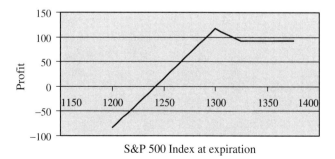

Figure 15.21 Put ratio spread.

The maximum profit is $+\$11,700$, which is realized if $S_T = 1300$. At all $S_T \geq 1325$, a profit of $\$9200$ is realized. This is represented by the horizontal line segment to the right of $K_H = 1325$. Note that the slope of the line to the left of $K_L = 1300$ is 2. That is, for every dollar below $S_T = 1300$, the strategy loses two additional dollars. This bullish strategy breaks even at $S_T = 1241.50$.

15.11 RATE-OF-RETURN DIAGRAMS

In a rate-of-return diagram, the rate of return on an investor's initial outlay is on the y axis, and S_T is on the x axis. You should prepare rate-of-return diagrams only if there is an initial cash outflow.[12]

EXAMPLE 15.1   Consider an investor who writes a covered call. The initial parameters are $S_0 = 38$, $K = 40$, $C_0 = 3$, and $T =$ three months. Thus, the initial cash flows are as follows:

Buy 100 shares of stock	-38 (per share)
Write 1 call	$+3$ (per share)
Initial cash flow at time 0	-35 (per share)

At expiration, we have the following results:

Sell Stock for S_T	Buy Call for C_T	Total Cash Flow at Time T	Profit/Loss $CF_0 + CF_T$	Rate of Return
$+34$	0	$+34$	-1	-2.86%
$+35$	0	$+35$	0	0%
$+36$	0	$+36$	$+1$	$+2.86\%$
$+37$	0	$+37$	$+2$	$+5.71\%$
$+38$	0	$+38$	$+3$	$+8.57\%$
$+39$	0	$+39$	$+4$	$+11.43\%$
$+40$	0	$+40$	$+5$	$+14.29\%$
$+41$	-1	$+40$	$+5$	$+14.29\%$
$+42$	-2	$+40$	$+5$	$+14.29\%$

The profit diagram is depicted in Figure 15.22a, and the rate-of-return diagram in Figure 15.22b. Note that the rate of return is over a three-month holding period. It can be annualized in one of two ways: simple interest (multiply each return by 4, since there are four 3-month periods in a year), or compounded interest (add 1.0 to each decimal return and take the number to the fourth power, then subtract 1.0). These two approaches are illustrated as follows:

Three Month Unannualized Rate of Return	Annualized Rate of Return, Simple	Annualized Rate of Return, Compounded
-2.86%	$(-.0286)(4) = -11.43\%$	$(0.9714)^4 - 1 = -10.95\%$
0%	0%	0%
$+2.86\%$	$+11.43\%$	$+11.93\%$

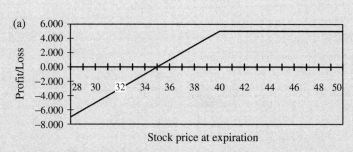

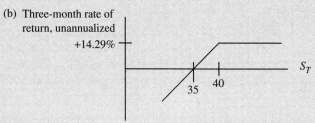

Figure 15.22 Writing a covered call: (*a*) profit diagram and (*b*) rate-of-return diagram.

+5.71%	+22.86%	+24.89%
+8.57%	+34.29%	+38.95%
+11.43%	+45.71%	+54.17%
+14.29%	$(14.29)(4) = +57.14\%$	$(1.1429)^4 - 1 = +70.60\%$

Also note that the unannualized rate of return of 14.29% is achieved if the stock price rises from 38 to as little as 40. In contrast, the unannualized rate of return on the stock if $S_0 = 38$ and $S_T = 40$ is only $(40 - 38)/38 = 5.263\%$.

15.12 PROFIT DIAGRAMS FOR DIFFERENT HOLDING PERIODS

Investors do not have to hold their positions until expiration. Profit diagrams for shorter holding periods can be created, though you must *estimate* what each option will be worth at different times to expiration. Option pricing models are used to estimate future option values, but they will not be presented until Chapters 17 and 18. FinCAD provides two option strategy simulators that illustrate the "decay process" of option strategies. Click on FinCADXL, and look under the "Options–vanilla" menu. The two choices for illustrating strategy decay diagrams are Option Strategy Simulator–New and Option Strategy Simulation–Two Options. Figure 15.23a shows how the new Option Strategy Simulator diagrams the time-evolving profits and losses from a bull vertical spread. The price of the underlying asset on the day that the strategy is first created is 68.75. Figure 15.23b depicts the same "decay process" for a purchased straddle. Figure 15.23c gives the values that were entered into the "option details" portion of the FinCAD spreadsheet for the straddle. The put and the call were purchased on the start date. The options expire on the expiry date. The value date is the date on which the profits and losses are computed. The decay of a strategy shows how profits and losses change at different stock prices as time passes, all else equal.

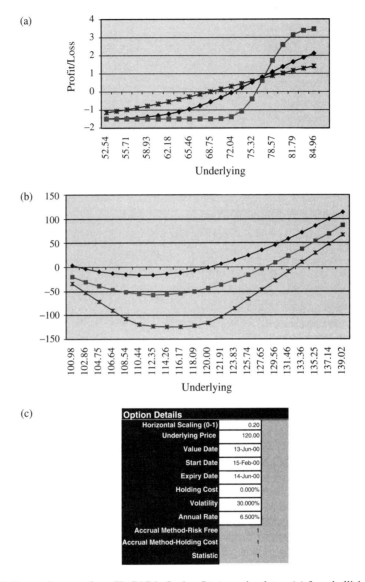

Figure 15.23 Decay diagrams from FinCAD's Option Strategy simulator: (*a*) for a bullish money spread with calls, and (*b*) for a purchased straddle. (*c*) Values entered as "option details" for the straddle. Curves show profit and loss as follows: asterisks, one day later (assuming no change in the implied volatility); diamonds, one month later; squares, seven weeks later (i.e., one day before options expire).

15.13 SEVERAL CAVEATS

Before using the strategies described in the preceding sections, you must be aware of several factors that will affect the profit or loss ultimately realized.

a. First, there is no reason that these positions must be held until expiration. They can be closed out early, and doing so will affect the nature of the profit diagram. For example,

EXAMPLE 15.2 Today is June 2. July 155 puts are priced at $3\,^1/_8$. July 150 puts have a premium of $1^1/_2$. For an investor who wishes to create a bullish vertical spread with puts, the initial cash flows on June 2 are as follows:

Sell 1 July 155 put	$+3\,^1/_8$
Buy 1 July 150 put	$-1\,^1/_2$
Initial cash flow, CF_0	$+1\,^5/_8$

Now, suppose that the investor wishes to observe the profit diagram as it would look if the strategy was closed out on June 25, which is 22 days before the expiration date of July 17. The values of the puts must be estimated for a range of stock prices, and assuming that the puts have 22 days remaining to expiration. It is possible that the June 25 cash flow table would be as follows[13]:

$S(T)$	Buy One July 155 Put	Sell One July 150 Put	Cash Flow on June 25	Total Cash Flow $(+1\,^5/_8+$ June 25 Cash Flow)
143	−9.2131	6.4931	−2.7201	−1.0951
145	−7.5760	5.1348	−2.4412	−0.8162
147	−6.0458	3.9155	−2.1303	−0.5053
149	−4.6361	2.8408	−1.7953	−0.1703
151	−3.3576	1.9110	−1.4466	0.1784
153	−2.2172	1.1221	−1.0951	0.5299
155	−1.2175	0.4658	−0.7517	0.8733
157	−0.3567	−0.0695	−0.4262	1.1988
159	0.3710	−0.4974	−0.1263	1.4987
161	0.9750	−0.8327	0.1423	1.7673
163	1.4670	−1.0904	0.3765	2.0015
165	1.8603	−1.2846	0.5757	2.2007
167	2.1689	−1.4281	0.7408	2.3658
169	2.4067	−1.5322	0.8745	2.4995
171	2.5866	−1.6064	0.9803	2.6053
173	2.7203	−1.6582	1.0621	2.6871
175	2.8179	−1.6938	1.1241	2.7491
177	2.8880	−1.7179	1.1701	2.7951
179	2.9374	−1.7339	1.2036	2.8286
181	2.9717	−1.7443	1.2274	2.8524
183	2.9951	−1.7510	1.2441	2.8691

Figure 15.24 shows the June 25 cash flows (not profits) to this strategy, assuming that all positions are held only until June 25th.

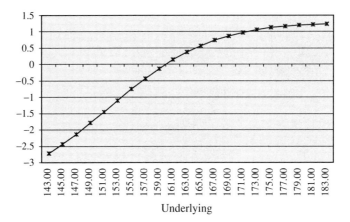

Figure 15.24 A FinCAD Option Strategy simulator diagram for *payoffs* of bullish vertical spread created in Example 15.2.

Figures 15.23a and 15.23b show how the profit diagrams for a bullish vertical spread and purchased straddle might change if they were closed out prior to expiration.

b. Keep in mind that bid–ask spreads exist for options. Thus, an investor buys at a higher asked price and sells at a lower bid price. Bid–ask spreads are a cost of trading and will reduce profits (or increase losses). Sometimes, an investor will have to pay more than $S_T - K$ for a call purchased at expiration, or receive less than that amount if sold, because the bid price is below the call's intrinsic value and the asked price is above it. Indeed, when the expiration day is near, bid prices of deep in-the-money calls and puts are frequently less than $S - K$ and $K - S$, respectively. Floor traders arbitrage under these conditions.

c. Brokerage commissions can be substantial.

d. We have ignored dividend payments on the stock.

e. Perhaps most important, we have ignored the risk of early exercise. Most of the options traded in the United States are American options. As such, a written put that is in the money might be exercised early at any time. Written in-the-money calls are most likely to be exercised just prior to an ex-dividend date, though transactions costs and tax considerations might induce the in-the-money call owner to exercise even when there are no dividends. We will cover the topic of early exercise in greater detail in Chapter 16. Keep in mind, however, that early exercise can add to the investor's transactions costs, margin requirements, and risk.

f. We have ignored the margin requirements required for written option positions.

g. We have ignored the timing of the cash flows, and the time value of money.

h. Most of the examples in this chapter had 100 shares of stock as the underlying asset. The profit diagrams from these strategies can also be realized when one is trading foreign exchange options and futures options.

15.14 RESEARCH ON OPTION STRATEGIES

Several empirical papers have attempted to measure the risks and rewards to investors who use some of the strategies discussed in this chapter. When reading any of these, keep in mind the caveats of Section 15.13. Many of the early papers used closing daily option prices and did not account for market frictions such as transactions costs, bid–asked spreads, and nonsynchronous trading. Also, the realized results of any strategy can be time specific. For example, writing covered calls will provide superior results in a neutral market but will underperform many strategies when the market rises sharply. Be cautious in interpreting strategy results obtained over a short time period. Black (1975) is an insightful early article on using options.

Another important fact to remember is this:

> If options are correctly priced, no option strategy should offer superior returns, given its level of risk. The different strategies should appeal to different investors based on their beliefs and on their levels of risk aversion.

A related issue entails evaluating the performance of portfolio managers when they use options. Options create highly skewed returns distributions, so that the usual method of comparing the expected return to a risk measure such as the variance of the returns distribution is not advised. See Bookstaber and Clarke (1984), Galai and Geske (1984), and Ferguson (1987) for some of the issues in performance evaluation when portfolio managers use options.

15.15 SUMMARY

In this chapter, we demonstrate how profit tables and profit diagrams can be prepared for any simple or complex option strategy. There are six elementary strategies: long and short stock, buy and write a call, and buy and write a put. All complex strategies are combinations of these six basic positions.

When option positions are held until expiration, the payoff patterns differ considerably from those that can be achieved by using only the underlying security. Thus, the payoffs can be patterned according to an investor's beliefs and level of risk aversion. Indeed, this is often cited as an economic rationale for the existence of options.

In Chapter 17, however, we will see that over shorter periods of time (e.g., one day), and for a specified probability distribution of stock price movements, a call option is equivalent to a levered position in the stock. In other words, the payoff pattern of a long call position will be seen to be identical to the one provided by a long position in the stock financed in part by borrowed funds. A long put is equivalent to the short sale of stock and lending. In the absence of transactions costs, the payoffs provided by an option can be replicated by adjusting the investment in stocks and bonds as time passes, and as the price of the stock changes. Therefore, realizing the payoff patterns of the strategies in this chapter should not necessarily be cited as a reason for the existence of options. However, one reason that options exist is reduced transactions costs.

McMillan (1992) provides additional details on the different strategies covered in this chapter.

References

Black, Fischer. 1975. "Fact and Fantasy in the Use of Options." *Financial Analysts Journal*, Vol. 31, No. 4, July/August, pp. 36–41, 61–72.

Bookstaber, Richard M., and Roger Clarke. 1984. "Option Portfolio Strategies: Measurement and Evaluation." *Journal of Business*, Vol. 57, No. 4, October, pp. 469–492.

Brown, Keith C. and Scott L. Lummer. 1986. "The Cash Management Implications of a Hedged Dividend Capture Strategy." *Financial Management*, Vol. 15, No. 2, Summer, pp. 7–17.

Brown, Keith C. and Scott L. Lummer. 1988. "A Reexamination of the Covered Call Option Strategy for Corporate Cash Management." *Financial Management*, Vol. 17, No. 4, Winter, pp. 45–58.

Ferguson, Robert. 1987. "A Comparison of the Mean-Variance and Long-Term Return Characteristics of Three Investment Strategies." *Financial Analysts Journal*, Vol. 43, No. 4, July–August, pp. 55–66.

Galai, Dan, and Robert Geske. 1984. "Option Performance Measurement." *Journal of Portfolio Management*, Vol. 10, No. 3, Spring, pp. 42–46.

McMillan, Lawrence G. 1992. *Options as a Strategic Investment*, 3rd ed. New York: New York Institute of Finance.

Zivney, Terry L, and Michael J. Alderson. 1986. "Hedged Dividend Capture with Stock Index Options." *Financial Management*, Vol 15, No. 2, Summer, pp. 5–12.

Notes

[1]Recall that the subject of short selling is covered in detail in Appendix A of Chapter 5.

[2]An investor who is very bearish should buy puts.

[3]An investor who is very bullish should buy calls. The writer of an at-the-money naked put, or an out-of-the-money naked put, can be neutral on the stock.

[4]If the AMAT put was only slightly in the money at expiration (e.g., $S_T = 49.80$), a put owner might not exercise because transactions costs might exceed the in-the-money amount. Some brokers will automatically exercise puts that are in the money by some minimum amount on the expiration day.

[5]In a horizontal spread, the investor typically writes a call with a short time to expiration and buys a call with a longer time to expiration. The same can be done with puts.

[6]The covered call writer would likely be assigned the written call by the call holder. In this case, he receives the strike price of 20 upon delivery of the shares. The profit diagram is the same as the example in the body of the text. In practice, when deciding whether to close an in-the-money option position early, a call writer should consider commissions, dividends, whether he wishes to continue owning a particular stock (here, Cisco), and his subjective perceived probability that this stock will decline in price before expiration.

[7]The six basic positions are long stock, short stock, long call, short (written) call, long put, and short put. All the more complex strategies consist of combinations of the basic positions.

[8]See Brown and Lummer 1986, 1988, and Zivney and Alderson (1986).

[9]The basic put–call parity theorem is $C - P = S - PV(K)$. In other words, the difference between a call and a put on the same stock with the same strike price and time to expiration equals the value of the stock less the present value of K. Rearranging, $(-S + C) - P = -PV(K)$, which says that the difference between the cost of a covered call $(-S + C)$ and the cost of a long position in a put $(-P)$ equals the investment of $\$PV(K)$.

[10]If another option with a different strike price and a different time to expiration were to be sold, it would be called a **diagonal spread**.

[11]As will be discussed in Chapter 16, if in-the-money calls will ever be exercised early, it will be optimal to do so only on the day before the stock trades ex-dividend.

[12]Rate-of-return diagrams are tricky to interpret when the initial cash flow is positive (i.e., an initial cash inflow). You might, however, consider the interest rate you compute to be a borrowing cost, because you are effectively borrowing money when you initially have a cash inflow. Then, your goal is to borrow that money at the lowest possible rate.

[13]The put values were estimated using the Black–Scholes put option pricing model, with no dividends. The volatility is 30%, and the riskless interest rate is 6.5%. See Section 18.10.1 of Chapter 18 for discussion of this model.

PROBLEMS

15.1 You buy a call for 2 5/8. The strike price is 60. What is the maximum loss you can possibly realize? What is the maximum profit? At what expiration day stock price will you break even?

15.2 You write a naked call. The call premium is 4 3/4. The strike price is 40. What is the maximum loss you can possibly realize? What is the maximum profit? At what expiration day stock price will you break even?

15.3 Refer to Figure 14.5. Suppose you buy the Broadcom June 40 put option. Prepare the profit table and profit diagram. What is the breakeven expiration day stock price?

15.4 Refer to Figure 14.5. Suppose you sell the AmOnline (America Online) July 50 put option. Prepare the profit table and profit diagram. What is the breakeven expiration day stock price? Why would an investor write this put? What are the benefits and costs of writing this naked put compared with placing a limit order to buy the stock at a price of $50/share?

15.5 Figure 15.8 uses Cisco common stock to illustrate a covered call strategy. It shows that the losses from this strategy can be significant if the stock price declines sharply. These losses can be capped by purchasing a put. Using the data from Figure 14.5, prepare a profit table and a profit diagram for a strategy in which you buy 100 shares of Cisco, sell one July 20 call, and buy one July 15 put.

15.6 An investor wishes to buy a bullish spread using calls on eBay. Refer to Figure 14.5. Construct the profit diagram if the May 50 and May 55 calls are used. Then construct the profit diagram if the May 55 and May 60 calls are used. Compare the two diagrams.

Discuss the advantages and drawbacks of each.

15.7 Define C_H as the premium of a call with a high strike price, K_H. Define C_L as the premium of a call with a low strike price, K_L. What is the maximum profit that can be realized from a bullish spread with calls? What is the maximum loss from a bullish spread with calls?

15.8 Prepare the profit table for the strangle strategy shown in Figure 15.16.

15.9 Prepare a profit table and a profit diagram for a strangle strategy in which the Swiss franc June 5700 call and the June 5650 put are purchased. Compare the result with that for the strangle strategy in Figure 15.16. How is it different?

15.10 Use the data from Figure 14.5 to prepare a profit table and a profit diagram sketch for the following strategy, assuming that all positions are held until expiration. The underlying security is General Electric (Gen El).

> Sell short 200 shares
>
> Buy 2 June 50 calls
>
> Sell 1 June 50 put
>
> Sell 1 June 55 call

15.11 Some floor traders will "leg into two ratio spreads." This strategy is used when a great deal of near term volatility is expected, followed by a large price increase or a large price decrease. For example, suppose a floor trader believed that Qualcomm was going to announce a surprise earnings figure at the end of June 2000, at which time the stock would move to either $180 or $140 per share. Until then, the trader believed that the stock would likely exhibit considerable volatility between

$155 and $165 per share. Reflecting this uncertainty, he observed that the July 160 puts and calls were overpriced relative to their "normal" values. Assume the July 160 put sold for 7 and the July 160 call sold for 8 on June 3, 2000.

The investor could have bought the high-priced puts and calls (a straddle), thereby profiting if his beliefs were correct. To realize a profit, the stock would then have had to move 15 points either up or down, from its current value of $159.375 share.

Instead, the trader could have legged into two ratio spreads. Legging into a position involves piecemeal trades over time, with the risk that one leg (or more) might not get executed. First, he could have sold one July 160 put (for 7) and one July 160 call (for 8). At this stage, if Qualcomm's price had remained stable (i.e., the trader was wrong), he likely would have profited as the time value of the July 160 options decayed.

Suppose instead, that two days later, Qualcomm had made a move to 165, such that one leg of the back spread would be entered by buying two out-of-the-money July 155 puts. Assume that at this time the July 155 puts sold for 3 $1/8$ each. Now, the trader's belief of considerable short-term volatility would be tested. Assume that the trader was correct and that four days after the July 155 puts were bought, Qualcomm indeed fell to 155. The last leg of the back spread would be entered by buying two out-of-the-money July 165 calls. Assume that they sell for 3 $3/4$ each.

Prepare the profit table and profit diagram for this strategy.

Note that it is unlikely that individual investors could ever profitably employ this strategy because they must buy the options at the ask price and sell at the bid. They also must pay high commissions on the options. Finally, be cognizant of the great risk that exists until all the legs have been entered.

15.12 Suppose that on an airplane flight you overhear one businessman talking excitedly to another about Dell. You also think that you hear the terms "financial distress" and "takeover candidate." Finally, you hear one of the businessmen say, "Dell's stock price will really move when this becomes public." However, because the pilot rudely interrupted your eavesdropping, you do not know whether your unwitting informant expects Dell's stock price to move up or move down. Suppose that the date of the flight is May 10, 2001, which also happens to be the date of the price data in Figure 14.5. Discuss the options trades you would make based on your information.

15.13 Using the July 20 and July 25 puts and calls for Cisco in Figure 14.5, construct a long "box spread." That is, prepare a profit table and a profit diagram for the following positions:

> Buy 1 July 20 call
>
> Sell 1 July 20 put
>
> Sell 1 July 25 call
>
> Buy 1 July 25 put

What do you notice about this strategy? Suppose you *reverse* the positions in each of the four options. What do you notice now about this strategy?

Use FinCAD's "Option Strategy Simulator–New" to analyze how this strategy changes over time, all else equal.

15.14 Use call data from Figure 14.5 for AmOnline to construct a "long butterfly." That is, prepare a profit table and a profit diagram for the following positions:

> Buy 1 July 50 call
>
> Sell 2 July 55 calls
>
> Buy 1 July 60 call

Use FinCAD's "Option Strategy Simulator–New" to analyze how this strategy changes over time, all else equal.

Now, suppose you had read the data from the wrong column and used puts instead of calls. Redo the profit table and profit diagram using the put data. What do you notice?

Finally, reverse the positions in each call option and redo the profit table and profit diagram for this "short butterfly."

15.15 Use call data from Figure 14.6 for S&P 500 (SPX) options to construct a "long condor." That is, prepare a profit table and a profit diagram for the following positions:

> Buy 1 May 1250 call
>
> Sell 1 May 1275 call
>
> Sell 1 May 1300 call
>
> Buy 1 May 1325 call

Use FinCAD's "Option Strategy Simulator–New" to analyze how this strategy changes over time, all else equal.

Suppose you had read the data from the wrong column and used puts instead of calls (Duh!). Redo the profit table and profit diagram using the put data. What do you notice?

Finally, reverse the positions in each of the four case options, (this is known as a "short condor.") Redo the profit table and profit diagram.

15.16 A stop-loss order works like this. You tell your broker to sell some stock that you own if its price ever declines to some lower level. If the stock reaches that level, your stop-loss order will automatically become a market order to sell (or a limit order to sell). Compare the benefits and costs of these two alternative strategies: (a) buy stock and place a stop-loss order at a price $5 below the current stock price and (b) buy an in-the-money call option, with the strike price $5 below the current stock price.

15.17 Fill in the two blanks in the following, which is based on a *Wall Street Journal* article dealing with LEAPS on a different stock.

The new long-term options could also be used to protect profits on stock bought earlier. For example, suppose an investor owned 100 shares of America Online purchased several years ago at $65 a share. The stock is currently selling for around $144. Suppose the nervous investor is worried about losing some of the gain if the market goes into the soup. To sleep better, the investor could try a "hedge wrapper." To construct a hedge wrapper, sell a call with a strike price above the current price of the stock and purchase a put with a strike price below the stock's price. In the AOL case, the worried investor could sell a call with a strike price of $155, while buying a put with a $130 strike price. Both options expire in January 2000. The investor would receive a brokerage credit of $1012.50 for selling the call and would pay $725 for the put—a net credit of $287.50, not counting commissions.

This strategy would not only offer protection against a stock price slide, it would ensure a profit—again, not counting commissions—of at least __ % on the combined stock and stock options positions. The investor's downslide protection comes from the put, which gains in value if the stock price drops below the put's strike price.

The trade-off is that the return would be capped at __%, no matter how high the stock rallied. That's because the investor could expect to have the stock "called" away at the $155 strike price once AOL's stock price rose above $155 a share.

15.18 In the late 1980s, two companies, Marion Merrill Dow and Rhône-Poulenc, issued **contingent value rights** (CVRs) that traded on the American Stock Exchange. To describe a CVR, two useful definitions are as follows:

BP = base price

TP = target price

If S_T is the stock price at expiration, then a CVR pays off as follows at time T:

0   if $S_T \geq TP$

$TP - S_T$ if $BP \leq S_T \leq TP$

$TP - BP$ if $S_T \leq BP$

Here are the relevant parameters, assuming that the companies do not elect to extend the expiration date (which they could do):

	BP	TP	T
Marion Merrill Dow	$30.00	$45.77	September 30, 1991
Rhône-Poulenc	$52.00	$98.26	July 31, 1993

On January 10, 1991, the Rhône-Poulenc CVR sold for $8.25, and the common stock sold for $67.75. Prepare a profit table and profit diagram for the Rhône-Poulenc CVR. What other strategy offers the same type of payoff structure as a CVR?

Also prepare a profit table and profit diagram for a strategy in which one share of Rhône-Poulenc and one CVR are bought. What rate of return would an investor earn if Rhône-Poulenc's stock price on July 31, 1993 was unchanged from what it was on January 10, 1991? What are the rates of return if $S_T = BP$ and if $S_T = TP$? What is the breakeven point?

What is the minimum rate of return this strategy can realize?

15.19 Use FinCAD's "Option Strategy Simulator–New" template to analyze how a written strangle decays over time.

15.20 You buy a call option with a strike price of 40. The price of the call is 3. The price (today) of the underlying asset is 39. At what price would the underlying asset have to sell (S_T) for you to break even?

a. 36
b. 37
c. 40
d. 42
e. 43

15.21 You write a put with a strike price of 40. The price of the put is 3. The price of the underlying asset is 39. At what price would the underlying asset have to sell (S_T) for you to break even?

a. 36
b. 37
c. 40
d. 42
e. 43

15.22 The profit diagram for writing a covered call looks like

a. Buying a call
b. Writing a naked call
c. Buying a put
d. Writing a naked put
e. Buying the underlying asset

CHAPTER 16

Arbitrage Restrictions on Option Prices

In Chapter 15, we presented option strategies based on the value of options at expiration. In Chapters 17 and 18, we will discuss two particularly important models that can be used to calculate option prices before the option expiration date.

However, before those two specific models are presented, it is important to realize that basic option values before expiration must obey a set of pricing restrictions, regardless of the specific option-pricing model employed. Therefore, in this chapter, we present the upper and lower boundary prices for call and put options.

We close this chapter with a particularly important relationship is known as *put-call parity*. Note that this important relationship, the subject of Section 16.4, can be studied independently of the other pricing restrictions.

To begin, recall that a fundamental assertion of modern finance is that arbitrage cannot persist. Arbitrage is a trade, or a set of trades, that produces a positive cash flow at one or more dates and zero cash flows at all other dates. In well-functioning markets, options, like any other security, cannot be priced such that arbitrage opportunities exist. If the chance to realize a riskless arbitrage profit were to appear, investors would immediately move to exploit it, and in the process, prices would correct themselves. This chapter also establishes important concepts concerning the early exercise decision for American options on equities.[1]

We make the following assumptions in deriving the arbitrage restrictions described in this chapter:

a. No commissions or transactions costs.

b. All trades take place at a single price (i.e., there is no bid–ask spread, and trading does not affect the market price).

c. No taxes.

d. No margin requirements and no short sale restrictions. Investors receive the full amount of written options and shares sold short.[2]

e. Investors can trade in the stock and options markets instantaneously. Investors get immediate notice of option assignments.

f. Dividends are received on the ex-dividend day, and the ex-day stock price decline equals the dividend amount.

g. Investors prefer more wealth to less, and they are quick to take advantage of any arbitrage opportunities that appear.

h. The underlying asset is 100 shares of common stock, or an index option. (Some of the results do not apply to futures options or options on foreign exchange.)

If an option or options appear to violate any of the following derived restrictions, do not believe that *you* can exploit the apparent mispricing. The foregoing assumptions probably do not hold for you unless you are a low cost trader (i.e., an institutional trader or an individual with substantial capital who has seats on the appropriate options and stock exchanges). Floor traders also have the advantage of buying at the bid price and selling at the ask price. Finally, even if you observe that an option's *closing* price appears to be violating a pricing restriction, remember that prices in the financial press are always suspect owing to nonsynchronous trading and bid–ask spreads.

16.1 NOTATION

16.1.1 Time

Some notation must be introduced. Today is defined as time zero (0). The expiration date is time T. Any intermediate dates are denoted $t1$, $t2$, etc., with $t1$ the closest to time 0. Figure 16.1 depicts a time line that should make these concepts easier to picture. At time 0, the time left until expiration equals T. At time $t1$, the time left until expiration equals $T-t1$.

16.1.2 Interest Rates

The present value, as of today, of $\$Z$ to be received at time T is $Z(1+r)^{-T}=Z/(1+r)^{T}$. Thus if $T=1$ year, $K=\$50$, and the yearly interest rate is r is 8%, the present value is $50/(1.08)^{1}=\$46.2963$. An annual 8% interest rate can be converted to a rate applicable for a shorter period of time by using either the simple interest method (so that an annual rate of 8% is a 4% semiannual rate and a 2% quarterly rate) or the compound interest method. With the latter, one solves for the periodic rate that, if compounded, yields 8% per year. That is, in this example, the semiannual rate is 3.923% (because $1.03923^{2}-1=8\%$) and the quarterly rate is 1.943% (because $1.01943^{4}-1=8\%$).

You might ask whether the interest rate is a borrowing rate or a lending rate. Under the assumptions in this chapter, the two rates are equal. However, if you were ever to try to arbitrage, use your own borrowing rate if the trades call for borrowing and your own lending rate if they require lending. If markets are functioning properly, the pricing restrictions will incorporate the borrowing and lending rates of the most advantageously situated investors (the one with the lowest borrowing rate and the one with the highest riskless lending rate).

16.1.3 Dividends

Although we assume that corporations pay dividends on the ex-dividend day, that rarely happens in reality. On average, firms actually pay their dividends about a month after the ex-day. The error

```
/------------/------------/------------/------------/
```

Date	0	$t1$	$t2$	T
Time to expiration	T	$T-t1$	$T-t2$	0

Figure 16.1

created by assuming that a dividend payment of $0.50 is made on the ex-day, rather than on the actual payment day, equals the interest that could be earned on that amount between the ex-day and payment day. If the annual interest rate is 6%, this is about $0.50 \times 0.06 \times \frac{1}{12} = 0.0025. The error of a quarter of a cent per share can be safely ignored.

Announcements of the ex-date and the dividend amount are usually made well in advance of the ex-date. Thus, dividends can be frequently regarded as certain, or riskless, particularly when we are dealing with short-term options. In some cases, however, there is significant probability that a dividend will be raised, lowered, or eliminated altogether. Moreover, the dividends associated with long-term options such as LEAPS should be treated as random variables.

When dividends are uncertain, we must have some new notation. Define the maximum dividend amount expected as $\overline{D}$. When we discuss the present value of $\overline{D}$, we mean the maximum present value of the largest possible dividend. Therefore, you must assess (a) the closest date you believe that the stock will trade ex-dividend (a closer date increases the present value) and (b) the largest dividend you believe the company will pay. The latter will frequently equal the most recent quarterly dividend, with some added amount to account for a possible dividend increase.

Similarly, define the smallest dividend amount you believe possible as $\underline{D}$. If you believe there is some probability that the company will actually skip its dividend payment, then $\underline{D}$ equals zero. Most of the time, $\underline{D}$ will equal the current quarterly dividend. This is because dividends are infrequently reduced or suspended. When discussing the present value of $\underline{D}$, we mean the minimum present value of the smallest dividend believed possible, which is $\underline{D}$, paid at the latest date you believe possible.

For the remainder of the chapter, we generally follow the following format. First, a proposition is made and then the proposition is proven. Then, the proposition is intuitively discussed and examples are frequently given. Moreover, each proof follows the same format. Following the proposition, we ask, "What if the proposition is violated?" If it is violated, an inequality in the form $A > 0$ is created, where A defines certain trades that will lead to a cash inflow today. Then, we will demonstrate that no matter what happens in the future, only nonnegative cash flows will be realized. The proof is then complete because arbitrage profits are earned if the proposition is violated.

The arbitrage restrictions create the smallest distance possible between the highest permitted option value and the lowest permitted option value. To say that an option's lowest value (lower bound) is zero and that its highest value (upper bound) is infinity does not provide us with much information. If we can show that an option must sell between 4 and 7, or better still, between 5.2 and 5.7, then we have better information. At the limit, the upper and lower bounds will converge, in which case we can say we have an option pricing model. Option pricing models are the subject of the next two chapters.

We are now ready to establish pricing restrictions for option prices. In Section 16.2 we set boundary conditions for calls. Upper bounds, or maximum prices, for calls will be determined first. Then, we derive lower bounds, or minimum prices, given other factors such as the stock price, strike price, and dividends. You will learn that the bounds for American calls frequently differ from those for European calls. After establishing the upper and lower pricing boundaries, we will prove that two calls that differ only in their times to expiration or only in their exercise price must satisfy certain pricing restrictions. In Section 16.3 we determine the analogous pricing restrictions for puts.

Along the way, important statements about the possibility of early exercise of American calls and puts will be made, given the pricing restrictions that were proven.

16.2 PRICING RESTRICTIONS FOR CALLS

16.2.1 Upper Bound

The highest no-arbitrage price for a call is the current value of the underlying asset. That is,

Proposition I: $C \leq S$

What if $C > S$

If Proposition I is violated, $C - S > 0$. The form of this inequality is $A > 0$. To arbitrage, we wish to trade today so that we receive a cash inflow of C and pay a cash outflow of S. Therefore, we sell the call and purchase the stock.

Today		**At Any Date Before Expiration, the Written Call May Be Assigned**[3]	**At Expiration (if not exercised early)**	
			$S_T > K$	$S_T < K$
Sell call	$+C$	Deliver stock that you own	$-(S_T - K)$	0
Buy stock	$-S$	and receive K	$+S_T$	$+S_T$
	>0	$+K > 0$	$+K$	$+S_T$

Thus, if a call price exceeds the stock price, an investor can arbitrage by writing a covered call. By purchasing the stock at a price that is lower than the written call premium, the arbitrageur is causing a cash inflow to occur at time zero. Subsequently, only positive or zero cash flows will occur. This is arbitrage.

It is important to account for the possible early assignment of a written American option. Thus, we include the center column of our arbitrage tables. If the written call had been European, only the initial and expiration day cash flows would have been relevant.

16.2.2 Lower Bounds

The lower bound for call prices depends on whether the call is American or European and on whether there will be ex-dividend days between today and the expiration date.

16.2.2.1 American and European Calls, No Dividends

Proposition II: $C \geq \max[0, S - K(1+r)^{-T}]$

Proposition II says that any call on a stock that pays no dividends (or will not pay any dividends until after the call has expired) must sell for more than zero if $S < K(1+r)^{-T}$. If $S > K(1+r)^{-T}$, the call must sell for more than the stock price minus the present value of K, $S - K(1+r)^{-T}$.

It should be intuitively obvious why option premiums must be nonnegative. If an option has a negative price, the buyer receives a cash inflow when he purchases the option. Obviously, if that situation ever presented itself, an investor could "buy" the option and throw it away. By doing so, he would realize a cash inflow. Therefore, we have proven that a call premium cannot be negative.

Now, we complete the proof by showing that a call must sell for more than the difference between S and the present value of K, that is, $C \geq S - K(1+r)^{-T}$.

What if	$C < S - K(1+r)^{-T}$
Then	$C - S + K(1+r)^{-T} < 0$
Or	$-C + S - K(1+r)^{-T} > 0$

		At Expiration	
Today		$S_T > K$	$S_T < K$
Buy call	$-C$	$+(S_T - K)$	0
Sell stock	$+S$	$-S_T$	$-S_T$
Lend	$-K(1+r)^{-T}$	$+K$	$+K$
	>0	0	$-S_T + K > 0$

This proof holds for American or European calls because the arbitrage involves the purchase of the call. Thus, because he owns the option, the arbitrageur does not have to worry about being assigned the exercise.

There is a weaker lower bound for American calls (not European calls) that would allow an arbitrageur to immediately realize the profit.

Proposition II′: $C \geq \max[0, S - K]$

What if	$C < S - K$
Then	$C - S + K < 0$
Or	$-C + S - K > 0$

Today	
Buy call	$-C$
Exercise call (acquire the stock for $\$K$)	$-K$
Sell stock that you bought from the exercise	$+S$
	>0

Proposition II′ states that an American call must always sell for at least its intrinsic value. This is a weaker bound than Proposition II, for in-the-money calls. To illustrate why it is weaker, consider the case of: $S = 44$, $K = 40$, $r = 10\%$, and $T = 1$ year. Proposition II says that for American or European calls on non-dividend paying stocks, $C \geq S - K(1+r)^{-T}$, that is, $C \geq 44 - 40/1.1 = 7.636$. Proposition II′, however, merely states that $C \geq S - K$, or $C \geq 44 - 40 = 4$.

Proposition II′ is a weaker bound than Proposition II because stating that the call premium must exceed 7.636 is stronger than saying that it exceeds a price of only 4. However, the proof of proposition II′ is interesting because all cash flows from the arbitrage are realized immediately. Also, Proposition II′ holds for all American calls, even if there will be ex-dividend days prior to expiration.[4]

We have now established upper and lower pricing bounds for American and European calls on non-dividend-paying stocks. Figure 16.2 illustrates the nature of these bounds. The upper

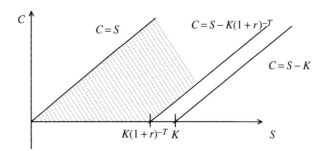

Figure 16.2 Boundaries on call option values before expiration, non-dividend paying stocks.

bound is the line $C=S$. The lower bound is the greater of 0 (if the call is out of the money), or $S-K(1+r)^{-T}$. The latter line dominates the $C=S-K$ line.

Before expiration, calls on non-dividend-paying stocks can sell only in the shaded region in Figure 16.2 We can now make some important statements.

1. *Before expiration, in-the-money calls on non-dividend-paying stocks will always have some time value.* We know this because $C \geq S-K(1+r)^{-T}$. In Figure 16.2, note that in-the-money calls will always sell for more than their intrinsic value (if there are no dividends). On day T, there is no time to expiration, so $C_T=S_T-K$ if the call is in the money, and $C_T=0$ if the call is out of the money.

2. *An American call on a non-dividend-paying stock will never be exercised before expiration.* If an investor exercises an American call before expiration, an investor pays \$$K$ for stock worth \$$S$. That is, the "profit" is the call's intrinsic value, $S-K$. We know, however, that if the investor sells the call, he receives at least $S-K(1+r)^{-T}$. This latter amount is always greater than the call's intrinsic value. If the call is out of the money (i.e., $K<S$), it is irrational for an investor to exercise it early because the investor pays \$$K$ for the stock when exercising, but the market price is \$$S$. The only time an American call on a non-dividend-paying stock will be rationally exercised is on its expiration day.

3. *An American call on a non-dividend paying stock will sell for the same price as a European call on the same stock, all else equal.* If an American call will never be exercised early (under the assumptions made at the start of the chapter), then an American call is effectively the same as a European call. There is no value to the option to exercise early if it will never be used. Note that in the "real world," in-the-money American calls might be exercised early before expiration, even if the stock will not pay dividends prior to expiration. This is because of the market imperfections we assumed away at the start of the chapter. Example 16.1 illustrates how the bid-ask spread can lead to early exercise.

Taxes and commissions might also induce an investor to exercise early.[5] Finally, suppose an investor is short the stock and long an in-the-money call. To close the short position and eliminate the costly margin tied up in the short position, an investor might elect to exercise early.

EXAMPLE 16.1   The existence of bid–ask spreads might lead an investor to exercise early. Suppose $S=72$, $K=60$, and the bid and ask prices on the call are $11\,{}^3/_8$ and $12\,{}^1/_8$, respectively. If a market order to sell were placed, an investor would realize only $11\,{}^3/_8$. The investor might be better off exercising and selling the stock, even after commissions.

16.2.2.2 European Calls on Dividend-Paying Stocks

For simplicity, assume that there is just one ex-dividend day between today and the expiration day. Today is time 0, and the ex-day is time $t1$.[6] Under this assumption, we can state:

Proposition III: $\quad C \geq \max[0, S - \overline{D}(1+r)^{-t1} - K(1+r)^{-T}]$

What if $\qquad C < S - \overline{D}(1+r)^{-t1} - K(1+r)^{-T}$

Then $\qquad C - S + \overline{D}(1+r)^{-t1} + K(1+r)^{-T} < 0$

Or $\qquad -C + S - \overline{D}(1+r)^{-t1} - K(1+r)^{-T} > 0$

Today		At Time $t1$	At Expiration $S_T > K$	At Expiration $S_T < K$
Buy call	$-C$		$+(S_T - K)$	0
Sell stock	$+S$	$-D$ (actual)	$-S_T$	$-S_T$
Lend	$-\overline{D}(1+r)^{-t1}$	$+\overline{D}$		
Lend	$-K(1+r)^{-T}$		$+K$	$+K$
	> 0	≥ 0	0	> 0

Note that there are two loans being made. First, a loan of $\$\overline{D}(1+r)^{-t1}$ is made from time 0 to time $t1$. This guarantees that the investor will receive the maximum dividend believed possible on the ex-day. The second loan is a loan of $\$K(1+r)^{-T}$ from time 0 to time T. Thus, the investor receives $\$K$ at time T.

At time $t1$, the stock trades ex-dividend. The arbitrageur is short the stock, so he must pay out the dividend. However, he had earlier made a loan so that he would be repaid an amount equal to the greatest dividend for which he believed he would be liable. Thus, at time $t1$, there is a positive cash flow (if the actual dividend is less than $\overline{D}$) or a zero cash flow (if the actual dividend equals $\overline{D}$).

EXAMPLE 16.2   As an example of a European call on a dividend paying stock that can sell below its intrinsic value, consider:

$S = 60$

$K = 20$

$T = 1$ year

$r = 10\%$

$K(1+r)^{-T} = 20/1.1 = 18.18$

Present value of dividends $= 3$

Note that while the intrinsic value of the call is 40, the lower bound of this call is only $60 - 18.18 - 3 = 38.82$. The reason for this is that the European call owner has a call only on the stock's value at time T, which equals the present value of all dividends subsequent to time T. The European call owner has no claim to any dividends paid between times 0 and T.

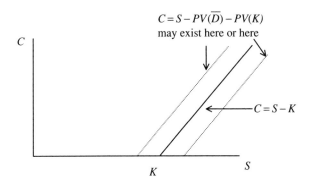

Figure 16.3 The lower bound for a European call on a dividend-paying stock can be to the left or the right of the intrinsic value line.

At expiration, the call must be sold for its intrinsic value if it finishes in the money, or else it expires worthless. The stock originally sold short must be covered (i.e., repurchased), creating a cash outflow of $\$S_T$. Finally, the original loan of $K(1+r)^{-T}$ is repaid, resulting in a cash inflow of $\$K$.

Proposition III creates an interesting phenomenon for European calls on dividend-paying assets. They can sell for below their intrinsic value. In other words, the restriction can lie to the left or the right of the $C = S - K$ line, as shown in Figure 16.3. Example 16.2 illustrates this phenomenon.

American calls, however, can never sell below their intrinsic value, regardless of dividends. If a dividend before the expiration date of the call is significant, the American call owner will exercise and capture the dividend.

16.2.2.3   American Calls on Dividend-Paying Stocks

As stated in Proposition IV, to prevent arbitrage the value of an American call on a dividend paying stock must equal or exceed four values. That is, the lower bound on the value of such a call is given by the maximum of the four values. In Proposition IV, we assume that times $t1$ and $t2$ are the nearby and more distant ex-dividend dates, respectively. If there is only one ex-date, or more than two ex-dates, Proposition IV must be appropriately modified (see page 451–2 for an example using three ex-dates).

$$\textbf{Propositions IV: } \quad C \geq \max \begin{cases} \text{a.} & 0 \\ \text{b.} & S - K(1+r)^{-t1} \\ \text{c.} & S - \overline{D1}(1+r)^{-t1} - K(1+r)^{-t2} \\ \text{d.} & S - \overline{D1}(1+r)^{-t1} - \overline{D2}(1+r)^{-t2} - K(1+r)^{-T} \end{cases}$$

We have already demonstrated that a call cannot sell for a negative value. Thus, Proposition IVa has been proven.

Proof of Proposition IVb proceeds as follows.

$$\begin{array}{ll} \text{What if} & C < S - K(1+r)^{-t1} \\ \text{Then} & C - S + K(1+r)^{-t1} < 0 \\ \text{Or} & -C + S - K(1+r)^{-t1} > 0 \end{array}$$

Today		Just Before the Stock Trades Ex-Dividend at Time $t1$
Buy call	$-C$	Exercise call: acquire stock and pay K
Sell stock	$+S$	Long stock and short stock offset each other
Lend	$-K(1+r)^{-t1}$	$+K$
	>0	0

The arbitrageur exercises the call an instant before the stock trades ex-dividend. In reality, if the stock traded ex-dividend on, say, January 12, then the call would be exercised at the close of trading on January 11. By exercising, the arbitrageur pays $K for the long stock position. However, because the stock was also sold short, the two positions offset each other.

Proof of Proposition IVc involves the exercise of the call just before the stock trades ex-dividend at time $t2$. It is left as an exercise for the student. However, the proof of Proposition IVd should provide a guide to prove Proposition IVc.

Proposition IVd proceeds as follows.

What if	$C < S - \overline{D1}(1+r)^{-t1} - \overline{D2}(1+r)^{-t2} - K(1+r)^{-T}$
Then	$C - S + \overline{D1}(1+r)^{-t1} + \overline{D2}(1+r)^{-t2} + K(1+r)^{-T} < 0$
Or	$-C + S - \overline{D1}(1+r)^{-t1} - \overline{D2}(1+r)^{-t2} - K(1+r)^{-T} > 0$

				Time T	
Today		Time $t1$	Time $t2$	$S_T > K$	$S_T < K$
Buy call	$-C$			$+(S_T - K)$	0
Sell stock	$+S$	$-D1$(actual)	$-D2$(actual)	$-S_T$	$-S_T$
Lend	$-\overline{D1}(1+r)^{-t1}$	$+\overline{D1}$			
Lend	$-\overline{D2}(1+r)^{-t2}$		$+\overline{D2}$		
Lend	$-K(1+r)^{-T}$			$+K$	$+K$
	>0	≥ 0	≥ 0	0	>0

Let's work an example of Proposition IVd. On March 20, 1997, IBM stock closed at $146 $^{1}/_{8}$ per share. The January 1998 IBM LEAP call with $K = 130$ closed at 27. The last dividend amount was $0.35/share, and the last ex-dividend date was February 6, 1997. The option expires on the third Friday of January 1998, which is January 16. The riskless interest rate is 6%. Assume that the earliest next three ex-dates will be on May 6, August 6, and November 6, 1997, and that the highest dividend amounts possible are $0.40, $0.45, and $0.45 per share on those three dates, respectively. Thus,

$S = 146\,^{1}/_{8}$

$K = 130$

$T = 302\text{ days} = 0.8274\text{ year}$

$r = 6\%/\text{year}$

$t1 = 47$ days $= 0.1288$ year

$t2 = 139$ days $= 0.3808$ year

$t3 = 231$ days $= 0.6329$ year

$\overline{D1} = 0.40$

$\overline{D2} = 0.45$

$\overline{D3} = 0.45$

Because there are three dividend dates, Propositions IV state that the call must sell for more than the greatest value of the following *five* amounts (note that to account for three dividend dates, we must modify Proposition IV on page 450).

a. 0

b. $S - K(1+r)^{-t1} = 146.125 - 130/(1.06)^{0.1288} = 17.097$

c. $S - \overline{D1}(1+r)^{-t1} - K(1+r)^{-t2} = 146.125 - 0.40/(1.06)^{0.1288} - 130/(1.06)^{0.3808} = 18.5808$

d. $S - \overline{D1}(1+r)^{-t1} - \overline{D2}(1+r)^{-t2} - K(1+r)^{-t3}$

$= 146.125 - 0.40/(1.06)^{0.1288} - 0.45/(1.06)^{0.3808} - 130/(1.06)^{0.6329} = 19.9947$

e. $S - \overline{D1}(1+r)^{-t1} - \overline{D2}(1+r)^{-t2} - \overline{D3}(1+r)^{-t3} - K(1+r)^{-T}$

$= 146.125 - 0.40/(1.06)^{0.1288} - 0.45/(1.06)^{0.3808} - 0.45/(1.06)^{0.6329}$

$- 130/(1.06)^{0.8274} = 20.973$

The greatest value of these four amounts is 20.973, and the actual call value was 27. Thus, there were no arbitrage opportunities. However, suppose the actual call value was 20. Then the price would violate Proposition IVe. To arbitrage, do the following:

| | | | | | Jan. 16, 1997 | |
| | | | | | $S_T > 130$ | $S_T < 130$ |
March 20		**May 6**	**Aug. 6**	**Nov. 6**		
Buy call	-20				$+(S_T - 130)$	0
Sell stock	$+146.125$	$-D1$(actual)	$-D2$(actual)	$-D3$(actual)	$-S_T$	$-S_T$
Lend	-0.3970	$+0.40$				
Lend	-0.4401		$+0.45$			
Lend	-0.4337			$+0.45$		
Lend	-123.88				$+130$	$+130$
	$+0.9742$	≥ 0	≥ 0	≥ 0	0	≥ 0

Note that the arbitrage does not require early exercise of the call. There will be no cash outflows at any date. There is a cash inflow of $0.9742 on March 20. If the actual dividend on May 6 is less than 0.40, there will be another cash inflow on that date because $0.40/share was the highest dividend the arbitrageur thought possible on May 6. If the stock price on the expiration date is greater than 130, the arbitrageur gets a zero cash flow on that day. It is also possible that if $S_T < 130$, an additional cash inflow will be earned at expiration.

Now we can make some important statements

1. *An in-the-money American call on a dividend-paying stock will always have some time value, except (possibly) on the day before it trades ex-dividend and (always) on its expiration day.* This statement can be made because of Proposition IVb. An American call that is in the money will always sell for at least $S - K(1+r)^{-t1}$, and this amount always exceeds $S - K$ (its intrinsic value) except on the last with-dividend day, when $t1$ approaches 0. If Proposition IVb is the lower bound of an American call on a dividend-paying stock, then it might have no time value on the day before it trades ex-dividend.

2. *An in-the-money American call will never be exercised early, except on the day before it trades ex-dividend.* By exercising an American call early, the call owner realizes only the call's intrinsic value. Before the stock's last "with-dividend" day, it is preferred to sell the call under our assumptions. This is because the intrinsic value *and* some time value will be realized. However, on the day before the stock trades ex-dividend, it may have only intrinsic value. This is a necessary condition for it to be exercised early. Again, it must be stressed that market imperfections such as transactions costs and taxes might result in some investors exercising in the money calls earlier than the day before it trades ex-dividend.

16.2.3   Early Exercise of American Calls[7]

Before expiration, the only possible time that an American call will (theoretically) have zero time value is the last day before an ex-dividend date. Therefore, we can conclude that American options will never be exercised except immediately before any ex-dividend dates, and at expiration. Recall that when the call owner sells the option, he receives its intrinsic value plus some time value. If the owner exercises the option, however, he receives only its intrinsic value.

Someone who exercises too early forfeits the option's time value and also, if he continues to retain ownership in the stock, may regret having exercised. The regret comes from a sudden and unexpected large decline in the stock price. That is, if the stock price is below K at expiration, the owner of the call has realized the benefits of a call's limited liability because he loses the same amount if S_T is a dollar below K or if S_T drops to zero. A stock owner, however, bears the entire loss.

Finally, funds must be used to pay K for the stock, and these funds will no longer be able to earn a rate of return for the early exerciser. One condition for optimal early exercise is for the dividend amount to exceed the present value of the interest that could be earned on K between the ex-date and the option's expiration date. An investor who is considering early exercise on the last with-dividend date will receive the dividend but will lose the interest he could have earned on the K that he is effectively saving in the bank until expiration.

Thus, we have stated three reasons for not exercising until just before the stock trades ex-dividend (in practice, just before the close of trading on the last with-dividend day). The benefit of exercising on this day is that the call owner will receive the dividend. Exercising early on any day other than the day before the ex-day has the three costs just stated, but no benefits. For American calls, the early exercise privilege is valuable only on the last with-dividend date. On that date, the call owner captures the dividend by exercising early. We next show that by exercising early when it is optimal, he will also avoid a decline in the value of the call on the ex-dividend day.

Assume the following: (a) an investor owns an in-the-money American call on a stock that is about to trade ex-dividend; (b) the stock will fall in price by the amount of the ex-dividend amount; and (c) the call is selling at its minimum price boundary condition defined by Proposition IVb (i.e., it has no time value). On the ex-day, the call may trade at a lower price because the stock price will fall, and because the lower pricing boundary has fallen from

$$C \geq S(\text{with-div}) - K$$

an instant before it trades ex-dividend to

$$C \geq S(\text{ex-div}) - K(1+r)^{-T}$$

where T is the time to expiration and $S(\text{ex-div}) = S(\text{with-div}) - \text{div}$.

In other words, the lower pricing boundary actually shifts on the ex-dividend day. The possibility of arbitrage keeps the American call value high (just equal to, or just above, its intrinsic value) on the last with-dividend day, when an otherwise equivalent European call would have sold at less than its intrinsic value because of the impending dividend. After the stock trades ex-dividend, and if there are no more ex-dates, the European and American calls will sell for the same price, and both must sell for more than intrinsic value.

Figure 16.4 shows how an American call can fall in value on the ex-dividend day. On the last with-dividend day, the stock price is $S(\text{with-div})$, and the call is selling at its lowest possible price, $C(\text{with-div}) = S(\text{with-div}) - K$. This is the lower bound by Proposition IVb, when $t1$ is zero. Figure 16.4 shows the stock price falling on the ex-dividend day to $S(\text{ex-div})$. If there are no further dividends, the new lower boundary for the call is $S - K(1+r)^{-T}$ (by Proposition II). Figure 16.4 shows a range of possible ex-day call values that are below $C(\text{with-div})$. No investor who expected the ex-dividend call price to be in this range would hold the call. If all investors shared the same belief that the call will decline in value to be in this range, no other investors would be willing to buy options from the call owners. Thus, early exercise is the only way to avoid the loss.

Let's make a general demonstration of the early exercise logic. A call owner will exercise her call early if the realized wealth from exercising exceeds the value of the call if it is held another day (on which the underlying asset will trade ex-dividend). If the call is exercised early, her wealth will be $S(\text{with-div}) - K$. Thus, the call owner will exercise early on the day before the stock trades ex-dividend if the call's intrinsic value on that day is greater than the call price expected on the ex-date:

$$S(\text{with-div}) - K > E[\tilde{C}(\text{ex-dividend})] \tag{16.1}$$

The tilde (˜) above the ex-dividend call value denotes it as a random variable. Note also that on the day before a stock trades ex-dividend, deep in-the-money calls will often sell for their lower bound of $S(\text{with-div}) - K$.

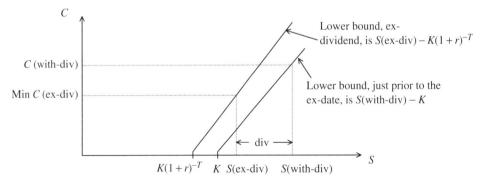

Figure 16.4 American calls on dividend-paying stocks should be exercised early (on the last with-dividend day) when the value of the call will decline on the ex-dividend day.

The ex-dividend call value will sell for its lower bound, perhaps plus an unknown amount, $\tilde{z}$:

$$E[\tilde{C}(\text{ex-div})] = E[\tilde{S}(\text{ex-div}) - K(1+r)^{-T} + \tilde{z}] \qquad (16.2)$$

Substitute Equation (16.2) into (16.1). We conclude that the call owner will surely exercise if:

$$S(\text{with-div}) - K > E[\tilde{S}(\text{ex-div}) - K(1+r)^{-T} + \tilde{z}] \qquad (16.3)$$

The variable $\tilde{z}$ allows the call to sell for more than its minimum bound on the ex-dividend day. Now assume that the stock price is expected to decline by the dividend amount on the ex-dividend day and write

$$E[\tilde{S}(\text{ex-div})] = S(\text{with-div}) - \text{div} \qquad (16.4)$$

Substituting Equation (16.4) into (16.3), we conclude that early exercise is optimal if

$$S(\text{with-div}) - K > S(\text{with-div}) - \text{div} - K(1+r)^{-T} + E[\tilde{z}] \qquad (16.5)$$

After simplifying this expression, we have:

$$\text{div} > K - K(1+r)^{-T} + E[\tilde{z}] \qquad (16.6)$$

This expression must hold for early exercise to be optimal. Note that if the call is sufficiently deep in the money and/or close to expiration, it is likely that the ex-dividend call will sell for its lowest possible value of $S - K(1+r)^{-T}$, which means that for deep in-the-money, short-term calls, $E[\tilde{z}]$ often will be zero. If $E[\tilde{z}] = 0$, then the condition for optimal early exercise is:

$$\text{div} > K - K(1+r)^{-T} \qquad (16.7)$$

The right-hand side of Equation (16.7) equals the interest that could be earned by investing the present value of $\$K$ until expiration. Thus, we have shown that a deep in-the-money call should be exercised just before it trades ex-dividend if it is expected to decline in value when the stock trades ex dividend, and this will occur when condition (16.7) exists. Equivalently, we can say that early exercise is optimal when the proceeds from early exercise exceed the expected ex-day price of the call.

EXAMPLE 16.3 If $K=50$, $r=10\%$/year, and $T=2$ months, then $K - [K/(1+r)^T] = 50 - [50/(1.1)^{0.1667}] = 0.7880$, which is the present value of the interest on $50. If (a) the dividend exceeds this amount, (b) the call owner believes that the stock price will fall by the dividend amount, and (c) the call owner believes that the call will sell at its lower bound on the ex-day, the call should be exercised.

Consider the data more specifically. Let the with-dividend stock price be $60 and the dividend equal $2. If the American call is selling at its lower bound, with-dividend, it sells for $10. If you expect the call, ex-dividend, to sell at its lower bound of $S(\text{ex-div}) - K(1+r)^{-T}$, then you expect it to be worth only $58 - 49.212 = 8.788$. In other words, holding the call will produce a loss. If all investors have the same beliefs as you, no one will buy the call from you, with-dividend, for $10. The only rational action for all owners of this call is to exercise the calls, with-dividend.

Summing up, early exercise of American calls will occur only on the day before an ex-dividend date and is more likely to occur

The greater the dividend

The lower the interest rate

The more the call is in the money

The lower the strike price

The shorter the remaining time to expiration

The lower the time value of the call on the last with-dividend day

16.3 PUTS

16.3.1 Upper Bounds

16.3.1.1 American Puts

	Proposition V:	$P \leq K$
	What if	$P > K$
	Then	$P - K > 0$

Today		**At Any Later Date if the Written Put Is Assigned**
Sell put	$+P$	Pay K to acquire the stock, $-K$
		Immediately sell the stock, $+S$
Lend	$-K$	$+K +$ interest
	> 0	$+S +$ interest > 0

Even if S is zero, the arbitrageur realizes a cash inflow equal to the interest on the loan of \$$K$. If the written put is never exercised, the arbitrageur receives a positive cash flow at time T of \$$K +$ interest.

16.3.1.2 Upper Bound for European Puts

For European puts, we can obtain an even tighter upper boundary for prices:

	Proposition VI:	$P \leq K(1+r)^{-T}$
	What if	$P > K(1+r)^{-T}$
	Then	$P - K(1+r)^{-T} > 0$

		At Expiration	
Today		$S_T > K$	$S_T < K$
Sell put	$+P$	0	$-(K - S_T)$
Lend	$-K(1+r)^{-T}$	$+K$	$+K$
	> 0	$+K > 0$	$+S_T > 0$

EXAMPLE 16.4   Consider the following data:

$K = 20$

$K(1+r)^{-T} = 19$

American put premium $= 19.50$

This situation does *not* offer an arbitrage opportunity. Suppose an investor tried to arbitrage by selling the put (cash inflow of 19.50) and lending (cash outflow of 19). Then, the next day, the stock falls to zero and the put is exercised early. The investor receives worthless stock and pays K (cash outflow of 20). However, the loan of 19 will have earned only one day's interest. The cash flow on the early exercise date is then negative (19 + one day's interest + 0.50 − 20). Thus, a violation of Proposition VI does not lead to arbitrage profits for American puts.

It is important to note that Proposition VI holds for European puts. If an investor tried to arbitrage with an American put when $K(1+r)^{-T} < P < K$, the written American put could be assigned before expiration at a time that the stock price was very low (consider the case if the stock were worthless). In this case, interest earned on the loan of $K(1+r)^{-T}$ might not be sufficient to fund the required payment, which is equal to the strike price. As a result, this could lead to a negative cash flow on the early exercise date.

16.3.2   Lower Bound for Puts on a Non-Dividend-Paying Stock

16.3.2.1   American Puts

Proposition VII: $P \geq \max[0, K-S]$

Like calls, puts cannot be worth a negative amount. If a put option "sold" for less than zero, an investor could buy the put, receive a cash inflow equal to the negative premium, and then throw the put away.

What if $P < K - S$?
Then: $P - K + S < 0$
Or: $-P + K - S > 0$

Today

Buy put $-P$
Buy stock $-S$
Exercise put $+K$
_____
                 >0

Note that this arbitrage can be done only with American puts because the purchased put is immediately exercised. Moreover, the transaction could be done at any time, regardless of dividend payments. Thus, the following statement can be made:

An American put can never sell below its intrinsic value. It will always have zero or positive time value.

16.3.2.2 European Puts

For European puts on a non-dividend-paying stock, we have a weaker lower pricing boundary:

Proposition VIII: $\qquad P \geq \max\,[0,\,K(1+r)^{-T}-S]$

What if	$P < K(1+r)^{-T}-S$
Then	$P - K(1+r)^{-T}+S<0$
Or	$-P+K(1+r)^{-T}-S>0$

		At Expiration	
Today		$S_T>K$	$S_T<K$
Buy put	$-P$	0	$+(K-S_T)$
Borrow	$+K(1+r)^{-T}$	$-K$	$-K$
Buy stock	$-S$	$+S_T$	$+S_T$
	>0	≥ 0	0

Thus, from Proposition VIII:

A European put on a non-dividend-paying stock can sell for less than its intrinsic value.

In fact, in-the-money European puts will frequently sell for less than their intrinsic value. These puts will also rise in value as time passes, since we know that at expiration, they must sell for their intrinsic value, $\max[0,\,K-S_T]$. American puts can never sell for less than their intrinsic value and can never rise in value as the expiration date nears.

Summarizing what we have learned for puts on non-dividend-paying stocks, there are different boundaries for American puts and for European puts. They are depicted in Figure 16.5.

Note that American puts have a higher price range than European puts. This is intuitive when the value of the right to exercise early is high. Because in-the-money American puts are, in fact, frequently exercised early, they will often sell for more than otherwise equivalent European puts.

At least two factors induce an owner of an in-the-money American put to exercise early. If the put is deeply in the money, its owner can begin to earn a return on the K he receives from exercising the put. Also, as S declines, the range of "good" outcomes for the put owner narrows. After all, the stock can only go to zero. For example, why would one want to buy a put with a $10 strike

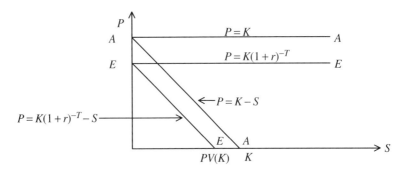

Figure 16.5 Pricing boundaries for puts on non-dividend-paying stocks: *AAA*, American put boundaries; *EEE*, European put boundaries.

price if the stock were selling for only $0.50 per share? There is very limited additional profit to be earned if the stock price fell to zero.

16.3.3 Lower Price Boundaries for Puts on Dividend-Paying Stocks

16.3.3.1 European Puts

Proposition IX: $P \geq \max[0, K(1+r)^{-T} - S + \underline{D}(1+r)^{-t1}]$

Recall that $\underline{D}$ is the smallest dividend believed possible. If there is more than one dividend, the present value all the smallest dividends believed possible must be added to Proposition IX.[8]

	What if	$P < K(1+r)^{-T} - S + \underline{D}(1+r)^{-t1}$
	Then	$P - K(1+r)^{-T} + S - \underline{D}(1+r)^{-t1} < 0$
	Or	$-P + K(1+r)^{-T} - S + \underline{D}(1+r)^{-t1} > 0$

				At Expiration	
Today		**At Time $t1$**	$S_T > K$	$S_T < K$
Buy put	$-P$		0	$+(K - S_T)$
Borrow	$+K(1+r)^{-T}$		$-K$	$-K$
Buy stock	$-S$	$+\underline{D}(\text{actual})$	$+S_T$	$+S_T$
Borrow	$+\underline{D}(1+r)^{-t1}$	$-\underline{D}$		
	>0	≥ 0	≥ 0	0

Dividends increase the lower bound of European put prices. The minimum price is raised by the present value of the smallest dividend that the arbitrageur believes will be paid ($\underline{D}$ equals zero if there is a probability that the dividend will be skipped altogether). This result is intuitive, since on a stock's ex-dividend day, the price falls by the amount of the dividend. The price decline will make the put more valuable. The boundary of Proposition VIII can never be weaker than the boundary of Proposition IX.

16.3.3.2 American Puts

The lower bound for American puts on dividend-paying stocks is the greatest of several possible amounts. Let us assume that there are two ex-dividend dates before the expiration date of the put. Then, the put must be worth the maximum of four values:

Proposition X: $P \geq \max \begin{cases} \text{a.} & 0 \\ \text{b.} & K - S \\ \text{c.} & K(1+r)^{-t1} - S + \underline{D1}(1+r)^{-t1} \\ \text{d.} & K(1+r)^{-t2} - S + \underline{D1}(1+r)^{-t1} + \underline{D2}(1+r)^{-t2} \end{cases}$

We already know that an American put must sell for more than zero and for more than $K - S$ (Proposition VII). In proving parts Propositions Xc and Xd, the arbitrageur would exercise the put an instant *after* the stock trades ex-dividend. To facilitate understanding of the proof, we will use the notation $t1+\varepsilon$ to denote "an instant after the ex-dividend time." In practice, it refers to the opening of trading on the ex-day. There is no difference, however, between the present value of \$1 received at time $t1$, and \$1 received at time $t1+\varepsilon$ because ε is "an instant."

Proof of proposition Xc proceeds as follows.

$$\begin{array}{ll} \text{What if} & P < K(1+r)^{-t1} - S + \underline{D1}(1+r)^{-t1} \\ \text{Then} & P - K(1+r)^{-t1} + S - \underline{D1}(1+r)^{-t1} < 0 \\ \text{Or} & -P + K(1+r)^{-t1} - S + \underline{D1}(1+r)^{-t1} > 0 \end{array}$$

Today		At Time $t1$	At Time $t1 + \varepsilon$ (exercise the put and deliver the shares owned)
Buy put	$-P$		$+K$
Borrow	$+K(1+r)^{-t1}$		$-K$
Buy stock	$-S$	$+D1$(actual)	
Borrow	$+\underline{D1}(1+r)^{-t1}$	$-\underline{D1}$	
	>0	≥ 0	0

If the put has any time value at time $t1+\varepsilon$, it will be better to sell the put, sell the stock, and repay the loan principal of K (verify this for two cases: if the put at time $t1+\varepsilon$ is in the money and if it is out of the money). This would still generate additional cash inflows.

The proof of Proposition Xd is essentially identical to that of Xc and is left as an exercise. The arbitrageur would exercise the put at time $t2+\varepsilon$, an instant after the second ex-dividend date.

Any of the three lower bounds Proposition (Xb, Xc, or Xd) may apply for an in-the-money put. Consider the following three-part example:

$$S = 20$$
$$K = 30$$
$$t1 = \text{first ex-dividend date} = 1 \text{ month} = 0.08333 \text{ year}$$
$$t2 = \text{second ex-dividend date} = 4 \text{ months} = 0.3333 \text{ year}$$
$$r = 10\%/\text{year}$$

Case I: $\underline{D1} = \underline{D2} = $ smallest dividend amount at times $t1$ and $t2 = 1.0$
Case II: $\underline{D1} = \underline{D2} = $ smallest dividend amount at times $t1$ and $t2 = 0.3$
Case III: $\underline{D1} = \underline{D2} = $ smallest dividend amount at times $t1$ and $t2 = 0.1$

Given that P must exceed zero and must be equal to or exceed the maximum of the values computed in Xb, Xc, and Xd above, we have:

For Case I:

$$P \geq \max[0, 30 - 20, 30(1.1)^{-0.0833} - 20 + 1(1.1)^{-0.0833},$$
$$30(1.1)^{-0.3333} - 20 + 1(1.1)^{-0.0833} + 1(1.1)^{-0.3333}] \qquad \text{(Xd is boundary)}$$
$$= P \geq \max[0, 10, 10.7548, 11.0227] = P \geq 11.0227$$

For Case II:

$$P \geq \max[0, 30 - 20, 30(1.1)^{-0.0833} - 20 + 0.3(1.1)^{-0.0833},$$
$$30(1.1)^{-0.3333} - 20 + 0.3(1.1)^{-0.0833} + 0.3(1.1)^{-0.3333}] \qquad \text{(Xc is boundary)}$$
$$= P \geq \max[0, 10, 10.0603, 9.6501] = P \geq 10.0603$$

For Case III:

$$P \geq \max[0, 30 - 20, 30(1.1)^{-0.0833} - 20 + 0.1(1.1)^{-0.0833},$$

$$30(1.1)^{-0.3333} - 20 + 0.1(1.1)^{-0.0833} + 0.1(1.1)^{-0.3333}] \qquad \text{(Xd is boundary)}$$

$$= P \geq \max[0, 10, 9.8619, 9.2580] = P \geq 10$$

Now, suppose that the conditions cited in Case I held, and a put expiring in five months sold for 10.50. An arbitrageur could buy the stock and buy the put, for an initial cash outlay of 30.50. He can borrow that amount for four months (because he plans on exercising immediately after receiving the second dividend), agreeing to repay $[30.5(1.1)^{0.333} =]$ \$31.485 at time $t2 + \varepsilon$. Thus, there is no initial cash outlay required for the arbitrage. At time $t1$, he would receive the first dividend of \$1 and invest it to earn 10% for three months. On the option's expiration day, this will be worth $[1(1.1)^{0.25} =]$ \$1.024. At time $t2$, he will receive another dollar in dividends, and immediately thereafter, he will exercise the put and receive the strike price of 30. His outflow at time $t2 + \varepsilon$ is the repayment of the initial loan principal, and interest of \$31.485. However, he will also have three sources of cash inflows at time $t2 + \varepsilon$: the strike price from exercising the put (\$30), the first dividend and interest earned on it (\$1.024), and the second dividend (\$1), for a total cash inflow of \$32.024. Thus, there is an arbitrage opportunity. If the stock price were to rise above \$30/share by time $t2 + \varepsilon$, even more profits would be earned. Likewise, if dividend payments are actually more than \$1/share at times $t1$ or $t2$, the arbitrage profits will increase.[9]

16.3.4 Early Exercise of American Puts

Frequently, it is optimal for owners of in-the-money American puts to exercise their options early. Consider the decision facing the owner of an in-the-money put who is also very bearish. He believes with certainty (i.e., probability = 1.0) that the expiration day stock price will be below the strike price. Suppose the put is selling for its intrinsic value, $K - S$. The investor has three possible courses of action: he can hold, sell, or exercise the option. Clearly, holding the put option for another day is an inferior strategy in comparison to exercising. By exercising, the investor receives $K today, and he can immediately invest it to earn interest. By waiting one day, or waiting until the expiration day, he is forgoing interest that could be earned on the $K.

Now, all we have to do is add the assumption that all investors agree that there is no chance that the put will finish out of the money. In that case, no one would ever want to buy the put for $K - S$ and hold it. The put essentially becomes a "hot potato." In other words, an investor may be unable, at certain times, to sell a deep in-the-money American put for its intrinsic value.[10]

In Chapter 17 (Section 17.4), we will use the binomial option pricing model to demonstrate that an investor can frequently use stocks and bonds to replicate a deep in-the-money American put at a cost less than the price of the American put. In other words, an investor could arbitrage by exercising an American put (realizing its intrinsic value of $K - S$), and then proceeding to create an equivalent put for a cost less than $K - S$.

Summarizing, early exercise of American puts will be more likely:

- The higher the strike price
- The lower the stock price
- The higher the interest rates

- The smaller the time value
- The more deeply the put is in the money

Dividends will tend to reduce the likelihood of early exercise.[11] One reason is that dividends may increase the lower bound of American put prices (see Section 16.3.3.2). Thus, ex-dividend dates might create more time value for a put. Moreover, even the bearish owner of both a put and the underlying stock (a protective put) might decide to wait to receive the next dividend before exercising his put. If the present value of the next dividend exceeds the present value of the interest that could be earned on K between today and the ex-date, an investor might decide not to exercise early but to wait for the dividend.

Even an American put with time value could be exercised early. Exercising early does destroy the put's time value. But the interest earned on K (more accurately, the interest earned on the present value of K) could exceed the time value that is killed if it is exercised early. Thus, the following statement can be made:

An in-the-money American put can rationally be exercised at almost any time before expiration.

16.4 PUT–CALL PARITY

Put–call parity establishes a no-arbitrage pricing condition between a call and a put premium. This pricing boundary of a call relative to a put on the same stock requires that both options have the same strike price and time to expiration. Put–call parity also has importance in obtaining an exact European put option pricing model in subsequent chapters and provides, as well, some insights into certain attributes of options. Although put–call parity has long been known to option traders, Stoll (1969) formalized its proof. In this section, all the assumptions previously made on the first page of this chapter still apply.

16.4.1 European Options; No Dividends

The most basic put–call parity proposition applies to European puts and calls on stocks that will pay no dividends before option expiration. In words, the difference between the price of a call and a price of a put on the same stock, with the same strike price and time to expiration, equals the price of the underlying asset minus the present value of the strike price. That is:

$$\textbf{Proposition XI:} \qquad C - P = S - K(1+r)^{-T}$$

We divide the proof into parts A and B.

Part A

$$\text{What if} \qquad C - P > S - K(1+r)^{-T}$$
$$\text{Then} \qquad C - P - S + K(1+r)^{-T} > 0$$

		At Expiration	
Today		$S_T < K$	$S_T > K$
Sell call	$+C$	0	$-(S_T - K)$
Buy put	$-P$	$+(K - S_T)$	0
Buy stock	$-S$	$+S_T$	$+S_T$
Borrow	$+K(1+r)^{-T}$	$-K$	$-K$
	>0	0	0

Part A of the proof illustrates a **conversion** trade. In a conversion, an arbitrageur exploits the violation of the put–call parity relationship by buying the stock, selling the overpriced call, buying the underpriced put, and borrowing. However, quite often no money is borrowed. Instead, the arbitrageur realizes a riskless rate of return in excess of what can be earned on other riskless investments.

Part B

$$\text{What if} \quad C - P < S - K(1+r)^{-T}$$
$$\text{Then} \quad C - P - S + K(1+r)^{-T} < 0$$
$$\text{Or} \quad -C + P + S - K(1+r)^{-T} > 0$$

Today		$S_T < K$	$S_T > K$
		At Expiration	
Buy call	$-C$	0	$+(S_T - K)$
Sell put	$+P$	$-(K - S_T)$	0
Sell stock	$+S$	$-S_T$	$-S_T$
Lend	$-K(1+r)^{-T}$	$+K$	$+K$
	> 0	0	0

Part B of the proof illustrates a **reverse conversion**, or **reversal** trade. In this part of the proof, we assume that the arbitrageur receives full use of the proceeds of the short sale. However, most individuals will not have this advantage. However, "quasi-arbitrageurs" already own the stock, and they have the ability to sell the stock and receive the proceeds.

There is some additional useful discussion of Proposition XI. First, arrange it to read:

$$-C = -S - P + K(1+r)^{-T}$$

$$\text{buy call} = \text{buy stock} + \text{buy put} + \text{borrow } K(1+r)^{-T}$$

EXAMPLE 16.5 Suppose an April 45 Dell Computer call sells for $4\,{}^7/_8$, the April 45 put is at $2\,{}^7/_8$, and Dell stock price is 47. Assume that the riskless interest rate is 6%/year and that there are 39 days to expiration (i.e., 0.10685 year). Do these option prices obey put–call parity? From Proposition XI we write:

$$C - P = S - K(1 + r)^{-T}$$
$$4.875 - 2.875 = 47 - 45(1.06)^{-0.10685}$$
$$2 < 2.287$$

This is close, but not exact. The violation of Proposition XI signals that the call is "cheap" relative to the put. Thus, the arbitrage trades are to buy the call, write the put, sell the stock, and lend the proceeds. However, the following conditions are essential: (1) these must be European options, or (2) it must be known that Dell Computer will pay no dividends in the next 39 days. To conditions 1 or 2 we add two others: (3) we were sure that we could trade at these prices, and (4) we could cover all trading costs (whew!).

You may have heard that a call option has properties similar to a levered purchase of stock (i.e., buying stock on margin). For example, consider two alternatives: (a) buy a call on 100 shares for $300, or (b) buy 100 shares of stock for $30/share by borrowing $2400 from your broker and investing $600 of your own money. Now, what would happen if the very next day, the stock rose to $31/share? The value of a typical at-the-money call might rise to $350, which represents a 16.667% rate of return (note that the stock itself rose only 3.333%). Under alternative (b), the investor would repay the loan to the broker. Ignoring the one day of interest, the investor is left with ($3100 − $2400 =) $700. Thus, the investor has also earned a return of 16.667% [(700 − 600)/600]. This example illustrates that a call purchase has similar characteristics to a levered purchase of the underlying asset.[12]

However, the call owner also effectively owns a put. The put gives the call owner limited liability. If the price of the underlying asset were to fall below the strike price, and finish out of the money, the call owner would not lose any additional capital beyond what he originally paid for the call. This is unlike the levered equity position, where the investor could lose more than the initial investment of $600 if the stock price were to decline below $24/share.

A second interesting result is obtained by studying put–call parity in the form $C - P = S - K(1 + r)^{-T}$. For an interest rate $r = 0$, this equation reduces to $C - P = S - K$. However, for positive interest rates, the value of an at-the-money call will always exceed the value of a put if the two European options are on the same underlying asset and have the same K and T, and there are no dividends to be paid prior to expiration.

A third implication of the basic put–call parity proposition is that floor traders and other exchange members (who have low transactions costs) can use the principles behind put–call parity to create their own puts. Before June 1977, there were no exchange-traded put options. Thus, put positions *had* to be used to create conversions and reversals. At times it may be cheaper to replicate an option via a conversion or reversal than by buying or selling the actual option.

Finally, there is an implication from put–call parity for the role of market expectations in determining option values. When investors are bullish, one would intuitively expect call values to rise. Similarly, you might expect put values to rise if investors are bearish. Under the perfect market conditions used to derive put–call parity, market expectations cannot influence option values. Even if investors were wildly bullish about the prospects for the underlying stock, $C - P$ must equal $S - K(1 + r)^{-T}$. That is, given S, K, r, and T, there is an explicit relationship between European call and put values that must exist, regardless of market expectations. Note, however, that investors' bullish or bearish beliefs will influence S. But, given S, C cannot rise or fall relative to P.

In subsequent put–call parity propositions we introduce unknown dividends and/or American options. In these cases, boundaries are created within which $C - P$ can lie without permitting arbitrage. Within these boundaries, call prices can rise somewhat relative to put prices when investors are bullish, and put prices can rise somewhat rise relative to call prices when investors are bearish. The term "somewhat" is used because there are still put–call pricing restrictions even for options of these types.

16.4.2   European Options on Stocks That Pay Unknown Dividends

If the cash flows of the underlying assets are unknown, put–call parity becomes an inequality, and option prices can lie within a range of values that would preclude arbitrage.

Proposition XII:
$$S - \underline{D1}(1+r)^{-t1} - \underline{D2}(1+r)^{-t2} - K(1+r)^{-T} \geq C - P$$
$$\geq S - \overline{D1}(1+r)^{-t1} - \overline{D2}(1+r)^{-t2} - K(1+r)^{-T}$$

In Proposition XII, $\underline{D1}$ and $\underline{D2}$ are the smallest dividends the arbitrageur believes possible at times $t1$ and $t2$. $\overline{D1}$ and $\overline{D2}$ are the largest dividends possible at those dates.[13] The present values of the smallest dividend amounts possible are subtracted from the price of the underlying asset on the left-hand side (LHS) of the inequality, while the present values of the largest possible dividends are subtracted from the price of the underlying asset on the right-hand side (RHS). You are encouraged to prove the RHS. The proof of the LHS proceeds as follows:

What if $\qquad S - \underline{D1}(1+r)^{-t1} - \underline{D2}(1+r)^{-t2} - K(1+r)^{-T} < C - P$

Then $\qquad\quad S - \underline{D1}(1+r)^{-t1} - \underline{D2}(1+r)^{-t2} - K(1+r)^{-T} - C + P < 0$

Or $\qquad\quad\;\; -S + \underline{D1}(1+r)^{-t1} + \underline{D2}(1+r)^{-t2} + K(1+r)^{-T} + C - P > 0$

	Today	Time $t1$	Time $t2$	At Expiration $S_T < K$	At Expiration $S_T > K$
Buy stock	$-S$	$+D1$(actual)	$+D2$(actual)	$+S_T$	$+S_T$
Borrow	$+\underline{D1}(1+r)^{-t1}$	$-\underline{D1}$			
Borrow	$+\underline{D2}(1+r)^{-t2}$		$-\underline{D2}$		
Borrow	$+K(1+r)^{-T}$			$-K$	$-K$
Sell call	$+C$			0	$-(S_T - K)$
Buy put	$-P$			$+(K - S_T)$	0
	>0	≥ 0	≥ 0	0	0

Note that the *borrowings* include the present value of the *smallest* dividend believed possible at the *farthest* ex-dividend dates believed possible. In proving the RHS of Proposition XII, one *lends* the present value of the *largest* dividend believed possible at the *nearest* ex-dates believed possible.

16.4.3 American Options on Non-Dividend-Paying Stocks

For American options, put–call parity pricing restrictions become wider, and the proofs become more complicated, since either a put or a call must always be written (and thus exposed to possible early exercise). If a call is written on a stock that does not pay dividends, or if the stock will not trade ex-dividend before the options' expiration date, early exercise is not a factor (under our assumptions). But early exercise of in-the-money American puts is always a possibility, and the arbitrage proofs must account for this when the put is written (see the proof of the RHS of Proposition XIII shortly).

Proposition XIII: $\quad S - K(1+r)^{-T} \geq C - P \geq S - K$

Proof of the LHS of Proposition XIII proceeds as follows:

What if $\qquad S - K(1+r)^{-T} < C - P$

Then $\qquad\quad S - K(1+r)^{-T} - C + P < 0$

Or $\qquad\quad\;\; -S + K(1+r)^{-T} + C - P > 0$

	Today	At Expiration	
		$S_T < K$	$S_T > K$
Buy stock	$-S$	$+S_T$	$+S_T$
Borrow	$+K(1+r)^{-T}$	$-K$	$-K$
Write call	$+C$	0	$-(S_T-K)$
Buy put	$-P$	$+(K-S_T)$	0
	>0	0	0

Because there are no dividends, we do not have to guard against the possibility of the call's early exercise. However, this possibility cannot be ignored in the following proof of the RHS of Proposition XIII.

What if $\quad C-P<S-K$

Then $\quad C-P-S+K<0$

Or $\quad -C+P+S-K>0$

	Today	If the Put Could Be Assigned Before T	At Expiration (if the put was not assigned earlier)	
			$S_T<K$	$S_T>K$
Buy call	$-C$	$+$ Time value (if any)[14]	0	$+(S_T-K)$
Sell put	$+P$	Assigned: long stock; pay K	$-(K-S_T)$	0
Sell stock	$+S$	The short position offsets the long position	$-S_T$	$-S_T$
Lend	$-K$	$+K+$ interest	$+K+$ interest	$+K+$ interest
	>0	≥ 0	>0	>0

The key feature to the proof of the RHS is to guard against the possibility that the stock could plummet in value the day after the arbitrage transactions are made. In this proof, at the very least, the arbitrageur will earn one day's interest if the put is exercised early one day after the initial trades. This guarantees that there will never be a cash outflow at any date.

Note that is important that the loan of $\$K$ be made only on an overnight basis and be renewed daily. Otherwise, if the stock should plummet at the same time that interest rates soared, the call might be worthless if the put were exercised early, and the value of the loan might be less than $\$K$. For example, suppose that the arbitrage requires a loan of $K=\$40$ and that this is made for a period of $T=30$ days at an annual rate of 10%. The loan contract stipulates that $40(1.1)^{0.08219}=40.3146$ will be repaid one month hence. Then, the next day, interest rates rise to an annual rate of 12% and the put is assigned. When trying to sell the loan contract, the arbitrageur will find that other investors who will be willing to pay only the present value of $40.3146, at the prevailing interest rate of 12%. With 29 days remaining, the selling value is then only $40.3146(1.12)^{-0.07945}=\$39.9532$. If the call was worthless, the cash flow on the early exercise date would be negative. By lending one day at a time, positive interest will always be earned.

16.4.4   American Options on Stocks That Pay Unknown Dividends

To enforce the following proposition, arbitrageurs must be sure that nonnegative cash flows are earned at all times, including those just before and after any ex-dividend dates. In performing a conversion, a written call could be exercised just before any ex-dates. If the arbitrageur performs a reversal, then the written put can be assigned anytime (as early as "tomorrow"). To make the proof of proposition XIV easier, we will assume that only one ex-dividend day exists prior to the options' expiration date.[15]

Proposition XIV: $S - K(1+r)^{-T} \geq C - P \geq S - \overline{D1}(1+r)^{-t1} - K$

Proof of the LHS of Proposition XIV proceeds as follows:

What if $S - K(1+r)^{-T} < C - P$

Then $S - K(1+r)^{-T} - C + P < 0$

Or $-S + K(1+r)^{-T} + C - P > 0$

Today		At Time $t1$ the Call Could Be Assigned	If the Call Is Not Assigned Early at $t1$
Buy stock	$-S$	Deliver stock to the exerciser of the call	$+D1$
Borrow	$+K(1+r)^{-T}$	$-K(1+r)^{-T} -$ interest	
Sell call	$+C$	$+K$	
Buy put	$-P$	$+$ Time value (if any)	
	>0	>0	>0

If the call is exercised an instant before the first ex-dividend date, time $t1$, the arbitrageur delivers the stock and receives payment of $\$K$. The receipt of $\$K$ is sufficient to pay off the loan plus interest on the loan. The put is sold if it has any value. If the call is not assigned early, the arbitrageur receives the dividend.[16]

If the call is not exercised at time $t1$, and if there is only one ex-dividend day, only the expiration day needs to be considered to complete the proof. This was done for the LHS of Proposition XIV. Thus, the LHS of Proposition XIV is complete, and we present the proof of the RHS.

What if $C - P < S - \overline{D1}(1+r)^{-t1} - K$

Then $C - P - S + \overline{D1}(1+r)^{-t1} + K < 0$

Or $-C + P + S - \overline{D1}(1+r)^{-t1} - K > 0$

Today		(1) The Put Could Be Assigned Before $t1$	(2) If the Put Is Not Assigned at Time $t1$	(3) The Put Could Be Assigned After $t1$ but Before T	(4) If the Put Has Not Been Assigned by Time T	
					$S_T < K$	$S_T > K$
Buy call	$-C$	+Time value (if any)		+Time value (if any)	0	$+(S_T - K)$

Sell put	$+P$	Put assigned: acquire stock and pay K		Put assigned: acquire stock and pay K	$-(K-S_T)$	0
Sell stock	$+S$	Long position offsets short position	$-D1(\text{actual})$	Long position offsets short position	$-S_T$	$-S_T$
Lend	$-\overline{D1}(1+r)^{-t1}$	$+\overline{D1}(1+r)^{-t1}$ +interest	$+\overline{D1}$			
Lend	$-K$	$+K+\text{interest}$		$+K+\text{interest}$	$+K+\text{int}$	$+K+\text{int}$
	>0	>0	≥ 0	>0	>0	>0

EXAMPLE 16.6 Consider the following actual market data for GM at 3 P.M. on February 15, 2000:

$$S = 74\,{}^1/_2$$
$$K = 75$$

$C = 9$ for the Sept 75 call

$P = 8\,{}^3/_4$ for the Sept 75 put

$r = 6\%$ per year

$T = 221$ days $= 0.6055$ year

$$K(1+r)^{-T} = 75(1.06)^{-0.6055} = 72.40$$

The last ex-dividend date was on February 7, 2000, and the dividend amount was $0.50 per share. Thus, the arbitrageur might assume:

$$\overline{D1} = 0.55$$

$t1 = 90$ days $= 0.2466$ year

$$\overline{D1}(1.06)^{-0.2466} = 0.5422$$

$$\overline{D2} = 0.60$$

$t2 = 182$ days $= 0.4986$ year

$$\overline{D2}(1.06)^{-0.4986} = 0.5828$$

When there are two ex-dividend days prior to expiration, Proposition XIV states that:

$$S - K(1+r)^{-T} \geq C - P \geq S - \overline{D1}(1+r)^{-t1} - \overline{D2}(1+r)^{-t2} - K$$
$$74.5 - 72.4 \geq 9 - 8.75 \geq 74.5 - 0.5422 - 0.5828 - 75$$
$$2.1 \geq 0.25 \geq -1.625$$

As you can see, when dividends are substantial, and the American options have a long time to expiration, the put–call parity pricing restriction is not very strong. Look closely at Proposition XIV. As the dividends are paid off, and as T shrinks, the range of prices implied by the proposition will shrink. Here, market expectations will likely affect option values. If investors are bullish, we might observe $C-P$ to be about 2.1. If investors are bearish, we might see $C-P$ to be about -1.625.

The put, if it is in the money, could be exercised as early as tomorrow. Even if the call is worthless tomorrow, the arbitrageur still will earn one day's interest on the two loans made. This is demonstrated in column (1). If the put is not exercised before the next ex-dividend date, the arbitrageur pays the actual dividend due on the short sale of stock, but receives $\overline{D1}$. Then there is a nonnegative cash flow at time $t1$, as shown in column 2.

Then, the arbitrageur must ask, What if the written put is assigned after time $t1$, but before expiration? As shown in column 3, he is again assured of a positive cash inflow. Finally, column 4 presents the positive cash flows the arbitrageur receives if the written put is never assigned before it expires. This completes the proof of Proposition XIV.

The arbitrageur could take some risks (though by definition, he would no longer be an arbitrageur), and narrow the bounds he believes should exist around put and call prices. For example, he might assess the probability of early exercise of the call at time $t1$ to be so small that it can be safely ignored. Or he might believe there is little probability that the stock will fall so much that the put will be exercised in the next month. These assumptions will narrow the bounds implied by American put–call parity on stocks paying unknown dividends.[17]

16.5 BOX SPREADS USING EUROPEAN OPTIONS

From Proposition XI, we know $C-P=S-K(1+r)^{-T}$. Given the price of an underlying security, Proposition XI holds for all put–call pairs with the same time to expiration. As such, define $C(K1)$ and $P(K1)$ as a call and a put with a low strike price, $K1$. Further, define $C(K2)$ and $P(K2)$ as a call and a put with a higher strike price, $K2$. Thus,

$$C(K1) - P(K1) = S - K1(1+r)^{-T} \tag{16.8}$$

and

$$C(K2) - P(K2) = S - K2(1+r)^{-T} \tag{16.9}$$

Subtracting Equation (16.9) from Equation (16.8) yields:

$$C(K1) - C(K2) - P(K1) + P(K2) = (K2 - K1)(1+r)^{-T} \tag{16.10}$$

Note that the stock price does not appear in (16.10). To prove that equation (16.10) must hold, we proceed with a two-part proof.[18]

What if $C(K1) - C(K2) - P(K1) + P(K2) > (K2 - K1)(1+r)^{-T}$

Then $C(K1) - C(K2) - P(K1) + P(K2) - (K2 - K1)(1+r)^{-T} > 0$

Today		At Expiration		
		$S_T < K1$	$K1 < S_T < K2$	$K2 < S_T$
Sell call	$+C(K1)$	0	$-(S_T - K1)$	$-(S_T - K1)$
Buy call	$-C(K2)$	0	0	$+(S_T - K2)$
Buy put	$-P(K1)$	$+(K1 - S_T)$	0	0

Sell put	$+P(K2)$	$-(K2-S_T)$	$-(K2-S_T)$	0
Lend	$-(K2-K1)(1+r)^{-T}$	$+(K2-K1)$	$+(K2-K1)$	$+(K2-K1)$
	>0	0	0	0

The four option positions and lending today generates a cash inflow. This is because the call with the lower strike price, $K1$, will have more intrinsic value than a call with the higher strike price, $K2$. Therefore, the call with the lower strike price is more valuable. Similarly, the put with the higher strike price, $K2$, will be more valuable than the put with the lower strike price. In the end-of-chapter problems, you are asked to prove these two relationships.

Note that the underlying stock price does not appear in Equation (16.10). In words, Equation (16.10) says that a risk-free asset is created by selling a call with strike $K1$, buying a call with strike $K2$, buying a put with strike $K1$, and selling a put with strike $K2$.[19] This option combination is known as a "short box spread." One lends risklessly by purchasing a call with strike $K1$, selling a call with strike $K2$, selling a put with strike $K1$, and buying a put with strike $K2$. This position is known as a "long box spread." The box spread is a popular and convenient way for option traders to borrow and lend through the options markets.

16.6 SUMMARY

In this chapter, we established certain relationships concerning the pricing of calls relative to the underlying stock price, relative to time to expiration, and relative to the calls' strike prices. Then, analogous boundary relationships were derived for puts.

By mastering the techniques for deriving the propositions, you should now be able to understand the process of arbitrage. If markets are working well, there should not be any arbitrage opportunities. However, some investors, such as traders on the floors of the different exchanges, have such low transactions costs that they can buy at the bid price and sell at the asked price, hence they may be able to arbitrage. Arbitrage is the price-setting mechanism in options markets as well as in the financial futures markets.

From these pricing restrictions, we were also able to establish that an American call on a non-dividend-paying stock would never be exercised early. The only time an American call would be exercised early is on the day before the stock trades ex-dividend. On the other hand, in-the-money American puts could frequently be exercised early.

Finally, we established put–call parity, which creates no-arbitrage pricing relationships between puts and calls. The propositions differ, depending on whether the options are American or European, and on whether the underlying asset will have a cash distribution such as a dividend prior to the options' expiration.

References

Cox, John C., and Mark Rubinstein. 1985. *Option Markets*. Englewood Cliffs, NJ: Prentice-Hall.

Geske, Robert, and Kuldeep Shastri. 1985. "The Early Exercise of American Puts." *Journal of Banking and Finance*, Vol. 9, No. 2, pp. 207–219.

Jarrow, Robert A., and Andrew T. Rudd. 1983. *Option Pricing*. Homewood, IL: Dow Jones Irwin.

Klemkosky, Robert C., and Bruce G. Resnick. 1980. "An Ex Ante Analysis of Put–Call Parity." *Journal of Financial Economics*, Vol. 8, No. 4, pp. 363–378.

Merton, Robert C. 1973. "Theory of Rational Option Pricing." *Bell Journal of Economics and Management Science*, Vol. 4, pp. 141–183.

Roll, Richard. 1977. "An Analytic Valuation Formula for Unprotected American Call Options on Stocks with Known Dividends." *Journal of Financial Economics*, Vol. 5, No. 2, pp. 251–258.

Smith, Clifford. 1976. "Option Pricing: A Review." *Journal of Financial Economics*, Vol. 3, March, pp. 3–51.

Notes

[1]Many of the results of this chapter were originally stated in Merton (1973). Further development occurred in Cox and Rubinstein (1985, Chapter 4) and Jarrow and Rudd (1983, Chapters 4–6).

[2]Note that there arbitrageurs who own the stock *prior* to the arbitrage trades might exist. Rather than selling the stock short, they can just sell the stock they own. For them, selling actually does yield full use of the proceeds from the required sale. Sometimes this is referred to as "quasi-arbitrage." Quasi-arbitrageurs switch one investment for another that dominates the original.

[3]The terms "exercised" and "assigned" are used interchangeably in this book. However, "assigned" usually refers to what is experienced by the option writer. The option owner exercises her option. The writer is assigned the exercise.

[4]Floor traders frequently exploit violations of Proposition II′ when there is only a short time to expiration. Their bid prices will often be $1/8$ or $1/4$ below the intrinsic values of in-the-money options.

[5]Whenever long-term capital gains are taxed at a lower marginal rate than short-term capital gains, investors must consider the trade-offs of a realizing a certain short-term capital gain versus holding onto a risky investment to (hopefully) realize a long-term capital gain because the latter would be taxed at a lower rate. If an investor exercises a call, the holding period for the stock begins on the day after the exercise date. Thus, in early December, an investor might have a large unrealized profit on a call that expires in December. If she sells it, she would have to pay taxes on the profit at her high marginal tax rate. However, if she was still bullish on the stock, she might exercise it and (a) defer the taxes on the profit until the following year, and (b) by holding the stock for the required period (perhaps six months or a year), possibly stretch the short-term gain into a long-term gain. By exercising the call early, the investor would begin the holding period earlier.

[6]If there were two ex-days the proposition would read:

$$C \ge \max[0, S - \overline{D1}(1+r)^{-t1} - \overline{D2}(1+r)^{-t2} - K(1+r)^{-T}].$$

$\overline{D1}$ is the greatest dividend that will be paid at the next ex-date, and $\overline{D2}$ is the maximum dividend at the following ex-date. In effect, think of stock value as consisting of two components: the present value of dividends that will be paid between today and the option's expiration date, and the present value of all dividends subsequent to the expiration date. When you buy a European call, you are buying a call on the latter only. Thus, in setting the arbitrage boundary, the dividends that are to be paid prior to expiration are subtracted from the stock's current value.

[7]See Smith (1976, pp. 13–14) and Roll (1977) for additional discussion on the early exercise of American calls on dividend-paying stocks.

[8]For the case of two dividends, Proposition IX would be as follows:

$$P \ge \max[0, K(1+r)^{-T} - S + \underline{D1}(1+r)^{-t1} + \underline{D2}(1+r)^{-t2}]$$

[9]The example presented in this paragraph is different from the methods of the proofs in that a zero cash flow at time zero, and time $t1$, is achieved, and the arbitrage profit is realized at time $t2$. The setup could have been presented just as easily to realize the profit at the initiation of the trades by borrowing the present values of the dividends and also borrowing the present value of the strike price; you are encouraged to work it out in this way, too.

[10]Market makers will buy the deep in-the-money American puts, but only at bid prices below intrinsic value; they will then earn arbitrage profits.

[11]This is demonstrated by Geske and Shastri (1985).

[12]Leverage is a double-edged sword. If the stock price was to decline to $29/share, which is a mere 3.33% decline in value, both the call owner and the buyer of stock on margin would suffer much greater percentage declines in wealth.

[13]If the underlying asset is paying a *known* dividend amount, Proposition XII collapses to be $C - P = S - D1(1+r)^{-t1} - D2(1+r)^{-t2} - K(1+r)^{-T}$. You are also encouraged to prove this version of the proposition.

[14]The put will be exercised early only if it is in the money. Thus the call will not have any intrinsic value.

[15]If the underlying asset pays a known dividend, then Proposition XIV becomes $S - K(1+r)^{-T} \geq C - P \geq S - PV(\text{divs}) - K$, and $PV(\text{divs}) = $ present value of all dividends that will be paid prior to the options' expiration day.

[16]If there were two dividends, the same logic would apply on day $t2$. Should the written call be assigned early, the receipt of K still will suffice to repay the loan plus interest.

[17]If interest rates are known at every date, the bounds for American put–call parity can be narrowed. See Jarrow and Rudd (1983, pp. 72–75).

[18]Part B of the proof simply reverses all the option positions and includes borrowings. We leave this as an exercise for the reader.

[19]One can also begin this proof by using Proposition XII. You are encouraged to do so.

PROBLEMS

16.1   Suppose there is only one ex-dividend date between today and the expiration day of a call. State Proposition IV.

16.2   Suppose there are three ex-dividend dates between today and the expiration day of a call. State Proposition IV.

16.3   Prove Proposition IVc.

16.4   Prove Proposition Xd.

16.5   Discuss the factors that increase the likelihood that an American put will be exercised early.

16.6   Discuss the factors that increase the likelihood that an American call will be exercised early.

16.7   Why should an American call never be exercised early, except perhaps just before it trades ex-dividend?

16.8   Given the following data, what is the lowest price of an American call?

$S = 60$
$K = 50$

$S = 55$
$K = 50$
$T = 3$ months
$r = 10\%$/year

The next ex-dividend date will be two months hence. You have established the following probabilities for the dividend amount:

Probability	Dividend Amount
0.01	$0.15
0.10	$0.17
0.50	$0.19
0.38	$0.21
0.01	$0.23

16.9   Assume that $S = 44$, and use all the other data in Problem 16.8. Compute the lowest value of an American put.

16.10   Given the following information, should the call be exercised early?

$S = 60$
$K = 50$

$C=10$

$T=2$ months

$r=10\%$/year

The stock will trade ex-dividend tomorrow. The dividend amount will be $1/share. You believe that the stock price will decline by the dividend amount.

16.11 Is the following statement true, false, or uncertain? "The time value of any American option is never negative. The time value of a European option might be negative." Provide an explanation for your answer.

16.12 Discuss why an American put will increase in value the longer the time to expiration, but a European put can increase or decrease in value as time to expiration lengthens.

16.13 Suppose you are completely indifferent between exercising early a call that you own and holding onto it for another day. Tomorrow, the underlying stock trades ex-dividend. You are fully knowledgeable about when, if at all, to rationally exercise your call. Then, you receive new information: interest rates have just sharply risen. Given that you were previously indifferent about exercising your call early, and now, interest rates are higher than they were before, would the interest rate rise cause you to exercise early, or to hold onto the call for another day? Explain your answer.

16.14 Suppose that on February 2, 2001, ZZZ Corp. common stock closes at 39.40, and the April 45 put option on ZZZ closes at 5.50. You believe that ZZZ will trade ex-dividend on March 21. Also, you have formed the following probabilities concerning the possible dividend amounts:

Probability	Amount per Share
0.01	$0.10
0.80	$0.30
0.18	$0.32
0.01	$0.35

Assume that the riskless interest rate is 8%. Do the April 45 ZZZ puts violate Proposition X?

16.15 Today is the last with-dividend day for the common stock of Miss Molly's Buggy-whips (MMB). Today's stock price is $47/share. Tomorrow, MMB trades ex-dividend. The dividend that will be paid is one dollar. On the ex-dividend day, you expect MMB's stock price to decline by the dividend amount.

You own a call option with a strike price of 40. It has two months until expiration. The riskless interest rate is 10%/year.

a. If the call is selling at its lower bound today, what is its premium?

b. If you expect the call to sell at its lower bound tomorrow, what will be its premium tomorrow?

c. Based on your answers to parts a and b, is it rational and optimal for you to exercise your call? Why or why not?

16.16 Suppose $S=40$ and $r=10\%$/year. The stock pays no dividends. A European call with a strike of 40 and time to expiration of 6 months sells for 7. A European put with the same K and T sells for 4. What riskless rate of return can an investor realize over the six-month period by writing the call, buying the put, and buying the stock?

16.17 Prepare a profit diagram for each of the following two strategies: (a) buy a put with a strike price of 45 and (b) buy a call with a strike of 45 and sell 100 shares of the stock short. The put is selling for 3.8, the call is selling for 1.5, and the stock sells for 42.5. Discuss the similarities and the differences between the two profit diagrams.

16.18 Define $C(T1)$ as a call expiring at nearby date $T1$, and $C(T2)$ as a call expiring at a more distant date, $T2$. $C(T1)$ and $C(T2)$ have the same underlying asset and the same strike price. If the underlying asset will not trade ex-dividend before time $T2$, or if the calls are American, prove that $C(T2) \geq C(T1)$. To get you started on this question:

What if $C(T2) < C(T1)$
Then $C(T2) - C(T1) < 0$
Or $-C(T2) + C(T1) > 0$

a. Assume that at any date before the first expiration date, $T1$, the nearby American call could be assigned. Today, you would buy $C(T2)$ and sell $C(T1)$. What trades do you make if you are assigned $C(T1)$?

b. Assume that the first expiration date, T1, comes and goes but the nearby American call was not assigned. What trades do you make at $T2$?

c. Now, define $P(T1)$ as the price of an American put expiring at nearby time $T1$ and $P(T2)$ as the price of a put expiring at a more distant date $T2$. Each put has the same underlying asset and the same strike price. Prove that $P(T2) \geq P(T1)$. In your proof, make sure you account for the possibility that a put could be assigned.

16.19 Suppose:

$S = 20$

$K = 20$

$T1 = $ expiration date for nearby call $= 2$ months
$T2 = $ expiration date for distant call $= 5$ months
$t1 = $ next ex-dividend date $= 3$ months

Under what conditions would it be possible for the short-term European call to sell for *more* than a longer term European call? How about European puts? Can a long-term European put sell for less than an otherwise identical European put with less time to expiration?

16.20 Define $C(K1)$ as an American call with a low strike price $K1$, and $C(K2)$ as an American call with a higher strike price $K2$. Each call

has the same underlying asset and the same time to expiration. Prove that $C(K1) \geq C(K2)$. To get you started:

What if $C(K1) < C(K2)$
Then $C(K1) - C(K2) < 0$
Or $-C(K1) + C(K2) > 0$

a. As an additional hint, today you would buy $C(K1)$ and sell $C(K2)$. Assume that the written American call could be assigned at any date before the expiration date. What trades do you make if you are assigned $C(K2)$?

b. Assume that the expiration date comes and goes, but the written American call was not assigned. What trades do you make at expiration?

c. Suppose the calls are European. Can you still prove that $C(K1) \geq C(K2)$?

d. Suppose the stock pays dividends. Can you still prove that $C(K1) \geq C(K2)$?

e. Now, define $P(K1)$ as an American put with a low strike price $K1$, and $P(K2)$ as an American put with a higher strike price $K2$. Each put has the same underlying asset and the same time to expiration. Prove that $P(K2) \geq P(K1)$. In your proof, make sure you account for the possibility that a put could be assigned.

16.21 Consider an American put with a strike price of 65. The price of the put is 4. The price of the underlying asset is 60. Which of the following would you do to arbitrage?

a. Buy the put, buy the underlying asset, exercise the put.

b. Buy the put, sell the underlying asset, exercise the put.

c. Sell the put, buy the underlying asset, exercise the put.

d. Sell the put, sell the underlying asset, exercise the put.

CHAPTER 17

The Binomial Option Pricing Model

At expiration, we know that an option is worth its intrinsic value. Thus, at expiration, an option's intrinsic value serves as an exact option pricing model. However, it is also important to be able to value options before expiration. While the put–call parity relationship does generate put and call option price boundaries before expiration, an important condition of the put–call parity relationship is that a put price must be known before a call price can be generated. Thus, although put–call parity and other pricing bounds shown in Chapter 16 narrowed the range of possible option prices, we still do not have a model that provides an exact option price before expiration.

In this chapter, we derive a model that provides an exact option price before expiration. This model is called the binomial option pricing model (BOPM). One of the advantages of this particular model is its flexibility.[1] The binomial option pricing model can be used to value complex options of many types, including American puts, American calls on dividend-paying stocks, options on debt instruments and interest rates, and exotic options. It can also accommodate changing conditions over time. For example, if interest rates are believed likely to change during the life of the option, or if the volatility of the underlying asset is believed likely to change, the BOPM can handle these situations quite easily. Even more, the BOPM can account for different assumed stock price movement processes, such as one in which the variance of the stock's returns is greater at lower price levels (constant elasticity of variance), or if there is a probability of a "jump" (a discontinuity, perhaps due to a possible tender offer for the stock) in the stock's price at each date.[2]

Studying the BOPM in detail also allows us to achieve additional understanding of several aspects of options that we have already learned. For example, the BOPM clarifies conditions under which options will be exercised early. Moreover, it validates the concept that buying a call is like buying stock and borrowing, and the concept that buying a put is like selling stock short and lending. The idea that options can be replicated with portfolios of stocks and bonds, which has revolutionized the field of finance, permits institutions to hedge their option portfolios. Option replication gave rise to the portfolio insurance industry that had an estimated size of $80 billion in September 1987 and has even been blamed for the stock market crash of October 1987.[3] Finally, under certain assumptions, the BOPM can be shown to converge to several different option pricing models. These include the Black–Scholes option pricing model (BSOPM), which is the most widely used option pricing model, and the subject of the next chapter.

17.1 A QUIZ

Before beginning with the details of the BOPM, take about 30 minutes and answer the following questions. Doing so will make the subsequent material easier to follow. The answers are at the end of the quiz, but try to work through the questions independently.

Consider a European call option on a stock. The call has one period (say one month) until expiration. The current stock price, S_{T-1}, is \$40. At the expiration date, time T, the stock will sell for one of only two possible prices: either $S_{T,u} = \$50$, or for $S_{T,d} = \$35$. The strike price is \$45.

1. If the stock rises to \$50 on the expiration date, what is the price of the call option? If $S_{T,u} = (1+u)S_{T-1}$, then u is the rate of return on the stock if there is an uptick. What is the value of u?

2. If the stock falls to \$35 at time T, what will the call be worth at that time? If $S_{T,d} = (1+d) \times S_{T-1}$, what is the value of d?

As will soon be discussed, we can create a levered portfolio (consisting of a long position in stock, financed in part by borrowed funds) that will duplicate the payoffs of the call. Suppose the riskless interest rate is $r = 1\%$ per period (e.g., 1% per month) and that investors can borrow and lend at that rate. Consider a portfolio, created at time $T-1$, consisting of a third of a share of stock and \$11.551155 in borrowed funds. This is a levered portfolio financed at the riskless interest rate.

3. If the stock were to rise to \$50, how much would the levered portfolio be worth at time T? Be sure to pay the interest on the borrowed funds.

4. If the stock were to fall to \$35 at time T, what would the levered portfolio be worth?

Your answers to 3 and 4 should be identical to the call values you computed in 1 and 2. The call offers the exact same payoffs (at time T) as the levered portfolio. Therefore, at time $T-1$, the call should sell for the same price as the amount invested in the levered portfolio. If it did not, all investors would buy the cheaper assets and sell short the more expensive ones.

5. How much of the investor's money was invested in the levered portfolio at time $T-1$? This must also equal the price of the call at time $T-1$. In other words:

$$0.333333 S_{T-1} - 11.551155 = C_{T-1}$$

The left-hand side expresses the amount invested in the levered portfolio: a third of a share of stock, and \$11.551155 in borrowed funds.

6. If the call sells for \$2 at time $T-1$, how can an investor earn an arbitrage profit? Prepare an arbitrage table like those shown in Chapter 16 by finding the positive cash inflow at time $T-1$ and showing that no matter what S_T is, there is a zero cash flow at time T.

7. If the call sells for \$1.50 at time $T-1$, how can an investor earn an arbitrage profit? Prepare an arbitrage table like those in Chapter 16 by finding the positive cash inflow at time $T-1$, and showing that no matter what S_T is, there is a zero cash flow at time T.

8. Would your answer to any of the foregoing questions change in any way if you knew that the probability of the stock rising was 90%? Would your answers change if the probability was only 5% that the stock would rise?

9. It is generally agreed that arbitrage cannot exist in well-functioning markets, simply because investors maximize wealth. That is, they prefer more to less. In other words, if an arbitrage opportunity came along, investors would quickly exploit it to the maximum extent possible. Do any of the foregoing results depend on the level of investors' risk aversion? Do they change if investors are risk neutral or risk seekers?

You might be wondering how the third of a share of stock and the $11.551155 in debt were chosen. They were computed because they are the unique numbers that equated the payoffs of the call with the payoffs of the levered portfolio, and they will be algebraically defined by a set of equations in the next section.

The answers to the quiz are presented next. However to get maximum benefit out of the exercise, you should work out the solutions before proceeding with the rest of the chapter.

Answers to the Quiz

1. $C_{T,u}=5$; $u=0.25$
2. $C_{T,d}=0$; $d=-0.125$
3. $50(0.333333)-11.551155(1.01)=5$
4. $35(0.333333)-11.551155(1.01)=0$
5. $S_{T-1}/3-11.551155=C_{T-1}=1.782178$, given $S_{T-1}=40$

6.

		Time T	
Time $T-1$		$S_T=35$	$S_T=50$
Sell call	+2	0	−5
Buy $1/3$ share of stock	−13.333333	+11.66667	+16.66667
Borrow	+11.551155	−11.66667	−11.66667
	+0.217822	0	0

7.

		Time T	
Time $T-1$		$S_T=35$	$S_T=50$
Buy call	−1.50	0	+5
Sell $1/3$ share of stock	+13.333333	−11.66667	−16.66667
Lend	−11.551155	+11.66667	+11.66667
	+0.282178	0	0

8. No
9. No

17.2   DERIVING THE BINOMIAL OPTION PRICING MODEL FOR CALLS ON NON-DIVIDEND-PAYING STOCKS

17.2.1   Assumptions

To begin, we assert that investors prefer more to less. This assertion is important because we can be sure that all arbitrage opportunities will be instantaneously exploited under this assertion. In addition, we make the following sets of assumptions.

1. Markets are perfect and competitive. This means that there are no transactions costs, no margin requirements, and no taxes. In addition investors receive full use of the proceeds from short sales, and, if they wish, investors can trade fractions of securities (i.e., securities are infinitely divisible). Also they can trade all they want at the market prices at every date. Finally, there is only one interest rate, r, and investors can risklessly borrow and lend at that rate.

2. The periodic interest rate r, and the sizes of the uptick u and downtick d are known in every future period. The stock can move only according to this "geometric random walk" (up by $u\%$ per period, or down by $d\%$ per period). It is not necessary for u, d, and r to be constant in every period. It is only necessary for them to be known. In other words, u, d, and r are deterministic.

Note that there are some "assumptions" that you might think are necessary. For example, there are no assumptions about the expected or required return on the stock. Also, there are no assumptions about the investors' degree of risk aversion, if any. Moreover, nothing is assumed about the probability of the uptick or the downtick. Note well, however, that we do assume that the pricing process of the underlying asset is known. That is, we assume that we know the sizes of u and d in each period.

Before we derive the single-period BOPM in the next section, we present an overview of how call option prices are calculated using the BOPM. Today is time $T-1$, and the option expires at the end of the single period, i.e., at time T. To calculate a call option price today using the BOPM, follow these steps:

1. Define the stock price process. Given today's price, the stock can take on one of only two possible prices at the next date: $(1+u)$ times the current stock price, or $(1+d)$ times the current stock price.

2. Determine the terminal prices of a call option. There will be two possible call prices, one for each possible stock price. These prices are equal to the intrinsic value of the call option at expiration.

3. Equate the payoffs of an unknown "equivalent portfolio" of stocks and bonds with the payoffs of the call. There will be two equations (one for each stock price) and two unknowns (the number of shares of stock to be bought and the amount of debt). Thus, the composition of the equivalent portfolio can be determined.

4. Apply the law of one price: if two assets offer identical payoffs for every possible future outcome (here, there are two possible outcomes that will occur at the next date: the stock will change by either $u\%$ or $d\%$), then today's prices of the two assets must be equal. Since the equivalent portfolio and the call offer the same payoffs, they must be worth the same today.

17.2.2   The Derivation of the One-Period Binomial Option Pricing Model

We start with a one-period, two-date model. At time $T-1$, the stock price is S_{T-1}. At the option's expiration date, time T, the stock price can take on one of only two values. If there is an uptick at time T, then $S_{T,u}=(1+u)S_{T-1}$. If there is a downtick at time T, then the stock will take on the lower value, $S_{T,d}=(1+d)S_{T-1}$. Graphically, this is depicted as follows:

$$S_{T-1} \begin{cases} S_{T,u}=(1+u)S_{T-1} \\ \\ S_{T,d}=(1+d)S_{T-1} \end{cases}$$

The parameters u and d are the possible rates of return on the underlying asset. For stocks, it is realistic to expect u to be greater than zero and d to be less than zero. However, this might not be the case for all underlying assets. For example, if pure discount Treasury bill prices were being modeled, it might be more realistic to have both u and d greater than zero.

The parameter r equals the riskless interest rate during the single period. To preclude arbitrage opportunities, u must exceed r and r must exceed d. If u and d were both greater than r, investors could arbitrage by borrowing as much as possible to invest in the risky stock. At time T, it would then be certain that the risky stock price will be high enough to repay the loan and still have some cash left over. In other words, if $u>d>r$, then

	Time T	
Time $T-1$	**Uptick**	**Downtick**
Borrow $1	$-\$1(1+r)$	$-\$1(1+r)$
Invest $1 in the stock	$+\$1(1+u)$	$+\$1(1+d)$
Net cash flow=$0	$\overline{u-r>0}$	$\overline{d-r>0}$

Similarly, we cannot have $r>u>d$, for in this case, no rational person would ever buy the risky stock. After all, no matter what outcome occurs at time T, the investor would have been better off buying the riskless asset. Equivalently, we could demonstrate how an arbitrage profit could be earned by selling the stock short and using the proceeds to invest in riskless securities. Problem 17.1 at the end of the chapter illustrates the arbitrage process if $r>u>d$.

Returning to the binomial model, if time T is the expiration date of a call option with a strike price of K, the call will be worth $C_{T,u}=\max(0, S_{T,u}-K)$ if the stock price rises. If the stock price falls in value at time T, the call would be worth $C_{T,d}=\max(0, S_{T,d}-K)$. Graphically, we have

$$C_{T-1} \left\{ \begin{array}{l} C_{T,u} = \max(0, S_{T,u}- K) = \max[0,(1 + u)S_{T-1} - K] \\ \\ C_{T,d} = \max(0, S_{T,d} - K) = \max[0,(1 + d)S_{T-1} - K] \end{array} \right.$$

Now consider the possibility of forming a portfolio that will make the same payoffs at time T as the call. We will buy a fraction of a share of stock, denoted by Δ, and invest $\$B$ in riskless bonds (debt instruments). We will see that for a portfolio that is equivalent to a call, Δ will always be positive or zero (nonnegative) and B will always be negative or zero (nonpositive). This means that a call is equivalent to a portfolio consisting of a long position in stock and borrowing. This is a levered portfolio (i.e., a purchase of stock made on margin). On the other hand, for a put, Δ will always be nonpositive and B will always be nonnegative. Thus, a put is equivalent to a short position in the underlying asset, combined with lending.

The debt–equity equivalent portfolio will require an investment of $\Delta S_{T-1}+B$. In the case of a call, $B\leq0$, $\Delta\geq0$, and $\Delta S_{T-1}\geq|B|$.[4] The debt–equity portfolio will either be worth $\Delta S_{T,u}+(1+r)B$ if there is an uptick in the stock, or $\Delta S_{T,d}+(1+r)B$ if there is a downtick in the stock. Graphically, this is

$$\Delta S_{T-1} + B \left\{ \begin{array}{l} \Delta(1 + u)S_{T-1} + (1+r)B = \Delta S_{T,u} + (1+r)B \\ \\ \Delta(1 + d)S_{T-1} + (1+r)B = \Delta S_{T,d} + (1+r)B \end{array} \right.$$

Now, equate the payoffs of the equivalent portfolio with the values of the call at time T:

$$\Delta(1+u)S_{T-1} + (1+r)B = C_{T,u}$$
$$\Delta(1+d)S_{T-1} + (1+r)B = C_{T,d}$$

This is a set of two simultaneous equations with two unknowns, Δ and B. Our goal is to find the values of these unknowns, in which case we will have defined a levered portfolio that pays off the same as the call. Solving the system of simultaneous equations, we get:

$$\Delta = \frac{C_{T,u} - C_{T,d}}{(u-d)S_{T-1}} = \frac{C_{T,u} - C_{T,d}}{S_{T,u} - S_{T,d}}; \quad \Delta \geq 0 \qquad (17.1)$$

$$B = \frac{(1+u)C_{T,d} - (1+d)C_{T,u}}{(u-d)(1+r)}; \quad B \leq 0 \qquad (17.2)$$

The general formulation for Δ and B merely alters the notation of Equations (17.1) and (17.2):

$$\Delta = \frac{C_u - C_d}{(u-d)S} = \frac{C_u - C_d}{S_u - S_d} \qquad (17.3)$$

$$B = \frac{(1+u)C_d - (1+d)C_u}{(u-d)(1+r)} \qquad (17.4)$$

The value of Δ tells us the fraction of one share of stock to buy in order to replicate one call.[5] That is, $0 \leq \Delta \leq 1$. The value of B, where $B \leq 0$, specifies how much to borrow to finance the investment in the stock.

If the call and the debt–equity portfolio both offer exactly the same payoffs at time T, then the price of the call at time $T-1$ must equal the investment in the equivalent portfolio at time $T-1$:

$$C_{T-1} = \Delta S_{T-1} + B \qquad (17.5)$$

The general statement that a call is equivalent to a unique levered position in the underlying asset is thus[6]:

$$C = \Delta S + B \qquad (17.6)$$

If the call sold for less than the equivalent portfolio, an arbitrageur would buy the call and sell the equivalent portfolio (i.e., sell the stock and lend). This would lead to a positive cash inflow at time $T-1$, with a zero cash flow at time T, regardless of whether the stock rises or falls. Question 7 in the quiz at the start of the chapter illustrates this.

If the call sold for a price higher than $\Delta S_{T-1}+B$, an arbitrage profit could be earned by selling the call and buying the equivalent portfolio (buy the stock and borrow). Question 6 in the quiz illustrates this.[7]

Next, substitute the expressions for Δ [Equation (17.1)] and B [Equation (17.2)] into the expression for the call value [Equation (17.5)]. After simplifying, we get:

$$C_{T-1} = \frac{[(r-d)/(u-d)]C_{T,u} + [(u-r)/(u-d)]C_{T,d}}{1+r}$$

or

$$C_{T-1} = \frac{pC_{T,u} + (1-p)C_{T,d}}{1+r} \qquad (17.7)$$

where

$$p = \frac{r-d}{u-d} \quad \text{and} \quad 1-p = \frac{u-r}{u-d}$$

From this, we derive the general binomial option pricing model equation for the value of a call option on a non-dividend-paying stock:

$$C = \frac{pC_u + (1-p)C_d}{1+r} \tag{17.8}$$

Equation (17.8) defines the BOPM single-period value of a call option. This must be the value of the call if we know the process of stock price movements (the u and the d), if we know the riskless interest rate, if we can trade without frictions such as commissions, if assets are infinitely divisible (i.e., we can trade fractions of assets), and if investors prefer more to less. Nowhere did we ever mention risk aversion. Investors can be extremely risk averse, not very risk averse, risk neutral, or even risk seekers, and we would get the same result. Furthermore, nowhere did we mention the probabilities of an uptick and downtick. It does not matter if investors assign a probability of 0.98 to an uptick, or if the probability of an uptick is 0.01.

If time T is not an ex-dividend date, it can be demonstrated that the formula for the call value in Equations (17.7) and (17.8), C_{T-1}, will always exceed or equal $S_{T-1} - K$. Thus, we do not have to worry that Equation (17.8) will produce a value that permits an arbitrage opportunity by violating Proposition II′ in Chapter 16. If it is certain that the call will finish in the money [i.e., $(1+d)S_{T-1} > K$], then $C_{T-1} \geq S_{T-1} - K$ (if time T is not an ex-dividend day).

17.2.3   Risk Neutrality

Looking at Equation (17.8), it is tempting to view p as a probability measure, in which case the value of the call equals the present value of the expected value of the call:

$$C_{T-1} = \frac{\begin{array}{l}[(\text{probability of an uptick} \times \text{value of the call if the stock has an uptick}) \\ + (\text{probability of a downtick} \times \text{value of the call if the stock has a downtick})]\end{array}}{1+r}$$

Of course in deriving Equation (17.8), we never considered probabilities.

Nevertheless, the parameter p does have one element of being a probability measure, since $0 \leq p \leq 1$, and there is one interesting case in which p *is* a probability. That occurs when investors are *risk neutral*. If investors are risk neutral, they do not care about risk. All assets will be priced to yield the same risk-free rate of return. If any asset had an expected return above the riskless rate of interest, all investors would buy it, regardless of its risk (we are continuing to assume that investors prefer higher expected returns to lower ones).

Define q as the probability of an uptick. If investors are risk neutral, the stock (like any asset) must be priced to yield the riskless rate of return:

$$S_{T-1} = \frac{q(1+u)S_{T-1} + (1-q)(1+d)S_{T-1}}{1+r} = \frac{qS_{T,u} + (1-q)S_{T,d}}{1+r}$$

$$= \frac{\text{the expected stock price at time } T}{1+r} = \frac{E(S_T)}{1+r}$$

Solving $S_{T-1}=[q(1+u)S_{T-1}+(1-q)(1+d)S_{T-1}]/(1+r)$ for q, we have:

$$q = \frac{r-d}{u-d}$$

This is the same value we found for p. In a risk-neutral economy, the call must also be priced to yield the riskless rate of return:

$$C_{T-1} = \frac{qC_{T,u}+(1-q)C_{T,d}}{1+r} = \frac{pC_{T,u}+(1-p)C_{T,d}}{1+r} = \frac{E(C_T)}{1+r}$$

Thus, the binomial option pricing model solution for the value of a call equals the value of a call in a risk-neutral economy. The parameter p is the probability of an uptick in an economy characterized by risk-neutral investors. However, keep in mind that p need not be the probability of an uptick if investors are risk averse. In any type of market environment, it will always be the case that $p=(r-d)/(u-d)$.

The idea that options are valued the same in a risk-neutral economy as in any economy has led to the simplification of what were previously very complicated solutions of option pricing problems.[8]

17.2.4 The Two-Period Binomial Option Pricing Model

Now we will extend the BOPM to a two-period world. We will assume that the process guiding the price of the underlying asset is stationary over time. This means that we assume that u and d are constant in every period. This assumption is *not* necessary to derive a multiperiod option model; u and d are assumed to be constant only to obtain a "nice" call option pricing formula for a multiperiod case.

In a two-period world, time progresses as shown in Figure 17.1. Time T is the expiration date of the call option. We continue to assume that there are no ex-dividend days.

The stock price process is:

$$
\begin{array}{ccc}
 & & S_{T,uu}=(1+u)^2 S_{T-2} \\
 & S_{T-1,u}=(1+u)S_{T-2} & \\
S_{T-2} & & S_{T,ud}=(1+u)(1+d)S_{T-2} \\
 & S_{T-1,d}=(1+d)S_{T-2} & \\
 & & S_{T,dd}=(1+d)^2 S_{T-2}
\end{array}
$$

$$T-2 \qquad\qquad T-1 \qquad\qquad\qquad\qquad T$$

The current stock price is S_{T-2}. At the end of the next period, time $T-1$, the stock price can take on one of two values, depending on whether there is an uptick or a downtick. At the end of the second period, time T, the stock price can be one of three values. Note that the time T stock price is the same regardless of whether an uptick follows a downtick or a downtick follows an uptick. This will always be the case if u and d are constants over time. Thus, there are two ways of realizing the stock price $S_{T,ud}$, which equals $S_{T,du}$.

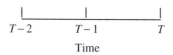

Time

Figure 17.1

The pricing process of the call is:

$$C_{T,uu} = \max[0,(1+u)^2 S_{T-2} - K]$$

$C_{T-1,u}$

C_{T-2}

$$C_{T,ud} = \max[0,(1+u)(1+d)S_{T-2} - K]$$

$C_{T-1,d}$

$$C_{T,dd} = \max[0,(1+d)^2 S_{T-2} - K]$$

$T-2 \qquad T-1 \qquad\qquad\qquad T$

We use a recursive process to solve for C_{T-2}. To do this, we start at the option expiration date and work our way back to the present. Thus, we can compute the value of $C_{T-1,u}$ by the one-period analysis we already learned. In other words, pretend we are at time $T-1$ and the stock just had an uptick. In this case, we are in the following situation:

$$S_{T,uu} = (1+u)^2 S_{T-2}$$

$$S_{T-1,u} = (1+u)S_{T-2}$$

$$S_{T,ud} = (1+u)(1+d)S_{T-2}$$

$$C_{T,uu} = \max[0,(1+u)^2 S_{T-2} - K] = \max[0,(1+u)S_{T-1,u} - K]$$

$C_{T-1,u}$

$$C_{T,ud} = \max[0,(1+u)(1+d)S_{T-2} - K] = \max[0,(1+d)S_{T-1,u} - K]$$

In this case, it is as if we are in a single-period world. Equation (17.9) defines the value of the call at time $T-1$, given that there was an uptick during the first period:

$$C_{T-1,u} = \frac{pC_{T,uu} + (1-p)C_{T,ud}}{1+r} \tag{17.9}$$

Equation (17.9) is just a restatement of the general single period BOPM call pricing model on a non-dividend-paying stock, Equation (17.8). The only difference is a slight change in the notation.

Now, let us assume instead that we are at time $T-1$, but instead of an uptick, there was just a downtick realized in the first period. Thus, the situation facing us is:

$$S_{T,ud} = (1+u)(1+d)S_{T-2}$$

$$S_{T-1,d} = (1+d)S_{T-2}$$

$$S_{T,dd} = (1+d)^2 S_{T-2}$$

$$C_{T-1,d} \Bigg\langle \begin{array}{l} C_{T,ud} = \max[0,(1+u)(1+d)S_{T-2} - K] = \max[0,(1+u)S_{T-1,d} - K] \\[2ex] C_{T,dd} = \max[0,(1+d)^2 S_{T-2} - K] = \max[0,(1+d)S_{T-1,d} - K] \end{array}$$

Again, once we know that there was a downtick in the first period, we are in a single period world, and we can use the general equation, (17.8), to find the value of the call:

$$C_{T-1,d} = \frac{pC_{T,ud} + (1-p)C_{T,dd}}{1+r} \tag{17.10}$$

At this stage, we know the value of the call if there is an uptick in the first period, and we also know the value of the call if there is a downtick in the first period. In the recursive process, we now move back to time $T-2$, and again apply the single period BOPM principles:

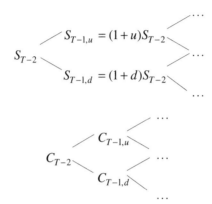

At time $T-2$, we can invest in a levered portfolio that will provide the same payoffs at time $T-1$ as the call. The initial investment of $\Delta S_{T-2}+B$ will take on one of two values, depending on whether there is an uptick or a downtick during the first period:

$$\Delta S_{T-2} + B \Bigg\langle \begin{array}{l} (1+u)\,\Delta S_{T-2} + (1+r)B = \Delta S_{T-1,u} + (1+r)B \\[2ex] (1+d)\,\Delta S_{T-2} + (1+r)B = \Delta S_{T-1,d} + (1+r)B \end{array}$$

Now, equate the time $T-1$ payoffs of the equivalent portfolio with the values of the call at time $T-1$:

$$\Delta(1+u)S_{T-2} + (1+r)B = C_{T-1,u}$$

$$\Delta(1+d)S_{T-2} + (1+r)B = C_{T-1,d}$$

These consist of two simultaneous equations with two unknowns, Δ and B. Solving them, we get:

$$\Delta = \frac{C_{T-1,u} - C_{T-1,d}}{(u-d)S_{T-2}} = \frac{C_{T-1,u} - C_{T-1,d}}{S_{T-1,u} - S_{T-1,d}} \tag{17.11}$$

$$B = \frac{(1+u)C_{T-1,d} - (1+d)C_{T-1,u}}{(u-d)(1+r)} \tag{17.12}$$

Note that the equations are identical to Equations (17.3) and (17.4). These equations define the investment in Δ shares of stock and bonds (but remember that for calls, $B \le 0$) at time $T-2$, that creates a portfolio having payoffs that are the same as those from the call at time $T-1$.

If two assets or portfolios offer the exact same payoffs at time $T-1$, they must sell for the same price at time $T-2$. We have

$$C_{T-2} = \Delta S_{T-2} + B \tag{17.13}$$

where Δ and B are defined as in Equations (17.11) and (17.12). Now, substitute Equations (17.9) and (17.10) into (17.11) and (17.12), and then substitute the resulting expressions into Equation (17.13). The result is the value of a call when there are two periods before its expiration date:

$$C_{T-2} = \frac{p^2 C_{T,uu} + 2p(1-p)C_{T,ud} + (1-p)^2 C_{T,dd}}{(1+r)^2} \tag{17.14}$$

All the variables on the right-hand side of Equation (17.14) are known. The value of p is $(r-d)/(u-d)$. The time T value of the call can take on one of three values:

$$C_{T,uu} = \max[0, S_{T,uu} - K] = \max[0, (1+u)^2 S_{T-2} - K]$$

$$C_{T,ud} = \max[0, S_{T,ud} - K] = \max[0, (1+u)(1+d)S_{T-2} - K]$$

$$C_{T,dd} = \max[0, S_{T,dd} - K] = \max[0, (1+d)^2 S_{T-2} - K]$$

There is one more important concept to be learned in this theory. A portfolio of stocks and bonds can offer the same payoffs as any option. In other words, any option can be replicated by using stocks and bonds. However, the replication is a dynamic process. The values of Δ and B that we compute at time $T-2$ will not be the same as the values that exist at time $T-1$. Thus, at the end of every period, the composition of the equivalent portfolio changes. When you buy an option, there is a one-time cash outflow, and no other cash flow takes place until the option is sold or expires. If we are to claim that a dynamically adjusted portfolio of stocks and bonds is equivalent to an option, it must be the case that no other cash flows occur at all the equivalent portfolio's intermediate dates, when Δ and B change.

It turns out that the equivalent portfolio offers this property, which is called **self-financing**. Although Δ and B change over time, there are no additional cash requirements needed to continue the replicating process. If Δ increases, more shares must be bought at the new, higher stock price. However, there will be an increase in B equal to the product of the change in Δ and the new stock price. The value of the new shares to be purchased equals the increase in required borrowing.

Likewise, if the price of the underlying asset declines, Δ will decline, and shares will have to be sold to continue the replicating process. However, the proceeds from the sale of shares, at the new stock price, will exactly equal the decline in borrowing needed to maintain an equivalent portfolio. The self-financing property is illustrated in the example developed in Section 17.2.5.

17.2.5   A Numerical Example of the Two-Period Binomial Option Pricing Model

EXAMPLE 17.1   The current stock price be $20 per share. The stock can either rise by 20% per period or fall by 10% per period. The riskless interest rate is 10% per period. Find the value of a call option with a strike price of 20, having two periods until expiration. Also, at times $T-2$ and $T-1$, find the composition of the portfolio of stocks and riskless debt that is equivalent to the call, and demonstrate that the payoffs of this equivalent portfolio are indeed the same as the payoffs of the call. Finally, show that the equivalent portfolio is self-financing.

Solution   Since $u=0.2$, $d=-0.1$, and $r=0.1$, the value of p is

$$p = \frac{0.1-(-0.1)}{0.2-(-0.1)} = \frac{2}{3} = 0.66667$$

Next, map out the stock price process (sometimes, this is called the "binomial tree"):

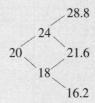

The pricing process for the call is

$$C_{T-2} \begin{array}{c} C_{T-1,u} \\ C_{T-1,d} \end{array} \begin{array}{c} C_{T,uu} = \max[0, 28.8 - 20] = 8.8 \\ C_{T,ud} = \max[0, 21.6 - 20] = 1.6 \\ C_{T,dd} = \max[0, 16.2 - 20] = 0 \end{array}$$

From here, the problem is solved recursively, moving from right to left, using the single-period BOPM pricing model at each step. If there is an uptick during the first period, Equation (17.9) determines the price of the call:

$$C_{T-1,u} = \frac{pC_{T,uu} + (1-p)C_{T,ud}}{1+r} = \frac{(2/3)(8.8) + (1/3)(1.6)}{1.1} = 5.\overline{8181}\ldots$$

If there is a downtick during the first period, Equation (17.10) determines the value of the call:

$$C_{T-1,d} = \frac{(2/3)(1.6) + (1/3)(0)}{1.1} = 0.969697$$

To find the value of the call at time $T-2$, we can use one of two approaches. First, since we know the value of the call at time $T-1$ if there is an uptick in the first period, and we also know the value of the call at time $T-1$ if there is a downtick in the first period, we are in a single-period situation that looks like:

$$C_{T-2} \begin{cases} 5.\overline{8181} = C_{T-1,u} \\ 0.969697 = C_{T-1,d} \end{cases}$$

The general single-period BOPM equation (17.8) can be used to value the call at time $T-2$:

$$C_{T-2} = \frac{(2/3)(5.\overline{8181}) + (1/3)(0.969697)}{1.1} = 3.8200184$$

Alternatively, we could use Equation (17.14) directly to find C_{T-2}:

$$C_{T-2} = \frac{(2/3)^2(8.8) + 2(2/3)(1/3)(1.6) + (1/3)^2(0)}{1.1^2} = 3.8200184$$

Next, we will find the composition of the equivalent portfolio at each date, using general formulas (17.3) and (17.4). At time $T-2$, Equations (17.11) and (17.12) are the versions of (17.3) and (17.4) that are used:

$$\Delta = \frac{C_{T-1,u} - C_{T-1,d}}{S_{T-1,u} - S_{T-1,d}} = \frac{5.\overline{8181} - 0.969697}{24 - 18} = 0.8080808$$

$$B = \frac{(1+u)C_{T-1,d} - (1+d)C_{T-1,u}}{(u-d)(1+r)} = \frac{(1.2)(0.969697) - (0.9)(5.\overline{8181})}{(0.3)(1.1)} = -12.341598$$

This says that an investor who bought 0.8080808 share of stock at its time $T-2$ price of \$20/share, and borrowed (because of the negative sign) \$12.341598, will have created a levered portfolio that pays off the same as the call, regardless of whether there is an uptick or a downtick.

The cost of the levered portfolio is:

$$\Delta S + B = (0.8080808)(20) - 12.341598 = 3.820018$$

This is the same as the value of the call we just computed, except for a small rounding error. If the stock has an uptick in the first period, then the levered portfolio will be worth:

$$\Delta S_{T-1,u} + (1+r)B = (0.8080808)(24) - (1.1)(12.341598) = 5.818182$$

which is the same value as the call if the stock rises at time $T-1$. If the stock declined in the first period, the levered portfolio would be worth:

$$\Delta S_{T-1,d} + (1+r)B = (0.8080808)(18) - (1.1)(12.341598) = 0.969697$$

which, again, is the same as the payoff provided by the call. Thus, we have shown that the portfolio consisting of 0.8080808 share of stock, financed in part with \$12.341598 in borrowed funds, offers the same payoffs as the call. Also, since the call and the levered portfolio offer identical payoffs at time $T-1$, they must be valued the same at time $T-2$, and they are.

Next, we must determine the composition of the two possible equivalent portfolios at time $T-1$. We will also verify that each is self-financing, so that no additional cash flows occur when replicating the option. Because there are two possible states of the world at time $T-1$, we must find the equivalent portfolio given that there was an uptick in the first period, and then repeat the calculations given that there was a downtick in the first period.

If there was an uptick in the first period, then by Equations (17.3) and (17.4) we find the composition of the new equivalent portfolio:

$$\Delta = \frac{C_u - C_d}{S_u - S_d} = \frac{8.8 - 1.6}{28.8 - 21.6} = 1$$

$$B = \frac{(1+u)C_d - (1+d)C_u}{(u-d)(1+r)} = \frac{(1.2)(1.6) - (0.9)(8.8)}{[0.2 - (-0.1)](1.1)} = -18.181818$$

What this means is that although the equivalent portfolio at time $T-2$ consisted of 0.8080808 share of stock and −\$12.341598 in bonds, if the stock had an uptick in the first period, the new equivalent portfolio consists of one share of stock and $B=$−\$18.181818.[9] The equivalent portfolio is self-financing, though, because an additional 0.1919192 share of stock must be purchased at \$24/share, for a total additional investment in stock of \$4.60606. The old indebtedness was \$12.341598. After one period of interest, the option replicator owes \$13.575758 (1.1 × 12.341598). Since the new B in the equivalent portfolio is −\$18.181818, this means that (\$18.181818−\$13.575758=) \$4.60606 must be additionally borrowed!

What if the stock had a downtick in the first period? Then the composition of the equivalent portfolio would be:

$$\Delta = \frac{C_u - C_d}{S_u - S_d} = \frac{1.6 - 0}{21.6 - 16.2} = 0.296296$$

$$B = \frac{(1+u)C_d - (1+d)C_u}{(u-d)(1+r)} = \frac{(1.2)(0) - (0.9)(1.6)}{[0.2 - (-0.1)](1.1)} = -4.363636$$

To continue replicating the option, (0.8080808 − 0.296296 =) 0.5117848 share of stock must be sold, at the new price of \$18/share. This provides \$9.212126 (0.5117848 × 18).

However, the new replicating portfolio also requires the borrowing of less money. The loan established at time $T-2$ was $12.341598. Including interest, the total loan at time $T-1$ is then $13.575758. If the proceeds from the sale of stock are used to repay the loan, the remaining loan balance is ($13.575758 − $9.212126 =) $4.3636316. Note that this equals the new $-B$ value for the replicating portfolio (except for a small rounding error).

Thus, we have shown that at each date and possible stock price, there is a portfolio of stocks and bonds that will offer the same payoffs as the call. The dollar value of this portfolio equals the price of the call, at each date and possible stock price. Finally, the equivalent portfolio was shown to be self-financing. The final time path solution to the call values and composition of the equivalent portfolio is shown in Figure 17.2.

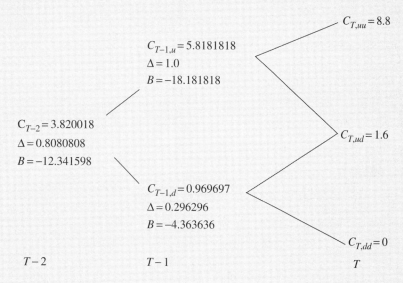

Figure 17.2 Call values and composition of the equivalent portfolio of Example 17.1. (Here and in other figures in this chapter, dollar signs are omitted for clarity.)

17.2.6   The Multiperiod Binomial Option Pricing Model

Equation (17.15), the three-period version of the BOPM, can be derived using the same logic as in Section 17.2.4:

$$C_{T-3} = \frac{p^3 C_{T,uuu} + 3p^2(1-p)C_{T,uud} + 3p(1-p)^2 C_{T,udd} + (1-p)^3 C_{T,ddd}}{(1+r)^3} \quad (17.15)$$

We can rewrite this in a different way. First, we want to know how many ways a stock price can reach a terminal value in a binomial process. In other words, in n periods [in Equation (17.15), $n=3$], how many ways can the stock realize j upticks, where $j=0, 1, 2, 3$? Recall that if the stock pricing process is stationary over time, the order in which the upticks occur does not matter: uud, *udu*, and *duu* will all result in the same time T stock price. The answer is given by the binomial coefficient:

$$\binom{n}{j} = \frac{n!}{j!(n-j)!}$$

Thus, if $n=3$, how many ways can we get two upticks and one downtick? The answer is:

$$\frac{3!}{2!(3-2)!} = \frac{3 \times 2 \times 1}{(2 \times 1) \times (1)} = \frac{6}{2} = 3 \text{ ways}$$

How many ways can a stock realize 6 upticks in 10 periods? The answer is:

$$\frac{10!}{6!(10-6)!} = \frac{10 \times 9 \times 8 \times 7 \times 6 \times 5 \times 4 \times 3 \times 2 \times 1}{(6 \times 5 \times 4 \times 3 \times 2 \times 1) \times (4 \times 3 \times 2 \times 1)} = \frac{10 \times 9 \times 8 \times 7}{4 \times 3 \times 2 \times 1} = 210 \text{ ways}$$

Equation (17.15) can be rewritten as follows:

$$C_{T-3} = \frac{\binom{3}{3} p^3 C_{T,uuu} + \binom{3}{2} p^2 (1-p) C_{T,uud} + \binom{3}{1} p(1-p)^2 C_{T,udd} + \binom{3}{0} (1-p)^3 C_{T,ddd}}{(1+r)^3}$$

where

$$C_{t,uuu} = \max[0, (1+u)^3 (1+d)^0 \, S_{T-3} - K]$$

$$C_{t,uud} = \max[0, (1+u)^2 (1+d)^1 \, S_{T-3} - K]$$

$$C_{t,udd} = \max[0, (1+u)^1 (1+d)^2 \, S_{T-3} - K]$$

$$C_{t,ddd} = \max[0, (1+u)^0 (1+d)^3 \, S_{T-3} - K]$$

We can also write Equation (17.15) as follows:

$$C_{T-3} = \frac{1}{(1+r)^3} \sum_{j=0}^{3} \binom{3}{j} p^j (1-p)^{3-j} \max[0, (1+u)^j (1+d)^{3-j} S_{T-3} - K]$$

Thus, letting n equal the number of periods and j equal the number of upticks, the general multi-period BOPM for a call with n periods until expiration is:

$$C = \frac{1}{(1+r)^n} \sum_{j=0}^{n} \binom{n}{j} p^j (1-p)^{n-j} \max[0, (1+u)^j (1+d)^{n-j} S_{T-n} - K] \qquad (17.16)$$

Now, let a be the minimum number of upticks needed to result in the call finishing in the money. This means that we will ignore all the outcomes in which the call's time T value is 0. If $j < a$, then the call is worthless. Then the model becomes:

$$C = \frac{1}{(1+r)^n} \sum_{j=a}^{n} \binom{n}{j} p^j (1-p)^{n-j} [(1+u)^j (1+d)^{n-j} S_{T-n} - K] \qquad (17.17)$$

Note that $(1+u)^j(1+d)^{n-j}S_{T-n}=S_{T|j}=$ the time T stock price, given that there are j upticks (and $n-j$ downticks). Furthermore, $(1+u)^j(1+d)^{n-j}S_{T-n}-K=C_{T|j}=$ the time T call value, given that there are j upticks.

Equation (17.17) is a formidable-looking formula, but Example 17.2 will illustrate just how easy it is to use. Remember, this formula is to be used to value calls only when there are no ex-dividend days between today and the option's expiration date.

It is critical to learn the steps and logic behind the derivation of the multiperiod BOPM for two reasons. First, the model can be used to value calls on dividend-paying stocks, and in particular, to determine the times at which early exercise will be optimal for the call owner. And second, sometimes the user will believe that the pricing process behind the underlying asset will change over time (the u, d, and r need not be stationary over time). In both these cases, there is no simple model to determine the call's value. Rather, the recursive, step-by-step solution to the BOPM must be worked out. Fortunately, computers can do the job for us.

Cox and Rubinstein (1985) show that carving the time to expiration into as few as five intervals provides estimated call values reasonably close to those found by using the continuous time Black–Scholes option pricing model (BSOPM). However if great accuracy is important, and computation time (using a computer) is relatively unimportant, Cox and Rubinstein (1985) and Jarrow and Rudd (1983) recommend carving the time to expiration into 150 intervals. More intervals are needed when early exercise is a consideration.

17.2.7 A Numerical Example of the Multiperiod Binomial Option Pricing Model

EXAMPLE 17.2 Find the value of a call option on a non-dividend-paying stock that has the following parameters:

$n=6$ months

$u=0.05$/month

$d=-0.04$/month

$r=0.01$/month

$K=25$

$S_{T-6}=30$

This problem was developed when a class was asked: "Given that the common stock of XYZ sells for $30/share, what is the highest reasonable stock price at which it might sell six months hence?" A typical answer was $40–$45 per share. The students were also asked to estimate the lowest stock price at which it could reasonably sell in six months. A typical answer was in the range of $20–$25 per share.

Solution When estimating u and d, it should always be the case that $u>|d|$, since stocks should always be priced to increase in value. They are risky assets, and in well-functioning markets ought to be priced to provide positive returns, almost always in excess of the riskless rate of interest. As you will see, we made the arbitrary selection of $u=0.05$ and

$d=-0.04$ to generate a highest price (given 6 upticks) and a lowest price (given 6 downticks) in the ranges believed possible. This is a reasonable approach to obtaining an estimate for u and d.

Table 17.1 presents the number of upticks (j), the number of ways that j upticks can be realized ($\binom{n}{j}$), the resulting time T stock price (S_T), and the resulting expiration day call value ($C_T=S_T-K$).[10] Additionally, we can determine the value of p as follows:

$$p = \frac{r-d}{u-d} = \frac{0.01-(-0.04)}{0.05-(-0.04)} = 0.55556$$

The parameter a is the minimum number of upticks needed to ensure that the call finishes in the money. When $K=25$, the value of a is 1. That is, if there is one uptick, then the call will finish in the money. If we were evaluating a call with a strike price of 30, then $a=3$.

TABLE 17.1   Computation of S_T and C_T in a Binomial Framework

j	$\binom{n}{j}$	S_T	C_T
6	$\dfrac{6!}{6!0!}=1$	$30(1.05)^6=40.2029$	15.2029
5	$\dfrac{6!}{5!1!}=6$	$30(1.05)^5(0.96)^1=36.7569$	11.7569
4	$\dfrac{6!}{4!2!}=15$	$30(1.05)^4(0.96)^2=33.6063$	8.6063
3	$\dfrac{6!}{3!3!}=20$	$30(1.05)^3(0.96)^3=30.7258$	5.7258
2	$\dfrac{6!}{2!4!}=15$	$30(1.05)^2(0.96)^4=28.0921$	3.0921
1	$\dfrac{6!}{1!5!}=6$	$30(1.05)^1(0.96)^5=25.6842$	0.6842
0	$\dfrac{6!}{0!6!}=1$	$30(1.05)^0(0.96)^6=23.4827$	0.0

Therefore, the multiperiod BOPM estimates the call's value to be:

$$C_{T-6} = \frac{1}{(1.01)^6}\left[\binom{6}{6}p^6(1-p)^0 C_{T|6} + \binom{6}{5}p^5(1-p)^1 C_{T|5} + \binom{6}{4}p^4(1-p)^2 C_{T|4} + \cdots\right]$$

which is:

$$C_{T-6} = \frac{1}{1.01^6}\begin{bmatrix}(1)(0.556)^6(0.444)^0(15.2029) + (6)(0.556)^5(0.444)^1(11.7569)\\ + (15)(0.556)^4(0.444)^2(8.6063) + (20)(0.556)^3(0.444)^3(5.7258)\\ + (15)(0.556)^2(0.444)^4(3.0921) + (6)(0.556)^1(0.444)^5(0.6842) + 0\end{bmatrix}$$

$$= \$6.4599$$

17.3 USING THE BINOMIAL OPTION PRICING MODEL TO VALUE CALLS ON DIVIDEND-PAYING STOCKS

17.3.1 European Calls on Stocks That Pay a Discrete Percentage Dividend

The BOPM formula [Equation (17.17)] can be used to value European calls or American calls on non-dividend paying stocks. In this section, the equation is modified to treat the case in which the underlying stock pays a percentage of its value out in dividends at the end of one (or more) periods before the expiration date of the European call option. Here this percentage is assumed to be constant.

Saying that a stock will pay out a constant fraction of its value in dividends is just another way of saying that the stock has a constant dividend yield. For example, if the dividend yield is 1% and if the stock price is $10/share, the dividend amount is $0.10, and we assume that the stock will fall in value by that amount whenever it trades ex-dividend. Stocks do not pay dividends in this way. Firms almost always pay a fixed dollar amount, occasionally increasing that dollar amount when earnings increase.[11] But if foreign exchange, a well-diversified stock index, or a futures contract[12] is the underlying asset, the constant dividend yield model may be applicable.

Define δ as the constant dividend yield of the stock and assume that the dollar dividend amount (= δS) is paid at the end of one or more periods before the call's expiration date. Further assume that the stock price declines by the dividend amount when paid. The stock's ex-dividend date and dividend payment date are assumed to be the same. If there are m ex-dividend dates before expiration, n periods to expiration, and j upticks, then the time T stock price is:

$$S_T = (1+u)^j(1+d)^{n-j}(1-\delta)^m S_{T-n}$$

Suppose there are $n=5$ periods until expiration and that the stock will trade ex-dividend at the end of the first and fourth periods. Let the stock price today equal $S_{T-5}=20$, $u=0.1$, $d=-0.05$, and $\delta=0.02$. Then, Figure 17.3 shows the time path of possible stock prices.

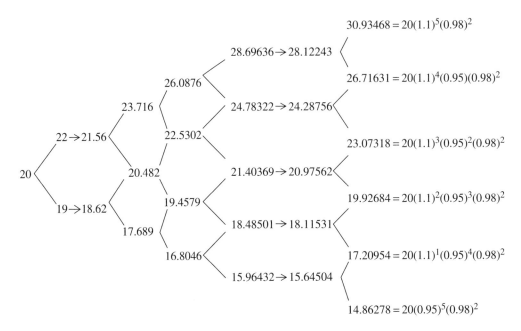

Figure 17.3

The arrows ($\rightarrow$) denote that the stock trades ex-dividend. The stock never actually trades at the cum-dividend price. For example, in the first period, the stock either rises from 20 to 21.56 or falls from 20 to 18.62.

Note that in this constant dividend yield model, it does not matter *when* the ex-dividend days occur. We have specified that they occur at times $T-4$ and $T-1$, but the same time T stock prices would result if we specified *any* two dates.

Since the options are European, the expiration day value of the call, given j upticks, is $\max[0, (1+u)^j(1+d)^{n-j}(1-\delta)^m S_{T-5}-K]$. The multiperiod BOPM is:

$$C = \frac{1}{(1+r)^n} \sum_{j=a}^{n} \binom{n}{j} [p^j(1-p)^{n-j}][(1+u)^j(1+d)^{n-j}(1-\delta)^m S_{T-n} - K] \qquad (17.18)$$

The single-step, recursive process that leads to Equation (17.18) is the same as the one used in the no-dividend model. Let us just examine the upper right portion of the foregoing pricing process for the stock:

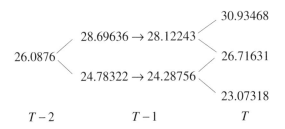

We will find the value of a call with a strike price of 25 at time $T-2$. At time $T-2$, S_{T-2} $=26.0876$. Since $C_T=\max[0, S_T - K]$, we have the following call pricing process:

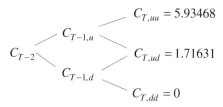

$$C_{T,uu} = 5.93468$$
$$C_{T-1,u}$$
$$C_{T-2}$$
$$C_{T,ud} = 1.71631$$
$$C_{T-1,d}$$
$$C_{T,dd} = 0$$

If we assume that $r=0\%$ per period, the value of p is:

$$p = \frac{r-d}{u-d} = \frac{0.00-(-0.05)}{0.10-(-0.05)} = 0.33333$$

Equation (17.18) can be used to find C_{T-2} in one easy step. Expanded, Equation (17.18) says:

$$C_{T-2} = \frac{1}{(1+r)^2} \{[1][p^2(1-p)^0][(1+u)^2(1+d)^0(1-\delta)^1 S_{T-2} - K]$$
$$+[2][p^1(1-p)^1][(1+u)^1(1+d)^1(1-\delta)^1 S_{T-2} - K]$$
$$+[1][p^0(1-p)^2][(1+u)^0(1+d)^2(1-\delta)^1 S_{T-2} - K]\}$$

There must be at least one uptick for the call to finish in the money. Thus, $a=1$, and the last term in brackets, for $j=0$ upticks, equals zero. Substituting values in for the symbols, we have:

$$C_{T-2} = \frac{1}{(1+0)^2} \{[1][(0.3333)^2(0.6667)^0][(1.1)^2(0.95)^0(0.98)^1(26.0876) - 25]$$
$$+[2][(0.3333)^1(0.6667)^1][(1.1)^1(0.95)^1(0.98)^1(26.0876) - 25]+[0]\}$$

$$C_{T-2} = 1\{[1][0.1111][30.93468 - 25] + [2][0.22222][26.71631 - 25]\} = 1.4222131$$

Alternatively, we could use the recursive method to find call values at each date and state of the world. First, use general equation (17.8) to compute $C_{T-1,u}$, and $C_{T-1,d}$:

$$C_{T-1,u} = \frac{(0.33333)(5.93468) + (0.66667)(1.71631)}{1.0} = 3.1224333$$

$$C_{T-1,d} = \frac{(0.33333)(1.71631) + (0.66667)(0)}{1.0} = 0.5721033$$

Then compute C_{T-2}:

$$C_{T-2} = \frac{(0.33333)(3.1224333) + (0.66667)(0.5721033)}{1.0} = 1.4222133$$

The compositions of the equivalent portfolios are found by using general equations (17.3) and (17.4). At time $T-2$, the call is in the following situation:

$$C_{T-2} \nearrow \begin{array}{l} C_{T-1,u} = 3.1224333 \\ \\ C_{T-1,d} = 0.5721033 \end{array}$$

The equivalent portfolio will follow the following pricing process[13]:

$$\Delta S_{T-2} + B \nearrow \begin{array}{l} \Delta S_{\text{ex},T-1,u} + \Delta \text{div}_u + (1+r)B = \Delta S_{\text{with-div},T-1,u} + (1+r)B \\ \\ \Delta S_{\text{ex},T-1,d} + \Delta \text{div}_d + (1+r)B = \Delta S_{\text{with-div},T-1,d} + (1+r)B \end{array}$$

Equate the payoffs of the equivalent portfolio to those of the call:

$$\Delta S_{\text{with-div},T-1,u} + (1+r)B = C_{T-1,u}.$$
$$\Delta S_{\text{with-div},T-1,d} + (1+r)B = C_{T-1,d}$$

Compare these equations to those that led to general equations (17.3) and (17.4). They are identical, except that here, the with-dividend stock prices are used. This will always be the case if we assume that the stock price is expected to decline by the dividend amount. Consequently, when the two simultaneous equations in ΔS are solved, the solution for Δ uses the *with-dividend* stock price in the denominator:

$$\Delta = \frac{C_u - C_d}{S_u - S_d} = \frac{3.122433 - 0.5721033}{28.69636 - 24.78322} = 0.6517349$$

Equation (17.4) is used to find the value of B at time $T-2$:

$$B = \frac{(1+u)C_d - (1+d)C_u}{(u-d)(1+r)} = \frac{(1.1)(0.5721033) - (0.95)(3.1224333)}{[0.1 - (-0.05)](1)} = -15.57999$$

Thus, if you buy 0.6517349 share of stock at the $T-2$ price of 26.0876 and borrow $15.57999 (at zero percent interest), the payoffs are equal to the call. If the stock price rises, the dividend is $0.57393/share. Because you own 0.6517349 share, you get a dividend of $0.37405. Add this to the new ex-dividend value of your shares, which is $(0.6517349 \times 28.12243 =)18.3282369, and you have $18.70242. Repay the loan of $15.57999, and the time $T-1$ ex-dividend value of the equivalent portfolio is $3.12243. Except for a miniscule rounding error, this equals $C_{T-1,u}$.

Given there is an uptick in the first period, at time $T-1$, the equivalent portfolio's composition is:

$$\Delta = \frac{C_u - C_d}{S_u - S_d} = \frac{5.93468 - 1.7631}{30.93468 - 26.71631} = 1.0$$

$$B = \frac{(1+u)C_d - (1+d)C_u}{(u-d)(1+r)} = \frac{(1.1)(1.71631) - (0.95)(5.93468)}{[0.1 - (-0.05)](1)} = -25.0$$

The payoffs of the equivalent portfolio are identical to the call's payoffs. If there is an uptick in the second period, the value of the single share rises to $30.93468. Subtract the (interest-free) loan of $25.0, and the equivalent portfolio is worth $5.93468. The latter equals $C_{T,uu}$.

Furthermore, the equivalent portfolio is self-financing if there is an uptick in the first period. At time $T-2$, you had 0.6517349 share. You also received a dividend of $0.37405, which can be used to buy 0.0133008 additional share of stock at the time $T-1$ ex-dividend price of $28.12243/share. Thus, you have 0.6650357 share, ex-dividend, and the new equivalent portfolio requires that you have 1.0 share. Therefore, you must spend $9.420011 to buy the additional 0.3349643 share of stock at $28.12243/share. However, you originally had borrowed $15.57999 at an interest rate of zero, but now the equivalent portfolio requires you to borrow $25. The additional borrowing of $9.42001 will exactly pay for your additional shares of stock (except for a small rounding error).

Finally, the same analysis can be applied if there is a downtick in the first period. This is left as an exercise for the student (see Problem 17.8 at the end of the chapter).

In summary, if we assume the stock has a constant dividend yield, the multiperiod BOPM is easily modified to value European calls. You must, however, know the number of times the stock will trade ex-dividend before option expiration. Then, the possible time T stock prices are

$$S_T = (1+u)^j (1+d)^{n-j} (1-\delta)^m S_{T-n}$$

when there are n periods to expiration and m ex-dividend dates prior to that date. Just let $j=0$, $1,\ldots, n$ upticks to find each possible stock price at expiration. The formulas to find the equivalent portfolio are the same as we found earlier, except that if the stock trades ex-dividend at the next date, you must remember to use the with-dividend stock prices to find Δ.

17.3.2 European Calls on Stocks Paying a Discrete, Known Dividend Amount

Here, we assume that we know the dates at which the stock will trade ex-dividend, paying a known dollar dividend amount. The model can even be extended to assume that if the stock has an uptick, there will be a known dividend amount, div_u, and if the stock has a downtick, it will pay a different known amount, div_d. This provides additional realism to the stock pricing process being modeled, since if the stock rises, it is likely that the company's profits have risen and a higher dividend will be paid. One of the great advantages of the BOPM is that such situations can be easily handled. All you need to understand is the basic single-period BOPM logic.

Unlike the constant dividend yield BOPM, there is no "simple" equation, such as Equation (17.18), that provides a call value. This is because when the stock pays a dividend *amount*, it becomes important to know the exact ex-dividend dates. In the constant dividend yield example of Section 17.3.1, it mattered only that the stock was going to trade ex-dividend twice before the expiration date. Now, it matters *when* those dividends will be paid. For example, consider Figures 17.4 and 17.5, in which $n=3$, $u=0.1$, and $d=-0.05$. In Figure 17.4 the stock trades ex-dividend in the amount of $1 at time $T-2$. In Figure 17.5, the stock trades ex-dividend in the amount of $1 at time $T-1$. As you can see, the time T stock prices differ. Also, the number of possible time T stock prices differ depending on when the ex-dividend day occurs. The impact of this is that to use the BOPM to value a European call, it is necessary to use the single-period model recursively.

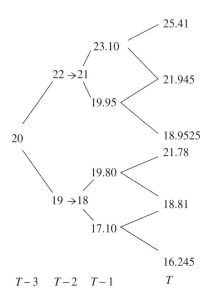

Figure 17.4 The stock trades ex-dividend at time $T-2$.

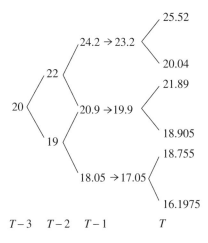

Figure 17.5 The stock trades ex-dividend at time $T-1$.

You should be able to work out all steps in the recursive single-period BOPM. For each outcome at each date, you should be able to find the value of the call, find the composition of the equivalent portfolio, verify that the payoffs of the equivalent portfolio and the call are equal, and verify that the equivalent portfolio is self-financing.

17.3.3 American Calls on Stocks Paying a Given Dollar Dividend Amount

The recursive single-period approach must be used when American calls on stocks paying a given dollar dividend are to be valued by means of BOPM. One benefit of the model is that the dates and outcomes in which the call will be exercised early will be specified. In fact, you can even estimate the probability of early exercise.

At each date and state of the world, the value of the American call is:

$$\max\left[\frac{pC_u + (1-p)C_d}{1+r}, S - K\right] \tag{17.19}$$

In other words, you first use Equation (17.7) to find the value of the call. If the resulting value is less than the intrinsic value, Proposition II′ from Chapter 16 has been violated. Therefore, in these cases, the American call will sell for its intrinsic value instead of the value from Equation (17.7).

For any outcome at any date before expiration, the American call will be exercised early by rational investors whenever it sells for $S-K$. This is because investors can use the equivalent portfolio of stocks and bonds to replicate the American call's payoffs at a lower cost than the price of the call (its intrinsic value). In other words, an investor who wished to own the call could replicate it at the lower cost of $[pC_u + (1-p)C_d]/(1+r)$, rather than buy the call for $S-K$. Likewise, if an investor currently owned the call, and wished to continue owning it, it would be rational to exercise it and then replicate it using stocks and bonds. Again, the cost of replication is less than $S-K$.

To illustrate, consider the example in Figure 17.5. We will value both an American call and a European call; the strike price is 20. First, use Equation (17.7) to value the call at each date and state of the world. We work from right to left. The values of u, d, r, and p are 0.1, −0.05, 0.0, and 1/3, respectively.

Time $T-1$

$$C_{T,uuu} = 5.52$$

$$C_{T-1,uu}$$

$$C_{T,uud} = 2.04$$

$$C_{T-1,uu} = \frac{pC_{T,uuu} + (1-p)C_{T,uud}}{1+r} = 3.20$$

$$C_{T,udu} = 1.89$$

$$C_{T-1,ud}$$

$$C_{T,udd} = 0.0$$

$$C_{T-1,ud} = \frac{pC_{T,udu} + (1-p)C_{T,udd}}{1+r} = 0.63$$

$$C_{T,ddu} = 0.0$$

$$C_{T-1,dd}$$

$$C_{T,udd} = 0.0$$

$$C_{T-1,dd} = \frac{pC_{T,ddu} + (1-p)C_{T,ddd}}{1+r} = 0.0$$

Time $T-2$

$$C_{T-1,uu} = 3.20$$

$$C_{T-2,u}$$

$$C_{T-1,ud} = 0.63$$

$$C_{T-2,u} = \frac{pC_{T-1,uu} + (1-p)C_{T-1,ud}}{1+r} = 1.486667 \ \text{(European)}$$

Because this value is less than the call's intrinsic value, the American call sells for $S_{T-2,u} - K$, which is 2. At this price, all rational owners of the call will exercise it, because the same call can be replicated with an equivalent portfolio of stocks and bonds at a cost of only \$1.486667 (which is the value of the European call). The American call owner can exercise the call, paying \$20 for a stock that he then sells for \$22, resulting in a cash inflow of \$2. Then, he can invest in a levered portfolio that offers the same payoffs as the call but requires a cash outlay of only \$1.486667. The final result is a cash inflow of \$0.51333 at time $T-2$. However, the cash flows at time $T-1$ are the same regardless of whether the investor owns the call or invests in the levered portfolio.

Continuing with the call value computations, we write:

$$C_{T-1,du} = 0.63$$

$$C_{T-2,d}$$

$$C_{T-1,dd} = 0.00$$

$$C_{T-2,d} = \frac{pC_{T-1,du} + (1-p)C_{T-1,dd}}{1+r} = 0.21$$

There are two values (one American, and one European) for the call to be determined at time $T-3$. The American call is valued by using the American call values at time $T-2$:

$$C_{T-2,u} = 2$$

$$C_{T-3}$$

$$C_{T-2,d} = 0.21$$

$$C_{T-3} = \frac{pC_{T-2,u} + (1-p)C_{T-2,d}}{1+r} = 0.806667 \ \text{(American)}$$

Because 0.806667 is greater than $S-K$, the American call will not be exercised early at time $T-3$. The value of the European call at time $T-3$ utilizes the European call values at time $T-2$.

$$C_{T-2,u} = 1.486667$$

$$C_{T-3}$$

$$C_{T-2,d} = 0.21$$

$$C_{T-3} = \frac{pC_{T-2,u} + (1-p)C_{T-2,d}}{1+r} = 0.635556 \ \text{(European)}$$

Next, find the equivalent portfolios at each date and possible outcome. In each case, we use Equations (17.3) and (17.4).

$$\Delta = \frac{C_u - C_d}{S_u - S_d} \tag{17.3}$$

$$B = \frac{(1+u)C_d - (1+d)C_u}{(u-d)(1+r)} \tag{17.4}$$

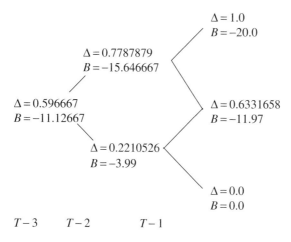

Figure 17.6 American call.

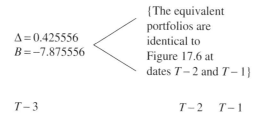

Figure 17.7 European call.

Use the American call values in the numerator of Equation (17.3) when solving for the number of shares needed to replicate American calls. Use European call values when solving for European deltas. Finally, use cum-dividend values of the stock in the denominator of Equation (17.3).

Here again, remember to use the appropriate (American or European) call values in the numerator in Equation (17.4) when solving for the amount to be invested in bonds as part of the call replication process.

Figure 17.6 depicts the time path of the equivalent portfolio for the American call. Figure 17.7 shows that only the time $T-3$ equivalent portfolio is different when one is examining European calls.

At each date, the payoffs of the equivalent portfolio are identical to the values of the call.

At time $T-3$ for an American call:

$$\Delta S + B = 0.596667(20) - 11.12667$$
$$= 0.806667$$
$$= C_{T-3}(\text{American})$$

$$0.596667(22) - 11.12667 = 2 = C_{T-2,u} \text{ (American)}$$

$$0.596667(19) - 11.12667 = 0.21 = C_{T-2,d}$$

At time $T-3$ for a European call:

$$0.425556(22) - 7.875556 = 1.48667 = C_{T-2,u} \text{ (European)}$$

$$\Delta S + B = 0.425556(20) - 7.875556$$
$$= 0.635556 = C_{T-3}\text{(European)}$$

$$0.425556(19) - 7.875556 = 0.21 = C_{T-2,d}$$

Additionally, if the stock has an uptick in the first period, then:

$$0.7787879(24.2) - 15.646667 = 3.2 = C_{T-1,uu}$$

$$\Delta S + B = 0.7787879(22) - 15.646667$$
$$= 1.486667 = C_{T-2,u}$$

$$0.7787879(20.9) - 15.646667 = 0.63 = C_{T-1,ud}$$

Note that if the call is American, it is cheaper to replicate the call than it is to buy it. At time $T-2$, after an uptick, the American call must sell for its intrinsic value of $2 to prevent arbitrage opportunities. Yet there will be no buyers for the call if its market price is $2. An investor can instead buy 0.7787879 share of stock at $22/share and borrow $15.646667. The payoffs of this levered portfolio are identical to those of the call, and it is cheaper to buy the levered portfolio, so why pay $2 for the call? The call owner will not find buyers for the call, and it will be rational for him to exercise it, thereby acquiring the stock for $20, sell it for its market price of $22, and then buy the equivalent portfolio. This point can be illustrated using an arbitrage table:

	Time $T-2$		Time $T-1$ (ex-dividend)	
			Stock=$23.2	Stock=$19.9
Exercise call; pay K	−20			
Sell stock acquired	+22			
Buy 0.7787879 share		Dividend	+0.7787879	+0.7787879
of stock at $22/share	−17.133333	Sell stock	+18.067879	+15.497879
Borrow	+15.646667	Repay loan	−15.646667	−15.646667
	+0.513333		+3.2	+0.63

The table illustrates that if there is an uptick in the first period, the call holder will be better off at time $T-2$ by exercising the call and then using stocks and bonds to replicate it. The payoffs at time $T-1$ are the same regardless of whether he replicates or owns the call.

The student will be asked to verify that the remaining equivalent portfolios offer the same payoffs as the call at each date and state of the world (Problem 17.9 at the end of the chapter).

Finally, we must verify that the equivalent portfolio is self-financing at each date and state of the world. At time $T-3$ the American call replicator owns 0.596667 share of stock that sells for $20/share and has borrowed $11.126667. If the stock has a downtick in the first period, the new Δ is 0.2210526, and the new B is −3.99. The equivalent portfolio requires the sale of $(0.596667 - 0.2210526=)$ 0.3756141 share of stock at $19/share, providing proceeds of $7.136667. This amount is exactly the amount needed to pay down the debt from $11.126667 to $3.99. Thus the equivalent portfolio for the American call is self-financing if the stock has a downtick.[14]

Now consider the equivalent portfolio for the European call at time $T-3$. It consists of 0.425556 share of stock and borrowing of \$7.875556. If the stock has an uptick in the first period, the equivalent portfolio then consists of 0.7787879 share of stock that sells for \$22/share and \$15.646667 in debt. The additional cash needed to buy the additional 0.3532323 share of stock at \$22/share is \$7.771111. However, because the riskless interest rate is 0%, the additional borrowing required to continue with the replication is (\$15.646667 − \$7.875556=) \$7.771111. Thus the equivalent portfolio is self-financing if the stock has an uptick in the first period.

If the stock has a downtick in the first period, the European Δ declines from 0.425556 to 0.2210526. The sale of 0.204503 share of stock at \$19/share provides \$3.885556. This equals the decline in required borrowing from the B value of \$7.875556 at time $T-3$ to the B value of 3.99 at time $T-2$.

Demonstrating that the equivalent portfolio is self-financing at all subsequent dates and outcomes is left as an exercise for the student (Problem 17.10 at the end of the chapter).

17.4 PUTS

17.4.1 Simple Binomial Put Pricing

The derivation of the equations that define the single-period BOPM equivalent portfolio for a put is similar to the one for calls explained in Section 17.2.2. To start, define the pricing process for the underlying asset to be:

$$S_{T-1} \nearrow \begin{array}{l} S_{T,u} = (1+u)S_{T-1} \\[1em] S_{T,d} = (1+d)S_{T-1} \end{array}$$

As with calls, time T is the expiration date of a put option. If the stock rises, the put will be worth $P_{T,u}=\max(0,\ K-S_{T,u})$. If the stock declines in value at time T, the put is worth $P_{T,d}=\max(0,\ K-S_{T,d})$. Graphically, we have

$$P_{T-1} \nearrow \begin{array}{l} P_{T,u} = \max(0, K - S_{T,u}) = \max(0, K - (1+u)S_{T-1}) \\[1em] P_{T,d} = \max(0, K - S_{T,d}) = \max(0, K - (1+d)S_{T-1}) \end{array}$$

The portfolio making the same payoffs at time T as the put requires an investment in Δ shares of stock and B in riskless bonds (debt instruments). We will see that for a portfolio equivalent to a put, Δ will always be negative or zero (in other words, Δ is nonpositive) and B will always be positive or zero (nonnegative). This means that a put is equivalent to a portfolio consisting of a short position in stock and lending. We assume that the put replicator receives full use of the proceeds from the short sale of stock.

Graphically, the equivalent portfolio follows the same process as for calls:

$$\Delta S_{T-1} + B \nearrow \begin{array}{l} \Delta(1+u)S_{T-1} + (1+r)B = \Delta S_{T,u} + (1+r)B \\[1em] \Delta(1+d)S_{T-1} + (1+r)B = \Delta S_{T,d} + (1+r)B \end{array}$$

Now, equate the payoffs of the equivalent portfolio with the values of the put at time T:

$$\Delta(1+u)S_{T-1} + (1+r)B = P_{T,u}$$

$$\Delta(1+d)S_{T-1} + (1+r)B = P_{T,d}$$

These two equations are simultaneous equations with two unknowns, Δ and B. When we achieve our goal of finding the values of these unknowns, we will have defined a levered portfolio that always pays off the same as the put. Solving the system of simultaneous equations, we get:

$$\Delta = \frac{P_{T,u} - P_{T,d}}{(u-d)S_{T-1}} = \frac{P_{T,u} - P_{T,d}}{S_{T,u} - S_{T,d}}; \quad \Delta \leq 0 \tag{17.20}$$

$$B = \frac{(1+u)P_{T,d} - (1+d)P_{T,u}}{(u-d)(1+r)}; \quad B \geq 0 \tag{17.21}$$

Note that Equations (17.20) and (17.21) are identical to equations (17.1) and (17.2) except that put values are substituted for call values and that the signs for Δ and B have changed. The change in signs stems from differences in intrinsic value for the put versus the call.

The general formulation for the put Δ and B are:

$$\Delta = \frac{P_u - P_d}{(u-d)S} = \frac{P_u - P_d}{S_u - S_d} \tag{17.22}$$

$$B = \frac{(1+u)P_d - (1+d)P_u}{(u-d)(1+r)} \tag{17.23}$$

The values of Δ and B define the number of shares of stock to sell and the amount to lend to replicate a put. If the put and the debt–equity portfolio both offer exactly the same payoffs at time T, then the price of the put at time $T-1$ must equal the investment in the equivalent portfolio at time $T-1$:

$$P_{T-1} = \Delta S_{T-1} + B \tag{17.24}$$

Next, substitute the expressions for Δ [Equation (17.22)], and B [Equation (17.23)] into the expression for the put value [Equation (17.24)]. After simpifying, we get:

$$P_{T-1} = \frac{[(r-d)/(u-d)]P_{T,u} + [(u-r)/(u-d)]P_{T,d}}{1+r}$$

or

$$P_{T-1} = \frac{pP_{T,u} + (1-p)P_{T,d}}{1+r} \tag{17.25}$$

where

$$p = \frac{r-d}{u-d} \quad \text{and} \quad 1-p = \frac{u-r}{u-d}$$

The general BOPM equation for the value of a European put option is given by Equation (17.26):

$$P = \frac{pP_u + (1-p)P_d}{1+r} \qquad (17.26)$$

There will be many cases in which Equation (17.26) yields a value for P that is less than intrinsic value. This is permissible for a European put. Indeed, recall from Chapter 16 that in-the-money European puts will frequently sell for less than $K-S$.

If we are valuing an American put, the BOPM formula is:

$$P = \max\left[K - S, \frac{pP_u + (1-p)P_d}{1+r} \right] \qquad (17.27)$$

In other words, if the value of $(pP_u + (1-p)P_d)/(1+r)$ is less than $K-S$ (intrinsic value of the put), the American put will be worth $K-S$. Recall that by Propositions X of Chapter 16, an American put can never sell for less than its intrinsic value.

Whenever the American put sells for $K-S$ before expiration, the put owner will find it rational to exercise it early. By doing so, he will realize the intrinsic value of $K-S$ and also find that he can replicate the put's payoffs for a cost less than $K-S$.

Because of the possibility of early exercise, there is no "simple" formula to value an American put in a multiperiod BOPM framework. You must use the single-period put BOPM to solve for its value recursively, starting at the expiration date. In this way, you can identify the dates and situations in which the put will be exercised early.

17.4.2 A Numerical Example of Binomial Put Pricing

EXAMPLE 17.3 Consider a four-date, three-period world with time T representing the expiration date. The stock price at time $T-3$ is 60. If the stock rises, the size of the uptick is 10% per period. If the stock declines, the downtick per period is −5%. The riskless interest rate is 2% per period. The stock pays no dividends. Suppose there is a put option with a strike price of 65. Then:

    a. Find the value of the stock for each possible outcome at every date.

    b. Find the value of the European put for each possible outcome at every date.

    c. Find the value of the American put for each possible outcome at every date.

    d. Find the composition of the equivalent portfolio for the European and American put for each possible outcome at every date.

    e. Verify that the payoffs of each equivalent portfolio is identical for the put, regardless of whether there is an uptick or a downtick.

    f. Verify that the equivalent portfolios are self-financing.

Use the recursive, single-period approach, computing the necessary values for each possible outcome at every date.

Solution: First, the stock price process is:

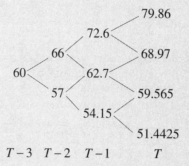

$$T-3 \quad T-2 \quad T-1 \qquad T$$

Next, we compute the value of p to be $(r-d)/(u-d)=(0.02-(-0.05))/(0.1-(-0.05))=0.466667$. Using Equation (17.26), recursively, we find that the values of the European puts are as follows:

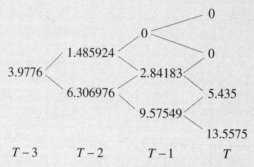

$$T-3 \qquad T-2 \qquad T-1 \qquad T$$

Then we use Equation (17.27) to find the value of the American put. In the following diagram, the outcomes in which early exercise will occur contain two values: one for the value of $[pP_u + (1+p)P_d]/(1+r)$, and, since this value is less than the put's intrinsic value at that date, the put's intrinsic value at each time before T is presented in bold type. When $[pP_u + (1-p)P_d]/(1+r)$ is less than $K-S$, the value of the American put equals its intrinsic value.

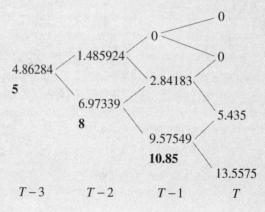

$$T-3 \qquad T-2 \qquad T-1 \qquad T$$

This put should be exercised immediately, at time $T-3$. The put holder can exercise the put, realizing its intrinsic value of 5 and then replicate the put's payoffs for 4.86284.

For the European put, the composition of the equivalent portfolio at each date is defined by Equations (17.22) and (17.23):

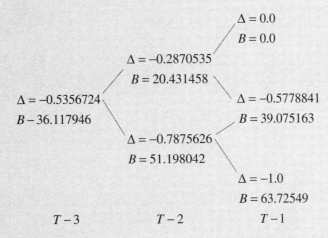

Thus, if there was an initial downtick in the first period, then at time $T-2$, $\Delta = (P_u - P_d)/(S_u - S_d) = (2.84183 - 9.57549)/(62.7 - 54.15) = -0.7875626$, and $B = [(1+u)P_d - (1+d)P_u]/[(u-d)(1+r)] = [(1.1)9.57549 - (0.95)2.84183]/[(0.1 - (-0.05))(1.02)] = 51.198042$.

For the American put, Equations (17.22) and (17.23) are again used to define the equivalent portfolio, but the American values for the puts are used in the numerators:

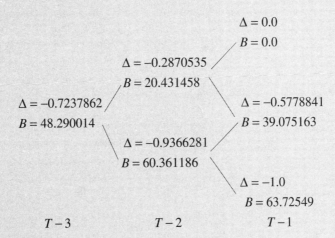

For example, at time $T-3$, $\Delta = (P_u - P_d)/(S_u - S_d) = (1.485924 - 8)/(66 - 57) = -0.7237862$, and $B = [(1+u)P_d - (1+d)P_u]/[(u-d)(1+r)] = [(1.1)8 - (0.95)1.48592]/[(0.1 - (-0.05))(1.02)] = 48.290014$.

We now must verify that the payoffs of the equivalent portfolios equal those of the put. For the European put at time $T-3$, we have:

$$(-0.5356724)(66)+(36.117946)(1.02)$$
$$=1.485927=P_{T-2,u}$$

$$\Delta S+B=(-0.5356724)(60)+36.117946$$
$$=3.9776=P_{T-3}$$

$$(-0.5356724)(57)+(36.117946)(1.02)$$
$$=6.306978=P_{T-2,d}$$

Verification that the remaining equivalent portfolios pay off amounts identical to the European puts is left as an exercise for the student (Problem 17.11 at the end of the chapter).

For the American put at time $T-2$, given that there was an uptick in the first period, we have:

$$(-0.2870535)(72.6)+(20.431458)(1.02)$$
$$=0.0=P_{T-1,uu}$$

$$\Delta S+B=(-0.2870535)(66)+20.431458$$
$$=1.48593=P_{T-2,u}$$

$$(-0.2870535)(62.7)+(20.431458)(1.02)$$
$$=2.84183=P_{T-1,ud}$$

Verification that the remaining equivalent portfolios pay amounts that are identical to the American puts is again left as an exercise for the student (Problem 17.11).

Finally, we can verify that the equivalent portfolios are self-financing. For the European put, if there was a downtick in the first period, the equivalent portfolio at time $T-2$ consists of $\Delta=-0.7875626$ and $B=51.198042$. The required changes in the equivalent portfolio depend on whether there is an uptick or downtick at time $T-1$:

$\Delta=-0.5778841$ Repurchase 0.2096785 share at $62.70 per share.
$B=39.075163$ This costs $13.146842. The original loan of
                     $51.198042 is worth ($51.198042)(1.02)=
                     $52.222003. The reduction in the required loan to
$\Delta=-0.7875626$ $39.075163 is $13.14684.
$B=51.198042$

$\Delta=-1.0$ Sell short an additional 0.2124374 share at $54.15
$B=63.72549$ per share. This provides $11.503485. This is also
                     the increase in required lending. You originally
                     lend $51.198042. Now you are owed $52.222003.
                     The required equivalent B is $63.72549.

For the American put, we will demonstrate that the equivalent portfolio will be self-financing only if there is an uptick.[15] At time $T-3$, the equivalent portfolio for the American put is $\Delta=-0.7237862$ and $B=48.290014$. If there is an uptick, the new equivalent portfolio is $\Delta=-0.2870535$ and $B=20.431458$. Thus, the replicator must repurchase 0.4367327 share of stock at $66 per share, which requires $28.824358. After interest, the new loan amount is $(1.02)(48.290014)=\$49.255814$. The required equivalent portfolio loan amount of $20.431458 is $28.824356 less than the outstanding loan balance, and this reduction in lending pays for the repurchase of shares that were originally sold short.

17.5 PORTFOLIO INSURANCE AND DYNAMIC TRADING

Dynamic trading is synonymous with option replication using equivalent portfolios. Insuring portfolios with dynamic trading techniques has received considerable blame for the stock market "break" of October 1987. Since the foundations of insuring via dynamic trading lie in the BOPM, it seems appropriate to illustrate this investment technique now, and to show how it acted to accentuate market momentum (on the upside and then on the downside) and may indeed have contributed to the events of October 1987.

Portfolio insurance is a strategy used by traders who seek to eliminate the possibility of losses during some interval of time. Actually, users of this strategy can insure that portfolio returns will not fall below a minimum target rate of return, as long as that return is less than the riskless rate of return during the insurance horizon. For example, suppose the riskless rate of return is 10% per year, or 33.1% over the three-year insurance horizon. The insurer can guarantee that he will do no worse than earn a chosen return of $x\%$, where $x \le 33.1\%$. If he wishes to avoid losses, he selects $x=0\%$. Depending on their strategies, other insurers might select values of $x +10\%$ (+3.228% per year), or -14.26% (-5% per year).

If, in our example $x=33.1\%$, the insurer would invest 100% of his portfolio's funds in riskless assets. Usually, $x<33.1\%$, in which case the insurer effectively sells some of his upside profits in exchange for truncating his minimum rate of return at $x\%$. If the return on the underlying asset is less than $x\%$, the insurer will earn the minimum rate of return. If the return on the underlying assets exceeds $x\%$, the insurer will participate in some of the increase in value. For example, suppose $x=0\%$ for the insurance horizon. Then, the insured portfolio earns 0% if the market return is negative or zero. However, if the market rises, the insured portfolio will not profit by the full extent of the rise. If the market were to rise by 50% over a three-year insurance horizon, an insured portfolio might earn only 40%. Thus, the portfolio insurer pays for insurance with reduced upside capture.

The easiest way to implement portfolio insurance is to purchase a European put on the underlying asset. A European put will usually be cheaper to purchase than an otherwise equivalent American put, so the insurer will be better off buying the former, with a time to expiration equal to his insurance horizon. Let us assume that European puts with a wide range of strike prices exist, with times to expiration long enough to meet an insurer's horizon, and that the insurer's portfolio and the underlying asset are identical. We know that deep in-the-money European puts will frequently sell for less than intrinsic value. Thus, given the current portfolio value, there will be some strike price for which a put will have zero time value. For now, this is the put of interest to us.

As an example, suppose an investor wants to create a portfolio of stocks that mimics the semi-conductor index (SOX). Let the SOX spot price S_0 be 810. Suppose the value of the portfolio is $5 million, and there exists a three-year European put on the SOX with a strike price of $K=830$ selling for $P=\$20$ (note that this put has no time value). The insurer must buy one put (on 100 shares of the SOX) for each hundred shares of the SOX purchased. Effectively, 100 shares of the SOX costs $81,000, and one put costs $2000. With $5 million, the insurer can buy 5,000,000/83,000=60.24 units of the SOX, where each unit covers 100 shares (i.e., 100 shares of stock and 1 put). Each put on 100 shares costs $2000, meaning that 60.24 puts will cost $120,480. Thus, $4,879,520 is invested in stocks, and $120,480 in puts. We ignore transactions costs and dividends and assume the stock and puts are infinitely divisible.

If $S_T \leq 830$ three years hence, the puts finish in the money. Because index options are cash settled at expiration, the put owner receives the in-the-money amount in cash. For example, if $S_T=798$, the put owner receives $3200 for each put ($K-S_T=830-798=32$). He sells his 60.24 shares of the SOX for $79,800 each and receives $3200 for each of the 60.24 puts. The total cash received is $5 million if $S_T \leq 830$.

If $S_T>830$, the puts expire worthless, and the insurer sells the portfolio of stocks for S_T. For example, if $S_T=861$, the cash received is $60.24 \times \$86,100 = \$5,186,664$. Note that the SOX index rose by 6.296%, but the insured portfolio's return was only 3.73%. The insured portfolio did not fully participate in the market's gains because the puts, which expired worthless, initially cost $20.

Thus, investment in stock and the purchase of protective puts will insure a portfolio. Because the puts are purchased at time 0, the cost of the insurance is known up front.

Instead of buying puts, an insurer can replicate the puts by dynamically trading stocks and bonds. In other words, the insurer first invests 100% of his funds in the risky underlying asset (stock). Then he finds the equivalent portfolio for a put with the desired strike price and time to expiration. We know that the equivalent portfolio for a put is short stock ($-1 \leq \Delta \leq 0$) and lending ($B \geq 0$). The portfolio insurer need not sell stock short. Rather, the insurer sells the necessary stock from his portfolio and lends the proceeds.

For example, let $S=810$, $u=0.1259$, $d=-0.11$, $r=0.06$, $T=3$ years, and $K=830$. The stock pricing process is as follows:

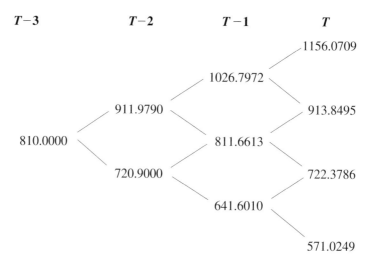

$T-3$	$T-2$	$T-1$	T
			1156.0709
		1026.7972	
	911.9790		913.8495
810.0000		811.6613	
	720.9000		722.3786
		641.6010	
			571.0249

The values of the European put, and the equivalent portfolios are as follows:

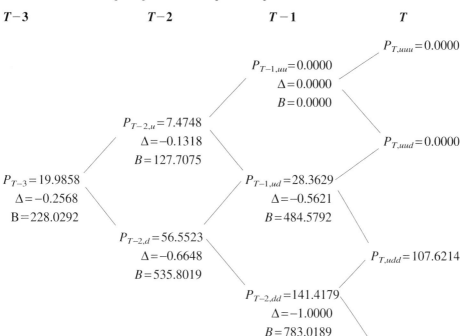

| $T-3$ | $T-2$ | $T-1$ | T |

$P_{T,uuu}=0.0000$

$P_{T-1,uu}=0.0000$
$\Delta=0.0000$
$B=0.0000$

$P_{T-2,u}=7.4748$
$\Delta=-0.1318$
$B=127.7075$

$P_{T,uud}=0.0000$

$P_{T-3}=19.9858$
$\Delta=-0.2568$
$B=228.0292$

$P_{T-1,ud}=28.3629$
$\Delta=-0.5621$
$B=484.5792$

$P_{T-2,d}=56.5523$
$\Delta=-0.6648$
$B=535.8019$

$P_{T,udd}=107.6214$

$P_{T-2,dd}=141.4179$
$\Delta=-1.0000$
$B=783.0189$

$P_{T,ddd}=258.9751$

As an exercise, verify that the equivalent portfolios pay off identical amounts to the puts and that the equivalent portfolio is self-financing [You should also use Equations (17.22) and (17.23) to check the values of Δ and B in the above diagram.]

Note that the put at time $T-3$ is selling just below its intrinsic value of 20. The difference between the put's price and its intrinsic value will create some slight deviations from perfect portfolio insurance in the subsequent analysis.

The dynamic trader who wishes to insure his portfolio will first invest \$4,879,602 in 60.242 units of the SOX at \$81,000/unit.[16] Each unit has 100 shares of the SOX. Then, he will replicate the purchase of 60.242 puts, using the equivalent portfolio at each date.

Thus, to replicate the long put position at time $T-3$, the insurer must sell 0.256844×60.242 units of the SOX at \$81,000/unit. This is because the put delta at time $T-3$ is –0.256844. This is \$1,253,296 of stock. He lends these proceeds and the remaining \$120,398[17] of his starting wealth to earn the riskless rate of return. Note that the amount lent, which is (\$1,253,296+120,398=) \$1,373,694, equals the value of B at time $T-3$ times 100 times 60.242. The portfolio equivalent to a long stock plus long put position at time $T-3$ is \$3,626,306 in stock and \$1,373,694 in riskless debt.

The same analysis proceeds at each date. The insurer will buy shares if Δ rises (Δ becomes less negative) or sell additional shares if Δ declines (Δ becomes more negative). The required loan at each date equals $B\times100\times60.242$. The dynamic trading is self-financing, so that shares bought are financed by a reduction in lending, and shares sold are accompanied by an increase in lending. The time path of the equivalent portfolio for the long stock plus long put strategy is:

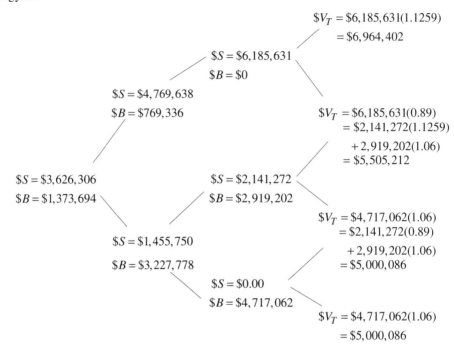

$$\$V_T = \$6,185,631(1.1259)$$
$$= \$6,964,402$$

$$\$S = \$6,185,631$$
$$\$B = \$0$$

$$\$S = \$4,769,638$$
$$\$B = \$769,336$$

$$\$V_T = \$6,185,631(0.89)$$
$$= \$2,141,272(1.1259)$$
$$+ 2,919,202(1.06)$$
$$= \$5,505,212$$

$$\$S = \$3,626,306$$
$$\$B = \$1,373,694$$

$$\$S = \$2,141,272$$
$$\$B = \$2,919,202$$

$$\$V_T = \$4,717,062(1.06)$$
$$= \$2,141,272(0.89)$$
$$+ 2,919,202(1.06)$$
$$= \$5,000,086$$

$$\$S = \$1,455,750$$
$$\$B = \$3,227,778$$

$$\$S = \$0.00$$
$$\$B = \$4,717,062$$

$$\$V_T = \$4,717,062(1.06)$$
$$= \$5,000,086$$

As stated earlier, because this put sold at time $T-3$ for less than its intrinsic value, some errors would emerge. They are most obvious when the stock has either 3 or 2 downticks, and the final portfolio value is $5,000,086. Had the put initially sold for exactly $20, perfect insurance on the downside would have been realized, and the terminal value of the portfolio would have been exactly $5 million. The unobserved cost of insuring against a terminal value of $5,000,086 is reduced upside capture if the SOX has 2 or 3 upticks.

If the market has three upticks, it will rise 42.725%. However, the insured portfolio rises only 39.288%. Similarly, the portfolio does not participate fully in the market rise if it has two upticks: the market rise is 12.821%, but the insured portfolio rises only 10.104%. Thus, the cost of insuring the portfolio is limited upside capture. Unlike the traded put (which has a one-time, up-front insurance cost equal to the price of the put), the dynamic trading approach pays for the insurance over time. Note also that the cost for insurance is unknown when dynamic trading is used to replicate the put. If market volatility increases (higher u and a more negative d), the degree of upside capture declines and there will also be greater risk that the final return will be less than the target minimum return.

Just before October 1987, an estimated $80 billion in equity portfolios was insured by means of the dynamic trading approach just described. Traded puts were inadequate for insurance purposes for several reasons. First, their times to expiration were too short. Second, only American puts traded in 1987, which meant that the insurers would have to overpay for the protection that they wanted. Only since 1987 have European-style LEAPS begun trading, but even so, the liquidity of these long-term puts has been insufficient to satisfy the needs of many large investors. Finally, there has been, and currently is, an inadequate strike price range for the insurers. Thus, in 1987, dynamic trading was the preferred method for portfolio insurance.

For the first eight months of 1987, the market, measured by the Dow Jones Industrial Average, rose from 1896 to 2722 (a gain of almost 44%). Because put deltas become less negative as the market rises, insurers bought more stock as the market rose. Some observers believe that buying for insurance purposes helped to cause the stock market to rise to an unrealistic level by August 1987.

Then, in September and early October, the DJIA declined from a peak of 2722 on August 25, 1987 to 2505 on October 13. By the close of trading on October 16, the Dow had tumbled to 2247. As the foregoing diagrams illustrate, portfolio insurers sell stocks as the market declines. To reestablish their replicated protective puts, insurers had to sell enormous amounts of stock and stock index futures.[18] According to the Presidential Task Force on Market Mechanisms (1988), the so called the Brady Report, on three days, October 14, 15, and 16, insurers sold $3.7 billion in stock and stock index futures. On October 19 and 20, insurers sold an additional $5.2 billion and $2.1 billion more, respectively.

With such sustained selling by dynamic portfolio insurers, is it any wonder that the technique was blamed for exacerbating the decline? The Dow fell to 1738 on October 19, and the intraday low of 1709 was reached on October 20.

The purpose of placing the discussion of portfolio insurance and the crash in this chapter is the tie-in between dynamic trading and the BOPM. We close with two comments. First, there is still disagreement about just how much dynamic portfolio insurance contributed to the October 1987 crash. Large market declines occurred worldwide in October 1987, and portfolio insurance was nonexistent in many countries. Also, insurance-related selling on the crash days was only about 25% of the total NYSE volume. Obviously, others also sold stock and futures on those days. Finally, to the extent dynamic selling pressure lowered prices, other traders should have stepped up their buying to capitalize on the resulting unrealistic low prices.

Second, note that the unexpectedly high market volatility increased the "cost" of insurance. Shares had to be sold at prices well below those implied by the downtick returns. If a portfolio insurer who uses dynamic replication of options seriously misestimates volatility (the u and d parameters), the result will either be missed floors or forgone upside gains (see Rendleman and O'Brien, 1990). In response to the unexpectedly poor performance of insured portfolios, the size of the portfolio insurance industry greatly declined after October 1987. Jacobs (1999) claims that hundreds of billions of dollars of dynamic option replication still exists and could create financial crises in the future.

17.6   OTHER REFERENCES ON THE BINOMIAL OPTION PRICING MODEL AND DYNAMIC TRADING

The following references should be consulted for additional information about the binomial option pricing model (BOPM): Cox, Ross, and Rubinstein (1979), Rendleman and Bartter (1979), Rubinstein and Leland (1981), Jarrow and Rudd (1983, Chapter 13), Cox and Rubinstein (1985, Chapters 5 and 7), Boyle (1988), and Schroder (1988).

Papers on portfolio insurance using dynamic trading techniques include Rubinstein (1985, 1988), Abken (1987), O'Brien (1988a, 1988b), and Rendleman and O'Brien (1990).

Reports by the U.S. Commodity Futures Trading Commission (1988), the U.S. Securities and Exchange Commission (1988), and the Presidential Task Force on Market Mechanisms (1988) contain detailed information about the October 1987 stock market crash. More crash information is contained in Miller, Scholes, Malkiel, and Hawke (1988), Harris (1989), Kamphius, Kormendi, and Watson (1989), and Kleidon and Whaley (1992).

17.7   SUMMARY

A substantial portion of this chapter was devoted to the mechanics of applying the single-period BOPM to options. Besides ordinary European calls, we used the BOPM to value American calls on dividend paying stocks and European and American puts. The BOPM is extremely flexible. It can be used to value any kind of option and to incorporate possible early exercise as well as changing economic conditions (changing interest rates and changing stock volatility).

The single most important lesson to be learned is that if you know the binomial pricing process of the underlying stock, you can replicate any option, or indeed, any strategy covered in Chapter 15, with a portfolio of stocks and bonds. In a multiperiod world, the composition of this portfolio changes over time, thus the replicator must buy or sell stock every period[19]. However, the equivalent portfolio is self-financing, so that any stock purchase is accompanied by an increase in borrowing (for calls) or a decrease in lending (for puts).

Thus, we have an option pricing model, a method for valuing complicated options. To obtain accurate estimates of option values, however, the time to expiration must be carved into many intervals. The multiperiod BOPM for European calls can be cumbersome to use in this case, and the recursive single-period BOPM method is also time-consuming, even with a computer.

In the next chapter, we make some additional assumptions and obtain the Black–Scholes option pricing model. This model is easy to use, though at the cost of reduced flexibility.

References

Abken, Peter A. 1987. "An Introduction to Portfolio Insurance." *Federal Reserve Bank of Atlanta Economic Review*, November, pp. 2–25.

Boyle, Phelim. 1988. "A Lattice Framework for Option Pricing with Two State Variables." *Journal of Financial and Quantitative Analysis*, Vol. 23, March, pp. 1–12.

Brenner, Menachem, ed. 1983. *Option Pricing*. Lexington, MA: Lexington Books.

Cox, John C. and Stephen A. Ross. 1976. "The Valuation of Options for Alternative Stochastic Processes." *Journal of Financial Economics*, Vol. 3, January/March, pp. 145–166.

Cox, John C., Stephen A. Ross, and Mark Rubinstein. 1979. "Option Pricing: A Simplified Approach." *Journal of Financial Economics*, Vol. 7, September, 229–263.

Cox, John C., and Mark Rubinstein. 1985. *Option Markets*. Englewood Cliffs, NJ: Prentice-Hall.

Harris, L. 1989. "The October 1987 S&P 500 Stock-Futures Basis." *Journal of Finance*, Vol. 44, March, pp. 77–99.

Jacobs, Bruce I. 1999. *Capital Ideas and Market Realities: Option Replication, Investor Behavior, and Stock Market Crashes*. Oxford: Blackwell Publishers.

Jarrow, Robert A., and Andrew T. Rudd. 1983. *Option Pricing*. Homewood, IL: Dow-Jones Irwin.

Jarrow, Robert, and Stuart Turnbull. 2000. *Derivative Securities, 2nd ed*. Stamford, CT: South-Western College Publishing, Thomson Learning.

Kamphius, R. W. Jr., R. W. Kormendi, and J. W. H. Watson, eds. 1989. *Black Monday and the Future of Financial Markets*. Homewood, IL: Dow-Jones Irwin.

Kleidon, A. W., and Robert E. Whaley. 1992. "One Market? Stocks, Futures, and Options During October 1987." *Journal of Finance*, Vol. 47, July, pp. 851–877.

Miller, Merton, Myron Scholes, Burton Malkiel, and J. Hawke, Jr. 1988. *Final Report of the Committee of Inquiry Appointed by the Chicago Mercantile Exchange to Examine the Events Surrounding October 19, 1987*. Chicago: Chicago Mercantile Exchange.

O'Brien, Thomas J. 1988a. "The Mechanics of Portfolio Insurance." *Journal of Portfolio Management,"* Vol. 14, Spring, pp. 40–47.

O'Brien, Thomas J. 1988b. "How Option Replicating Portfolio Insurance Works: Expanded Details," New York University and Salomon Brothers Center for the Study of Financial Institutions, Monograph 1988-4.

Presidential Task Force on Market Mechanisms. 1988. *Brady Report.* Washington, DC: U.S. Government Printing Office.

Rendleman, Richard J. and Brit J. Bartter. 1979. "Two-State Asset Pricing." *Journal of Finance*, Vol. 34, December, pp. 1093–1110.

Rendleman, Richard J., and Thomas J. O'Brien. 1990. "The Effects of Volatility Misestimation on Option-Replication Portfolio Insurance." *Financial Analysts Journal*, Vol. 46, May/June, pp. 61–70.

Rubinstein, Mark. 1985. "Alternative Paths to Portfolio Insurance." *Financial Analysts Journal*, Vol. 41, July/August, pp. 42–52.

Rubinstein, Mark. 1988. "Portfolio Insurance and the Market Crash." *Financial Analysts Journal*, Vol. 44, January/February, pp. 38–47.

Rubinstein, Mark, and Hayne E. Leland. 1981. "Replicating Options with Positions in Stock and Cash." *Financial Analysts Journal*, Vol. 37, July/August, pp. 63–72.

Schroder, Mark. 1988. "Adapting the Binomial Model to Value Options on Assets with Fixed-Cash Payouts." *Financial Analysts Journal*, November/December, pp. 54–62.

U.S. Commodity Futures Trading Commission. 1988. *Final Report on Stock Index Futures and Cash Market Activity During October 1987.* Washington, DC: U.S. Government Printing Office.

U.S. Securities and Exchange Commission. 1988. *The October 1987 Market Break: Report by the Division of Market Regulation.* Washington, DC: U.S. Government Printing Office.

Notes

[1] The foundations for this chapter were developed in Cox, Ross, and Rubinstein (1979, pp. 229–263). Other articles that further developed the BOPM are listed at the end of the chapter.

[2] See Cox and Rubinstein (1985, Chapter 7) for applications of the BOPM to other stock pricing processes. A similar exposition by those authors is contained in Brenner (1983, Chapter 1). More advanced treatments of option valuation when the underlying asset follows different stochastic pricing processes are in Cox and Ross (1976) and Jarrow and Rudd (1983, Chapters 11 and 12).

[3] On one day, October 19, 1987, the Dow Jones Industrial Average fell 508 points, an unprecedented decline of 22.6% from the day before. Shortly after the crash, the size of stock portfolios covered by some form of insurance declined by about 50%. Portfolio insurance using replicated protective puts did not work as well as those who used the strategy had expected because the volatility of the market was greater than ever imagined. Still, option replication is widely employed today.

[4] $|B|$ is the absolute value of B. The statement means that the amount invested in the stock must exceed or equal the amount borrowed. This makes sense because we know that call values cannot be negative.

[5] Note that the formula for Δ may be read as the difference in call values divided by the difference in stock values. The time to expiration can be carved into as many subperiods (months, days, minutes, etc.) as you wish. As the length of the period shrinks toward zero, and the number of periods that make up the time to expiration increases to infinity, it can be shown that

$$\Delta = \frac{C_u - C_d}{S_u - S_d} \rightarrow \frac{\partial C}{\partial S}$$

which is the call's delta. It measures how much the call's value changes if the price of the underlying asset changes by a small amount, all else equal.

[6]This presentation can be rearranged to read $C - \Delta S = B$. This says that an investor who bought a fraction of one share of stock, denoted by Δ, and wrote one call, has created a riskless asset. Thus, Δ is frequently referred to as the call's **hedge ratio**, because Δ shares of stock plus one written call creates a riskless portfolio, or a "riskless hedge."

[7]One caveat must be made, however, if $C_{T-1} > \Delta S_{T-1} + B$. If we are dealing with American calls, the arbitrageur must be aware of the possibility of early exercise, since a call has been written as part of the arbitrage process. If the next date is not an ex-dividend date, there is no problem. A call owner will never exercise it early, and any that are irrationally early exercised would only mean greater profits for our arbitrageur. Nevertheless, we must be careful about writing a call in an attempt to arbitrage if the next day is an ex-date. This point will be covered in Section 17.3.3 on American calls on dividend-paying stocks.

[8]See Cox and Ross (1976) and Jarrow and Rudd (1983, pp. 88–95), and Jarrow and Turnbull (2000). Many authors call p and q "martingale probabilities".

[9]Recall that at any date, if the probability of a call on a non-dividend-paying stock finishing in the money is 1.0, then $\Delta = 1.0$.

[10]Recall that $0! = 1$.

[11]Dividend decreases occur much less frequently than do dividend increases.

[12]Since $F = Se^{rT}$, you should see the analogy between a futures or forward contract and a stock paying a continuous dividend.

[13]Note that the dividend amount if the stock rises is different from the amount if the stock falls. This will always be the case in the constant dividend yield model.

[14]Because the American call is exercised at time $T - 2$ if there is an uptick in the stock's price, the self-financing demonstration does not apply.

[15]See also note 14. If the American put will be exercised early the next period, the self-financing property does not hold for the equivalent portfolio.

[16]The insurer must buy 60.242 units of the SOX and 60.242 puts with his $5 million. One protective put is needed for each unit of the underlying stock purchased. The value of one put on 100 shares (P_{T-3}) is $1998.58.

[17]The insurer began with $5 million and invested $4,879,602 in stocks. Thus, $120,398 remained. Had the insurer used actual puts (rather than the replication process described here), he would have used the $120,398 to buy 60.24 protective puts.

[18]Actually, most portfolio insurance is done with stock index futures, rather than the actual stock.

[19]The exception to this statement occurs when the call will finish out of the money with certainty (then $\Delta = 0.0$) or in the money with certainty (then $\Delta = 1.0$).

PROBLEMS

17.1 A stock sells for $35 per share. One year from today, it will sell for either $36/share or $38/share. The riskless interest rate for the next year is 10%. Demonstrate how an arbitrage profit can be earned.

17.2 Let x and y be unknowns. Solve the following system of simultaneous equations:

$$5x + 3y = 13$$
$$3x + 2y = 9$$

17.3 In a binomial model framework, equate the payoffs of a call with the payoffs of a portfolio of Δ shares of stock and B in riskless debt. Algebraically solve the resulting set of simultaneous equations to obtain the definitions for Δ and B as they are given in Equations (17.1) and (17.2).

17.4 A stock currently sells for \$23/share. At the end of a single period, it can sell for either \$19/share or \$30/share. The riskless interest rate is 5%/period. You wish to find the value of a call with a strike price of 20. Set up the equations that equate the end-of-period payoffs of the call with the end-of-period payoffs of a portfolio of x shares of stock and y riskless bonds. The riskless bonds have a face value (maturity value) of \$1, and they mature at the end of the period. Solve the system of equations for x and y. Check your answers using Equations (17.1) and (17.2).

17.5 What is the "self-financing" requirement? Why is it necessary for the equivalent portfolio of stocks and bonds to be self-financing?

17.6 Use the data in Example 17.2, the multiperiod BOPM problem of Section 17.2.7, to find the value of a call with a strike price of 30.

17.7 Section 17.3.1 stated that if a stock has a constant dividend yield δ, it does not matter *when* the dividends are paid. What matters is *how many* ex-dividend dates there are prior to expiration. In the example in that section, the stock traded ex-dividend at times $T-4$ and $T-1$. Prepare the stock price path if the stock instead trades ex-dividend at times $T-3$ and $T-2$, and verify that the time T stock prices are the same as those in Figure 17.3.

17.8 Section 17.3.1 presented a two-period example of a stock paying a constant dividend yield:

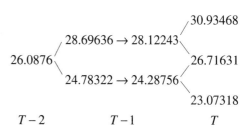

$$
\begin{array}{ccc}
 & & 30.93468 \\
 & 28.69636 \rightarrow 28.12243 \\
26.0876 & & 26.71631 \\
 & 24.78322 \rightarrow 24.28756 \\
 & & 23.07318 \\
T-2 & T-1 & T
\end{array}
$$

Assume that $r=0\%$. If the stock has a downtick at time $T-1$, find the composition of the equivalent portfolio at that time. Verify that the payoffs of that equivalent portfolio at time T are identical to $C_{T,du}$ and $C_{T,dd}$. Also verify that the equivalent portfolio was self-financing when moving from time $T-2$ to $T-1$.

17.9 In the examples in Sections 17.3.2 and 17.3.3 (Figures 17.5 and 16.6), verify that the equivalent portfolios have the same payoffs as the call at each date and state of the world. Be sure to verify this property for both upticks and downticks.

17.10 In the example in Section 17.3.2 (Figure 17.5), verify that the equivalent portfolio for the European call is self-financing at every date and state of the world. In the text, this was demonstrated for the passage of time from time $T-3$ to time $T-2$ at the end of section 17.3.3. Be sure to verify this property for both upticks and downticks.

17.11

a. Verify that all the equivalent portfolios pay off amounts that are identical to the puts at every date and every state of the world, for the example given in Section 17.4.2. Do this for both American and European puts.

b. Verify that the equivalent portfolios for the European put example of Section 17.4.2. are self-financing.

17.12 A stock currently sells for $61.20. A call exists with a strike price of 60 and has four months until expiration. The stock can either rise by 2% each month or fall by 1% each month. The riskless interest rate is 0.5%/month. A dividend of $1.50 per share will be paid two months hence (i.e., at time $T-2$). For each date and state of the world:

   a. Plot out the time path of possible stock prices.

   b. Recursively solve for the value of a European call.

   c. Find the composition of the equivalent portfolio.

   d. Pick one node, and verify that the payoffs of the equivalent portfolio are identical to those of the call.

   e. Pick one node, and verify that the equivalent portfolio is self-financing.

17.13

   a. Answer parts a–d of Problem 17.12, for an American call.

   b. Assume a risk-neutral world. What is the probability of the stock having an uptick and a downtick? What is the probability that the stock will be exercised early at time $T-3$? Find the probability of early exercise at each subsequent date.

17.14 In the context of the BOPM, discuss how American puts are priced. In particular, focus on the possibility and rationality of early exercise.

17.15 In the context of the BOPM, discuss how American calls on dividend-paying stocks are priced. In particular, focus on the possibility and rationality of early exercise. When and how does exercising early dominate the strategy of holding on to the call?

17.16

   a. Consider the problem posed as a quiz in Section 17.1. Suppose that the data are only part of a larger pricing process as follows:

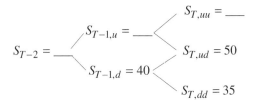

Assume that the stock pricing process is stationary over time. Find the values of $S_{T,uu}$, $S_{T-1,u}$, and S_{T-2}.

   b. Find the value of $C_{T-1,u}$.

   c. *Solve for* the equivalent portfolio for $C_{T-1,u}$. In other words, set up the system of simultaneous equations that equate the payoffs of an unknown equivalent portfolio to those of the call. Solve for Δ and B. Use Equations (17.3) and (17.4) to check your answer. Verify that the payoffs of the equivalent portfolio are identical to those of the call.

   d. Use the multiperiod BOPM to find the value of C_{T-2}

   e. Use the single-period BOPM, and the two possible call values at time $T-1$ to find the value of C_{T-2}.

   f. Find the equivalent portfolio for C_{T-2}. Verify that the payoffs of the equivalent portfolio are identical to those of the call. Verify that the equivalent portfolio is self-financing.

17.17 Use the multiperiod BOPM to estimate the value of a call that has four months to expiration and a strike price of 30. The stock sells for $35.50/share. The size of an uptick is 10%/month, and the size of a downtick is 7%/month. The riskless interest rate is 0.583%/month.

17.18

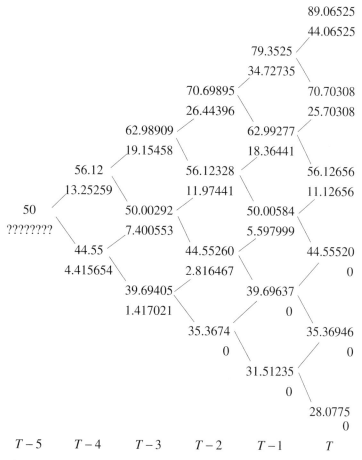

					89.06525
					44.06525
				79.3525	
				34.72735	
			70.69895		70.70308
			26.44396		25.70308
		62.98909		62.99277	
		19.15458		18.36441	
	56.12		56.12328		56.12656
	13.25259		11.97441		11.12656
50		50.00292		50.00584	
????????		7.400553		5.597999	
	44.55		44.55260		44.55520
	4.415654		2.816467		0
		39.69405		39.69637	
		1.417021		0	
			35.3674		35.36946
			0		0
				31.51235	
				0	
					28.0775
					0

$$T-5 \qquad T-4 \qquad T-3 \qquad T-2 \qquad T-1 \qquad T$$

The accompanying tree diagram is for a stock following a binomial pricing process. The risk-free interest rate is 0.84% per period. The upper number in each "box" is the stock price. The lower number is the price of a call. Time T is the expiration date of the call.

a. Compute the value of the call at time $T-5$.

b. Suppose the stock has had two upticks, so the stock sells for $62.98909 at time $T-3$. Find the composition of the equivalent portfolio of stocks and bonds at that "node." Then verify that regardless of whether there is an uptick

or a downtick at time $T-2$, the payoffs of the equivalent portfolio and the call are the same.

c. Now, suppose time T is an ex-dividend date, and the dividend amount is $6 per share. Suppose the stock is selling for $62.99277 at time $T-1$. The ex-dividend prices at time T will be either $64.70308 or $50.12656. Will an American call be exercised early at time $T-1$? Why or why not?

17.19 Today's stock price is $100. At the end of the upcoming single period, the stock will sell, ex-dividend, for either $140 or $65. The dividend amount is $10. The riskless interest rate for the single period is 10%.

a. Find the theoretical value of an **American** call with a strike price of 90; the call expires at the end of the single period.

b. If the market price of the call at time $T-1$ is actually $12, then clearly and thoroughly demonstrate how an arbitrage profit could be earned, given your answer to part a.

17.20   The diagram shows some data as part of a lengthy binomial process. The riskless interest rate is 1% per period.

a. Verify that the payoffs of the call at time $T-66$ are the same as the payoffs of the equivalent portfolio.

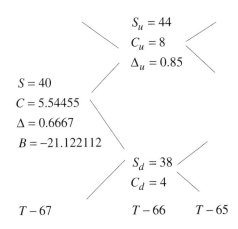

$$S_u = 44$$
$$C_u = 8$$
$$\Delta_u = 0.85$$

$$S = 40$$
$$C = 5.54455$$
$$\Delta = 0.6667$$
$$B = -21.122112$$

$$S_d = 38$$
$$C_d = 4$$

$$T-67 \qquad\qquad T-66 \qquad T-65$$

b. Compute B_u at time $T-66$, when $S_u = 44$. (Hint: the equivalent portfolio is self financing).

CHAPTER 18

Continuous Time Option Pricing Models

The binomial option pricing model (BOPM), produces reasonably accurate option values if the user has accurate beliefs about the values of u and d. Also, the BOPM is extremely flexible. For example, the BOPM can be used to value both European and American puts and calls, either with or without dividend payments. The possibility of early exercise can be accounted for in each period, and the values of u, d, and r can change over time. The primary drawback of the BOPM is that a computer must be used to estimate option values when the time to maturity is carved into many small periods.

18.1 THE BLACK–SCHOLES OPTION PRICING MODEL

Under certain assumptions and when time to maturity is carved into an infinite number of subintervals, the BOPM will converge to the option pricing model attributed to Fischer Black and Myron Scholes. The Black–Scholes call option pricing model (henceforth, the BSOPM) provides an explicit solution to the problem of option pricing.[1] By "explicit," we mean that an equation is obtained.

Although the BSOPM is relatively simple to use, it is important to be aware that the model can accurately value only European options, or American calls on non-dividend-paying stocks. As the possibility of early exercise becomes more likely, the BSOPM produces increasingly inaccurate values. Moreover, an important assumption of the BSOPM is that the wanderings of the stock price through time follow one particular type of pricing process, which cannot change over time.

In this chapter, we first present a set of sufficient assumptions that will lead to the derivation of the BSOPM. Then, the model itself is stated, and a numerical example is shown in detail. Following that, we examine a few details concerning the assumed stochastic process guiding the value of the underlying asset. It is important to realize that a model generally will produce useful results only if the assumptions behind it are realistic. If the assumptions are violated in the real world, the model will frequently provide poor predictions.

18.1.1 Assumptions Behind the Black–Scholes Option Pricing Model

Although other sets of assumptions have been used to derive the BSOPM, the following assumption list is sufficient.

1. Capital markets are perfect. That is, there are no transactions costs or taxes. There are no short selling constraints, and investors get full use of the proceeds from short sales. All assets are infinitely divisible.
2. All investors can borrow and lend at the same riskless interest rate, which is constant over the life of the option.[2]
3. The stock pays no dividends. This means that the model can value European or American calls, since the latter will be exercised only at the expiration date, if and only if the call finishes in the money.
4. Markets are always open, and trading is continuous.
5. The wanderings of the stock price through time follow the rules of a specific type of stochastic process called a geometric Brownian motion. This pricing process is discussed in the chapter appendix.

18.1.2 A Quick Discussion of the Importance of Lognormal Returns

If the stock price follows a geometric Brownian motion, then the distribution of the stock's returns will be lognormally distributed.[3] The chapter appendix contains additional material on Brownian motion and returns distributions.

Lognormal returns are realistic for two reasons. First, if returns are lognormally distributed, the lowest possible return in any period is –100%. In contrast, if returns are normally distributed, there is some probability that returns will be less than –100%. Second, lognormal returns distributions are "positively skewed," that is, skewed to the right. This is realistic because while the lowest return in any period is –100%, the highest return will likely be in excess of 100%, particularly when measured over a year. Thus, a realistic depiction of a stock's returns distribution would have a minimum return of –100% and a maximum return well beyond +100%. The longer the time interval under consideration, the more valid the latter statement becomes. Therefore, annual returns will be more positively skewed than monthly returns, and monthly returns will be more skewed than daily returns. Returns distributions will not be symmetric. They will be skewed to the right.

18.1.3 The Variance of the Stock's Return Is Proportional to Time

Two comments must be made about the implications of this lognormal distribution assumption. First, although the price of the underlying asset (such as a stock) may be a function of its expected rate of return, the value of an option predicted by the BSOPM is independent of the expected return. In other words, all else equal, the value of an option on a stock that has a high expected rate of return is the same as the value of an option on an otherwise equivalent stock with a low expected rate of return.

Second, if the stock price follows a geometric Brownian motion process, the variance of the stock's returns is proportional to time. Correspondingly, the standard deviation of the stock's returns is proportional to the square root of time. Thus, define a subscript, l, to denote a long period of time, and define another subscript, s, to denote a short period of time. Then,

$$\sigma_l^2 = \left(\frac{l}{s}\right)\sigma_s^2 \tag{18.1}$$

EXAMPLE 18.1 If $s=1$ day and $l=1$ week, then

$$\sigma_{weekly}^2 = (7)\sigma_{daily}^2$$

This means that the variance of weekly returns is seven times greater than the variance of daily returns. If $s=1$ month and $l=1$ year, the variance of yearly returns is 12 times the variance of monthly returns:

$$\sigma_{yearly}^2 = (12)\sigma_{monthly}^2$$

The corresponding relationship for standard deviations is:

$$\sigma_l = \sqrt{\frac{l}{s}}\,\sigma_s$$

(18.2)

The standard deviation of a stock's returns is proportional to the square root of time. For example, if $s=1$ week, and $l=1$ year, then

$$\sigma_{yearly}\sqrt{52}\sigma_{weekly} = 7.2111\sigma_{weekly}$$

This says that if the stock follows the stochastic pricing process that has been described, the standard deviation of a stock's yearly returns distribution will be 7.2111 times the standard deviation of its weekly returns distribution.

where σ_s^2 is the variance of the stock's returns measured over the longer interval of time, σ_s^2 is the variance of the stock's returns measured over the shorter period of time, and l/s is the number of short intervals in a long interval.

Perhaps an analogy will help make this important concept clear. Consider a person who starts to stagger along a straight line. Place him at point zero. After one day, he will have staggered back and forth, but will likely not have strayed too far from point zero. After one month, he may have wandered much further from point zero. After a year, he may be miles from it.

A stock's price behaves like this person. If today's stock price is \$100/share, and it follows the pricing process described, then after one day has passed, it may be priced between \$98 and \$103 per share. After one month, it may sell between \$90 and \$115 per share. One year hence, it may sell for as low as \$60 and as high as \$160. The variance of the returns distribution grows larger as longer time intervals are considered. The variance of the annual returns distribution should be 365 times as great as the variance of the daily returns distribution. Figure 18.1 depicts the nature of the returns distributions as longer time intervals are considered.

18.2 THE BLACK–SCHOLES OPTION PRICING MODEL AND A DETAILED NUMERICAL EXAMPLE

Under the preceding assumptions, the value of a European call, or an American call on a non-dividend-paying stock, is as follows:[4]

$$C = SN(d_1) - Ke^{-rT}N(d_2)$$

(18.3)

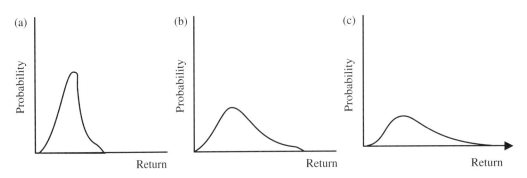

Figure 18.1 Probability distributions of returns. (a) Daily, (b) monthly, and (c) annual. Each return distribution is lognormal.

where

S = price of the underlying asset

K = strike price of the call option

r = risk-free interest rate

T = time to expiration

$N(d)$ = the cumulative standard normal distribution function[5]

$$d_1 = \frac{\ln(S/K) + (r + \sigma^2/2)T}{\sigma\sqrt{T}}$$

$$d_2 = d_1 - \sigma\sqrt{T}$$

σ = standard deviation of the underlying asset's returns

$\ln(S/K)$ = natural logarithm of S/K

e^{-rT} = exponential function of $-rT$. Thus, e^{-rT} is the present value factor when r is continuously compounded for time period T. The present value of K, therefore, is Ke^{-rT}.

An important aspect of the BSOPM is that both r and σ are assumed to be known and constant. In the BSOPM, r is generally stated as an annual interest rate; T, the time to expiration, is stated in years; and σ should be defined as the standard deviation of the stock's annual returns. However, any consistent interval of time can be used. For example, you may wish to define r as the monthly riskless interest rate, T as the number of months until expiration, and σ as the standard deviation of the stock's monthly returns.

For the value of r, some users employ the bond equivalent yield[6] on Treasury bills that mature near the option's expiration date. Other users believe that a more realistic rate is the Eurodollar interest rate, which incorporates a small default risk premium. For valuing options that expire more than one year in the future, r is typically the yield on the zero-coupon Treasury strip that matures on a date near the option's expiration date.

You might be surprised to see that the expected return on the stock does not appear in the formula. The value of an option is independent of the expected return of the stock.[7] However, the volatility of the stock returns, σ, is an important determinant of an option's value. In addition, σ is the only determinant of the call option value that is not directly observable. Users of the BSOPM must estimate σ, just as users of the BOPM had to estimate values for u and d.

Finally, note that there are no variables in the BSOPM that reflect the level of risk aversion in the economy. Under the stated assumptions, option values are invariant to investors' attitudes to risk.

EXAMPLE 18.2   Example of the BSOPM: A stock is currently selling for 58.875. The riskless interest rate is 8% per year. Estimate the value of a call with a strike price of 60 and a time to expiration of three months. The standard deviation of the stock's annual returns is 0.22. Thus, $S=58.875$, $K=60$, $T=0.25$ year, $r=0.08$/year, $\sigma=0.22$/year, and $\sigma^2=0.0484$. To find the Black–Scholes call option price, first calculate:

$$d_1 = \frac{\ln(S/K) + (r + \sigma^2/2)T}{\sigma\sqrt{T}} = \frac{\ln(58.875/60) + (0.08 + 0.0484/2)0.25}{0.22\sqrt{0.25}}$$

$$= \frac{\ln(0.98125) + 0.02605}{(0.22)(0.5)} = \frac{-0.018928 + 0.02605}{0.11} = 0.064745$$

and

$$d_2 = d_1 - \sigma\sqrt{T} = 0.064745 - 0.22\sqrt{0.25} = 0.064745 - 0.11 = -0.045255$$

Next, values for $N(d_1)$ and $N(d_2)$ are needed, and they are found by using the cumulative standard normal distribution function table found in the appendix to this chapter[8]:

$$N(d_1) = 0.525812$$

and

$$N(d_2) = 0.481952$$

The discounted strike price is given by:

$$Ke^{-rT} = 60e^{-(0.08)(0.25)} = (60)e^{-0.02} = (60)(0.9802) = 58.81192$$

Finally, recall that the stock price is 58.875. Therefore the call option price is:

$$C = SN(d_1) - Ke^{-rT}N(d_2) = 58.875(0.525812) - 58.81192(0.481952) = 2.6127$$

This is the theoretical value of this call, and its accuracy depends critically on the estimate of σ. Later in this chapter, methods for estimating σ will be presented.

FinCAD provides the same solution, as shown in Figure 18.2. To generate the same solution for the call value, it is necessary to enter the value date as "today( )" and the expiration (expiry) date as "today( )+(365/4)." In addition, the annually compounded interest rate is $\exp(0.08)-1=8.3287068\%$. The meaning of the Greeks (delta, gamma, theta, vega, and rho) will be explained in the next chapter.

AaBS		
Underlying price	58.875	
Exercise price	60	
Expiry date	24-Jun-98	= TODAY()+(365/4)
Value (settlement) date	3/25/98	= TODAY()
Volatility	0.22	
Risk free interest rate	0.083287068	= exp(0.08)-1
Option type	1	Call
Statistic	1	fair value
Discounting method	1	annually compounded rate
Accrual method	1	actual/ 365 (fixed)

Fair value	2.612634856	1
Delta	0.5258117	2
Gamma	0.061471836	3
Theta	-0.020339844	4
Vega	11.71927424	5
Rho	6.541324504	6

Figure 18.2 The FinCAD function aaBS can be used to determine Black–Scholes prices for call and put options.

18.3   AN INTUITIVE LOOK AT THE BLACK–SCHOLES OPTION PRICING MODEL

By assuming a world of certainty, we can gain an insightful view of the structure of the BSOPM. In such a world, all assets, including stock and all options, must be priced to yield the same riskless rate of return. If any asset was priced to yield more (and in a certain world, everyone would know this), then many investors would rush to buy the asset until its price rose enough to provide the same riskless return as all other assets. If any asset was priced so that its known rate of return was less, no investor would buy it, and its price would decline.

In a certain world, if investors knew that a call was going to finish out of the money, $S_T \leq K$, then the price of the call at every date would always be zero. On the other hand, suppose that investors know that a call will finish in the money. At expiration, everyone knows that C_T will sell for its intrinsic value, $S_T - K$. Because the call must be priced to yield the riskless return, today's price will equal the present value of C_T. In other words, $C_0 = [S_T - K](1+r)^{-T}$, given that $S_T > K$. The discount rate, r, is the riskless interest rate.

In addition, the stock must also be priced to yield a riskless rate of return, r. Thus $S_0 = S_T(1+r)^{-T}$. This is equivalent to saying that $S_T = S_0(1+r)^T$. Substitute this into today's call value, and

$$C_0 = [S_0(1+r)^T - K](1+r)^{-T}$$

or

$$C_0 = S_0 - K(1+r)^{-T}$$

Compare this value of a call with the BSOPM. To convert the call value just given to the Black–Scholes call value, simply multiply S_0 by $N(d_1)$ and multiply $K(1+r)^{-T}$ by $N(d_2)$. Smith (1976, footnotes 20 and 22), and Jarrow and Rudd (1983, pp. 93–94) point out an interesting feature of the Black–Scholes model. They explain that if the Black–Scholes model is the correct option pricing model to use, the term $N(d_2)$ is the probability that the call will finish in the money in a risk-neutral world.[9]

18.4   THE BLACK–SCHOLES OPTION PRICING MODEL AND EUROPEAN PUT PRICES

One easy approach to estimate the value of a European put on a non-dividend-paying stock starts by calculating a call option price using the basic BSOPM. Then, a put value is obtained by using the basic put–call parity theorem. For example, in Section 18.2 we computed the theoretical value of a call with the following inputs:

$S = 58.875$

$K = 60$

$T = 0.25$ year

$r = 0.08$

$\sigma = 0.22$

Using the BSOPM, we found that the value of a European call is $2.6127.

The basic put–call parity theorem is Proposition XI in Chapter 16:

$$C - P = S - K(1+r)^{-T}$$

If interest is compounded continuously, put–call parity can be restated as follows:

$$C - P = S - Ke^{-rT} \tag{18.4}$$

Rearranging, and solving for P:

$$P = C - S + Ke^{-rT} = 2.6127 - 58.875 + 60e^{-(0.08)(0.25)} = \$2.5496$$

Alternatively, the BSOPM formula can be restated to value European puts on non-dividend-paying stocks by using the continuous time version of the put–call parity theorem. That is, we start with the BSOPM

$$C = SN(d_1) - Ke^{-rT}N(d_2)$$

and rearrange the put–call parity proposition to be

$$C = P + S - Ke^{-rT} \tag{18.5}$$

This yields, after substituting Equation (18.5) into the BSOPM,

$$SN(d_1) - Ke^{-rT}N(d_2) = P + S - Ke^{-rT} \tag{18.6}$$

Solving Equation (18.6) for P results in

$$P = SN(d_1) - S + Ke^{-rT} - Ke^{-rT}N(d_2)$$

or

$$P = S[N(d_1) - 1] - Ke^{-rT}[N(d_2) - 1] \tag{18.7}$$

Note that in Equation (18.7), the terms $[N(d_1) - 1]$ and $[N(d_2) - 1]$ are negative because the area under the normal density function has a maximum of 1. Thus, Equation (18.7) can be restated as follows:

$$P = Ke^{-rT}[1 - N(d_2)] - S[1 - N(d_1)]$$

In addition, because of the symmetry of the normal density function, that is, because $[1 - N(d)] = N(-d)$, the put price can also be expressed as follows:

$$P = Ke^{-rT}N(-d_2) - SN(-d_1) \tag{18.8}$$

Now, let's use Equation (18.8) to value the put directly. Recall that in Example 18.2 we found that $d_1 = 0.064745$ and $N(d_1) = 0.525812$. Therefore, $1 - N(d_1) = N(-d_1) = 0.474188$. Furthermore, since $d_2 = -0.04525$ and $N(d_2) = 0.481952$, we have $1 - N(d_2) = N(-d_2) = 0.518048$. The value of the put equals:

$$P = Ke^{-rT}N(-d_2) - SN(-d_1) = (58.81192 \times 0.518048) - (58.875 \times 0.474188) = 2.5496$$

Note that this is the same value that we estimated by using the BSOPM call formula along with the put–call parity proposition. Intuitively, this makes sense because the put–call parity proposition was used to derive Equation (18.8).

18.5 TWO HANDY EXTENSIONS OF THE BLACK–SCHOLES OPTION PRICING MODEL

As you know, the BSOPM is designed to provide prices for European options on a security that does not pay dividends. Financial economists have modified and extended the BSOPM to allow its use to value options on securities of other types. We now turn our attention to an examination of two extensions to the BSOPM. These two variants of the BSOPM value European calls on stocks that will trade ex-dividend before the expiration date. Note that these two variants could also be used to value American calls if the user is highly confident that the call will not be exercised before expiration.

18.5.1 Variant One: The Black–Scholes Option Pricing Model on Securities Paying Known, Discrete Dividends

If the stock will trade ex-dividend before expiration, then the holder of a European call owns an option only on the stock price at expiration because he has no claim on dividends before the expiration date. The stock's theoretical value at expiration is the present value of all dividends after the expiration date. However, today's stock price is the present value of all dividends after today. Thus, the difference between the stock price today and the stock price at expiration is the present value of dividends received between tomorrow and the option expiration date. Therefore, a European call option on a dividend paying stock is really a call option on an asset price adjusted for the present value of all dividends received after today and prior to expiration.

To use this variant of the BSOPM, define

$$S^* = S - PV(\text{divs}) = S - \sum_{i=1}^{N} \text{div}_i (1+r)^{-t_i}$$

That is, S^* is today's stock price minus the present value of all dividends received after today and prior to the option expiration date. In this notation, div_i is the dividend amount at time t_i, and T is

---

EXAMPLE 18.3   Given the following information, what is the value of a European call option?

$S = 44$

$K = 40$

$r = 0.08/\text{year}$

$T = 67$ days

$\sigma = 0.30/\text{year}$

A dividend of \$1.10 will be paid 39 days from today, i.e., in 0.10685 of a year.

$$S^* = 44 - 1.10e^{-0.08(0.10685)} = 44 - 1.091 = 42.909$$

$$d_1 = \frac{\ln(S^*/K) + (r + \sigma^2/2)T}{\sigma\sqrt{T}} = \frac{\ln(42.909/40) + [0.08 + 1/2(0.09)]0.184}{0.3\sqrt{0.184}}$$

$$= \frac{\ln(1.0727) + 0.023}{(0.3)(0.42844)} = \frac{0.07018 + 0.023}{0.1285} = 0.7247$$

$$N(d_1) = 0.7658$$

$$d_2 = d_1 - \sigma\sqrt{T} = 0.725 - 0.30\sqrt{0.184} = 0.7247 - 0.1285 = 0.5962$$

$$N(d_2) = 0.7245$$

$$Ke^{-rT} = 40e^{-(0.08)(0.18356)} = 40 \times 0.9854 = 39.4169$$

Therefore,

$$C = S^* N(d_1) - Ke^{-rT} N(d_2) = (42.909 \times 0.7658) - (39.4169 \times 0.7245) = 4.299$$

The FinCAD function aaBSdcf computes the same result, as shown in Figure 18.3.

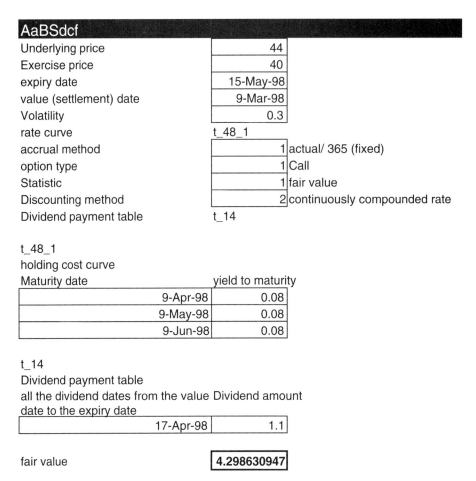

AaBSdcf		
Underlying price	44	
Exercise price	40	
expiry date	15-May-98	
value (settlement) date	9-Mar-98	
Volatility	0.3	
rate curve	t_48_1	
accrual method	1	actual/ 365 (fixed)
option type	1	Call
Statistic	1	fair value
Discounting method	2	continuously compounded rate
Dividend payment table	t_14	

t_48_1
holding cost curve

Maturity date	yield to maturity
9-Apr-98	0.08
9-May-98	0.08
9-Jun-98	0.08

t_14
Dividend payment table
all the dividend dates from the value Dividend amount
date to the expiry date

17-Apr-98	1.1

fair value	4.298630947

Figure 18.3 Using the FinCAD function aaBSdcf to compute option valuation when the underlying asset pays a discrete dividend.

the expiration date. Here, it is assumed that the ex-dividend day and the payment day are the same, that the dividends are known with certainty, and that the stock price will decline by the dividend amount on the ex-day. Thus, to value a European call option on a dividend-paying stock, merely use S^* in place of S in the standard BSOPM.[10]

18.5.2 Variant Two: The Black–Scholes Option Pricing Model on Securities Paying a Continuous Dividend Stream

Although individual stocks do not pay dividends continuously, a continuous dividend flow model can be used to approximate the dividend stream paid by a well-diversified stock portfolio. The approximation model is particularly inviting if the option has a long time to expiration. However, if the call has a short time to expiration, this model is less adequate. This is because many stocks in the portfolio will trade ex-dividend on the same date during the option's remaining life. At other dates, however, no stock in the portfolio will trade ex-dividend.

This continuous dividend flow model is also valid when one is valuing European calls on futures contracts, on foreign exchange, or on a pure discount debt instrument such as a T-bill. Interest accrues on the T-bill daily, a process that is analogous to a continuous dividend stream.

To use the continuous dividend model, define

$$S^* = Se^{-dT}$$

where d is the annual *constant* dividend yield and T is the time to option expiration, in years. Thus, if a stock index is currently at $S = 156$, the dividend yield is 4%, and the call has nine months to expiration, then

$$S^* = 156e^{-(0.04)(0.75)} = 151.3895$$

Therefore, to value a European call on a stock that pays a constant dividend yield, one would simply substitute the value of S^* for S in the BSOPM.

The FinancialCAD function aaBSG computes the value of a European option on an asset paying a continuous dividend (called a "holding cost" on the FinCAD example).

18.5.3   European Puts with Known Dividends

To value a European put on a stock that will pay known dividends, you can first use the method explained in Section 18.5.1 to value a European call on a dividend-paying stock. Then, you could use the version of put–call parity that applies to European options on stocks that pay known dividends.[11] Alternatively, define S^* as the current stock price minus the present value of all dividends between today and expiration. Then, substitute S^* into the BSOPM put pricing model, Equation (18.8).

The FinCAD functions described earlier typically have an "option switch" button that toggles between a call and a put. For example, aaBS has such a switch on line 8, and aaBINdcf has it on line 10.

18.6   THE RELATION BETWEEN THE BINOMIAL AND THE BLACK–SCHOLES OPTION PRICING MODELS

Under certain conditions, the BOPM will converge to the BSOPM. Let the number of intervals in the BOPM become infinitely large. The length of each time interval in the BOPM thus shrinks to approach zero. Then, we must choose specific values of u, d, and q (the probability of an "uptick"). These values will result in the stock following a geometric Brownian motion. Thus, let the following define u, d, and q:

$$u = e^{\sigma\sqrt{T/n}} - 1$$

$$d = e^{-\sigma\sqrt{T/n}} - 1$$

$$q = \frac{1}{2} + \frac{1}{2}\left(\frac{\mu}{\sigma}\right)\sqrt{\frac{T}{n}}$$

where T is the time to expiration and n is the number of subintervals in T. The parameters μ and σ define the expected return on the stock and the standard deviation of the stock's return distribution, respectively. If u, d, and q take on these specific values, it can be shown that as $n \Rightarrow \infty$, the stock price will be lognormally distributed, and the BSOPM will result.

EXAMPLE 18.4   Suppose $T=4$ months $=0.3333$ year, and $n=4$. If the stock's standard deviation of annual returns is 0.60 and the expected return is 0.20 per year, then choosing the following will make the BOPM and BSOPM mutually consistent:

$$u = e^{\sigma\sqrt{T/n}} - 1 = e^{(0.60)\sqrt{0.0833}} - 1 = e^{0.1732051} - 1 = 0.18911$$

$$d = e^{-\sigma\sqrt{T/n}} - 1 = e^{(-0.60)\sqrt{0.0833}} - 1 = e^{-0.1732051} - 1 = -0.159035$$

$$q = \frac{1}{2} + \frac{1}{2}\left(\frac{\mu}{\sigma}\right)\sqrt{\frac{T}{n}} = \frac{1}{2} + \frac{1}{2}\left(\frac{0.20}{0.60}\right)\sqrt{0.08333} = 0.5481125$$

If u, d, and q are defined in this way, the stock price will become lognormally distributed as $n \Rightarrow \infty$.[12]

Sometimes, you may wish to use the BOPM, when you are uncertain of the choice of u and d. If you have estimates of the required return on the stock and the volatility of the stock's returns, these formulas can be used to obtain reasonable estimates for u and d. The value of q in the BOPM is only important when you are not assuming a risk-neutral world.

18.7   THE NETTLESOME TASK OF ESTIMATING A SECURITY'S VOLATILITY, σ

18.7.1   Historical Volatility

The estimate of a call option value made by using the BSOPM is only as good as the estimate of σ that is used in the formula. No one knows what the standard deviation of stock returns will be during the life of the option. Thus, it must be estimated. One way to estimate future volatility is to use historical price data To do this, follow this easy procedure.

1. Decide on the length of the interval for which you will use historical prices. You may wish to select daily, weekly, or monthly prices. Also record any ex-dividend days and any ex–stock distribution days during the estimation period.

2. How many price observations should you gather? There is a trade-off between obtaining too many and too few observations. Assuming no major changes in the company, an estimate of the standard deviation will be more reliable (efficient) as more observations are used. However, as you move further back in time to obtain price data, there will be an increasing likelihood that the risk of the company's stock was different from what it is today. Thus, perhaps a good compromise is to use about 60–200 daily price observations, 40–60 weekly price observations, or 30–50 monthly price observations.

3. Compute the continuously compounded rate of return for each interval. That is, compute daily, weekly, or monthly log price relatives. To do this, find

$$r_{t2} = \ln\left[\frac{S_{t2}}{S_{t1}}\right]$$

or, if there was an ex-dividend day during the interval,

$$r_{t2} = \ln\left[\frac{S_{t2} + \text{div}}{S_{t1}}\right]$$

where div is the dividend amount. You must also adjust these returns for any stock dividends or stock splits.[13]

4. Compute the average of the time series of the n returns, $\bar{r}$:

$$\bar{r} = \left(\frac{1}{n}\right)\sum_{t=1}^{n} r_t$$

where n is the number of log price relatives you have.

5. Estimate the variance of the stock's returns:

$$\text{var}(r) = \left(\frac{1}{n-1}\right)\sum_{t=1}^{n}(r_t - \bar{r})^2 \tag{18.9}$$

Finally, use Equations (18.1) or (18.2) to obtain an estimate of the variance or standard deviation of the stock's returns for any desired interval of time. For example, if you used daily log price relatives, you can estimate the variance of the stock's annual returns by multiplying the variance of daily returns by 365.

EXAMPLE 18.5   Estimating the Variance of a Stock's Monthly Returns

Month	Stock Price	Div	$\dfrac{S_{t2} + \text{div}}{S_{t1}}$	$\ln\left[\dfrac{S_{t2} + \text{div}}{S_{t1}}\right]$	$\ln\left[\dfrac{S_{t2} + \text{div}}{S_{t1}}\right] - \bar{r}$	$\left(\ln\left[\dfrac{S_{t2} + \text{div}}{S_{t1}}\right] - \bar{r}\right)^2$
0	40.00					
1	42.00	0	1.050000	0.048790	0.041735	0.001742
2	41.125	0	0.979166	−0.021050	−0.028100	0.000790
3	42.375	0	1.030395	0.029942	0.022887	0.000524
4	39.75	0	0.938053	−0.063940	−0.071000	0.005042
5	40	0	1.006289	0.006269	−0.000790	0.000001
6	40	1	1.025000	0.024692	0.017638	0.000311
7	41	0	1.025000	0.024692	0.017638	0.000311

$$\bar{r} = 0.007055 \qquad\qquad \sum_{\text{month}=1}^{7} = 0.008720$$

$$\sigma^2 = \left(\frac{1}{6}\right)\sum_{t=1}^{7}(r_t - \bar{r})^2 = 0.001453$$

Thus, the estimated variance of the stock's monthly returns is 0.001453. The variance of the stock's annual returns is 12 times as great: 0.017436. As stated earlier in practice, you would use between 30 and 50 observations to obtain a good estimate of the stock's monthly volatility.

Historical volatility estimates for CBOE-traded options are available at the board's website (www.cboe.com/MktData/HistoricalVolatility.asp).

18.7.2   Improving on the Estimate from Historical Data

The series of closing prices is not the only kind of data that can be used to estimate stock return volatility. For example, you can utilize the information in the stock's ending price, as well as its high, low, and beginning price that occur during the interval.[14]

You can also estimate the historical variances of the stocks of other companies that are in similar businesses and have similar capital structures to compare the stock's historical volatility to that of these firms. If there are significant differences, you may wish to adjust your estimated volatility to be closer to the other firms. Similarly, firm-specific information such as capital structure, liquidity, and fixed versus variable operating costs might aid in estimating a stock's variance. If any of these last data are used, you should generally make only small adjustments to your initial estimated volatility obtained from historical data.

18.7.3   Implied Volatility (IV)

Up until now, you have placed an estimated variance into the BSOPM to obtain an estimated call value. However, it is also possible to take the market price of the call as given and "back out" a variance (or standard deviation) that is consistent with that option price. This variance is called an option's implied variance (implied standard deviation), or, more commonly, implied volatility, VOL, or IV.

The primary advantage of an implied standard deviation over a historical volatility is that an implied standard deviation represents an ex-ante market assessment of risk. For this reason, option-implied forecasts of return volatility have frequently been regarded as superior to estimates based on historical data. Generally, a computer is used to perform a trial-and-error routine to search for the unique σ that provides a model price equal to the observed price.[15]

FinCAD has functions that allow implied volatility to be calculated for options of many different types. For example, the FinCAD function aaBS_iv can be used to compute the implied volatility of a European call or put option. Figure 18.4 illustrates how the implied volatility for Example 18.6 is computed.

EXAMPLE 18.6   On February 19, 1998, the S&P 500 Index closed at 1028.28. The March call options with a strike price of 1030 had a closing price of 20. The short-term interest rate was 5.25%. The option had 28 days until expiration.

Solution   A standard deviation of 16.23% is consistent with this option price, as shown in Figure 18.4.

aaBS_iv		
Underlying price	1028.28	
Exercise price	1030	
Expiry date	20-Mar-98	
Value (settlement) date	19-Feb-98	
Price	20	
Risk free interest rate	0.0525	
Option type	1	call
Discounting method	1	annually compounded rate
accrual method	1	Actual/365 (fixed)
implied volatility	0.162318349	

Figure 18.4 The FinCAD function aaBS_iv can be used to determine the implied volatility of a call option.

If you use yesterday's option price data to obtain an IV to use in valuing options today, an obvious question is: Which option price should be used? There have been several techniques suggested for making the best use of information contained in a set of implied volatilities. Despite the widespread use of implied volatility, there is no generally accepted method to estimate implied volatility.[16]

18.7.4   Using Implied Volatility Estimates

Finding the implied volatilities of options is useful for determining which option is the most undervalued or the most overvalued. Relative to the other options on the same stock, the option with the lowest IV is most undervalued. This statement assumes that the assumptions behind the BSOPM are valid. However, there could be good reasons for one option to have a higher or lower IV than another option. For example, the stock's volatility might be expected to change over time, causing calls with longer times to expiration and calls with shorter times to expiration to have different IVs. In addition, there could be a perceived probability of a jump (a discontinuity) in the stock price, which would cause calls with different strikes to differ in their IVs. Ex-dividend dates can cause IVs to differ across options' times to expiration. Finally, refer to Section 18.7.6, which discusses the "volatility smile."

Computing an IV that is drastically different from one you believe ought to be incorporated in an option's price is tantamount to holding the belief that the option is mispriced. Suppose you calculate an IV for a call to be 30% (based on its asked price). However, you believe that the true volatility is 60%. In other words, you believe the call is undervalued. You could just buy the call. On average, if your beliefs are correct, you should earn an above-average rate of return for the risks you bear.

Alternatively, you can try to arbitrage by purchasing the undervalued call and selling the equivalent portfolio of stock and T-bills. The proportions allocated to stock and T-bills in the latter portfolio should reflect the estimated volatility of 60%. The equivalent portfolio must be revised frequently over time, to reflect changes in the required proportions that are needed to replicate the call. If your beliefs about volatility are correct, you should end up with a profit equal to the difference between the value of the call with a volatility of 30% (its actual price), and the value of the call if it were selling with a volatility of 60%.

Merville and Pieptea (1989), analyzed the time series properties of the IVs of 25 stocks. They disclosed at least two interesting findings: changes in IV are correlated across stocks; and there appear to be one or more forces that pull IVs back to their long-term average values (this is called **mean reversion**). These findings imply that the IV of one stock provides information about the IV of another stock. In addition, if a recent IV is considerably different from its long-run average IV (perhaps calculated over the past year), then a "better" estimated volatility might be a weighted average of the recent IV and its long-term mean.

Many traders use the mean reverting property of implied volatility to improve their trading performance. For example, suppose a bullish trader believes that a certain stock price is about to rise. If the current IV is below its long-term average value, the trader will buy calls. As such, he is effectively buying the underlying asset and buying volatility. Note that the trader might be wrong and the price of the underlying asset might *not* rise substantially, but he can still profit. If the IV of the option does increase, the trader will benefit, because all else equal, the call price will increase as its IV increases.

If the IV is above its long-term average value, option prices are "high," so the trader will write puts, rather than buy calls. Here, he is selling volatility. If the puts' IV declines to its long-run average value, the put prices will decline, and the put seller will profit even if the stock price does not rise.

18.7.5 Market Volatility Index (VIX)

The volatility implied in option prices is important financial information. Beginning in 1993, the Chicago Board Option Exchange began computing and disseminating a real-time, market-wide implied volatility index. Thus, during the trading day, investors can monitor the market's assessment of expected stock market risk by looking up the symbol (VIX). By its construction, the Market Volatility Index, is a 30-day forward-looking measure of the dispersion of expected returns of the Standard & Poor's 100 Index (OEX).

Whaley (1993) describes in detail how the VIX is constructed as well and discusses how the VIX can be used. Briefly, however, the VIX is calculated as follows. Each minute during the trading day, the implied volatility from eight OEX options is calculated. These eight options are divided into two groups, one group representing options with the nearest expiration date and the other representing options with the second-nearest expiration date. Both groups of options consist of the two calls and two puts with strike prices immediately above and below the current OEX level. After the implied volatilities have been calculated, they are weighted such that the VIX represents an implied volatility of an at-the-money OEX option with 30 calendar days to expiration. Data on the VIX can be found at the exchange's website (www.cboe.com/MktData/vix.asp).

18.7.6 The Volatility Smile and the Term Structure of Volatility

If the Black–Scholes model is correct, then all options with the same underlying asset should have the same implied volatility, regardless of their strike prices or times to expiration. If options systematically differ in their implied volatilities, then either the BSOPM is wrong (perhaps because of flawed assumptions behind the model) or the market is mispricing the options.

Given actual trade prices, there is often a structure to volatilities implied by the BSOPM. This volatility structure is generally divided into two parts: a **volatility smile** (also known as the "skew") and a **term structure of volatility**. The volatility smile describes the way implied volatility varies across strike prices for a given expiration date. The "term structure of volatility" is the relationship among implied volatility across expiration dates for a given strike price.[17]

As an example of the volatility smile, consider the data in Table 18.1. where the option premium column gives average bid–ask prices for June 2000 S&P 500 Index call and put options at the close of trading on May 16, 2000. Such data are available each day at the CBOE website (www.cboe.com). Then, taking the May 16, 2000, closing S&P 500 Index level of 1466.04, a riskless interest rate of 5.75%, an estimated dividend yield of 1.5%, and $T=0.08493$ year (31 days to expiration), we can use the FinCAD function, aaBSG_iv, to generate implied volatilities.

The columns of Table 18.1 present the strike price, the call price, the call's implied volatility, and the call price, computed with a standard deviation of 0.22 (which is approximately the implied volatility of the around-the-money options). Then the put price, the put's implied volatility, and the put price computed with a standard deviation of 0.22 are presented in the last three columns.

From Table 18.1, one can see that implied volatility is not constant across strike prices. In addition, comparing columns 2 and 4 shows that if you use the constant at-the-money implied volatility of 0.22 to price *all* the calls, there are systematic pricing errors. That is, the in-the-money call options appear to be overpriced (their actual prices are above their theoretical prices) and the out-of-the-money call options appear to be underpriced (their actual prices are below their theoretical prices).

The implied volatilities of put prices are also not the same for all strike prices. But interestingly, the *out*-of-the money puts have higher implied volatilities than the in-the-money puts. For calls, the reverse is generally true. That is, for strikes up to 1600, the out-of-the-money calls have

TABLE 18.1   Implied Volatility Across Strike Prices

Strike Price	Call Price	Call IV	Theoretical Call Price with $\sigma = 0.22$	Put Price	Put IV	Theoretical Put Price with $\sigma = 0.22$
1225				1.5625	0.3360	0.054
1250				2.34375	0.3283	0.153
1275				2.625	0.3021	0.390
1300				3.8125	0.2920	0.904
1325				5.75	0.2855	1.919
1350	129.5	0.2834	124.335	8.25	0.2762	3.753
1375	107.625	0.2689	102.510	11.375	0.2641	6.809
1400	86.625	0.2534	82.353	14.875	0.2463	11.533
1425	67.625	0.2423	64.288	20.0625	0.2315	18.350
1450	50.6875	0.2324	48.648	29	0.2285	27.592
1475	35.625	0.2201	35.612	38.625	0.2152	39.437
1500	22.5	0.2036	25.178	50.875	0.2016	53.885
1525	14	0.1982	17.173	66.75	0.1923	70.762
1550	7.875	0.1912	11.291	85.375	0.1826	89.761
1575	4.375	0.1896	7.154	106.875	0.1788	110.505
1600	2.28125	0.1881	4.367	129.5	0.1668	132.600
1625	1.21875	0.1897	2.569	153.375	0.1512	155.684
1650	0.625	0.1912	1.457			

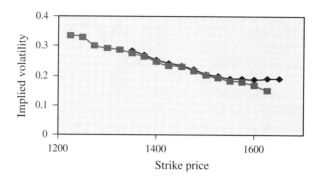

Figure 18.5 Volatility smiles: diamonds, call IV; squares, put IV.

lower implied volatilities than in-the-money calls. But the "smile" appears for the calls when strikes exceed 1600.

Figure 18.5 graphs the volatility smile data presented in Table 18.1. Actually, only the calls exhibit a slight smile (perhaps a smirk?). Puts show only a decline in their implied volatilities as strike prices rise.

Traders should account for any relationship between σ and K when they use the BSOPM to value options. Otherwise, if they use just one constant volatility to value all options, they will conclude that options are systematically over-or undervalued, depending on how far they are in or out of the money. One way to account for the volatility smile uses the following quadratic regression equation:

$$IV = \alpha + \beta_1 \ln\left(\frac{S}{K}\right) + \beta_2 \ln\left(\frac{S}{K}\right)^2 + \varepsilon \qquad (18.10)$$

This model states that the implied volatility in option prices is a quadratic function (U-shaped, if β_2 is positive) of S/K, which measures the extent to which the option is in or out of the money. Using the call data in Table 18.1 to estimate Equation (18.10) results in the following information:

$$\alpha = 2.169318 \ (t = 6.639)$$
$$\beta_1 = -4.47227 \ (t = -6.727)$$
$$\beta_2 = 2.522705 \ (t = 7.484)$$
$$R^2 = 0.988$$

These coefficients are unlikely to be constant over time. Therefore, traders should use the most recently available price data to estimate the model. This method is a simpler approach than estimating a stochastic volatility model.[18]

Volatility smiles may occur if volatility itself is stochastic. In other words, an assumption behind the BSOPM is that the volatility of the underlying asset is constant, right through expiration. But a more accurate depiction of security markets is that the volatility of returns changes from day to day. Many individuals in the market spend considerable time trying to accurately predict future volatility. Volatility may trend up and down, and it may randomly fluctuate around the trend. Occasionally, jumps (discontinuities) in the time series of prices occur. Volatility that changes over time, and/or jumps, can create volatility smiles.

18.8   GENERALIZING THE BLACK–SCHOLES OPTION PRICING MODEL

It is important to understand that many option pricing models are related. For example, you will see in Chapter 20 that many exotic options are simply parts of the BSOPM. The BSOPM itself, however, can be generalized to encapsulate several important pricing models. All that is needed is the addition of a cost-of-carry term, b. Then, one can use this generalized model to price European options on non-dividend-paying stocks (Black and Scholes, 1973), options on stocks that pay a continuous dividend (Merton, 1973), currency options (Garman and Kohlhagen, 1983), and options on futures (Black, 1976). The formulas for the generalized options are as follows:

$$C_{\text{gen}} = Se^{(b-r)T}N(d_1) - Ke^{-rT}N(d_2) \tag{18.11}$$

and

$$P_{\text{gen}} = Ke^{-rT}N(-d_2) - Se^{(b-r)T}N(-d_1) \tag{18.12}$$

where, S, K, r, T, $N(d)$, σ, ln, and e are as defined in Section 18.2. However, in the generalized BSOPM, we have

$$d_1 = \frac{\ln(S/K) + (b + \sigma^2/2)T}{\sigma\sqrt{T}} \tag{18.13}$$

$$d_2 = \frac{\ln(S/K) + (b - \sigma^2/2)T}{\sigma\sqrt{T}} = d_1 - \sigma\sqrt{T} \tag{18.14}$$

and

$$b = \text{cost-of-carry rate of holding the underlying asset}$$

By altering the 'b' term in Equations (18.11) through (18.14), four option pricing models emerge.

Setting	Yields This European Option Pricing Model
$b = r$	Stock option model (i.e., the BSOPM)
$b = r - \delta$	Stock option model with continuous dividends, δ
$b = r - r_f$	Currency option model where r_f is the foreign risk-free rate
$b = 0$	Futures option model

18.9   OPTIONS ON FUTURES CONTRACTS

Because we have spent considerable time examining options and futures, it is natural to spend a bit of time learning about options on futures contracts. A futures option is an option on a futures contract. A call futures option gives the owner the right but not the obligation to assume a long position in a futures contract. The buyer of a futures call pays a premium to the seller (writer). The writer of a futures call has the obligation to deliver a futures contract should the call owner decide to exercise it. The strike price is the futures price at which the long position is assumed. Upon exercising a futures call, the positions are marked to market. Thus, whereas the exerciser of an "ordinary" call must pay $K to acquire the asset, the exerciser of a futures call is actually paid the intrinsic value of the option. That is, the futures contract is immediately marked to market, and the exerciser is paid $(F-K)$ to go long a futures contract, where F is the futures settle price on the exercise day, and K is the striking price.

Futures options trade on many different exchanges, with underlying assets consisting of virtually every successful futures contract. The *Wall Street Journal* presents their prices in tables that are based on the underlying commodity. For example, see Figure 14.8. Different conventions exist for interpreting futures options price data. Therefore, before you ever trade futures options, be sure to learn how to read the data!

Many futures options have expiration dates in months that are not delivery months for the futures contracts that underlie them. For example, there are January, February, and March S&P 500 futures options (in fact, you can trade S&P 500 futures options with any of 12 expiration months). But S&P 500 futures contracts expire quarterly: in March, June, September, and December. The same situation exists for all foreign exchange futures that trade on the IMM. What this means is that January, February, and March futures options have March futures underlying them. April, May, and June futures options require the delivery of June futures contracts, and so on. An investor who exercises a *February put* on a Japanese yen futures contract, will go short one *March* yen futures contract at the strike price.

The last trading day of futures options differs from contract to contract, and it can differ for a given contract, depending on whether the option expires in the futures' delivery month or in a non-delivery month. Always contact the exchange on which a futures option (or futures contract) trades for current contract specifications, as these can change at any time.

18.9.1 Valuing European Futures Options

Black (1976) derived a formula for computing the value of a European call option on a forward or futures contract. Black made all the assumptions that were behind the BSOPM, including constant interest rates. This last assumption is critical because if interest rates are known, a futures price is equivalent to a forward price.[19]

From Equations (18.11) through (18.14), by setting $b=0$, and using F to denote the underlying asset, Black's model for call options is generally written as follows:

$$C = e^{-rT}\left[FN(d_1) - KN(d_2)\right] \tag{18.15}$$

and for puts, it is

$$P = e^{-rT}\left[KN(-d_2) - FN(-d_1)\right] \tag{18.16}$$

The delta of a European futures call is

$$\Delta_c = e^{-rT}N(d_1); \quad 0 \le \Delta_c < 1$$

and the delta of a European futures put is

$$\Delta_p = -e^{-rT}[1 - N(d_1)]; \quad -1 < \Delta_p \le 0$$

Note the similarity to the BSOPM. The only difference is that Fe^{-rT} is substituted for S. Intuitively, this makes sense because Fe^{-rT} is the present value of F, in continuous time. Thus, the Black model combines the BSOPM with the cost-of-carry futures pricing model.

Observe Equations (18.15) and (18.16). Suppose that a futures call is very deep in the money so that $N(d_1) = N(d_2) = 1.0$. Then Equation (18.15) yields a theoretical call value of

$$C = e^{-rT}[F - K]$$

This is the present value of its intrinsic value, which is less than its intrinsic value of $F - K$. This means that a deep in-the-money European futures call can sell for less than its intrinsic value (unless r or T is zero), regardless of whether there are payouts such as dividends on the underlying asset. Similarly, if a futures put is very deep in the money, then

$$P = e^{-rT}[K - F]$$

which is the present value of $K - F$. Thus, we can conclude that like calls, European futures puts can also sell for less than their intrinsic value.

Finally, it is logical to expect the Black model to underprice exchange-traded futures options because it is a European futures options pricing model. However, all futures options that trade in the United States are American futures options. We will see next that both American futures calls and puts can exercised early if they are sufficiently in the money. Therefore, the prices of American futures options will almost always have an early exercise premium above that of their European equivalents.

18.9.2 Valuing American Futures Options

All the futures options that trade in American markets are American-style contracts. Accordingly, the owners of these options can exercise them at any time before expiration. Because owners might find it optimal to exercise early, American futures options cannot be worth less than otherwise identical European futures options. Also, an American futures option cannot sell for less than its intrinsic value.

There will always exist a critical futures price, F^*, for which early exercise will be optimal. For American futures calls, it is the futures price at which the call sells for its intrinsic value. If $F > F^*$, then the futures call owner will find it optimal to exercise early. The owner of an American futures call might find it optimal to exercise early even when there are no dividends or carry returns. Note that this is different from a call on a spot good, which will be exercised early only just before an ex-dividend date. For American futures puts, F^* is the price at which the put sells for $K - F$ (its intrinsic value); if F is below F^*, it will be rational to exercise the American futures put early.

We see intuitively, that deep in-the-money futures options are exercised early because when an investor exercises them, he receives a cash inflow, since the futures position is marked to market. By not exercising early, the investor is missing out on interest income on the futures option's intrinsic value.

Because deep in-the-money futures puts and calls might be exercised early, American futures options will almost always be worth more than European futures options.[20]

18.9.3   Put–Call Parity for Options on Futures Contracts

For European futures options, the put–call parity proposition is:

$$C - P = (F - K)(1 + r)^{-T} = PV(F - K) \tag{18.17}$$

Note that Equation (18.17) combines the standard cost-of-carry pricing model [$(F = S(1 + r)^T = S + \text{carry costs})$] with the standard put–call parity theorem.[21]

For American futures options, the put – call parity proposition is:[22]

$$F(1 + r)^{-T} - K \leq C - P \leq F - K(1 + r)^{-T} \tag{18.18a}$$

or

$$PV(F) - K \leq C - P \leq F - PV(K) \tag{18.18b}$$

18.9.4   Strategies That Use Options on Futures Contracts

Any option strategy covered in Chapter 15 can be replicated with futures options and futures contracts. Note, however, that when one is going long or short futures, there is no initial cash flow; in contrast, when one is buying and selling stock, there are initial cash outflows and inflows, respectively.

For example, a bullish stock market investor can use S&P 500 futures options to speculate on that belief. He can buy futures calls. Alternatively, he can reduce his initial outlay by buying a vertical futures call spread. These strategies offer one significant advantage over simply going long the March S&P 500 futures contract: there is a limited loss if the bullish investor is wrong.

A crude oil producer might purchase put options on crude oil futures contracts as insurance against the risk that the spot price of crude oil will decline below the price at which the firm will no longer earn a sufficient profit.

For another example, consider an investor who believes that the $/¥ exchange rate will be stable in the near future. The investor can sell a strangle on the Japanese yen by selling a futures call and selling a futures put.

Next, suppose a manager of a portfolio of Treasury bonds expects interest rates to remain stable, or perhaps rise somewhat. He can use T-bond futures options to his advantage. He might consider writing futures calls as a way to increase income. Note that this is not exactly a covered call position because instead of being long T-bond futures contracts, the manager is long spot bonds.

Consider an equity portfolio manager who would commit funds to the market if the S&P 500 fell another 10 points. He might consider writing out-of-the money naked futures puts as a way of increasing income. Here, the sale of the futures puts serves as a substitute for placing limit buy orders.

Thus, we see that futures options offer market participants opportunities to speculate on their beliefs, and to hedge against adverse price changes.

18.10   AMERICAN CALL OPTIONS

If there are no dividends, the basic BSOPM values American calls as well as European calls. The reason for this is that absent dividends, we know that rational investors will not exercise American call options early. If the underlying asset does pay dividends, however, there are several methods of estimating the value of an American call. These include the following:

1. The BOPM
2. Pseudo-American call valuation model
3. Roll–Geske–Whaley compound option model
4. Numerical methods and simulation

We have already covered the BOPM (Chapter 17). The BOPM provides estimates as accurate as those of methods 3 and 4 at no greater effort or computer time. Refer to Jarrow and Turnbull (2000, pp. 257–258), and Hull (2000, Appendix 11B) to learn about the Roll–Geske–Whaley model. Chapter 16 of Hull (2000) and Part Six of Wilmott (1998) cover numerical methods and simulation. Here, we will discuss only the pseudo-American approximation model.

18.10.1 Pseudo-American Call Model

Recall that an American call will be exercised before expiration on a day before the underlying stock trades ex-dividend, if at all. Suppose there are two ex-dividend days before expiration, $t1$ and $t2$:

As with the discrete dividend pricing model for European options (see Section 18.5.1), we assume that we can decompose today's stock value into two components: a riskless component that equals the present value of the dividends at times $t1$ and $t2$, and a risky component that consists of the present value of all dividends after time T.

Suppose you knew that the call was going to be exercised immediately before time $t1$, that is, at time $t1 - \varepsilon$ (ε represents an instant). Then the life of the option is only from time 0 to time $t1$. Although the call exerciser pays $\$K$ for the stock at time $t1 - \varepsilon$, she also will immediately receive the dividend, div1. Moreover, by owning the stock at time $t1 - \varepsilon$, she will also be entitled to receive the present value of the second dividend, $\text{div}2(1+r)^{-(t2-t1)}$. Thus, define the following values:

$$S^* = S - PV(\text{divs}) = S - \text{div}(1+r)^{-t1} - \text{div}2(1+r)^{-t2}$$

$$K^* = K - \text{div}1 - \text{div}2(1+r)^{-(t2-t1)}$$

$$T^* = t1$$

To find the value of this option, which we will refer to as C_S (S stands for "short"), substitute the S^* for S, K^* for K, and T^* for T into the BSOPM.

Suppose instead that you knew that the call was going to be exercised just before the second dividend, that is, at time $t2 - \varepsilon$. Now, the exerciser pays $\$K$ for the stock, and she will immediately receive the dividend, div2. Define:

$$K^{**} = K - \text{div}2$$

$$T^{**} = t2$$

To find the value of this option, denoted as C_M (M stands for "medium"), substitute S^* for S, K^{**} for K, and T^{**} for T, into the BSOPM.

Finally, suppose you knew that the option would not be exercised early. Then the value of the option equals the value of a European call on a dividend-paying stock expiring at time T. As explained in Section 18.5.1., such a call can be valued by substituting S^* into the basic BSOPM. Refer to this option as C_L (L stands for "long").

EXAMPLE 18.7 Suppose the call in the example of Section 18.5.1. was American. Because there is only one ex-dividend date, we need consider only the values of a short-lived option C_S and a long-lived option C_L. The example in Section 18.5.1 provides the value of C_L: $4.298. The value for C_S is computed as follows:

$S = 44$

$K = 40$

$r = 0.08$/year

$T = 67$ days = time until expiration day

$\sigma = 0.3$/year

A dividend of $1.10 will be paid 39 days from today.

$S^* = 44 - 1.10e^{-0.08(0.10685)} = 44 - 1.091 = 42.909$

$K^* = 40 - 1.1 = 38.90$

$T^* = 39/365 = 0.10685$ year

$$d_1 = \frac{\ln(S^*/K^*) + (r + \sigma^2/2)T^*}{\sigma\sqrt{T^*}} = \frac{\ln(42.909/38.9) + [0.08 + 1/2(0.09)]0.10685}{0.30\sqrt{0.10685}}$$

$$= \frac{\ln(1.10306) + 0.0134}{(0.30)(0.3269)} = \frac{0.098087 + 0.013356}{0.098064} = 1.13644$$

$N(d_1) = 0.8721$

$d_2 = d_1 - \sigma\sqrt{T^*} = 1.13644 - 0.30\sqrt{0.10685} = 1.13644 - 0.098064 = 1.0384$

$N(d_2) = 0.85045$

$K^* e^{-rT^*} = 38.90e^{-(0.08)(0.10685)} = 38.90 \times 0.9915 = 38.5689$

Therefore,

$$C_s = S^*N(d_1) - K^*e^{-rT^*}N(d_2) = (42.909 \times 0.8721) - (38.5689 \times 0.85045) = 4.6205.$$

You are encouraged to use the FinCAD function aaBS to check this answer. In this example, because the pseudo-American call model in Equation (18.19) states that the call will be the greater of C_S and C_L, the value of the American call is max(4.298, 4.6205), or $4.6205.

According to the pseudo-American call valuation model, the value of an American call on a dividend-paying stock is the greatest of C_S, C_M, and C_L:[23]

$$C = \max(C_S,\ C_M,\ C_L) \tag{18.19}$$

FinancialCAD offers two programs to compute the value of American options: aaBIN2 for continuous dividends and aaBINdcf for discrete dividends. If aaBINdcf is used to value the pseudo-American call option example in Section 18.10.1, a theoretical value of 4.709 is found. As predicted, the pseudo-American model underpriced this option. Figure 18.6 shows the results from aaBINdcf.

18.10.2 American Puts

Because they might be exercised early, American puts present the same valuation difficulties as American calls on dividend-paying stocks. Actually, the problem is worse, because American puts may be exercised anytime. In contrast, American calls will be exercised only just before an ex-dividend date.

Geske and Shastri (1985) discuss the factors that increase the likelihood that American puts will be exercised early. They find that American puts will most likely be exercised early immediately after an ex-dividend date. This is logical because a put holder would typically expect the stock price to decline on the ex-dividend date, so he will be inclined to wait until after the next ex-dividend date before exercising. Furthermore, some investors own the underlying stock plus protective puts. These investors will frequently wish to receive any dividends that are forthcoming.

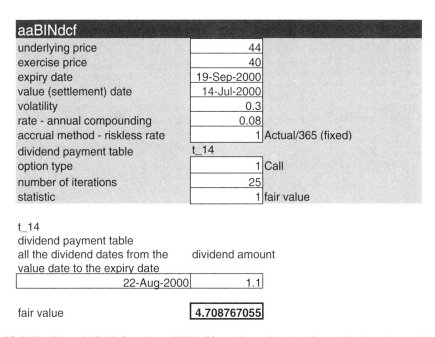

Figure 18.6 The FinancialCAD function aaBINdcf is used to value American calls when the underlying asset pays a discrete dividend.

If so, they may be inclined to wait until after the ex-date before exercising their puts. Lower interest rates and transactions costs will also discourage early exercise.

In the absence of dividends, there will always exist some critical stock price below which the holder of an American put will exercise. That critical stock price is the price at which an American put sells for exactly its intrinsic value, $K-S$. In many cases, the critical stock price is not too much below the strike price. For example, for an option with the parameters $K=\$20$, $r=10\%$, $\sigma=0.4$/year, and $T=3$ months, the critical stock price is \$14.75. At that stock price, an otherwise equivalent European put is valued at less than its intrinsic value, while the American put is worth its intrinsic value of 5.25. Figure 18.7 illustrates the pricing of an American and a European put given the foregoing parameter values.

The BSOPM works reasonably well for short term, out-of-the-money puts because the probability of early exercise is low. However, when the probability of early exercise is non trivial, several other methods exist to value American puts. These include the following:

1. The BOPM

2. Numerical methods

3. Approximation techniques

The BOPM was applied to the valuation of American puts in Section 17.4. The FinCAD functions aaBIN2 and aaBINdcf can be used to value American puts; these functions employ the binomial option pricing model. Numerical methods lie beyond the scope of this book. However, several approximation methods to value American puts exist. These methods include a technique introduced by Johnson (1983), the compound option approach of Geske and Johnson (1984), and quadratic approximations derived by MacMillan (1986) and Barone-Adesi and Whaley (1987).

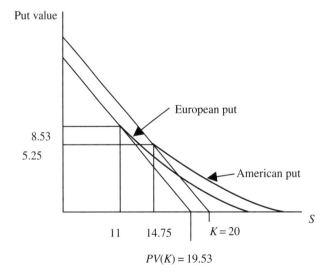

Figure 18.7 Relative pricing of an American and a European put when $K=\$20$, $T=3$, months, $r=10\%$, and $\sigma=40\%$/year. At prices below the critical stock price, $S^*=\$14.75$, the American put is worth its intrinsic value. At and below S^*, the American put will be exercised early.

18.11 Summary

This chapter provides a summary of some of the continuous time option pricing models that have been developed. The BSOPM is the easiest to use because it is a formula that can be solved by hand. However, the BSOPM is developed under critical assumptions. Figlewski (1989a, 1989b), who studies the impact of real markets (in which the cited assumptions do not hold) on option pricing, has concluded that in practice, the BSOPM will provide only guidelines for option values. Figlewski finds that option prices can lie within rather wide bounds without permitting any arbitrage profits from trading the underlying asset, bonds and the options. In particular, he cites the importance of accurately predicting the underlying asset's volatility and the problems caused by indivisibilities, brokerage fees, and bid–asked spreads. These factors make call replication (hence arbitrage) difficult. In other words, the BSOPM ignores many real considerations that also affect actual option prices. As such, the model should be used only to compare prices of different options, not to establish definitive option values.

Even when the BSOPM is used as an approximation, remember that the model is developed under a specifically assumed stochastic process for the underlying asset, and thus it may not provide accurate values for American options that are likely to be exercised early. In contrast, the more flexible BOPM can always be used to value an option on an asset that follows any type of stochastic pricing process, and also can value American options. Other option pricing models have been derived to value options when the underlying asset follows specific pricing processes. Other techniques have been developed to aid us in valuing American options. However, these techniques almost always require the use of a computer.

References

Barone-Adesi, Giovanni, and Robert E. Whaley. 1987. "Efficient Analytic Approximation of American Option Values." *Journal of Finance,* Vol. 42, No. 2, pp. 301–320.

Black, Fischer. 1976. "The Pricing of Commodity Contracts." *Journal of Financial Economics*, Vol. 3, pp. 167–179.

Black, Fischer, and Myron Scholes. 1973. "The Pricing of Options and Corporate Liabilities." *Journal of Political Economy*, Vol. 81, pp. 637–654.

Brenner, M., and M. G. Subrahmanyam. 1988. "A Simple Formula to Compute the Implied Standard Deviation." *Financial Analysts Journal*, Vol. 44, pp. 80–83.

Cho, D. Chinhyung, and Edward W. Frees. 1988. "Estimating the Volatility of Discrete Stock Prices." *Journal of Finance*, Vol. 43, No. 2, pp. 451–466.

Chriss, Neil A. 1997. *Black–Scholes and Beyond: Option Pricing Models*. New York: Irwin Professional Publishing.

Corrado, C. J., and T. W. Miller Jr., 1996a. "A Note on a Simple, Accurate Formula to Compute Implied Standard Deviations." *Journal of Banking and Finance*, Vol. 20, pp. 595–603.

Corrado, C. J., and T. W. Miller Jr. 1996b. "Efficient Option–Implied Volatility Estimators." *Journal of Futures Markets*, Vol. 16, pp. 247–272.

Cox, John C., and Mark Rubinstein. 1985. *Options Markets*. Englewood Cliffs, NJ: Prentice-Hall.

Figlewski, Stephen. 1989a. "What Does an Option Pricing Model Tell Us About Option Prices." *Financial Analysts Journal*, Vol. 45, No. 5, pp. 12–15.

Figlewski, Stephen. 1989b. "Options Arbitrage in Imperfect Markets." *Journal of Finance*, Vol. 44, No. 5, pp. 1289–1311.

Garman, Mark, and S. W. Kohlhagen. 1983. "Foreign Currency Option Values." *Journal of International Money and Finance,* Vol. 2, pp. 231–237.

Geske, Robert, and H. E. Johnson. 1984. "The American Put Option Valued Analytically." *Journal of Finance*, Vol. 39, No. 5, pp. 1511–1524.

Geske, R., and K. Shastri. 1985. "The Early Exercise of American Puts." *Journal of Banking and Finance*, Vol. 9, No. 2, pp. 207–219.

Hull, John. 2000. *Options, Futures and Other Derivative Securities*. 4th ed. Englewood Cliffs; Prentice Hall.

Jarrow, Robert A., and Andrew Rudd. 1983. *Option Pricing*. Homewood, IL: Irwin.

Jarrow, Robert A., and Stuart Turnbull. 2000. *Derivative Securities*, 2nd ed. Cincinnati, OH: South-Western.

Johnson, H. E. 1983. "An Analytic Approximation for the American Put Price." *Journal of Financial and Quantitative Analysis* Vol. 18, No. 1, pp. 141–148.

MacMillan, Lionel W. 1986 "Analytic Approximation for the American Put Option." *Advances in Futures and Options Research*, Vol. 1, Part A, pp. 119–139.

Merton, Robert. 1973. "Theory of Rational Option Pricing." *Bell Journal of Economics and Management Science,* Vol. 4, pp. 141–183.

Merville, Larry J., and Dan R. Pieptea. 1989. "Stock-Price Volatility, Mean-Reverting Diffusion, and Noise." *Journal of Financial Economics*, Vol. 24, No. 1, pp. 193–214.

Ramaswamy, Krishna, and Suresh M. Sundaresan. 1985. "The Valuation of Options on Futures Contracts." *Journal of Finance,* Vol. 40, No. 5, pp. 1319–1340.

Shimko, David. 1993. "Bounds of Probability." *Risk*, Vol. 6, No. 4, pp. 33–37.

Smith, Clifford W. 1976. "Option Pricing: A Review." *Journal of Financial Economics*, Vol. 3, pp. 3–51.

Whaley, Robert E. 1986. "Valuation of American Futures Options: Theory and Empirical Tests." *Journal of Finance,* Vol. 41, pp. 127–150.

Whaley, Robert. 1993. "Derivatives on Market Volatility: Hedging Tools Long Overdue." *Journal of Derivatives,* Vol. 1, Fall, pp. 71–84.

Wilmott, Paul. 1998. *Derivatives: The Theory and Practice of Financial Engineering*. West Sussex, England: John Wiley & Sons, Ltd.

Yang, D., and Q. Zhang. 2000. "Drift-Independent Volatility Estimation Based on High, Low, Open, and Close Prices." *Journal of Business*, Vol. 73, pp. 477–491.

Notes

[1] See Black and Scholes (1973). Many papers contributed to the development of the Black–Scholes option pricing model. See Smith (1976, footnote 3 and section 3), for a summary of several of these models.

[2] Ramaswamy and Sundaresan (1985) incorporate stochastic (i.e., randomly changing) interest rates into a stock index futures option pricing model.

[3] If a stock's returns are lognormally distributed, the log of the stock's relative prices, that is, $\ln(S_t/S_{t-1})$, is normally distributed. Note that the log of the stock's relative prices equals the stock's continuously compounded returns.

[4] It is also frequently written as $C = SN(d_1) - K(1+r)^{-T}N(d_2)$. This version assumes discrete discounting to permit computation of the present value of the strike price.

[5] See the appendix to this chapter for a table of the cumulative standard normal distribution function.

[6] See Chapter 10.

[7] However, the current price of the stock is a function of its expected return. Thus, if new information were suddenly revealed that caused investors to expect a stock to double in price (i.e., its expected return is 100%), we would expect that S would quickly be revalued to reflect its equilibrium required rate of return. The latter is a function of the stock's risk.

[8]Several numerical approximation formulas exist to compute the values of $N(d_1)$ and $N(d_2)$. For example, a handy approximation, accurate to two decimal places if $0 < d < 2.20$ is given by:

$$N(d) \approx 0.5 + \frac{d(4.4 - d)}{10}$$

For $d_1 = 0.064745$, $N(d_1)$ is approximately 0.528068. The same formula works for d_2, when $0 < d_2 < 2.20$. Thus, to compute $N(d_2)$, where $d_2 = -0.045255$, one must take advantage of the symmetry of the normal distribution. That is, $N(-d_2) = 1 - N(d_2)$. Therefore, to compute $N(-0.045255)$, we would write

$$N(-d_2) = 1 - N(d_2)$$
$$\approx 1 - \left(0.5 + \frac{0.045255(4.4 - 0.045255)}{10} \right)$$
$$\approx 0.48029$$

Chriss (1997) provides additional numerical approximations accurate to four, six, and more decimal places.

[9]A similar intuitive interpretation of $N(d_1)$ does not exist. However, the whole term, $S_0 N(d_1)$, can be interpreted as the expected value (using risk-neutral probabilities) of the stock price conditional on the stock price exceeding the exercise price times the probability that the option will expire in the money.

[10]An implicit assumption for this model is that σ is the volatility of only the portion of today's stock price that consists of the present value of dividends after expiration. The model essentially says that S consists of two components: a riskless part, which is the present value of dividends between today and expiration, and a risky part, which is S^*. The volatility of S^* is described by σ.

[11]The version is $C - P = S - PV(\text{divs}) - Ke^{-rT}$.

[12]These definitions of u, d and q are given in Cox and Rubinstein (1985, p. 200), but they are not unique. Using a slightly different technique, Jarrow and Turnbull (2000, p. 135) define the appropriate values of u, d, and q to be

$$q = \frac{1}{2}$$
$$u = e^{\left[\left(r - (\sigma^2 / 2) \right)(T/n) + \sigma \sqrt{T/n} \right]}$$
$$d = e^{\left[\left(r - (\sigma^2 / 2) \right)(T/n) - \sigma \sqrt{T/n} \right]}$$

In the example just presented in the text, if $r = 12\%$ per year, then Jarrow and Turnbull's formulas would result in $u = 1.183173$ and $d = -0.836775$. Then $S_u = Se^u$ and $S_d = Se^d$ using the Jarrow and Turnbull notation.

[13]For example, if S_{t2} is an ex-stock split price of 40.625, S_{t1}, the last price before the ex-day, is 80, and the split size is 2, then the return is:

$$\ln\left[\frac{(2)(40.625)}{80} \right] = 0.0155042$$

[14]For a discussion of these extreme value methods, see Yang and Zhang (2000). Cho and Frees (1988) develop a variance estimator that employs every observed trade during some intraday time interval. Their estimator makes use of bid and ask prices and the length of time between price changes.

[15]However, some closed-form estimators exist. For example, see Brenner and Subrahmanyam (1988) and Corrado and Miller (1996a).

[16]For a discussion of various methods, see Corrado and Miller (1996b).

[17]Plotting both effects simultaneously in a three-dimensional picture results in a **volatility surface**.

[18]Shimko (1993) offers a similar approach to account for the volatility smile.

[19]Recall that this is because the effects of the daily resettlement of futures contracts can be negated if interest rates are known.

[20]They will be worth the same only if investors perceive no chance that the futures option will ever be so deep in the money that it will be exercised early. This might occur for futures options that are very deep out of the money.

[21]One proves this equation by first assuming $C - P < (F - K)(1 + r)^{-T}$ and showing that this implies an arbitrage. Then repeat the exercise by demonstrating that arbitrage profits can be earned if $C - P > (F - K)(1 + r)^{-T}$.

[22]See Whaley (1986) for the proof of the American futures options' put–call proposition.

[23]The pseudo-American call value will usually *under* estimate the actual worth of an American call on a dividend-paying stock. This is because the owner of an American call has the option of deciding which of the three times he will exercise (if at all).

PROBLEMS

18.1 A call has 91 days until it expires. The risk-free interest rate is 8% per year. The strike price of the call is 60. The stock price is 64. The standard deviation of the stock's *monthly* returns is 0.144. Compute the value of the call using the BSOPM. Use FinCAD to compute the call's value.

18.2 Suppose that the call in Problem 18.1 is European and that 27 days from today the stock will trade ex-dividend in the amount of $1/share. Estimate the value of the call. Use FinCAD to compute the call's value.

18.3 Determine the value of a European put with the parameters stated in Problem 18.1. Check your answer with FinCAD.

18.4 Discuss the meaning of the following statement: "The Black–Scholes option pricing model is an arbitrage pricing model. If an option's price differs from the BSOPM value, a dynamic riskless arbitrage strategy is possible."

18.5 Ten monthly closing prices for a stock are given. In addition, note that on March 4 the stock traded ex-dividend in the amount of $1/share on July 10 the stock split 3 for 1, and on July 11 the stock traded ex-dividend in the amount of $0.40/share. Compute the variance of monthly returns, the standard deviation of daily returns, and the standard deviation of annual returns.

Month	Stock Price on Last Day of Month
January	80.125
February	76.625
March	79.00
April	84.50
May	86.125
June	86.125
July	29.875
August	28.5
September	31.125
October	30.0

18.6 Use the FinCAD function aaBS_iv to compute implied volatilities given the following information. Assume that no dividends are paid, the riskless interest rate is 4.75%, and there are 32 days until expiration.

Stock	Stock Price	Option Strike	Call Price
Mother Aircraft	83 $1/4$	80	4 $5/8$
		85	1 $3/4$
Generous Motors	52 $7/8$	50	3 $1/2$
		55	$7/8$

18.7 Use the BSOPM to value the following call option:

Stock price = $200

Strike price = $210

Time to expiration = 156 days

Risk-free interest rate = 11%/year

Variance of monthly stock returns = 0.02

Given your answer, what is the composition of an equivalent portfolio of stocks and bonds? What is the value of a put with the same strike price and time to expiration? Use FinCAD to check your answers.

18.8 Why might two calls on the same stock have two different implied volatilities?

18.9 When, if ever, should the BSOPM be used to value American calls? Explain your answer.

18.10 How can option traders use options on the VIX index to improve their trading profits?

18.11 As an example of the volatility smile, consider the accompanying data. The option premium column is the average bid–ask price for April 2000 S&P 500 Index options at the close of trading on April 6, 2000. Using the April 6, 2000, closing S&P 500 Index level of 1501.34, a riskless rate of 5.87%, a dividend yield of 1.12%, and 14 days to expiration, calculate the implied volatility for each strike. Then calculate a BSOPM value for all the strikes using the closest to the money IV. What do you notice about the predicted BSOPM prices and the observed prices? Plot these two data series. Finally, estimate a quadratic regression relationship like the one in Equation (18.10).

Option Strike	Option Premium
1400	109.875
1425	87.625
1445	70.875

1450	67.000
1455	62.750
1460	59.000
1465	55.250
1470	51.625
1475	48.000
1480	44.500
1485	41.250
1490	38.000
1495	35.000
1500	32.125
1520	21.250
1525	19.000
1540	13.375
1550	10.250
1555	9.000
1560	7.745
1565	6.875
1570	5.750
1575	4.313
1600	1.500

18.12 Put option A has a strike price of 40 and put option B has a strike price of 60. Both puts are American. The price of the underlying asset is 58. Which put, A or B, is the BSOPM more likely to provide an accurate estimate of value? Explain your choice.

18.13 You wish to estimate a stock's u and d to use in the BOPM. In your BOPM framework, you will divide the time to expiration of six months into 12 half-month periods ($n=12$). If your computer tells you that the standard deviation of the stock's annual returns distribution is 32%, what u and d should you use?

18.14 The price of the underlying asset of a call option is 156. The underlying asset pays a continuous dividend yield of 4%. The option has nine months until expiration. The strike price of the option is 160. The volatility of the underlying asset is 40%, and the riskless interest rate is 6%. Compute the value of the call option. Use the FinCAD functions aaBSG and aaGK to verify your answer.

18.15 You may wonder whether there is a difference between the implied volatility of a European call on a dividend-paying stock and the implied volatility of an American call on the same dividend-paying stock. FinCAD may provide a clue to this question. Use aaBSdcf_iv and aaBINdcf_iv to compute the implied volatility for the situation in which the stock sells for $60/share and it will trade ex-dividend one month from "today"; the dividend amount is $1/share. The call option itself has a strike price of 55, it expires two months from today, and the call premium is 7. The riskless interest rate is 6% for all maturities on the yield curve. Explain your results.

Partial answer: The implied volatility for the European call is 47.225%. You should work with FinCAD until you come up with this answer. Then proceed to compute the implied volatility for the American call.

18.16 Look in a recent *Wall Street Journal*. Choose an option that satisfies the following:

a. There must be a put and a call with the same underlying asset and the same strike price.

b. At least 100 puts and 100 calls must have traded.

c. The time to expiration is greater than two weeks and less than three months.

Find the ticker symbol for your underlying asset (www.cboe.com/tools/symbols/ can help you here). Find the historical volatility for your underlying asset (go to www.cboe.com/tools/historical/ and click on the most recent textfile with the data). Then use the FinCAD function aaBS to compute the theoretical fair value for your put and for your call.

18.17 A deep in-the-money European put can sell for less than its intrinsic value. An otherwise equivalent American put must sell for at least its intrinsic value. Use the FinCAD function aaBS to find the price at which a European put sells for less than its intrinsic value. Start

with an at-the-money put, with the underlying asset and the strike price both equal to 50. The option expires two months from today. The volatility of the underlying asset is 35%. The riskless interest rate is 6%. You should find, using aaBS, that the fair value of the European put is 2.602122697. Continue to work with the inputs (lines 2–11) for aaBS until you come up with this solution. *Then*, start reducing the price of the underlying asset by $1 at a time, until the fair value of the put is less than intrinsic value. Print the page at which this happens.

Partial Answer

Price of Underlying Asset	Intrinsic Value	Fair Value of Put
49	1	3.074543875
48	2	3.603770217
47	3	4.190380375

Note how the put's theoretical value is approaching its intrinsic value. Continue with this process until you find the price of the underlying asset that produces a put value that is less than its intrinsic value. *Finally*, use aaBIN to find the theoretical value of an American put, taking as the underlying asset price the one that produced a fair value for the European put that was less than its intrinsic value.

18.18 Lets check how closely put–call parity holds for index LEAPS (long-term equity appreciation security). Go to http://quote.cboe.com/QuoteTable.htm. Click on "all options and LEAPS for this underlying (complete file)". The underlying index is SPX (the S&P 500 Index option). Scroll down the resulting file (which may take a minute or two to get) until you see "XX DEC" options, where XX are the last two digits of next year (e.g., in November 1999, XX=00). Choose the at-the-money strike and record the midpoint of the bid–ask spread for the put and the call. For example, on November 19, 1999, the S&P was at 1422, so the following data were observed.

Calls				**Puts**		
	Bid	**Ask**			**Bid**	**Ask**
00 Dec 1425 SXG LQ-E	151 $^1/_4$	155 $^1/_4$		00 Dec 1425 SXG XQ-E	95 $^5/_8$	99 $^5/_8$

Use the basic put–call parity proposition, $C - P = S - PV(K)$ to determine how closely put–call parity holds when actual prices are used. Then, use the FinCAD function aaBSG to estimate the theoretical fair values for your put and your call. Note that the "holding cost" is the dividend yield on the index, which you should estimate from recent information (*Barron's* presents this information each week). Estimate the riskless interest rate from data in a recent *Wall Street Journal*. The volatility of the S&P 500 is typically about 22%. Options expire on the third riday of the month. Print the aaBSG output files.

18.19   The Black–Scholes option pricing model will often underprice the true value of American options. Explain why.

18.20   Suppose that Mr. Bull buys a call option on a December, 2001, S&P 500 futures contract. The call costs him $1750, has a strike price of 1375, and expires on the third Friday of December. The December futures price on that day is 1318.

a. At what price does Mr. Bull have the right to go long a December futures?

b. Does Mr. Bull have to hold the futures call option until expiration? Explain.

c. Suppose that before the third Friday of December, the December S&P 500 futures price rises to 1395.45 and the futures call premium rises to $2750. Mr. Bull decides to exercise the futures call option. Calculate his cash inflow.

d. On subsequent days, his long futures position is marked to market daily. Calculate Mr. Bull's cash flow if the S&P 500 futures price rockets to 1400.

18.21   Suppose the December corn futures price is 333.75. Calculate the value of an option on this futures contract, assuming $K = 350$, the riskless interest rate is 7.50%/year, there are 79 days to expiration, and $\sigma = 20\%$/year.

APPENDIX   Notes on Continuous Compounding and Stock Return Distributions

A18.1   CONTINUOUS COMPOUNDING

Suppose you have $1.00 today, and a bank pays interest of 6%, compounded annually. Then one year from today, you will have $1.06, and two years hence, you will have $1(1.06)(1.06) = \$1.1236$.

If the bank pays interest of 6%, compounded monthly, then it is paying $^1/_2$% interest each month. Thus, after one month, you will have $1.005. After two months, you will have $1(1.005)(1.005) = \$1.010025$. After 12 months, you will have $1(1.005)^{12} = \$1.06168$. Thus, a 6% interest rate, compounded monthly, provides you with a 6.168% annual rate of return. After 24 months, your original dollar will be worth $1.12716.

Define the following terms:

F = future value
P = present value
r = interest rate

m = number of times interest is compounded per year (e.g., m = 12 if interest is compounded monthly).

t = number of years

The general formula for determining the future value of a present amount, if interest is compounded is:

$$F = P\left(1 + \frac{r}{m}\right)^{mt}$$

In this example, if m = 12 and t = 2, we would have

$$F = 1\left(1 + \frac{0.06}{12}\right)^{(12)(2)} = \$1.12716$$

Interest can be compounded at smaller intervals of time. For example, interest can be compounded daily, or by the second. As m gets larger, the more frequently interest is compounded. As m approaches infinity (∞), it can be shown that

$$F = Pe^{rt} \qquad\qquad\qquad\qquad\qquad\qquad (A18.1)$$

Like π, which equals $3.1415927\ldots$, e is a specific number, namely, 2.7182818. Thus, if you deposit \$1.00 into a bank that pays 6% interest, compounded continuously, then after one year, you will have

$$F = 1e^{(0.06)(1)} = \$1.0618$$

and after two years, you will have

$$F = 1e^{(0.06)(2)} = \$1.1275$$

If your calculator has an "e^x" button, then verify that $e^{0.06} = 1.0618$ and that $e^{0.12} = 1.1275$. If your calculator has a "y^x" button verify the foregoing equation by using $y = 2.7182818$.

If you are told that you are earning $c\%$ on your money, compounded continuously, then you can compute the effective annual rate of return, $a\%$, by using this relationship:

$$e^c - 1 = a$$

For example, $e^{0.06} - 1 = 0.0618$. In other words, 6% compounded continuously is equivalent to 6.18% compounded annually. See example A18.1 for an application.

Given an annual rate of $a\%$, you can reverse the procedure to find the equivalent continuously compounded rate, $c\%$:

$e^c - 1 = a$
$\quad e^c = 1 + a$
$\ln(e^c) = \ln(1 + a)$
$\quad\quad c = \ln(1 + a)$

EXAMPLE A18.1   What is the effective annual rate that is equivalent to earning 15% compounded continuously?

Answer $e^{0.15} - 1 = 16.1834\%$.

Thus if you earn a rate of return of $a\%$ per period, finding the natural logarithm of $(1+a)$ will provide you with the equivalent continuously compounded rate of return.

If a stock rises from \$14/share to \$18/share, its rate of return is $(18-14)/14 = 0.2857143 = 28.57143\%$. Its continuously compounded rate of return is $\ln(S_{t2}/S_{t1}) = \ln(18/14) = \ln(1.2857143) = 0.2513144$. This 25.13144% continuously compounded rate of return is equivalent to an "uncompounded" rate of return of 28.57143%.

It is stated later (Section A18.2.2) that if a stock follows geometric Brownian motion, the distribution of its returns will be lognormally distributed. If returns are lognormally distributed, the log of the stock's relative prices are normally distributed. The log of relative prices are equal to the stock's continuously compounded returns.

A18.2   Stock Returns Distributions

A18.2.1   Geometric Brownian Motion

One assumption used in deriving the BSOPM is that the stock price randomly wanders through time following a price path called geometric Brownian motion. Although much of the background material necessary to understand geometric Brownian motion is mathematically quite difficult, the implications of the stock price following this particular *stochastic process* is important for a discussion of the BSOPM. Thus, what follows is a discussion that is aimed at helping users of option models decide whether the value of the underlying stock or asset moves randomly according to geometric Brownian motion or some other stochastic process.

The stochastic process that the underlying asset must follow in order to derive the BSOPM is called geometric Brownian motion, and it is defined by:[1]

$$\frac{\Delta S}{S} = \mu \Delta t + \sigma \Delta z$$

(A18.2)

where

$\Delta S/S = (S_{t+\Delta t} - S_t)/S_t =$ rate of return on the stock

$\mu =$ expected (constant) return on the stock per unit of time

$\Delta t =$ a unit of time

$\sigma =$ the (constant) standard deviation of the stock's return during the unit of time

$z =$ a normally distributed random variable with a mean of zero and a variance of t.

The random variable z, is called a Wiener process. Over small intervals of time, changes in z, Δz, are normally distributed random variables, with $E(\Delta z) = 0$, and $\text{var}(\Delta z) = \Delta t$. The covariance of any two Δz is zero; in other words, $\text{cov}(\Delta z_{t2}, \Delta z_{t1}) = 0$.

Note that Δz is just a normally distributed random variable, with a mean of zero and a variance of Δt. Suppose Δt is one day. We draw a value of Δz out of a probability distribution that has a mean of zero and a variance of one. If, instead, we are interested in Δz over one week, and Δt is one day, then Δz is drawn out of a probability distribution having a mean of zero and a variance of 7 (because there are seven days in a week). The mean is always zero and the variance is proportional to time. In addition, any two realizations of Δz are independent.

EXAMPLE A18.2 Suppose Δt is one day. A stock has an expected return of $\mu = 0.0005$ per day.[2] The standard deviation of the stock's daily return distribution is 0.0261725.[3] The return generating process is such that each day the return consists of a nonstochastic component, 0.05%, and a random component. The latter equals the stock's daily standard deviation times the realization of Δz, which is drawn from a normal probability distribution with a mean of zero and a variance of one.

Table A18.1 depicts one particular realization of the stochastic process driving this stock's price over a 60-day period. The first column is the day number. The second column is the realization of Δz, a random number drawn from a normal distribution with a mean of zero and a variance of one. The third column illustrates how the stock price would move if there were no stochastic component to its return. That is, each day, the stock's return is 0.05%. The fourth column gives the stochastic component, $\sigma \Delta z$, where $\sigma = 0.0261725$/day. The daily return, R, is $\mu \Delta t + \sigma \Delta z$. Column five lists each day's stock price, where $S(T) = S(T-1)[1+R]$.

TABLE A18.1 An Example of a Stock Price Path Over a 60-day Period Driven by Geometric Brownian Motion

Day	Δz	Nonstochastic Trend Price $S(T) = S(T-1)[1.0005]$	Stochastic Component $(0.0261725)\Delta z$	$S(T) = S(T-1)[1.0+R]$ $R = \mu \Delta t + \sigma \Delta z$ $\Delta t = 1$ Day
0		1.000000		1.000000
1	−2.48007	1.000500	−0.064910	0.935590
2	−0.87537	1.001000	−0.022911	0.914623
3	−0.80587	1.001501	−0.021092	0.895789
4	−1.03927	1.002002	−0.027200	0.871871
5	0.10523	1.002503	0.002754	0.874709
6	0.66993	1.003004	0.017534	0.890483
7	−0.21137	1.003505	−0.005532	0.886002
8	2.19733	1.004007	0.057510	0.937398
9	−0.82807	1.004509	−0.021673	0.917551
10	0.58783	1.005011	0.015385	0.932126
11	−1.25487	1.005514	−0.032843	0.901978
12	−0.26827	1.006017	−0.007021	0.896096
13	1.28023	1.006520	0.033507	0.926569
14	0.56773	1.007023	0.014859	0.940800
15	−0.03447	1.007526	−0.000902	0.940422
16	1.29413	1.008030	0.033871	0.972745
17	0.06143	1.008534	0.001608	0.974795
18	0.79553	1.009038	0.020821	0.995578
19	1.66593	1.009543	0.043601	1.039485
20	−0.44497	1.010048	−0.011646	1.027899
21	−0.03137	1.010553	−0.000821	1.027569
22	0.36873	1.011058	0.009650	1.037999

TABLE A18.1 Continued

Day	Δz	Nonstochastic Trend Price $S(T)=S(T-1)[1.0005]$	Stochastic Component $(0.0261725)\Delta z$	$S(T)=S(T-1)[1.0+R]$ $R=\mu\Delta t+\sigma\Delta z$ $\Delta t=1$ Day
23	−0.20397	1.011563	−0.005338	1.032977
24	−0.13357	1.012069	−0.003496	1.029882
25	0.34653	1.012575	0.009069	1.039737
26	0.20593	1.013082	0.005390	1.045861
27	−0.04727	1.013588	−0.001237	1.045090
28	−0.64737	1.014095	−0.016943	1.027905
29	−0.41207	1.014602	−0.010785	1.017333
30	−0.06837	1.015109	−0.001790	1.016021
31	−0.20927	1.015617	−0.005477	1.010964
32	−0.55077	1.016125	−0.014415	0.996897
33	−0.38087	1.016633	−0.009968	0.987458
34	0.27863	1.017141	0.007292	0.995152
35	−0.44457	1.017650	−0.011636	0.984071
36	−1.07717	1.018158	−0.028192	0.956819
37	0.17163	1.018667	0.004492	0.961596
38	0.50863	1.019177	0.013312	0.974877
39	0.78913	1.019686	0.020653	0.995499
40	−0.49757	1.020196	−0.013023	0.983033
41	1.32373	1.020706	0.034645	1.017582
42	0.83613	1.021217	0.021884	1.040359
43	−1.82237	1.021727	−0.047696	0.991258
44	−0.38177	1.022238	−0.009992	0.981849
45	−1.17227	1.022749	−0.030681	0.952215
46	1.26993	1.023261	0.033237	0.984341
47	0.35793	1.023772	0.009368	0.994054
48	1.84673	1.024284	0.048333	1.042597
49	−1.35187	1.024796	−0.035382	1.006229
50	−0.76187	1.025309	−0.019940	0.986668
51	−0.47267	1.025821	−0.012371	0.974955
52	−0.22147	1.026334	−0.005797	0.969791
53	−1.20347	1.026847	−0.031498	0.939730
54	0.41413	1.027361	0.010839	0.950385
55	−0.78127	1.027875	−0.020448	0.931427
56	1.59143	1.028388	0.041652	0.970688
57	0.44953	1.028903	0.011765	0.982594
58	1.48893	1.029417	0.038969	1.021376
59	−0.72487	1.029932	−0.018972	1.002509
60	−0.50337	1.030447	−0.013175	0.989803

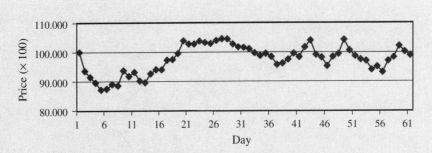

Figure A18.1 A stock price following geometric Brownian motion.

Figure A18.1 shows how the stock price (times 100) in column 5 of Table A18.1 changes in value over the 60-day period. The graph very much looks like a typical stock's price movements, doesn't it?

A18.2.2   Lognormal Stock Returns

You may have noticed that the three returns distributions shown earlier (Figure 18.1a–c) are not normally distributed. In fact, one result of the stock following a geometric Brownian motion is that returns are "lognormally" distributed. Specifying that returns are lognormally distributed is equivalent to saying that the natural logarithm of the relative prices, $\ln(S_{t2}/S_{t1})$, are normally distributed.

Lognormal returns are realistic for two reasons. First, if returns are lognormally distributed, then the lowest possible return in any period is –100%. In contrast, if returns are normally distributed, there is some probability that returns will be less than –100%. The difference between normally distributed returns and lognormally distributed returns is illustrated in Figure A18.2.

If a security's return during a period is –100%, the terminal stock price at the end of the period, S_{t2}, is zero. Then, $\ln(S_{t2}/S_{t1})=\ln(1+R)=\ln(0)=-\infty$, which is the "left tail" of any normal distribution. But the left tail of a lognormal distribution is anchored at 0 when R, the return, is -100%.

Second, lognormal returns distributions are "positively skewed." Positive skewness is characterized by the extended right tail in Figures 18.1 and A18.2. This is realistic because while the lowest return in any period is –100%, the highest return will likely be in excess of 100% when measured over a year. Thus, a realistic depiction of a stock's returns distribution would have a minimum return of –100% and a maximum return well beyond +100%. The longer the time interval under consideration, the more valid the latter statement becomes. Therefore, annual returns will be more positively skewed than monthly returns, and monthly returns will be more skewed than daily returns. Returns distributions will not be symmetric. They will be skewed to the right.

There is one last point to consider. It was stated that the natural logarithm of a stock's relative prices will be normally distributed if the stock follows the pricing process we are describing. The natural logarithm of relative prices, $\ln(S_{t2}/S_{t1})=\ln(1+R)$, is a continuously compounded return. In other words, if a stock price follows a geometric Brownian motion, its continuously compounded returns are normally distributed. Its returns measured over any longer interval of time are lognormally distributed.

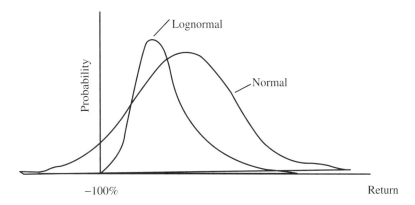

Figure A18.2 Lognormal and normal probability distributions.

To summarize, then, three important concepts of this section are:

1. An important assumption of the BSOPM is that the stock price follows a geometric Brownian motion.
2. As a result of this assumed stock price behavior, returns over a given interval of time are lognormally distributed and continuously compounded returns are normally distributed.
3. If the stock's price follows a geometric Brownian motion, its returns variance is proportional to time and the standard deviation of its returns is proportional to the square root of time (see Section 18.1.3).

Assuming that geometric Brownian motion governs the movements of the underlying stock price is important. In particular, in some instances the geometric Brownian motion is restrictive. For example, in the geometric Brownian motion process, the stock price changes by just a little bit every instant. While this is an adequate description for most stocks at most times, it does not fit the stock's situation in all cases. For instance, suppose a stock is a target of an unfriendly takeover that is being resisted. Suppose the stock price is midway between the offer price and the stock price before the tender offer. If the acquisition is successful, it is likely that the stock price will jump, instantaneously, by $10/share. However, if the target defends itself, it is likely that the stock price will decline by $5/share. Under these circumstances, the stock price would be well described as usually following a continuous diffusion process. However, at random times, the stock price "jumps" a random amount up or down. If there is a nontrivial probability of a jump in the price of the underlying asset, the BSOPM may not be adequate when valuing options on that asset.[4]

Another problem is that in the geometric Brownian motion model, the variance of the stock's returns is assumed to be constant regardless of the stock's price. However, there is considerable evidence that stock prices are more volatile at lower prices than at higher prices. In addition, considerable research has concluded that returns variances themselves change randomly over time; that is, they are stochastic. This seems reasonable, because both the nature of the firm and its environment randomly change over time. The variance of a stock's returns distribution will likely be greater on a day that an earnings report is released, a dividend announcement made, or a government statistic on the economy released, than on other days. Several models have been developed to price options under conditions of stochastic volatility. These papers also cite considerable research that supports, both theoretically and empirically, the idea that stock returns variances randomly change over time.[5]

A18.3 CUMULATIVE PROBABILITIES FOR THE STANDARD NORMAL DISTRIBUTION

TABLE A18.2a Cumulative Probabilities for the Standard Normal Distribution: Negative Values of z

z	Second Digit of z									
	0.00	0.01	0.02	0.03	0.04	0.05	0.06	0.07	0.08	0.09
−3.5	0.0002	0.0002	0.0002	0.0002	0.0002	0.0002	0.0002	0.0002	0.0002	0.0002
−3.4	0.0003	0.0003	0.0003	0.0003	0.0003	0.0003	0.0003	0.0003	0.0003	0.0002
−3.3	0.0005	0.0005	0.0005	0.0004	0.0004	0.0004	0.0004	0.0004	0.0004	0.0003
−3.2	0.0007	0.0007	0.0006	0.0006	0.0006	0.0006	0.0006	0.0005	0.0005	0.0005
−3.1	0.0010	0.0009	0.0009	0.0009	0.0008	0.0008	0.0008	0.0008	0.0007	0.0007
−3.0	0.0013	0.0013	0.0013	0.0012	0.0012	0.0011	0.0011	0.0011	0.0010	0.0010
−2.9	0.0019	0.0018	0.0018	0.0017	0.0016	0.0016	0.0015	0.0015	0.0014	0.0014
−2.8	0.0026	0.0025	0.0024	0.0023	0.0023	0.0022	0.0021	0.0021	0.0020	0.0019
−2.7	0.0035	0.0034	0.0033	0.0032	0.0031	0.0030	0.0029	0.0028	0.0027	0.0026
−2.6	0.0047	0.0045	0.0044	0.0043	0.0041	0.0040	0.0039	0.0038	0.0037	0.0036
−2.5	0.0062	0.0060	0.0059	0.0057	0.0055	0.0054	0.0052	0.0051	0.0049	0.0048
−2.4	0.0082	0.0080	0.0078	0.0075	0.0073	0.0071	0.0069	0.0068	0.0066	0.0064
−2.3	0.0107	0.0104	0.0102	0.0099	0.0096	0.0094	0.0091	0.0089	0.0087	0.0084
−2.2	0.0139	0.0136	0.0132	0.0129	0.0125	0.0122	0.0119	0.0116	0.0113	0.0110
−2.1	0.0179	0.0174	0.0170	0.0166	0.0162	0.0158	0.0154	0.0150	0.0146	0.0143
−2.0	0.0228	0.0222	0.0217	0.0212	0.0207	0.0202	0.0197	0.0192	0.0188	0.0183
−1.9	0.0287	0.0281	0.0274	0.0268	0.0262	0.0256	0.0250	0.0244	0.0239	0.0233
−1.8	0.0359	0.0351	0.0344	0.0336	0.0329	0.0322	0.0314	0.0307	0.0301	0.0294
−1.7	0.0446	0.0436	0.0427	0.0418	0.0409	0.0401	0.0392	0.0384	0.0375	0.0367
−1.6	0.0548	0.0537	0.0526	0.0516	0.0505	0.0495	0.0485	0.0475	0.0465	0.0455
−1.5	0.0668	0.0655	0.0643	0.0630	0.0618	0.0606	0.0594	0.0582	0.0571	0.0559
−1.4	0.0808	0.0793	0.0778	0.0764	0.0749	0.0735	0.0721	0.0708	0.0694	0.0681
−1.3	0.0968	0.0951	0.0934	0.0918	0.0901	0.0885	0.0869	0.0853	0.0838	0.0823
−1.2	0.1151	0.1131	0.1112	0.1093	0.1075	0.1056	0.1038	0.1020	0.1003	0.0985
−1.1	0.1357	0.1335	0.1314	0.1292	0.1271	0.1251	0.1230	0.1210	0.1190	0.1170
−1.0	0.1587	0.1562	0.1539	0.1515	0.1492	0.1469	0.1446	0.1423	0.1401	0.1379
−0.9	0.1841	0.1814	0.1788	0.1762	0.1736	0.1711	0.1685	0.1660	0.1635	0.1611
−0.8	0.2119	0.2090	0.2061	0.2033	0.2005	0.1977	0.1949	0.1922	0.1894	0.1867
−0.7	0.2420	0.2389	0.2358	0.2327	0.2296	0.2266	0.2236	0.2206	0.2177	0.2148
−0.6	0.2743	0.2709	0.2676	0.2643	0.2611	0.2578	0.2546	0.2514	0.2483	0.2451
−0.5	0.3085	0.3050	0.3015	0.2981	0.2946	0.2912	0.2877	0.2843	0.2810	0.2776
−0.4	0.3446	0.3409	0.3372	0.3336	0.3300	0.3264	0.3228	0.3192	0.3156	0.3121
−0.3	0.3821	0.3783	0.3745	0.3707	0.3669	0.3632	0.3594	0.3557	0.3520	0.3483
−0.2	0.4207	0.4168	0.4129	0.4090	0.4052	0.4013	0.3974	0.3936	0.3897	0.3859
−0.1	0.4602	0.4562	0.4522	0.4483	0.4443	0.4404	0.4364	0.4325	0.4286	0.4247
−0.0	0.5000	0.4960	0.4920	0.4880	0.4840	0.4801	0.4761	0.4721	0.4681	0.4641

Example: $N(-0.22) = 0.4129$

TABLE A18.2b   Cumulative Probability for the Standard Normal Distribution: Positive Values of z

z	0.00	0.01	0.02	0.03	0.04	0.05	0.06	0.07	0.08	0.09
0.0	0.5000	0.5040	0.5080	0.5120	0.5160	0.5199	0.5239	0.5279	0.5319	0.5359
0.1	0.5398	0.5438	0.5478	0.5517	0.5557	0.5596	0.5636	0.5675	0.5714	0.5753
0.2	0.5793	0.5832	0.5871	0.5910	0.5948	0.5987	0.6026	0.6064	0.6103	0.6141
0.3	0.6179	0.6217	0.6255	0.6293	0.6331	0.6368	0.6406	0.6443	0.6480	0.6517
0.4	0.6554	0.6591	0.6628	0.6664	0.6700	0.6736	0.6772	0.6808	0.6844	0.6879
0.5	0.6915	0.6950	0.6985	0.7019	0.7054	0.7088	0.7123	0.7157	0.7190	0.7224
0.6	0.7257	0.7291	0.7324	0.7357	0.7389	0.7422	0.7454	0.7486	0.7517	0.7549
0.7	0.7580	0.7611	0.7642	0.7673	0.7704	0.7734	0.7764	0.7794	0.7823	0.7852
0.8	0.7881	0.7910	0.7939	0.7967	0.7995	0.8023	0.8051	0.8078	0.8106	0.8133
0.9	0.8159	0.8186	0.8212	0.8238	0.8264	0.8289	0.8315	0.8340	0.8365	0.8389
1.0	0.8413	0.8438	0.8461	0.8485	0.8508	0.8531	0.8554	0.8577	0.8599	0.8621
1.1	0.8643	0.8665	0.8686	0.8708	0.8729	0.8749	0.8770	0.8790	0.8810	0.8830
1.2	0.8849	0.8869	0.8888	0.8907	0.8925	0.8944	0.8962	0.8980	0.8997	0.9015
1.3	0.9032	0.9049	0.9066	0.9082	0.9099	0.9115	0.9131	0.9147	0.9162	0.9177
1.4	0.9192	0.9207	0.9222	0.9236	0.9251	0.9265	0.9279	0.9292	0.9306	0.9319
1.5	0.9332	0.9345	0.9357	0.9370	0.9382	0.9394	0.9406	0.9418	0.9429	0.9441
1.6	0.9452	0.9463	0.9474	0.9484	0.9495	0.9505	0.9515	0.9525	0.9535	0.9545
1.7	0.9554	0.9564	0.9573	0.9582	0.9591	0.9599	0.9608	0.9616	0.9625	0.9633
1.8	0.9641	0.9649	0.9656	0.9664	0.9671	0.9678	0.9686	0.9693	0.9699	0.9706
1.9	0.9713	0.9719	0.9726	0.9732	0.9738	0.9744	0.9750	0.9756	0.9761	0.9767
2.0	0.9772	0.9778	0.9783	0.9788	0.9793	0.9798	0.9803	0.9808	0.9812	0.9817
2.1	0.9821	0.9826	0.9830	0.9834	0.9838	0.9842	0.9846	0.9850	0.9854	0.9857
2.2	0.9861	0.9864	0.9868	0.9871	0.9875	0.9878	0.9881	0.9884	0.9887	0.9890
2.3	0.9893	0.9896	0.9898	0.9901	0.9904	0.9906	0.9909	0.9911	0.9913	0.9916
2.4	0.9918	0.9920	0.9922	0.9925	0.9927	0.9929	0.9931	0.9932	0.9934	0.9936
2.5	0.9938	0.9940	0.9941	0.9943	0.9945	0.9946	0.9948	0.9949	0.9951	0.9952
2.6	0.9953	0.9955	0.9956	0.9957	0.9959	0.9960	0.9961	0.9962	0.9963	0.9964
2.7	0.9965	0.9966	0.9967	0.9968	0.9969	0.9970	0.9971	0.9972	0.9973	0.9974
2.8	0.9974	0.9975	0.9976	0.9977	0.9977	0.9978	0.9979	0.9979	0.9980	0.9981
2.9	0.9981	0.9982	0.9982	0.9983	0.9984	0.9984	0.9985	0.9985	0.9986	0.9986
3.0	0.9987	0.9987	0.9987	0.9988	0.9988	0.9989	0.9989	0.9989	0.9990	0.9990
3.1	0.9990	0.9991	0.9991	0.9991	0.9992	0.9992	0.9992	0.9992	0.9993	0.9993
3.2	0.9993	0.9993	0.9994	0.9994	0.9994	0.9994	0.9994	0.9995	0.9995	0.9995
3.3	0.9995	0.9995	0.9995	0.9996	0.9996	0.9996	0.9996	0.9996	0.9996	0.9997
3.4	0.9997	0.9997	0.9997	0.9997	0.9997	0.9997	0.9997	0.9997	0.9997	0.9998
3.5	0.9998	0.9998	0.9998	0.9998	0.9998	0.9998	0.9998	0.9998	0.9998	0.9998

Example: $N(0.64) = 0.7389$

References

Ball, Clifford A., and Walter N. Torous. 1985. "On Jumps in Common Stock Prices and Their Impact on Call Option Pricing." *Journal of Finance,* Vol. 40, No. 1, pp. 155–173.

Cox, John C., and Stephen A. Ross. 1976. "The Valuation of Options for Alternative Stochastic Processes." *Journal of Financial Economics,* Vol. 3, No. 1/2, pp. 145–166.

Cox, John C., Stephen A. Ross, and Mark Rubinstein. 1979. "Option Pricing: A Simplified Approach." *Journal of Financial Economics,* Vol. 7, pp. 229–263.

Finucane, Thomas J. 1989. "Black–Scholes Approximations of Call Option Prices with Stochastic Volatilities: A Note." *Journal of Financial and Quantitative Analysis,* Vol. 24, No. 4, pp. 527–532.

Heston, S. 1993. "A Closed-Form Solution for Options With Stochastic Volatility with Application to Bond and Currency Options." *Review of Financial Studies,* Vol. 6, pp. 327–343.

Hull, John, and Alan White. 1987. "The Pricing of Options on Assets with Stochastic Volatilities." *Journal of Finance*, Vol. 42, No. 2, pp. 281–300.

Jarrow, Robert A., and Andrew Rudd. 1983, *Option Pricing.* Homewood, IL: Irwin.

Johnson, Herb, and David Shanno. 1987. "Option Pricing When the Variance Is Changing." *Journal of Financial and Quantitative Analysis*, Vol. 22, No. 2, pp. 143–151.

Merton, Robert C. (1976a). "Option Pricing When Underlying Stock Returns Are Discontinuous." *Journal of Financial Economics,* Vol. 3, pp. 125–144.

Merton, Robert C. (1976b). "The Impact on Option Pricing of Specification Error in the Underlying Stock Price Returns." *Journal of Finance*, Vol. 31, No. 2, pp. 333–350.

Scott, Louis O. 1987. "Option Pricing When the Variance Changes Randomly: Theory, Estimation and an Application." *Journal of Financial and Quantitative Analysis*, Vol. 22, No.4, pp. 419–438.

Wiggins, James B. 1987. Option Values Under Stochastic Volatility: Theory and Empirical Estimates. *Journal of Financial Economics*, Vol. 19, No. 2, pp. 351–372.

Wilmott, Paul, 1998. *Derivatives. The Theory and Practice of Financial Engineering.* West Sussex, England: John Wiley & Sons, Ltd.

Notes

[1] Actually, the stochastic process exists in continuous time. Thus, Δt is an "instant", μ is the instantaneous expected rate of return, σ is the standard deviation during one instant of time, and the returns process is:

$$\frac{dS}{S} = \mu dt + \sigma dz$$

[2] A return of 0.0005/day is 0.05%/day. If this were compounded over 365 days, the expected annual return would be $(1.0005)^{365} - 1 = 0.20016$, or 20.016% per year.

[3] If the standard deviation of the stock's daily returns is 0.0261725, the variance of the stock's daily returns is 0.000685, the variance of the stock's annual returns is $(365)(0.000685) = 0.250025$, and the standard deviation of the stock's annual returns is $(0.250025)^{0.5} = (0.0261725)(365)^{0.5} = 0.500025$.

[4] For additional detailed discussions on jump process option pricing models, see Cox and Ross (1976), Merton (1976a, 1976b), Cox, Ross and Rubinstein (1979), Jarrow and Rudd (1983, Chapter 12), Ball and Torous (1985), and Wilmott (1998, Chapter 26).

[5] For additional detailed discussions on stochastic volatility models, see Hull and White (1987), Johnson and Shanno (1987), Scott (1987), Wiggins (1987), Finucane (1989), Heston (1993), and Wilmott (1998, Chapter 23).

CHAPTER 19

Using Options for Risk Management

Volume in option trading continues to remain robust. In this chapter, we focus on the details of how options provide price insurance. That is, how can a risk manager protect an underlying portfolio from adverse price changes using options? As you learned in earlier chapters, options can be used to limit downside risk while still allowing upside participation. These results can be provided by either the fiduciary call strategy (purchase calls and debt instruments) or the protective put strategy (the owner of an asset buys puts). Also, options can be used to limit upside risk while reaping any benefits from declines in the price of an underlying asset. This can be achieved by buying calls to provide insurance against a short position.

Also in this chapter, we will present some necessary technical details concerning how option values change as the factors that influence option values (S, K, r, T, σ) change. Risk managers must be aware of these details to use options effectively. Although option contracts are indispensable tools for risk management, market participants use options for other reasons. These include the following.

- *Options can generate additional cash flow*. The sale of covered calls provides additional cash flow. Of course, the writer of a covered call also hopes that the underlying asset price does not rise much above the strike price. Writing naked puts is a revenue-providing strategy that is used as a substitute for placing limit orders to buy an asset.

- *Options can be used to exploit tax-related situations*. Writing a covered call as a substitute for the outright sale of the asset might defer a capital gain, or stretch a short-term gain into a long-term gain. Many other tax-driven strategies exist, but users should always obtain an opinion from tax accountants or tax attorneys before attempting to use options to reduce taxes.

- *Options provide leverage*. Because the purchase of a call is equivalent to buying the underlying asset and borrowing, the leverage provided by options may exceed that available to many market participants who purchase only the underlying asset. The initial premium of an option is generally only a small fraction of the cost of buying the underlying asset.

- *Options can circumvent short selling difficulties*. If an asset cannot be easily sold short, the purchase of a put may be the most efficient method for generating profits from a price decline in the underlying asset.

An important question every risk manager faces is whether to buy options to insure against adverse price moves or to use forwards, futures, or swaps to hedge against price risks. Unfortunately, there is no easy answer to this question. However, here are some important considerations.

When options are used to buy insurance, there is an initial cash outflow, the option premium. This is often a negative factor in the decision to use options to manage risk. By contrast, forwards, futures, and swaps can often be used with no initial cash outflow. Recall that forwards, futures, and swaps can often lock in a price. That is, these contracts can sometimes reduce price uncertainty to zero. However, this might be a negative factor in the decision to use these derivatives to manage risk. Using forwards, futures, and swaps instead of options means that in 50% of the cases, the risk manager will be likely to regret having hedged a spot position. This occurs when an unhedged position would have benefited from the subsequent price change. When used as insurance, options hedge only downside risk. The insurer will capture the upside, less the cost of insurance (the option premium). These differences are illustrated in Figure 19.1 for the situation in which a firm has a long position in the underlying asset and faces the risk that prices will fall.[1]

In Figure 19.1a, the sale of futures or forwards hedges the long position in the underlying asset. The result is the horizontal line with a zero change in profit, regardless of price changes. Figure 19.1b illustrates how the purchase of a protective put insures against downside risk, but allows for profitable participation should the price of the underlying asset rise. Thus, risk managers must understand the trade-off of having to *pay* for insurance vs the alternative of hedging, which has zero initial cost. Given this trade-off, the risk manager must next consider his beliefs about the direction of prices and his tolerance for taking risks of adverse price movements.

Suppose the policy of a firm is to have a continuous hedging strategy.[2] This firm's risk manager expects prices to move in a way that would actually benefit the firm if it was unhedged. This risk manager may wish to use options, so that the firm will benefit from the beneficial subsequent price change. Under the situation in Figure 19.1, she might want to buy the protective put. This will cost an initial put premium, but if she is correct and prices do rise (by an amount large enough to offset the cost of the put), the firm will be better off than it would have been, had it hedged by selling forwards or futures.

Furthermore, the risk manager is not bound to just one strategy. It is possible to initially buy the put and, if prices rise, later sell the put (at a loss), and sell futures or forwards to lock in the value of the spot position at a higher price.

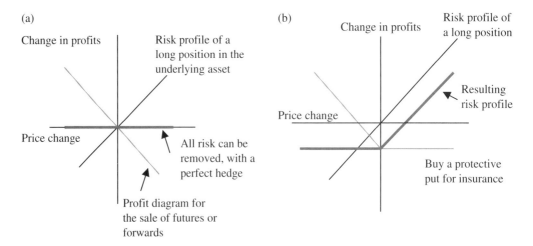

Figure 19.1 Profit diagrams illustrate the difference between (a) hedging and (b) insurance.

Next we discuss "the Greeks," which refer to the analysis of how an option's value changes if there is a change in one of the factors that determines its value (σ, S, r, T, or K). These sensitivities are determined by taking the partial derivative of the Black–Scholes option pricing model (BSOPM) with respect to one of these determinants of value, and each result has traditionally been assigned a Greek letter. Understanding these measures is extremely important for everyone who uses options, particularly those who use them in risk management programs.

19.1   THE GREEKS

A risk manager cannot make a well-informed decision to use options without knowing how option values change as the factors that influence those values change. This knowledge is necessary for the risk manager to understand how the value of a portfolio consisting of the underlying asset and options will change during the life of the hedge.

The theoretical call value determined by the BSOPM can be partially differentiated with respect to each of its five parameters, K, T, r, σ, and S.[3] The results are formulas that predict how much a call option value will change if only *one* input parameter changes by a small amount, all else equal. That is, no other input parameter values are allowed to change. Economists call such an analysis "comparative statics," or sensitivities. Because each of the sensitivities is commonly known by a Greek letter, the BSOPM comparative statics are also known as "the Greeks." Each of the Greeks has a "sign." A positive sign means that the option value will increase when the factor increases, all else constant. A negative sign means that the option value will decrease when that factor increases, all else equal. To begin, let us look at the Greeks for call options.

19.1.1   The Greeks for Black–Scholes Calls (a.k.a. "No-Name," Theta, Rho, Vega, Delta, and Gamma)

The formulas for the Greeks for Black–Scholes calls are as follows.[4]

Partial Derivative Notation	Greek Letter	Brief Interpretation	Formula	Sign
$\dfrac{\partial C}{\partial K}$		By how much will a call price change, given a change in the strike price?	$-e^{-rT}N(d_2)$	<0
$\dfrac{\partial C}{\partial T}$	theta[5] (θ)	By how much will a call price change, given a change in the time to expiration?	$Ke^{-rT}\left[\dfrac{\sigma N'(d_2)}{2\sqrt{T}} + rN(d_2)\right]$	>0
$\dfrac{\partial C}{\partial r}$	rho (ρ)	By how much will a call price change, given a change in the riskless interest rate?	$TKe^{-rT}N(d_2)$	>0
$\dfrac{\partial C}{\partial \sigma}$	vega (v)	By how much will a call's value change, given a change	$S\sqrt{T}N'(d_1)$	>0

in the volatility of the
underlying asset?

$\dfrac{\partial C}{\partial S}$	delta (Δ)	Hedge ratio: By how much will a call price change given a change in the value of the underlying asset?	$N(d_1)$	>0, but $0 \le \Delta \le 1$
$\dfrac{\partial \Delta}{\partial S}=\dfrac{\partial^2 C}{\partial S^2}$	gamma (Γ)	By how much will a call's delta change, given a change in the price of the underlying asset?	$\dfrac{N'(d_1)}{S\sigma\sqrt{T}}$	>0

In these formulas, note that there are terms for $N(d_1)$ and for $N'(d_1)$, where $N'(d)$ is the height of the standard normal density at d (and d can represent any value of d_1 or d_2). It can also be thought of as the incremental change in the area under standard normal distribution at d. It is given by

$$N'(d) = \frac{\partial N(d)}{\partial d} = \frac{e^{-d^2/2}}{\sqrt{2\Pi}}$$

Recall that the normal distribution function sums the area under the normal curve from $-\infty$ to d. The normal density measures the height of the normal curve at d. Thus, if there is a small change from d to d', the distribution function increases by the value of the density at d.

EXAMPLE 19.1   Comparative Statics
Compute the values of each of the foregoing partial derivatives for the following call option:

$S=47$
$K=50$
$T=0.5$ year
$r=10\%$/year
$\sigma=0.40$/year

Then use the BSOPM to calculate the theoretical call value as follows. First, obtain a value for d_1.

$$d_1 = \frac{\ln(S/K)+(r+\sigma^2/2)T}{\sigma\sqrt{T}} = \frac{\ln(47/50)+[(0.10+(1/2)(0.16)]0.5}{0.4\sqrt{0.5}}$$

$$= \frac{\ln(0.94)+0.09}{(0.4)(0.7071)} = \frac{-0.061875+0.09}{0.28284} = 0.099435$$

Then, using the table of the cumulative standard normal distribution function in the appendix to Chapter 18 (Table A18.2), we can finish the calculation:

$$N(d_1) = 0.539604$$

$$d_2 = d_1 - \sigma\sqrt{T} = 0.099435 - 0.40\sqrt{0.5} = 0.099435 - 0.28284 = -0.18341$$

$$N(d_2) = 0.427239$$

$$Ke^{-rT} = 50e^{-0.05} = 50 \times 0.9512 = 47.5615$$

$$C = SN(d_1) - Ke^{-rT}N(d_2) = (47 \times 0.539604) - (47.5615 \times 0.427239) = 5.0413$$

Now use the same formulas to find the sensitivity of the option's value to each of the parameters. First,

$$\frac{\partial C}{\partial K} = -e^{-rT}N(d_2) = -\left[e^{-(0.10)(0.50)}\right](0.4272) = -0.4064$$

That is, if you were to compare two calls that were identical in every way except that their strike prices were \$1 apart (e.g., $K = 49$ vs $K = 50$), the one with the lower strike should be worth \$0.4064 more than the one with the higher strike price.

$$\frac{\partial C}{\partial T} = Ke^{-rT}\left[\frac{\sigma N'(d_2)}{2\sqrt{T}} + rN(d_2)\right]$$

$$= (50)\left(e^{-(0.1)(0.5)}\right)\left[\frac{(0.4)(0.3923)}{2\sqrt{0.50}} + (0.1)(0.4272)\right] = 7.3093$$

The value of N' (d2) in this partial derivative formula is given by

$$\frac{e^{-d_2^2/2}}{\sqrt{2\Pi}} = \frac{e^{-(-0.1834)^2/2}}{\sqrt{2(3.1416)}} = 0.3923$$

If the call's time to expiration had been one year longer, the call price would have been about \$7.3093 greater. That is, if the call had had $1\frac{1}{2}$ years to expiration instead of $\frac{1}{2}$ year, it would have been worth about \$12.3506. Actually, because the partial derivative evaluates changes in call values for small changes in T, it is more accurate to estimate that the rate of time decay is about \$0.020025/day (7.3093/365), all else equal. Theta is greatest for at-the-money (or just-in-the-money) options that are close to expiration. Any time value rapidly disappears as the expiration date nears.

$$\frac{\partial C}{\partial r} = TKe^{-rT}N(d_2) = (0.50)(50)\left[e^{-(0.1)(0.50)}\right](0.4272) = 10.159$$

This means that if interest rates were to rise from 10% to 110%, the value of the call would rise by \$10.159. Again, however, it is more accurate to interpret the number as meaning that an increase in the riskless interest rate from 10% to 11% would result in an increase in the value of the call equal to $0.10159, or about 10 cents. This example illustrates that it is *not* critical to have a precise value for the riskless interest rate.

$$\frac{\partial C}{\partial \sigma} = S\sqrt{T}N'(d_1) = (47)\left(\sqrt{0.50}\right)(0.3971) = 13.193$$

The value of $N'(d_1)$ in the foregoing equation is:

$$\frac{e^{-d_1^2/2}}{\sqrt{2\Pi}} = \frac{e^{-(0.0994^2/2)}}{\sqrt{2(3.1416)}} = 0.39697$$

Thus, if σ were to increase by 1.0, from 0.40 to 1.40, the value of the call would rise by about $13.193. More realistically, if the volatility increased from 0.40 to 0.50, the call's value would be $1.3193 greater than originally estimated. Also, note that the call price would be lower by $1.3193 if the volatility fell to 0.30. Because σ is the only parameter that is not observable, it must be estimated. This example illustrates just how critical an accurate estimate of σ must be! It also demonstrates the potential rewards from buying options when implied volatility is low and expected to rise, and from selling options when implied volatility is high and expected to decline.

Next, let us calculate

$$\frac{\partial C}{\partial S} = N(d_1) = 0.5396$$

This means that if the stock price were to rise by one dollar, we would expect the call value to increase by about $0.54, all else equal. The delta of a call option must be greater than or equal to 0 but less than or equal to 1. Note that for an at-the-money call option, where $d_1 \approx 0$, the delta is about 0.50. We will discuss the importance of delta in detail later in the chapter.

$$\Gamma = \frac{\partial \Delta}{\partial S} = \frac{\partial^2 C}{\partial S^2} = \frac{N'(d_1)}{S\sigma\sqrt{T}} = \frac{0.39697}{47 \times 0.40 \times \sqrt{0.50}} = 0.02986$$

Given the example just discussed, an increase in the stock price of $1 will increase the call delta by 0.02986. In other words, currently, the delta of the call is 0.5396. If the stock were to rise in price from $47/share to $48/share, the delta would rise to about 0.56946. This Greek is known as gamma, and we will also discuss the importance of gamma later in the chapter.

The FinCAD function AsBS will compute the Greeks for our example, as shown in Figure 19.2. Note that FinCAD follows convention by presenting theta as a negative number for the *one-day* decay in the call price. The actual value (from FinCAD) of -0.020025318 is very close to the value we computed ($7.3093/365 = -0.020025$ per day). FinCAD's value for vega of 0.131930711

AaBS		
underlying price	47	
exercise price	50	
expiry date	29-Jan-2001	
value (settlement) date	31-Jul-2000	
Volatility	0.4	
risk free interest rate	0.1	
option type	1	Call
Statistic	1	Fair value
discounting method	2	Continuously compounded rate
accrual method	1	Actual/365 (fixed)

fair value	5.041250976
Delta	0.539603796
Gamma	0.029862089
Theta	-0.020025318
Vega	0.131930711
Rho	0.101600637

Figure 19.2 The FinCAD function AaBS computers the Greeks.

is the amount the call value will change if the volatility of the underlying asset increased from 0.40 to 0.41. Use FinCAD to compute the value of the call if $\sigma=41\%$ and check this result. Finally, FinCAD's value for rho is 0.101600637, which is the amount that the theoretical call value will rise if the interest rate rises from 10% to 11%.

19.1.2 The Greeks for Black–Scholes Option Pricing Model: Puts

The following equations define how the value of a European put changes, given that any one of the five underlying determinants of option values changes, all else equal. Once the Greeks for calls have been obtained, the Greeks for puts can be obtained by differentiating the variable P in the put–call parity formula $P=C-S+Ke^{-rT}$. (The key is to remember that both P and C are *functions* of K, T, r, S, and σ.)

Partial Derivative Notation	Greek Letter	Brief Interpretation	Formula	Sign
$\dfrac{\partial P}{\partial K}$		By how much will a call price change, given a change in the strike price?	$\dfrac{\partial C}{\partial K}+e^{-rT}$	>0
$\dfrac{\partial P}{\partial T}$	theta[5] $(\theta)^5$	By how much will a put price change, given a change in the time to expiration?	$\dfrac{\partial C}{\partial T}-rKe^{-rT}$	$\lessgtr 0$
$\dfrac{\partial P}{\partial r}$	rho (ρ)	By how much will a put price change, given a change in the riskless interest rate?	$\dfrac{\partial C}{\partial r}-TKe^{-rT}$	<0

$\dfrac{\partial P}{\partial \sigma}$	vega (v)	By how much will a put's value change, given a change in the volatility of the underlying asset?	$\dfrac{\partial C}{\partial \sigma} = S\sqrt{T}N'(d_1)$	> 0
$\dfrac{\partial C}{\partial S}$	delta (Δ)	Hedge ratio: By how much will a put price change given a change in the value of the underlying asset?	$\dfrac{\partial C}{\partial S} - 1 = N(d_1) - 1$	< 0, but $-1 \le \Delta \le 0$
$\dfrac{\partial \Delta}{\partial S} = \dfrac{\partial^2 P}{\partial S^2}$	gamma (Γ)	By how much will a put's delta change, given a change in the price of the underlying asset?	$\dfrac{N'(d_1)}{S\sigma\sqrt{T}}$	> 0

There are some interesting features about the put sensitivities. First, note that the sign of theta for a put is indeterminate. Mathematically, this is because in absolute value, the second term in the equation can be less than or greater than the theta of a call.[6] Second, the influence of volatility is the same for puts as it is for calls. Third, the delta of a put equals the delta of a call minus one. Consequently, the gamma value of a put equals the gamma value for a call.

19.2   THE IMPORTANCE OF DELTA

Delta is vital in formulating and evaluating option strategies. Therefore, addition to what has been said thus far in this chapter, as well as in Chapters 17 and 18, Section 19.2.1 is devoted entirely to the concept of an option's delta.

19.2.1   What Is Delta?

The delta, Δ, of a call is $\partial C/\partial S = N(d_1)$. The delta of a put is $\partial P/\partial S = N(d_1) - 1$. Option deltas are also frequently called hedge ratios. Delta describes the change in the value of the option, given a small change in the value of the underlying security, all else equal.

Some insight into delta is gained by a graphical analysis. In Figure 19.3, the value of a call on a non-dividend-paying stock is graphed as a function of the stock price. The call's delta is the slope of the call pricing line at any point. Thus, if the call is deep out of the money, its delta is about zero. The delta of a call increases as the stock price increases. When the call is deep in the money, it sells for about its intrinsic value and the delta of the call approaches one. The delta of an American call that sells for exactly its intrinsic value is one. This should occur only when there is an ex-dividend date before expiration.

The delta of an in-the-money call will typically be above 0.50. On the expiration date, an in-the-money call will be priced on the S–K line, which is a 45° straight line. That is, the delta of an in-the-money call at expiration is 1. Thus, we can state that as the expiration date nears, the delta of an in-the-money call rises toward 1, all else equal. Similarly, the delta of an out-of-the money call will usually be below 0.50, and it will fall toward zero as time passes, all else equal. At expiration, the delta of an out-of-the-money call is 0.

Figure 19.4 shows how American puts are valued as a function of the price of the underlying asset. The delta of a put is the slope of the put pricing line at any stock price. When $S \gg K$, a put is deep out-of-the-money, and its delta is about zero. As the stock price falls, delta declines. A deep in-the-money put will have a delta of -1. The American put price curve eventually coincides with the $K-S$ line. As shown in Figure 19.4, S^* is the critical stock price. At and below S^*, the American put should be exercised early, and its delta will have declined to -1.0. The delta of a European put will not become -1.0 until its price has declined to equal $K(1+r)^{-T} - S$.

The delta of an out-of-the-money put will rise toward zero as time passes, all else equal. The delta of an in-the-money put will fall toward -1 as the expiration date nears, all else equal. A useful rule of thumb is that at-the-money call deltas are about 0.50, and at-the-money put deltas are about -0.50.

Understanding delta is fundamental to understanding what you are buying or selling when you trade options. The purchase of a call with a delta of 0.50 is tantamount to buying half a share of stock, mostly with borrowed funds. Buying a put with a delta of -0.20 is essentially equivalent to selling short 0.20 share of stock and lending the proceeds of the short sale plus some additional sum.

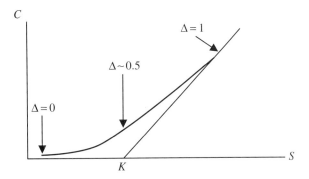

Figure 19.3 A call's delta ranges from about 0 (for a deep out-of-the-money call) to about 1.0 (for a deep out-of-the-money call) as the stock price increases.

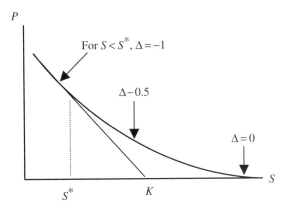

Figure 19.4 The delta of an American put declines from about 0 (for a deep out-of-the-money put) to -1.0 (for a deep out-of-the-money puts for which $S < S^*$ as S declines, where S^* is the critical stock price at which an American put sells for its intrinsic value).

Delta measures the investor's exposure to changes in the price of the underlying asset. If a call has a delta of 0.70 and if the price of the underlying asset increases by one dollar, the price of the call will likely increase by 70 cents ($70 for a call on 100 shares), all else equal. As the price of the underlying asset, its volatility, the time to expiration, or the riskless interest rate changes, so does the delta of an option.

19.2.2   What Is Gamma?

An option's gamma, Γ, measures how delta changes as the stock price changes. Recall that the delta of a put equals the delta of a call minus one. Thus, because the differentiable terms in a call delta and a put delta are the same, the gamma for a put equals the gamma for a call:

$$\Gamma = \frac{\partial \Delta}{\partial S} = \frac{\partial^2 C}{\partial S^2} = \frac{\partial^2 P}{\partial S^2} = \frac{N'(d_1)}{S\sigma\sqrt{T}}$$

Consider a deep out-of-the-money call. The delta of such a call is about 0. If the stock price were to change by a small amount, delta would still be 0. Thus, the gamma for a deep out-of-the-money call is about 0. Similarly, because the delta of a deep in-the-money call is about 1.0, delta will not change if S changes by a small amount. Thus, the gamma of a deep in-the-money call is also about 0. Similar logic applies for the put gamma.

The gamma for a call and a put is maximized when the option is at the money. In other words, if S changes by a small amount, the delta of an at the money call will change by a great amount. How great? If the call has a long time to expiration, the change in delta will not be much, perhaps gamma will equal 0.1 (this value will still be greater for at the money calls than for in-the-money or out-of-the-money calls with the same time to expiration). If the call has a short time to expiration and is at the money, gamma will be higher. Imagine an at-the-money call late on its expiration day. If the stock rises by one cent, the call is in the money and its delta will be 1. But if the stock declines by a penny, the call is out of the money and its delta will be 0. What this means is that deltas of at-the-money calls with short lives are quite unstable. Thus, the gammas of calls (and puts) that are exactly at the money on their expiration day are very high.

Figures 19.5 and 19.6 depict how a call's delta and gamma are functions of the price of the underlying asset, all else constant.

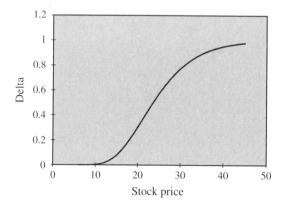

Figure 19.5 Call delta as a function of stock price.

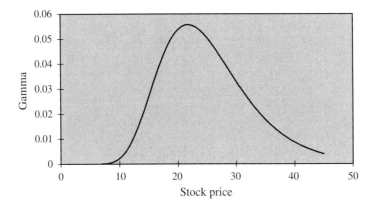

Figure 19.6 Call gamma as a function of stock price.

19.3   RISKLESS HEDGING

One of the great insights of Black and Scholes (1973) was the realization that by holding the proper combination of stock and calls, an investor could create a riskless hedge. This statement is nothing more than a restatement of the idea that a call (or any option or portfolio of options) can be replicated with a portfolio of stocks and riskless bonds. In other words, we know that

$$C = \Delta S + B$$

where $0 \leq \Delta \leq 1$ and $B \leq 0$. The equation says that buying a call is equivalent to buying stock and borrowing. Now, rearrange the equation to read

$$C - \Delta S = B$$

or

$$-C + \Delta S = -B$$

This says that buying Δ shares of stock and selling a call is like riskless lending.

The delta of a call defines a "hedge ratio" for creating a riskless hedge. If Δ shares of stock are bought and one call written, the position is riskless. Strictly speaking, the riskless hedge exists only for small changes in the stock price and over very small time intervals. As time passes and/or the stock price changes, the delta of the call changes (as measured by gamma). As Δ varies, shares of stock must be bought or sold to maintain the riskless hedge.

Now, suppose you were to find what you believe is a mispriced option. You can use the riskless hedging concept to "arbitrage." Quotes are used because the arbitrage profit will be realized only if you are correct in the estimate of volatility that went into your theoretical option price. Recall that the BSOPM assumes that volatility and interest rates are constant for the life of the option. Thus, unexpected changes in volatility and/or interest rates create risk. Note that these changes can work in your favor or against you.

Suppose you found a call option that you believed was overpriced in the market. To take advantage of your opinion, you would sell the call and buy Δ ($0 \leq \Delta \leq 1$) share of stock. Similarly, if, in your opinion, a call was underpriced, you would buy the call and hedge the purchase by selling a fractional amount (Δ) of a share of stock. In either case, your "riskless hedge" will provide you with a rate of return in excess of the riskless interest rate, regardless of what the stock does.[7]

The term "riskless hedge" appears in quotes because, in reality, there is still risk with this strategy. The risk stems from the fact that the fractional share bought or sold is given by Δ. In turn, Δ is based on the BSOPM, and, as a consequence, Δ reflects an estimate for volatility, σ. Believing that an option is underpriced is equivalent to believing that the implied volatility (IV) is too low while believing that an option is overpriced is equivalent to believing that its implied volatility (IV) is too high. A trader whose volatility assessment is incorrect will fail to realize the profit he expected. Of course, if his volatility assessment is very inaccurate, he could even lose money.

A "purer" form of arbitrage (an initial cash inflow, and a zero cash flow at expiration, regardless of S_T) can be earned if you were to borrow or lend the funds needed to set up the riskless hedge. Compare the BSOPM:

$$C = SN(d_1) - Ke^{-rT}N(d_2)$$

to the BOPM:

$$C = S\Delta + B$$

In each equation, the first term on the right-hand side defines the amount of money to invest in the stock: $N(d_1)$ shares $= \Delta$ shares of stock, at a price of $\$S$/share. The second term on the right-hand side defines the appropriate amount to borrow or lend, as necessary, to complete the replication of the call: $B = -Ke^{-rT}N(d_2)$. You would borrow when, as in Example 19.2, you are buying Δ shares of stock and selling an overpriced call. You lend when selling Δ shares of stock and buying an undervalued call. It is important to note that what you are actually doing is either buying an undervalued call and, at the same time, selling a replicated call, or selling an overvalued call and, at the same time, buying a replicated call.[8]

EXAMPLE 19.2[9] Consider an option trader who believes that the return volatility of Applied Materials (AMAT) will decrease over the 70 days remaining before an option expiration date. Suppose AMAT is currently selling for 86 $^3/_8$, and the appropriate risk-free borrowing and lending rate is 6%. There exists a call option with a strike price of 85 with an observed price of $7.25. At this price, the market's expectation of AMAT's return volatility until expiration (i.e., the implied volatility) is about 40.5% (use the FinCAD function aaBS_iv to verify this). However, the trader believes that the market's estimate of volatility is too high and that a volatility of about 32.7% is more accurate. Thus, in the opinion of the trader, the AMAT 85 call option should theoretically sell for about $6.127. The trader can conduct an "arbitrage" to try to profit from his expectations. The arbitrage involves borrowing to buy the appropriate number of shares of AMAT and selling the appropriate number of "overpriced" call options. Put another way, the cheap replicated option is bought with $\sigma = 32.7\%$ and dynamically adjusted as time passes and prices change, and the equivalent overpriced call is sold with $\sigma = 40.5\%$. If the investor is correct in his volatility assessment, he will profit.

Column one in Table 19.1 is the days until call expiration. The second column is AMAT share prices. Following that is the weekly return and the delta for a call option with an 85 strike computed using the trader's belief that $\sigma = 32.7\%$. For ease of presentation, Table 19.1 provides weekly information.[10]

Note that in Table 19.1 there are two entries at expiration. In Case I, the AMAT final stock price is such that the trader's volatility estimate 10 weeks earlier turns out to

TABLE 19.1   Replicating a Call: Delta Changes as the Stock Price Changes and as the Expiration Date Nears

Days to Expiration	AMAT Price	Weekly Return[1]	Delta of an 85 AMAT Call ($\sigma = 32.7\%$)
70	86.375		0.604
63	89.500	0.0355	0.700
56	94.000	0.0491	0.822
49	93.125	−0.0094	0.813
42	90.250	−0.0314	0.745
35	85.375	−0.0555	0.560
28	86.625	0.0145	0.620
21	93.125	0.0724	0.894
14	93.750	0.0067	0.945
7	90.625	−0.0339	0.928

Case I: Closing Price Such That Trader's Volatility Estimate was Correct[2]

0	97.625	0.0744	1.000

Average weekly return	0.0122
Weekly return standard deviation	0.0453
Annualized	0.3270

Case II: Closing Price Such That Market's Volatility Estimate was correct[3]

0	80.375	−0.1200	0.000

Average weekly return	−0.0072
Weekly return standard deviation	0.0561
Annualized	0.4047

[1] This is the continuously compounded rate of return, $\ln(P2/P1)$. Thus, $\ln(89.5/86.375) = 0.0355$, and $\ln(90.625/93.75) = -0.0339$.

[2] Note that if the expiration day closing price is 85, the trader's estimate of volatility (32.7%) will also be correct.

[3] Note that if the expiration day closing price is 103.5, the market's implied volatility (40.5%) will also be correct.

be correct (i.e., 32.7%). In Case II, the AMAT final stock price is such that the market's implied volatility estimate 10 weeks earlier turns out to be correct (i.e., 40.5%).

Let us return to the moment in time with 10 weeks to option expiration. Suppose a trader wants to try to arbitrage the overvalued (in his opinion) AMAT 85 call. Although the market price of this call is $7.25, the trader believes that the call option should sell for $6.127 because he thinks the market has overestimated AMAT's future return volatility. To assist in the understanding of the arbitrage, recall the BSOPM,

$$C = SN(d_1) - Ke^{-rT} N(d_2)$$

long call = long stock − short T-bills (i.e., borrowing)

That is, an actual long call position equals a theoretical portfolio consisting of a long stock position funded by a short position in T-bills (i.e., borrowing). In this arbitrage case, because the trader writes overpriced calls, he must "hedge" this position with a purchase of a theoretical (replicated) call. The trader replicates the call using his belief that σ is only 32.7%. Thus, the cost of replicating the call (6.127) is less than the price he receives from selling the overpriced call (7.25). The difference ($1.123) is the theoretical arbitrage profit, if the trader is correct about his volatility beliefs. Thus, with 70 days to expiration, the trader sells a call for $7.25, and borrows money ($46.043) to finance the purchase of $\Delta = 0.604$ shares of stock. At the time of the arbitrage, the trader realizes a cash inflow of $1.123:

Sell (overpriced) call	+ $7.25	
Buy 0.604 shares of stock at $86.375/share:	−$52.17 ⎤	Buy replicated
Borrow	+ $46.043 ⎦	call
Net inflow	+ $1.123	

If the trader is correct, the "mispricing" she has identified has an expected profit of $1.123 per share (before commissions).

In this example we assume that readjustment of the equivalent (or "hedge") portfolio occurs every seventh day. In practice, there is a trade-off between letting the required composition of the equivalent portfolio stray too far from the current position and incurring the transactions costs to rebalance. Here, every seventh day, the trader takes one of two actions, either purchasing more shares and financing the purchase by increasing the amount borrowed, or selling shares and investing the proceeds (i.e., reducing the amount borrowed). The details of rebalancing the hedge portfolio appear in Table 19.2. The first column is the days until expiration, and the second column is the AMAT stock price. Column three is the delta of an AMAT 85 call (calculated by using the trader's volatility estimate of 32.7%). The fourth column shows how many shares are bought or sold, column five represents the cost of additional shares or the proceeds from selling shares. Column six is the interest expense or income from the subsequent share transactions.

Suppose the trader decides to sell 100 AMAT 85 call options with 70 days to expiration, each on 100 shares of stock. The trader initially hedges a short position in the calls by purchasing 6040 shares. The number of shares to purchase is obtained by multiplying the initial hedge ratio (i.e., Δ) by the number of shares underlying the options i.e., (10,000). To complete the synthetic long call position, the trader must also borrow $460,430. The interest expense will be $460,430 \times (e^{(0.06)(70/365)} - 1) = \$5329$.

Seven days later, $\Delta = 0.700$ for the 85 call. Given this new delta, the equivalent portfolio requires that the trader be long 7000 shares. Because the trader originally bought 6040 shares on day 0, this indicates a need to purchase 960 additional shares at the new AMAT market price of $89.50/share. This will cost ($89.50 \times 960 =$) $85,920. The trader finances the purchase by borrowing this amount at 6% for 63 days. Thus, the trader will (ultimately) incur an interest expense of $894 $[(e^{(0.06)(63/365)} - 1)\,\$85,920 = \$894]$ on this new borrowing. As Table 19.2 illustrates, this rebalancing process occurs every seven days until option expiration.

In Table 19.2, there are two cases at expiration. Case I has the AMAT stock price at expiration that is consistent with the trader's forecast for return volatility, and the call finishes in the money. Case II has the price at expiration that is consistent with the implied volatility 70 days earlier, and the call finishes out of the money. Note that in Case I, the delta of the option increases to 1.000 (from 0.928) while the delta plummets to zero in Case II because the call has finished out of the money. In both cases, all the shares that had been purchased as part of the option replication strategy (3240) are sold on the expiration day of the call option. Now, let us use Table 19.3 to show the profitability of the trader's strategy under Case I and Case II.[11]

In Case I, the realized profit of $10,961 is very close to the expected profit of $11,233. But why was the realized total *loss* of $22,869 different from the total profit projected in Case II? The problem lies in the decision to rebalance every seventh day. As the option's expiration day nears, Δ becomes more volatile (Γ is high), particularly for around-the-money options such as this one. It is necessary to rebalance more frequently when Γ is high. The lesson to be learned is that the riskless hedge requires monitoring and frequent adjustment. The more volatile Δ is, the more frequently you should adjust. In general, traders who delta hedge should close out their positions early when gamma is high. Also bear in mind that changing interest rates will affect option prices and deltas, and that the underlying asset can be more or less volatile than originally believed. An option's delta will change not only as S and T change, but also if there are changes in σ and/or the riskless interest rate. Finally, the example ignored commissions. All these factors introduce risk and costs into the "riskless" hedge.

TABLE 19.2 Delta Hedging for Initial Position

Days to Exp.	AMAT Price	Δ for $K=85$ Call ($\sigma=0.327$)	Shares Bought (Sold)	Share Proceeds (Cost)	Interest Income (Expense)
63	89.500	0.700	960	(85,920)	(894)
56	94.000	0.822	1220	(114,680)	(1061)
49	93.125	0.813	(90)	8,381	68
42	90.250	0.745	(680)	61,370	425
35	85.375	0.560	(1850)	157,944	911
28	86.625	0.620	600	(51,975)	(240)
21	93.125	0.894	2740	(255,163)	(882)
14	93.750	0.945	510	(47,813)	(110)
7	90.625	0.928	(170)	15,406	18
Case I					
0	97.625	1.000	(3240)	316,305	0
Case II					
0	80.375	0.000	(3240)	260,415	0

TABLE 19.3   Profitability of Trader's Strategy for Cases I and II

	Intrinsic Values	
Initial Price-Expiration	**Case I**	**Case II**
Profit (Loss) on call position	(53,750)	72,500
(Initial price – exp. day intrinsic value)[1]		
Profit (Loss) on initial stock position	67,950	(36,240)
(ending price – purchase price)[2]		
Interim gain (loss) from trading shares	3,855	(52,035)
(Sum of column 5, Table 19.3)		
Total interest income (expense)	(1,765)	(1,765)
(Sum of column 6, Table 19.3)		
Financing original position	(5,329)	(5,329)
(interest on $460,430 for 70 days at 6%)		
Realized total profit (loss)	$10,961	($22,869)
Projected total profit	$11,233	$11,233
$[(\$7.25 - 6.127) \times 10,000]$		

[1]The initial proceeds in both cases is $72,500 because 100 calls are sold at a price of $725 per call. The expiration day value of each call in Case I is $1262.50 because $C_T = S_T - K = 97.625 - 85 = 12.625$, and $72,500 - 126,250 = -53,750$. The calls expire worthless in Case II.

[2]6040 shares were initially bought at $86.375/share. In Case I, these shares are sold for $97.625/share. In Case II, they are sold at a price of $80.375/share.

Note that it is not necessary to hold onto the arbitrage portfolio for the entire life of the option. Indeed, when an option has a short time to expiration and is near the money, so that gamma is high, the arbitrage trades should be unwound. Failure to unwind early created the problem for our trader in Case II. Moreover, the trader should unwind her trades, and maybe even reverse them in the event that the option over- or under valuation is ever reversed. Here, initially, the option was overvalued at $7.25. Suppose it remained overvalued until 21 days before expiration, at which time it became undervalued. From the BSOPM, the theoretical value of this call with 21 days to expiration, σ of 0.327, a riskless rate of 6%, and a stock price of $93.125, is $8.80 (use the FinCAD function aaBS to verify this). Suppose the actual call price with 21 days to expiration was $8.00 (i.e., it became undervalued). Then, with 21 days to expiration, the trader could close the position and realize a profit of almost $39,000:

Profit (loss) on call position	(7,500)
Profit (loss) on initial stock position	40,770
Interim gain (loss) from trading shares	9,980
Total interest income (expense)	(739)
Financing original position	(3,724)
(Interest on $460,430 for 49 days at 6%)	
Realized total profit	$38,787

19.4 POSITION DELTAS AND GAMMAS

19.4.1 Position Deltas

The position delta determines how much a portfolio changes in value if the price of the underlying stock changes by a small amount. The portfolio might consist of several puts and calls on the same stock, with different strikes and expiration dates, and also long and short positions in the stock itself. The delta of one share of stock that is owned equals $+1.0$. The delta of a share of stock that is sold short is -1.0.

Assuming that each option covers one share of stock, the position delta Δ_Π is calculated as a weighted sum of individual deltas. That is,

$$\Delta_\Pi = \sum_{i=1}^{N} n_i \Delta_i$$

where n_i is the number of options of one particular type, or the number of shares of stock. The sign of n_i is positive if the options or stock is owned, and negative if the options have been written or the stock sold short. The delta of the ith option or stock is given by Δ_i.

Position deltas measure the change in the value of a portfolio, given a small change in the value of the underlying stock. Knowing your portfolio's position delta is as essential to intelligent option trading as knowing the profit diagrams of your portfolio. For example, suppose you buy a vertical spread using around-the-money calls. From Chapter 15, you know that you will profit if both calls finish in the money. Both calls will be in the money if the stock price at expiration is above the higher of the two strikes. Thus, the time T cash inflow equals the difference in the strike prices, $K_H - K_L$. However, the position delta for the vertical spread might only be 0.30 when the spread is purchased. The position delta for a 1:1 vertical spread equals the difference in the two

EXAMPLE 19.3 Suppose you have positions in the following assets:

Long or Short, Number of Options or Shares	n_i	Asset	Delta/Unit	Total Deltas $= n_i \Delta_i$
Long 300 shares	+300	Stock	1.00	300.00
Long 40 contracts	+40	Puts	−0.46	−18.40
Short 150 contracts	−150	Calls	0.80	−120.00
Long 62 contracts	+62	Calls	0.28	17.36
				$\Delta_\Pi = 178.96$

In this example, the position delta of 178.96 is positive. This means that if the stock price were to increase by one dollar, the value of this portfolio would rise by $178.96. If the stock price were to decline by one dollar, the value of this portfolio would fall by $178.96. This example assumes that the underlying asset of an option is one share of stock.

calls' deltas. Thus, if the stock price were to rise or fall by one dollar immediately after purchasing the spread, your profit or loss is only 30 cents.

A *delta-neutral* position is a portfolio that is immune to changes in the stock price. That is, the portfolio of options and stock has a position delta of 0.0. However, arbitrageurs are not the only users of delta-neutral positions. Many market makers trade options and try to maintain a delta-neutral position. These market makers are not speculating on movements of the stock price. Instead, they can concentrate on capitalizing on the bid–ask spread and trade what they perceive to be mispriced options. Being delta neutral allows them to sleep at night. Delta-neutral hedging is not totally effective, Since there is always a chance that the stock will jump unexpectedly. Recall that delta estimates the change in the value of an option for a *small* change in the price of the underlying asset. A large change in the price of the underlying asset will create a change in the value of a delta-neutral portfolio.

Many institutions are also delta hedgers, including investment bankers and commercial bankers, who sell nontraded (over-the-counter) options to their clients or purchase them from their clients. For example, a customer who owns a large block of shares of a stock on which no options trade might wish to write covered calls or buy protective puts on those shares. As another example, consider a corporate client who anticipates the purchase (or sale) of a number of government bonds, or some foreign exchange, in the near future. This client would like to insure that the firm pays a price for the purchase of the asset that is no higher than some maximum tolerable amount, or to insure that the price it will receive for the bonds or foreign exchange is no lower than some tolerable minimum.

These are examples of customers who would like to modify the risk exposure they face in some way. The bank can buy or sell custom-designed options to the client at a price that reflects the current price of the underlying asset, the riskless interest rate, the strike price, the time to expiration, and the estimated volatility of the underlying asset *plus a profit premium*. Then, the bank will enter into a delta-neutral position by trading the underlying asset and riskless securities, reflecting the underlying asset's estimated volatility. As long as the estimated volatility is correct, the bank will earn a profit by providing the service to the customer. The bank will often also be willing to allow the customer to offset his position early, for a price, of course.

19.4.2 Position Gammas

Similar to position deltas, a position gamma Γ_Π is the weighted sum of the gammas of the elements of the portfolio:

$$\Gamma_\Pi = \sum_{i=1}^{N} n_i \Gamma_i$$

where n_i is the number of options of one particular type. The sign of n_i is positive if the option is owned, and negative if the option has been written. The gamma of the ith option is given by Γ_i. Note that the gamma of a stock is zero, because the delta of a stock is always to one.

Ideally, a delta-neutral hedger would like to maintain a portfolio with a positive gamma. Recall from Sections 19.1.1 and 19.1.2 that the gamma of both a call and a put is given by the same formula and that gammas cannot be negative. However, a *portfolio* can have a positive or negative gamma. It is important to note that a portfolio with a positive gamma increases in value if the underlying stock value *changes*. Further, a portfolio with a negative gamma decreases in value if the underlying stock value *changes*.

EXAMPLE 19.4 Suppose $S = K = \$100$, $r = 8\%$, $\sigma = 30\%$, and $T = 180$ days. Then, by using the BSOPM, one can generate the following information.

Variable	Call Option	Put Option	Stock
Price	$10.30	$ 6.44	$100
Delta	0.6151	− 0.3849	1
Gamma	0.0181	0.0181	0

Now, suppose a trader is considering the use of either calls or puts to maintain a delta-neutral portfolio. This can be accomplished with the purchase of puts or by writing calls. The impact of a positive or negative gamma can be seen by the following information, presented on a per-share basis.

Using Puts

Delta-neutral strategy: long 1 put at $6.44; long 0.3849 share at $100/share.

Positive position gamma: $(1 \times 0.0181) + (0.3849 \times 0) = 0.0181$.

Stock Price	Put Price	Value of 0.3849 Share	Portfolio Value	Percent Change (from $S = 100$)
90	11.25	34.64	45.89	2.14
100	6.44	38.49	44.93	
110	3.41	42.34	45.75	1.83

Using Calls

Delta-neutral strategy: short 1 call at $10.30; long 0.6151 share at $100/share.

Negative position gamma: $(-1 \times 0.0181) + (0.3849 \times 0) = -0.0181$.

Stock Price	Call Price	Value of 0.6151 Share	Portfolio Value	Percent Change (from $S = 100$)
90	5.12	55.36	50.24	−1.89
100	10.30	61.51	51.21	
110	17.28	67.66	50.38	−1.62

Note that when the delta hedger uses puts to construct a portfolio, the value of the portfolio increases, regardless of the direction of the change in the underlying asset price. When calls are used, however the portfolio value falls whether the underlying asset price increases or decreases.

From a cost standpoint, a delta-neutral hedger would like to have a portfolio with a low, but positive gamma. Recall that gamma measures changes in delta, and that deltas change as S, T, σ, and/or r change. Thus, a portfolio that is delta-neutral today may not be delta neutral tomorrow. A low position gamma will mean that the delta-neutral investor will conserve on the transactions costs of readjusting his portfolio delta back to zero if S changes. But a positive gamma at least compensates a trader for bearing the risk of fluctuating delta, as the value of his portfolio will increase if the underlying asset's price changes, all else equal.

19.4.3 Generalized Portfolio Sensitivities

Traders can create portfolios that are neutral (insensitive) to any single "Greek" or combination of "Greeks." From the foregoing examples, you can see that a trader needs one option to remove one effect. In Example 19.4 the trader used a delta-neutral strategy to make the portfolio insensitive to changes in the stock price (i.e., recall that traders can use either calls or puts in a delta-neutral strategy). To neutralize additional effects, traders must add additional options to their portfolios.

Given a strike price (which never changes), we know the value of a call option is a function of the time to expiration, the underlying stock price, the riskless interest rate, and the volatility of the returns on the underlying asset. That is,[12]

$$C = C(T, S, r, \sigma) \tag{19.1}$$

A major concern to hedgers is how call prices change as the underlying asset price changes. Using calculus, changes in the call price, dC, can be approximated by

$$dC = \frac{\partial C}{\partial T} dT + \frac{\partial C}{\partial S} dS + \frac{\partial C}{\partial r} dr + \frac{\partial C}{\partial \sigma} d\sigma + \frac{1}{2} \frac{\partial^2 C}{\partial S^2} (dS)^2 \tag{19.2}$$

Equation (19.2) may look a little intimidating. However, when the "Greeks" are substituted into Equation (19.2), it becomes:

$$dC = \Theta \, dT + \Delta \, dS + \rho \, dr + \upsilon \, d\sigma + \frac{1}{2} \Gamma (dS)^2 \tag{19.3}$$

Quite often, it is assumed that the riskless interest rate and volatility are constant (even though they are not). That is, the dr and $d\sigma$ terms in Equation (19.3) are assumed to be zero, so

$$dC = \Theta dT + \Delta dS + \frac{1}{2} \Gamma (dS)^2 \tag{19.4}$$

What is important for risk managers is that Equation (19.4) also holds for portfolios, denoted by Π, comprised of options and the underlying asset. That is, because position thetas, deltas, and gammas are weighted sums of these sensitivities for the constituent assets, the change in the value of the portfolio can be written as follows:

$$d\Pi = \Theta_\Pi dT + \Delta_\Pi dS + \frac{1}{2} \Gamma_\Pi (dS)^2 \tag{19.5}$$

Equation (19.5) says that the change in the value of a portfolio $d\Pi$, (which comprise options and the underlying stock) depends on the portfolio's time decay, Θ_Π, the passing of time, dT, sensitivity to changes in the underlying asset price, Δ_Π, changes in the underlying asset price, dS, and changes in Δ_Π, i.e., Γ_Π. The value of Equation (19.5) to risk managers is shown next.

Suppose the trader in Example (19.4) wants to hedge a stock position with call options but also wants to make sure that the portfolio value does not decline by much if the price of the underlying asset changes, all else equal. Such a position is commonly known as delta–gamma hedging. Delta–gamma hedging is a popular strategy to employ when the underlying asset price tends to exhibit big moves, causing losses in portfolios that are only delta neutral.[13] Example 19.5 illustrates delta-gamma hedging.

EXAMPLE 19.5 Delta–Gamma Hedge To use options to remove delta effects via a delta-neutral hedging strategy, the trader employed one option. To remove another effect (i.e., gamma), the trader will need to use a second option. Suppose $S = K_1 = \$100$, $r = 8\%$, $\sigma = 30\%$, $T = 180$ days, and $K_2 = 110$. Then, one can use the BSOPM to generate the following information.

Variable	Call Option ($K=100$)	Call Option ($K=110$)	Stock
Price	$10.30	$6.06	$100
Delta	0.6151	0.4365	1
Gamma	0.0181	0.0187	0

Suppose the trader decides to sell 200 call options with the strike of 100, each on 100 shares of stock. Because the trader wants to create a delta–gamma-hedged portfolio, she must simultaneously solve for the number of shares to purchase, S, and the number of $K = 110$ calls to purchase, K_{110}. This is straightforward because the gamma of the stock is zero, and the portfolio gamma is a weighted sum of the constituent gammas. The trader wants a gamma of zero. That is,

$$0 = (-200 \times 100 \times 0.0181) + (S \times 0) + \left(K_{110} \times 100 \times 0.0187\right)$$

which yields $K_{110} = 193.583$ for any value of S. Assuming the trader buys 194 of the calls having a strike price of 110, solving for the number of shares is accomplished by noting that the delta of a share is 1 and that the trader also wants to hold a delta-neutral portfolio. Accordingly,

$$0 = (-200 \times 100 \times 0.6151) + (S \times 1) + (194 \times 100 \times 0.4365)$$

yields $S = 3834$. To examine the performance of the delta–gamma hedge, suppose the stock price were to change to either $101 or to $99.

Stock Price	Call Price		Portfolio Value	Percent Change (from $S=100$)
	$K=100$	$K=110$		
99	9.6984	5.6310	$294839.4	0.0007
100	10.3044	6.0580	$294837.2	
101	10.9285	6.5040	$294841.6	0.0015

Note how the value of the portfolio remains (virtually) unchanged, even when the stock price changes up or down by 1%. At the same time, the portfolio delta of zero remains (virtually) unchanged:

Original delta, at $S = 100 = (3834)(1) + (194)(100)(0.4365) + (-200)(100)(0.6151) = 0.1$

At $S = 99$, delta $= (3834)(1) + (194)(100)(0.4178) + (-200)(100)(0.5967) = 5.32$

At $S = 101$, delta $= (3834)(1) + (194)(100)(0.4552) + (-200)(100)(0.6330) = 4.88$

Note that like most concepts dealing with options, delta and gamma hedging (and vega hedging discussed next) are calculus concepts that work best when there are very small changes in the price of the underlying asset.

Example 19.6 Delta–Gamma–Vega Hedge   In Equation (19.4), an important effect has been assumed to be constant. This effect, which stems from the volatility of the underlying asset, is known as "vega."

Now suppose $S=K_1=\$100$, $r=8\%$, $\sigma=30\%$, $T=180$ days, $K_2=110$, and $K_3=90$. Then, one can use the BSOPM to generate the following information.

	Call Option			
Variable	$K=90$	$K=100$	$K=110$	**Stock**
Price	$16.33	$10.30	$6.06	$100
Delta	0.7860	0.6151	0.4365	1
Gamma	0.0138	0.0181	0.0187	0
Vega	0.2046	0.2684	0.2766	0

Suppose the trader is long 200 call options with the 100 strike. Each option is on 100 shares of stock. Because the trader wants to create a portfolio that is delta-gamma-vega neutral, he must simultaneously solve for the number of shares to purchase, S, the position in the 110 calls, K_{110}, and the position in the 90 calls, K_{90}. That is, he must choose the position in these securities so that the portfolio's delta, gamma, and vega all equal zero (at least initially). To solve this problem, we begin by noting that the gamma and the vega of the stock are zero and that the position in the option with the 100 strike is given (i.e., $K_{100}=-200$). Thus, to be gamma neutral and vega neutral implies

$$0 = (-200 \times 100 \times 0.0181) + (S \times 0) + (K_{110} \times 100 \times 0.0187) + (K_{90} \times 100 \times 0.0138)$$

and

$$0 = (-200 \times 100 \times 0.2684) + (S \times 0) + (K_{110} \times 100 \times 0.2766) + (K_{90} \times 100 \times 0.2046)$$

This becomes:

$$362 = 1.87 K_{110} + 1.38 K_{90}$$
$$5368 = 27.66 K_{110} + 20.46 K_{90}$$

Solving these two equations simultaneously yields $K_{110}=14.76$ and $K_{90}=-282.33$ for any value of S. Then, solving for the number of shares is accomplished by noting that the delta of a share is 1 and that the trader also wants to hold a delta-neutral portfolio. Accordingly,

$$0 = (-200 \times 100 \times 0.6151) + (S \times 1) + (14.76 \times 100 \times 0.4365) +$$
$$\cdot (-282.33 \times 100 \times 0.7860)$$

yields $S = 9244.86$. Assume the trader buys 9245 shares (and buys 15 of the $K = 110$ calls and sells 282 of the $K = 90$ calls). To examine the performance of the delta–gamma–vega hedge, suppose an earnings announcement makes the volatility of the underlying asset jump to 35 or 25%. Letting $r = 8\%$, $T = 180$ days and $S = 100$, we have the following.

Stock Volatility	Call Price			Portfolio Value	Percent Change in Portfolio Value (from $\sigma = 30\%$)
	$K = 90$	$K = 100$	$K = 110$		
25%	15.36	8.97	4.68	$677,763	−0.1938%
30%	16.33	10.30	6.06	$679,084	
35%	17.39	11.65	7.45	$678,277	−0.1188%

Therefore, the portfolio, as constructed, hedges the portfolio against instantaneous changes in the volatility of the underlying asset. It is important to note, however, that a delta–gamma–vega hedge may outperform or underperform a delta–gamma hedge when the underlying stock price changes.

19.4.4 Time Spreads

Time spreads are also sometimes called calendar spreads or horizontal spreads. Time spreads are identified by the ratio of options written and purchased.

19.4.4.1 1:1 Time Spreads

To create a 1:1 time spread, the investor buys one option and sells one option. The two options must be either both calls or both puts, and must share the same strike price on the same underlying asset. However, unlike most of the option portfolios discussed thus far, the time spread portfolio of options has options with different maturity dates.

Traders like to hold long positions in time spreads. A long time spread position involves selling the option with a short time to expiration and buying the longer term option. This is done for two reasons. First, the trader typically wishes to exploit the higher theta of the nearby option. Options, particularly if they are at the money, will usually lose any time value at a fast and increasing rate as the expiration date nears. At-the-money options usually have more time value than other options, all else equal. Thus, a hypothetical at-the-money call with one month to expiration might be sold for $2, and a call with two months to expiration might be bought for $3. If the stock price remains unchanged, the former will expire worthless (creating a profit of $2), and the latter (which now has one month to expiration) might be sold for $2 (creating a loss of 1). Thus, the net profit is $1. The second reason for the tendency of traders to sell the nearby option is sold is that many empirical studies have found that options with short lives are usually overvalued relative to options with a longer time to expiration, all else equal.[14]

The maximum profit on a time spread occurs when the stock price equals the strike price on the expiration date of the nearby call. The short-term written option expires worthless, and the longer term option can be sold with some time value remaining. An important risk to be kept in mind is that if the written, short-term option is in the money as its expiration date nears, it could be exercised early. To preclude this possibility, therefore, in-the-money time spreads using American options often must be closed out early.

EXAMPLE 19.7 Time Spread   On August 1, the following are observed:

$S = 42.875$

$K = 45$

$r = 11\%/\text{year}$

Price of a call expiring on September 21 = 2

Price of a call expiring on December 21 = 3.375

Prepare the profit diagram for a long time spread.

Solution

On August 1:

Sell 1 Sep 45 call	+2
Buy 1 Dec 45 call	−3.375
	−1.375

Thus, the initial outlay for a call on 100 shares is $137.50.

The profit table is prepared based on the closing prices of September 21. Using the BSOPM to estimate the September 21 prices of the December call given a range of stock prices on September 21. A volatility of $\sigma = 40\%$ is used because this is the implied volatility of the September call on August 1. Finally, remember that on September 21, the December call will have a time to expiration of 0.25 year.

	On September 21		Time T	Profit/Loss
S_T	Buy Sept 45 call	Sell Dec 45 call	Cash Flow, CF_T	$CF_0 + CF_T$
37	0	+0.893	+0.893	−0.482
38	0	+1.143	+1.143	−0.232
39	0	+1.436	+1.436	+0.061
40	0	+1.775	+1.775	+0.400
41	0	+2.161	+2.161	+0.786
42	0	+2.594	+2.594	+1.219
43	0	+3.074	+3.074	+1.699
44	0	+3.601	+3.601	+2.226
45	0	+4.173	+4.173	+2.800
46	−1	+4.788	+3.794	+2.419
47	−2	+5.450	+3.450	+2.075

48	−3	+6.144	+3.144	+1.769
49	−4	+6.874	+2.874	+1.499
50	−5	+7.637	+2.637	+1.262
51	−6	+8.429	+2.429	+1.054
52	−7	+9.248	+2.248	+0.873
53	−8	+10.091	+2.091	+0.716
54	−9	+10.956	+1.956	+0.581
55	−10	+11.840	+1.840	+0.465

The profit diagram for the long time spread appears in Figure 19.7.

The maximum loss is of $1.375 is realized if the stock price plummets until both options are worthless on September 21, or if the stock price rises so high that both options sell for their intrinsic value $(S_T - K)$ on September 21. However, the range of stock prices for which a profit is earned is quite wide: from $39/share to a price above $55/share.

The strategy described in Example 19.7 is usually called a bullish time spread because the stock price must rise for the maximum profit to be reached. If both calls were in the money, a bearish time spread would be purchased.

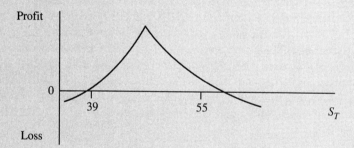

Figure 19.7 Profit diagram for a long time spread.

19.4.4.2 Neutral Time Spreads

A neutral time spread is a strategy designed to capitalize on two options that are somehow mispriced relative to each other. The two options differ only in their times to expiration. As discussed earlier, usually the short-term option is written and the longer option is purchased. The number of each option traded is designed to create a delta-neutral portfolio.

In Example 19.7, the implied standard deviations was 0.4043 for the September call and 0.3262 for the December call. Thus, assuming that the BSOPM is the proper pricing formula, the short-term call is overvalued relative to the December call.

Assume that the "true" volatility is 0.40/year. Then the hedge ratios of the two options are $\Delta = 0.4439$ for the September call and $\Delta = 0.5415$ for the December call. A delta-neutral portfolio of these two options is

$$\Delta_p = 0 = n_1 \Delta_1 + n_2 \Delta_2$$

Rearranging, we have

$$\frac{n_1}{n_2} = \frac{-\Delta_2}{\Delta_1}$$

Using these deltas, and naming the September and December calls as assets 1 and 2, respectively, we write

$$\frac{n_1}{n_2} = \frac{-0.5415}{0.4439} = -1.22 \qquad\qquad (19.6)$$

Equation (19.6) says that to create a delta-neutral position, 1.22 September calls should be sold for each December call purchased. This allows the investor to arbitrage the relative mispricing of the two options and not speculate on price movements. As time passes and as the price of the stock changes, the deltas will change, and the relative number of options needed to maintain the delta neutral position also will change. Thus, the position must be monitored. The investor typically rebalances the portfolio when it is necessary to buy or sell some threshold number of options to maintain a delta-neutral position. When rebalancing, the investor should, of course, always buy the more undervalued option, or sell the more overvalued option.

As usual, there are real risks and costs that must be included. For example, we have ignored transactions costs. In practice, the position will have to be closed out early if the options are in the money as September 21 nears, because the September call could be exercised early. If they are exercised, the trader will bear additional transactions costs of having to purchase the stock and making delivery. In addition, there are rebalancing costs of trading options to maintain delta neutrality. For this reason, neutral hedgers prefer low gamma positions, if possible. We assumed there are no ex-dividend dates between August 1 and September 21. Dividends would affect the computed deltas and also would introduce early exercise risk. We assumed constant interest rates and constant volatility. These also affect the computed deltas and, indeed, may be the source of the apparent mispricing.

19.5   CAPS, FLOORS, AND COLLARS: USING OPTIONS TO MANAGE INTEREST RATE RISK

19.5.1   Caps

Many firms, financial institutions, and individuals borrow and/or lend money at variable interest rates. This means that the interest rate on the loan balance changes at prespecified dates. The magnitude of the change in the interest rate on the loan is typically tied to a publicly available index such as LIBOR or a commercial paper index.

A **cap** is a clause or product that effectively places a maximum interest rate on a variable-rate loan. With a cap, a borrower will pay the lesser of the rate that is pegged to the index, or the cap rate. Sometimes caps are called **ceilings**. An interest rate **floor** effectively sets a *minimum* interest rate on a variable-rate loan. A **collar** effectively sets both a maximum and a minimum interest rate on a variable-rate loan. Many variable-rate mortgages have collars. For example, a home buyer might be offered a $100,000 mortgage with an interest rate of 8.5% for the first year. Each subsequent year, a new interest rate is applied to the remaining loan balance. The new interest rate

EXAMPLE 19.8 Consider a notional principal of $8 million with a cap of 10%. The interest rate is reset quarterly, and interest payments are made quarterly. Suppose that on one of the rate-fixing dates, the underlying index (LIBOR) is 12%.

With an annual rate of 10%, the quarterly rate is 2.50%, and the quarterly payment would be ($8,000,000)(0.0250) = $200,000. Instead, because the new interest rate is 12%, the actual payment based on the quarterly market interest rate is ($8,000,000)(0.0300) = $240,000. If the borrower had purchased a 10% cap on a notional principal of $8 million, he would be paid the difference in these amounts, $40,000, by the financial institution that sold him the cap. This effectively sets the maximum annual interest rate of 10%.

What this means is that if this call finishes 200 basis points in the money (because 12% is 200 basis points above the strike price of 10%), the payoff to the call owner (the borrower) is $40,000.

might equal the prevailing rate on one-year T-bills plus 225 basis points. However the interest rate can never exceed 12.5% (a cap), or be below 5.5% (a floor).[15]

Hundreds of billions of dollars of loans in the United States have caps, floors, or collars. It is important to note, however, that caps, floors, and collars apply only to the loan payments. In a cap, floor, or collar, there is no default risk concerning the loan principal. However there is default risk concerning the loan payments. The loan principal is frequently called **notional principal**. The dollar payment with a cap and floor is a function of the difference between the market interest rate and the cap/floor rate times the notional principal.

A cap can be viewed as a call option on an interest rate. Assume that a loan has an interest rate cap of 10% (the strike price). If, on the interest rate reset date, the new interest rate is 10% or less, the call expires worthless. However, if the new interest rate is greater than 10%, the call pays off the difference between the new interest rate that would exist in the absence of the cap and 10%, times the notional principal. This amount must then be adjusted for the timing of the loan repayments at the new loan rate.

More generally, define:

NP = notional principal

R_c = interest rate cap

R = new interest rate (determined by some interest rate index, such as LIBOR)

d = days until the next interest rate reset date

Then, a cap's payoffs[16] on each interest rate reset date are as follows:

$$0 \qquad \text{if } R < R_c$$
$$(NP)(R - R_c)\frac{d}{360} \quad \text{if } R > R_c$$

In Example 19.8, the cap's payoff is ($8,000,000)(0.12 − 0.10)(90/360) = $40,000, because 12% > 10%.

Financial institutions sell caps to their clients. The latter are usually firms that have borrowed money at variable interest rates and wish to insure against the possibility that at some future interest rate reset date, they will have to pay more than the interest rate cap.

Because most cap agreements have a series of interest rate reset dates, a cap is actually a series, or portfolio, of call options, each expiring on a reset date. The term **caplet** refers to any one of the options making up a cap.

19.5.2   Floors

An interest rate floor is a put option on an interest rate. Floors represent insurance for the lending institution that it will never receive less than the floor interest rate on a variable loan rate that it has made. If the new interest rate is above the strike (the floor), the put expires worthless. If the market interest rate (e.g.,three month LIBOR) is below the interest rate floor (the strike price), the put pays off to the lender. Borrowers sell floor agreements to lenders, and borrowers must make payments to the lending institution if interest rates decline below the floor rate.

Define the following:

NP = notional principal

R_f = interest rate floor

R = new interest rate (determined by some interest rate index, such as LIBOR)

d = days until the next interest rate reset date

Then, a floor's payoffs on each interest rate reset date are as follows

$$0 \qquad \text{if } R \geq R_f$$
$$NP(R_f - R)\frac{d}{360}; \quad \text{if } R < R_f$$

19.5.3   Collars

An interest rate collar combines a cap and a floor. Equivalently, the lending institution sells an interest rate call to the borrower and buys an interest rate floor from the borrower. A collar's payoffs on each interest rate reset date are as follows:

$$NP\ (R - R_f)\frac{d}{360} \quad \text{if } R < R_f \qquad \text{(borrower pays lender)}$$
$$0 \qquad\qquad \text{if } R_f < R < R_c$$
$$NP(R - R_c)\frac{d}{360} \quad \text{if } R > R_c \qquad \text{(lender pays borrower)}$$

The profit diagram for a collar from the lender's viewpoint (Figure 19.8a) shows that if $R < R_f$, the lender profits because he owns an interest rate put. If $R > R_c$, the lender loses because he has sold an interest rate call. In Figure 19.8b, the profit diagram for a collar from the borrower's viewpoint, the borrower benefits from owning a cap (an interest rate call) if $R > R_c$. The borrower loses if interest rates decline below the floor rate.

Figure 19.9 shows that a collar effectively sets a minimum and a maximum interest rate for a variable-rate borrower who has also purchased a collar.

Typically, caps, floors, and collars are out of the money when they are originated. By choosing the cap and floor rates appropriately, the lender can create what is known as a "zero-cost collar." That is, the value of the call sold by the lender equals the value of the put the lender purchases.[17]

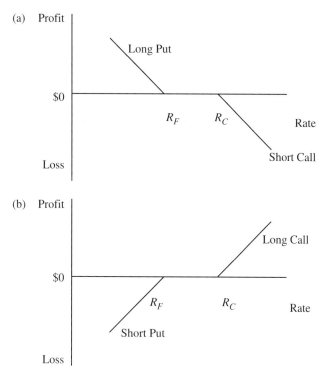

Figure 19.8 (a) A collar's payoff profile to the lender, where "Rate" is the interest rate on the reset date and R_f and R_c are the interest rate floor and cap, respectively. (b) A collar's payoff profile to the borrower.

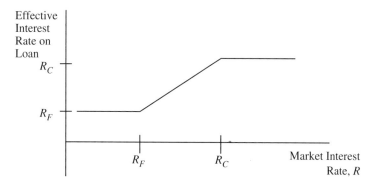

Figure 19.9 A borrower who has borrowed at a variable interest rate and has also bought a collar will never pay an interest rate below the floor rate or above the cap rate.

19.5.4 Valuing Caps, Floors, and Collars

There is a secondary, OTC, market for caps, floors, and collars. Generally, these products trade in multiples of $5 million notional principal, with maturities ranging from three months to 10 or more years. While the traded caps, floors, and collars usually have interest rates based on three-month LIBOR, they can have monthly, quarterly, or semiannual reset dates. Because financial institutions trade these products to adjust their net risk exposure, it is important to be able to value these products.[18]

Consider the following information. Suppose a two-year variable-rate loan in the amount of $10 million exists with reset dates on March 31, June 30, September 30, and December 31. The reset rate is LIBOR. Let today be March 1, 2001. Define $r(0, t)$ as spot LIBOR from March 1, 2001 (day 0) until time t. Define $r(t1, t2)$ as the forward LIBOR from time $t1$ until time $t2$. This forward interest rate might be inferred from Eurodollar futures prices, or from current spot Eurodollar rates. Assume that the volatility of forward Eurodollar interest rates is 20%/year.

Recall that a cap, floor, or collar is a portfolio of options that expire on different reset dates. Thus, to value a cap, floor, or collar, an interest rate option pricing model is used to value each option that expires on each interest rate reset date. Although the more complex Heath, Jarrow, and Morton (1992) model yields more precise option prices, a common practice is to use a version of Black's (1976) forward option pricing model. Thus, to value a caplet or floorlet, use

$$\text{caplet value} = C = (NP)(t_2 - t_1)e^{-rt_2}[FN(d_1) - KN(d_2)] \qquad (19.7)$$

$$\text{floorlet value} = P = (NP)(t_2 - t_1)\, e^{-rt_2}[KN(-d_2) - FN(-d_1)] \qquad (19.8)$$

where

t_1 = the period of time until the start of the forward period = the time to expiration of the caplet, in years = the time until the loan reset date

t_2 = end of the forward period

$t_2 - t_1$ = length of the forward period

$r = (0, t_2)$ = the spot interest rate for the period ending at time $t2$

$F = r(t_1, t_2)$; thus F, the forward interest rate, is the underlying asset

K = cap or floor interest rate

σ = standard deviation of the percentage changes in the forward interest rate

$d_1 = [\ln(F/K)/\sigma\, t_1^{1/2}] + 0.5\sigma\, t_1^{1/2}$

$d_2 = d_1 - \sigma t_1^{1/2}$

Equations (19.7) and (19.8) take the values of Black's forward option pricing model and multiply them by the notional principal times the length of the forward period. The payment on the caplet is made at time t_2.

Table 19.4 presents a valuation example for caplets and floorlets. For times to expiration of less than one year, the riskless interest rate is approximately the T-bill bond equivalent yield. For expirations of more than one year, the riskless interest rate is approximated by the yield on a zero-coupon, or stripped, T-note (or T-bond). The forward rates are approximately equal to Eurodollar futures add-on yields and are presented as percentages. The latter represent F, the underlying asset, in Black's model. The notional principal is $10 million. Today is March 1, 2001. The strike price for the cap, R_c, is 10%. The strike price for the floor, R_f, is 5%. The volatility of each underlying asset (each caplet has its own unique forward rate; each *could* have a different volatility) is 20%. Each caplet and floorlet value is given in dollars.[19]

The value of the cap equals the sum of the eight call values (the individual caplets), or $4,314.23. By summing the values of the eight floorlets, you obtain the floor value of $7930.66. In a collar, the lender sells the cap and buys the floor, so the cost of the collar to the buyer is $3,616.42.

TABLE 19.4 Valuation of Caplets and Floorlets

Loan Reset Date	Time to Expiration, in Years	$r(0, t_1)$	$r(t_1, t_2)$	Cap Value for $R_c = 10\%$	Floor Value for $R_F = 5\%$
03/31/01	0.08219	0.055	6.2821	0.0000	0.0608
06/30/01	0.33151	0.062	6.2825	0.1341	139.1975
09/30/01	0.58356	0.063	6.4735	19.0599	387.8555
12/31/01	0.83562	0.064	6.6701	160.1481	594.3566
03/31/02	1.08219	0.065	6.8567	540.2025	779.6977
06/30/02	1.33151	0.066	6.4431	456.8923	2036.8952
09/30/02	1.58356	0.066	7.1376	1970.4166	1184.0161
12/31/02	1.83562	0.067	6.5372	1167.3808	2808.5782
03/31/03	2.08219	0.067			
				Sum: $4314.2343	$7930.6576

If the borrower wanted a zero-cost collar with a cap of 10%, then the lending institution would search for the interest rate floor that had a value of $4,314.23, the same as the cap.[20]

FinancialCAD can be used to solve for the value of a cap or floor. Before we do that, however, it is useful to first use aaConverR_DFcrv to convert the series of spot interest rates into a series of discount factors. This is shown in Figure 19.10. Then, in Figure 19.11, we use these discount factors and the function aaRatefwd_crv to compute the forward rates that exist in the spot yield curve. These are the same forward rates shown in Table 19.4.

We use the FinancialCAD function aaRcapBL_fs statv to solve for the value of a cap or floor, as shown in Figure 19.12. Note that the discount factors produced by aaConvertR_DFcrv (Figure 19.10) are used as in input in Figure 19.12. Other functions, such as aaRcap_BL_dgen and aaRcap_BL can also be used to value caps and floors.

There is a small difference between the total dollar value of the cap that is computed by FinancialCAD in Figure 19.12, $4330.66, and the cap value of $4314.23 generated in Table 19.4. The difference arises because FinancialCAD does not discount by e^{rt_2} like we do in equations 19.7 and 19.8. Click on FinancialCAD's "Show Math" button in its function finder for Rate Caps and Floors to learn how they discount.

19.6 SUMMARY

In this chapter, we focus on the details of how options provide insurance and some necessary technical details concerning how option prices change as the factors that influence option prices change.

The BSOPM can be differentiated with respect to each of its five parameters, K, T, r, σ, and S. In addition, the second derivative of the BSOPM with respect to S is quite useful. The results are useful formulas that predict how much an option value will change if only *one* input parameter changes by a small amount, and all other inputs are held constant.

A particularly important sensitivity is known as delta. Delta is also called an option hedge ratio. Delta measures the amount by which the option value changes, given a small change in the

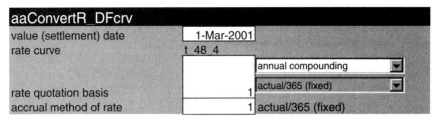

t_48_4
rate curve

maturity date	yield to maturity
31-Mar-2001	0.055
30-Jun-2001	0.062
30-Sep-2001	0.063
31-Dec-2001	0.064
31-Mar-2002	0.065
30-Jun-2002	0.066
30-Sep-2002	0.066
31-Dec-2002	0.067
31-Mar-2003	0.067

discount factor curve - aaConvertR_DFcrv

grid date	discount factor
1-Mar-2001	1
31-Mar-2001	0.995609058
30-Jun-2001	0.980256078
30-Sep-2001	0.964975317
31-Dec-2001	0.949482868
31-Mar-2002	0.934119588
30-Jun-2002	0.918419491
30-Sep-2002	0.903742602
31-Dec-2002	0.887770948
31-Mar-2003	0.873687812
#N/A	#N/A

Figure 19.10 The financialCAD function aaConvertR_DFcrv converts a series of spot interest rates into a series of discount factors.

value of the underlying asset and holding everything else equal. Delta and gamma, the rate at which delta changes, are important factors to consider when one is managing risk.

Portfolios consisting of the underlying asset and options also have deltas and gammas. These are commonly called position deltas and position gammas. We provide an example of how risk managers can immunize their portfolios against delta and gamma effects.

We also provide a discussion on time spreads. Time spreads are portfolios of options that do not have the same time to expiration. We present an example of how such a portfolio can be delta hedged.

Because many firms, institutions, and individuals borrow at variable interest rates, we discuss the use of options to manage interest rate risk. In particular, we show how a borrower can ensure

aaRatefwd_crv

date list	t_7		
discount factor curve	t_43_1		
interpolation method		1	linear ▼
			actual/365 (fixed) ▼
accrual method		1	actual/365 (fixed)
margin above or below a floating rate		0	

t_7
date list
effective and terminating date pairs

31-Mar-2001
30-Jun-2001
30-Sep-2001
31-Dec-2001
31-Mar-2002
30-Jun-2002
30-Sep-2002
31-Dec-2002
31-Mar-2003

t_43_1
discount factor curve

grid date	discount factor
1-Mar-2001	1
31-Mar-2001	0.995609058
30-Jun-2001	0.980256078
30-Sep-2001	0.964975317
31-Dec-2001	0.949482868
31-Mar-2002	0.934119588
30-Jun-2002	0.918419491
30-Sep-2002	0.903742602
31-Dec-2002	0.887770948
31-Mar-2003	0.873687812

forward rate list given date list and discount factors – aaRatefwd_crv
forward rate

0.062820965
0.062825192
0.064734825
0.066700917
0.068566618
0.064430912
0.071376297
0.065372252

Figure 19.11 The financialCAD function aaRatefwd_crv, converts a series of discount factors (based on spot interest rates), into forward rates.

that he will never pay a variable interest rate above a set level, known as a cap. In addition, we show how a lender can ensure that he will never receive less on a variable rate loan than predetermined amount, known as a floor. Finally, we present an example of how to calculate the value of a cap and a floor.

aaRcapBL_fs_statv		
value (settlement) date	1-Mar-2001	
interpolation method	1	linear
option type	1	rate cap
accrual method	1	actual/365 (actual)
current fixing of rate as of last reset day		actual/365 (actual)
rate cap payment table – using volatility	t_3	
discount factor curve	t_43_1	

t_3

rate cap payment table - using volatility

effective date	terminating date	notional principal amount	exercise rate	implied volatility
31-Mar-2001	30-Jun-2001	10,000,000.00	0.1	0.2
30-Jun-2001	30-Sep-2001	10,000,000.00	0.1	0.2
30-Sep-2001	31-Dec-2001	10,000,000.00	0.1	0.2
31-Dec-2001	31-Mar-2002	10,000,000.00	0.1	0.2
31-Mar-2002	30-Jun-2002	10,000,000.00	0.1	0.2
30-Jun-2002	30-Sep-2002	10,000,000.00	0.1	0.2
30-Sep-2002	31-Dec-2002	10,000,000.00	0.1	0.2
31-Dec-2002	31-Mar-2003	10,000,000.00	0.1	0.2

t_43_1

discount factor curve

grid date	discount factor
1-Mar-2001	1
31-Mar-2001	0.995609058
30-Jun-2001	0.980256078
30-Sep-2001	0.964975317
31-Dec-2001	0.949482868
31-Mar-2002	0.934119588
30-Jun-2002	0.918419491
30-Sep-2002	0.903742602
31-Dec-2002	0.887770948
31-Mar-2003	0.873687812
#N/A	#N/A

rate cap table - Black '76 - aaRcapBL_fs_statv

effective date	terminating date	notional principal amount	exercise rate	implied volatility	fair value	delta	gamma
31-Mar-2001	30-Jun-2001	10,000,000.00	0.1	0.2	-3.13037E-12	8.14E-14	1.82E-14
30-Jun-2001	30-Sep-2001	10,000,000.00	0.1	0.2	0.13427369	0.008424	0.000489
30-Sep-2001	31-Dec-2001	10,000,000.00	0.1	0.2	19.09125701	0.670891	0.020825
31-Dec-2001	31-Mar-2002	10,000,000.00	0.1	0.2	160.49948	3.8818	0.079043
31-Mar-2002	30-Jun-2002	10,000,000.00	0.1	0.2	541.7054766	9.996654	0.148473
30-Jun-2002	30-Sep-2002	10,000,000.00	0.1	0.2	458.4045613	8.378268	0.123284
30-Sep-2002	31-Dec-2002	10,000,000.00	0.1	0.2	1978.204807	25.14651	0.23784
31-Dec-2002	31-Mar-2003	10,000,000.00	0.1	0.2	1172.616137	16.35053	0.173722

4330.655993

Figure 19.12 The financialCAD function aaRcapBL_fs_statv, solves for the value of a cap or floor.

References

Abken, Peter A. 1989. "Interest Rate Caps, Collars and Floors." *Federal Reserve Bank of Atlanta Economic Review,* Vol. 74, pp. 3–24.

Black, Fischer. 1976. "The Pricing of Commodity Contracts." *Journal of Financial Economics,* Vol. 3, pp. 167–179.

Black, Fischer, and Myron Scholes. 1973. "The Pricing of Options and Corporate Liabilities." *Journal of Political Economy*, Vol. 81, pp. 637–654.

Boyle, Phelim, and Stuart Turnbull. 1989. "Pricing and Hedging Capped Options." *Journal of Futures Markets,* Vol .9, pp. 41–54.

Brown, Keith, and Donald J. Smith. 1988. "Recent Innovations in Interest Rate Risk Management and the Reintermediation of Commercial Banking." *Financial Management,* Vol. 15, pp. 45–58.

Conine, Thomas, and Maurry Tamarkin. 1984. "A Pedagogic Note on the Derivation of the Comparative Statics of the Option Pricing Model," *Financial Review,* Vol. 19, pp. 397–400.

Heath, D., R. Jarrow, and A. Morton. 1992. "Bond Pricing and the Term Structure of Interest Rates." *Econometrica,* Vol. 60, pp. 77–105.

Galai, Dan, and Ronald Masulis. 1976. "The Option Pricing Model and the Risk Factor of Stock," *Journal of Financial Economics,* Vol. 3, pp. 53–81.

Natenberg, Sheldon. 1994. *Option Volatility and Pricing*. Chicago: Probus Publishing.

Rubinstein, Mark. 1985. "Nonparametric Tests of Alternative Option Pricing Models Using All Reported Trades and Quotes on the 30 Most Active CBOE Option Classes from August 23, 1976, Through August 31, 1987," *Journal of Finance,* Vol. 40, pp. 455–480.

Stapleton, Richard and Marti Subrahmanyam. 1990. "Interest Rate Caps and Floors," In Stephen Figlewski, William L. Silber, and Marti G. Subrahmanyam, eds. *Financial Options: From Theory to Practice.* Homewood, IL: Business One-Irwin., pp. 281–313.

Notes

[1]Of course, tax, accounting, and legal factors may all affect the risk manager's decision to use options, futures, forwards, or swaps.

[2]Recall that in a continuous hedging strategy, the risk manager will always hedge, regardless of her beliefs or of price forecasts. In contrast, a selective hedging strategy will allow the risk manager to hedge only when she expects prices to move adversely.

[3]In addition, the second derivative of the BSOPM with respect to S is quite useful.

[4]Note that the partial derivative with respect to the strike price has no Greek name. This is most likely because the strike price of the option is not stochastic. For details on the derivations of these formulas, see Galai and Masulis (1976) and Conine and Tamarkin (1984).

[5]By convention, theta is frequently defined as the *negative* of $\partial C / \partial T$.

[6]See the discussion of theta in Chapter 14 for some intuition concerning this result.

[7]It is assumed that you can sell short the stock costlessly and receive full use of the proceeds. Also, note that under the assumptions of the BSOPM, Δ can asymptotically approach 0.0 and 1.0 but can never exactly equal those values. The tails of a normal curve stretch out to infinity, so that $N(d_1)$ can never exactly equal 0.0 or 1.0.

[8]The principles of call replication using the binomial option pricing model appear in Chapter 17.

[9]The seeds of this example stem from material presented in Natenberg (1994, Chapter 5).

[10]Note that the choice to present the data every week is arbitrary. In practice, investors monitor Δ daily, or even intra daily, and adjust their positions when their investment in the underlying asset is sufficiently different from the Δ that is prescribed by their option pricing model.

[11]Recall that there are many different possible paths through which the stock price can wander before option expiration. Vastly different results for such an example can be obtained depending on the interim volatility of the stock price (i.e, the volatility over the first nine weeks). You are encouraged to prepare a spreadsheet and experiment. One interesting aspect is that if the volatility over the first nine weeks is lower than the trader's forecast, it is possible to obtain a result closer to the projected profit than if the volatility over the first nine weeks is higher than the trader's forecast for subsequent return volatility.

[12]The reader should note that this logic applies to a wide variety of derivative securities (such as forwards, futures, and options on futures, as well as options on the underlying asset) and to the underlying asset.

[13]However, it is important to note that the portfolio value of a delta–gamma hedge can still change if the riskless interest rate changes, as time passes, and/or if volatility changes. Note that equation 19.4 can be derived by applying Itô's lemma to $C = C(S,t)$ where the underlying price, S, is assumed to follow an Itô process. Then,

$$dC = \frac{\partial C}{\partial S} dS + \frac{\partial C}{\partial t} dt + \frac{1}{z} \frac{\partial^2 C}{\partial S^2} (dS)^2$$

which is (19.4), when the 'greeks' are substituted for $\frac{\partial C}{\partial S}$, $\frac{\partial C}{\partial t}$, and $\frac{\partial^2 C}{\partial S^2}$.

[14]Rubinstein (1985) employs actual transaction data and bid–asked spreads, accounts for dividends and early exercise, and considers several different option pricing models in his tests of option market efficiency. He finds that implied volatilities for out-of-the-money calls grow significantly higher, the shorter the time to expiration. He also finds that the market began to overprice at the money calls with a short time to expiration in his later subperiod, October 1977–September 1978. The empirical phenomenon may be explained in one of two ways: (a) all our option pricing models are incorrect, or (b) investors like to play "long shots" that offer a small chance of a large percentage payoff, and their purchase of options that offer this feature results in higher prices for these options.

[15]Another common clause is that the yearly adjustment can never exceed a preset amount. For example, while a variable-rate mortgage might specify a cap of 12.5% and a floor of 5.5%, it might also restrict the yearly change in the interest rate to be no more than 200 basis points. From Example 19.8, this would mean that one year after the loan is originated, the new interest rate could range between 6.5 and 10.5%.

[16]The payoff to the cap or floor is often negotiated to be discounted [i.e., the present value of $NP(R - R_c)(d/360)$].

[17]In foreign exchange transactions, a zero-cost collar is called a **range forward**.

[18]Instead of trading caps, floors, and collars, financial institutions could insure the risk of their net interest rate exposure by using Eurodollar futures options, or by using Eurodollar futures contracts and dynamic hedging methods (i.e., delta hedging to dynamically create an option).

[19]By convention, the forward rate in a cap, $r(t_1 t_2)$, is computed using $[1 + r(0, t_2)]^{t_2} = [1 + r(0, t_1)]^{t_1} [1 + r(t_1, t_2)(t_2 - t_1)]$. The forward rates are then said to be computed on a "money market basis". You are encouraged to use Equation (19.7) to verify the cap values, and Equation (19.8) to verify the floor values.

[20]For more details on caps, floors, and collars, see Brown and Smith (1988), Abken (1989), Boyle and Turnbull (1989), and Stapleton and Subrahmanyam (1990).

PROBLEMS

19.1   Toastcoil is a firm in an enviable position. It has a monopoly in the United States. in the business of manufacturing heating elements that are put into toasters. No other firm in the country manufactures these elements. While other firms in Europe and Japan make the products, they do not export to the United States. Toastcoil does not export its product and none of its raw materials are imported. On the surface, Toastcoil faces no currency risk. It has no revenues, expenses, assets, or liabilities that are based on any foreign currency.

But this is an erroneous view of Toastcoil's position. If the ¥/$ exchange rate rises, then Japanese manufacturers may find it profitable to enter the U.S. market. If any Eurocurrency price of the dollar rises, European manufacturers may decide to export their products to the United. States. Therefore, Toastcoil does indeed face foreign exchange risk. If the dollar rises in value, the firm's profitable monopoly position may erode from foreign competitors.

How can Toastcoil use options to protect itself against this exchange rate risk?

19.2 In the winter of 1997, several Asian currencies dropped drastically in value against the U.S. dollar. Several currencies, including the Indonesian rupiah, fell by more than 50% in value.

    a. One small Indonesian firm had in an earlier year borrowed $800 million because U.S. interest rates were lower than Indonesian interest rates. Then, in July, this firm used foreign currency options to hedge part of its dollar-denominated debt. Explain how the firm could use options for this purpose.

    b. If the $/rupiah exchange rate began to decline, how would the Indonesian firm maintain its hedge?

19.3 You are given the following information:

$S = 93$

$K = 100$

$T = 0.25$ year

$r = 7.5\%/$year

$\sigma = 0.75/$year

No dividends

    a. Use the BSOPM to calculate the put and call prices. Use FinCAD and put–call parity to verify your answer.

    b. Use the formulas in Section 19.1.1 to calculate values for delta, gamma, vega, rho, and theta for calls and puts. Use FinCAD to verify your answers.

19.4 Consider a call option with a strike price of $K = 90$, and 70 days until expiration. The price of the underlying asset is 86.375, and the volatility of the underlying asset is 32.7%. The riskless interest rate is 6%. The actual market price of the option is 3. You might refer to Section 19.3 to answer the following questions.

    a. Explain what trades you would make to arbitrage this mispriced option, assuming that your estimate of volatility, 32.7%, is correct.

    b. Suppose that the subsequent weekly prices of the underlying asset are those shown in Table 19.1. Dynamically maintain your arbitrage. Create a table similar to Table 19.2, and use the Case I price for the stock price at expiration ($S_T = 97.625$). What is the actual arbitrage profit, and how does it compare to the arbitrage profit you expected?

19.5 Suppose you have positions in the following assets:

Long or Short, Number of Options or Shares	Delta/Unit
Short 1,300 shares	1.00
Long 400 puts	−0.46
Short 150 calls	0.80
Long 72 calls	0.28

Calculate the position delta. Explain what will happen to the value of the portfolio if the stock price increases by $1.

19.6 An options trader has several long and short positions in many puts and calls on a given stock. The computed position delta of the portfolio is −12,456. Each option is on one share of stock. How many shares of stock should be bought or sold in order to be delta neutral?

19.7   Suppose you bought 100 undervalued puts with a Δ (that reflects your estimated volatility) of -0.30. You wish to create a delta-neutral position by using in-the-money puts that are correctly valued (or overvalued) and have a Δ of -0.85. How many of the latter should you trade, and should they be bought or sold?

19.8   An options market maker has the following positions in options:

Long or Short Number of Options	Put/Call	Option Delta
Long 20	Calls	0.2
Long 48	Calls	0.6
Short 16	Calls	0.82
Long 120	Puts	-0.12
Short 30	Puts	-0.51

a. What is his position delta? How can we use trades in the underlying shares, to go home delta neutral?

b. Suppose instead that he anticipates a weak opening in this stock and wants to have a position delta of -0.50 overnight. How many shares of stock should he buy or sell to achieve this?

19.9   An investor wishes to enter into a delta-neutral position with two options that, given the current price of the underlying asset, have the following prices and deltas:

Option	Price	Delta
A	14	-0.4300
B	14	+0.3300

a. Suppose an investor writes eight contracts of option A. To be delta neutral, how many contracts of option B should be traded? Should they be bought or sold?

b. The investor estimates that if the price of the underlying asset increased by one dollar, the delta of option A would become -0.4200, and the delta of option B would become 0.3340. Using this information, estimate the position gamma for the delta-neutral position you formed in part a.

c. If the underlying asset does increase in value by \$1, and the investor wishes to reestablish the delta-neutral position using the underlying asset, how many shares must he buy or sell?

19.10   Suppose $S = K_1 = \$90$, $r = 6\%$, $\sigma = 50\%$, $T = 90$ days, and $K_2 = 110$. Then, by using the BSOPM or the FinCAD function aaBS, fill in the following table:

Variable	Call Option K=90	K=110	Stock
Price			
Delta			
Gamma			

a. Suppose an investor writes 400 of the 90 calls. What positions does he need in the stock and the 110 calls to be delta–gamma neutral?

b. Instead, suppose the investor buys 250 of the 90 calls. What positions does he need in the stock and the 110 calls to be delta–gamma neutral?

19.11   In Section 19.4.4.2, our computations yielded 1.22 as the initial ratio of calls written per call purchased needed to create a delta-neutral position. If the stock price remained unchanged, what will happen to that ratio as the expiration date nears? Provide an intuitive answer (i.e., do not compute new deltas). If the stock price were to rise immediately after entering the neutral spread, what would happen to that ratio? Again, do not compute new deltas. Provide an intuitive answer.

19.12 Consider the following information. Suppose an 18-month variable-rate loan exists with reset dates on March 31, June 30, September 30, and December 31. The reset rate is LIBOR. Let today be February 1, 2001. The notional principal is $25 million. The volatility of interest rates is 15%.

Loan Reset Date	Time to Expiration (years)	$r(0,t1)$	$r(t1,t2)$	Cap Value for R_c= 8%	Floor Value for R_F= 3%
03/31/01	0.035				
06/30/01	0.042				
09/30/01	0.048				
12/31/01	0.053				
03/31/02	0.055				
06/30/02	0.057				
09/30/02	0.058				

Calculate the dollar value of the cap and the floor. Use the FinCAD function aaRcapBL_fs_statv to check your solution.

19.13 Use the FinCAD function aaRcap BL_fs_statv to compute the theoretical value of the 5% floor in the example shown in Section 19.5.4.

PART 5

DERIVATIVE FRONTIERS

CHAPTER 20

Current Topics in Risk Management

In this chapter, we discuss several currently important risk management topics: value at risk (VaR), credit derivatives, options on debt instruments, swaptions, and exotic options.

20.1 VALUE AT RISK (VaR)

20.1.1 Background

One goal of active risk management is to reduce the variability of uncertain cash flows. As you have seen, however, risk management cannot eliminate this variability. Further, many examples that we have presented in this textbook have presented risk management vehicles dealing with a single risk, such as interest rate risk, foreign currency risk, commodity price risk, or stock market risk. However, the modern corporation could have hundreds, or thousands, of sources of uncertainty that are being hedged (or not being hedged).

Value at risk (VaR) is the name of a risk management concept by means of which senior management can be informed, via a single number, of the short-term price risk faced by the firm. The origin of "value at risk" stems from a request by J. P. Morgan's chairman, Dennis Weatherstone, for a simple report, to be made available to him every day, concerning the firm's risk exposure. Since then, VaR has rapidly become the financial industry's standard for measuring exposure to financial price risks. Today, few financial firms fail to make VaR part of their daily reporting to senior management.

Use of the VaR concept has become pervasive.[1] The Bank for International Settlements (BIS), which is essentially the central bank of the world's major central banks, proposed in April 1995 that major banks use VaR to determine their capital adequacy requirements. These requirements became effective January 1, 1998. The U.S. Federal Reserve Bank and the International Swaps and Derivatives Association (ISDA) basically endorsed the BIS's recommendations about VaR. In December 1995, the U.S. Securities and Exchange Commission (SEC) proposed rules that would require corporations to disclose information concerning their use of derivatives. Firms would be directed to use one of three methods that would provide information about the risk exposure of their portfolios of financial assets and derivatives. One of the methods was VaR.[2] In April 1996, eleven individuals from the institutional investment community formed the Risk Standards Working Group (1996) and charged themselves to "create a set of risk standards for institutional investment managers and institutional investors." Risk Standard 12 states that money managers "should regularly measure relevant risks and quantify the key drivers of risk and return." The standard proceeds to suggest VaR as one possible method for measurement of risk.[3]

The website www.gloriamundi.org/ is devoted to the concept of VaR.

20.1.2 The VaR Concept

The VaR concept is an attempt to encapsulate an estimate of the price risk possessed by a portfolio of derivatives and other financial assets. The statistic that VaR provides is the dollar amount by which the value of a portfolio might change with a stated probability during a stated time horizon; the time horizon might be one day, one week, or longer. For example, a financial institution might estimate that there is a 1% probability that its portfolio will decline by more $15 million during the next week. The decline in value might be caused by changes in the prices of fundamental risk factors such as changes in foreign exchange rates, interest rate changes, commodity price fluctuations, changes in stock prices, and/or increases in volatility.

It is important to note that the price risk number obtained from a VaR model summarizes risk exposure into a dollar figure that purportedly represents the estimated maximum loss over an interval of time. That is, a dollar loss greater than the VaR estimate will occur with a smaller probability than the VaR estimate.

20.1.3 Computing VaR

There is no standard method to compute VaR. However, several accepted methods for computing VaR have emerged. These methods are the variance–covariance approach, the historical simulation method, and the Monte Carlo simulation method. It is important to note that VaR is sensitive to the assumptions made and to the method used. In other words, your VaR number will differ depending on your assumptions and which method you have chosen to compute it. Risk managers should understand both these sources of sensitivity when choosing a method to compute VaR.

20.1.3.1 The Variance–Covariance Approach

The **variance–covariance approach** is also known as the "delta-normal method." The variance–covariance approach is used by J. P. Morgan's *RiskMetrics* model.[4]

The important assumption of this approach to estimate VaR is that the returns for each of the institution's assets are normally distributed. Recall from your investments course that the variance of a portfolio's returns are computed using the following formula:

$$\mathrm{Var}(\tilde{R}) = \sum_i \sum_j w_i w_j \sigma_{ij} = \sum_i \sum_j w_i w_j \sigma_i \sigma_j \rho_{ij} \tag{20.1}$$

where

w_i = fraction of the total portfolio value consisting of asset i, where $\Sigma w_i = 1.0$
σ_{ij} = covariance of asset i's returns with asset j's returns
σ_i = standard deviation of asset i's returns
ρ_{ij} = correlation of asset i's returns with asset j's returns

For two assets, equation (20.1) becomes

$$\mathrm{Var}(\tilde{R}) = w_1^2 \sigma_1^2 + w_2^2 \sigma_2^2 + 2 w_1 w_2 \sigma_{12} = w_1^2 \sigma_1^2 + w_2^2 \sigma_2^2 + 2 w_1 w_2 \sigma_1 \sigma_2 \rho_{12}. \tag{20.2}$$

Suppose the risk manager assumes that the return distribution of his portfolio is normal with a mean of zero. Then, the first step to obtain a VaR estimate is to obtain an estimate of the variance of his portfolio's periodic returns. These periodic returns could be calculated daily, weekly, or for any other interval.

After one has obtained a portfolio mean return and return variance, it becomes a simple statistical procedure to estimate what the loss in value of the portfolio will be during that period. Further note that this estimate can be calculated with any desired probability. For example, the value at risk, VaR, will equal 1.645 times the portfolio's standard deviation with a probability of 5%. The maximum loss with a 1% probability will equal 2.327 times the portfolio's standard deviation.

In one approach for using the variance–covariance method to estimate VaR, the variance of each asset's returns and each pairwise covariance are estimated. These variance estimates can be calculated from historical data, the implied volatilities contained in option prices, and/or volatility forecasts, or they can be generated from the risk manager's subjective beliefs. If the risk manager has only two assets in his portfolio, w_1 and w_2 in Equation (20.2) are the fractions invested in each asset, σ_1 and σ_2 are the standard deviations of the returns of each asset, and ρ_{12} is the correlation between the returns of the two assets.

In practice, many VaR users employ changes in value instead of using rates of return. That is, let V_t represent the value of an asset on day t. Then, the change in value is simply $V_2 - V_1$. The percentage change in value (i.e., the rate of return) is given by $(V_2 - V_1)/V_1$.

There are a few reasons to use value changes instead of percentage changes in value. First, many derivatives, such as futures contracts, are marked to market. In these cases, their values are zero after they have been marked to market, and the percentage rate of return cannot be computed. Second, many derivatives will have a negative value; that is, they are liabilities. Regardless of whether a contract is an asset or a liability, the user of VaR is interested in the change of the value of the contract over the period of interest. Thus, the standard deviations of value changes are of greater use than the standard deviations of rates of returns.

EXAMPLE 20.1   Using the Variance–Covariance Approach to Calculate VaR:
Consider a portfolio consists of these three assets:

   a. *A currency swap*. Because of changes in the exchange rate since the swap was first entered into, the swap now has a value of $2 million, or 8.7% of the portfolio's total value.

   b. *A bond*. The market value of the bond is $17 million, which is 73.9% of the portfolio's total value.

   c. *A stock*. The 10,000 shares are worth $4 million, or 17.4% of the portfolio's total value.

Assume the variance–covariance matrix[5] of the assets' daily returns is

	Swap	Bond	Stock
Swap	0.00090	–0.00008	0.00007
Bond		0.00040	–0.00010
Stock			0.00300

Then the variance of the portfolio's daily returns distribution is then found by using Equation (20.1):

$$\mathrm{Var}(\tilde{R}) = w_1^2\sigma_1^2 + w_2^2\sigma_2^2 + w_3^2\sigma_3^2 + 2w_1w_2\sigma_{12} + 2w_1w_3\sigma_{13} + 2w_2w_3\sigma_{23}$$

$$= (0.087)^2(0.00090) + (0.739)^2(0.00040) + (0.174)^2(0.00300)$$

$$+ 2\ (0.087)(0.739)(-0.00008) + 2(0.087)\ (0.174)(0.00007)$$

$$+ 2\ (0.174)(0.739)(-0.00010)$$

$$= 0.0002822$$

The standard deviation of the daily returns distribution is $(0.0002822)^{1/2} = 0.0168$, or 1.68%. One standard deviation of dollar loss from the portfolio value of $23 million is $386,375 (1.68% of $23 million is $386,375). To calculate the VaR, multiply the number of standard deviations for a stated probability level by one standard deviation of dollar loss. Thus, there is a 5% probability that a one-day loss of (1.645)($386,375) = $635,587 will be realized. There is a 1% probability that a one-day loss of (2.327)($386,375) = $899,095 will be realized.

An important assumption we made was that returns, or value changes, are normally distributed. Option returns are, of course, not normally distributed. The lack of normality becomes most obvious when options are held until expiration, as the returns distribution of a long put or long call is truncated at –100% and there is a great deal of positive skewness.

One way to avoid the "nonlinear" payoff pattern of options is to assume that the options are equivalent to delta units of the underlying asset. Recall from Chapter 16, that the BOPM teaches us that a call is equivalent to owning delta shares of stock and borrowing. Thus, the risk manager can substitute $\Delta S + B$ for any option. The returns distributions for stocks and bonds are closer to normal than are those for options. Remember, however, that the concept of delta is applicable only when all else is held equal. Thus, substituting $\Delta S + B$ for an option works best when one is calculating a daily VaR. For periods longer than one day, the time to expiration is definitely not being held constant, and it is unlikely that the riskless interest rate and the implied volatility of the underlying asset will remain constant. Option deltas change when any fundamental determinant of option value changes, such as time to expiration. Moreover, deltas are unstable when gammas are high.

Another approach for using the variance–covariance approach to estimate VaR requires the decomposition of asset value volatility into its most fundamental sources. This is the approach taken by J.P. Morgan's *RiskMetrics* model. The fundamental factors behind the changes in asset values are interest rates in each relevant country and for several times to maturity, spot exchange rates, country stock market factors, and commodity prices. Think of a forward exchange contract. The basic factors that cause it to change in value are the domestic interest rate for a zero-coupon bond maturing on the same day as the forward contract's delivery date, the foreign interest rate for the same time to maturity, and the spot exchange rate.

There are several potential problems with the variance–covariance approach for estimating VaR. First, if historical data are used to estimate the variance–covariance matrix of asset returns, it is highly likely that the future will not replicate the past. In particular, the estimation period might not include an "event" that happens only once every 'N' years, such as the 1987 stock market crash or the 1997 collapse of the Asian stock markets and currency values. Similarly, the recent past may actually include a period in which an "event" occurred that is unlikely to ever occur again. Then, the probability of a large loss will be overstated.

VaR figures that are calculated from historical data will differ, depending on how far back in the past the historical data are gathered. If one year of daily historical data were gathered on January 1, 1989, these data would not include the very unusual financial events of October 1987. But if two years of data are gathered, the estimated variances and covariances are very different from those estimated using only one year of data from 1988 only. Consider a $23 million portfolio that mimics the S&P 500 Index. The mean daily return and standard deviation of daily returns for the S&P 500 Index were as follows:

	1988 Only	**1987 and 1988**
Mean	0.000284	0.000237
Standard deviation	0.010613	0.016858
5% VaR	$401,543	$637,822
1% VaR	$568,018	$902,257

As you can see, the effect on the VaR calculation is dramatic. For example, assuming a mean of zero, if one were using 1988 data only to calculate VaR on January 1, 1989, the 1% VaR is $568,018. However, if two years of daily data are used, the 1% VaR is $902,257, about 60% higher. Recall that the purpose of VaR is to encapsulate risk into one number so that senior management can ascertain the firm's price risk. Senior risk managers must be aware of this type of data effect on VaR.

Another shortcoming that is somewhat related to the foregoing discussion is that return distributions may not be normal. The return distribution might be skewed, or it may possess what is called "fat tails." A fat-tailed distribution is said to possess leptokurtosis and is characterized by too many observations (relative to a normal distribution) in the tails. That is, unusual events occur more frequently than a normal distribution would predict.

Finally, as we have already noted, options, and assets with optionlike characteristics, possess nonnormal return distributions. Their sensitivities to changes in their determinants of value (S, r, σ, and T) are themselves unstable and unpredictable. Moreover, their sensitivities (e.g., their deltas) are estimated only for infinitesimal changes in their fundamental determinants of value.

20.1.3.2   The Historical Simulation Approach

In the historical simulation approach, the risk manager determines how each relevant price has changed during each of the past 'N' time periods. For example, the relevant prices might be the dollar price of the Japanese yen and euro, short-term U.S. interest rates, and the dollar price of oil. It is possible to use a historical database to find the price changes for each of these four variables on each of the last 300 days. The risk manager then estimates how each of the 300 sets of price changes would affect the value of his current portfolio of spot assets and derivatives. Assuming that each of these outcomes is equally likely, he will then rank the resulting estimated value changes from most positive (value increases) to most negative (value decreases). If the risk manager is interested in the VaR at the 95% confidence level, he will find the 15th worst outcome out of the 300. The VaR at the 99% confidence level is the 3rd worst outcome. These are the losses that will be exceeded only 5% of the time and 1% of the time, respectively.

Institutions might be interested in their VaR for the next day, or for longer intervals of time. The more actively the portfolio is traded, the shorter the time interval of interest. If the portfolio is turned over frequently, then estimating the monthly VaR for today's portfolio provides little information. Thus, tomorrow's portfolio is likely to be very different from today's portfolio.

Institutions might also wish to use the last 100, 250, and 500 days to estimate their daily VaR. Note that there is no assurance that any given amount of historical data is "correct." The risk manager must decide whether the distant past or the recent past more accurately predicts what tomorrow will bring.

It is important to note that using the historical simulation approach implicitly incorporates the correlations among asset price changes. To the extent that, say, price changes of the yen and the euro are highly correlated, this correlation will show up in the historical set of price changes.

20.1.3.3   The Monte Carlo Simulation Approach

In the Monte Carlo simulation approach, the risk manager specifies probability distributions or stochastic processes for prices in the future. A different probability distribution can be assumed for each pricing determinant. For example, changes in interest rates might be skewed right, while changes in oil prices might be drawn from a uniform distribution and changes in the price of a currency might be normally distributed.

After the distributions or processes are defined, random realizations of outcomes can be simulated. Each randomly chosen outcome is a set of prices. Correlations are explicitly incorporated in the simulation. The change in value of each asset in the portfolio is estimated for each randomly selected set of prices, thereby producing a probability distribution of future value changes of the portfolio. The risk manager can then determine what the worst outcome will be with a desired confidence level.

20.1.4   Stress Testing

For any VaR calculation method, it is important for the risk manager to perform *stress testing*. The purpose of stress testing is to assess the valuation impact of worst-case scenarios, regardless of whether these outcomes were realized during the recent past.

One benefit of stress testing is that economic variables can be ranked in order of their effect on portfolio value. If, say, the risk manager discovers that his portfolio's value is most sensitive to a rise in short-term U.S. interest rates, he could decide to hedge that price risk specifically. Stress testing also allows the risk manager to examine the effect of economic conditions other than price changes. For example, changes in the shape of one country's yield curve, changes in options' implied volatilities, or changes in correlations might be important VaR determinants.

20.1.4.1   Stress Testing: The Importance of Skewness and Leptokurtosis

It is well recognized that financial asset returns are not distributed normally. are widely known In fact, the distributions of asset returns exhibit skewness and leptokurtosis. These exotic-sounding terms are merely ways of describing how asset returns are distributed.

Measures of central tendency and dispersion (i.e., the mean and the variance) are widely known. In statistical terms, the expected value, or mean, is known as the first moment of a probability

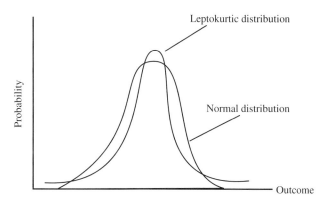

Figure 20.1 Normal distribution and leptokurtic distribution. Relative to the normal distribution, the leptokurtic distribution has a greater probability that an observation near the mean will occur (the distribution in more peaked) and a greater probability that observations far from the mean will occur (the distribution possesses fat tails).

distribution and the variance is the second moment. Skewness, a measure of symmetry, is known as the third moment, and kurtosis is known as the fourth moment. Kurtosis can best be described in terms of the well-known symmetric, normal distribution. In comparison to a normal distribution, a distribution that possesses *leptokurtosis* is one that has too many observations near the mean and too many observations far from the mean (in the so-called tails of the distribution). Figure 20.1 illustrates the difference between a normal distribution and a distribution that exhibits leptokurtosis.

The risk manager must realize that financial asset returns display leptokurtosis and build this fact into a stress testing system. If returns are normally distributed, the probability of the event occurring might be 0.000001, or one in a million. But, because actual returns distributions are leptokurtic, or fat-tailed, low probability events occur more frequently than predicted by normal distributions.

20.1.4.2   The 1987 Stock Market Crash: A Lesson in Leptokurtosis

Imagine the following scenario. It is October 1, 1987. Suppose an extremely creative risk-managing group calculates the mean and standard deviation of the daily returns on the S&P 500 Index to calculate a portfolio VaR. They find the following.

Time Period	Mean	Standard Deviation
1/1/1987–9/30/1987	0.001505	0.009840
1/1/1986–9/30/1987	0.000952	0.009538
1/1/1983–9/30/1987	0.000690	0.008385
1/1/1950–9/30/1987	0.000309	0.007841

In addition, for the period between January 1, 1950, and September 30, 1987, the risk-managing team has uncovered the following information. Of the 9571 trading days, the market was down on 4430 days. Because the members of the risk managing team are concerned about down days, they rank the returns from lowest to highest, which allows them to prepare the following table.

Market Falls by	Number of Days	Percentage of Down Days
>7%	0	0.0000
6–7%	2	0.0451
5–6%	3	0.0677
4–5%	6	0.1354
3–4%	19	0.4289
2–3%	103	2.3251
1–2%	757	17.0880

The risk management team also finds that there are 222 days when the market fell by more than 1.60% (4430×0.05) and 44 days when the market fell by more than 2.50% (4430×0.01). The three worst one-day losses occurred on May 28, 1962, September 26, 1955, and June 26, 1950. However, the fourth worst one-day loss (–4.9%) occurred on September 11, 1986.

Armed with the data, the risk-managing team uses the time period January 1, 1950, through September 30, 1987 to calculate the one-day VaR for the firm's $100 million portfolio.

VaR Calculation Method	VaR Level	VaR in Dollars
Variance–covariance	5%	–$1,289,845
Variance–covariance	1%	–$1,824,600
Historical simulation	5%	–$1,600,000
Historical simulation	1%	–$2,500,000

After filing their report with senior management, the risk management team embarks on its well-deserved one-month vacation. Lolling on the beach on October 19, 1987, they hear that the market fell that day by 22.90%. The team is stunned. Their diversified portfolio has suffered a terrific blow. They quickly convene and ask themselves the following question:

If financial asset returns are normally distributed, what is the probability of observing a market crash like the one that occurred on October 19, 1987?

Because the daily mean return is not statistically different from zero, the 22.90% decline represents

$$\frac{22.90}{0.7841} = 29.205$$

standard deviations from the mean. If asset returns are normally distributed, statistically speaking, the 1987 stock market crash essentially should not have occurred. In fact, given the foregoing data, if asset returns are normally distributed, 4% market declines should occur about once in every 5.9 million trading days. Yet, there were 11 days in 9571 with a market decline of 4% or more. Events like the 1987 stock market crash defy probability, yet they do occur. Further, it is quite possible that a similar event will occur again in your lifetime, because stock return distributions possess leptokurtosis.

It is important to recognize that the value-at-risk concept is designed for "normal" market conditions. However, sometimes the risk management team is interested in analyzing the performance of the portfolio under extreme market conditions. This demand has given rise to *CrashMetrics*, a data set and methodology that can be used to estimate the exposure of a portfolio to extreme market movements. Basically, the *CrashMetrics* method assumes that the effects of a crash cannot be hedged and then proceeds to predict the worst outcome for the portfolio.[6]

20.1.5   Back Testing

Because of the statistically perverse nature of asset returns, it is important that risk managers perform *back testing*. In back testing, the risk management team examines the performance of their VaR estimates of extreme losses with respect to realized losses. That is, back testing allows the risk manager to determine whether the VaR methods employed are adequate.

When back testing, the risk manager must be aware that there will be periods in which actual losses will exceed those predicted by VaR. For example, the risk manager must realize that statistically speaking, actual losses will exceed a 5% VaR, 5% of the time. Over a 250-day trading year, this will occur on about 12 days (i.e., $0.05 \times 250 = 12.50$).

On the days that actual losses exceed VaR predictions, the risk management team must perform a postmortem of sorts. What went wrong? Was the VaR employed appropriate? Was it defective? Or, was it "one of those days" when economic events simply overpower the portfolio? Regardless, the risk manager must remain vigilant and ask whether the extreme events merely represent an extreme, or whether they signal that the return distribution assumption must be modified. Of particular importance to the risk manager is the degree to which the VaR is exceeded. That is, it is one thing to post actual losses just a shade lower than a 5% VaR but something quite different to find that actual losses are 1.5 times the prediction by a 5% VaR.

Sometimes, the composition of the portfolio can drive actual losses beyond VaR. If selling an asset in one day can be accomplished only by accepting a large price discount, the value change caused by an adverse set of price changes should reflect this. Accordingly, bid prices should be used for the computation of VaR, particularly if the risk manager believes that parts of the portfolio will be liquidated after adverse price movements. For this reason, institutions will often adjust their VaR for the liquidity of their positions.

20.1.6   Which VaR Calculation Is Best?

Unfortunately, this obvious question has no simple answer. Each institution has a portfolio with some unique characteristics. Each VaR calculation method has its strengths and weaknesses. Under some conditions the variance–covariance model is superior, in other instances the historical simulation is quite handy; and the Monte Carlo simulation technique is the best for complex cases. Thus the risk manager must be familiar with all three methods.[7]

20.2   CREDIT DERIVATIVES AND OPTIONS ON DEBT INSTRUMENTS

20.2.1   Credit Derivatives Background

Credit risk permeates market economies. Credit risk incorporates several types of "credit events," including changes in credit spreads or relative prices, changes in bond ratings or credit ratings, and outright default. As the chance of default increases, the prices of an issuer's bonds decline, and their yields to maturity rise. It is also true that the interest rate that must be paid by bond issuers on any floating rate debt and newly issued debt will also rise. However, in no way do increased interest payments protect the bondholder from the chance of default by the bond issuer. Indeed, higher coupon payments actually increase the probability of default.

Because changes in credit worthiness, most notably default, can result in material losses, financial institutions look to protect themselves against credit risk. Traditionally, these firms have tried to construct a portfolio composed of geographically diversified low risk loans. However, a complete shifting of default risk generally cannot be accomplished through portfolio selection. Credit derivatives, which are also contracts, have emerged to fulfill the important economic function of shifting credit risk. Credit derivatives first appeared in 1991 and have grown into an important component of the risk management function. By the end of 2001, the size of the credit derivatives market was estimated to be as much as $1 trillion.[8]

The risk of default is difficult to measure. However, in the spirit of VaR, J. P. Morgan created *CreditMetrics*, which is composed of data sets and models that attempt to help measure default risk.[9]

20.2.2   Major Types of Credit Derivative

There are many different types of credit derivative and more are being invented each year. Thus, it is impossible to describe every possible credit derivative. A credit derivative has payments made contingent on a well-defined credit event: changes in credit spreads or relative prices (hence periodic rates of return), changes in bond ratings or credit ratings, or default. Credit derivatives exist as forward contracts, swaps and options; all are OTC contracts. The underlying debit instruments (also called the "reference credit") might be a sovereign (i.e., made by a foreign government) loan or bond, a corporate loan or bond, or a bank loan. Often, the reference credit is a portfolio of these credits. Credit derivatives might be cash settled, or settled with physical delivery of the bond or loan.

A risk manger should be aware of the two types of credit derivatives described below.

20.2.2.1   Total Return Swaps

A **total return swap** is a widely used credit derivative. In a common form of a total return swap, the party wishing to shift default risk agrees to receive a floating riskless reference rate, perhaps based on LIBOR or a Treasury security, and to pay the total return on a debt instrument.[10] The buyer of credit risk receives the return on the risky underlying credit and pays the rate based on LIBOR.

The total return on the risky debt instrument can be decomposed into a component identifiable as a return for bearing interest rate risk and a return for bearing credit risk. Because the swap can be structured to eliminate interest rate risk through the variable riskless interest payments, a total return swap can isolate credit risk.

As an example, suppose a manager of a bond portfolio want to reduce his exposure to a decline in the credit worthiness of MissMolly.com. The portfolio manager owns a bond issued by MissMolly.com, which is selling at par, matures in 10 years, and has a coupon payment.[11] Instead of simply selling the bonds in his portfolio, the fund manager decides to enter into a total return swap with a 24-month tenor. Most credit derivatives have a tenor that is less than the time to maturity of the underlying asset.

Under the terms of the swap agreement, the fund manager agrees to receive a floating payment of LIBOR + 125 basis points and pay the swap dealer the total return on the bond (i.e., the coupon and capital gain return). Payments are made every six months, and the notional principal is set equal to the fund's investment in Miss Molly.com bonds. Note that if the total return on the bonds is negative due to a rating downgrade, the total return payer (i.e., the bond fund manager) will actually *receive* two payments: the negative return on the risky bond plus LIBOR + 125 bp. If the total return on the risky bond is positive, the bond portfolio manager pays that return to the swap dealer and receives LIBOR + 125 bp.

Thus, you can see that the bond fund manager is protected from a decline in the credit quality of the issuer. Without the swap in place, the bond fund manager would have suffered major losses due to the loss in bond value caused by the rating downgrade.

In another feature of some total return swaps, if the bond issuer defaults, the total return payer can deliver the bond and receive its face value in return.

20.2.2.2   Credit Default Swaps

Suppose a bank has lent money to a major corporation and fears that the borrower will default. This bank could purchase a credit default swap. A credit swap is really an option. Under the terms of a credit swap, the credit swap buyer (i.e., the bank) pays a lump sum[12] to the credit swap seller. The credit swap buyer has shifted the risk of default of the bond in question to the credit swap seller. If there is a default later during the credit swap tenor, the credit swap buyer will receive a default payment for the credit swap seller. If there is no default, the bank will receive nothing. Unlike traditional swaps, the credit buyer receives a payment only if there is a default.

20.2.3   Other "Event" Derivatives

Traditionally, derivative securities were designed to shift price risk. Further, this price risk was traditionally thought to evolve gradually. That is, even though dramatic price moves were sometimes encountered, the security was not designed around a catastrophic event. However, as already discussed, derivative securities have evolved to shift risk occurring from a dramatic set of circumstances, such as a "credit event," like a default.

The OTC credit derivative market is not the only market in which the risk of dramatic events can be hedged. Two innovative contracts were developed at the CBOT in corn yield insurance futures and catastrophe insurance options, although both failed. At the CME, weather derivatives now trade.

The purpose of the corn yield insurance futures was to allow farmers to hedge against quantity risk. Coupled with the CBOT corn futures contracts that allow price risk reduction, these new contracts attempted to permit further overall risk reduction for corn growing enterprises in terms of both price and quantity (the elements of total revenue).

Catastrophe insurance options were designed to allow insurance companies to shift the dollar losses resulting from such natural disasters such as tornadoes, floods, earthquakes, and hurricanes. The underlying assets for these options were a set of "loss indexes" published daily by Property Claim Services (PCS). Each loss index tracks PCS estimates for insured industry losses resulting from catastrophic events.[13]

A significant portion of the U.S. economy is directly affected by weather. Because the Chicago Mercantile Exchange lists Weather Futures and Options, firms are no longer obliged to stand by and let the weather dictate revenues, costs, and profits. These contracts are based on indexes of heating degree-days and cooling degree-days. A degree-day is defined as how much a day's temperature deviates from the benchmark of 65 degrees. Thus, these derivative contracts are designed to shift the risk of adverse temperatures (either too hot or too cold). The Merc's website, (www.cme.com/products/index/weather/products_index_weather.cfm) contains a full description of these new exchange-traded derivatives. Many private companies also offer weather derivatives. These include Koch Industries (www.entergykoch.com/index.asp) and Aquila (www.aquila.com/solutions/weather/).

Finally, degree-days have a direct impact on electricity demand and, as such, on electricity prices. To hedge against fluctuations in electricity prices, the NYMEX and IPE introduced electricity futures and options. A remarkable aspect of electricity is that it is not storable. Thus, the cost-of-carry relationship (which is based on storage) does not have to hold for electricity prices. This means that electricity traders have to face a whole new set of pricing factors. For more information on these markets, see the NYMEX (www.nymex.com) and IPE (www.IPEmarkets.com) website.

20.2.4 Options on Debt Instruments and Interest Rate Options

Options on debt instruments and interest rate options differ significantly from options on equities. Because they can be thought of in any of four ways, options on debt instruments and interest rate options can be ambiguous contracts.

1. *They are options on cash debt instruments such as spot T-bills, T-notes, or T-bonds.* However, under this interpretation, one must confront the fact that as time passes, there will be changes in the nature of the underlying asset; that is, the security's time to maturity will change. As this occurs, the interest rate that is appropriate for discounting the debt instrument's cash flows will change. For example, consider a call option today on a pure discount bond that has six years to maturity. Its price equals the present value of its face value, where the discount rate is the six-year rate. One year hence, the appropriate discount rate will be the five-year rate. Today's six-year rate will likely differ from next year's five-year rate. In addition, we can see from the appendix to Chapter 9 that longer duration bonds have greater price volatility than shorter duration bonds. Therefore, as the underlying asset's time to maturity declines, its price volatility will also decline.

2. *They are options on forward contracts on the underlying asset.* This characterization is definitely appropriate for European options on debt instruments, or for situations in which early exercise of American options is unlikely. The underlying asset is what will exist on the delivery date. That is, if a European call option on a spot six-year bond has one year to expiration, it is essentially a call option on a forward five-year bond.

3. *They are options on spot interest rates.* The spot interest rate is the one that discounts the cash flows of the cash debt instrument described in item 1.

4. *They are options on forward interest rates.* The appropriate rate is then the forward discount rate appropriate for the forward security in item 2.

Standardized options on spot T-bills and specific T-notes were once traded on the AMEX. However, because these contracts did not generate sufficient volume, they failed. Options on specific T-bonds, and on interest rates themselves, continue to trade on the CBOE, in what must be described as very thin markets.

One reason for the failure of options on long-term spot debt instruments as viable trading contracts, while options on long-term interest rate futures have succeeded, is that there is a limited supply of any given T-bond or T-note. Because of this limited supply, traders who control the available supply of a particular T-bond or T-note could possibly manipulate the option price on a specific security. In contrast, the underlying asset behind CBOT Treasury note and Treasury bond futures options are the futures contracts themselves.

Potential problems will arise when the liquidity of one particular debt security is poor. An option contract requires a liquid underlying asset. Since most futures contracts are more liquid than any specific spot debt instrument, options on Treasury futures have thrived, while options on the spot debt instruments themselves have not.[14]

A tremendous demand has emerged for custom-made interest rate options, such as caps, floors, and collars. Banks and other financial institutions offer these products to their clients, who either have portfolios of debt securities or have borrowed money (frequently at variable rates). The banks' customers often desire the payoff patterns offered by options or combinations of options such as spreads. Government securities dealers also buy and sell specialized debt instrument option contracts. The banks that buy and/or sell these options protect themselves by using exchange-traded options, or by the dynamic option replication techniques covered in Chapter 17.

In the next section, we describe some of the varied approaches that might be used to price options on debt instruments and interest rates.

20.2.4.1 Why the Black–Scholes Option Pricing Model Is Not Really Appropriate for Pricing Options on Debt Instruments and Interest Rates

As a first approximation, the Black–Scholes option pricing model can be used to estimate the value of European calls and puts on debt instruments. Let S represent the price of the cash bond. Therefore, S is the present value of the future cash flows to the bondholder, discounted at the appropriate discount rate, R. The cash flows include the coupon payments and principal.

$$S = \sum_{t=1}^{T} \frac{CF_t}{(1+R)^t} \tag{20.3}$$

Then, S is the price of the underlying asset in the BSOPM:

$$C = SN(d_1) - Ke^{-rT} N(d_2)$$

where all the parameters are as defined in Chapter 17.

Because of the severe violations of the BSOPM assumptions, however, the BSOPM is not well specified for the bond as an underlying asset. Specifically, these violations include the following.

1. Most bonds pay semiannual coupons. The true value of the underlying asset is the total price of the bond, which equals the quoted price plus accrued interest. This value will be discontinuous around the coupon payment date, which means that the bond's spot price cannot follow a continuous diffusion process. Still, we can make adjustments similar to those that were made to handle discrete dividend payments in Chapter 17. That is, we cannot reduce the total spot price (today's quoted price plus today's accrued interest) by the present value of coupons and accrued interest between today and the option's expiration date. This is appropriate for European options, and effectively makes the underlying asset a forward bond. If a forward price is readily available, just use that price in the BSOPM as the underlying asset. This also means that Black's model [Equations (18.15) for calls and (18.16) for puts] should be used to value interest rate options.

Summarizing, use $S^* = S + AI - PV(C)$ in the BSOPM as the underlying asset. The total price of the bond (quoted price plus accrued interest) is $S + AI$, and $PV(C)$ is the present value of any coupons between today and the option's expiration date.

2. The price of a cash debt instrument will not follow the diffusion process assumed by the BSOPM because a bond's price is always drawn to its face value. As time passes, there will always be a force that brings discount bond prices up to face value, even if interest rates rise. The same force draws the prices of premium bonds down to face value, even if interest rates decline. At maturity, a bond's price equals its face value.

3. If bond *prices* followed a diffusion process, negative yields to maturity might be implied at sufficiently high prices. Negative bond yields are highly unlikely to exist, so there must be bounds on bond prices that preclude such yields from occurring. But with the imposition of such limits, the bond price will no longer follow a diffusion process that allows the use of the BSOPM to value an option on the bond. If you assume that interest rates follow a diffusion process, the interest rate becomes the underlying asset of the model. Better still, it could be argued that the forward interest rate should follow the diffusion process, and that *it* should be the underlying asset for Black's models. But if interest rates follow a diffusion process, then again, negative interest rates could exist.

4. The BSOPM assumes that interest rates are constant (or at least nonstochastic). However, this cannot be the case for options on debt instruments, whose prices change because interest rates change. One way around this when one is valuing options on *bonds* is to assume that the short-term interest rate between today and expiration is constant, but the long term rate driving the bond's price is stochastic. This assumption becomes less appealing when one is pricing options on short-term debt instruments.

5. The BSOPM assumes that the volatility of the underlying asset is constant. However, the volatility of bond prices is a function of its duration, which is related to its maturity. All else equal, bond price volatilities decline as they near maturity. Estimating the bond's volatility is difficult because it changes both as time passes and as interest rates change. If a spot interest rate is serving as the underlying asset, its volatility will generally increase as time passes (short-term interest rates are more volatile than long-term interest rates). The use of a forward interest rate as the underlying asset keeps constant its duration and volatility.

Despite these shortcomings, however, a variation of the BSOPM developed by Black (1976) is often used to price European-style interest rate options, as well as interest rate caps, interest rate floors, and European options on swaps. However, users of this model are implicitly making one of two assumptions. Either they are assuming that interest rates are constant or they are assuming a lognormal probability distribution for the underlying asset (an interest rate or a bond price).

20.2.4.2 Alternative Models Used to Price Interest Rate Derivatives

Given the problems and complications just outlined, those who need accurate values of debt options generally do not use the BSOPM. Instead, numerical methods are chosen. In particular, many use a "lattice" approach. That is, the user builds a "tree" that represents the various evolutionary paths of the interest rate, bond price, or the term structure of interest rates. To help picture this approach, think of how the binomial option pricing model creates a "tree" of prices.[15]

One class of models used in pricing interest rate derivatives is known as the equilibrium class. The models in this class use continuous time mathematics to describe how the "short rate" evolves over time. In these models, the "short rate" is very short. Indeed, it is sometimes called the instantaneous short rate because it is over an infinitely small interval. These models differ from one another in their assumptions of how the short rate evolves over time (i.e., what stochastic process does the short rate follow?).[16] Examples of such models are those of Vasicek (1977), Rendleman and Bartter (1980), and Cox, Ingersoll, and Ross (1985).

A significant weakness of the equilibrium class of models is that they sometimes fail to describe the term structure of interest rates observed in the market. Traders find this shortcoming to be frustrating. Thus, a second class of models has won a much wider acceptance. These models start with the assertion that the current term structure of interest rates contains no arbitrage opportunities. These models are known as no-arbitrage models. It is important to note that as the term structure of interest rates changes over time, the no-arbitrage model parameters must be reestimated accordingly.

Ho and Lee (1986, 1990) developed the first no-arbitrage model. Hull and White (1990) present a very important no-arbitrage model that extended the Vasicek (1977) equilibrium model while maintaining relative ease of use. The no-arbitrage model that is probably used the most by market participants to price interest rate derivatives is the Heath–Jarrow–Morton (HJM) model, introduced in 1992. It can be shown that most other no-arbitrage models are special cases of the HJM model. An important distinction of the HJM model is that this approach is based on the evolution of forward interest rates (as opposed to spot interest rates). The HJM model allows for wide flexibility. Fortunately, software such as FinancialCAD is available to those wishing to use the no-arbitrage approach to value interest rate derivatives.

20.2.5   Options on Swaps

While trading volume in all derivative markets has grown dramatically in recent years, perhaps one of the most explosive growth areas has been in the market for options on swaps. Much of the growth is probably attributable to the increased recognition that these instruments provide considerable risk-shifting capability. In addition, these instruments, while sophisticated and apparently rather complex, are relatively simple.

An option to enter an interest rate swap at some later date is called a swaption.[17] That is, a swaption is based on a forward-start interest rate swap. For example, a six-month into a three-year swaption is an option to enter into a three-year interest rate swap six months from now. One key to understanding swaptions is that the right to enter the swap can be viewed in two ways:

a. Call swaptions. These swaptions are also called **payer swaptions**. The holder of a payer swaption has the right, but not the obligation, to enter the swap as the fixed rate *payer*. Here, holders of the swaption are looking to protect themselves against subsequent increases in the fixed rate. A likely candidate to purchase this type of swap is a firm that will be borrowing at a floating rate at some future date but wants to swap to a fixed rate. A call swaption is similar to a call option on an interest rate or a put on a debt instrument.

b. Put swaptions. These swaptions are also called **receiver swaptions**. The holder of a receiver swaption has the right, but not the obligation, to enter the swap as the fixed-rate *receiver*. Here, holders of the swaption want to protect themselves against subsequent decreases in the fixed rate. A firm would purchase this type of swaption if it currently holds a portfolio of floating-rate securities but is thinking about swapping to receive a fixed rate. A put swaption is similar to a put on an interest rate or a call on a debt instrument.

As with any option, the purchaser of a swaption must pay a premium to receive the rights conferred by the swaption. The swaption premium is expressed as basis points per dollar of notional principal. Various factors influence the value of a swaption. First, note that a swaption can have American-style or European-style exercise. The time to expiration of the swaption refers to the time from now until the time the swap can be entered. The fixed rate on the swaption is called the strike price. The underlying rate is the fair fixed rate on a forward-start interest rate swap. The volatility of this fair fixed rate is also required.

20.2.5.1   European Swaption Valuation

Because a swap can be viewed as a collection of forward contracts, a European option on a swap can be valued by Black's (1976) version of the BSOPM presented in Chapter 18.

A swaption has a strike rate K_x that is the fixed rate that will be swapped against the floating rate if the option is exercised. In a call swaption, or payer swaption, the buyer has the right to become the fixed-rate payer. The pricing model is

$$\text{call swaption} = (N \times B)[F_r N(d_1) - K_x N(d_2)] \qquad (20.4)$$

In Equation (20.4), N represents the notional principal, and B represents the present value of a security that pays $1/n$ at all i payment dates of the swap. The underlying asset of the call is a T-year forward-start swap where payments are made every nth interval. Thus, if b_i represents the present value of one dollar received at time i, we write

$$B = \frac{1}{n}\sum_{i}^{nT} b_i(0,i) \qquad (20.5)$$

Also, in Equation (20.04), F_r represents today's fair fixed rate on a forward swap, and:

$$d_1 = \frac{\ln(F_r/K_x) + (\sigma^2/2)T}{\sigma\sqrt{T}} \qquad (20.6)$$

$$d_2 = \frac{\ln(F_r/K_x) - (\sigma^2/2)T}{\sigma\sqrt{T}} = d_1 - \sigma\sqrt{T} \qquad (20.7)$$

In a put swaption, or receiver swaption, the buyer has the right to receive the fixed rate. Using the notation of Equation (20.4), the value of a put swaption is given by:

$$\text{put swaption} = (N \times B)[K_x N(-d_2) - F_r N(-d_1)] \qquad (20.8)$$

20.2.5.2   Pricing a Call Swaption: Example

Recall the example of a forward swap from Chapter 13 (Section 13.1.4). Assume that in that example, the forward swap will begin in 47 days. The notional principal is $50 million. Assume a 360-day year. If the forward swap is executed today, both parties, the fixed-rate payer and the receive-fixed party, are obligated to the terms of the forward swap. That is, in any forward contract, including a forward swap, both parties have the right *and* the obligation to enter into the swap. An alternative for the fixed-rate payer would be to purchase a payer swaption, in which case the fixed-rate payer would have the right, but not the obligation, to enter the swap.

To begin the process of valuing a payer swaption, recall the Eurodollar futures settlement prices from Table 10.2. For example, on July 28, 1999, the September Eurodollar futures contract settled at 94.555, implying a borrowing rate of 5.445% from the expiration of the September contract to the expiration of the December contract, a period assumed here to be 90 days. Thus, the first swap payment would occur in 137 days. The value of b_1 is given by

$$b_1 = e^{-0.05445(137/365)} = 0.979770.$$

The other elements of b are computed in accordance with Table 20.1.

TABLE 20.1 Computing the Value of b for a Payer Swaption from Price Data Observed on July 28, 1999

Month	Settle Yield	Days Until First Swap Payment[1]	Unannualized Rate[2]	b
Sept. 1999	0.05445	137	0.020437397	0.979770
Dec. 1999	0.0581	228	0.036292603	0.964358
Mar. 2000	0.05815	320	0.050980822	0.950297
June 2000	0.0605	412	0.068290411	0.933989
Sept. 2000	0.06235	503	0.085923425	0.917664
Dec. 2000	0.06465	593	0.10503411	0.900294
Mar. 2001	0.0645	685	0.121047945	0.885991
June 2001	0.0651	777	0.13858274	0.870591

[1] Days between July 28, 1999 and the twelfth day of the following contract month. For example, there are 137 days between July 28, 1999 and December 12, 1999. There are 777 days between July 28, 1999 and September 12, 2001.
[2] Settle yield×(days until first swap payment/365).

Using these values for b_i, and noting that $n=4$ and $T=2$, the value for B as stated in equation (20.5) is:

$$B = \frac{1}{4}(0.979770 + 0.964358 + 0.950297 + 0.933989$$
$$+ 0.917664 + 0.900294 + 0.885991 + 0.870591) = 1.85073$$

Suppose the strike price is set equal to the fair fixed rate on the forward swap, 6.09%. The time to maturity of the swaption equals the time when the swap would start (i.e., 47 days hence or 47/360 year). The final, and important input, is the volatility of the swap rate. Assume, for this example, that it is 20% per year, or 0.20. The values for d_1 and d_2 are calculated as follows[18]:

$$d_1 = \frac{\ln(0.0609/0.0609) + (0.20^2/2)47/360}{0.20\sqrt{47/360}} = 0.036132$$

$$d_2 = d_1 - \sigma\sqrt{T} = 0.036132 - 0.20\sqrt{47/360} = -0.036132$$

From the cumulative normal distribution, $N(d_1)=N(0.036132)=0.514417$ and $N(d_2)=N(-0.036132)=0.485588$. Combining this information yields a call swaption value of

$$\text{call swaption} = (N \times B)[F_r N(d_1) - K_r N(d_2)]$$
$$= (50,000,000 \times 1.85073)[0.0609 \times 0.514417 - 0.0609 \times 0.485588]$$
$$= \$162,465, \text{ or } \$0.0032493 \text{ per dollar of notional principal}$$
$$(\text{i.e., } 0.32493 \text{ basis point})$$

This is an example of how to price a European swaption. In practice, swaptions can be American or European, or an exotic combination of the two, which is known as a *Bermuda* option. For example, consider a swaption with a maturity of four years. It may be European during the first year and American thereafter. To value an American swaption or a Bermudan swaption, it is necessary to use lattice techniques that make normality assumptions (see Jarrow and Turnbull, 2000, Chapter 15) or a lattice technique that approximates the Heath–Jarrow–Morton model (the HJM model does not make normality or lognormality assumptions.) For more details see, Jarrow (1995) or Buetow and Fabozzi (2001). The next section discusses exotic options of other types.

20.3 EXOTIC OPTIONS

From about the late 1980s, options have evolved that allow hedgers to shift risks in ways that ordinary, traded options cannot accomplish. These options have become known as exotic options.

Exotic options are generally divided into two broad groups. One group is widely known as **path-dependent** options and the other group is often called **path-independent**, or **free-range**, options. We begin with a discussion of free-range options.[19]

20.3.1 Free-Range Exotic Options

Recall from Chapter 18 that the BSOPM formulas for calls and puts are

$$C = SN(d_1) - Ke^{-rT}N(d_2) \tag{18.3}$$

and

$$P = Ke^{-rT}N(-d_2) - SN(-d_1) \tag{18.8}$$

where we use the following definitions:

S = price of the underlying asset
K = strike price of the call option
r = risk-free interest rate
T = time to expiration
$N(d)$ = cumulative standard normal distribution function

$$d_1 = \frac{\ln(S/K) + (r + \sigma^2/2)T}{\sigma\sqrt{T}}$$

$$d_2 = d_1 - \sigma\sqrt{T}$$

σ = the standard deviation of the underlying asset's returns
$\ln(S/K)$ = the natural logarithm of S/K
e^{-rT} = the exponential function of $-rT$.

20.3.1.1 European Digital Options

Digital options, also known as binary options, are important to financial engineers as building blocks in the construction of more complex options. At expiration, a digital call option is worth $1 if $S_T > K$ and zero otherwise. For binary puts, the expiration value is $1 if $K > S_T$ and zero otherwise. Thus, the payoff from digital call put options is discontinuous at the strike price.[20] Before expiration, the values of digital options (C_{digital} and P_{digital}) are given by:

$$C_{\text{digital}} = e^{-rT} N(d_2) \tag{20.9}$$

and

$$P_{\text{digital}} = e^{-rT} N(-d_2) \tag{20.10}$$

If the payoff of the digital option is multiplied by the strike price, the digital option is known as a strike-or-nothing (son) option. Thus, at expiration, a strike-or-nothing call option is worth $K if $S_T > K$ and zero otherwise. For strike-or-nothing puts, the expiration value is $K if $K > S_T$ and zero otherwise. As such, before expiration, the value of these options is:

$$C_{\text{son}} = K e^{-rT} N(d_2) \tag{20.11}$$

and

$$P_{\text{son}} = K e^{-rT} N(-d_2) \tag{20.12}$$

Asset-or-nothing (aon) options, a natural companion to strike-or-nothing options, are also useful to financial engineers. The payoff at expiration for an asset-or-nothing call is S_T if $S_T > K$ and zero otherwise. For asset-or-nothing puts, the expiration value is S_T if $K > S_T$ and zero otherwise. Before expiration, these options are valued as follows:

$$C_{\text{aon}} = S N(d_1) \tag{20.13}$$

and

$$P_{\text{aon}} = S N(-d_1) \tag{20.14}$$

Note that the formulas for asset-or-nothing and strike-or-nothing options are simply parts of the BSOPM. Thus, one can see that the call option value given by the BSOPM represents a portfolio comprising a long position in an asset-or-nothing call option and a short position in a strike-or-nothing call option. Also, a put option value given by the BSOPM represents a portfolio made up of a long position in a strike-or-nothing put option and a short position in an asset-or-nothing put option.

20.3.1.2   European Gap Options

Gap options also have a discontinuous payoff profile. However, unlike the payoff to the ordinary digital option, the payoff to a gap option is not flat on both sides of the strike price. The payoff to a gap call option is $S_T - G$ if $S_T > K$ and zero otherwise. Note that this is the same payoff as that of an ordinary call option if $G = K$. Thus, to make a gap call option different from an ordinary call, G must be greater than or less than K. Before expiration, the value of a gap option can be thought of as the value of an ordinary call plus an adjustment for the difference between K and G. That is, for a gap call, we write:

$$C_{\text{gap}} = \left[SN(d_1) - Ke^{-rT} N(d_2) \right] + (K - G)e^{-rT} N(d_2) \tag{20.15}$$

Equation (20.15) shows that the value of a gap call equals the value of a long position in an asset-or-nothing call when $G = 0$.

The payoff to a gap put option is $G - S_T$ if $K > S_T$ and zero otherwise. Note that this is the same payoff as that of an ordinary put option if $G = K$. Again, to make a gap put option different from an ordinary put option, G must differ from K. Before expiration, the value of a gap put option can be thought of as the value of an ordinary put plus an adjustment for the difference between G and K. That is, a gap put is expressed thus:

$$P_{\text{gap}} = \left[Ke^{-rT} N(-d_2) - SN(-d_1) \right] + (G - K)e^{-rT} N(-d_2) \tag{20.16}$$

Equation (20.16) shows that the value of a gap put equals the value of a short position in an asset-or-nothing put when $G = 0$.

20.3.1.3   European Paylater Options

Paylater options provide a means to protect the holder of the option against a disastrous move in the underlying asset—at zero initial cost. However, the premium of $\$L_c$ is paid if the option expires in the money, even if the option does not expire sufficiently in the money to pay the premium. Thus, the payoff at expiration for a paylater call option is $S_T - K - L_c$ if $S_T > K$ and zero otherwise. Note that a paylater call option will have a negative payoff if $K < S_T < K + L_c$.

Because a paylater call option can be viewed as a combination of an ordinary call option less a payment of $\$L_c$ times the value of a digital call option, one can solve for the premium at initiation (i.e., at time 0) by stating

$$[C_{\text{paylater}}]_0 = \left[SN(d_1) - Ke^{-rT} N(d_2) \right]_0 - \left[L_c e^{-rT} N(d_2) \right]_0 \tag{20.17}$$

Because the value of a paylater call option is set to zero at time 0, the premium amount L_c is

$$0 = \left[SN(d_1) - Ke^{-rT} N(d_2) \right]_0 - \left[L_c e^{-rT} N(d_2) \right]_0$$

$$L_c = \frac{\left[SN(d_1) - Ke^{-rT} N(d_2) \right]_0}{\left[e^{-rT} N(d_2) \right]_0}$$

After time zero, say at arbitrary time t, the value of a paylater call option is

$$[C_{\text{paylater}}]_t = \left[SN(d_1) - Ke^{-rT} N(d_2) \right]_t - \left[L_c e^{-rT} N(d_2) \right]_t \tag{20.18}$$

Similarly, for puts,

$$0 = \left[Ke^{-rT}N(-d_2) - SN(-d_1) \right]_0 - \left[L_p e^{-rT}N(-d_2) \right]$$

$$L_p = \frac{\left[Ke^{-rT}N(-d_2) - SN(-d_1) \right]_0}{\left[e^{-rT}N(-d_2) \right]_0}$$

and

$$[P_{\text{paylater}}]_t = \left[Ke^{-rT}N(-d_2) - SN(-d_1) \right]_t - \left[L_p e^{-rT}N(-d_2) \right]_t \tag{20.19}$$

Although the holder of a paylater option does not have to pay for the option if it expires out of the money, the premium the holder must pay if the option finishes in the money is significant. For example, if $S = K = 100$, $r = 6\%$, $T = 90$ days, $\sigma = 30\%$, and there are no dividends, the BSOPM yields a call option value of about \$6.67. Equation (20.18) shows that a paylater call option premium is about \$13.29. Thus, if $S_T = 100.01$, the holder of the ordinary call option has lost \$6.66 while the cost to a paylater holder is \$13.28, about twice as much. In percentage terms, the difference is even higher for out-of-the-money options.

20.3.1.4 European Chooser Options

Chooser options are sometimes known as "as you like it" options or "options for the undecided" (Rubinstein, 1991). This is because at purchase, the chooser option is neither a call option nor a put option. The buyer of a chooser option has the right, at a prespecified time, to "choose" whether the option finishes its life as an ordinary call option or as an ordinary put option. Chooser options are a lower cost alternative to purchasing a straddle.[21]

Pricing a chooser option is surprisingly straightforward. First, let the chooser option expire at time T, but the holder of the chooser must "choose" at time t. The exercise price equals K. Of course, the holder of the chooser will convert the option into a call if, at time t, a call with strike equal K expiring at time T is more valuable than a put with the same strike and expiration date. That is, the holder will chose "call" if

$$C_t(S, T-t, K) > P_t(S, T-t, K) \tag{20.20}$$

By using a continuous time version of put–call parity, equation (20.20) can be written as follows:

$$C_t(S, T-t, K) > C_t(S, T-t, K) - S_t + Ke^{-r(T-t)} \tag{20.21}$$

Therefore, from Equation (20.21), you can see that the holder of a chooser option will chose call if, at time t, the stock price is greater than the discounted strike price.

At initiation, the payoffs to a chooser option can be replicated by the following portfolio:

A long position in an ordinary call option with a strike price equal to K and a time to maturity of T

A long position in an ordinary put with a strike price equal to $Ke^{-r(T-t)}$ and a time to maturity of t (the choice date)

20.3.1.5   Compound Options

A compound option is an option written on another option. There are four basic types of compound option: a call on a call, a put on a call, a call on a put, and a put on a put. A call option on a call is a cacall. A caput is a call on a put.[22]

Many securities and contracts can be modeled as compound options. Both Black and Scholes (1973) and Galai and Masulis (1976) point out that ordinary calls on 100 shares of stock are actually compound options. The owner of a call has an option on a firm's stock, but stock represents a call on the assets of a levered firm. When a firm's debt matures, the firm will either repay the principal due to the bondholders (if the firm's value is sufficient to repay this amount), leaving the residual amount for the stockholders, or default, in which case the bondholders take over the firm's assets and the stockholders get nothing (this will occur if the value of the firm's assets is less than the amount due to the bondholders). Thus, owning a call is a compound option on the underlying firm's assets.

Coupon-paying bonds and sinking fund bonds are compound options (Geske, 1977). For example, the stockholders of a firm that has issued a coupon bond own a stream of compound European options. At each coupon date, the firm has the option of defaulting or paying the bondholders off with the coupon in exchange for another European option that expires at the next coupon payment date. The underlying assets of each option are the firm's assets. When the stockholders pay the last coupon and principal, they then own the residual value of the firm's assets.

"Split-fee options" exist in the mortgage-backed securities market. These, too, are actually compound options in which the buyer initially buys the right (but not the obligation) to later buy an option to subsequently make or take delivery of bonds that are collateralized with mortgages.

20.3.1.6   Options on the Minimum or Maximum of Two Unknown Outcomes

Stulz (1982) introduced formulas for the pricing of options on the minimum or maximum of two risky assets. These options are exotic because, unlike ordinary options, there are two different underlying assets. [23]

There are call options on the maximum of two stochastic values, put options on the minimum of two stochastic values, call options on the minimum of two stochastic values, and put options on the maximum of two stochastic values.

20.3.2   Path-Dependent Options

Unlike the free-range options discussed earlier, one group of options has a value that depends on the path of the price of the underlying asset before option expiration. These exotic options are called path-dependent options.

20.3.2.1   European Barrier Options with One Barrier and No Dividends

Barrier options are now heavily traded in the over-the-counter markets. One appealing feature of these options is that they are less expensive than ordinary options. This is because the payoff to a barrier option depends on whether the price of the underlying asset reaches a critical level, known as the barrier, before option expiration. Intuitively, then, barrier options are less expensive than ordinary options because there are fewer positive payoff opportunities for barrier options.[24]

Call and put barrier options can both be divided into two groups. These two groups are "out-barrier" options (also known as knock-outs or outs) and "in-barrier" options (knock-ins or ins). A knock-out option ceases to exist when the value of the underlying asset touches the barrier level. By contrast, a knock-in option comes into existence when the underlying asset price reaches the barrier level. The name of a barrier option also depends on the price path of the underlying asset. Thus, an upward price path of the underlying asset leads to "up and in" and "up and out" barrier options, while a downward price path of the underlying asset leads to "down and out" and "down and in" barrier options. Thus, although there are eight basic categories of barrier options, we will present only the cases involving call options.

Barrier options sometimes contain a rebate feature. Under the terms of the rebate, the holder of an "out" option receives part of the premium paid for the option if the option is "knocked out." Similarly, the holder of an "in" option would receive a portion of the option premium if the option expires without being "knocked in."[25]

Merton (1973) and Reiner and Rubinstein (1991) have developed formulas used to price barrier options.[26] An interesting feature of barrier options is that in the absence of a rebate provision and given identical payoffs and barrier levels, the value of a European down-and-in barrier option plus the value of a European down-and-out barrier option equals the value of a call option value given by the BSOPM. That is,

$$C_{BSOPM} = C_{down-out} + C_{down-in} \qquad (20.22)$$

The following pricing relationship also holds:

$$C_{BSOPM} = C_{up-out} + C_{up-in} \qquad (20.23)$$

To proceed, add the following definitions to those in Section 20.3.1:

$$H = \text{barrier level}$$

$$w = \frac{\ln(S/H)}{\sigma\sqrt{T}} + (1+\mu)\sigma\sqrt{T}$$

$$y = \frac{\ln(H^2/SK)}{\sigma\sqrt{T}} + (1+\mu)\sigma\sqrt{T}$$

$$z = \frac{\ln(H/S)}{\sigma\sqrt{T}} + (1+\mu)\sigma\sqrt{T}$$

$$\mu = \frac{r - 0.5\sigma^2}{\sigma^2}$$

Given these definitions, if the barrier level H is less than the strike price K the value of a down-and-in call is given by:

$$C_{down-in} = S(H/S)^{2(\mu+1)} N(y) - Ke^{-rT}(H/S)^{2\mu} N(y - \sigma\sqrt{T}) \qquad (20.24)$$

We can use Equations (20.22) and (20.24), to show that the value of a down-and-out call is given by $C_{\text{BSOPM}} - C_{\text{down-in}}$.[27]

If the barrier level H is greater than the strike price K, the value of an up-and-in call is given by

$$
\begin{aligned}
C_{\text{up-in}} = {} & SN(w) - Ke^{-rT}N(w - \sigma\sqrt{T}) \\
& + S(H/S)^{2(\mu+1)}[N(z) - N(y)] \\
& - Ke^{-rT}(H/S)^{2\mu}[N(z - \sigma\sqrt{T}) - N(y - \sigma\sqrt{T})]
\end{aligned}
\tag{20.25}
$$

and the value of an up-and-out call is computed by using Equations (20.23) and (20.25). Note that when the barrier level is less than or equal to the strike price, the value of an up-and-out call is zero because this barrier option cannot expire with a positive intrinsic value. Consequently, when the barrier level is less than or equal to the strike price, the value of an up-and-in call equals the value of a Black–Scholes call.

20.3.2.2 Lookback Options

The payoff to a lookback option depends on the value of the extreme stock price during the life of the option. Sometimes these options are called "no regrets" options. This is because, for example, the holder of a lookback call can buy the underlying asset at its lowest price between option initiation and option expiration.

There are several types of lookback option. A standard lookback call option yields proceeds at exercise equal to the stock price at exercise less the minimum stock price observed during the life of the option. These standard lookback options are sometimes known as "floating-strike" options. By contrast, a fixed-strike lookback call option gives proceeds at exercise equal to the difference between the highest stock price observed during the life of the option and the exercise price. These options are also known as "extreme" lookback options.

Goldman, Sosin, and Gatto (1979) developed a formula for pricing floating-strike, or standard lookback, options. For a floating-strike lookback call, their formula is

$$
\begin{aligned}
C_{\text{floating-strike}} = {} & SN(g) - S_{\min}e^{-rT}N(g - \sigma\sqrt{T}) \\
& + Se^{-rT}\frac{\sigma^2}{2r}\left[\left(\frac{S}{S_{\min}}\right)^{-2r/\sigma^2} N\left(-g + \frac{2r}{\sigma}\sqrt{T}\right) - e^{rT}N(-g)\right]
\end{aligned}
\tag{20.26}
$$

where

$$
g = \frac{\ln(S/S_{\min}) + (r + \sigma^2/2)T}{\sigma\sqrt{T}}.
$$

Conze and Viswanathan (1991) developed formulas for extreme lookback options. For example, in cases of strike prices less than or equal to the maximum price achieved by the underlying asset, their formula for call options is

$$C_{\text{fixed-strike}} = SN(f) - S_{\text{max}}e^{-rT}N(f - \sigma\sqrt{T}) + e^{-rT}(S_{\text{max}} - K)$$

$$+ Se^{-rT}\frac{\sigma^2}{2r}\left[-\left(\frac{S}{S_{\text{max}}}\right)^{-2r/\sigma^2}N\left(f - \frac{2r}{\sigma}\sqrt{T}\right) + e^{rT}N(f)\right] \qquad (20.27)$$

where

$$f = \frac{\ln(S/S_{\text{max}}) + (r + \sigma^2/2)T}{\sigma\sqrt{T}}$$

While we have presented formulas only for European lookback call options, formulas exist for European lookback put options (see, e.g., Haug, 1998). In addition, there are many variants of lookback options. For example, "partial-time" lookback options exist. The unique feature of these options is as follows. For a partial-time, floating-strike lookback option, the end of the lookback period occurs before option expiration. For a partial-time fixed-strike lookback option, the beginning of the lookback period starts a predetermined time after option initiation. Also, there are **Russian** options, which are like an infinite-life lookback option. After initiation, the holder of a Russian option can wait as long as desired before exercising the option. Of course, upon exercising during the finite lookback period, the option ceases to exist.

20.3.2.3 Average Options

Average price options are quite popular and are used in many different over-the-counter markets. The payoff to average options, also known as "Asian" options, depends on the average price of the underlying asset during the life of the options.

There are two basic types of average option, average price and average strike. At expiration, an average price call option pays the maximum of zero or $S_{\text{avg}} - K$. The payoff to an average price put option is the maximum of zero or $K - S_{\text{avg}}$. At expiration, an average strike call pays the maximum of zero or $S_T - S_{\text{avg}}$. Accordingly, the expiration payoff to an average strike put is the maximum of zero or $S_{\text{avg}} - S_T$.

Average price options are cheaper than ordinary call options. This is because volatility is dampened when averaging the prices of the underlying asset. Generally, a simple arithmetic average is used to calculate the average price. In this case, however, it is not possible to use a formula to price these options. Thus, these options must be priced by means of analytical approximations or with computer simulations.[28]

20.3.3 Shouts and Ladders

Shouts and ladders can best be described by means of a short example. Consider the case of an option holder who has an in-the-money option that still has some time left to maturity. The option holder would like to guarantee a profit on this position. For traded options, the option holder could use a stop-loss order. However, for over-the-counter options, stop-loss orders may be unavailable. Shout options provide a substitute. A **shout option** gives the option holder the right to capture the intrinsic value portion of the option premium before expiration and keep the time value.

For example, suppose a three-month, one-shout call option exists on Intel Corporation. At the time the option was purchased, $S = K = \$75$. After one month, Intel stock stands at $100. The option holder may "shout" and lock in the $25 intrinsic value. The option holder still holds a two-month call option, but the strike price is adjusted to $100.

If a shout option has numerous shouting opportunities, it is known as a **ladder**.

20.4 SUMMARY

In this chapter, we present three currently important risk management topics: value at risk (VaR), credit derivatives, and exotic options.

VaR is an attempt to condense into a single figure an estimate of the price risk possessed by a portfolio of derivatives and other financial assets of a single firm. The price risk number obtained from a VaR model summarizes risk exposure into a dollar figure that purportedly represents the estimated maximum loss over an interval of time. As yet, there is no standard method to compute VaR. However, several accepted methods for computing VaR have emerged. These methods are the variance–covariance approach, the historical simulation method, and the Monte Carlo simulation method. For any VaR calculation method, it is important for the risk manager to assess the valuation impact of worst-case scenarios, such as the market crash of 1987.

The second major topic presented in this chapter is credit risk. Credit risk permeates market economies. In its most basic form, credit risk is the chance that a bond issuer will not make every coupon payment, that is, the chance that the bond issuer will default. Because default on a contract can result in material losses, financial institutions look to protect themselves against credit risk. There are many different types of credit derivative, and more are being invented each year. However, the two most popular credit derivatives are total return swaps and credit swaps.

The third topic in this chapter is exotic options. From about the late 1980s, options have evolved that allow hedgers to shift risks in ways that ordinary, traded options cannot accomplish. These options have become known as exotic options. Exotic options are generally divided into two broad groups. One group of exotic options is known as path-independent, or free-range options. Options in this group include digitals, gaps, and paylater, chooser, and compound options. The other group is widely known as path-dependent options. Examples of path-dependent options include barrier, lookback, and average options.

References

Abken, Peter A. 1990. "Innovations in Modeling the Term Structure of Interest Rates." *Federal Reserve Bank Economic Review*, Vol. 75, No. 4, pp. 2–27.

Black, Fischer. 1976. "The Pricing of Commodity Contracts." *Journal of Financial Economics*, Vol. 3, pp. 167–179.

Black, Fischer, and Myron Scholes. 1973. "The Pricing of Options and Corporate Liabilities." *Journal of Political Economy*, Vol. 81, pp. 637–654.

Buetow, Gerald, and Frank Fabozzi. 2001. *Valuation of Interest Rate Swaps and Swaptions*. New Hope, PA: Frank J. Fabozzi Associates.

Conze, A., and Viswanathan. 1991. "Path Dependent Options: The Case of Lookback Options." *Journal of Finance*, Vol. 46, pp. 1893–1907.

Cox, J. C., J. E. Ingersoll, and S. A. Ross. 1985. "A Theory of the Term Structure of Interest Rates." *Econometrica*, Vol. 53, pp. 385–407.

Galai, Dan and Ronald Masulis. 1976. "The Option Pricing Model and the Risk Factor of Stock." *Journal of Financial Economics*, Vol. 3, pp. 53–81.

Geske, Robert. 1977. "The Valuation of Corporate Liabilities as Compound Options." *Journal of Financial and Quantitative Analysis*, Vol. 12, No. 4, pp. 541–552.

Goldman, B. M., H. B. Sosin, and M. A. Gatto. 1979. "Path Dependent Options: Buy at the Low, Sell at the High." *Journal of Finance*, Vol. 34, pp. 1111–1127.

Haug, Espen Gaarder. 1998. *The Complete Guide to Option Pricing Formulas*. New York: McGraw-Hill.

Heath, D., R. Jarrow; and A. Morton. 1992. "Bond Pricing and the Term Structure of Interest Rates; A New Methodology." *Econometrica*, Vol. 60, pp. 77–105.

Ho, Thomas and Allen Abrahamson. 1990. "Options on Interest Sensitive Securities." In Stephen Figlewski, William L. Silber, and Marti G. Subrahmanyam, eds., *Financial Options: From Theory to Practice* Homewood, IL: Business-One, Irwin, Chapter 8, pp. 314–356.

Ho, Thomas and Sang-bin Lee. 1986. "Term Structure Movements and Pricing Interest Rate Contingent Claims," *Journal of Finance*, Vol. 41, pp. 1011–1030.

Ho, Thomas and Sang-bin Lee. 1990. "Interest Rate Futures Options and Interest Rate Options." *Financial Review*, 25, pp. 345–370.

Hull, John. 2000. *Options, Futures and Other Derivative Securities*, 4th ed. Englewood Cliffs, NJ: Prentice Hall.

Hull, John, and Alan White. 1990. "Pricing Interest-Rate-Derivative Securities." *The Review of Financial Studies*, Vol. 3, pp. 573–592.

Jarrow, Robert. 1995. *Modeling Fixed Income Securities and Interest Rate Options*. New York: McGraw-Hill.

Jarrow, Robert, and Stuart Turnbull. 2000. *Derivative Securities*, 2nd ed. Cincinnati, OH: South-Western College Publishing.

Kemna, A, and A. Vorst. 1990. "A Pricing Method for Options Based on Average Asset Values." *Journal of Banking and Finance*, Vol. 14, pp. 113–129.

Labuszewski, John, and John Nyhoff. 1988. *Trading Options on Futures: Markets, Methods, Strategies, and Tactics*. New York: John Wiley Sons.

Merton, Robert C. 1973. "Theory of Rational Option Pricing." *Bell Journal of Economics and Management Science*, Vol. 4, No. 1, pp. 141–183.

Reiner, Eric, and Mark Rubinstein. 1991. "Breaking Down the Barriers." *Risk*, Vol. 4, No.8.

Rendleman, Richard J., and Brit J. Bartter. 1980. "The Pricing of Options on Debt Securities." *Journal of Financial and Quantitative Analysis*, Vol. 15, pp. 11–24.

Rich, Don. 1994. "The Mathematical Foundation of Barrier Option-Pricing Theory." *Advances in Futures and Options Research*, Vol. 7, pp. 267–311.

Rubinstein, Mark. 1991. "Options for the Undecided." *Risk*, Vol. 4, No. 4.

Risk Standards Working Group (S. Brenner, K. Byrne, C. Campisano, M. Cottrill, M. deMarco, J. Lukomnik, R. Rose, D. Russ, J. Seymour, K. Wassmann, G. Williamson, T. Styblo Beder, and M. Nederlof). 1996. "Risk Standards for Institutional Investment Managers and Institutional Investors," (Can be viewed at www.gloriamundi.org/var/bestprac.html)

Smithson, Charles W. 1998. *Managing Financial Risk: A Guide to Derivative Products, Financial Engineering, and Value Maximization*, 3rd ed. New York: McGraw-Hill.

Stulz, R. 1982. "Options of the Minimum or the Maximum of Two Risky Assets," *Journal of Financial Economics*, Vol. 10, pp. 161–185.

Vasicek, O. A. 1977. "An Equilibrium Characterization of the Term Structure," *Journal if Financial Economics*, 5, pp. 177–188.

Wilmott, Paul. 1998. *Derivatives: The Theory and Practice of Financial Engineering*. New York: John Wiley & Sons.

Notes

[1]For a voluminous source of regulatory and other documents concerning risk management, see the group web site www.riskinstitute.ch. This site, maintained by the International Financial Risk Institute (IFCI), contains many documents prepared by, among others, various committees of the Bank of International Settlements (BIS) and the International Organization of Securities Commissions (IOSCO).

[2]The other two methods were a table that disclosed the terms and expected future cash flows arising from a firm's derivatives portfolio, and a sensitivity analysis that reported the magnitude of losses that would be incurred if financial prices changed. VaR is a form of sensitivity analysis that incorporates probabilities and also considers different time horizons.

[3]Besides VaR, other risk measures presented by the standard are duration, beta, standard deviation, semivariance, tracking error, and drawdown size. The standard states that the risk measure should capture the relevant risks for the portfolio, strategy or instrument. The document "Risk Standards for Institutional Investment Managers and Institutional Investors" can be retrieved at www.rogerscaseyassoc.com/ghrisk-ds.html.

[4]For detailed information concerning *RiskMetrics*, including downloads of various software packages, visit www.riskmetrics.com or follow the link from www.jpmorgan.com.

[5]A variance–covariance matrix for n assets has n rows and n columns. The diagonal elements are the variances of each asset; e.g., the variance of the swap's returns in this example is 0.00090. Each off-diagonal element is the covariance of the asset of that row with the asset of that column. In this example, the covariance of the bond's returns with the swap's returns is –0.00008.

[6]The *CrashMetrics* method can also suggest ways in which derivatives that are not part of the current portfolio can be bought (or sold) to offset crash risk. This is known on the street as "platinum hedging." For a detailed description of the *CrashMetrics* technique, refer to www.crashmetrics.com.

[7]Smithson (1998, Chapter 19) presents the results of empirical studies that examine the VaR techniques and Wilmott (1998, Chapter 42) presents technical discussions.

[8]Many types of financial arrangements that were similar to credit derivatives existed long before 1991. These include municpal bond insurance and letters of credit. However unlike these early tools for managing credit risk, credit derivatives permit the credit risk to be unbundled from the underlying debt instrument and be traded.

[9]One can obtain a detailed description of *CreditMetrics* at the company's website (www.jpmorgan.com). Another firm active in the credit modeling business is KMV; you can learn more about them, and also read several technical papers, by visiting their website (www.kmv.com).

[10]In chapter 12, you learned about *equity swaps*. Recall that in an equity swap, the fixed-price payer makes periodic fixed interest payments on a notional principal. The floating-price payer makes periodic payments that are determined by the total return on a given stock index. This basic swap structure can easily be adapted to shift credit risk. This is accomplished as follows. First, the total return on a given stock index is replaced with the total return on a debt instrument. Second, the fixed-floating swap structure is changed to a floating-floating swap structure.

[11]The coupon payment might be fixed or floating.

[12]Sometimes the up-front cost is amortized periodic payments, making this credit derivative more like a swap.

[13]For further information on the PCS indexes, see the website (www.iso.com/AISG/pcs/pcs.html).

[14]Labuszewski and Nyhoff (1988) offer other reasons for the failure of options on spot T-bonds and spot T-bills despite the success options on interest rate futures. First, they note that interest rate futures option traders at the CME and the CBOT were able to easily hedge themselves by trading futures in a pit adjacent to their own. In contrast AMEX and CBOE spot interest rate option traders had to offset their risks either by trading the cash T-bonds or T-bills or by trading interest rate futures, since spot securities and spot interest rate options do not trade

at the same physical location. In addition, hedging with the cash securities is costly because bid-asked spreads in the cash market are wider than those in the futures market. The authors also note that institutions find it easier to make or take delivery of a futures contract, in comparison to having to make or take delivery of one specific cash bond. After delivery, if it takes place, the institution will also find it easier to offset the futures position, versus to trading out of the cash instrument.

[15]Chapters 20–22 in Hull (2000), Part IV in Jarrow and Turnbull (2000), and Part 4 of Wilmott (1998) are excellent, but highly technical, sources of information on the various models used to value interest rate derivatives. Abken (1990), and Ho and Abrahamson (1990) provide an intuitive, easy-to-read, explanation of the rather complex Ho and Lee (1986, 1990) model.

[16]See the appendix to Chapter 18 for a discussion and example of a price following a stochastic process.

[17]Although we will not discuss them here, an option on a floor is called a "floortion" and an option on a cap is called a "caption." No kidding.

[18]Here, note that $d_2 = -d_1$. This is because the fair fixed forward rate equals the strike.

[19]For an excellent discussion of hedging with exotic options, see Chapter 19 in Jarrow and Turnbull (2000).

[20]Recall from Chapter 15 that a similar payoff profile exists for a vertical spreads using ordinary calls and puts.

[21]Recall that in a straddle, the trader purchases a call option and a put option. Both options have the same strike price and time to maturity.

[22]The actual formula for valuing a compound option involves a standardized bivariate normal distribution function, which is a three-dimensional analogue to the usual two-dimensional univariate normal distribution. Picture a mountain, with the volume under it equal to 1.0. The value of the standardized bivariate normal distribution function is the volume under the mountain found by defining two coordinates of the mountain in the x and y (surface) dimensions. Two random variables, X and Y, have a bivariate normal distribution if, given any value of X, the Y is normally distributed; and given any value of Y, the X is normally distributed. A computer algorithm is necessary to find the values of standardized multivariate normal distribution functions.

[23]The term **rainbow option** is often used to describe an option with many underlying assets. Not all rainbow options are exotic options. One important example of a rainbow option is the T-bond futures contract traded at the CBOT. As described in Chapter 9, the short has the option to select from many T-bonds when making delivery.

[24]Although we will discuss only single-barrier European options, it is really the additional features that make these options truly exotic. For example, barrier options could have an early exercise feature, a barrier that is in effect only during certain intervals of the option's life, or a provision to reset the barrier.

[25]In part, rebates for barrier options arose from the following. Because out-barrier options cease to exist when the barrier is hit, the party that is short the barrier option has the incentive to attempt to manipulate the underlying asset price level so that the barrier is hit. While it is possible to initiate a large short position in the underlying asset to temporarily drive down the underlying price, in a well-functioning market it is impossible to keep an underlying asset price below the barrier level for a long interval. Consequently, another type of barrier option exists. **Parisian options** are barrier options for which the barrier feature is triggered only if the underlying asset price has spent a prespecified amount of time in violation of the barrier.

[26]Rich (1994) also contains some useful barrier option formulas. Also, see Haug (1998).

[27]Barrier option formulas for down-and-in and down-and-out options also exist for cases where the barrier level H is greater than or equal to the strike price K (see, e.g., Haug, 1998).

[28]Kemna and Vorst (1990) have shown that if the average of the underlying asset is calculated by a geometric average, it is possible under certain assumptions to use the BSOPM, but with modified volatility and interest rate terms, to price an average option.

PROBLEMS

20.1 Consider a portfolio consists of these three assets: a currency swap (because of changes in the exchange rate since the swap was first entered into, the swap now has a value equal to 12% of the portfolio's total value), a bond (the market value of the bond is 53% of the portfolio's total value), and shares of a stock whose value comprises the remaining value of the portfolio.

Assume the variance–covariance matrix of the assets' daily returns is as follows:

	Swap	Bond	Stock
Swap	0.0010	−0.0060	0.0002
Bond		0.0025	−0.0001
Stock			0.0053

a. Use Equation (20.1) to calculate the variance and standard deviation of the portfolio's daily returns distribution.

b. Calculate the 1 and 5% VaR for this portfolio.

c. Are there any assumptions underlying your analysis?

20.2 It is August 10, 2000. You have just found out that your very, very wealthy (and eccentric) aunt has a portfolio consisting of 3,010,005 shares of IBM (and nothing else). She is willing to give you the "extra" 10,005 shares! In the middle of your daydream of whether you should order a silver or a black M3, she tells you the catch. Because of her lack of portfolio diversification, she spends time visiting various finance websites and has stumbled across VaR. She instructs you to use the variance–covariance method and the historic simulation method to calculate her 1 and 5% VaR. She instructs you to use data from January 2, 1962 if possible, through August

10, 2000. Prepare a table for you aunt. *Hints*: (1) Use Yahoo! to download an Excel file. (2) See Section 20.1.4.2. (3) Do not lecture your aunt on "portfolio diversification."

20.3 Suppose $S=K=100$, $r=6\%$, $T=90$ days, $\sigma=30\%$, and no dividends.

a. Calculate the values of calls and puts for digital options, strike-or-nothing options, and asset-or-nothing options.

b. By recalculating the value of an asset-or-nothing option by holding constant everything except the strike price, use $S=100.50$ and $S=99.50$, to estimate the delta of an asset-or-nothing option. Compare this estimate to the delta from an ordinary Black–Scholes option. What do you notice?

20.4 Suppose $S=100$, $K=110$, $r=6\%$, $T=180$ days, $\sigma=45\%$, and no dividends. Calculate the value of a paylater call option and the value of an ordinary Black–Scholes option. At expiration, suppose $S=110.125$. What is the loss for the holder of a paylater call option versus the loss for a holder of an ordinary Black–Scholes option? What is it in percentage terms?

20.5 Prove that at initiation, the payoffs to a chooser option can be replicated by the following portfolio: (a) a long position in an ordinary call option with a strike price equal to K and a time to maturity of T, and (b) a long position in an ordinary put with a strike price equal to $Ke^{-r(T-t)}$ and a time to maturity of t (the choice date).

20.6 Once again, suppose $S=100$, $K=110$, $r=6\%$, $T=180$ days, $\sigma=45\%$, and no dividends. However, $H=90$. H? Yes, H is the barrier level. Calculate the value of a down-and-in call and a down-and-out call.

20.7 Use the information from problem 20.6 to calculate the value of a up-and-in call and an up-and-out call assuming $H = 100$.

20.8 Rework Problem 20.7 with $H=90$. Verify that the answers you obtain equal Black–Scholes option prices.

20.9 Consider the purchaser of the payer swaption in Section 20.2.5.2. What is the breakeven fixed rate for this swaption? That is, the hedger (i.e., the purchaser of the payer swaption) could have entered a forward start swap instead. If the fixed-swap rate subsequently increases, the holder of this payer swaption would exercise the option. Calculate how far the fair fixed rate must increase for the hedger to be indifferent between purchasing a payer swaption today (and waiting) or entering a forward start swap today.

20.10 Given the information in Section 20.2.5, calculate the value of the receiver swaption.

Index

Note: Page numbers followed by *f*, *t*, or *n* indicate figures, tables, and notes respectively.

Derivatives: Valuation and Risk Management

Companion Software by

FinancialCAD®

Fincad® *XL — Dubofsky/Miller Edition* (**www.fincad.com/oxford**) turns Microsoft® Excel into a powerful financial engineering application. Designed to be used in conjunction with this book, *Fincad XL — Dubofsky/Miller Edition* is based on FinancialCAD's industry-leading financial instrument modeling kit, *Fincad XL*. Thousands of financial professionals at leading Wall Street firms and banks, as well as thousands of other companies, use *Fincad XL* every day.

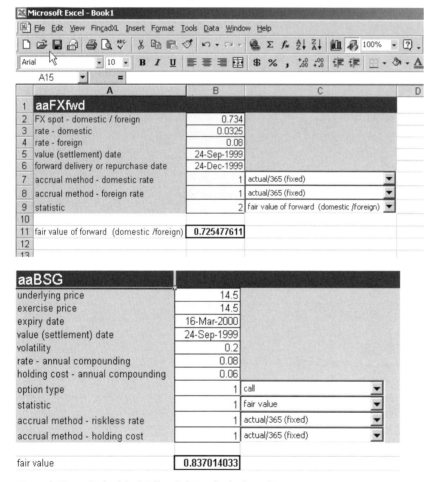

Fincad XL — Dubofsky/Miller Edition is designed to:

- Provide you with a powerful analytic/computational tool to solve the vast array of problems covered in the text
- Enable you to gain "hands-on" experience with the same technology used by thousands of industry professionals every day
- Provide a "real-world" application of industry standard models for derivatives valuation and risk assessment